Characters in
20th-
CENTURY
LITERATURE

Characters in
20th-
CENTURY
LITERATURE

Laurie Lanzen Harris

 Gale Research Inc. • DETROIT • LONDON

The paper used in this publication meets the minimum requirements of American National Standard for Information Sciences—Permanence Paper for Printed Library Materials, ANSI Z39.48-1984. ∞™

While every effort has been made to ensure the reliability of the information presented in this publication, Gale Research Inc. neither guarantees the accuracy of the data contained herein nor assumes any responsibility for errors, omissions, or discrepancies. Gale accepts no payment for listing; and inclusion in the publication of any organization, agency, institution, publication, service, or individual does not imply endorsement of the author or publisher.

Errors brought to the attention of the publisher and verified to the satisfaction of the publisher will be corrected in future editions.

Library of Congress Catalog Card Number
ISBN 0-8103-1847-4

Printed in the United States of America.

Published simultaneously in the United Kingdom
by Gale Research International Limited
(An affiliated company of Gale Research Inc.)

To Dan

Contents

Preface   xi

Preface

Characters are the medium through which the author speaks to the world. The character may represent a philosophy, reflect the author's artistic intent, or illuminate his or her vision of humanity. The literature of the twentieth century is brimming with beloved literary characters who seem to transcend the books in which they appear, acquiring lives of their own. Huckleberry Finn, Leopold Bloom, Clarissa Dalloway, Holden Caulfield, Nick Adams, Jay Gatsby, Sherlock Holmes—such characters as these have become archetypal figures of the modern era, yet they also embody a timeless statement on the human condition. The rich heritage of modern world fiction, as seen through the characters who bring a work of art to life, is the focus of this book.

The Scope of the Work

Characters in 20th-Century Literature presents essays that elucidate the function and significance of the most important literary characters from more than 600 works of twentieth-century literature. Descriptions of over 2,000 characters, drawn from 250 of the twentieth century's major novelists, dramatists, and short story writers, are included. Students and general readers will find that an author's most representative and widely discussed works are featured in *Characters in 20th-Century Literature.* The term "twentieth century" used in the title refers to all authors now living or who have died since 1899. To augment existing reference sources that concentrate on the interpretation of characters, over half the volume is devoted to authors of the post-1960 era, with special emphasis given to minority writers and authors from emerging nations. Thus, discussions of *The Color Purple,* by Pulitzer Prize-winning author Alice Walker, and *Miramar,* by 1988 Nobel Laureate Naguib Mahfouz, are included.

The Organization of the Work

The book is arranged alphabetically by author. Each author entry begins with the following elements: the author's name, birth and death dates, nationality, and principal genres. The author's works are chronologically arranged beneath the author heading, and the title heading offers the full title, genre, and date of publication; in the case of dramas, the date of first performance is given. The essay on each work contains a brief plot synopsis as well as commentary on thematic and stylistic aspects of the work and the way in which the characters illustrate the central themes and aesthetics of the author. A student will thus be better prepared to understand the ethical or philosophical points of view expounded by an author and to discover trends and patterns in a writer's major works. The names of all characters mentioned in the essay are boldfaced for easy reference. If the character is known by more than one name—for example, "Molly Bloom" and "Marion Tweedy Bloom"—both are included and boldfaced. The length of the essays varies, reflecting the magnitude and complexity of individual works.

A list of critical essays and articles for further reading on titles discussed concludes each author entry. This section also includes references to several literary series published by Gale Research, including *Contemporary Authors, Contemporary Authors New Revision Series, Contemporary Literary Criticism, Twentieth-Century Literary Criticism, Short Story Criticism,* and *Dictionary of Literary Biography.*

The book concludes with an index to characters and titles. If a character appears in more than one work by an author, the character name is followed by the title in which he or she appears. If a character name is used by more than one author, the author's name appears in parentheses after the character name.

Acknowledgments

I would like to thank Dedria Bryfonski and Chris Nasso of the New Publication Development group at Gale for the opportunity to edit *Characters in 20th-Century Literature,* Dennis Poupard and Daniel Marowski of the Literary Criticism Series for their assistance, and Jay P. Pederson, Norma Jean Merry, Madeline Gleason, Kathleen Aro, Christine Norris, Jane Thacker, Claire Rewold, and Kevin P. Decker, who helped in the composition of this volume. I would especially like to thank my husband, Dan Harris, for his tireless support and encouragement.

Chinua Achebe

1930-

Nigerian novelist, poet, short story writer, and essayist.

Things Fall Apart (novel, 1958)

Achebe's first novel is set in the Nigerian Ibo village of Umuofia during the late 1800s. The central character, **Okonkwo,** is a respected village leader whose inability to change brings about tragedy. The first half of *Things Fall Apart* portrays traditional village life and customs before British colonization. The Ibo's ancient rites, including human sacrifices, are presented as part of a viable, well-ordered culture which is destroyed by the coming of the white man. Okonkwo's troubles begin when he accidentally kills a young member of his tribe. The punishment for his crime is exile from the clan for seven years. When Okonkwo returns to his village, he discovers that the European missionaries have already begun to change the people. Okonkwo and a few other older members of the tribe resist the changes the white men try to enforce and are sent to jail. After their release, Okonkwo strikes out in anger and kills a messenger from the British authorities. Okonkwo then commits suicide, a crime worse than any other in the Ibo culture.

Thing Fall Apart is considered the beginning of contemporary African literature because of Achebe's fusion of the Ibo language and its rhythms with conventional Western novelistic techniques. Achebe was praised for depicting both the good and bad aspects of a previously unknown culture and its destruction by Europeans who forced their values and beliefs upon the native Africans.

Arrow of God (novel, 1964)

This novel is set in the Ibo village of Umuaro during the 1920s, after British rule of Nigeria had been established. At this point in Nigerian history, the native struggle was not against the encroaching white man's civilization, but was instead an effort to maintain aspects of the tribal past. The main character is **Ezeulu,** the chief priest for the god Ulu and a powerful man in his Ibo community who understands the importance of adapting to the changes instigated by the British. He even sends one of his sons to be taught by the missionaries. On the other hand, Ezeulu still strongly believes in the village gods and his own powers and responsibilities as the representative of Ulu. He subsequently refuses, when asked by the white District Officer, to become a warrant chief, a representative of a decentralized Ibo government. Through a series of misunderstandings, Ezeulu is imprisoned. Upon his return to the village, he realizes that the people no longer look to him as their sole spiritual and tribal leader. In an effort to punish them, Ezeulu refuses to name the day of the all-important yam feast and the villagers are unable to begin the yam harvest. In desperation, the villagers take it upon themselves to gather the yams with the blessing of the Christian missionaries. These events, coupled with the death of one his sons, leads Ezeulu to question his own faith

1

in the tribal gods, which in turn creates a breakdown of Ezeulu's mental processes, leaving him out of touch with reality for the remainder of his life.

Arrow of God is marked by Achebe's attention to the detail of tribal life and values. His story is about the changes wrought by European colonization and the erosion of traditional, tribal religion. Achebe's insistence on educating his readers about the Ibo past has been noted by critics, who generally find this work difficult but enlightening.

FURTHER READING

Contemporary Authors, Vols. 1-4, rev. ed.; *Contemporary Authors New Revision Series,* Vol. 6. Detroit: Gale Research Co.

Contemporary Literary Criticism, Vols. 1, 3, 5, 7, 11, 26, 51. Detroit: Gale Research Co.

McDougall, Russell. "Okonkwo's Walk: The Choreography of the Things Falling Apart." *World Literature Written in English* 26 (Spring 1986): 24-33.

Nwongo, D. Ibe. "The Igbo World of Achebe's *Arrow of God.*" *Literary Half-Yearly* 27 (January 1986): 11-42.

Olorounto, Samuel B. "The Notion of Conflict in Chinua Achebe's Novels." *Obsidian II* 1 (Winter 1986): 17-36.

Henry Adams

1838-1918

American autobiographer, historian, essayist, and novelist.

Democracy (novel, 1880)

The greater of Adams's two novels, *Democracy* is set in post-Civil War Washington, D.C., during a time of political turmoil and reconstruction. Recently widowed, **Madeleine Lee** has come to Washington seeking the companionship of some distinguished elder statesman with whom she can help chart her nation's future. In her arsenal are money, social position, beauty, charm, and a wellspring of fresh ideas. **John Carrington,** a lawyer and Confederate veteran, immediately falls for her. His cynical attitude of defeat and inferior standing, however, preclude any romantic attachment. For a time, Madeleine pursues **Senator Ratcliffe.** A villainous figure from Illinois with colossal political sway, Ratcliffe gains control of the new administration before the president has taken office. Gradually, with the aid of Carrington, Madeleine discovers that the senator's career has been founded on a bribe. She has, furthermore, learned the distressing truth about the symbiotic relationship between political dealing and human imperfectability. For her, the climate of Washington, devoid of idealism and conscience, rife with graft and corruption, becomes intolerable. Rather than succumbing to the allure of POWER (so capitalized in the novel) and ally herself with Ratcliffe, Madeleine leaves Washington for Europe.

Popular in its day as a political roman à clef, *Democracy* is important primarily for its pioneering exposure of governmental evils in Washington. Adams's work in general is less pertinent to the history of literature than it is to the history of ideas. In the latter context Adams embodies for many a particularly modern viewpoint, one which sees the world becoming less stable and coherent and which predicts this trend will continue, never to be arrested. Adams developed this doctrine most thoroughly in his best-known work, *The Education of Henry Adams.*

FURTHER READING

Auchincloss, Louis. *Henry Adams*. Minneapolis: University of Minnesota Press, 1971.

Blackmur, R. P. *Henry Adams*. New York: Harcourt Brace Jovanovich, 1980.

Contemporary Authors, Vol. 104. Detroit: Gale Research Co.

Dictionary of Literary Biography, Vols. 12, 47. Detroit: Gale Research Co.

Levenson, J. C. *The Mind and Art of Henry Adams*. Boston: Houghton Mifflin, 1957.

Twentieth-Century Literary Criticism, Vol. 4. Detroit: Gale Research Co.

James Agee
1909-1955
American novelist, journalist, critic, and essayist.

A Death in the Family (novel, 1957)

The autobiographical novel is set in Knoxville, Tennessee, in 1915. Much of the lyrical narrative's four-day action is seen through the eyes of **Rufus Follet,** a lonely, sensitive, intelligent six-year-old boy. After viewing a wonderfully touching Charlie Chaplin film with his father, **Jay Follet,** Rufus is put to bed. During the night Jay and his wife, **Mary ,** are awakened by a phone call summoning Jay to his father's deathbed. On his return drive, a loose cotter pin in the automobile causes Jay's instantaneous death. Mary's overwhelming grief is shared by other family members, each holding differing religious views and interpretations of the death, as they make preparations for Jay's funeral. Reality and fantasy converge with Jay's brief, mysterious visitation and Rufus's later verbal encounter with his ghost. The final day of the novel concerns Jay's burial. At the conclusion of the ceremony, **Uncle Andrew Lynch,** Mary's bitter, agnostic brother, takes Rufus aside and explains that he has witnessed something miraculous, perhaps enough to make him believe in God. He describes a butterfly that alighted on the casket as it was being lowered into the ground; when the casket reached bottom the sun burst dazzlingly from behind the clouds and the butterfly flew high into the sky. Rufus feels privileged that Uncle Andrew has chosen to tell him the story; he wonders at the end about the difference between love and hate and the unspoken feelings that surround him.

Agee wrote that he intended *A Death in the Family* to be "chiefly a remembrance of my childhood, and a memorial to my father." Left unfinished at his death, the novel was pieced together by editors who inserted several passages from outside the time frame of the story. While some critics maintain that the interpolations detract from the narrative by creating internal contradictions and by further complicating Agee's attempt to present the event from a variety of viewpoints, others contend that the inserted passages surpass the main narrative in the quality of their prose and contribute to the cohesiveness of the novel by focusing the narrative more exclusively on Rufus. For its unmatched poetic style and sympathetic portrayal of the human struggle against fear, loneliness, and death, Agee's novel was awarded a posthumous Pulitzer Prize in 1958.

FURTHER READING

Barson, Alfred T. *A Way of Seeing: A Critical Study of James Agee*. Amherst: University of Massachusetts Press, 1972.

Contemporary Authors, Vol. 108. Detroit: Gale Research Co.

Dictionary of Literary Biography, Vols. 2, 26. *Concise Dictionary of American Literary Biography, 1941-1968*. Detroit: Gale Research Co.

Doty, Mark A. *Tell Me Who I Am: James Agee's Search for Selfhood*. Baton Rouge: Louisiana State University Press, 1981.

Kramer, Victor A. *James Agee*. Boston: Twayne, 1975.

Seib, Kenneth. *James Agee: Promise and Fulfillment*. Pittsburgh: University of Pittsburgh Press, 1968.

Twentieth-Century Literary Criticism, Vols. 1, 19. Detroit: Gale Research Co.

Alain-Fournier
1886-1914

French novelist.

The Wanderer (novel, 1913)

The novel takes place in rural France during the nineteenth century. It is narrated by one of the main characters, **François Seurel,** a young schoolboy, crippled and withdrawn, who idolizes his strong and adventurous friend, **Augustin Meaulnes.** With his friends Meaulnes and **Frantz de Galais,** Seurel forms a trio whose idealistic quests are imbued with allusions to the journeys depicted in medieval romance.

As the story opens, Meaulnes is sent to the train station to meet Seurel's grandparents, but instead decides to embark on an adventure. He loses his way and happens upon a great and seemingly enchanted manor where a party is in progress. Here he meets **Yvonne de Galais,** a figure of beauty and purity, and he falls deeply in love with her. He also learns that the party was to be in honor of Yvonne's brother, Frantz, and his bride-to-be, **Valentine Blondeau.** But Valentine has run away, and the grief-stricken Frantz becomes a wanderer with a band of gypsies.

Meaulnes returns home and relates his adventures to Seurel. Soon afterward, Frantz arrives in the town and both Seurel and Meaulnes swear to help Frantz in his search for Valentine. Meaulnes, also in search of the elusive ideal embodied in Yvonne, is unlucky in his quest.

Later, living in Paris, Meaulnes begins an affair with Valentine, unaware of her identity as Frantz's lost love. But Seurel has found Yvonne and brings her and Meaulnes together; they marry, but their union is plagued with unhappiness. Meaulnes becomes disillusioned and deserts her, devoting himself to the quest to reunite Frantz and Valentine. In his absence, Yvonne gives birth to a daughter and dies, leaving Seurel to grieve for her and care for the infant. Having brought Frantz and Valentine together, Meaulnes returns to learn of his wife's death. Overcome with grief, he dedicates himself to his child.

Alain-Fournier's novel is infused with a dream-like atmosphere, reminiscent of a fairy-tale and evoking the fantastic ambience of childhood. Critics often note the dualities represented in the novel, such as the idealism of childhood and the disillusionment of adulthood, and the sacred and profane nature of love, as embodied in the characters of Yvonne and Valentine.

FURTHER READING

Brosman, Catherine Savage. "Alain-Fournier's Domain: A New Look." *The French Review* 44, No. 3 (February 1971): 499-507.

Contemporary Authors, Vol. 104. Detroit: Gale Research Co.

Locke, Frederick W. *"Le grand Meaulnes:* The Desire and Pursuit of the Whole." *Renascence* 11, No. 3 (Spring 1959): 135-46.

Twentieth-Century Literary Criticism, Vol. 6. Detroit: Gale Research Co.

Turnell, Martin. "Alain-Fournier and *Le grand Meaulnes." The Southern Review* 2, No. 3 (Summer 1966): 477-98.

Edward Albee

1928-

American dramatist.

The Zoo Story (drama, 1959)

Set in New York's Central Park, the play depicts the encounter of **Jerry** and **Peter** on a Sunday afternoon. Peter, a man in his forties and a publishing executive, is a self-contained and reticent man, seemingly conservative and middle-class. Jerry, an articulate man in his thirties, is described by Albee in the stage directions as having a great "weariness." He appears as Peter sits reading on a park bench, announcing to this perfect stranger, "I've been to the Zoo!" He dominates the conversation, pouring out his deepest thoughts and feelings, wanting to connect with another human being, to know everything about Peter. Peter doesn't know what to make of Jerry's effusiveness and spends most of the play responding to Jerry's queries or listening to his stories with a mixture of wonder and uneasiness, as Jerry chides him for wanting to bring order out of the chaos of Jerry's rambling.

Jerry wants to know the direction he is heading and says to Peter, in a phrase that will be repeated throughout the play, "sometimes a person has to go a very long distance out of his way to come back a short distance correctly." He tells Peter about the rooming-house he lives in and about its strange and lonely inhabitants, focussing particularly on his grotesque landlady and her equally repulsive dog. In a long monologue, he describes how the landlady harbors a pathetic passion for him, and how he tried to poison her dog, a tale that proves to be an allegory for Jerry's own inability to relate to others. Although the dog does not die, he and Jerry harbor "sadness, suspicion, and indifference" for one another, paralleling the relationship that Jerry appears to have with other human beings. Although Peter claims not to understand the import of Jerry's tale, he is clearly agitated. Jerry provokes him into a fight over his park bench, throws him a knife and slaps him, goading him on until Peter holds the knife out towards him. Jerry impales himself on the knife and dies, thanking Peter.

Jerry, searching for meaning in life, for the chance to relate to others and to understand, has ended his quest in death. Although the meaning of the conclusion is debated by critics, most agree that Albee seeks to reveal the isolation and lack of communication that characterizes contemporary life. The work is noted for its simple but vivid language and dramatic intensity.

The American Dream (drama, 1961)

The play is set in an apartment living room and begins with a conversation between **Mommy** and **Daddy** that reveals the emptiness of the characters and their lives. They speak in banalities, yet the audience can see the dominance of Mommy and the subservience of Daddy and learns quickly that there is no love in their marriage, and that Mommy married Daddy for his money. **Grandma** offers a refreshing candor, speaking her mind in language that is clear and simple and accurately accessing the situation. Mommy and Daddy are waiting for someone to discuss their lack of "satisfaction" with something they bought. As Grandma relates the story, the two had been unable to have children and so had bought a baby. But they began to destroy it, plucking out its eyes and genitals and cutting off its hands; the baby eventually died.

Now the **Young Man** arrives on the scene, who, in Grandma's words, looks like "the American Dream" because of his good looks. He appears to be an empty, shallow young man, fixated on his looks and willing to do anything for money. His true character is shown in a conversation with Grandma in which he reveals that he is a twin who had lost his brother when they were infants. As the brother of the child destroyed by Mommy and Daddy, he claims that he is "incomplete" and he has suffered symbolically the physical mutilation endured by his brother. Thus, because his brother lost his eyes, he no longer sees with pity; because his brother lost his hands, he is now unable to touch with love and feeling. The conclusion indicates that the Young Man has been accepted by Mommy and Daddy as recompense for their earlier, "defective" product.

As he was to do in such later works as *Who's Afraid of Virgina Woolf?* Albee explores the emptiness of family relationships in this play, focussing on the physical and emotional barrenness of modern life. Daddy, Mommy, and Grandma reappear in his brief play *The Sandbox.*

Who's Afraid of Virginia Woolf? (drama, 1962)

The play is set in the fictional college town of New Carthage and centers on an evening spent at the home of **George,** a professor of history, and his wife, **Martha.** Their guests of the evening are **Nick,** a new biology professor, and his wife, **Honey.** The relationship between George and Martha is characterized by mutually destructive cruelty and rage, tempered with a childish delight in fantasy and humor. Their bitter, acrimonious association—their names ironically suggest George and Martha Washington—is marked by occasional moments of humor and tenderness; their marriage is anything but shallow, built on the knowledge of how to nurture and how to wound. They have not been able to have children, and, to compensate, have created a fantasy child, now twenty-one. Nick, a young man in his middle twenties, seems to function as an embodiment of their created son, but in negative ways. Martha lures him upstairs to her bedroom, where he plays out an Oedipal role, albeit unsuccessfully.

To George, Nick as a biology professor represents the new order, the son rebelling against the father, promoting the values of science and technology over the study of the history of thought. Nick himself is a ruthless man, willing to do almost anything to enhance his career, which is what is behind his sexual interlude with Martha. He does not particularly love his wife, and during the course of the evening George divulges that they married thinking Honey was pregnant, only to find out that it was a false, or hysterical, pregnancy. Thus, they too had a fantasy child. At the end of the second act, George decides to end the game: he announces that their son is dead. Martha, chastened by this change, retreats into docility and fear. The ambiguous conclusion appears to indicate a mood of reconciliation; with the fantasy child dead, the struggle for dominance that characterized their relationship is momentarily dormant.

Critics have noted Albee's social and political themes in this work, particularly in the contrast between George and Nick, one attracted to the variety and multiplicity of human behavior, the other a man who would control humanity through science, as George indicates through his vision of a dystopic future in which Nick and men like him would control the genetic makeup of society. As he has in several of his plays, Albee examines the nature of truth and fantasy as well as the sterility of the American family in his two childless couples. He depicts the generations at war, where the children (Nick and Honey) reject the world of the parents, and the parents (George and Martha) destroy their own children.

FURTHER READING

Amacher, Richard E. *Edward Albee*. New York: Twayne, 1969.

Bigsby, C.W.E. *Edward Albee*. Edinburgh: Oliver and Boyd, 1969.

Clurman, Harold. *The Naked Image: Observations on the Modern Theater*, pp. 13-24. New York: Macmillan, 1966.

Cohn, Ruby. "The Verbal Murders of Edward Albee." In *Dialogue in American Drama*, pp. 130-69. Bloomington: Indiana University Press, 1971.

Contemporary Authors, Vols. 5-8, rev. ed.; *Contemporary Authors New Revision Series*, Vol. 8. Detroit: Gale Research Co.

Contemporary Literary Criticism, Vols. 1, 2, 3, 5, 9, 11, 13, 25. Detroit: Gale Research Co.

Dictionary of Literary Biography, Vol. 7; *Concise Dictionary of American Literary Biography, 1941-1968*. Detroit: Gale Research Co.

Esslin, Martin. In *The Theatre of the Absurd*, pp. 266-70. Garden City: Doubleday, 1969.

Evans, Gareth Lloyd. "American Connections—O'Neill, Miller, Williams, and Albee." In *The Language of Modern Drama*, pp. 177-204. London: J. M. Dent & Sons, 1977.

Gilman, Richard. "The Drama Is Coming Now." *Tulane Drama Review* 7 (Summer 1963): 27-42.

Kerr, Walter. "Albee, Miller, Williams." In *Thirty Plays Hath November: Pain and Pleasure in the Contemporary Theater*, pp. 203-30. New York: Simon and Schuster, 1969.

Rutenberg, Michael E. *Edward Albee: Playwright in Protest*. New York: Avon, 1969.

Sholom Aleichem

1859-1916

Yiddish novelist, dramatist, and short story writer.

"Modern Children" (short story, 1946)

"Modern Children," one of several stories written by Aleichem in which **Reb Tevye** is the main character, is a humorous short story dealing with a father's befuddled attempts to marry off his eldest daughter to everyone's satisfaction. The tale is told by Tevye, the dairy man, a poor Eastern European Jew living with his strong-willed wife and several daughters. As the story opens, Tevye's wife, **Golda,** urges Tevye to pay a visit to a prosperous neighbor and widower, **Lazer-Wolf,** who recently had been asking after Tevye. Assuming that Lazer-Wolf was interested in purchasing the family cow, Tevye proceeds to bargain with his neighbor only to find that, after some discussion, Lazer-Wolf is interested in Tevye's eldest daughter, **Tzeitl,** not the cow. Upon enlightenment, Tevye agrees to discuss the matter with his wife, who is delighted, and his daughter, who is not. Tevye, anxious over his daughter's happiness, learns of her love for a poor local tailor, **Motel Kamzoil,** and sympathetic but confused over the breach of tradition, specifically, his own lack of control in the situation, contrives to win his wife's support of Tzeitl's marriage to the tailor.

Late at night, when the family is asleep, Tevye sits up in bed and causes a great uproar, waking Golda. He tells her that he has had a nightmare in which Lazer-Wolf's former wife appeared and threatened to choke both Tzeitl and Lazer-Wolf if they married. Tevye also claims that Golda's grandmother appeared in the dream and congratulated Tevye on his daughter's marriage to a tailor. Golda, a great believer in dreams, particularly those in which her grandmother appears, is more than willing to accept the tailor as her son-in-law.

Aleichem was one of the first writers to introduce a light-hearted humor into Yiddish literature. Some of the techniques he used to reinforce this effect are the many comic situations, demonstrated in the misuse of language by his characters. Tevye, for instance, considers himself a scholarly man but his dialogue is rife with malapropisms, inappropriate allusions, and misquoted bits and pieces from the Bible, the Talmud, and other lofty sources.

Aleichem's characters are painfully aware of their stations in society but, like Tevye, accept their fates, often with much complaint, as the will of God. Although Tevye is insignificant in his world, he is given heroic proportions, and the reader sees beyond the humor and recognizes the grievous problems with which the Jewish people had to struggle while still holding to their faith and dignity in a world over which they had little control.

FURTHER READING

Howe, Irving. "Sholom Aleichem: Voice of Our Past." In *A World More Attractive: A View of Modern Literature and Politics,* pp. 207-15. New York: Horizon Press, 1963.

Kazin, Alfred. "Sholom Aleichem: The Old Country." In *Contemporaries,* pp. 271-78. Boston: Atlantic-Little, Brown and Co., 1962.

Samuel, Maurice. *The World of Sholom Aleichem.* New York: Knopf, 1943.

Twentieth-Century Literary Criticism, Vol. 1. Detroit: Gale Research Co.

Kingsley Amis

1922-

English novelist, poet, and essayist.

Lucky Jim (novel, 1954)

Set in an unnamed provincial university college in England, the novel depicts the end of the academic career of **Jim Dixon,** a lecturer in history in his mid-twenties. It is a blend of seriousness and satire, as Amis reveals the pretensions and snobbery of provincial academic life as well as his young protagonist's quest for self-knowledge and his final liberation to pursue the life he wants.

As the novel begins, Dixon is in the last weeks of his first year as a lecturer, unhappy with his job and the prospect of years in an academic community he finds moribund. He is a young man of the lower-middle classes and a graduate of a provincial university. The history professor he works for, **Neddy Welch,** pompous and complacent, represents all that he loathes in academic life. Dixon also finds himself involved with a neurotic young woman, **Margaret Peel,** for whom he feels compassion but not love. At Welch's suggestion, he is preparing a public lecture on the insipid topic of "Merrie England."

He meets two people who offer him an escape from his situation. He falls head over heels in love with **Christine Callaghan,** a beautiful girl who is unfortunately involved with Welch's son **Bertrand.** Christine's uncle **Julius Gore-Urquhart,** a patron of the arts, takes an immediate interest in Dixon and helps him to secure a good job in London. In a series of humorous episodes, Dixon takes on Bertrand in a fist fight and severs connections with Margaret. When it comes time to give his lecture, Dixon uses the occasion to end his academic career on a tumultuous note, for as he delivers the lecture, it is clear that he is using the opportunity to reveal his contempt for the artificiality of the provincial world of the university. At last he and Christine disentangle themselves from their previous lives and are depicted in the conclusion in the city of London, free at last to explore what life has to offer.

When the novel was first published, Amis was linked to the group of writers known as the "Angry Young Men," who, like Amis, portrayed the ambivalent, often troubled lives of university-educated young men of working-class origins confronted with the gap between their educations and their prospects in an England still dominated by the power of the middle-and upper-class elite. Since then, Amis has explored a variety of other issues and areas in his art, but *Lucky Jim* remains his most famous, and for some critics, his best novel.

The Old Devils (novel, 1986)

This much-acclaimed novel has been called Amis's best fiction since *Lucky Jim*. It is set in South Wales and centers on the lives of a group of characters, friends since their youth and now old pensioners, whose lives revolve around drink and the endless discussion of their Welshness. The men—**Malcolm Cellan-Davies, Charlie Norris,** and **Peter Thomas**—spend most of their time in their favorite pub, The Bible and Crown, or at each other's houses drinking enormous amounts of whiskey and gin. Their wives—**Gwen Cellan-Davies, Sophie Norris,** and **Muriel Thomas**—occupy themselves in similar pursuits, drinking bottle after bottle of wine at their morning "coffees." The catalyst for the main action arrives in the persons of **Alun Weaver** and his wife, **Rhiannon,** who, after Alun's success in the literary world of London, have returned to Wales. A good deal of Alun's success has come from his writings on **Brydan,** a Dylan Thomas figure, a poet, drunk, and local hero. The Weavers's return sparks the group to reminiscence about their past, particularly Malcolm and Peter, who were once in love with Rhiannon and who learn that they are still susceptible to her charms. Alun, an aging lothario, also tries to pick up where he left off with several of the wives.

Amis draws a compassionate and humorous portrait of the infirmities of old age in this fiction, presenting a moving depiction of aging and interdependence. These people, whose lives are given over to the daily pursuit of drunkenness, are also capable of humane understanding and the sympathies if not the vigor of youth. In one memorable scene, Malcolm declares his love for Rhiannon and takes her on a walk filled with vivid recollections of his former passion for her; although she remembers none of it, she accepts his lovingly etched memories as her own.

Alun, who has spent a lifetime presenting himself as the quintessential Welshman to the English television public, sees a financial opportunity in a new series called "In Search of Wales"; in these and other actions, Amis reveals him to be a self-centered fraud. The concern with "Welshness" that consumes the characters seems deliberately artificial, for Amis shows how any real sense of national identity has been lost in that country, replaced with the phony commercialism embodied in Alun.

As many commentators have noted, the atmosphere of death permeates the work, and in the conclusion one of the group, Alun, dies. Yet the finale of the novel is a wedding between the Weavers's daughter and the Thomas's son, a closing symbol of hope and rebirth in this poignant ensemble piece on the effects of the passing of the years.

FURTHER READING

Burgess, Anthony. "Ending Up in Wales." *The Observer* (14 September 1986): 27.

Contemporary Authors, Vols. 9-12, rev. ed.; *Contemporary Authors New Revision Series,* Vol. 8. Detroit: Gale Research Co.

Contemporary Literary Criticism, Vols. 1, 2, 3, 5, 8, 13, 30, 44. Detroit: Gale Research Co.

Dictionary of Literary Biography, Vols. 15, 27. Detroit: Gale Research Co.

Everett, Barbara. "Philistines." *London Review* 9, No. 7 (2 April 1987): 3, 5-8.

Fallis, Richard. *"Lucky Jim* and Academic Wishful Thinking." *Studies in the Novel* 9, No. 1 (Spring 1977): 65-72.

Hurrell, John D. "Class and Conscience in John Braine and Kingsley Amis." *Critique* 2, No. 2 (1958): 39-53.

Lodge, David. "The Modern, the Contemporary, and the Importance of Being Amis." In *The Language of Fiction,* pp. 242-67. London: Routledge and Kegan Paul, 1966.

Wolcott, James. "Do Not Go Sober." *The New Republic* 196, No. 3767 (30 March 1987): 33-5.

Sherwood Anderson
1876-1941
American short story writer.

Winesburg, Ohio (short stories, 1919)

Winesburg, Ohio is a collection of short stories that deal with the alienation and loneliness of people living in a small, pre-industrial midwestern town. The stories, each describing a crucial episode in the life of an individual, are linked together thematically and through the character of **George Willard.**

Anderson was one of the first American writers to delve into the psyche of his characters, and he explains their motivations with compassion. Each story describes a grotesque: an individual so obsessed with a given truth that he loses his identity to it, resulting in isolation from others and a distorted perception of reality. In the story "Hands," for instance, **Wing Biddlebaum,** a former school teacher, had been run out of a small town in Pennsylvania twenty years prior to the time of the story, after having been falsely accused of child molestation. He was in fact a gifted teacher who had a natural inclination to communicate with his hands. Biddlebaum never feels a part of the community and is an unhappy, lonely figure. He is ashamed of his hands, trying to hide them in his pockets or ball them into fists, but finds that even after twenty years he can neither master nor trust them. In "Godliness," a four-part story, **Jesse Bentley** is so obsessed with religious fervor that he unwittingly looses the child he had yearned for, which leads to his madness. The character of **Wash Williams** in "Respectability" allows the bitterness and hatred that he feels towards his unfaithful wife and her family to dramatically change his lifestyle and color his relationship with the rest of humanity.

Many of the characters are allowed a brief period of enlightenment, and most attempt to communicate their "truths" to George Willard, a reporter on the local newspaper and a person they find to be interested, honest, insightful, and compassionate. A focal point of the stories is George's growth from boyhood to maturity. His family is discussed in "Mother"; his relationships with women are described in the stories "Nobody Knows," "An Awakening," and "Sophistication"; and he grapples with the idea of his own mortality in

"Death." He leaves Winesburg for the city in "Departure," taking the town's truths with him.

Winesburg, Ohio was Anderson's most important work and is considered a masterpiece of twentieth-century American fiction. His tales, related in a simple prose style and noted for their bittersweet tone, provide eloquent insight into lives compromised by loneliness and insensitivity and tempered only occasionally by the beauty of love and hope.

FURTHER READING

Anderson, David D. *Sherwood Anderson: An Introduction and Interpretation.* New York: Holt, Rinehart & Winston, 1967.

Burbank, Rex. *Sherwood Anderson.* Boston: Twayne, 1964.

Contemporary Authors, Vol. 104. Detroit: Gale Research Co.

Dictionary of Literary Biography, Vols. 4, 9; *Dictionary of Literary Biography Documentary Series,* Vol. 1. Detroit: Gale Research Co.

Geismar, Maxwell. "Sherwood Anderson: Last of the Townsmen." In *The Last of the Provincials: The American Novel, 1915-1925,* pp. 223-84. Boston: Houghton, 1947.

Rideout, Walter B. "The Simplicity of *Winesburg, Ohio.*" *Shenandoah* (Spring 1962): 20-31.

Taylor, Welford Dunaway. *Sherwood Anderson.* New York: Ungar, 1977.

Twentieth-Century Literary Criticism, Vols. 1, 10. Detroit: Gale Research Co.

Jean Anouilh
1910-1987
French dramatist.

Antigone (drama, 1942)

The play, based on the Greek tragedy of Sophocles, is set in Thebes and recounts the story of **Antigone.** It is one of Anouilh's *pièces noires,* a classification he gave to works adapted from classical myth. In the drama's prologue, we learn the tragic story of Oedipus and his family. The former king, having learned that he had killed his father and married his mother, blinded himself and was banished from Thebes. His two sons, **Eteocles** and **Polynices,** were to rule in one-year intervals, but after his first year on the throne, Eteocles had refused to yield to his brother, and in the fight that ensued the brothers had killed each other. As the action begins, their uncle **Creon,** now king, has decided that Eteocles could receive a full burial, but that the corpse of Polynices is to be left for the vultures. Antigone, the sister of Polynices and Eteocles, pleads with her uncle for a burial for her brother. When he refuses, she buries him anyway, knowing that the punishment is death. She is caught and confesses. Her situation is further complicated by her love for Creon's son, **Haemon,** to whom she is engaged. In the central portion of the drama, Antigone and Creon debate the conflict of God's law, as embodied in the actions of Antigone, and civil law, represented by Creon. Antigone is an idealistic, uncompromising figure, and she chides her uncle for his life of compromise and pragmatism. He argues with her, painting an unflattering portrait of her brother, even offering to pardon her, but she is unrelenting in her purpose: to die for what she believes. She is placed in a cave and left to die, where she hangs herself and is found by Haemon, who commits suicide out of grief. His mother, **Eurydice,** also kills herself upon learning of her son's death.

11

Like many of Anouilh's heroes and heroines, Antigone embodies the concept that fidelity to one's ideals is more important than life. The author makes it clear that Antigone chooses her death and her role of heroine, for she realizes that she is a rebel and unable to live in the commonplace world of compromise and corruption.

The Lark (drama, 1953)

This play is a retelling of the life and death of **Joan of Arc.** It is grouped in Anouilh's category of *pièces costumes,* which are based on historical personages of heroic proportions. As with *Antigone,* the play presents a heroine who is steadfast in her convictions when forced to confront the forces of conformity even though she is ultimately vanquished by them. Joan is secure in her vision to liberate France and to be true to the voices that guide her actions. Although others—her parents and the representatives of the Church and State—try to dissuade her from her task, she remains firm in her resolve although she knows it means she will lose her life.

Like Antigone, Joan is governed by a belief in absolutes and disdains compromise. Her goals are to serve God by driving the English out of France; her sense of God is pure, unsullied by the pretense, mediocrity, and compromise that characterize the world around her. One of the representatives of the Church, **Cauchon,** aware of his limitations, realizes that he does not have the moral courage necessary to save Joan. In her trial for heresy, Anouilh focuses once again on an individual whose beliefs are so firmly held that not even the fear of death can dissuade her from her purpose. Anouilh makes us aware of the loneliness and the burden that Joan bears, as her friends desert her and she admits to her father her feelings of isolation and the weight of her responsibility. Thus, she faces her death alone: she is a lonely, proud rebel, and even her voices abandon her as she faces the stake.

Becket, or the Honor of God (drama, 1959)

The play is set in the twelfth century at the court of **King Henry II** of England, and, like *The Lark,* is one of Anouilh's *pièces costumes.* **Thomas Becket,** a Saxon, is the friend and confidant of King Henry II, and the two feel a deep loyalty and devotion to one another that is undermined when Henry makes Becket Archbishop of Canterbury so that he can control the power of the Church. Becket changes under the mantle of his new responsibility: like Antigone and Joan of Arc, he sees his lonely task as one in which he must defy his former friend and king and do what he believes is right. He is now answerable to God and not a monarch and must champion God's laws even if they run counter to those of his king and former friend. He is not motivated by any deep and abiding love of God, but rather by the necessity to remain faithful to his conception of the honor of God. Henry, baffled and angered at the change in his friend, pleads with him, but to no avail. After openly defying Henry, Becket is forced to flee to France for his own safety. Still feeling the remnants of their former love for one another, the two meet secretly on the coast of France, but their efforts to reconcile are futile. They return separately to England, where Henry has Becket murdered by four of his knights, silencing the man of honor.

The play begins and ends in Canterbury Cathedral, where Henry is forced to pay penance for his role in Becket's death. He begins to think about his friend and to recount their lives together. Thus, the story of their friendship and its tragic consequences unfolds. In the play's conclusion, with his penance complete, Henry announces that he has decided to make Becket a saint and to round up and punish his murderers—entrusting the task to one of the assassins—so that no one will doubt his devotion to the honor of God. Unlike Becket, a heroic individual and a man unwilling to compromise, Henry seems vague in his commitment to anyone except Becket, lacking the moral courage evident in his beloved friend.

As in many of his other works, Anouilh here explores the individual who bravely remains faithful to himself and his ideals, even in the face of death. He once again explores the conflict between God's honor and laws and those of king and state. Becket, his uncompromising hero, faces the world of corruption and compromise and is destroyed by it, facing death alone and aware of the heavy responsibility of the honor of god.

FURTHER READING

Archer, Marguerite. *Jean Anouilh.* New York: Columbia University Press, 1971.

Champigny, Robert. "Theatre in a Mirror: Anouilh." *Yale French Studies,* No. 14 (Winter 1954-55): 57-64.

Contemporary Authors, Vols. 17-20, rev. ed. Detroit: Gale Research Co.

Contemporary Literary Criticism, Vols. 1, 3, 8, 13, 40, 50. Detroit: Gale Research Co.

Curtis, Anthony. *New Developments in the French Theater: A Critical Introduction to the Plays of Jean-Paul Sartre, Simone de Beauvoir, Albert Camus, and Jean Anouilh.* New York: The Curtain Press, 1948.

Falb, Lewis W. *Jean Anouilh.* New York: Ungar, 1977.

Fazia, Alba della. *Jean Anouilh.* New York: Twayne, 1969.

Knapp, Bettina L. and Alba della Fazia. "Introduction." *Becket ou l'Honneur de Dieu* by Jean Anouilh, pp. v-xv. New York: Appleton-Century-Crofts, 1969.

Lenski, B.A. *Jean Anouilh: Stages in Rebellion.* New York: Humanities Press, 1975.

McIntyre, H.G. *The Theater of Jean Anouilh.* New York: Barnes and Noble, 1981.

Stroupe, John H. "Familial Imagery in Anouilh's *Becket.*" *Romance Notes* (Fall 1978): 16-21.

Sholem Asch

1880-1957

Polish-born Yiddish novelist, dramatist, short story writer, and journalist.

"The Christological Trilogy": *The Nazarene* (novel, 1939); *The Apostle* (novel, 1943); *Mary* (novel, 1949)

Asch's trilogy chronicles the beginnings of Christianity and traces its origin in Judaic tradition. **Pan Viadomsky** is a scholar of Roman history who gains the reputation of a trickster during the 1930s in Warsaw when he claims to possess an ancient manuscript which is an eyewitness account of **Yeshua's** (Jesus's) sojourn on Earth. Although an avowed anti-Semitic, Pan Viadomsky agrees to have a young Jewish student, **Jochanan,** come to work for him. Jochanan marvels at Pan Viadomsky's detailed knowledge of Yeshua and gradually the two become friends. One day, Pan Viadomsky reveals to Jochanan the source of his knowledge: he explains that he is the reincarnation of the Hegemon of Jerusalem, Pontius Pilate's right-hand man. He tells Jochanan how they came to be in Jerusalem at that time and describes events leading up to the crucifixion of Yeshua. Pan Viadomsky allows Jochanan to see the manuscript in question, which was supposedly written by **Judah Ish-Kiriot.** Jochanan is startled to realize that he remembers, through his racial heritage, many of the same events recorded in the manuscript. Together, through their memories of the ancient past, Pan Viadomsky and Jochanan are able to piece together the remainder of Yeshua's story. Pan Viadomsky further confesses that since his story has been told he is ready to die, but the spirit of the Hegemon, condemned by Yeshua at his crucifixion to remain forever on earth, will live on in another body.

Asch's second installment of the trilogy follows the growth of Christianity after the crucifixion and focuses on the mission work of **Simon Bar Jonah** and **Saul of Tarshish**. While Simon spread the gospel of Christ's resurrection and plan of salvation for humanity, Saul was commissioned by the Roman government to seek out the Christians and have them arrested. Meanwhile, Simon was performing miracles in the name of the Messiah and even escaped from prison with divine aid. Saul was on his way to Damascus to find more Christians when a vision of the Lord appeared to him demanding to know, "Why dost thou persecute me?" Saul then accepted Christ as his savior and later went to Antioch on his first mission. Until then, the gospel had been preached mainly to the Jews, but Saul realized that he had been chosen by God to spread the word to the Gentile nations. To signify his new mission, Saul was thereafter known as **Paul**. He and Simon endured many hardships as they taught the gospel, but it was a fulfilling and successful undertaking. Both men lost their lives in Nero's widespread purging of the Christians after Rome burned. Their martyrdom, however, served to strengthen the resolve of the early Christians and to ensure Christianity's survival in the next centuries. Although *Mary* concludes the trilogy, it actually covers the beginning and end of Christ's story, and repeats some episodes from *The Nazarene*. It starts when **Miriam** is chosen to bear the Messiah and records her fear and excitement at such a momentous endeavor. The story follows Yeshua's childhood in Nazareth and the climactic events of his adult life. In the course of the novel, Asch presents the emotions and thoughts of Miriam and attempts to answer questions raised by many readers of the Bible about the divinity of Christ.

The novels of Asch's Christological trilogy generated considerable controversy among Jewish readers for his sympathetic portrayal of Christ. Many thought Asch was betraying his Jewish heritage in appearing to accept Jesus as the Messiah. Asch, however, explained that his purpose was to portray the intricate relationship between Jewish and Christian beliefs, which he believed was the root of contemporary Western culture. Asch's understanding of biblical matters is widely admired, and these works have been consistently praised for their realistic depictions of characters and settings.

FURTHER READING

Cargill, Oscar. "Sholem Asch: Still Immigrant and Alien." *College English* 12 (November 1950): 67-74.

Contemporary Authors, Vol. 105. Detroit: Gale Research Co.

George, Ralph W. "Sholem Asch—Man of Letters and Prophet." *Religion in Life* 20 (Winter 1950-1951): 106-113.

Lieberman, Chaim. *The Christianity of Sholem Asch: An Appraisal from the Jewish Viewpoint*. Translated by Abraham Burstein. New York: Philosophical Library, 1953.

Madison, Charles A. "Sholem Asch: Novelist of Lyric Intensity." In *Yiddish Literature: Its Scope and Major Writers*, pp. 221-61. New York: Ungar, 1968.

Twentieth-Century Literary Criticism, Vol. 3. Detroit: Gale Research Co.

Margaret Atwood

1939-

Canadian novelist, short story writer, poet, and essayist.

Lady Oracle (novel, 1976)

The novel is set in England and Canada and relates the story of **Joan Foster**'s adolescence

and maturation into womanhood. She is bright and talented; she is also, however, grossly overweight, and she uses her obesity as a shield against the world. Eventually, she feels the need for independence, but is financially destitute. When her adored **Aunt Louisa K. Delacourt** dies, Joan learns that she has left her a large sum of money, but she must reduce before receiving any of her inheritance. Surprisingly, Louisa's mandate is inspirational, and Joan quickly loses weight. Afterwards, Joan adopts her aunt's name and begins to write novels. She also meets **Arthur Foster,** a political activist, whom she marries. Joan then develops another alter ego—**Lady Oracle,** the mystic poet, whose work meets with overwhelming success. Despite her accomplishments, Joan is undone by her identities, her new appearance, and the pressures of fame. A frustrated Joan stages her suicide by pretending to drown in Lake Ontario. She then moves to Italy to start a new life.

Lady Oracle is a humorous novel with a feminist theme in which Atwood closely analyzes the concept of appearances. Joan is ashamed of her obesity, but alarmed by the reaction of others when she is slim. As a famous author, she is fawned over, but she realizes she is not "Lady Oracle"; she is still, in her heart, the homely Joan Foster who is self-conscious and insecure. She knows, too, that the attention she garners is not directed at her, but towards her image. When she stages her death, she is actually killing the false Joan—Lady Oracle, the authoress and media darling.

The Handmaid's Tale (novel, 1985)

Set in Massachusetts, this dystopian novel takes place several decades in the future. After the assassination of the president and the suspension of the Constitution, the United States is no longer operating as a democracy; rather, it is a religious dictatorship called the Republic of Gilead. **Offred,** the narrator and protagonist, is a married woman and a mother who, while trying to escape the country, has been taken as a government hostage. Her daughter has been kidnapped and her husband is presumed dead. Offred, whose name derives from the name of her Commander, **Fred,** is to be a Handmaid, forced into surrogate motherhood for Fred and his wife, who is now too old to bear children. In the totalitarian theocracy of Gilead, terror and fear reign; public executions are commonplace and secret police control the state. Women's roles are defined by their ability to breed, for infertility is on the rise in the country. Thus Offred is indoctrinated at the Rachel and Leah Centre and sent to Fred's home to do her duty. Should she not become pregnant, she will be sent to a toxic waste site for the remainder of her days. Should she break the many laws that control all aspects of women's lives in the society, she will face death. Although she is forbidden to read, Offred revels in the joy of language and loves word play, and as her consciousness of her situation develops, her narrative voice grows in complexity and depth.

Offred is haunted with memories of the way life used to be, of what was lost in the apocalypse that turned the nation into a misogynist nightmare. She remembers her mother, a devoted feminist who crusaded against pornography, yet is instructed by the Aunts, a group of thought-police who educate the women in the new way of thinking, that there was too much "choice." Yet the new regime has forgotten about the necessity of love, and it is through love that Offred attempts to make her escape. She begins an affair with **Nick,** the chauffeur of the Commander, who is involved with the underworld that seeks to subvert the theocracy, and together they plot their flight.

The Handmaid's Tale is a cautionary tale offering an insightful, disturbing warning against political and religious extremism. Once again, Atwood depicts a woman who is victimized by men and literally held captive by their expectations and desires. Although the work was controversial, it is considered by many critics to be Atwood's finest novel to date.

FURTHER READING

Cameron, Elspeth. "Margaret Atwood: A Patchwork Self." *Book Forum* 4, No. 1 (1978): 35-45.

Contemporary Authors, Vols. 49-52; *Contemporary Authors New Revision Series,* Vol. 3. Detroit: Gale Research Co.

Contemporary Literary Criticism, Vols. 2, 3, 4, 8, 13, 15, 25, 44. Detroit: Gale Research Co.

Dictionary of Literary Biography, Vol. 53. Detroit: Gale Research Co.

Ehrenreich, Barbara. "Feminism's Phantom." *The New Republic* 194, No. 11 (17 March 1986): 33-5.

Glendinning, Victoria. "Lady Oracle." *Saturday Night* 101, No. 1 (January 1986): 39-41.

Grace, Sherrill. *Violent Duality: A Study of Margaret Atwood.* Montreal: Vehicule Press, 1980.

McCarthy, Mary. "Breeders, Wives, and Unwoman." *The New York Times Book Review* (9 February 1986): 1, 35.

McPherson, William. "New Lives for Old." *Book World—The Washington Post* (26 September 1976): 1.

Rosengarten, Herbert. "Urbane Comedy." *Canadian Literature* (Spring 1977) 84-7.

Isaac Babel

1894-1941?

Russian short story writer, dramatist, and essayist.

"My First Goose" (short story, 1924)

This brief, image-laden story, from Babel's famous *Red Cavalry* collection, is set in a Cossack cavalry camp somewhere in Poland. **Kiril Liutov** has newly arrived, sent as a propaganda officer to bolster morale in the 1920 Russian campaign. **Commander Savitsky** receives Liutov with disdain, for Liutov is an intellectual, wears "specs," and is Jewish. As the quartermaster escorts Liutov to the soldiers' hut, he offers the following advice in order that the newcomer might assimilate with the coarse, anti-Semitic division: "go and mess up a lady, and a good lady too, and you'll have the boys patting you on the back." After enduring tirelessly rude treatment from the Cossacks, Liutov puts aside his issue of *Pravda* and approaches the partially blind landlady sitting on the porch. He demands food and, unsuccessful, pushes the woman aside, grabs a nearby sword, and overtakes a goose waddling in the yard. After brutally killing the bird, Liutov has the landlady clean and cook it. The Cossacks, "stiff as heathen priests at a sacrifice," now invite him to join their circle. Liutov eats their pork and cabbage soup and favors them by reciting Lenin's latest speech. Later, Liutov and the men huddle together to keep warm as they sleep. "I dreamed: and in my dreams saw women. But my heart, stained with bloodshed, grated and brimmed over."

Morally unable to harm another human, Liutov, through his sacrifice of the goose, symbolically commits the rape recommended to him. The ambivalence of his perceptions and the fact that he regards his deed as deplorable is typical of the protagonists in the *Red Cavalry* stories. Babel himself, though a proponent of and participant in the Russian campaign, could never reconcile the violence he witnessed with the political theories he espoused. Considered his masterpiece, *Red Cavalry* is praised for the emotional depth of its

stories: vivid war sketches that have earned Babel a prominent reputation as both a brilliant stylist and a sophisticated observer of human nature.

"Di Grasso" (short story, 1937)

The last work Babel published in his lifetime, "Di Grasso" is set in prewar Odessa, circa 1908. The narrator reminisces about a time when he was fourteen and in the employ of an unscrupulous ticket scalper, **Nick Schwarz.** A Sicilian theatrical company has arrived in town to perform a hackneyed folk pastoral. The narrator condescendingly details the plot which, surprisingly, soars dramatically in the final act when the tragedian **Di Grasso** magnificently leaps across the stage and plunges downward onto his arrogant rival, piercing his throat and sucking the gushing blood as the curtain closes.

The story returns to the boy, who had earlier pawned his father's watch and now despairs of having it returned, for despite his repayment, Schwarz refuses to surrender the watch. However, when Schwarz's wife views the final performance of the play, she is overcome with emotion. Upon hearing the boy's sobs while walking home, she discovers her husband's viciousness and forces him to return the watch immediately. Left alone in the moonlight to consider his change of fate, the boy "saw for the first time the things surrounding [him] as they really were—frozen in silence and ineffably beautiful."

Written two years before Babel's arrest and disappearance, "Di Grasso" has been studied as the writer's parting shot at the Stalin regime for its suppression of artistic works that did not wholly serve its proletarian cause. This interpretation is supported by Schwarz's character, his "enormous silky handle bars" and violent disposition, and multiple references to unwelcome regulation and confinement. Yet, "Di Grasso" is primarily a story which affirms the power of art to transform reality, to create freedom. For the narrator, Di Grasso confirmed "with every word and movement that there is more justice and hope in the frenzy of noble passion than in all the joyless rules of the world." Although Babel produced a relatively small body of work, his fiction has been widely praised by Western readers and critics, and today he is recognized as one of the masters of the Russian short story.

FURTHER READING

Andrew, J. M. "Structure and Style in the Short Story: Babel's 'My First Goose'." *The Modern Language Review* 70, No. 2 (April 1975): 366-79.

Carden, Patricia. *The Art of Isaac Babel.* Ithaca: Cornell University Press, 1972.

Contemporary Authors, Vol. 104. Detroit: Gale Research Co.

Ehre, Milton. *Isaac Babel.* Boston: Twayne, 1986.

Falen, James E. *Isaac Babel: Russian Master of the Short Story.* Knoxville: University of Tennessee Press, 1974.

Trilling, Lionel. Introduction to *The Collected Stories,* by Isaac Babel, edited and translated by Walter Morison, pp. 9-37. New York: Criterion Books, 1955.

Twentieth-Century Literary Criticism, Vols. 2, 13. Detroit: Gale Research Co.

Yarmolinsky, Avrahm. "Isaac Babel (1894-1941)—An Odessa Maupassant?" In *The Russian Literary Imagination,* pp. 131-86. New York: Funk & Wagnalls, 1969.

James Baldwin
1924-1987

American novelist and essayist.

Go Tell It on the Mountain (novel, 1953)

Set in Harlem in the 1930s, the novel is divided into three parts and is concerned with the religious conversion of **John Grimes.** In Part I, John is fourteen years old and is beset with feelings of guilt and ambivalence about sex, his relationship with his parents, and his growing hatred for whites. In Part II, we learn about the Grimes family in a series of flashbacks, a narrative technique that Baldwin was to employ extensively in his later fiction. This section offers insight into John's character with background information on his mother, **Elizabeth,** who gave birth to John before her marriage to his father, **Gabriel.** Gabriel is a storefront preacher whose cruelty to his bastard son is revealed as indicative of his harsh, unloving nature. In this section Baldwin also explores the deadening effects of racism on generations of blacks. The third section of the novel deals with John's conversion. As he lies on the floor before the altar of the Temple of the Fire Baptized, he is surrounded with visions of saints and demons, a truly surrealistic state from which he emerges cleansed, whole, and certain about the direction his life will take.

Like much of Baldwin's work, *Go Tell It on the Mountain* has distinctive autobiographical overtones, and many of the themes that characterize his later works, among them the nature of the father-son relationship, the meaning of religion in black life, and the importance of suffering, were first voiced in this novel. Like John, Baldwin was also the bastard son of a cruel storefront minister, and he, too, wrestled with the problems of familial love and identity inherent in this theme. Baldwin posits that religion is a deluding rather than a liberating force for blacks and depicts it as a means by which the enslavement of black culture by whites is perpetuated. His recurrent theme of suffering as a means to salvation and a sense of identity is also evoked in this novel, which has been called a *bildungsroman* of sorts as it chronicles the maturity of John Grimes. Stylistically, the work is characterized by Baldwin's cadenced, almost Biblical prose style and controlled narrative presentation.

Giovanni's Room (novel, 1956)

The novel chronicles the quest for sexual identity of the protagonist, **David.** A white American, David is confronted in early adulthood with his homosexual feelings and is appalled by them, for to give into them would be a rejection of the precepts of what it is to be a man in white, Western culture. He joins the Army hoping to resolve his concern, yet is still unable to come to grips with his sexual nature. Next, he journeys to Paris where he meets and proposes marriage to **Hella Lincoln.** Hella, unsure of her feelings for David, travels to Spain to contemplate their relationship. During her absence, David meets **Giovanni,** an Italian bartender. They begin a homosexual affair that is doomed from the start, for David cannot accept himself and therefore cannot give Giovanni the love that he needs. Despondent at David's rejection, Giovanni gives in to the sexual advances of his employer, then kills him. He is brought to trial, convicted, and sentenced to death for murder. In the novel's conclusion, Hella, having returned from Spain and discovered the truth about David, leaves him; Giovanni awaits execution, and David remains unresolved and alone.

Although the novel differs from Baldwin's other fiction in that all the characters are white, thematically the work explores many of the same subjects. Principal among these are the themes of sexuality and identity. Baldwin posits that it is through the honest expression of one's sexuality that identity is achieved. This theme is expanded and explored most notably in Baldwin's next novel, *Another Country*. Critics have praised Baldwin's courage in exploring a theme that was certainly taboo in the 1950s, and many found his treatment to be both sensitive and restrained.

Another Country (novel, 1962)

Another Country is an in-depth study of modern society and the malaise of modern urban life. Set in New York City, the work contains three sections and covers four narratives. Each of these narratives focuses on two characters, and all eight major characters interact throughout the novel. The pairs of characters represent the polarities of black/white and heterosexual/homosexual existence. The first narrative focuses on **Rufus Scott** and **Leona;** he is a black musician, she is his white mistress. Rufus's despair over his plight as a black man in a racist society eventually drives him to suicide and Leona to madness. The second narrative sequence covers **Ida Scott** and **Vivaldo Moore.** Ida is Rufus's sister, who makes it her goal to avenge her brother's death. Vivaldo, an Italian-American writer, feels somehow responsible for Rufus's death, and the knowledge haunts him. **Cass** and **Richard Selenski's** relationship form the third narrative. They are the only "conventional" couple in the novel, both white, married, and deeply troubled in their lives together. The fourth narrative involves **Eric Jones** and **Yves,** two white homosexuals whose relationship symbolizes sexual fulfillment and self-awareness.

During the course of the novel, the characters' lives are intertwined through a variety of sexual encounters— heterosexual, homosexual, and bisexual—played out against a social framework that represents social and sexual repression and that is hostile to their strivings for love and self-knowledge.

In this work, Baldwin explores his recurrent themes of isolation and the power of sexuality to overcome alienation and to lead to insight and the discovery of one's identity. He examines the traditional divisions of society, racial and sexual, depicting his characters as trapped and isolated within them. Through the exploration of one's sexuality Baldwin says, love and self-knowledge can be achieved.

FURTHER READING

Baker, Houston A., Jr. "The Embattled Craftsman: An Essay on James Baldwin." *Journal of Afro-American Affairs* 1, No.1 (1977): 28-51.

Bone, Robert. "The Novels of James Baldwin." *Tri-Quarterly* 2 (Winter 1965): 3-20.

Contemporary Authors, Vols. 1-4, rev. ed.; *Contemporary Authors New Revision Series,* Vol. 3; *Contemporary Authors Bibliographical Series,* Vol. 1. Detroit: Gale Research Co.

Contemporary Literary Criticism, Vols. 1, 2, 3, 4, 5, 8, 13, 15, 17, 42, 50. Detroit: Gale Research Co.

Dictionary of Literary Biography, Vols. 2, 7, 33; *Concise Dictionary of American Literary Biography, 1941-1968.* Detroit: Gale Research Co.

Gross, Barry. "The 'Uninhabitable Darkness' of Baldwin's *Another Country:* Image and Theme." *Black American Literature Forum* 6 (Winter 1972): 113-21.

Macebuh, Stanley. *James Baldwin: A Critical Study.* New York: Joseph Okpaku, 1973.

Newman, Charles. "The Lesson of the Master: Henry James and James Baldwin." *Yale Review* 56 (Oct. 1966): 45-59.

Pratt, Louis Hill. *James Baldwin.* Boston: Twayne, 1978.

Standley, Fred L. "*Another Country,* Another Time." *Studies in the Novel* 4 (Fall 1972): 504-12.

Sylvander, Carolyn Wedin. *James Baldwin.* New York: Ungar, 1980.

Wasserstrom, William. "James Baldwin: Stepping Out on the Promise." In *Black Fiction: New Studies in the Afro-American Novel since 1945,* edited by Robert Lee, pp. 74-96. New York: Barnes & Noble, 1980.

Djuna Barnes

1892-1982

American novelist, short story writer, and dramatist.

Nightwood (novel, 1936)

The novel is set variously in Paris, Berlin, and the countryside of New York and focuses on **Robin Vote** and her relationships with several characters. She represents the human psyche divided against itself, and the novel documents her search for unity and identity. Barnes's major theme in the work is the necessity to acknowledge the duality of human nature, both the primordial, bestial side and the reasoned elements. When we first encounter Robin, she is described in animal images, and we are told that she is "the infected carrier of the past." Throughout the work, she is associated with images of darkness, violence, and wild beasts.

Robin meets and marries **Felix Volbein,** a European obsessed with aristocracy and nobility who calls himself the Baron. The two have a child, but Robin leaves them soon after the birth. She is described walking the streets of Paris at night, like an animal stalking its prey. She meets and falls in love with **Nora Flood,** who, like Felix, is drawn to her animality. As their affair progresses, Nora comes to know that she is drawn to the depravity and bestiality that Robin represents, and that only in death would Robin be totally hers. Robin begins to roam again, and Nora is left in despair, seeking out the counsel of **Dr. Matthew O'Connor.** This occasions what for many is the central focus of the book, an extended section of Dr. O'Connor's thoughts on all aspects of life. His monologues, barely broken by Nora's brief questions or responses, provide a unifying focus for the novel, for he is the spokesman for Barnes's main theme of the need to unify the civilized and the primordial. A narrator of sorts, in his monologues he is speaking at once to other characters and to the reader. His conversations are characterized by their wit, humility, and insight into the despair of the other characters, particularly as they try to understand their attraction to Robin.

Robin has now ensnared **Jenny Petherbridge,** a character as desperately in love with her as Felix and Nora. The two of them leave Europe for America. Yet once in New York, Robin begins to wander again, this time seeking out animals in the wild, unable to communicate with humans. In the novel's enigmatic conclusion, it is evident that the love that Felix, Nora, and Jenny have had for Robin has destroyed them, and that she is slipping deeper and deeper into her animal self.

Stylistically, *Nightwood* represented a brilliant point of departure for American fiction. The disjointed narrative is unified through the repetition of images, particularly imagery associated with animals, darkness, and night. The tone of the novel is a blend of comedy and terror, enhanced by Barnes's authorial detachment. The prose style is noted for its lyrical and poetic qualities.

FURTHER READING

Burke, Kenneth. "Version, Con-, Per-, and In- (Thoughts on Djuna Barnes's Novel, *Nightwood*)." *Southern Review,* new series, 2 (1966-1967): 329-40.

Contemporary Authors, Vols. 9-12, rev. ed., 107. *Contemporary Authors New Revisions Series,* Vol. 16. Detroit: Gale Research Co.

Contemporary Literary Criticism, Vols. 3, 4, 8, 11, 29. Detroit: Gale Research Co.

Dictionary of Literary Biography, Vols. 4, 9, 45. Detroit: Gale Research Co.

Frank, Joseph. "Spatial Form in Modern Literature." *Sewanee Review* 53 (Summer 1945): 433-56.

Hawkes, John. "Notes on the Wild Goose Chase." *Massachusetts Review* 3 (Summer 1962): 784-88.

Scott, James B. *Djuna Barnes.* Boston: Twayne, 1976.

John Barth
1930-

American novelist, short story writer, and essayist.

The Floating Opera (novel, 1956; rev. ed. 1967)

Barth described *The Floating Opera* as the first of three nihilistic novels. **Todd Andrews** is a middle-aged lawyer living in Tidewater, Maryland, a recurrent setting for Barth, when the novel begins. The focus is Todd's decision to commit suicide. With this point of departure, Todd reflects on his life. Todd's story concerns the quest for self-knowledge as he grows from belief to despair to an awareness of the relativity of values. One of Barth's major motifs is masks and masking, and we see Todd revealed in a number of poses and personae as he seeks his identity. Todd's final decision to choose life over death is not described by Barth as a life-affirming action; instead, it is a simple, relative choice.

The Floating Opera of the title refers to a Maryland riverboat and its journeys, which parallel the wanderings of the hero. The narrative style of the novel, which critics note owes a great deal to Laurence Sterne's *Tristam Shandy,* is digressive, rambling, and discursive as its hero offers his stream-of-consciousness account of life.

The publisher of the first edition of *The Floating Opera* forced Barth to change the ending, making it more sentimental and less in keeping with his original, nihilistic tone. After the success of *Giles Goat-Boy* ten years later, Barth extensively revised his first novel, reinstated his original conclusion, and republished the work.

The Sot-Weed Factor (novel, 1966)

Although *The Sot-Weed Factor* shares the same Maryland setting of Barth's previous novels, stylistically the work proved to be a great departure. It is a pastiche of the eighteenth-century picaresque novel and is not only imitative but parodic. The story is based on a poem of the same title by a true historical figure, **Ebenezer Cooke,** who established himself as poet laureate of Maryland in the eighteenth century, and parts of the poem are reproduced throughout the text. Barth's approach here is to blend fact with fiction and authentic historical documents with falsifications to explore the nature of history and literary imagination. Ebenezer suffers from cosmopsis, the cosmic paralysis that afflicts those incapable of decision. His story is the hero's quest for identity, in this case played out against the New World. All the conventional literary allusions and historical associations involved in the hero's journey as well as the Edenic qualities of colonial America are parodied and exploited by Barth. An example of this is Barth's retelling of the story of Pocahontas and Captain Smith, which in his hands becomes a bawdy farce.

Another major character in this work is **Henry Burlingame,** tutor to Ebenezer and his twin sister **Anna.** Burlingame encourages his young charges to playact and experiment with masks, instructing them in creating a variety of identities. Burlingame himself is a foundling, and as such is free to create both his past and his current persona, and he appears in a number of disguises throughout the novel. As "tutor" to Ebenezer, his task is to inculcate in him an understanding that only "creation and faith" are worthy goals.

The Sot-Weed Factor is generally considered Barth's finest achievement, and critics have praised and examined Barth's parody of literary devices and historical perception. Several have noted the lack of depth in the characterizations that some attribute to the nature of parody.

Giles Goat-Boy; or, The Revised New Syllabus (novel, 1960)

The novel centers on **George Giles** as he chronicles his life and feeds it into WES-CAC, a computer whose acronym stands for West Campus Automatic Computer. Barth employs an allegorical structure, in which the University equals the Universe, West Campus is the Western powers, East Campus represents the Soviet and Eastern powers, the student body is humankind, and the sacred texts they study are the syllabi which Giles is developing.

This tale, which incorporates elements of fantasy, is also a *bildungsroman* of sorts, for it chronicles the development of Giles from a goat-boy to a man. In this the novel parallels Barth's other fictions in its depiction of the hero's quest for wisdom. As such, Giles is educated, embarks on a voyage, endures the temptations of the flesh, is executed and reborn.

Critical to Barth's narrative strategy in this work is his use of frame technique. Giles's story, the "Revised New Syllabus" of the title, is prefaced with a publisher's disclaimer and a cover letter to the editors and publisher, written by "J.B." (considered to be John Barth himself). The Syllabus is followed by a Postscript and Posttape by J.B., and a Footnote to the Postscript and the Posttape by the editor. In utilizing this device, Barth draws attention to the artifice of novel writing, a central theme in his work. Also important to an understanding of Barth's treatment of Giles is the author's study of myths and legends prior to composition of the novel. Although the hero's quest had been a major theme in his work prior to *Giles Goat-Boy,* the novel reveals a more studied approach to the archetype and its history in fiction.

FURTHER READING

Contemporary Authors, Vols. 1-4, rev. ed.; *Contemporary Authors New Revision Series,* Vol. 5; *Contemporary Authors Bibliographical Series,* Vol. 1. Detroit: Gale Research Co.

Contemporary Literary Criticism, Vols. 1, 2, 3, 5, 7, 9, 10, 14, 27, 51. Detroit: Gale Research Co.

Dictionary of Literary Biography, Vol. 2. Detroit: Gale Research Co.

Diser, Philip E. "The Historical Ebenezer Cooke." *Critique* 10, No. 3 (1968): 48-59.

Fiedler, Leslie. "John Barth: An Eccentric Genius." *New Leader* 44 (13 February 1961): 22-4.

Gross, Beverly. "The Anti-Novels of John Barth." *Chicago Review* 20 (November 1968): 95-109.

Helterman, Jeffrey. *John Barth's "Giles Goat-Boy": A Critical Commentary.* New York: Monarch, 1973.

Kennard, Jean E. "John Barth: Imitations of Imitations." *Mosaic* 3, No. 2 (1970): 116-31.

McDonald, James L. "Barth's Syllabus: The Frame of *Giles Goat-Boy.*" *Critique* 13, No. 3 (1972): 5-10.

Miller, Russell H. "*The Sot-Weed Factor:* A Contemporary Mock-Epic." *Critique* 8, No. 2 (Winter 1965-1966): 88-100.

Morrell, David. *John Barth: An Introduction.* University Park: Pennsylvania State University Press, 1976.

Noland, Richard W. "John Barth and the Novel of Comic Nihilism." *Wisconsin Studies in Contemporary Literature* 7 (Autumn 1966): 239-57.

Schickel, Richard. "*The Floating Opera.*" *Critique* 6, No. 2 (1963): 53-67.

Stubbs, John C. "John Barth as a Novelist of Ideas: The Themes of Value and Identity." *Critique* 8, No. 2 (Winter 1965-1966): 101-16.

Tanner, Tony. *City of Words: American Fiction, 1950-1970,* pp. 230-59. New York: Harper & Row, 1971.

Simone de Beauvoir
1908-1986
French philosopher, novelist, and essayist.

The Mandarins (novel, 1954)

Although best known as a philosopher and as the author of the highly influential feminist study *The Second Sex,* Beauvoir also wrote a number of novels, including *The Mandarins,* a *roman a clef* in which she depicted the lives of several prominent French intellectuals, including Jean-Paul Sartre and Albert Camus. The focus of the novel is the affair of the heroine, **Anne Dubreuilh,** with an American writer, based on Beauvoir's relationship with the American writer Nelson Algren. The novel was Beauvoir's first after she had completed *The Second Sex,* and in it she explores her insights into women's position in society.

The novel begins with the liberation of Paris in 1944. She shows the initial shock of a group of young intellectuals, the "mandarins" of the title, as they move from the exultation of liberation and freedom to an understanding of the world in flux around them. They argue and challenge one another's views as they confront the leading social, political, and philosophical issues of the era: the news of the horrors of the Stalin regime, the approach of the Cold War, and the political foment in their own country. Beauvoir explores the themes of art and its place in life, the conflict between the public and private persona among the politically engaged, and the desire for and commitment to social reform that motivates her characters. Seen through the eyes of Anne and her friend **Henri Perron,** these people are obsessed with language and philosophy, and Beauvoir shows them arguing among themselves, while outside the world is experiencing a whirlwind of change. Her female characters seem curiously unengaged with the politics that consume the male characters; they seem instead to be dominated by their dependency on men and their fear of aging and of losing their romantic attachments. Anne, a psychiatrist, has married a man much older than herself, a father figure. She allows her love affair and its consequences to dominate her life; when it ends, her life is in turmoil. As she approaches middle-age, she begins to fear age and death, and even contemplates suicide. A woman of intelligence, compassion, and strength, she at last comes to an awareness of the emptiness of her life and is determined to change.

Although the novel was awarded the Prix Goncourt, France's highest literary prize, it is not noted for its fine prose style. Rather, it is the panoramic sweep of history and the philosophic depth of the novel that have made it Beauvoir's most celebrated work of fiction. Beauvoir was opposed to the refinement of style and the lack of political and social import that she felt characterized most post-war fiction, and some critics believe that the rather pedestrian prose of her novel reflects this philosophy.

FURTHER READING

Contemporary Authors, Vols. 9-12, rev. ed., 118. Detroit: Gale Research Co.

Contemporary Literary Criticism, Vols. 1, 2, 4, 8, 31, 44, 50. Detroit: Gale Research Co.

Cottrell, Robert D. *Simone de Beauvoir.* New York: Ungar, 1975.

Dictionary of Literary Biography, Vol. 72; *Dictionary of Literary Biography Yearbook: 1986.* Detroit: Gale Research Co.

Harth, Erica. "The Creative Alienation of the Writer: Sartre, Camus, and Simone de Beauvoir." *MOSAIC* 8, No. 3 (Spring 1975): 177-86.

Leighton, Jean. *Simone de Beauvoir on Woman.* Rutherford: Fairleigh Dickinson University Press, 1975.

Samuel Beckett

1906-

Irish-born dramatist, novelist, short story writer, and essayist.

Molloy (novel, 1951); *Malone Dies* (novel, 1951); *The Unnamable* (novel, 1954)

These three works are generally understood to form a trilogy in which four characters— **Molloy, Moran, Malone,** and **The Unnamable**—form a single narrative consciousness.

As *Molloy* begins, we see a setting that is repeated throughout the trilogy, that of the narrator-protagonist in bed, writing. The works all focus on the act of creating, and it is not action but language, especially the playing with language, meaning, and the possibilities of knowing, that forms the essence of the work.

The first half of the novel is narrated by Molloy, who tells us of his quest, his journey to find his mother. He had set out on his bicycle to visit her, but had been distracted by a series of adventures that brought him into contact with a variety of characters and incidents. Now he sits in his mother's bed—she is dead—and waits for death. He catalogs what he has lost: he can't move his legs, the toes on one foot are gone, and so is the bike. He has been rescued and brought to this room by forces he does not know. Indeed, uncertainty abounds in his description of his journey, and an absurd, ambiguous, and self-negating atmosphere envelops the narrative, setting the reader on guard regarding the narrator's reliability.

Moran now takes over the narrative. He had also begun a quest, to look for Molloy. He also travels on bicycle, with his son. Also like Molloy, he returns home having deteriorated physically. His story had begun with definitive statements: "It's midnight. It's raining," which he contradicts in the conclusion. As in *Waiting for Godot,* nothing is determined in the novel; circularity rather than resolution ends the work.

In *Malone Dies* we see the protagonist in bed, writing, like Molloy and Moran. He, too, is recording his journey toward death, and is also at work on a piece of fiction. As in the other novels, we are aware of the artificiality of the form, as Malone comments on his problems with his stories. The novel is a satire on writing and on the concept of art imitating life. In

Malone's fiction, the character **Saposcat** changes into the character **Macmann,** whose name echoes the protagonists of the trilogy. Macmann is confined in an institution, and he and Malone die at the same time, as Malone is still relating his character's story. In common with his fellow protagonists, Malone is frustrated to the point of giving up, yet he goes on, for he can't do anything but write.

The Unnamable has for its protagonist a disembodied persona, only a voice. He is also writing, in a space that is described as opaque. The characters of the trilogy and other of Beckett's works are brought back in this novel, and the new characters—**Mahood, Basil,** and **Worm**—are introduced. In the opening sequence, the Unnamable wonders: "Where now? Who now? When now?" and the entire narrative offers an unstable point of view, as the reader is unsure who is speaking and which character is in control of the work. Fragmented syntax characterizes the novel, reflecting the Unnamable's own confusion, as the reader also wonders whether he blends with or creates his characters. Yet the indomitable spirit he shares with Beckett's prototypical figures is evident in the closing sequence, when he utters: "In the silence you don't know, you must go on, I can't go on, I'll go on."

These narratives have been called a sequence of four soliloquies in which Beckett explores language, meaning, and the creative act. The absurd existence is both suffered and chronicled in these works, as the aging, decaying protagonists are driven by their need to tell their story, in essence to create themselves. Although they all share a disgust for human existence, they are united in their need to "go on."

Waiting for Godot (drama, 1953)

This drama, considered one of the most influential of the modern theater, takes place on "a country road" where the only scenery is a tree. This simple, spare setting is the scene for the dialogues of **Estragon** and **Vladimir,** or Gogo and Didi, as they call one another, two tramps who are waiting for **Godot,** with whom they have an appointment. The play has been described as a work in which "nothing happens twice," for in the span of the two acts, we witness the characters in the act of waiting, going through an exercise in repetition whose meaning remains obscure. Variously interpreted as a Christian allegory, an indication of the despair and alienation that underlie human life, or the individual's triumph over the absurdity that governs existence, *Waiting for Godot* is ultimately an enigmatic play that refuses to yield to one single interpretation.

The play's tone ranges widely, as the protagonists move from slapstick comedy, reminiscent of the circus or music hall, to a bitter acknowledgment of the futility of existence, to an ironic insight into their plight, to a tender awareness of their mutual affection. Beckett's protagonists are at once clowns and grotesques—mocking themselves and the literary types they represent—and tormented everymen, embodying the hopelessness of the human condition in the modern world. Their relationship appears to mirror that of humankind, for they are torn between their mutual dependence and their isolation, alternately embracing and threatening to leave one another. They discuss their boots, their hats, philosophy, religion, and the prospect of hanging themselves, shifting topics as rapidly as the play changes tone.

Their dialogue is interrupted by the entrance of **Pozzo** and **Lucky.** Lucky appears to be Pozzo's slave and beast of burden, with a rope around his neck and his arms full of baggage. Pozzo seems to enjoy the sadomasochistic control he exerts over the other man, and for many critics they represent the cruelty that governs human relationships and are meant to be compared and contrasted to Estragon and Vladimir, who are at once attracted and repelled by this perverse couple. The first act ends with the appearance of a little boy who announces that Godot will not appear today, but surely tomorrow.

The second act is much like the first, with Gogo and Didi discussing the same topics as in

Act I, and with the reappearance of Pozzo and Lucky, although now Pozzo is blind and has no recollection of meeting them; Estragon, too, does not remember. Memory and repetition, themes that resonate throughout Beckett's work, are here the pronounced metaphors for the circularity of existence. This act ends, as did the first, with the boy reappearing to announce that Godot will not come today, but surely tomorrow; they agree to leave, but, as the stage direction tells us, they do not move. Repetition, not resolution, characterizes existence for these two figures, and by extension, for all humanity.

Endgame (drama, 1957)

Set in a seemingly post-apocalyptic world, this play focusses on another pair of Beckett characters, who, like Vladimir and Estragon, are embattled in the quest to determine meaning in existence. The atmosphere of the play is one of confinement and isolation: **Hamm** is blind and confined to a wheelchair; **Clov**'s eyes and legs are bad, but he "can move"; Hamm's parents, **Nell** and **Nagg,** live in trash cans. Their restricted existence takes place in a single room, while outside all is "death," and all nature is "corpsed." The longing for death is evident throughout, from the opening lines "Finished, it's finished, it must be nearly finished," to the concluding words: "you . . . remain." While a variety of interpretations have been set forth, this appears to be a despairing, agonizing vision of the individual's cosmic pain in confronting life. Yet the misery outlined in the work appears to be mitigated by the sense of the artificiality of the piece, by Hamm's and Clov's awareness that they are indeed in a play, evident in such lines as "an aside, ape!" and "not an underplot, I trust."

As in *Waiting for Godot,* the work is essentially plotless. The "endgame" of the title is taken from chess, and according to Beckett, Hamm plays the role of the king in a game already lost. The motif of games and of playing, which recurs throughout Beckett's work, is central to the play, for Hamm and Clov appear to be repeating roles in a game that they have played over and over again, with the same questions, answers, and "inanities." Their lives seem circumscribed by dependence and hostility, and Clov repeatedly claims to be leaving Hamm, yet it is all part of the "game," to be played indefinitely.

Krapp's Last Tape (drama, 1958)

In this play, **Krapp,** an old man of sixty-nine, sits listening to tapes of his earlier life. Set in Krapp's den, a room with a desk covered with boxes of tapes and a ledger, the play focusses on a character, who, like Vladimir and Estragon, is described as rather clown-like, with a red nose, white face, and tattered pants. In a mime that opens the play, he nearly slips on a banana peel, adding to the vaudeville-like atmosphere. He alternately listens to his tapes and goes off stage where we hear him open a bottle and drink. As he becomes more drunk, we learn of his earlier life through the tapes. The first recording he plays relates his recollections on life when he was thirty-nine, a man in the prime of life. This middle-aged Krapp refers to another tape, one done ten or twelve years earlier. Thus, we glimpse Krapp at three stages—youth, maturity, and old age. He recalls eating bananas, remembers an old lady singing, reminisces about living with a woman named Bianca, and talks about sex, drinking, family, and happiness. Krapp, as he listens to the tape, laughs at his former self, and at one point even goes to look up a word he used. He switches the tape on and off and moves it forward and backward in time, seeming to avoid those sequences in which his former self talks about the meaning of life, and referring to the younger voice as a "stupid bastard."

Beckett again returns to his themes of memory, isolation, and time in this brief work, examining through his protagonist the nature of identity.

FURTHER READING

Adams, Robert Martin. "Samuel Beckett." In *AfterJoyce: Studies in Fiction After "Ulysses,"* pp. 90-113. New York: Oxford University Press, 1977.

Bair, Deirdre. *Samuel Beckett.* New York: Harcourt Brace Jovanovich, 1978.

Brater, Enoch, ed. *Beckett at Eighty/Beckett in Context.* New York: Oxford University Press, 1986.

Cohn, Ruby. *Back to Beckett.* Princeton: Princeton University Press, 1973.

——. *Just Play: Beckett's Theater.* Princeton: Princeton University Press, 1980.

Contemporary Authors, Vols. 5-8, rev. ed. Detroit: Gale Research Co.

Contemporary Literary Criticism, Vols. 1, 2, 3, 4, 6, 9, 10, 11, 14, 18, 29. Detroit: Gale Research Co.

Dictionary of Literary Biography, Vols. 13, 15. Detroit: Gale Research Co.

Esslin, Martin. "Samuel Beckett: The Search for Self." In *The Theatre of the Absurd,* pp. 11-65. New York: Doubleday, 1969.

Friedman, Melvin J., ed. *Samuel Beckett Now.* Chicago: University of Chicago Press, 1970.

Kenner, Hugh. *Samuel Beckett: A Critical Study.* Berkeley: University of California Press, 1968.

Mayoux, Jean-Jacques. *Samuel Beckett.* London: British Council, 1974.

Mercier, Vivian. *Beckett/Beckett.* New York: Oxford University Press, 1977.

Sachner, Mark J. "The Artist as Fiction: An Aesthetics of Failure in Samuel Beckett's Trilogy." *The Midwest Quarterly* 18, No. 2 (January 1977): 144-55.

Schlueter, June. "Beckett's Didi and Gogo, Hamm and Clov." In *Metafictional Characters in Modern Drama.* New York: Columbia University Press, 1977.

Webb, Eugene. *The Plays of Samuel Beckett.* Seattle: University of Washington Press, 1974.

Wilcher, Robert. "'What's It Meant to Mean?': An Approach to Beckett's Theatre." *Critical Quarterly* (Summer 1976): 9-37.

Saul Bellow

1915-

American novelist, short story writer, and essayist.

The Adventures of Augie March (novel, 1953)

Augie March is the central figure of the novel that established Bellow as a major writer of American fiction and for which he received his first National Book Award. Augie's adventures are rendered in the picaresque tradition: we see him grow from a young boy in Chicago to adulthood and travel throughout the United States, Mexico, and Europe. Like all of Bellow's characters, Augie is searching for himself, and the novel chronicles his quest for identity. Along his way, Augie encounters a vast array of characters, and his response to them offers us further insight into his character, for he is a relatively passive character, which proves to be part of his charm as the young, innocent picaro but also part of the problem he must confront in himself. Augie has often been compared to Huck Finn, and the two share many similarities. Both are sensitive and compassionate, despite their difficult

27

young lives, and both are surprisingly resilient when the world tries to force them into its mold. And yet the central flaw in Augie appears to be his inability to commit—to another person or to a set of values. It is the quest, the endless adventure, and not the peace that comes with self-understanding that remains Augie's focus.

The adjectives "sprawling" and "exuberant" have often been used to describe Bellow's prose in *Augie March,* and some critics have complained that the novel could have ended several hundred pages before it does, or could have gone on indefinitely. The narrative style of this novel represents a clear break with the more compact form of his previous works. The novel is also written with great humor and lightheartedness, also in vivid contrast to the more somber earlier works.

Seize the Day (novella, 1956)

Tommy Wilhelm's story is encapsulated in a few hours on one day. He is depicted as a man at the nadir of his existence. He has been a failure at life—his career as a movie star, his marriage, his love affairs have all ended in shambles. The novella takes place in New York, and Tommy is shown as one of millions of lonely, isolated victims of urban life. As is the case with other Bellow heroes, Tommy seeks to find meaning in life, and his story is one of a quest for understanding of himself and the world around him. Also in common with other Bellow heroes, Tommy is drawn to the great ideas of the past, in this case the great literary figures, Shakespeare, Milton, Keats. Indeed, the central image of water and drowning reflects the influence of Milton's *Lycides.*

In the novel's conclusion, Tommy has finally found a oneness with humanity, and he experiences a spiritual awakening in a rush of tears at a stranger's funeral. Critics have been divided on the success of this conclusion and Tommy's apotheosis. Some find his transformation unbelievable, while others call the novel a masterpiece, finding in the novel's ending further evidence of Bellow's anti-pessimistic stance and allegiance with his characters' life-affirming beliefs.

Stylistically, *Seize the Day* signalled a return to the more measured prose of Bellow's earlier novels, *Dangling Man* and *The Victim,* unlike the sprawling, exuberant narrative style Bellow employed in *The Adventures of Augie March.* The narrative displays the same humor and energy of Bellow's previous fiction.

Henderson the Rain King (novel, 1959)

Eugene Henderson is one of only two gentile protagonists in the Bellow canon (the other is Arthur Corde of *The Dean's December*). As such, Henderson marks a departure from Augie March, Tommy Wilhelm, Herzog, and Charlie Citrine: he is wealthy, the product of privilege, and his milieu is not Chicago, but the suburbs of the East.

When the novel begins, we see Henderson's life in turmoil. He is pursued by the demands of ex-wives, children, and his business. In the face of this, Henderson decides to go to Africa, to embark on a quest for life's meaning, a trait he shares with other Bellovian heroes. Indeed, Henderson's famous cry; "I want, I want," could be applied to his fellow searchers on their individual voyages of discovery. During his quest he encounters several African tribes guided by **Romilayu,** who provides the hero with friendship and insight into the world of Africa. Another central figure, **Dahfu,** instructs Henderson in becoming a Rain King and represents fertility and renewal.

Bellow's Africa is metaphoric rather than realistic, and Henderson's quest is described in fantastic and mythic terms, rather than the realistic and naturalistic style of his previous novels. An important influence on the work is the philosophy of the German psychologist Wilhelm Reich, whose principles of primordial energy are embodied in the character of Dahfu. Commentators have praised the spirited prose and exuberant narrative pace of *Henderson the Rain King,* and it is considered one of Bellow's finest efforts.

Herzog (novel, 1964)

Moses Herzog is the central figure of what many critics consider Bellow's greatest novel, a work for which he was awarded his second National Book Award. In this work Bellow explored the situation of the intellectual in American society, a recurrent theme in his work.

The first line of the novel—"If I am out of my mind, it's all right with me"—indicates Herzog's state as we begin the story. We first encounter Herzog in collapse. Unhappily married for years, he is overwhelmed at the discovery of his ex-wife **Madeline**'s infidelity with his former best friend, **Valentine Gershbach**. Herzog, a man of depth and warmth, has lost faith in life and hope in humankind. He begins to write letters to friends, to the famous, to the living and the dead. Through these letters he seeks to understand, and like his fellow heroes in the Bellow canon, embarks on a quest for self-hood and a sense of purpose.

As with such Bellovian heroes as Charlie Citrine of *Humboldt's Gift,* we encounter in Herzog the wide-ranging philosophical discourses that so often characterize Bellow's novels. As he contemplates his life and tries to make sense of it, Herzog meditates and draws on his vast learning in literature and philosophy. Unlike Augie March or Henderson, whose quests for understanding and identity are played out across the map of the United States or Africa, Herzog's voyage of discovery is internal, and he has been called "the picaro flat on his back."

The novel has been called Bellow's most Jewish work, and the protagonist's meditative ramblings encompass a full range of thought on his faith. These focus particularly on the theme of Jewish suffering. Herzog is a modern American Jew dealing with problems of assimilation in a culture unaccommodating to his background.

In a pivotal scene, Herzog travels to Chicago, purportedly to murder his ex-wife and ex-friend. Poised to commit the crime, he finds himself unable to take life, and thus reaffirms his belief in the values he had questioned. The novel's conclusion presents Herzog at peace, cleansed of his sickness and affirming life.

Bellow's style in *Herzog* is marked by ironic presentation, particularly in his depiction of his hero's intellectual musings. Bellow blends third-person narration with the epistolary form of Herzog's letters to reveal Herzog's exploration of his own values as well as those of the philosophers and writers whose ideas he has accepted for so long. Considered by many to be his masterpiece, Bellow's *Herzog* displays the strong characterizations and intellectual power for which he is best known.

Humboldt's Gift (novel, 1975)

Like his fellow Bellovian heroes, **Charlie Citrine** is depicted in quest of answers to important philosophical questions, particularly the place of art and the artist in American society. Charlie is a character closely identified with his creator, for like Bellow, he is a Jewish intellectual, the son of immigrants, a celebrated writer, and resident of Chicago. The story revolves around Charlie's understanding of the life and death of his good friend, **Von Humboldt Fleisher,** a gifted poet who died in poverty and despair. As the novel begins, we see Charlie's life unravelling; he owes his publishers money, his marriage is finished, and he's having problems with his mistress, **Renata.** Amidst this mental and moral confusion, Charlie reflects on Humboldt.

Humboldt served as a mentor to the young Citrine, but later, as Charlie succeeded in the American literary scene, Humboldt sunk into madness and obscurity. Now his death inspires Citrine to think deeply about the nature of life and death, and about the plight of the artist in America. Reflecting on Humboldt's fate, Citrine bemoans the case of the poet in a nation that values monetary success over artistic striving and elevates the pragmatic over the spiritual.

Charlie insists that Humboldt speaks to him from the grave, and he does touch his former pupil literally and figuratively after death. In his will Humboldt has left Charlie a script that the two of them had written years ago, which will provide some financial security for Charlie. And Humboldt has left Charlie a spiritual legacy: a letter written shortly before his death, steeped in the theosophy of Rudolf Steiner, saying that ''we are not natural beings but supernatural beings,'' a message which provides Charlie with great comfort. Thus, Humboldt's ''gift'' to Citrine is a sense of hope in the despair and disarray of his life.

The character of Humboldt was based on the life of the American writer Delmore Schwartz, a close friend of Bellow's and a writer and intellectual who died tragically young. Thus, like Citrine, Humboldt is a character with autobiographical importance to Bellow.

The style of *Humboldt's Gift* is vibrant and expansive, and the broad canvas and vivid characterizations are reminiscent of Augie March and Henderson. One major influence on the novel is Rudolf Steiner's concept of anthromosophy, which informs Citrine's philosophical musings and has had a marked effect on Bellow. As he had done earlier in *Herzog,* Bellow here returns to a central thematic concern: the place of the intellectual in American culture. The novel, widely praised for its warmth, humor, and philosophic scope, won Bellow the Pulitzer Prize.

FURTHER READING

Aldridge, John W. ''The Complacency of Herzog.'' In *Time to Murder and Create: The Contemporary Novel in Crisis,* pp. 440-44. New York: McKay, 1966.

Alter, Robert. ''Heir of the Tradition.'' In *Rogues Progress: Studies in The Picaresque Novel,* pp. 106-132. Cambridge, Mass: Harvard University Press, 1964.

Axthelm, Peter M. ''The Full Perception: Saul Bellow.'' In *The Modern Confessional Novel,* pp. 128-77. New Haven: Yale University Press, 1967.

Bradbury, Malcolm. *Saul Bellow.* London: Methuen, 1982.

Chavkin, Allan. ''Bellow's Alternative to the Wasteland: Romantic Theme and Form in *Herzog.*'' *Studies in the Novel* 11 (Fall 1979): 326-37.

——. ''*Humboldt's Gift* and the Romantic Imagination.'' *Philological Quarterly* 62 (Winter 1983): 1-20.

Clayton, John J. *Saul Bellow: In Defense of Man.* Bloomington: Indiana University Press, 1968, 2nd ed. 1979.

Cohen, Sarah Blacher. *Saul Bellow's Enigmatic Laughter.* Urbana: University of Illinois Press, 1974.

——. ''Comedy and Guilt in *Humboldt's Gift.*'' *Modern Fiction Studies* 25 (Spring 1979): 47-57.

Contemporary Authors, Vols. 5-8, rev. ed.; *Contemporary Authors Bibliographical Series,* Vol. 1. Detroit: Gale Research Co.

Contemporary Literary Criticism, Vols. 1, 2, 3, 6, 8, 10, 13, 15, 25, 33, 34. Detroit: Gale Research Co.

Dictionary of Literary Biography, Vols. 2, 28; *Dictionary of Literary Biography Yearbook: 1982; Dictionary of Literary Biography Documentary Series,* Vol. 3.; *Concise Dictionary of American Literary Biography, 1941-1968.* Detroit: Gale Research Co.

Dutton, Robert R. *Saul Bellow.* New York: Twayne, 1971, rev. ed. 1982.

Fuchs, Daniel. *Saul Bellow: Vision and Revision.* Durham: Duke University Press, 1984.

Galloway, David D. ''The Absurd Man as Picaro: The Novels of Saul Bellow.'' *Texas Studies in Literature and Language* 6 (Summer 1964): 226-54.

Goldman, L. H. *Saul Bellow's Moral Vision: A Critical Study of the Jewish Experience.* New York: Irvington Publishers, 1981.

Guttmann, Allen. "Bellow's Henderson." *Critique* 7 (Spring-Summer 1965): 33-42.

Hassan, Ihab. "Quest and Affirmation in *Henderson the Rain King.*" In *The Modern American Novel: Essays in Criticism,* edited by Max Westbrook, pp. 223-29. New York: Random House, 1966.

Mudrick, Marvin. "Who Killed Herzog? Or, Three American Novelists." In *On Culture and Literature,* pp. 200-35. New York: Horizon, 1970.

Opdahl, Keith. *The Novels of Saul Bellow: An Introduction.* University Park: Pennsylvania State University Press, 1967.

Rodrigues, Eusebio L. *Quest for the Human: An Exploration of Saul Bellow's Fiction.* Lewisburg: Bucknell University Press, 1981.

Tanner, Tony. *Saul Bellow.* Edinburgh & London: Oliver & Boyd, 1965.

Arnold Bennett

1867-1931

English novelist, critic, and essayist.

The Old Wives' Tale (novel, 1908)

Set in the English Five Towns district made famous by Bennett in a highly successful series of novels, this work centers on **Sophia** and **Constance Baines,** two sisters whose lives are chronicled from childhood to death. The early lives of the two girls take place in the provincial town of Bursley, where their father, **John Baines,** a successful draper, has a tyrannical hold over the family. Sophia emerges as the rebel. Dominant and willful, she stands up to her father and eschews the life of a provincial housekeeper's wife, preferring instead a career as a teacher. She runs away to marry **Gerald Scales,** to the horror of her parents, and after their brief, unhappy marriage, settles in Paris where she begins a successful career in business. She returns to Bursley later in life and once again dominates the family, particularly the life of her sister Constance.

Constance's early life had always been overshadowed by her strong-willed sister. She is also the victim of her domineering mother, **Mrs. Baines,** as well as her demanding father, who, although an invalid, commands the family and the business. Unable to face her parent's wrath, she marries **Sam Povey,** a man they approve of, who later takes over the business after their deaths. In later life she continues to be dominated by Sophia, her family, and even her son, who grows to be a willful, spoiled boy.

The Old Wives' Tale established Bennett's place in English letters and is now considered among his most outstanding works of fiction. It is praised for its realistic, unsentimental evocation of everyday life, illuminated with the author's characteristic attention to detail in description of place and personality. He was especially interested in the organization of provincial society, and through his exploration of familial relations in the Baines family, weaves a credible and sensitive portrait of an era.

FURTHER READING

Contemporary Authors, Vol. 106. Detroit: Gale Research Co.

Dictionary of Literary Biography, Vols. 10, 34. Detroit: Gale Research Co.

Lodge, David. "Arnold Bennett: *The Old Wives' Tale.*" In *The Modes of Modern Writing: Metaphor, Metonymy, and the Typology of Modern Literature.* Ithaca: Cornell University Press, 1977.

Lucas, John. *Arnold Bennett: A Study of His Fiction.* London: Methuen, 1974.

Twentieth-Century Literary Criticism, Vols. 5, 20. Detroit: Gale Research Co.

Wain, John. *Arnold Bennett.* New York: Columbia University Press, 1967.

Thomas Berger
1924-

American novelist.

Little Big Man (novel, 1964)

Set in the Old West and covering the years 1852-1876, the novel is considered Berger's finest work and tells the story of **Jack Crabb,** a man who has experienced the Indian and the white world first-hand, and who, at the age of 100, relates his memoirs into a tape recorder for posterity. The novel is a satiric reworking of the western tradition in fiction and parodies the mythic and heroic stereotypes of that type of narrative. Crabbe is raised by the Cheyenne from the age of ten and he falls under the influence of **Old Lodge Skins,** a wise old Indian who teaches the boy about the ways of his culture and provides his insights into the clash of the white and the Indian worlds. He disdains the white man's contempt for nature and refers to Indians as "Human Beings," finding the white race to be savage. The whites are crafty, cruel, and insensitive to the natural world which the Indians revere, and the novel relates the collision of two cultures in which the white man is portrayed as the conqueror and destroyer who creates his own civilization on the ruins of an ancient world and way of life.

Berger has borrowed the picaresque tradition for his first-person narrative, and we follow his protagonist as he weaves his way between the two societies. He is variously a gunslinger, a buffalo hunter, and a gold miner, offering the perspective of a man who is at once inside and outside of two worlds. The work concludes with Crabb's description of Little Big Horn. He has been hired as a scout for **General George Armstrong Custer,** and he is the only white survivor of the debacle. This major conflict is handled with irony and sympathy, for although the Indians emerged as the victors of the battle, the vengeance of the white culture spelled the end of the Indian nation.

Berger satirizes both the white and the Indian perspectives in this work, particularly in his characterizations of Old Lodge Skins and Custer. Both are shown as complex individuals, capable of vision and narrow-mindedness, wisdom and foolishness, bravery and vanity. The work is comic, yet serious in its intent and savage in its satire.

FURTHER READING

Contemporary Authors, Vols. 1-4, rev. ed.; *Contemporary Authors New Revision Series,* Vol. 5. Detroit: Gale Research Co.

Contemporary Literary Criticism, Vols. 3, 5, 8, 11, 18, 38. Detroit: Gale Research Co.

Dictionary of Literary Biography, Vol. 2; *Dictionary of Literary Biography Yearbook: 1986.* Detroit: Gale Research Co.

Gurian, Jay. "Style in the Literary Desert: *Little Big Man.*" *Western American Literature* 3, No. 4 (Winter 1969): 285-96.

Lee, L. L. ''American Western, Picaresque: Thomas Berger's *Little Big Man.''* *The South Dakota Review* 5, No. 2 (Summer 1966): 35-42.

Wylder, Delbert E. ''Thomas Berger's *Little Big Man* as Literature.'' *Western American Literature* 3 (Winter 1969): 273-84.

Ambrose Bierce

1842-1914?

American short story writer, novelist, and essayist.

"An Occurrence at Owl Creek Bridge" (short story, 1891)

Set in Alabama during the Civil War, this gothic tale concerns the events surrounding the summary execution of a wealthy plantation owner, **Peyton Farquhar.** The opening of the story, the first of three distinct narrative sections, emotionlessly describes Peyton standing on a railroad bridge in northern Alabama; his wrists are bound, a noose is around his neck. The spectators consist of a company of Union Infantry. A single supporting plank, suspended by the weight of the company sergeant, lies between Peyton and death. At the close of the section the sergeant steps aside while Peyton simultaneously imagines how he might return home by throwing off the noose, springing into the stream below, and swimming to safety. Section two briefly narrates Peyton's prominent position and secessionist sympathies. A gray-clad soldier then arrives at the Farquhar estate asking for water. He informs Peyton that the Yanks are planning an advance and have secured the north bank of Owl Creek bridge. The soldier encourages Peyton in his scheme to single-handedly destroy the bridge and thwart the enemy. The narrator reveals at the close that the soldier was a Federal scout, an imposter. Section three, the longest and most impressionistic, records Peyton's regaining of consciousness following his fall through the bridge. In excruciating pain, he struggles beneath the current. With desperate, superhuman effort he frees himself of the snapped rope, still wound tightly about his neck. As his strength and reasoning return he realizes that he must not only swim vigorously but dodge the volleys of grapeshot that pursue him. His escape successful, he reaches land and travels by nightfall back to his wife and children. As he reaches his wife and is about to embrace her a stunning blow on his neck prevents him. The story closes: ''Peyton Farquhar was dead; his body, with a broken neck, swung gently from side to side beneath the timbers of the Owl Creek bridge.''

The best-known of Bierce's numerous stories, ''An Occurrence at Owl Creek Bridge'' is perhaps also the most representative. A writer of Civil War fiction, macabre tales, and sardonic anecdotal sketches, Bierce frequently dealt with the unusual and characteristically concluded his narratives with shocking, ironical twists. Often accompanying these technical traits is an intense exploration of psychological states, in this case the immediate moments preceding violent death. His most striking fictional effects depend on an adept manipulation of the reader viewpoint, which is nowhere better wrought than in this classic late nineteenth-century tale.

FURTHER READING

Contemporary Authors, Vol. 104. Detroit: Gale Research Co.

Cooper, Frederick Taber. ''Ambrose Bierce.'' *Some American Story Tellers,* pp. 331-53. New York: Henry Holt and Co., 1911.

Dictionary of Literary Biography, Vols. 11, 12, 23. Detroit: Gale Research Co.

Graffan, C. Hartley. *Bitter Bierce: A Mystery of American Letters*. New York: Cooper Square Publishers, 1966.

Grenander, M. E. *Ambrose Bierce*. New York: Twayne Publishers, 1971.

Twentieth-Century Literary Criticism, Vols. 1, 7. Detroit: Gale Research Co.

R. D. Blackmore

1825-1900

English novelist.

Lorna Doone (novel, 1869)

Set in Exmoor, England, during the late seventeenth century, this well-known novel is an adventure story relating the exploits of **John Ridd** and his love for **Lorna Doone.** As the novel opens, young John Ridd is returning home from school when he learns that his father has been killed by the villainous Doones, a band of outlaws. They have also kidnapped a young girl, whom they call Lorna. She becomes the ward of the head of the family, **Sir Ensor Doone,** and, as she grows older, the object of the affections of **Carver Doone,** the most cruel member of the bandit family and the murderer of Ridd's father. John, too, falls in love with Lorna, and he makes it his aim to save her from the clutches of the evil Carver. But John must face many adventures and death-defying ordeals before he can claim Lorna for his own. They are separated when it is discovered that she is actually **Lady Dugal,** an heiress, and she lives for a time at the court of King James II. John meanwhile continues to battle the Doone's and is also involved with Monmouth's rebellion. The novel's thrilling climax takes place in a church, where Carver has shot Lorna at the altar and he and John engage in mortal combat. John emerges victorious, and with his enemy vanquished, he and Lorna are happy at last.

Despite the melodrama and stock effects of the adventure mode, *Lorna Doone* remains a popular novel and has thrilled and delighted generations of readers. It is noted for its lively, lyrical style and for its vivid description of place and action.

FURTHER READING

Budd, Kenneth. *The Last Victorian: R. D. Blackmore and His Novel*. London: Centaur, 1960.

Contemporary Authors, Vol. 120. Detroit: Gale Research Co.

Dictionary of Literary Biography, Vol. 18. Detroit: Gale Research Co.

Dunn, Waldo Hilary. *R. D. Blackmore: The Author of "Lorna Doone."* London: Hale, 1956.

Sutton, Max Keith. *R. D. Blackmore*. Boston: Twayne, 1979.

Twentieth-Century Literary Criticism, Vol. 27. Detroit: Gale Research Co.

Heinrich Böll

1917-1985

German novelist, short story writer, and essayist.

Billiards at Half-Past Nine (novel, 1959)

This novel, set in contemporary Germany, spans the years 1907 to 1958 and relates the story of three generations of the Fähmel family. The present action described in the work takes place on the eightieth birthday of **Robert Fähmel**'s father, **Heinrich,** and through the extensive use of flashbacks Böll fills in the history of the family. The action of the novel is presented through a variety of characters with differing points of view, conveyed through third-person narration and interior monologue. Böll's central theme in this work is time as revealed in his characters' attempts to come to terms with their country's and their own history.

The first chapter provides a variety of perspectives on Robert; the focus then turns to the thoughts and feelings of Heinrich and his wife **Johanna,** as they reflect on their marriage, their family, and their past as Germans, particularly the effect of two world wars and the meaning of the Nazis. As in most of his work Böll here deals with the savagery of the capitalist system, the rise of fascism, and the inability of organized religion to deal with the moral crisis of twentieth-century Germany. We learn that as a young man Robert and his friend **Schrella** had become members of a pacifist sect called the "lambs," who represent peace and who see themselves in opposition to the "buffaloes" of the country, those given to power, violence, and destruction. Significantly, Hitler is never mentioned by name in the book, for Böll contends that the Nazis are only the most recent incarnation of the buffalo in humankind, and that anyone who perpetuates the lust for war and exploitation of the weak falls within their sphere. Robert and Schrella go into exile at the outbreak of war, but Robert returns and joins the army. He becomes a demolition expert, and in one of the novel's pivotal scenes, destroys the abbey that his father had built years before, an action meant to wound both national pride and the Catholic Church, who had tolerated the Nazis. In an ironic twist, Robert's son, **Joseph,** is restoring the abbey at the time of Heinrich's birthday.

The birthday is the scene of further action and revelation. Johanna, driven to violence over her despair at the state of modern Germany, shoots a high-ranking government official, whom she characterizes as a buffalo, an act which she feels will protect her grandchildren and the future of Germany from the cruelty and corruption he represents. She pleads insanity and is incarcerated in a mental institution. Despite his sympathetic portrait of the Fähmel family, Böll shows them as a wealthy, privileged group who chose a random act of violence instead of commitment to social change. In the novel's conclusion, the family is depicted as turning even more inward, dealing only with one another and isolating themselves from the outside world. They are at peace, but the buffaloes are still in control.

The work is noted for it structural complexity and its richly evocative descriptive passages and is considered by many critics to be one of Böll's finest achievements.

The Clown (novel, 1963)

The novel is set in the German city of Bonn after World War II. **Hans Schnier,** who makes his living as a clown, is a man who lives as an outsider in contemporary Germany. He is the son of wealthy parents who have made their fortune in coal, an industry that can serve the Nazis or the modern West German government. Rejecting their money and their way of life, Hans is uncompromising in his values and incapable of hypocrisy in a world riddled with deceit. As the novel opens, his girlfriend, **Marie Derkum,** has left him to marry a prominent Catholic. The experience devastates him and causes him to view his world from an intensely personal standpoint, rendered by Böll in a first-person method of narration. He is an isolated figure, and what little human contact he has with the outside world takes place over the phone. His thoughts revolve around Marie, and he desperately calls friends trying to locate her. Through flashbacks we learn about their life together. They had loved each other deeply, and had lived together as husband and wife outside the bonds of the Catholic

Church, which Hans always regarded as hypocritical. As in many of Böll's works, the Catholic Church is one object of his satire.

In his clown-protagonist, Böll presents a figure who stands aside and observes society, revealing its frailties. He also attacks the social malaise of contemporary Germany, which he depicts as devoted to militarism and capitalism, and he focuses especially on the opportunism of the ex-Nazis. Hans will not and cannot forget the Nazis, but other characters are not so vigilant. His mother, a racist, becomes head of a benevolent organization devoted to racial harmony; a fascist teacher who never joined the Nazi party becomes a figure lauded for his courage during the war. As in *Billiards at Half-past Nine,* it is not just the Nazis themselves, but all Germans who, without morals or values, change with the times to insure their best advantage that are the objects of scorn. In the novel's conclusion, Hans puts on makeup to act as a beggar, unwilling to compromise his values in a world of irresponsibility, immorality, and hypocrisy.

Böll's use of first-person narration heightens the subjective, isolated nature of Hans's experience and our understanding of him. Although the novel's tone is satiric, the overtones are tragic in this tale of the fate of the innocent in the world of the corrupt.

Group Portrait with Lady (novel, 1971)

The novel is set in a German city based on Cologne. Covering the years 1922 to 1970, the work relates the life of **Leni Gruyten-Pfeiffer** through a series of conflicting portraits offered by the people she has known. As the novel opens, Leni is forty-eight years old and a widow. The **Author,** who refers to himself as "Au.," is interviewing several of Leni's acquaintances with the purpose of gathering "factual" information about her, and he includes the transcripts of the interviews as well as letters and other documents in his "group portrait."

Through the various narrators, we learn about Leni, her family, and the devastation of the war. Described as a "whore" by the neighbors interviewed by the author, Leni is a sensuous, curious, and guileless woman, an individual of compassion and independence who is treated as an outcast for her way of life. Her brother **Heinrich Gruyten-Pfeiffer** is executed for selling arms to the Allies; he had sought to undermine the Hitler regime, which he loathed but was unable to stop. Her father, **Hubert Gruyten-Pfeiffer,** hates the Nazis as well, and in response to Heinrich's death, starts a dummy company staffed with fictitious workers whose names are drawn from Russian literature. Although the company is at first successful, Hubert is later found out and sent to prison. Leni's mother dies of despair. Leni is left alone and impoverished and finds work in a wreath factory, where she meets **Boris Lvovich Kolotovski,** a prisoner of war from Russia, and the two fall in love. Leni had been married for three days to a career soldier who was later killed, a union devoid of the love and passion she finds with Boris. Böll's satiric view of the folly of war is obvious in his setting of the novel's principal love affair, which takes place in a factory that creates monuments to the dead. Leni becomes pregnant and bears a son, but their happiness is short-lived, for Boris is captured—wearing a German uniform—and dies in an Allied work camp.

The action of the novel moves to the present, and the Author himself appears as a character, investigating the death of a Jewish nun, a confidant of Leni's early years, who had been allowed to starve to death during the war. He then joins Leni's friends who are trying to prevent her eviction from her flat. Always an idealist and an independent woman, Leni has become an advocate for the foreign workers in the city and has taken a Turkish lover. Once again, she is reviled by her neighbors. Her son by Boris, **Lev Gruyten,** is in prison for forging documents to save his mother's property, where he is known as a "deliberate under-achiever," a young man who has inherited his mother's disregard for what makes one a success in modern Germany. Leni's friends win their case, and the ending is a happy one.

Within his complex narrative framework Böll once again aims his satire at a social structure based on profit rather than on human welfare. The novel is considered by many critics to be his finest and was cited by the Nobel committee as Böll's ''most grandly conceived work'' when he received the prize in literature in 1972.

The Lost Honor of Katharina Blum (novel, 1974)

Set in contemporary Germany, the novel recounts the story of a young woman, **Katharina Blum**, who is driven to violence by the exploitive practices of the press. Böll's target in this novel is the irresponsibility of modern journalism, especially as practiced by the sensationalist ''yellow press,'' which ruins the lives of innocent individuals in the name of profit.

Katharina is hounded by the press because of her relationship with a known criminal, **Ludwig Götten.** Yet she is not the only person to befriend the man; a wealthy, influential member of the government has also been seen with Ludwig, but because of his power and position, the press leaves him alone. Thus Böll shows how the press, the police, and the courts conspire to undermine the lives of the insignificant in society, while protecting the privileged. For several days Katharina is ruthlessly attacked in the press by a journalist named **Werner Toetges,** who depicts her as an amoral gangster's moll and twists the words of his informants to create a woman whose character is based on falsehood and innuendo. He appears at Katharina's apartment, and believing his own lies about her nature, tries to force her to have sex; she shoots and kills him, destroying the man who had destroyed her honor.

Böll focuses on the nature of truth and the responsibility of the writer. Katharina is driven to violence because she has been debased and dehumanized by the power of language. Böll does not present her as an idealized figure; she is a simple young woman, honest and capable of love. Yet while she is not motivated by the greed that drives the press and politics, she is also apathetic about social injustice until she herself is the victim. Thus Böll continues his theme of the importance of social responsibility in this, the most political and polemical of his novels.

FURTHER READING

Conrad, Robert C. *Heinrich Böll.* Boston: Twayne, 1981.

Contemporary Authors, Vols. 21-24, rev. ed., 116. Detroit: Gale Research Co.

Contemporary Literary Criticism, Vols. 2, 3, 6, 9, 11, 15, 27, 39. Detroit: Gale Research Co.

Cunliffe, W. G. ''Heinrich Böll's Eccentric Rebels.'' *Modern Fiction Studies* (Autumn 1975): 473-79.

Dictionary of Literary Biography, Vol. 69; *Dictionary of Literary Biography Yearbook: 1985.* Detroit: Gale Research Co.

Friedrichsmeyer, Erhard. *The Major Works of Heinrich Böll: A Critical Commentary.* New York: Monarch Press, 1974.

Ley, Ralph. ''Compassion, Catholicism, and Communism: Reflections on Böll's *Gruppenbild mit Dame.*'' *University of Dayton Review* 10, No. 2 (1973): 25-40.

Myers, David. ''Heinrich Böll's *Gruppenbild mit Dame:* Aesthetic Play and Ethical Seriousness.'' *Seminar* 13, No. 3 (1977): 190-98.

Pikar, Gertrud B. ''The Symbolic Use of Color in Heinrich Böll's *Billard um halbzehn.*'' *University of Dayton Review* 12, No. 2 (1976): 41-50.

Pritchett, V. S. ''Grand Inquisitor.'' *New Statesman* 85, No. 2199 (11 May 1973): 694-95.

Reid, James Henderson. *Heinrich Böll: Withdrawal and Re-emergence.* London: Oswald, 1973.

Waidson, H. M. "The Novels and Stories of Heinrich Böll." *German Life and Letters* 12, No. 4 (July 1959) 264-72.

Warnke, Frank J. "Saeva Indignatio on the Rhine." *The New Republic* 152, No. 12 (20 March 1965): 17-19.

Yuill, W. E. "Heinrich Böll." *Essays on Contemporary German Literature: German Men of Letters, Vol. IV,* pp. 141-58, edited by Brian-Keith Smith. London: Oswald Wolff, 1966.

Ziolkowski, Theodore. "Heinrich Böll: Conscience and Craft." *Books Abroad* 34 (1960): 213-22.

Jorge Luis Borges
1899-1986

Argentinean short story writer, essayist, and poet.

"Tlön, Uqbar, Orbis Tertius" (short story, 1940)

This story, one of Borges's most ambitious, ambiguous, and well-known works of fantasy, presents and analyzes the blending of the real and the fictional worlds. It is related in the first person by Borges himself, who mentions that at dinner one evening his friend and collaborator **Adolfo Bioy Casares** alludes to the land of Uqbar. Neither atlases nor Borges's copy of the encyclopedia contain any reference to the country; only Bioy Casares's copy of *The Anglo-American Cyclopedia* gives information on the mysterious country.

Borges then describes how, after an interval of two years, he came upon what appears to be the only copy of *A First Encyclopedia of Tlön,* a book which he studies to learn about the planet, its people, their philosophical idealism, and their language. Since their philosophy does not acknowledge the constricting concepts of space and time, the language contains no nouns, no notion of causality, and science is reduced to a dialectical game. The search for rational truth so important to our culture is replaced on Tlön by a quest for theoretical structures. Crucially, the people of this seemingly perfect world of symmetry and order have learned to create objects by imagining them. Called hrönir, they are things that are at once imaginary and real.

In the postscript to the story, the origin of Tlön is explained as we learn that a cult from the 1600s devoted to the Kabbalah had invented the imaginary country. Their disciples had persisted for centuries and in the 1800s an American, **Ezra Buckley,** provided the financial assistance necessary to prepare the encyclopedia from which Borges learned of the planet. At this point in the narrative we also learn that objects from Tlön have begun to appear, the imaginary world having invaded the realm of reality. The narrator himself witnesses the discovery of a metal fragment from Tlön, engraved with an image of a god known only to "orbis tertius."

The closing section reveals the spread of the philosophy of Tlön as the world yields to what appears to be one of perfect order and consistency but is revealed to be a system of senseless paradigms. The narrator notes that Tlön is a "labyrinth devised by men, a labyrinth destined to be deciphered by men," also recognizing how our culture had so recently succumbed to the symmetry and order promised in the philosophies of dialectical materialism, anti-semitism, and Nazism. As the world slips into the mindless vision of Tlön, the narrator is at work on a translation of Sir Thomas Browne's *Urn Burial.*

This story contains many of the themes that Borges was to repeat throughout his fiction, most notably the blurring of the fictional and the real. The piece combines the elements of the essay and a work of imaginative literature: fictional and true facts are interspersed throughout the text, and the incorporation of the postscript and the use of lengthy footnotes in the text further contradicts our notion of the separation of the factual from the fictional. One of Borges's greatest works, "Tlön, Uqbar, Orbis Tertius" is widely acclaimed for its linguistic virtuosity, broad philosophical range, and irony.

"The Library of Babel" (short story, 1941)

One of Borges's most important stories, "The Library of Babel" was published in his collection *Ficciones* and is an allegorical tale of the futile nature of the human search for eternal truth. The "Library" of the title is the universe, described by the unnamed narrator as an "indefinite and perhaps infinite number of hexagonal galleries." Each geometric cubicle contains twenty shelves, with thirty-two books on each shelf, 410 pages in each book, forty lines on each page, and eighty letters on each line. As a young man, the narrator tells us, he wandered the vast holdings of the Library searching for the one book that would unlock the secrets of the universe. He tells of the "Men of the Library" who continue the search for truth, but rarely reach their goal, for the books contain writings that are incomprehensible to the reader. The narrator knows that he is now near death and that when he dies his body will be cast into the infinity of the central space in the Library's air shaft, where it will decay and he will, like dust, become one with the universe.

This story evinces Borges's fascination with the Kabbalah, mysticism, and other forms of philosophy. Critics interpret the work as the author's vision of the essentially inscrutable nature of the universe, which defies human comprehension.

"Death and the Compass" (short story, 1942)

The story centers on the last case of **Erik Lönnrot,** a police detective who prides himself on his use of logic. It has been described as a "metaphysical whodunit," and Borges utilizes the detective genre, imbued with his own recurrent motifs of numerology and mysticism. The story recounts Lönnrot's attempts to find a serial murderer. Three murders have been committed, each on the third day of three consecutive months. At the scene of the first murder, in the typewriter of the victim, **Rabbi Marcel Yarmolinsky,** is a note reading: "The first letter of the Name has been uttered." The second victim is **Daniel Simon Azevedo,** a thief and informer. The inscription at the scene of his death reads: "The second letter of the Name has been uttered." A man named **Ginzberg** calls police headquarters offering information on the "double sacrifice"; the call is traced to a bar and the owner identifies Ginzberg as **Gryphius,** who had recently left with two men dressed as harlequins, and who is apparently the third victim. Before leaving, one of the costumed men had written on a slate outside the bar: "The last letter of the Name has been uttered."

In the room of the rabbi, Lönnrot had found a number of books dealing with the Kabbalah and Hasidism concerned with the concept of speaking the unutterable name of God. A book in Gryphius's room indicates a passage of similar significance. The police receive a letter predicting that a fourth murder will not take place. It includes a map of the city, indicating an "equilateral and mystical triangle" formed by joining the sites of the three murders. Lönnrot, convinced by rational deduction that a fourth murder will take place, gets out his compass and goes on the trail of the murderer, a journey that leads him to the villa Triste-le-Roy. There he is caught by the notorious criminal **Red Scharlach,** who claims he set a trap for Lönnrot, the detective who had sent his brother to prison. In the mysterious, enigmatic conclusion, Lönnrot, knowing he is facing death, asks his executioner that when they meet in another incarnation, he wishes his nemesis to use a Greek maze to entrap him: a single straight line, invisible and unending. Scharlach agrees, then shoots him.

The story has received numerous critical explications, focussing on such topics as the recurrent theme of duality as well as the ironic tone in which the story is presented. It is considered one of Borges's finest works.

FURTHER READING

Barrenechea, Ana Maria. *Borges the Labyrinth Maker,* translated by Robert Lima. New York: New York University Press, 1965.

Barth, John. "The Literature of Exhaustion." *Atlantic Monthly* 220, No. 2 (August 1967): 29-34.

Christ, Ronald J. *The Narrow Act: Borges's Art of Illusion.* New York: New York University Press, 1969.

Contemporary Authors, Vols. 21-24, rev. ed.; *Contemporary Authors New Revision Series,* Vol. 19. Detroit: Gale Research Co.

Contemporary Literary Criticism, Vols. 1, 2, 3, 4, 6, 8, 9, 10, 13, 19, 44, 48. Detroit: Gale Research Co.

Dauster, Frank. "Notes on Borges's Labyrinths." *Hispanic Review* 30 (April 1962): 142-48.   '

Gardner, James. "Jorge Luis Borges, 1899-1986." *The New Criterion* 10, No. 2 (October 1986): 16-24.

Paz, Octavio. "In Time's Labyrinth," translated by Charles Lane. *The New Republic* 195, No. 18 (3 November 1986): 30-4.

Stark, John. "Jorge Luis Borges." In *The Literature of Exhaustion,* pp. 11-61. Durham: Duke University Press, 1974.

Sturrock, John. *Paper Tigers: The Ideal Fictions of Jorge Luis Borges.* Oxford: Oxford University Press, 1977.

Updike, John. "The Author as Librarian." *New Yorker* (31 October 1965): 223-46.

Elizabeth Bowen

1899-1973

Anglo-Irish novelist, short story writer, and essayist.

The Last September (novel, 1929)

Set in Ireland during the Anglo-Irish War of 1919-1921, the novel recounts the coming of age of **Lois Farquar,** set against the backdrop of war. Lois is a member of the Anglo-Irish gentry, a class of people who feel they can ignore the conflict raging outside their gates. Lois lives on her family's estate, Danielstown, and is a character isolated by her romantic notions of love and life. She is engaged to **Gerald Lesworth,** a British officer involved in the war, a man she does not necessarily love, but who is both an idealized vision of a suitor and a way out of her rather boring existence on Danielstown. Although Lois and her family continue their trivial social lives oblivious to the life and death struggle outside their homes, the war becomes real for all of them. Gerald is killed, and Danielstown and other estates are burned. Lois, once tired of her surroundings, is forced to mature and face a bleak reality, to acknowledge the encroachment of a national conflict on her personal life. Her romantic idealism is replaced with self-awareness.

In this work Bowen explores the workings of her heroine's mind as she faces the radical changes wrought by war. As so often in Bowen's works, we see here a young girl's awakening to life and to the world outside her class and consciousness, and her necessary loss of innocence. Bowen also parallels the development of Lois with the cataclysmic social and political change going on in Ireland.

The House in Paris (novel, 1935)

Set in Paris, the novel is divided into three parts. In the first section, we encounter two children, **Leopold Moody** and **Henrietta Mountjoy,** who have met at the home of **Naomi Fisher.** Leopold is waiting for his mother, whom he has never met. Henrietta is on her way to her grandmother's and has stopped for a visit. As they talk, they are revealed as sensitive, precocious children, more aware of the adult world around them than their age or experience would indicate. Their conversation dominates the first part of the work. At the conclusion of the first section, Leopold's mother has not appeared, but her husband, **Ray Forrestier,** has arrived to meet him. Leopold's identity is explained in the second section of the novel, which moves back in time ten years to the main story of **Karen Michaelis.** Wanting to escape from an arid family situation, Karen becomes engaged to Ray. She does not love Ray, but he is correct socially and of the proper class. While he is away, she meets **Max Ebhart,** the fiance of Naomi Fisher. She is drawn into an affair with him, which ends in her pregnancy and Max's suicide. A son, Leopold, is born, who is given to another couple to raise. Ray returns, and although aware of Karen's past, marries her. The third section returns the narrative to the present. Ray has decided to bring Leopold home to live with him and Karen.

Bowen portrays the loss of innocence in two of her characters in this novel, both Karen and her son, exploring the loneliness of the child and the shattered dreams of the mother. Bowen's thematic insistence on the fragmentariness of existence is enhanced by her disjointed use of time sequence in the work. The tone of the novel is dominated by the dark, claustrophobic atmosphere of the house and a tightly controlled narrative style.

The Death of the Heart (novel, 1938)

As the novel begins, **Portia Quayne,** sixteen, has been sent to live with her stepbrother, **Thomas Quayne** and his wife, **Anna,** following the death of her parents. Another of Bowen's innocents, she is a sensitive and naive girl. The Quaynes are childless and have lived a long and rather boring life together, and the sudden arrival of Portia creates conflict and change in their lives. **Matchett,** the Quayne's housekeeper, offers Portia the warmth and sense of security they are incapable of. Portia focuses her romantic yearnings on **Eddie,** a friend of the family and an employee of Thomas's. He is an irresponsible, immature young man and only toys with her affections. While on holiday, Portia tries to make Eddie live up to her idealized expectations of romance, but he rejects her rudely. This marks the death of her romantic view and the point at which she must confront reality. When she returns home, she learns that Anna has been reading her diary, and this, along with Eddie's rejection, crushes her and she runs away. She appeals first to Eddie, who rebuffs her, and then to another family friend, **Major Brutt,** whom she asks to marry her. He calls the Quaynes, who are brought to a greater understanding and sensitivity of Portia's predicament through the crisis. In the conclusion, Matchett is sent to retrieve Portia, and there is a sense that the innocence represented by Portia has affected the coldness of the Quaynes, and that the young girl has also been changed, acknowledging and accepting the ways of adulthood.

Stylistically, the work is noted for its use of multiple points of view, for we learn about the characters through their own thoughts and conversations, as well as through Portia's portraits of them in her diary. Bowen also makes use of narrators who provide both objective, detached description and more subjective analysis.

The Heat of the Day (novel, 1949)

Set in London during World War II, the novel recounts the story of **Stella Rodney**, who is in the British secret service. She is divorced and has a lover, **Robert Kelway,** who is also an agent. One of Stella's coworkers, a man named **Robert Harrison,** tells her that Kelway is a double agent, involved with providing secret documents to the Nazis. Harrison tries to blackmail her with the information, proposing to remain quiet if she will sleep with him. She refuses both his advances and his story. She confronts Kelway with the information, which he vehemently denies. He does eventually admit his treason, however, after which he falls to his death; whether he is the victim of an accident or a suicide is left unclear. His death forces Stella to reflect on her own life, and the novel relates her self-exploration, which takes place against the chaos and destruction of London at war, with bombing, violence, and death all around. Although the scene is London, the conflict is global, and Bowen examines through her heroine the political and moral ideologies motivating her characters. In the midst of the horrifying devastation, Stella is able to order and understand her experience, to gather the strength she needs to continue her life.

The tone of the novel is one of horror, destruction, and the insecurity bred of war. The motifs of conspiracy and betrayal illuminate Bowen's theme of the personal life shocked into reality through confrontation with the outside world. Yet faced with personal loss and surrounded with threats to her culture and way of life, Stella is able to affirm the will to live. The narrative is interspersed with accounts of historical events of the war, lending the work both poignancy and verisimilitude.

FURTHER READING

Austin, Allan E. *Elizabeth Bowen*. Boston: Twayne Publishers, 1971.

Blodgett, Harriet. *Patterns of Reality: Elizabeth Bowen's Novels*. The Hague: Mouton, 1975.

Brooke, Jocelyn. *Elizabeth Bowen*. London: Longmans Green, 1952.

Contemporary Authors, Vols. 17-18, 41-44, rev. ed.; *Contemporary Authors Permanent Series,* Vol. 2. Detroit: Gale Research Co.

Contemporary Literary Criticism, Vols. 1, 3, 6, 11, 15, 22. Detroit: Gale Research Co.

Daiches, David. "The Novels of Elizabeth Bowen." *English Journal* 38 (June 1949): 305-313.

Dictionary of Literary Biography, Vol. 15. Detroit: Gale Research Co.

Glendinning, Victoria. *Elizabeth Bowen: Portrait of A Writer*. London: Weidenfeld & Nicolson, 1977.

Hall, James. "The Giant Located: Elizabeth Bowen." In *The Lunatic Giant in the Drawing Room: The British and American Novel Since 1950, pp. 17-55*. Bloomington: Indiana University Press, 1968.

Heath, William. *Elizabeth Bowen: An Introduction to her Novels*. Madison: University of Wisconsin Press, 1961.

Kenney, Edwin J. *Elizabeth Bowen*. Lewisburg: Bucknell University Press, 1975.

Parrish, Paul A. "The Loss of Eden: Four Novels of Elizabeth Bowen." *Critique: Studies in Modern Fiction* 15, No. 1 (1973): 86-100.

Sullivan, Walter. "A Sense of Place: Elizabeth Bowen and the Landscape of the Heart." *The Sewanee Review* (Winter 1976): 142-49.

Ray Bradbury

1920-

American novelist and short story writer.

Fahrenheit 451 (novel, 1953)

Set in a futuristic society, this novel concerns the moral awakening of an individual pitted against the crushing social conformity imposed on him by a technologically advanced society. **Guy Montag** is a fireman whose job entails burning books. At first, Montag seems to take particular pleasure in his work, accepting the doctrine proffered by his fire chief, **Captain Beatty,** who suggests that books stimulate thoughtfulness leading to melancholy and malcontent. In short, books threaten the social order.

Early in the novel, Montag meets **Clarisse McClellan,** a young girl whose eccentric behavior and uncomfortable questions serve as a catalyst to Montag's moral transformation. By contrast, Montag's wife, **Mildred,** appears on the surface to be an ideal citizen. She enjoys the superfluous entertainment sanctioned by her society and tends to avoid introspective behavior and meaningful conversation. Montag is fully aware of the shallowness of their relationship; he realized that he would not mourn her death, nor could he even recall the circumstances of their original meeting. Her suicide attempt, however, alerts Montag to the possibility that the void he feels in his life may not be peculiar to himself. Similarly, near the end of the novel Montag realizes that Beatty welcomes death despite his former words in support of the prevailing state of affairs.

Gradually, the reader discovers that Montag has been hoarding books. His transgression is discovered by the authorities, and, aided by a retired English professor, he becomes a fugitive. He manages to leave the city before it is destroyed and joins a group of people who preserve books through memorization. Through this method, they in effect become the books; yet, they make no attempt to interpret them.

In *Fahrenheit 451,* Bradbury transcends the fantasy and science fiction element for which he is best known through his exploration of the universal theme of the individual seeking self-knowledge while grappling with a hostile environment. Stylistically, Bradbury is noted for his imagery, specifically his use of metaphor. In this novel, fire is revealed as both a constructive and cleansing element and as a destructive force.

FURTHER READING

Contemporary Authors, Vols. 1-4, rev. ed.; *Contemporary Authors New Revision Series,* Vol. 2. Detroit: Gale Research Co.

Contemporary Literary Criticism, Vols. 1, 3, 10, 15, 42. Detroit: Gale Research Co.

Dictionary of Literary Biography, Vol. 2. Detroit: Gale Research Co.

Nolan, William F. *The Ray Bradbury Companion.* Detroit: Bruccoli/Gale, 1975.

Slusser, George Edgar. *The Bradbury Chronicles.* San Bernardino: Borgo Press, 1977.

Watt, Donald. *Ray Bradbury.* New York: Taplinger, 1980.

Bertolt Brecht

1898-1956

German dramatist and poet.

The Threepenny Opera (drama, 1928)

This piece was written in collaboration with Kurt Weill, who provided the music, and was based on *The Beggar's Opera* by the eighteenth-century English writer John Gay, with verses from the fifteenth-century French poet François Villon. But while Gay set his satire among the English aristocracy, Brecht places his work in Victorian England, where he replaces the upper class with a middle class contaminated with capitalism. **Macheath** is portrayed as a scoundrel, a gangster with an unquenchable appetite for women and corruption. In the cynical atmosphere that pervades the work, depravity is everywhere. **Tiger Brown,** the police chief, embodies the corruption of the middle class, and **Mr. Peachum** directs the beggars of London almost as a guild. Yet despite Brecht's attempts to outline the play as a conflict between the bourgeoisie and the proletariat, his political stance remained too vague for the work to be remembered for its Marxist implications. The character of Macheath in particular appeared too vital and appealing to audiences to be interpreted solely on the basis of his representation as a corrupted capitalist, for he appears to be driven more by his animal desires than by societal forces. As in Gay's version, Macheath attracts first **Polly Peachum**, whose father is the head of the beggars, then after he is thrown in jail due to the machinations of Peachum and Tiger Brown, he wins the heart of Brown's daughter, who helps him to escape.

The work was one of the most popular of the German theater of the 1920s and is Brecht's best-known piece internationally. Many critics note that the play's cynical tone reflects the atmosphere of Weimar Germany in its last days. All positive and idealistic moral attitudes are ridiculed in the play, as love, marriage, and the family are derided by the underworld of crime and prostitution and the corruption of the middle class.

Galileo (drama, 1943)

The play is set in Italy during the early seventeenth century and depicts the life of **Galileo Galilei,** the famous astronomer. The work, particularly the character of Galileo, occupied Brecht for almost twenty years, and three versions of the play exist, each offering a slightly different interpretation of the character. For Brecht, Galileo was the representative of a new scientific age whose recantation of his belief in the Copernican theory of the universe made him a coward and a traitor to later generations.

As the play opens, Galileo is a highly respected scientist. He is portrayed as a sensuous man and a creature of appetites, voracious in the pursuit of knowledge, food, and pleasure. He is a complex figure, at once proud, cunning, greedy, and loving. Against the advice of friends, he moves to Florence, which is in the hands of the Church and a hostile environment for science. While there to serve as the mathematical adviser to the young prince, he is cautioned by the Church regarding his beliefs. In the face of disaster, he freely expounds his belief in Copernican theory—that the earth revolves around the sun—and is accused of heresy. The new pope, formerly a mathematician, is coerced into threatening Galileo with torture if he refuses to recant. To the surprise and dismay of his loyal students, Galileo does renounce his beliefs. He is placed under house arrest and spends the rest of his life writing his *Discoursi*, a statement of the beliefs he was forced to recant, which he smuggles out of the country through a former student, **Andrea Sarti,** in the final scene.

While Brecht was working on the second version of the play, the United States dropped the atomic bomb on Japan. This galvanized Brecht's intention to transform Galileo into a cowardly, traitorous figure who should have offered posterity a code of ethics regarding science that would have made such destruction through the powers of science impossible; instead, Galileo recanted his belief in what he knew to be the truth, committing, for Brecht, the "original sin" of science. In the second and third versions, the author tried to make Galileo appear even more cowardly, yet he was unable to alter the sympathy that the character evoked in the audience. For many critics, Galileo is the most complex and ambiguous character Brecht created, and despite his efforts to the contrary, audiences continue to find him a heroic, sympathetic character.

The Caucasian Chalk Circle (drama, 1948)

The play takes place in Soviet Georgia after World War II and is divided into three parts. As the first section of the drama opens, two peasant groups have returned to their lands, ravaged by the Nazis, and are involved in a dispute concerning how they will utilize it. One group wants to use the land for grazing herds, the other to grow fruit. Under the direction of the **Singer,** they reenact the ancient drama of the chalk circle. This forms the second section of the play, which takes place in Georgia during the Middle Ages and relates the story of **Grusha,** a kitchen maid who had taken care of an infant abandoned when the Grand Duke was overthrown, his Governor killed, and the Governor's wife had escaped, leaving her baby behind. Although she is betrothed to another, Grusha marries an old man to give the baby a name. When the Duke returns to power, the child's mother tries to claim the baby, bringing us to the third section of the play, the trial to determine the child's guardian. Presiding at the trial is **Azdak,** a corrupt, roguish character who nevertheless knows human nature. He places the child in the middle of a circle of chalk and tells each woman to take hold of the child and pull him towards her. Grusha, who will not harm the boy, lets him go; Azdak declares her the fit mother. In the conclusion, the peasants have learned that "what there is shall go to those who are good for it," and that as the child goes to the woman who is most "motherly," so the land goes to its best purpose, the production of fruit.

The play is considered to be one of Brecht's finest achievements in the epic mode, particularly in his use of the Singer. This character introduces action and characters and comments on the drama, raising questions and remarking on the play as it progresses. Through the Singer, the past and the present, the myth and its purpose, are made one. The work has a lyrical tone in the first sections, in vivid contrast to the realism of the final part, which relates the trial proceedings led by the vulgar but insightful Azdak.

Mother Courage and Her Children (drama, 1949)

This play, considered Brecht's masterpiece and a major work of twentieth-century literature, is set in Germany and surrounding countries during the seventeenth century at the time of the Thirty Years' War. **Mother Courage** makes her living off the war—she owns a canteen wagon that she and her children drag from camp to camp, following the destruction. Brecht's theme in this work is the absurdity of war, and Mother Courage, a character whose business is providing for soldiers, is an ambiguous, ironic presence. She is a woman of strength, cunning, and vitality, resilient in the face of the tragedy, loss, and waste that mark her life and provide the tone of the play. Yet her true nature remains uncertain, and whether or not she possesses the "courage" of her title is a topic disputed by critics.

As the play opens, we see Mother Courage with her three children, sons **Eilif** and **Swiss Cheese,** and daughter **Kattrin.** Eilif appears to have inherited his mother's cunning ways, Swiss Cheese is depicted as a sweet, docile young man, and Kattrin, who is mute, is a character of deep feeling and sensitivity. Mother Courage is a canny and sometimes ruthless businesswoman, always haggling over a deal with her eye on profit. During the first scene, as she dickers with a soldier, Eilif runs off to the war, captivated by tales of fortune. Mother Courage loses her second son in the third scene, when Swiss Cheese is accused of stealing a regimental cash box. She tries to raise the money necessary to bribe the officials and save her son, but she can't come up with the money in time, and Swiss Cheese loses his life.

Later scenes record the rise and fall of Mother Courage's fortunes as the war progresses. At one point, she cries that she will be ruined because of the declaration of peace. Eilif later returns in chains; he has been arrested for theft and murder during an interlude of peace. His mother, off at market, misses her son, who is taken away and executed. The characters of the **Chaplain** and the **Cook** travel at intervals with Mother Courage throughout the play, shown as comic rivals for her affections. The Cook offers to take Mother Courage to Utrecht with him to run an inn. She refuses when he makes it clear that he will not take Kattrin. The climax of the play occurs when Courage, having gone to town for barter, has left Kattrin with a peasant family. They are set upon by soldiers, who plan to raid the town and kill the inhabitants. In a desperate act of courage, Kattrin climbs onto the roof of the peasant's house and bangs a drum to wake the unsuspecting townsfolk. She succeeds, but pays with her life. The concluding scene depicts Mother Courage alone, all of her children the victims of war. But like the war, she survives and readies herself to carry on, saying: "I must get back into business."

In his plays, Brecht sought to replace the traditional forms of drama with what he termed "epic theater," designed to appeal to the intellect and the social conscience of the audience rather than to their emotions. In *Mother Courage,* he employed several examples of these effects, which distance, or "alienate," the viewer from the play, destroying the illusion of verisimilitude that characterizes traditional theater. Despite Brecht's efforts, he created in Mother Courage a character whose depth and complexity do indeed engage the audience's emotions, and she is considered one of the most significant characters of modern drama.

FURTHER READING

Bentley, Eric. "The Stagecraft of Brecht." In *In Search of Theater,* pp. 144-60. New York: Atheneum, 1953.

——. *The Brecht Commentaries: 1943-1980.* New York: Grove Press, 1981.

Brustein, Robert. "Bertolt Brecht." In *The Theatre of Revolt: An Approach to the Modern Drama,* pp. 231-78. Boston: Little, Brown, 1964.

Contemporary Authors, Vol. 104. Detroit: Gale Research Co.

Cook, Bruce. *Brecht in Exile.* New York: Holt, Rinehart and Winston, 1983.

Corrigan, Robert W. "Bertolt Brecht: Poet of the Collective." In *The Theatre in Search of a Fix.* New York: Delacorte, 1973.

Dictionary of Literary Biography, Vol. 56. Detroit: Gale Research Co.

Esslin, Martin. *Bertolt Brecht.* New York: Columbia University Press, 1969.

Ewen, Frederic. *Bertolt Brecht: His Life, His Art, and His Times.* New York: Citadel Press, 1967.

Gray, Ronald D. *Brecht the Dramatist.* Cambridge: Cambridge University Press, 1976.

Hill, Claude. *Bertolt Brecht.* Boston: Twayne, 1975.

Lyons, Charles R. *Bertolt Brecht: The Despair and the Polemic.* Carbondale: Southern Illinois University Press, 1968.

Twentieth-Century Literary Criticism, Vols. 1, 6, 13. Detroit: Gale Research Co.

Willet, John. *The Theater of Bertolt Brecht: A Study from Eight Aspects.* London: Methuen and Co., 1959.

Pearl S. Buck

1892-1973

American novelist, biographer, and essayist.

The Good Earth (novel, 1931)

Set in nineteenth century rural China, the novel begins with the marriage of the poor farmer **Wang Lung** to a slave girl named **O-Lan.** Together, the couple labor tirelessly on their small farm to increase their harvest, sell their surplus, and eventually buy more land. During this period of prosperity, O-Lan gives birth to two sons and a daughter. Before the birth of the couple's fourth child, however, a draught and famine strike the land. Withered and weak from starvation, O-Lan stoically kills the newborn after its first cry and the family, facing certain death if they stay in the country, leaves the land and travels to a city in the south. There, Wang Lung pulls a rickshaw while O-Lan and the rest of the family beg for copper in the streets. Among the city's destitute, there is a growing mood of insurrection and revolution. One day, the gates of a rich man's home are broken open by an angry mob and O-Lan and Wang Lung are swept along, acquiring the silver and jewels that enable them to return to their farm land. The drought ends and Wang Lung becomes idle as his fortune grows, hiring laborers and frequenting the village tea houses. Meanwhile, O-Lan continues in her selfless service to the family's needs and soon bears her husband twins, a son and a daughter. Wang Lung becomes enamored with a beautiful young concubine named **Lotus Blossom.** Insensitive to the strength and devotion of O-Lan, Wang Lung buys Lotus and brings her home, taking his wife's pearls as a gift for his new mistress. One fall, Wang Lung's love of the earth and of labor returns, and with his old friend **Ching,** he begins to work the fields again. At O-Lan's deathbed, Wang Lung first feels remorse for his treatment of his wife and arranges for her final wish, which is to see her oldest son married. After her death, the family moves into the great house in town where O-Lan had once been a slave before her marriage to Wang Lung.

Buck tells the story of Wang Lung's transition from diligence and faithfulness to self-indulgence and promiscuity simply and without judgment. This may be attributable to the author's many years of experience in China, where her view of the country and its people was colored by both the Christian teachings of her missionary parents as well as by the Confucian ideas of tranquility and acceptance. Unlike Buck's later works which are faulted for their stylistic weaknesses, *The Good Earth* maintains its fluidity through its simple language and melodic structuring. The tale is drawn from the tradition of the saga with its strong emphasis on story telling. Buck brings to this form her own concern with the personal and spiritual lives of ordinary people, stressing such universal themes and values as work, family, and the eternal nature of existence. She was awarded the Pulitzer Prize for the novel in 1932.

FURTHER READING

Bentley, Phyllis. "The Art of Pearl S. Buck." *English Journal* 24 (December 1935): 791-800.

Contemporary Authors, Vols. 1-4, 41-44, rev. ed. *Contemporary Authors New Revision Series*, Vol. 1. Detroit: Gale Research Co.

Contemporary Literary Criticism, Vols. 7, 11, 18. Detroit: Gale Research Co.

Dictionary of Literary Biography, Vol. 9. Detroit: Gale Research Co.

Harris, Theodore F. *Pearl S. Buck: A Biography.* New York: John Day Co., 1969.

Henchoz, Ami. "A Permanent Element in Pearl Buck's Novels." *English Studies* 25 (August 1943): 97-103.

Thompson, Dody Weston. "Pearl Buck." In *American Winners of the Nobel Literary Prize,* edited by Warren G. French and Walter E. Kidd, pp. 85-110. Norman: University of Oklahoma Press, 1968.

Mikhail Bulgakov

1891-1940

Russian novelist and dramatist.

The Master and Margarita (novel, 1969)

Because of its criticism of the Soviet government, this novel, Bulgakov's masterpiece, was not published until well after his death and was only available in censored form until 1969.

The novel is a difficult, complex work; it contains three narrative parts, all of them imbued with fantastic and realistic elements, embodying Bulgakov's satire of life under Soviet rule as well as his spiritual views and his deeply felt philosophy regarding the plight of the artist in society. The work is set in Moscow in the 1930s and spans the last four days of Holy Week, culminating in Easter. As the novel begins, the **Devil,** in the person of the black magician **Woland,** has come to Moscow, accompanied by his grotesque entourage. He is an enigmatic character, apparently sent to Moscow to create chaos, but he limits his meddling to those who already face punishment for their jealousy, bigotry, and greed. He meets the young aspiring poet **Ivan Bezdomny,** who is facing persecution for his poem on Jesus from the political writer and literary editor **Mikhail Alexandrovich Berlioz,** whose singular devotion to promoting Marxist thought in literature enjoins him in debate with Woland. Berlioz denies both the existence of Satan and the historical fact of Jesus's life. Woland repudiates him for his stupidity and predicts his death; later, Berlioz is decapitated by a streetcar.

Ivan is deemed mad by society and is confined to a mental institution where he meets the **Master,** a former historian turned writer who has committed himself voluntarily to avoid contact with the outside world and to devote himself to art. Ivan also meets the Master's beautiful mistress, **Margarita,** and the second part of the narrative deals with their lives. The Master is an artist who is victimized by the authorities because he dares to write the truth. Margarita is his faithful lover who helps him as he works on his book on the conflict between **Yeshua-ha-Nozri,** Jesus Christ, and **Pontius Pilate;** but the Master is the victim of scurrilous attacks in the press, and he burns his manuscript. Margarita visits the devil to try to win favor for the Master, and makes a Faustian pact with him that she hopes will guarantee the survival of the Master's novel.

The third narrative relates the arguments between Christ and Pilate that leads to Jesus's crucifixion and death. These sections are interwoven throughout the novel and, we come to learn, form the Master's novel. Jesus argues for the goodness in humankind before the magistrate whose role, which he discharges unwillingly, is to condemn and silence him. The themes of the artist's plight, the legend of Faust, the nature of good and evil, and the redemptive power of love are evident here and throughout the novel. Margarita bargains with a devil who appears to work with God rather than in opposition to him, and, in his ultimate recovery of the manuscript, acts as a savior to the Master and Margarita; although Margarita does bargain with the devil, she does so out of love and to preserve a work of art. The Master and Jesus are parallel characters, both victimized by a stupid and brutal system and both representing a message that is unadulterated and timeless. Bulgakov savagely satirizes the secular ideology represented in Berlioz and compares it to the true knowledge of good and evil that guide the lives of people like the Master and his beloved. In the conclusion, the Master and Margarita plead with the Devil to absolve Pilate and to let him meet with Jesus. Woland and his group of black riders leave the earth, and the Master and his beloved are granted the peace they desire.

FURTHER READING

Bagby, Lewis. "Eternal Themes in Mixail Bulgakov's *The Master and Margarita.*" *The International Fiction Review* 1, No. 1 (January 1974): 27-31.

Contemporary Authors, Vol. 105. Detroit: Gale Research Co.

Delaney, Joan. "*The Master and Margarita:* The Reach Exceeds the Grasp." *Slavic Review* 31, No. 1 (March 1971): 89-100.

Proffer, Elendea. *Bulgakov: Life and Work*. Ann Arbor: Ardis, 1984.

Twentieth-Century Literary Criticism, Vols. 2, 16. Detroit: Gale Research Co.

Wright, A. Colin. *Mikhail Bulgakov: Life and Interpretations*. Toronto: University of Toronto Press, 1978.

Ivan Bunin

1870-1953

Russian short story writer, novelist, and poet.

The Village (novel, 1910)

The novel is set in rural Russia in the early twentieth century. Divided into three parts, it tells of the life of **Tikhon Ilitch Krasoff** and his brother, **Kuzma Ilitch Krasoff,** who in their opposing temperaments encompass the duality of human nature. The first section is concerned with Tikhon. He is a rough, pragmatic man who is obsessed with making money and buying land. He begins his working life as a peddlar and becomes a prosperous innkeeper and landowner, although crop failures lead him to drink. In the second section, we learn about Kuzma. He is idealistic, sensitive and a poet, a wanderer and a tramp who is destined never to realize his dreams. As this section begins, Kuzma and Tikhon have quarrelled and parted ways, and we follow Kuzma on his journeys. In Part Three, Kuzma returns to the simple village, where he becomes an overseer on his brother's estate.

The novel is noted for its straight-forward, unidealized portrait of peasant life. Their existence is depicted as a monotonous cycle of brutality and poverty, and the peasants themselves are as harsh and unchangeable as the land they inhabit. Bunin himself called the work a poem, and many critics have noted that its three-part structure lends it the air of a triptych. The novel is essentially plotless, offering a realistic yet poetic representation of rural life.

"The Gentleman from San Francisco" (short story, 1916)

This short story, considered Bunin's masterpiece, relates the journey of the "gentleman" of the title, whose name is never known to us. As the story begins, he and his wife and daughter, who also remain nameless, are aboard the luxury ship *Atlantic* bound for Europe. The gentleman is a wealthy and powerful man who has decided he is ready, at the age of fifty-eight, to enjoy his money. He has planned the typical European "tour" for people of his class, and as they sail, it is obvious that the power structure that guides the world on shore is at work here, for the wealthy continue their lives of luxury, served by the underprivileged members of society: Chinese "boys," black waiters, and the nameless, faceless men who stoke the furnace of the great ship. The gentleman is snobbish and arrogant, used to having his orders obeyed; he is indifferent and insensitive to the needs of those around him and bent on satisfying his sensual pleasures. He is also an isolated man, devoid of love and leading a deadened and essentially meaningless existence. He is the representative of a decadent and dying culture and is described as a figure of decay, with false teeth, little hair, and yellow, sagging skin. When the family reaches Capri, they find themselves in the finest suite of a grand hotel. But when the gentleman suffers a heart attack, the hotel staff change their attitude from fawning deference to cold indifference: he has had the bad taste to disturb the other guests by dying in their midst, and his body is relegated to the cheapest room. From there he is transported, in an empty soda-water box, back aboard the *Atlantic,* this time in the hold of the ship, for his journey home.

Beneath the simple message of vanity and the corruption of wealth and power, the story has a deeper allegorical intent. Bunin draws parallels between the gentleman and the infamous Roman tyrant Tiberius, who had lived on Capri. Critics suggest that in their lust for power and devotion to debauchery the two men represent the decline and fall of their two cultures, doomed like Babylon to collapse. The story is given through the narrative perspective of an ironic, detached third-person narrator who provides commentary on the action.

FURTHER READING

Brooks, Cleanth, John Thibaut Purser, and Robert Penn Warren. "The Gentleman from San Francisco." In *An Approach to Literature,* pp. 174-77. New York: Appleton-Century-Crofts, 1952.

Contemporary Authors, Vol. 104. Detroit: Gale Research Co.

Gross, Seymour L. "Nature, Man, and God in Bunin's 'The Gentleman from San Francisco'." *Modern Fiction Studies* 6, No. 2 (Summer 1960): 153-63.

Murry, J. Middleton. "Ivan Bunin." *The Nation and The Athenaeum* 31, No. 13 (24 June 1922): 444.

Poggioli, Renato. "The Art of Ivan Bunin." In *The Phoenix and the Spider: A Book of Essays about Some Russian Writers and Their View of the Self,* pp. 131-57. Cambridge: Harvard University Press, 1957.

Strelsky, Nikander. "Bunin: Eclectic of the Future." *The South Atlantic Quarterly* 25, No. 3 (July 1936): 273-83.

Struve, Gleb. "The Art of Ivan Bunin." *The Slavonic Review* 11, No. 32 (January 1933): 423-36.

Twentieth-Century Literary Criticism, Vol. 6. Detroit: Gale Research Co.

Anthony Burgess

1917-

English novelist, essayist, and critic.

A Clockwork Orange (novel, 1962)

Set in a futuristic dystopia, the work is narrated by **Alex,** a teenage hoodlum. In this future world, tensions between Western and Eastern political powers appear to have subsided, but lawlessness and violence are the norm, and youth gangs terrorize the inhabitants. Alex, a character of monstrous savagery, speaks his own language, *nadsat,* which Burgess created using elements of English slang and Russian. Through Alex's eyes and immersed in his language, the reader experiences his career of brutal crime, encompassing all types of violence. A seemingly atypical aspect of his nature is his love for classical music, especially Beethoven and Mozart. How can this creature so full of viciousness and devoid of decency love music of such lofty origins and meanings? Yet it is central to Burgess's conception of Alex and of human nature that the character freely chooses both the evil acts he commits and the music he loves.

Alex is eventually caught, convicted, and is sentenced to prison. While he is imprisoned, there is a change in government that will dictate a chilling reversal in his fortunes, for the former liberal government has been thrown out and replaced with a more authoritarian power who punish criminal behavior in a particular way. Alex is subjected to behavior therapy designed to alter his violent urges. Using drugs and shock treatments, Alex is "taught" a new response to violence as he is forced to watch films depicting inhuman cruelty and savagery. Thus his treatment denies his self-hood and the freedom to choose; society deprives him of his individuality, and it is this that Burgess condemns in his novel.

Following his release, Alex becomes prey to his former victims; in one instance, he is beaten and left to the police, who, it turns out, now contains members of his former gang. Their violent behavior is now used by society to "protect" its members, and they, too, assault Alex. In this state, he reaches the home of **F. Alexander**, the prior victim of one of his most hideous acts of violence. Alexander is the author of a book entitled, ironically *A Clockwork Orange,* which reflects his liberal view of humanity. Yet Burgess shows him to be a hypocrite, for in his desire to revenge himself on Alex, he preys on his conditioned responses and tries to drive Alex to self-destruction. Now Alex has become an embarrassment to the government that had touted its reconditioning methods, and, because he is no longer useful to them, he is "reconverted" to his former, violent self.

Burgess's horrifying look into the future contains thematic elements that recur in much of his fiction. In his depiction of the opposing forms of government, he delineates the contrasting poles of the early philosophers Pelagius and Augustine, one representing the philosophy that humankind is capable of perfection, the other positing that humanity is by its very nature flawed and requires the kind of oppressive tactics used in *Clockwork Orange* to recondition the aberrant of society. Burgess's linguistic abilities are evident in his masterful creation of Alex's language, and his vast knowledge of music is also apparent as a unifying motif in the work.

Enderby (novel, 1968)

F.X. Enderby is the central character of a series of Burgess's novels, including *Inside Mr. Enderby* (later enlarged and republished as *Enderby*), *Enderby Outside, The Clockwork Testament; or, Enderby's End,* and *Enderby's Dark Lady, or, No End to Enderby.* He is one of Burgess's best-known and most humorous characters, and is, in the opinion of many critics, best represented in *Enderby.*

A middle-aged poet who is a recluse from society, Enderby is able to create only in the bathroom, a symbol for his obsession with isolation and with his own bodily functions. He is a man obsessed with food, always plagued by heartburn, flatulence, and guilt. His isolation is heightened by his sense of bereavement over his mother who died at his birth and who was replaced by a hideous stepmother who embodies all the cruelty and lack of sensitivity of her fairytale counterparts. Through Enderby Burgess also explores a recurrent theme in his work—the plight of the artist in modern society, which disregards poets and poetry.

The novels are filled with the madness of popular culture, which intrude upon the solitary life of the poet. Although Enderby is a man in mid-life, he is truly an innocent, which Burgess highlights when Enderby encounters a seductive widow who tries to lure him into an affair, and when he meets another artist, a failed poet who taunts him about the fleeting nature of a poet's fame. This encounter with the outside world nearly undoes Enderby; as a result, he loses his poetic gift and is driven to thoughts of suicide. But, like Alex, he is "reconditioned" by a psychiatrist, with Burgess once again parodying the behavioral scientists. Although he is transformed by this experience, losing his name and becoming **Piggy Hogg,** he reemerges from analysis with his mind and his poetic gift in tact, much to the dismay of his doctors.

Later volumes in the Enderby cycle deal with the state of the poet in our time, particularly with Enderby coming to grips with his competence as a poet. He is a man whose past makes him unable to reach out and to love other people. For Burgess, this signals his inability to recreate life in art, and his character remains stymied by his ineptitude, and doom him to mediocrity. Yet for the author and the reader he is a courageous character, not to be duped by the falseness of art in the modern era, dedicated to his poetry in the face of all the aridity and chaos of contemporary culture, and a hero. Philosophically, the work continues Burgess's exploration of the duality of existence, and he argues for the understanding that free will and evil are part of life, and that we possess the power of choice.

Earthly Powers (novel, 1980)

As the novel begins, **Kenneth M. Toomey** is an eighty-one year old man. His character is based on the life of W. Somerset Maugham, and like his prototype, he is a writer and a homosexual. It is through his eyes that we view the life of **Don Carlo Campanati,** a character based on Pope John XXIII. The two meet as young men, and their friendship over the years and their continuing debate on the nature of the human soul form the basis of the novel. Burgess depicts Don Carlo's rise to the papacy as the result of his pact with the devil, to whom he pledges allegiance for the power of the position. In Toomey, Burgess continues his examination of the position of the artist in contemporary society begun in such earlier works as the Enderby novels. Toomey is self-deprecating about his art and about the importance of the artist to society. As a homosexual, he is shown to be a lonely victim of his often vicious partners and outside the mainstream of society.

Once again Burgess addresses the Pelagian and Augustinian views of human nature. Here, the representative of Augustinian thought is Toomey, who believes in the fallen nature of humankind and sees his homosexuality as elemental to that state. The setting of the novel varies widely, and we follow Toomey as he travels the world. He functions as a witness for the reader to the horrors of the century, from World War I to the mass suicide at Jonestown. Don Carlo, the proponent of Pelagianism, believes that man is perfect, created in God's image, and that the devil is the source of all the evil in the world. As a young priest, he ironically builds his reputation on his powers as an exorcist, supposedly ridding the possessed of the devil which Burgess implies is permanently within all of us, and is the force behind Don Carlo's success.

Burgess creates a broad canvas in this novel, as he covers the historical, political, and literary world of the twentieth century through his protagonists. His vivid word play once again evinces his linguistic brilliance and his Joycean love of language.

FURTHER READING

Aggeler, Geoffrey. *Anthony Burgess: The Artist as Novelist.* Tuscaloosa: University of Alabama Press, 1979.

Bell, Pearl K. "Games Writers Play." *Commentary* 71, No. 2 (Februaray 1981): 69-72.

Coale, Samuel. *Anthony Burgess.* New York: Ungar, 1982.

Contemporary Authors, Vols. 1-4, rev. ed.; *Contemporary Authors New Revision Series,* Vol. 2. Detroit: Gale Research Co.

Contemporary Literary Criticism, Vols. 1, 2, 4, 5, 8, 10, 13, 15, 22, 40. Detroit: Gale Research Co.

DeVitis, A.A. *Anthony Burgess.* New York: Twayne, 1972.

Dictionary of Literary Biography, Vol. 14. Detroit: Gale Research Co.

Dix, Carol M. *Anthony Burgess.* London: Longman, 1971.

Mathews, Richard. *The Clockwork Universe of Anthony Burgess.* San Bernardino: Borgo Press, 1978.

Steiner, George. "Scroll and Keys." *The New Yorker* 57, No. 8 (13 April 1981): 159-62.

Sullivan, Walter. "Death Without Tears: Anthony Burgess and the Dissolution of the West." *The Hollins Critic* 6 (1969): 1-11.

Towers, Robert. "The Prince of Darkness Is Pope." *The New Republic* 184, Nos. 1 and 2 (3, 10 January 1981): 32-4.

William S. Burroughs

1914-

American novelist.

The Naked Lunch (novel, 1959)

This controversial work is an autobiographical account of Burroughs's fourteen-year addiction to morphine. The book's theme of addiction and its graphic depiction of drug use, homosexuality, and violence led to an obscenity case before the book was available in the United States. Through the plight of his protagonist, **William Lee,** Burroughs explores the causes behind addiction, which he uses as a metaphor for the dependence and obsession that mark the human condition in contemporary society.

The work has no single narrative viewpoint and is a loosely composed series of vignettes that depict Lee's feverish journeys around the world, always seeking out the company of other addicts. These scenes are interspersed with surreal, dream-like sequences that reveal horrifying, perverse, and violent activities. The novel is a pastiche of different narrative styles, drawn from science fiction and the detective story. As we follow Lee from New York to Chicago to Mexico to Tangier, we find a man driven to flight, trying to escape. His world is anarchic, amoral, and corrupt, but Burroughs indicates that the repression and horror of addiction traps anyone who is not free from the controlling elements of drugs, sex, societal and political structures, even language itself. In his highly experimental style, Burroughs seeks to break away from dependence on the rules of logic or grammar, that constrict meaning. The title is explained by Lee: a "naked lunch" is "a frozen moment when everyone sees what is on the end of every fork." The work frightens and repulses the reader, all according to Burroughs's plan, for he wanted to attack the reader's senses, beliefs, and attitudes toward life and toward what a literary work could be. Whether he succeeded remains arguable to some critics, but *Naked Lunch* has become known as a notorious statement of rebellion.

FURTHER READING

Contemporary Authors, Vols. 9-12, rev. ed.; *Contemporary Authors New Revision Series,* Vol. 20. Detroit: Gale Research Co.

Contemporary Literary Criticism, Vols. 1, 2, 5, 15, 22, 42. Detroit: Gale Research Co.

Dictionary of Literary Biography, Vols. 2, 8, 16; *Dictionary of Literary Biography Yearbook: 1981.* Detroit: Gale Research Co.

Hassan, Ihab. "The Subtracting Machine: The Work of William Burroughs." *Critique* 6, No. 1 (Spring 1963): 4-23.

McLuhan, Marshall. "Notes on Burroughs." *Nation* 199 (28 December 1964): 517-18.

Tanner, Tony. *City of Words: American Fiction,* 1950-1970, pp. 109-40. New York: Harper & Row, 1971.

Erskine Caldwell
1903-1987

American novelist and short story writer.

Tobacco Road (novel, 1932)

Tobacco Road depicts the degeneration of a poor white family living in Georgia during the Depression. The work shocked conventional literary tastes upon its publication for its stark, realistic depiction of poverty and the physical and erotic appetites of its characters.

The main character, **Jeeter Lester,** inhabits a ramshackle hut with his wife, **Ada,** his mother, and two of his twelve living children, **Dude,** an adolescent boy, and **Ellie May,** his harelipped daughter; the other children had fled the farm as soon as they were able. As the story opens, a hungry Jeeter is scheming to rob his son-in-law, **Lov Bensey,** of a sack of winter turnips. He is successful due to the sexual prowess of Ellie May. Lov had come to the farm to ask Jeeter's advice regarding Jeeter's daughter, **Pearl,** who had married Lov a year before. Lov complained that even after a year of marriage, Pearl, at fifteen, would neither speak nor sleep with him. Unconcerned, Jeeter explains that Ada had been much the same way. Later, **Sister Bessie Rice,** a widow and self-proclaimed preacher, arrives. She prays for Jeeter's soul and then, after fondling Dude, announces that her late husband had left her eight-hundred dollars which she planned to use to buy a new car, though she didn't drive. With an eye on Dude, she also says that she plans to remarry. Anxious for the car, Dude readily agrees, despite Bessie's advanced years and physical ugliness. After the marriage and the purchase of the car, the couple return to the Lester farm to live. Within one week, the car is as shabby and almost as useless as the farm itself.

Jeeter's mother continues to gather wood and start a fire every mealtime, just in case food should arrive. The rest of the family actively ignores and mistreats her. Near the end of the novel, Jeeter orders Bessie off the farm and Dude, while driving away, runs the car over his grandmother. The family, unconcerned, steps over and around her. In the conclusion, Jeeter, hoping to somehow borrow a mule and beg some cotton seeds, decides to burn the land in order to have it ready for planting. That night, the wind shifts, and Jeeter and Ada die in the burning hovel.

The characters of this notorious novel, deformed by their poverty and hopelessness to the level of grotesques, are portrayed as victims of a land that can no longer support them. Because of its vivid, explicit portrayal of sexuality, the novel met with problems of censorship and also proved to be a liberating influence on later writers.

FURTHER READING

Cantwell, Robert. "Caldwell's Characters: Why Don't They Leave?" *The Georgia Review* 11, No. 3 (Fall 1957): 252-64.

Contemporary Authors, Vols. 1-4, rev. ed.; *Contemporary Authors New Revision Series,* Vol. 2; *Contemporary Authors Autobiographical Series,* Vol. 1. Detroit: Gale Research Co.

Contemporary Literary Criticism, Vols. 1, 8, 14, 50. Detroit: Gale Research Co.

Dictionary of Literary Biography, Vol. 9. Detroit: Gale Research Co.

Frohock, W. M. "Erskine Caldwell—The Dangers of Ambiguity." In *The Novel of Violence in America,* pp. 106-23. Dallas: Southern Methodist University Press, 1957.

Gray, Richard. "The Good Farmer: Some Variations of a Historical Theme." In *The Literature of Memory: Modern Writers of the American South,* pp. 106-49. Baltimore: Johns Hopkins University Press, 1977.

Italo Calvino
1923-1985
Italian novelist, short story writer, and essayist.

Invisible Cities (novel, 1972)

Invisible Cities, based on the journals of thirteenth-century explorer Marco Polo, centers on a fictionalized **Marco Polo** describing fifty-five imaginary, symbolically related cities to an aged **Kublai Khan.** With elaborate, enchanting detail, the famous traveler, who has served as Khan's ambassador, patiently educates the legendary conqueror about his burgeoning empire. Conversation between the two men constitutes the sole action of the novel while the cities themselves, each assigned a woman's name, become the extended cast of characters. Each city—from Melania, a city of stereotypic inhabitants, to Zemrude, a city that alters according to the mood of each new observer—is unique, fantastic, and a rich subject for moral and philosophical speculation. Throughout the work Calvino playfully cautions that the cities are simply fleeting images, forever mutable, essentially invisible, and ultimately one. His depiction of such cities as Zemrude underscores his understanding of the chimerical possibilities of reality, an understanding inspired by the scientific notion that human perception is infinitely varied.

Calvino has acknowledged that his work is strongly influenced by the playful fantasy and moral content of the fable. Accordingly, he often creates fantastic settings, characters, and situations to comment on the modern world through such devices as allegory, irony, and satire. In all of his works Calvino displays his great knowledge of literature and the natural sciences, which he uses to extend the implications of his themes. Typical of his finest work, *Invisible Cities* supports several levels of interpretation beyond the immediate appeal of the fantastic. While the experiences of Marco Polo impart moral lessons on how to appreciate life, this work also focuses on the relationship between writer and reader. Kublai Khan serves as spokesman for the reader as he interprets, questions, argues, and attempts to find patterns that will yield meaning to the tales. Despite its intricate structure and intellectual density, the work was among the first to win for Calvino a wide-ranging international readership.

The Castle of Crossed Destinies (novel, 1973)

A semiotic fantasy, *The Castle of Crossed Destinies* consists of the intersecting tales of a group of travelers who lose their power of speech while passing through a mythical forest of self-loss. Calvino divided his work into two major parts: "The Castle of Crossed Destinies" and "The Tavern of Crossed Destinies." The chief difference between the two, other than setting, is the way in which the guests of the castle and the guests of the tavern—all of whom are confined to nonverbal communication—tell their various life stories. In the first setting the storytellers utilize a fifteenth-century tarot deck and, through gestures and connective, linear arrangement of the pictures, reveal pivotal personal events. In the second setting, the storytellers utilize a larger, eighteenth-century tarot deck but, rather than link their stories in crossword fashion, they arrange their histories in superimposed, irregular blocks. The narrator, an unnamed knight in the first section and a writer in the second, assumes central importance. His task is to intimately describe how each story evolves, present a marginal text depicting the chronological progression of the tarot cards, and offer the most likely interpretations of each person's tale. This forces the reader to become an active participant, for he must weigh what the cards signify with what the narrator has described. The characters are both stock and famous figures culled from literary tradition. They include **Roland,** the **Alchemist,** the **Grave Robber,** and the **Waverer.** The tavern section, especially, alludes to archetypal stories, including those of Faust, Parsifal, Oedipus, and Hamlet. At the center of each tale is a tragic flaw that leads the teller away from meaning and happiness and into the forest, where he experiences a disillusioning confrontation with himself. Yet none of the characters, including the narrator, arrive at any final sense of life's purpose.

Calvino, through use of the tarot deck, underscores the difficulty of precisely understanding the human condition. Although mythic, his narrative is nevertheless deeply concerned with life in the twentieth century. Considered both a structural and thematic triumph, *The Castle of Crossed Destinies* ranks among Calvino's best works. His experimentation in the novel form, from early neorealist works to the semiotic fantasies of his later years, has earned him high regard as one of Italy's most important and versatile modern authors.

FURTHER READING

Adler, Sara Maria. *Calvino: The Writer as Fablemaker.* Ediciones Jose Porrua Turanzas, 1979.

Calvino, Italo. *The Uses of Literature: Essays,* translated by Patrick Creagh. New York: Harcourt Brace Jovanovich, 1986.

Cannon, JoAnn. *Calvino, Writer and Critic.* Ravenna: Longo, 1981.

Carter, Albert H. *Italo Calvino: Metamorphoses of Fantasy.* Ann Arbor: UMI Research Press, 1987.

Contemporary Authors, Vols. 85-88, 116; *Contemporary Authors New Revision Series,* Vol. 23. Detroit: Gale Research Co.

Contemporary Literary Criticism, Vols. 5, 8, 11, 22, 33, 39. Detroit: Gale Research Co.

Olken, I. T. *With Pleated Eye and Garnet Wing: Symmetries of Italo Calvino.* Ann Arbor: University of Michigan Press, 1984.

Albert Camus

1913-1960

Algerian-born French novelist, essayist and dramatist.

The Stranger (novel, 1942)

This novel, considered one of the most important works of modern literature, relates the story of the life and death of **Meursault.**

Set in Algiers, the novel is rendered in the first person in a simple, detached tone. It begins with the brief sentence: "Mother died today," a fact that will define the course of the novel. Meursault is portrayed as a man governed by sensation; thus, at his mother's wake and funeral, he displays no feelings or actions of grief, and thinks instead about a cup of coffee and a cigarette. He is an unwitting nonconformist who does not abide by society's codes and rituals, as is evident when he returns home from his mother's funeral and begins an affair with a pretty young girl, **Marie.** Indeed, it is the sensation of Marie's body next to his, the heat and light of the sun, the taste of food, and the simple pleasures of the senses that seem to appeal to him. When Marie asks him if he loves her and if he will marry her, he replies that such concepts have no meaning for him, for he appears to have no opinions nor true feeling for such issues.

In the company of his friend **Raymond,** a pimp, he encounters two Arabs on a beach who are in pursuit of Raymond. His friend puts a revolver in his hand, and motivated more by the heat and glare of the sun than Raymond's plight, Meursualt discharges the gun into one of the Arabs, killing him. The aftermath of this incident forms the focal point of the novel. Meursault is tried for murder, but it is not the crime but the man who will not conform to society's rules, who is examined and judged. He is accused and condemned for not crying at his mother's funeral and is defined by the defense as "an inhuman monster wholly without moral sense"; for this he is convicted.

Condemned to death, Meursault spends the last days of his life exploring and trying to understand his relationship to the society that has rejected him. There is a change in the tone and the presentation of the protagonist at this point, as Meursault grows to understand the inherent absurdity of his situation. The conclusion reveals him able to remain faithful to himself, and to open himself to what he sees as the truth of the human condition: the "benign indifference of the universe"; in acknowledging the source of his being and his happiness, he faces his death.

The novel is noted for its presentation of Camus's concept of the absurd, as evidenced in his treatment of Meursault, who must face condemnation at the hands of a society that requires an illogical conformity to its rules. That Meursault is able to face the absurdity of his existence, to challenge it, and finally to accept his fate marks him as Camus's modern hero,

The Plague (novel, 1947)

The novel is set in the 1940s in the North African city of Oran and depicts the actions of a community as it battles the plague. The effect of the pestilence on the city transforms it from the ordinary, ugly place described in the preface to a site of extraordinary human endeavor, as the people, represented by **Dr. Bernard Rieux** and his group, unite to fight an evil and absurd enemy. It is this struggle against suffering and death and the effect it has on the characters, reflected particularly in their philosophical conversations, that forms the core of the novel.

The novel begins as Rieux finds a dead rat; later, the concierge of his building dies of symptoms that Rieux recognizes. Yet it is not until pages later that any of the characters can bear to utter the word "plague," a word that resonates with the horrifying fate of the city. The city is closed to the outside world, and a sense of exile and isolation overcomes the population. As the disease advances, Camus notes the growing interdependence and solidarity of the people, focussing especially on the doctor and the characters that surround him. Rieux, a man of compassion and deep respect for humankind, rejects orthodox religion and represents the philosophy that it is through human action that the disease can be contained and battled. Throughout the novel, he is shown in opposition to **Father Paneloux,** a Jesuit priest, who sees the plague as God's vengeance on the guilty people of Oran, and who represents the conviction that only through faith and divine intervention can the city be saved. **Jean Tarrou,** an idealistic young volunteer who rejects the ways of

Paneloux, aids Reiux during the pestilence and is claimed as one of its victims. **Raymond Rambert,** a journalist, is caught in Oran when the city is quarentined and at first thinks only of himself and his desire to escape the city. Unlike Rieux, he is unable to involve himself in the fate of the city until the doctor convinces him of the necessity of fighting in unison, however provisional the victory. For Rieux, it is not heroism but honesty that motivates the battle, and he defines honesty as "doing your job." The journalist is won over and becomes a volunteer; he loses his life to the plague at the end of the novel.

In the conclusion, we learn that Rieux himself is the author of the chronicle we have been reading. The plague has been vanquished, at least temorarily, and the city returns to its everyday routine. *The Plague* represents the development of Camus's philosophy of the absurd to embrace the collective actions of a community. In their confrontation and resistance of the forces that would deprive them of meaning and happiness in life, they triumph over the absurdity of suffering and death.

FURTHER READING

Bree, Germaine. *Camus.* New Brunswick: Rutgers University Press, 1959.

Champigny, Robert. *A Pagan Hero: An Interpretation of Meursault in Camus's "The Stranger."* Philadelphia: University of Pennsylvania Press, 1970.

Contemporary Authors, Vols. 89-92. Detroit: Gale Research Co.

Contemporary Literary Criticism, Vols. 1, 2, 4, 9, 11, 14, 32. Detroit: Gale Research Co.

Cruickshank, John. *Albert Camus and the Literature of Revolt.* London: Oxford University Press, 1960.

Dictionary of Literary Biography, Vol. 72. Detroit: Gale Research Co.

Hannah, Thomas. *The Thought and Art of Albert Camus.* Chicago: Henry Regnery Co., 1958.

Lazare, Donald. *The Unique Creation of Albert Camus.* New Haven: Yale University Press, 1973.

Rhein, Phillip H. *The Urge to Live.* Chapel Hill: University of North Carolina Press, 1964.

Truman Capote

1924-1984

American novelist, short story writer, and nonfiction writer.

Other Voices, Other Rooms (novel, 1948)

Capote's first novel is set in the contemporary South and concerns the quest of its thirteen-year-old protagonist, **Joel Knox,** for a father and for an identity. When the first search fails, the boy determines to find a niche in a world that frightens and rejects him. The central focus of the book is Joel's coming of age sexually. Raised by his mother and aunt, he has been enveloped in a feminine world and finds the society of men to be strange and threatening. The dilapidated southern mansion in which he lives is the home of a group of grotesque figures whose strange, remote characteristics reinforce the isolated, dreamlike world in which the protagonist dwells. Ultimately, he falls prey to the attentions of **Randolph,** a transvestite who, though grotesque, shares Joel's sense of utter alienation from conventional society. Although the young man chooses a life that most would consider deviant, he is satisfied with having gained an identity, however hard-won, and the novel ends on a note of guarded optimism.

Though the novel was faulted by some for its intensely decadent, spiritually hollow atmosphere, other critics consider it a respectable successor to the American Gothic romance. Many readers and critics ascribed Joel Knox's homosexual leanings to the twenty-three-year-old Truman Capote, and critics note the element of sensationalism and scandal this contributed to the book's notoriety and commercial success. The novel's dustjacket, with a photo of the author languidly reclining on a couch with an androgynous, insouciant look drew almost more attention than the novel itself and established Capote's reputation as an author drawn to self-promotion and celebrity.

Breakfast at Tiffany's (novella, 1958)

Regarded as one of Capote's most fresh and enduring works, *Breakfast at Tiffany's* is set in Manhattan in 1943. It is a portrait of **Holly Golightly,** an impulsive, outspoken, gamine who is in some ways worldly—she has no trouble, for example, accepting fifty dollar bills as "powder room change" from her escorts—but is fundamentally naive. Drawn to the social whirl of New York City, she lives in an apartment with a nameless cat and no furniture; bringing her gentleman friends home at all hours, she rings her neighbor's doorbells, seemingly oblivious to her acts of social indiscretion.

Her story is related in the first person by her devoted friend, **Buster,** a struggling writer and a neighbor in her apartment building. Both Buster and an elderly bartender become deeply attached to Holly, who avoids all close relationships. What she does love is Tiffany's, which is where she goes when she's depressed. It calms her down, she claims, and if she "could find a real-life place that made me feel like Tiffany's, then I'd buy some furniture and give the cat a name." While sharing with him her affection and appealing eccentricity, Holly ultimately draws Buster into trouble when she becomes embroiled with a criminal named **Sally Tomato,** a dope dealer whose exploits are depicted in a convoluted subplot.

But the secret of Holly's origins presents a facet of her that is unlike the person we have come to know. Unlike the urban sophisticate she appears to be, she is in truth a hillbilly from Texas, a child bride whose husband comes to fetch her and relates the story of her marriage at thirteen, her escape from a life of domestic banality, and her flight to New York.

Often compared with the character Sally Bowles from Christopher Isherwood's *Good-Bye to Berlin,* Holly is regarded as one of Capote's most important creations. Furthermore, critics consider *Breakfast at Tiffany's* a well-structured, beautifully paced portrait of 1940s New York that captures the manners and language of the time with an easy charm and grace.

FURTHER READING

Aldridge, John W. "Capote and Buechner—The Escape into Otherness." In *After the Lost Generation,* pp. 194-203. New York: McGraw-Hill, 1951.

Collins, Carvel. "Other Voices." *American Scholar* 25 (Winter 1955-1956): 108-16.

Contemporary Authors, Vols. 5-8, rev. ed.; *Contemporary Authors New Revision Series,* Vol. 18. Detroit: Gale Research Co.

Contemporary Literary Criticism, Vols. 1, 3, 8, 13, 19, 34, 38. Detroit: Gale Research Co.

Dictionary of Literary Biography, Vol. 2; *Dictionary of Literary Biography Yearbook: 1980, 1984; Concise Dictionary of American Literary Biography, 1941-1968.* Detroit: Gale Research Co.

Hassan, Ihab. "Truman Capote: The Vanishing Image of Narcissus." In *Radical Innocence: Studies in the Contemporary American Novel,* pp. 230-58. Princeton: Princeton University Press, 1961.

Hill, Pati. "The Art of Fiction XVII: Truman Capote." *Paris Review* 16 (Spring-Summer 1957): 34-51.

Hyman, Stanley Edgar. "Fruitcake at Tiffany's." In *Standards: A Chronicle of Books for Our Time*, pp. 148-52. New York: Horizon Press, 1966.

Kazin, Alfred. "Truman Capote and the Army of Wrongness." In *Contemporaries*, pp. 250-54. Boston: Little, Brown, 1962.

Nance, William L. *The Worlds of Truman Capote*. New York: Stein and Day, 1970.

Short Story Criticism, Vol. 2. Detroit: Gale Research Co.

Joyce Cary
1888-1957
Anglo-Irish novelist, critic, and poet.

Herself Surprised (novel, 1941); ***To Be a Pilgrim*** (novel, 1942); ***The Horse's Mouth*** (novel, 1944).

Sara Monday is the heroine of the first novel of Cary's first and best-known trilogy. She is the first-person narrator of the work, through whose personal perspective we view the first part of the sequence. The characters of the three novels are all interrelated, and the same themes resonate throughout. Sara is an earthy, passionate, loving woman, confounded by the world of men; yet it is through her relationships with men that she is defined for herself and for the reader. Central to her association with the three important men in her life is marriage. She is first married to **Matthew Monday,** who becomes jealous of her friendship with **Gulley Jimson,** an artist and the protagonist of the third novel in the series. Out of her love for Gulley, she steals items from the home of her employer, **Tom Wilcher,** the central figure of the second novel, a man who loves her and also wishes to marry her. Sara's actions land her in prison, where she indulges in a good deal of soul-searching, promising to mend her ways on her release.

The tone of the novel is richly comic, and many critics have noted parallels between Sara and Moll Flanders, seeing her as a modern-day picaro. Sara speaks with a voice distinctly her own, and her presence and point of view, displayed to particular effect through the use of interior monologue, dominate the work. She is revealed to the reader in different perspectives in the later novels of the trilogy. Thematically, Cary explores the freedom of the individual in conflict with the strictures of society, a topic central to all of his fiction.

Tom Wilcher, the first-person narrator of *To Be a Pilgrim,* is a man immersed in the past. He is opposed to change, seeing in the modern era a disregard for all authority—moral, religious, and governmental. The novel differs in tone from the earlier and later volumes of the sequence, for it is less humorous and more somber and reflective, indicating the character of the protagonist. Tom is concerned with history; he is an old man who has spent his life upholding the values and beliefs of the past. He is a "pilgrim" from another time misplaced in a modern world in a state of flux. His ruminations on the other characters of the novel reveal his shock and dismay at the actions of his family, who have in his mind turned their backs on the traditional moral code and fallen prey to the cold cynicism that has replaced religion in modern life. He loves Sara Monday, protagonist of the earlier novel in the series, and wishes to marry her when she is widowed. But his discernment of her as a representative of an older, traditional order is false, based solely on his perceptions; she rejects his ideas and rebuffs him.

In his examination of freedom and the individual in this work Cary explores the difficulties of a man out of step with his time. Tom does not share the exuberance of Sara or Gulley Jimson; rather, he is a man aware of his own failings, and doomed to be acutely affected by them in others. As in the other volumes in the sequence, the use of interior monologue brings the central character vividly to life.

Gulley Jimson, another of Cary's first-person narrators, is a self-obsessed artist, an ex-convict, and an anarchist. In *The Horse's Mouth* he is depicted in an ongoing battle with society, hating convention and fighting for his individual and artistic freedom. He lives by his own morality, stealing when necessary to buy supplies. He is driven to paint a masterpiece, a work on the Creation, even though his best-known works are the nudes he painted years ago of Sara Monday, a former lover and the protagonist of the first novel in the trilogy. He spends a good part of the novel trying to get his hands on them, but Sara and an art dealer have most of them. In an argument with Sara, he knocks her down the stairs, accidently killing her. Knowing that he will be caught and convicted, he returns home and feverishly works on his Creation. He falls off the scaffolding, suffering a stroke. He is last depicted on his way to prison in an ambulance.

Gulley is perhaps Cary's finest portrait of the individual in quest of freedom. He focuses on Gulley's struggle with a society that rejects him, describing the ruthless way the conventional world treats artists. He also deals with Gulley's personal battle to create, delineating the difficulties the artist faces in releasing the power of the imagination. Critics have noted that in this Cary appears to be revealing an autobiographical element in his character. Gulley's thoughts are rendered in a truncated manner, reflecting the vituperative, rebellious nature of the character.

Cary's first trilogy is considered to be his finest work, noted for its vivid characterization, exceptional handling of narrative stance, and variety of style and perspective.

FURTHER READING

Bloom, Robert. *The Indeterminate World: A Study of the Novels of Joyce Cary.* Philadelphia: University of Pennsylvania Press, 1962.

Contemporary Authors, Vol 104. Detroit: Gale Research Co.

Dictionary of Literary Biography, Vol. 15. Detroit: Gale Research Co.

Hall, James. "Directed Restlessness." In *The Tragic Comedians: Seven Modern British Novelists,* pp. 82-98. Bloomington: Indiana University Press, 1963.

Hoffman, Charles G. *Joyce Cary: The Comedy of Freedom.* Pittsburgh: University of Pittsburgh Press, 1964.

Karl, Frederick R. "Joyce Cary: The Moralist as Novelist." In *Contemporary English Novel,* pp. 131-47.

Larsen, Golden L. *The Dark Descent: Social Change and Moral Responsibility in the Novels of Joyce Cary.* London: Joseph, 1965.

Seltzer, Alvin J. "Speaking Out of Both Sides of *The Horse's Mouth:* Joyce Cary vs. Gulley Jimson." *Contemporary Literature* 15, No. 4 (Autumn 1974): 488-501.

Twentieth-Century Literary Criticism, Vols. 1, 29. Detroit: Gale Research Co.

Van Horn, Ruth G. "Freedom and Imagination in the Novels of Joyce Cary." *Midwest Journal* 5 (1952-1953): 19-30.

Wolkenfeld, Jack. *Joyce Cary: The Developing Style.* New York: New York University Press, 1968.

Wright, Andrew. *Joyce Cary: A Preface to his Novels*. London: Chatto and Windus, 1958.

Willa Cather
1873-1947
American novelist, short story writer, and essayist.

O, Pioneers! (novel, 1913)

Cather's second novel was the first of her many works to be set in the milieu of her own youth: the sweeping plains of Nebraska during the last decades of the nineteenth century. The book's heroine is the generous, high-spirited **Alexandra Bergson,** daughter of Swedish immigrants, who keeps her family whole after their father's early death. While she encourages and watches over all her brothers, her special love and high hopes are reserved for **Emil,** her sensitive, gifted younger brother. These dreams are destroyed, however, when Emil falls in love with **Marie Shabata,** a neighbor, and is murdered by her incensed husband, a Bohemian farmer. Alexandra bears the tragedy with characteristic stoicism, and in mid-life finds romantic love with **Carl Lindstrom,** with whom she can anticipate a rich old age on her beloved plains.

Cather herself acknowledged that in writing of the pioneer life and landscape of her childhood, she found a true "home pasture" for her burgeoning literary gift. Critics note that Alexandra, who with valor and great wisdom civilizes the new land, is the prototype of Cather's memorable "earth mother" heroines who reappear in later works, notably *My Antonia*.

My Antonia (novel, 1919)

Cather's fourth novel is widely considered to be her greatest work. Set on the Nebraska plains in the late nineteenth century, the story is told in the first person by **Jim Burden** as a warm reminiscence of his childhood. While Burden is an important character, thought by many critics to reflect Cather's persona, the novel's central character indisputably is the luminous **Antonia Shimerda,** a farm girl from a family of Bohemian immigrants.

In a lucid prose style graced with a nostalgic, nearly elegiac tone, Burden/Cather relates the life story of Antonia, whom Jim first meets when he is a small boy newly moved west. The gallant young Antonia helps her family survive after her father's suicide, hires herself out as household help, and eventually is abandoned by a lover and gives birth to a baby out of wedlock. In the novel's fifth and final "book," Jim, a successful East-coast lawyer, visits his old friend, now married to a Czech farmer with a brood of sturdy, loving children and a flourishing Nebraska farm. Antonia remains, despite the trials of her life, steadfastly joyous, nurturing, and indomitable, Cather's archetype for the noble pioneer woman and widely acknowledged as one of the most memorable characters in twentieth-century literature.

Death Comes for the Archbishop (novel, 1927)

Cather's ninth novel is set in the mid- to late-nineteenth century in the American West. Inspired by the letters of the real-life **Archbishop Lamy,** who first comes to America as a French missionary priest, the novel relates in episodic form his experiences serving in the territory of New Mexico. The narrative also centers on Lamy's childhood friend, **Joseph Vaillant,** who eventually becomes his vicar, tracing the founding of the enormous diocese through the death of the Archbishop at the end of a lengthy and fruitful religious tenure.

Along the way are interspersed episodes set dramatically against the rugged western mountains and deserts as well as in such locales as Durango, Mexico and the Vatican in Rome. The individual stories that comprise the novel range from the comic—such as Father Vaillant's parting of **Manuel Lujon** from his beloved white donkeys—to the tragic—as in the murder of a pathetic Mexican wife at the hands of her husband, **Buck Scales.**

In addition to Cather's characteristically vivid and majestic prose style in *Death Comes for the Archbishop*, critics note her masterful amalgamation of history, legend, character and dramatic incident, all set against the sweep of the Southwestern American landscape that Cather in adulthood had come to revere. For its successful rendering of ambitious elements and themes in the form of highest literary art, *Death Comes for the Archbishop* is regarded as one of Cather's greatest achievements.

FURTHER READING

Bennett, Mildred. *The World of Willa Cather.* Lincoln: University of Nebraska Press, 1961.

Bloom, Edward A. and Lillian D. Bloom. *Willa Cather's Gift of Sympathy*. Carbondale: Southern Illinois University Press, 1962.

Brown, E. K. and Leon Edel. *Willa Cather: A Critical Biography*. New York: Alfred A. Knopf, 1953.

Contemporary Authors, Vol. 104. Detroit: Gale Research Co.

Daiches, David. *Willa Cather: A Critical Introduction*. Boston: Twayne, 1975.

Dictionary of Literary Biography, Vols. 9, 54; *Dictionary of Literary Biography Documentary Series*, Vol. 1; *Concise Dictionary of American Literary Biography, 1865-1917*. Detroit: Gale Research Co.

O'Brien, Sharon. *Willa Cather: The Emerging Voice*. New York: Oxford University Press, 1987.

Randall, John H., III. *The Landscape and the Looking Glass: Willa Cather's Search for Value*. Boston: Houghton Mifflin, 1960

Rosowski, Susan J. *The Voyage Perilous: Willa Cather's Romanticism*. Lincoln: University of Nebraska Press, 1986.

Schroeder, James, ed. *Willa Cather and Her Critics*. Ithaca: Cornell University Press, 1967.

Short Story Criticism, Vol. 2. Detroit: Gale Research Co.

Slote, Bernice and Virginia Faulkner, eds. *The Art of Willa Cather*. Lincoln: University of Nebraska Press, 1974.

Twentieth-Century Literary Criticism, Vols. 1, 11, 31. Detroit: Gale Research Co.

Louis-Ferdinand Céline
1894-1961
French novelist and essayist.

Journey to the End of the Night (novel, 1932)

The novel recounts the life and travels of the picaresque protagonist-narrator, **Ferdinand Bardamu.** A deserter from the French forces during World War I, Bardamu is in flight throughout the novel, trying to escape from the reality of evil and horror he sees in existence. He is in turn a soldier, pimp, factory worker, doctor, and head of an insane asylum. Early episodes reveal his growing cynicism as he confronts the stupidity of war, of colonialism in Africa, of capitalism as a factory worker in the United Sates, and his disillusionment with his profession as a doctor as he cares for the poor in the slums of Paris. He is affected by spells of delirium, which form an escape from his painful existence. The mysterious figure of **Leon Robinson,** who functions in the novel as Bardamu's double, appears wherever he travels. He is present in Paris, where he tells Bardamu that he has been hired to kill an old woman. While planting the bomb to murder her, the weapon explodes and Robinson is blinded. The last section of the first part of the novel finds Bardamu as the head of an insane asylum, where, among the mad, he feels safe from the vagaries of the modern world.

Death is an omnipresent force in the novel, and Bardamu's disgust and cynicism toward life are vividly recounted in the second part of the work. This section includes Céline's vituperative attacks on contemporary society, particularly the constricting forces of poverty and the inequality between the classes that perpetuates the gulf between rich and poor. The work is dominated by symbols relating to vision and blindness, for to Céline, the evil in the world is so pervasive that it defies one's ability to see and comprehend. Robinson reappears and is later murdered by his mistress. His death appears as meaningless as his life; Bardamu continues on his cynical path toward death.

Céline's work was considered ground-breaking for his deliberate refutation of accepted literary styles. The work is episodic, composed of loosely arranged vignettes, and the narrative is fragmented, with phrases and conversations broken by ellipses. In rejection of stylized literary language, Céline employed the slang of the Parisian slums.

Death on the Installment Plan (novel, 1936)

Ferdinand, the protagonist of this novel, is a doctor and writer like Céline and claims to be the author of *Journey to the End of the Night.* The work is a *bildungsroman* of sorts, as Ferdinand relates the story of his youth and of his efforts to break out of the bourgeois background and the false values that constrain him. The novel's theme is the desolation at the heart of human existence, and Céline relates how maturity is only the process of disillusionment and abandonment of principles and faith.

In the first section of the novel, we see Ferdinand in the present, as a doctor in the slums of Paris. His patients are victims of poverty and despair, from which they seek solace in alcohol and sex. Ferdinand is also a victim of his "opera du deluge," a mental torment that afflicts him day and night. As he lays in bed, he recalls his youth, and his memories form the second section of the novel. The constricted social and familial atmosphere is dominated by his father, **Auguste,** who tries to force Ferdinand to accept his strict bourgeois values. Through the intervention of his kind uncle, **Edouard,** Ferdinand is sent to England to study a language that will help him in business. But Ferdinand refuses to learn, and his resistance symbolizes a rebellion against language as a tool of authority. For him, the family's pretense to honesty, culture and education is a sham. It is through him that they wish to live their pretentious dreams, and this he rejects. In a prominent scene, Ferdinand tries to kill his father; when this Oedipal rage subsides, he feels somehow liberated from his past. **Roger-Marin Courtial des Pereires,** inventor, publisher, and con man, becomes Ferdinand's new father. But when Courtial commits suicide, unable to realize his dreams, Ferdinand decides to leave home for good, and as the novel ends he is off to join the army in hopes of achieving a new life.

The fragmented syntax that characterized *Journey to the End of the Night* is also employed here, as is the argot of the Parisian working class, in a work that continues Céline's cynical view of modern existence begun in *Journey to the End of Night.*

FURTHER READING

Contemporary Authors, Vols. 85-88. Detroit: Gale Research Co.

Contemporary Literary Criticism, Vols. 1, 3, 4, 7, 9, 15, 47. Detroit: Gale Research Co.

Dictionary of Literary Biography, Vol. 72. Detroit: Gale Research Co.

Howe, Irving. "Céline: The Sod Beneath the Skin." In *A World More Attractive: A View of Modern Literature and Politics,* pp. 192-206. New York: Horizon, 1963.

Nettelbeck, Colin W. "Journey to the End of Art: The Evolution of the Novels of Louis-Ferdinand Céline." *PMLA* 87 (January 1972): 80-9.

Ostrovsky, Erika. *Céline and His Vision.* New York: New York University Press, 1967.

Owen, Carys T. "Networks of Symbol in *Voyage au bout de la nuit.*" *Forum for Modern Language Studies* (January 1975): 46-58.

Solomon, Philip H. "Céline's *Death on the Installment Plan:* The Intoxications of Delirium." *Yale French Studies* 50 (1974). 191-203.

Wicks, Ulrich. "Onlyman." *MOSAIC* 8, No. 3 (Spring 1975): 21-47.

John Cheever
1912-1982
American short story writer and novelist.

"The Enormous Radio" (short story, 1953)

Irene and **Jim Westcott**'s story takes place in their Manhattan apartment. A seemingly happy couple with the accepted trappings of success, the two share a love of music and purchase a radio. However, the radio doesn't tune in music, but rather the personal quarrels of their neighbors. Irene is first repelled and then strangely attracted to what she hears, and her compulsion to enter the private lives of others leads to the explosive conclusion of the story. Jim, disturbed by his wife's behavior to the point of rage, lashes out at her, revealing his repressed feelings of anger, frustration, and disappointment in her and in their life together. The respectability and happiness they share is a sham, their innocence a pose.

Irene and Jim are typical denizens of Cheever's fiction. Upwardly mobile, upper-middle-class with an eye on a suburban home, they represent the type of character Cheever so often wrote about. That they live a life seemingly happy which actually masks an existence of anxiety and chaos is also typical of Cheever's characters. Stylistically, the story also foreshadows Cheever's later work. The narrative stance is omniscient and ironic, and the narrator's position toward the characters is one of detachment. The work is praised for Cheever's effective narrative pace and for the ironic yet simple prose style.

The Wapshot Chronicle (novel, 1957)

The novel takes place in fictional St. Botolphs, a New England village. The story is told in four parts. Part I begins on the Fourth of July and depicts a typical summer in the Wapshot family—**Leander,** his wife, **Sarah,** his cousin **Honora,** and his sons, **Moses** and **Coverly.** At the end of the summer, the boys leave St. Botolphs to seek their fortune in the world of the city, Moses in Washington, D.C., and Coverly in New York. Honora, an overbearing and tenacious woman, controls the family and the family fortune. She has promised the boys their share of the family legacy if they can make their way in the world of business. Their adventures form the second part of the novel. In addition to their stories, Part II contains excerpts from Leander's journal. The Wapshots are a family in which the importance of tradition runs deep, and Leander, like his ancestors before him, keeps a journal for himself and his sons. This section reveals much about Leander's nature: he is a man of great vitality and imagination, one who loves life and celebrates the sensuous in human nature. His character is contrasted with Honora, who represents the narrow and circumspect in life. Part III depicts Moses and Coverly in search of wives, for Honora has stipulated that they must also marry and produce heirs to claim their money. In Part IV, Leander dies and is buried. As the novel closes, Coverly and his family have returned for the annual Fourth of July celebration, bringing the novel full circle and reaffirming the importance of family and tradition.

The novel, which won Cheever the National Book Award, has been described as episodic in structure, perhaps revealing the influence of Cheever's major prose format, the short story, on his first novel. The tone of the work is richly comic and its themes, which will be repeated in many of Cheever's later works, include the primacy of familial relationships and rituals. Cheever's depiction of Leander and Honora has been described as mythic for its treatment of two characters who represent the power of a family heritage that spans generations.

"The Country Husband" (short story, 1958)

As the story begins, **Francis Weed** has barely escaped death in a plane crash. The experience alters him completely. Like most of Cheever's characters, Francis is an upper-middle-class suburbanite, but his brush with death makes him see his life differently, and he is confronted with the poverty of existence in his affluent lifestyle. He can't even relate his harrowing tale to his family, who are too absorbed in their petty arguments to pay attention to him. As part of his transformation, Francis falls hopelessly in love with his children's baby-sitter, whom he feels embodies all the wonder and attraction of youth and promise. Yet the overwhelming changes prove to be too much for Francis, disrupting his and his family's predictable suburban existence. Ultimately, Francis goes to a psychiatrist to help him out of his trouble; the doctor prescribes woodworking, and in the closing of the story we see Francis at work in his cellar, apparently back to normal, grateful for the return to the rhythms of his former life.

Francis's story embodies Cheever's prototypical narrative approach, setting, and theme. Cheever tells the story with ironic detachment, yet with compassion for his troubled character. The setting is Shady Hills, one of Cheever's most typical suburban communities, depicted as a nightmare of rigid homogeneity—of well-kept lawns, cocktail parties, country club dances, and lonely, anxious people. Cheever's theme is the vapidness of the Shady Hills of the American landscape, yet he notes, too, how it offers beauty and comfort to its inhabitants.

Falconer (novel, 1977)

The Falconer of the title is Falconer prison, where **Ezekiel Farragut** has been incarcerated for the murder of his brother. Farragut, a former college professor, is forty-eight years old and a heroin addict as the novel begins. His story is one of redemption and rebirth as he suffers the brutalities of prison life and the confinement of body and spirit. His journey is one of painful self-knowledge relieved by the awakening of his homosexual feelings and his subsequent affair with another inmate, **Jody.** Farragut must also come to grips with his drug addiction and face further tests in his struggle for self-awareness and redemption. In the novel's conclusion, he has escaped from Falconer and is reborn.

Falconer was a great departure for Cheever in style, setting, and character. The language is sordid and crude, paralleling the cruel brutality of the prison setting. It is softened, however, by scenes of humor and human tenderness that can exist even in a prison. His protagonist is a murderer, in sharp contrast to the upper-middle-class suburban heroes of his previous short stories and novels. Cheever also deals explicitly with homosexuality in this novel, a subject only hinted at in his previous fiction. His theme is confinement, and the novel is replete with imagery revealing the effects of imprisonment on the human spirit.

Commentators have noted the autobiographical elements in *Falconer;* prior to its composition, Cheever had suffered a massive heart attack, and had faced and overcame his addiction to alcohol. He had also spent several years teaching at Sing Sing prison, an experience that surely influenced the novel. The work is considered his finest effort in the novel form, and critics singled out the tight narrative, and rich symbolism for praise.

FURTHER READING

Aldridge, John W. "John Cheever and the Soft Sell of Disaster." In his *Time to Murder and Create: The Contemporary Novel in Crisis,* pp. 171-77. Freeport: Books for Libraries Press, 1966.

Burhans, Clinton S., Jr. "John Cheever and the Grave of Social Coherence." *Twentieth Century Literature* 14 (January 1969): 187-98.

Coale, Samuel. *John Cheever.* New York: Ungar, 1977.

Contemporary Authors, Vols. 5-8, rev. ed, 106; *Contemporary Authors New Revision Series,* Vol. 5; *Contemporary Authors Bibliographical Series,* Vol. 1. Detroit: Gale Research Co.

Contemporary Literary Criticism, Vols. 3, 7, 8, 11, 15, 25. Detroit: Gale Research Co.

Dictionary of Literary Biography, Vol. 2; *Dictionary of Literary Biography Yearbook: 1980, 1982; Concise Dictionary of American Literary Biography, 1941-1968.* Detroit: Gale Research Co.

Didion, Joan. "Falconer." *New York Times Book Review* (6 March 1977): 1, 22, 24.

Donaldson, Scott. "The Machines in Cheever's Garden." In *The Changing Face of the American Suburbs,* edited by Barry Schwartz, pp. 309-22, 336-37. Chicago: University of Chicago Press, 1976.

Gardner, John. "On Miracle Row." *Saturday Review* 4 (2 April 1977): 20-3.

Hassan, Ihab. *Radical Innocence: Studies in the Contemporary American Novel,* pp. 187-94, 200. Princeton: Princeton University Press, 1961.

Kazin, Alfred. "O'Hara, Cheever & Updike." *New York Review of Books* 20 (19 April 1973): 14-18.

Kendle, Burton. "Cheever's Use of Mythology in 'The Enormous Radio.'" *Studies in Short Fiction* 4 (Spring 1967): 262-64.

Leonard, John. "Crying in the Wilderness." *Harper's* 254 (April 1977): 88-9.

O'Hara, James. "Cheever's *The Wapshot Chronicle:* A Narrative of Exploration." *Critique* 22, No. 2 (1980): 20-30.

Short Story Criticism, Vol. 1. Detroit: Gale Research Co.

Tyler, Anne. "Books Considered." *New Republic* 179 (4 November 1978): 45-7.

Waldeland, Lynne. *John Cheever.* Boston: Twayne, 1979.

Anton Chekhov

1860-1904

Russian dramatist and short story writer.

"Ward No. 6" (short story, 1892)

"Ward No. 6,' a story of madness and misery, begins in the mental ward of a hospital in a provincial Russian town. The narrator equates the harsh, unsanitary surroundings of the facility with the barbarous treatment the patients receive from the caretaker, **Nikita.** One patient, **Ivan Dmitrich Gromov,** appears unusually interesting, for he is remarkably learned and well-mannered. He suffers from a form of paranoia, believing that the foundation of rural Russian life is so seriously flawed that he will eventually be arrested and imprisoned through some miscarriage of justice. As the story progresses, the chief doctor of the institution, **Andrei Efimych Ragin,** begins visiting Gromov regularly. Once guided by altruism, Ragin, in the interests of self-preservation, has since abandoned attempts to improve hospital conditions through reform. In his view, the inherent obstacles present in a backward, directionless society are insurmountable. The one ideal to which Ragin clings is intellectual peace of mind. However, despite several philosophical discussions with Gromov, he cannot convince the patient that this peace can be obtained. Vehemently contradicting the doctor, Gromov contends that peace of mind is impossible within an environment so eminently capable of producing human pain. Ragin discovers this truth only after he is unexpectedly committed to the asylum. His subordinate, a mediocre doctor envious of Ragin's position, justified the incarceration after witnessing his superior's increasingly unsociable and erratic behavior. In his cell, Ragin suffers the same atrocities as the other patients and arrives at a chilling realization of the dark side of the human condition. Chekhov suggests, through the ephemeral image of a beautiful herd of deer, that Ragin has chosen a sterile, joyless life. The tale concludes with his sudden death following a stroke.

In comparison with the work of other great Russian authors, in particular the variety and vaulting ideological proportions of Tolstoy, Chekhov's stories are more uniform in mood and narrower in scope, frequently illustrating situations of hardship, boredom, and mundane suffering. Despite its dominant pessimism, "Ward No. 6" is considered one of Chekhov's most perfectly wrought and powerful stories. Many scholars esteem its profound social message, found in its direct opposition to Tolstoy's doctrine of nonresistance to evil. As in Chekhov's best work, the supreme emotional balance and stylistic control of the story exemplify the narrative talents of one of the most prominent authors in world literature.

The Seagull (drama, 1896)

The Seagull takes place during the nineteenth century on **Pyotr Sorin**'s country estate. Pyotr's sister, **Irina Arkadina,** a glamorous, selfish stage queen, is vacationing there with her twenty-five-year-old son, **Konstantin Treplyov.** Hopelessly in love with **Nina Zarechnaya,** Konstantin kills a seagull and presents it to the beautiful young actress, proclaiming that if she cannot reciprocate his love he will be lying like the seagull, dead at her feet. Nina is repulsed by Konstantin's melodramatic gesture; she is attracted, instead, to the famous novelist **Boris Trigorin,** a longtime admirer of Madame Arkadina. Konstantin, a zealous proponent of new dramatic forms that are abundantly expressive, socially relevant, and lacking in artifice, stages on the estate a play starring nineteen-year-old Nina. To Konstantin's bitter dismay, his work is largely unappreciated by either his mother or Trigorin, whom he jealously considers a trivial artist. Although Konstantin loves his mother despite her selfish neglect of his physical and emotional needs, he cannot quell his anger toward her. Trigorin, virtually unnoticed by Madame Arkadina, begins coldly pursuing Nina; he imagines himself the hunter and Nina seagull.

Nina lives with Trigorin in Moscow for nearly a year. After she gives birth to a child who soon dies, Trigorin deserts her. During this time Konstantin has relentlessly followed Nina, hoping that she will eventually return to him. Through occasional letters to him she has revealed her extreme emotional distress; she has suffered numerous disappointments in her career and in her one-sided relationship with Trigorin. Following a recuperative stay at the Sorin estate, Nina joins a repertory company, leaving Konstantin forever. True to his symbolic prediction, Konstantin kills himself, firing a bullet through his head.

Critics attribute the artistic success of *The Seagull* to a subtle interweaving of theme and character. The resulting scenario is one in which nuances of pacing and mood become paramount to the full realization of dramatic tension. Among Chekhov's major plays, this work remains particularly important for its intensive focus on the role of the creative artist in a society only superficially concerned with morality and truth.

"The Lady with the Dog" (short story, 1899)

One of the best of Chekhov's later stories, "The Lady with the Dog" is set in Yalta and Moscow during the 1890s. While vacationing, banker **Dmitrii Dmitrich Gurov** meets a young woman, **Anna Sergeevna von Diederitz,** strolling with her dog. A married man and veteran of numerous brief, meaningless affairs, Dmitrii determines that the woman is also married, bored, and searching for companionship. After a week of cautious flirtation, the two impulsively make love. Anna then becomes distraught, as much from guilt at her first infidelity as from the realization that her marriage is a sham and her love for her husband has long since vanished. Dmitrii comforts Anna, despite his irritation that the affair has now become complicated. Later, while gazing at the sea with Anna, he is overcome with a sense of the eternal. After spending several more days together, the two lovers reluctantly separate. Back in Moscow, Dmitrii realizes his attraction to Anna is unique; he decides to continue the relationship, for he can hardly contain his joy when thinking of her. The couple live from month to month in ecstatic anguish, miserable from the lies they must tell, immensely happy with the prospect of each new meeting. At the close of the story both Anna and Dmitrii are depicted as sufferers who find it morally impossible to continue their dual lives. They cannot find a solution to their dilemma, but the narrator avers that one will be discovered shortly, enabling the two, following a painful interim, to lead a pleasurable life together.

Inspired by Leo Tolstoy's *Anna Karenina,* Chekhov's story is a tale of adultery in which all moralizing has been omitted. With inimitable care, Chekhov depicted the inner conflicts of Anna and Dmitrii objectively, matching his style to the alternating emotions of the characters. As Beverly Hahn has written, the story, though by no means his most complex, stands as a remarkable testimony to Chekhov's belief in the worth of human love.

Uncle Vanya (drama, 1899)

Uncle Vanya is set in rural nineteenth-century Russia on the estate of a retired, ailing professor, **Alexandr Serebryakov.** Alexandr gained the estate through marriage to his first wife, now deceased. Except for periodic pain in his legs, he lives comfortably and with few worries, writing when he pleases and cared for by his nurse, **Marina,** and his new wife, twenty-seven-year-old **Yelena Andreevna.** Also living on the estate are **Maria Voynitskaya,** mother of Alexandr's first wife; **Sonya Alexandrovna,** Alexandr's daughter; and **Ivan Voynitsky,** Maria's son, whom Sonya knows as **Uncle Vanya.** Each suffers in a differing way from feelings of isolation, misunderstanding, and exploitation, which stem largely from the professor's increasingly tyrannical demands. The family doctor, **Mikhail Astrov,** has been summoned by Alexandr; yet, like the others, he is mistreated and reveals his discontentment, of both the present situation and his life as a whole. Only Marina remains detached from the drama of misplaced affections and deep emotions that follows: Yelena realizes her love for Alexandr is illusory, Sonya cannot communicate her love for the doctor, Ivan is infatuated with Yelena, and Mikhail, whose cynicism renders him incapable of love, kisses Yelena as Sonya looks on.

A strong need for reconciliation is obvious as the various characters' desires and resentments emerge. Uncle Vanya, who has tirelessly labored to produce a beautiful and prosperous estate for the professor, harbors the greatest bitterness, for he now perceives Alexandr's moral frailty, his egotism, and lack of compassion. Vanya realizes he has been serving a nonexistent ideal. When Alexandr announces his wish to abandon country living, sell the estate, and buy a small place in Finland, Vanya is outraged, as much for Sonya, the rightful heir, as for himself. Following a heated discussion between the two men, the professor tries to resolve their dispute only to have Ivan shoot at him. After a final reconciliation involving all the characters, Alexandr departs for the city with Yelena. Despite an atmosphere of taut emotion, Sonya assures Vanya that the future will be happier.

Through this major drama runs Chekhov's recurrent theme of human despair. Nearly all the characters appear helpless to control their destinies, for they are trapped in a frustrating world founded on illusions and false hopes. Clear communication, the final answer to the human dilemma, appears unattainable. Yet, the drama's final triumph is that it unites this turn-of-the-century pessimism with a timid note of hope, rightly sounded through the young, innocent voice of Sonya.

The Three Sisters (drama, 1901)

Set in a dull provincial town in Russia, Chekhov's drama revolves around the troubled marriage and middle-class life of **Andrey Prozorov** and **Natalya Ivanovna.** Intimately involved with Andrey's affairs are his three sisters, **Olga Prozorov, Masha Kuligin,** and **Irina Prozorov.** All of them disapprove of Natasha, an ill-bred, domineering woman. Following his precipitous marriage, Andrey has abandoned his ambition to become a professor. Instead, he gambles regularly, to obliterate the knowledge of his wife's shortcomings. His sisters had hoped that his career would lead the family back to Moscow, where they had lived until their father's army transfer eleven years ago. Both parents have since passed away. Of the sisters, Masha is perhaps most dissatisfied, for she must endure a lackluster marriage to **Fyodor Kuligin,** a well-meaning but dull man whom she once considered clever. The area's new battery commander, **Alexandr Vershinin,** periodically visits the sisters and unexpectedly falls in love with Masha. Also trapped in an unhappy marriage, he thinks that in several hundred years the world will be unimaginably beautiful and overflowing with happiness, but for now he cannot regard it as such.

Like Vershinin, the remaining characters are dissatisfied with the present but maintain some hope, however small, in the future. As the action progresses, Andrey's marriage continues to unsettle the sisters' lives. Everyone except Andrey realizes Natasha has been having an affair with the Chairman of the Rural Board. Near the end of the drama, the brigade, which has provided culture and diversion for the society-starved sisters, prepares to leave the small town. For a moment, Irina, who has promised to marry **Baron Nikolay Tuzenbakh** is content. Then she learns that her betrothed has been killed in a duel with **Vasily Solyony,** a rival suitor. In the final scene, the sisters lament their loneliness and wonder at the omnipresence of suffering in their world.

Among Chekhov's dramas, *The Three Sisters* is the closest to tragedy. It is the play which significantly contributes to his reputation as a portrayer of futile existences and a forerunner of the modernist tradition of the absurd. The thrust of his commentary is directed at the Russian middle class, who in his time appeared disastrously devoid of intellectual, emotional, and political depth. Chekhov's prominent position in world literature, however, is not so much a consequence of his philosophy or world view as it is based on fiction and dramas executed with phenomenal artistry which permanently altered the literary standards for these genres.

The Cherry Orchard (drama, 1904)

Chekhov's best-known play begins with the return of **Madame Lyubov Ranevskaya** to her country estate in Russia. She has been in France for five years, attempting to overcome the profound sense of loss that has plagued her since the deaths of her husband and young son. The sale of her villa at Mentone had become necessary to cover the huge expenses she has incurred. Now she realizes, albeit dimly, that her financial circumstances have become increasingly dire. **Yermolay Lopakhin,** a merchant whose father had been a serf on the estate, suggests that a regular income could be secured and a portion of the ancestral land saved if the cherry orchard, a majestic symbol of generations of toil, were cut down. The land could then be partitioned and either sold or rented to summer vacationers. Madame Ranevskaya cannot conceive of such destruction and futilely considers other possibilities with her daughters, **Anya** and **Varya,** and her indolent brother, **Leonid Gaev,** who has inexpertly managed the family property during her absence.

Lopakhin purchases the estate when it is eventually sold at public auction. Madame Ranevskaya receives the disturbing news while hosting a formal ball in the old mansion, where she has persisted in the notion that she can still live lavishly. The change in ownership, a monumental reversal for which Lopakhin exhibits immense pride, results in considerable changes for all the characters who are tied to the estate. Only **Firs,** an aging footman, can accept the news with equanimity, for his life as a servant has simply come to an end.

Controversy has arisen over the interpretation of Chekhov's last play, which he subtitled "A Comedy," genuinely intending it to be viewed as such. Often perceived as a nostalgic parable on the passing of the old order, this late work displays one of Chekhov's most important themes: the triumph of ignorance and vulgarity over the fragile traditions of elegance and nobility.

FURTHER READING

Bill, Valentine Tschebotarioff. *Chekhov: The Silent Voice of Freedom.* New York: Philosophical Library, 1987.

Bruford, W. H. *Anton Chekhov.* New Haven: Yale University Press, 1957.

Clyman, Toby, ed. *A Chekhov Companion.* Westport: Greenwood Press, 1985.

Contemporary Authors, Vols. 104, 124. Detroit: Gale Research Co.

Debreczeny, Paul and Thomas Eeckman, eds. *Checkhov's Art of Writing: A Collection of Critical Essays.* Columbus: Slavica Publishers, 1977.

Freidland, Louis S., ed. *Anton Chekhov, Letters on the Short Story, the Drama and Other Literary Topics.* 1924. Reprint. New York: Dover Publications, 1966.

Hahn, Beverly. *Chekhov: A Study of the Major Stories and Plays.* Cambridge: Cambridge University Press, 1977.

Hingley, Ronald. *A New Life of Chekhov.* New York: Alfred A. Knopf, 1976.

Jackson, Robert Louis, ed. *Chekhov: A Collection of Critical Essays.* Englewood Cliffs: Prentice-Hall, 1967.

Kramer, Karl D. *The Chameleon and the Dream: The Image of Reality in Cexov's Stories.* The Hague: Mouton, 1970.

Magarshack, David. *Chekhov the Dramatist.* New York: Hill & Wang, 1960.

Nabokov, Vladimir. "Anton Chekhov." In *Lectures on Russian Literature,* edited by Fredson Bowers, pp. 245-95. New York: Harcourt Brace Jovanovich, 1981.

Pritchett, V. S. *Chekhov: A Spirit Set Free.* New York: Random House, 1988.

Rayfield, Donald. *Chekhov: The Evolution of His Art.* New York: Barnes & Noble, 1975.

Short Story Criticism, Vol. 2. Detroit: Gale Research Co.

Smith, Virginia Llewellyn. *Anton Chekhov and the Lady with the Dog.* London: Oxford University Press, 1973.

Speirs, Logan. "Chekhov: The Stories" and "Chekhov: The Plays." In *Tolstoy and Chekhov,* pp. 137-82, 185-223. Cambridge: Cambridge University Press, 1971.

Tulloch, John. *Chekhov: A Structuralist Study.* New York: Barnes & Noble, 1980.

Twentieth-Century Literary Criticism, Vols. 3, 10, 31. Detroit: Gale Research Co.

Winner, Anthony. "Chekhov's Characters: True Tears, Real Things." In *Characters in the Twilight: Hardy, Zola, and Chekhov,* pp. 140-94. Charlottesville: University Press of Virginia, 1981.

Winner, Thomas. *Chekhov and His Prose.* New York: Holt, Rinehart & Winston, 1966.

Yermilov, Vladimir. *Anton Pavlovich Chekhov, 1860-1904.* Moscow: Foreign Languages Publishing House, 1956.

G.K. Chesterton

1874-1936

English novelist, short story writer, critic, essayist, and poet.

The Man Who Was Thursday (novel, 1908)

Set in London, the novel follows an episode in the life of **Gabriel Syme,** a Scotland Yard detective, formerly a poet, who is hired by a mysterious, cloaked figure to expose a group of seven anarchists who plan to destroy the world. Each member of the group, the Central Anarchist Council, is named for a day of the week, with Syme receiving the name Thursday. They are headed by the powerful and enigmatic **Sunday.** The anarchical philosophies they expound reveal Chesterton's thematic intent: to show the barrenness of the pessimism and nihilism that was a popular mode of thought during the early twentieth century. Through a series of revelations, the supposed anarchists learn that they are all in fact Scotland Yard detectives, hired by the mysterious Sunday. They pursue him in a chase sequence that is both bizarre and humorous, eventually tracking him to his mansion, where they are treated as honored guests, given refreshment and entertainment. Perplexed, they ask their host the reason behind his scheme. The detectives are shown a vision of the world in chaos, in "topsy-turvydom," which, although it doesn't clarify their experience, leaves them with a profound sense of mystery. The story is truly enigmatic and elliptical in meaning: the detectives are left in a state of wonder and awe at their encounter with Sunday, who some critics see as a God-figure.

Stylistically, many commentators note that the nightmarish atmosphere of the novel is similar to that created by Franz Kafka in his novels. The work is allegorical in content and intent: the detectives are given the names of the days of the week which also correspond to the days of creation; their commander, Sunday, represents the Sabbath, the day of peace. The themes that were to be repeated in much of Chesterton's fiction—the conflict between faith and reason, and between the teachings of the Catholic Church and the findings of modern science—are raised here, as is his abiding belief in the paradox and mystery of life.

"The Blue Cross" (short story, 1911)

Father Brown, Chesterton's well-known and popular priest-detective, is the central figure in this, the first of many short stories in which he figures.

The story involves the pursuit of **Flambeau,** master criminal and thief, by **Aristide Valentin,** Chief of the Paris Police, and, as Chesterton tells us, "the most famous investigator in the world."

Valentin has followed Flambeau from Europe to London, where his instincts tell him he will find his prey. He and Father Brown meet on a train to London; Valentin dismisses the round-faced cleric as a bumbling, provincial priest. Father Brown carries a relic to a Eucharistic Congress in London, a silver cross with sapphires. It is this, the "blue cross" of the title, that Valentin thinks has lured Flambeau to England. After arriving in London, Valentin embarks on his quest. He finds his first clue in a cafe, where he hears that prior to his arrival a pair of priests had dined, and one of them had thrown a bowl of soup at the wall. The trail is clear to Valentin, who subsequently encounters an irate grocer whose apple cart has been overturned by two clerics. Valentin enlists the help of the London police to follow the pair. Their tedious yet hilarious trail across London ends in Hampstead Heath, where Valentin at last catches up with the priests. To his shock he recognizes one as Flambeau and the other as Father Brown. He comes upon them discussing theology: Father Brown is outlining the religious argument against stealing when Flambeau demands the parcel containing the relic. But the little priest has caught the master criminal: recalling a confession of a thief, he had thought to exchange the parcel earlier in their journey. The one Flambeau now holds is empty. In the conclusion, both the renowned criminal and the famous investigator acknowledge Brown's mastery.

Father Brown, the child-like, seemingly innocent but all-knowing priest, is Chesterton's most enduring character. He has gained his knowledge of human nature and of crime from the confessional, which has taught him much about the evil in the human heart. For Father Brown, all criminal acts are at their basis human and call for human understanding. Believing in the inherent goodness of his fellow creatures, he is able to identify with the criminal, and this insight, rather than the supernatural powers with which most fictional detectives are endowed, is his weapon against crime. Both Flambeau and Valentin reappear in several Father Brown stories.

FURTHER READING

Barker, Dudley. "A Brief Survey of Chesterton's Work." In *G.K. Chesterton: A Centenary Appraisal*, pp. 3-15, edited by John Sullivan. New York: Barnes and Noble, 1974.

Belloc, Hilaire. *The Place of Gilbert Chesterton in English Letters*. New York: Sheed and Ward, 1940.

Boyd, Ian. *The Novels of G.K. Chesterton: A Study in Art and Propaganda*. New York: Barnes and Noble, 1975.

Contemporary Authors, Vol. 104. Detroit: Gale Research Co.

Dictionary of Literary Biography, Vols. 10, 19, 34, 70. Detroit: Gale Research Co.

Hunt, Peter R. "Dickens's Influence on Chesterton's Imaginative Writing." *The Chesterton Review* 7, No. 1 (Winter 1981): 36-49.

Kenner, Hugh. *Paradox in Chesterton*. New York: Sheed and Ward, 1947.

Short Story Criticism, Vol. 1. Detroit: Gale Research Co.

Twentieth-Century Literary Criticism, Vols. 1, 6. Detroit: Gale Research Co.

Youngberg, Karin. "Job and the Gargoyles: A Study of 'The Man Who Was Thursday'." *The Chesterton Review* 2, No. 2 (Spring-Summer 1976): 240-52.

Kate Chopin
1851-1904
American novelist.

The Awakening (novel, 1899)

Set in Louisiana, *The Awakening* is the story of **Edna Pontellier** and her coming of age as a woman. Edna, who is married to **Leonce Pontellier,** a pleasant but unexciting man, visits a summer resort where she discovers an altogether new atmosphere of exoticism and eroticism. This setting is conducive to Edna's heightened sexuality, and she becomes involved with **Robert LeGrun,** a younger man. Robert quickly abandons Edna because she is married, but she has been transformed by the experience. She returns to the New Orleans home she shares with Leonce and her children, but moves out shortly thereafter, and Leonce fears that Edna has suffered a nervous breakdown. Edna finds new friends to share the aesthetic interests she has developed, but despite her new unfettered lifestyle, she is still unfulfilled. Only when Robert returns to her does Edna feel a sense of happiness, and the two resume their romance. Though she tells him of her devotion, Robert leaves again, purportedly because he loves Edna too much. A devastated Edna drowns herself.

At the time of its publication, *The Awakening* was very controversial for its treatment of the provocative topic of female sexuality. Chopin did not judge Edna's behavior and, in fact, depicted her characters dispassionately. Chopin's prose is eloquent and simple in *The Awakening,* and her succinct writing emphasizes Edna's essential loneliness and tragic predicament.

FURTHER READING

Bogarad, Carley Rees. *"The Awakening:* A Refusal to Compromise." *The University of Michigan Papers in Women's Studies* 2, No. 3 (1977): 15-31.

Christ, Carol P. "Spiritual Liberation, Social Defeat: Kate Chopin." In *Diving Deep and Surfacing: Women Writers on Spiritual Quest,* pp. 27-40. Boston: Beacon Press, 1980.

Contemporary Authors, Vols. 104, 122. Detroit: Gale Research Co.

Dictionary of Literary Biography, Vol. 12; *Concise Dictionary of American Literary Biography, 1865-1917.* Detroit: Gale Research Co.

Twentieth-Century Literary Criticism, Vols. 5, 14. Detroit: Gale Research Co.

Wolff, Cynthia G. "Thanatos and Eros: Kate Chopin's *The Awakening."* *American Quarterly* 25, No. 4 (October 1973): 449-71.

Jean Cocteau
1889-1963
French dramatist, poet, novelist, and essayist.

The Holy Terrors (novel, 1929)

In this novel **Elisabeth** and her younger brother, **Paul,** are two adolescents isolated from the outside world who withdraw into their room, a created imaginary realm where, separated from reality, they indulge in the fantasy of the "game"—a ritual with its own rules, dialect, and rites. The threat to their world, jealously guarded by Elisabeth, is the reality outside the room, represented by the characters **Dargelos, Agathe,** and **Gérard.** Dargelos, strong, handsome, and aware of the power he exerts over his teachers and classmates, inspires the worship of the sensitive, withdrawn Paul. He is a callous, bullying type who strangely holds Paul's destiny in his hands. Early in the novel, he strikes Paul with a snowball, and Paul is taken back to the room by Gérard, his faithful friend, where he comes under the total influence of his dominant sister. Elisabeth meets Agathe, whose parents have committed suicide. Indeed, the presence and influence of adults is conspicuously absent from the realm of these children. Agathe and Gérard both move in and become part of the world of the ritual. Yet the powers of the outside world continue to impinge on the private domain, for Gérard falls in love with Elisabeth and Agathe with Paul. Elisabeth exercises her authority over her imaginary world by persuading Gérard and Agathe to marry, allowing her to remain in control of Paul.

Once again, the force of destiny appears in the form of Dargelos, as Agathe comes to resemble him in Paul's eyes. Paul's fascination with the outside world, which he can neither understand nor deny, finally takes the form of a ball of poison that Dargelos delivers to him through Gérard. Paul takes the poison, and Elisabeth, with her world of imagination and illusion about to end, shoots herself. As she falls, a screen hiding a window collapses with her, revealing the world of reality. Paul, in his last moments, searches for Dargelos.

Often interpreted as an allegory on fate, *The Holy Terrors* is considered Cocteau's finest novel. Its simple prose style, taut construction, and concern with the force of destiny have elicited comparisons to Greek drama. An aura of myth and mystery permeate the work, revealing the "grave, heroic, and mysterious" world of childhood fantasy as interpreted by Cocteau.

The Infernal Machine (drama, 1934)

This play is Cocteau's interpretation of the myth of **Oedipus.** While it is based on Sophocles's treatment of the story, Cocteau begins his version with Oedipus as he enters Thebes, driven by pride and ambition to destroy the **Sphinx.** Before the play begins, a voice outlines the main points of Oedipus's history. He was born the son of **Laius** and **Jocasta,** King and Queen of Thebes, but because an oracle had declared that Laius's son would kill his father and marry his mother, the infant was left on a mountain to die. Discovered by a shepherd, he was taken to the court of the **King** and **Queen of Corinth** and raised as their son. As the play begins, we learn that the ghost of Laius is about the city, attempting to warn Jocasta of the impending evil. Although she attempts to make contact with him, he cannot appear to her. Act Two relates the meeting of Oedipus and the Sphinx, who has brought pestilence to Thebes and whose destroyer will win the kingdom and the hand of the queen. Cocteau's Sphinx is a young girl of seventeen who falls in love with Oedipus and willingly gives him the answer to her riddle, hoping he will return her love and wish to marry her. But Oedipus is the picture of blind ambition, driven to annihilate the Sphinx and ascend the throne. In the third act, we see Jocasta and Oedipus in the incestuous marriage bed, where Oedipus's head touches the cradle Jocasta has kept by her bedside.

Each act is introduced by a voice whose speeches draw the audience's attention to the machine of fate, circling its mortal prey. Although we have seen the inexorable force of destiny at work throughout the play, the fourth act moves quickly, as Thebes is under the siege of plague and the oracle announces the gods' anger that the murderer of Laius was never brought to justice. The King of Corinth has died, admitting that Oedipus is not his son. The evidence mounts, and Oedipus must confront his crime and his fate. Jocasta hangs herself and Oedipus gouges out his eyes. The conclusion depicts the ghost of Jocasta as she appears to Oedipus, speaking to him as her son, acknowledging the stupidity and blindness of mortals and the pain of the temporal world. Yet their fate has transformed them into mythic characters, and the mortal world is no longer of consequence.

Cocteau's rendering of this ancient myth has been universally praised, especially for his ability to make his characters believable on both a contemporary and a cosmic level. Cocteau brought a relevance to his reworking of a story that deals with free will, identity, and the forces beyond mortal understanding or control.

FURTHER READING

Contemporary Authors, Vols. 25-28, rev. ed.; *Contemporary Authors Permanent Series,* Vol. 2. Detroit: Gale Research Co.

Contemporary Literary Criticism, Vols. 1, 8, 15, 16, 43. Detroit: Gale Research Co.

Crosland, Margaret. *Jean Cocteau.* New York: Knopf, 1956.

Fergusson, Francis. "Excursus: Poetry in the Theatre and Poetry of the Theatre, Cocteau's *Infernal Machine.*" In *Literary Criticism—Idea and Act: The English Institute, Selected Essays 1939-1972,* edited by W. K. Wimsatt, pp. 590-601. Berkeley: University of California Press, 1974.

Fowlie, Wallace. *Jean Cocteau: The History of a Poet's Age.* Bloomington: Indiana University Press, 1966.

Knapp, Bettina. *Jean Cocteau.* New York: Twayne, 1970.

Oxenhandler, Neal. *Scandal and Parade: The Theater of Jean Cocteau.* New Brunswick: Rutgers University Press, 1957.

Sprigge, Elizabeth and Jean-Jacques Kihm. *Jean Cocteau: The Man and the Mirror.* New York: Coward-McCann, 1968.

Colette
1873-1954
French novelist and short story writer.

Chéri (novel, 1920)

Set in Paris prior to World War I, *Chéri* and its sequel, *The Last of Chéri* present Colette's skillful depiction of the psychological ramifications of a love affair between an older woman, **Leonie Vallon,** called Léa, and her young lover, **Chéri (Fred Peloux),** the son of an old and intimate friend.

Léa and her friend **Mme. Peloux** are experienced women who inhabit the Parisian *demi-monde.* In a milieu where financial and social position can be brought about for women who make careful arrangements with gentlemen of the wealthy leisure class, each has been successful in her own way. They are at once both intimate and loyal friends as well as competitors. Thus, when Mme. Peloux has a son, Léa loves him as she might her own; she takes him under her guiding wing with full permission of his mother in order to prepare him for a life of luxury.

When he is nineteen years old, the maternal Léa takes Chéri away from Paris on holiday, and it is then that their passionate love affair begins. Since he is but one of many sensual relationships, Léa enjoys her interesting child-lover and recognizes that despite her relentless battle against aging, the affair will end, and she seems prepared for this, with equanimity.

After six years, a marriage of convenience is arranged for the now spoiled and arrogant Chéri to **Edmée,** a wealthy young woman of beauty and property. Chéri promises to remain Léa's lover despite his marriage, and Léa cheerfully acquiesces to what is an expected and logical turn of events.

But a new reaction sets in after the wedding, when Léa realizes that her passion for Chéri is stronger than any she has ever known. In despair, Léa leaves Paris for a year. Chéri is mystified at her abandonment; Edmée suffers his tantrums, accuses him of infidelity, and asks for a divorce. He refuses to divorce his wife, but spends the year haunting Léa's vacant house in Paris.

When she returns, Chéri begs Léa to remain his lover and she agrees, on condition that they will leave Paris and the influence of Mme. Peloux. However, the selfish Chéri now feels that life in seclusion with Léa will not be the same and rationalizes that since his aging mistress has lost the gracious and sophisticated ways which had made her so dependable, he must reject her terms. Sadder but wiser, Léa realizes that she has lost her *enfant terrible,* and bids Chéri a tender, loving farewell.

In this work Colette revealed the nature of love as a positive force, as it provides joy and elevation of spirit, and as a negative compulsion which brings despair and sadness at its renunciation. A sensitive stylistic ability is found in her descriptive passages which give, at times, only impressionistic glimpses of the nuances inherent in human relationships. This talent is combined with a precision of diction which presents exactly what Colette wants her reader to see, feel, and sense at a given moment in order to receive the full impact of her meaning.

The Last of Chéri (novel, 1926)

Written six years after Chéri, this novel shares the same settings, characters, and narrative voice. World War I has intervened, and the story begins upon **Chéri**'s return from duty.

He had served his country with the same indolent, detached attitude that he had maintained before the war. He had been patient and, insofar as he was able, uninvolved with life during his service, waiting only to be relieved of the boredom of a patriotism which he did not feel. He also finds himself bored with post-war Paris, since it has been irrevocably changed. He is disenchanted with **Edmée** and her volunteer work and disgusted with their vapid, inane socializing. He is victimized by the idleness which, before the war, had allowed him his varied, self-centered and interesting life. Now life seems to have little meaning; in an interview with his mother he confides his feelings, adding that he feels sensually impoverished, as well. **Mme. Peloux,** true to form, reacts as she did when he was child: she puts him in touch with his old mistress, whom he has not seen since the end of their affair.

His reunion with Léa appalls him. Now in her sixties, she is grey-haired, matronly, and nothing remains of her beautiful face and lovely figure. She has come to terms with her time in life; her romanticism is absent and she is pragmatic, direct, and genial. Only her voice and a pearl necklace, which Chéri had adored as a child as representative of her great beauty and charm, remain the same. She chides him for expecting life to be the same as before, and in the end adopts her earlier, motherly attitude towards him. He is relieved to leave her and "thinks himself happy."

But Chéri's feigned happiness is momentary. He cannot reconcile himself to what Léa has called the "disease of [his] generation." The old life is gone, and his disillusion with the ordinary existence which faces him is overpowering. What one critic has described as "a gradual suicide" begins. In deteriorating mental and physical health, Chéri leaves Edmée and spends long periods of time with **Desmond,** a shallow, self-serving friend of long standing. At times, he mourns Léa and regrets having left her before the war.

Finally, he finds an eerie comfort in the company of **Copine,** another aging courtesan who had been a friend of Léa's and one of her ardent admirers. It is in her seedy apartment, filled with photographs of Léa in her youth, that Chéri commits suicide, too tired and too stubborn to stay in a world that has no use for him, nor he for it.

FURTHER READING

Benet, Mary Kathleen. "The Style of Colette." In *Writers in Love,* pp. 237-54. New York: Macmillan, 1977.

Contemporary Authors, Vol. 104. Detroit: Gale Research Co.

Cottrell, Robert D. *Colette.* New York: Ungar, 1974.

Crosland, Margaret. *Colette: The Difficulty of Loving, a Biography.* London: Peter Owen, 1973.

Davies, Margaret. *Colette.* New York: Grove Press, 1961.

Stewart, Joan Hinde. *Colette.* New York: Twayne, 1983.

Twentieth-Century Literary Criticism, Vols. 1, 5, 16. Detroit: Gale Research Co.

Wescott, Glenway. "An Introduction to Colette." In *Images of Truth,* pp. 86-141. London: Hamish Hamilton, 1963.

Joseph Conrad
1857-1924

English novelist, novella and short story writer, essayist, and autobiographer.

Lord Jim (novel, 1900)

Conrad's first successful long novel takes place in the East Indies during the late nineteenth century. With his father's assistance, a young British sailor named **Jim** gains berth as chief mate aboard the *Patna,* a decrepit steamer scheduled to carry eight hundred Muslim pilgrims across the Indian Ocean. The voyage ends in misfortune when the ship strikes an unknown object. Under orders, Jim investigates the damage and reports that the forward hold is filling rapidly. The captain, a cowardly German, signals the crew to launch the lifeboats and leave the pilgrims behind. After a ponderous moment, Jim abandons his acquired code of honor and joins the departing men. Although a French gunboat eventually arrives and tows the sinking vessel and its passengers to safety, the *Patna* crew must stand trial for their negligence. **Marlow,** a fatherly captain who attends the inquiry, takes a keen psychological interest in Jim, wishing to understand, from the young sailor's point of view, the order and significance of the events that culminated in the tragedy. His intense curiosity compels him to narrate and scrutinize Jim's remaining life.

Eventually Jim becomes a trading post agent on the remote island of Patusan through the beneficence of Marlow and Marlow's business friend **Stein.** Plagued with self-hatred over his previous misdeed, Jim resolves to gain the islanders' trust and live a morally responsible life. He befriends the old native chief, **Doramin,** and his son, **Dain Waris.** Through them he receives the title **Lord Jim;** he accepts the role naturally, for it accords with the paternal, colonialist code of conduct that has been his since youth. The story ends when a fellow white outcast, **Gentleman Brown,** arrives during Jim's absence and with his gang rampages the island. Jim returns and, finding Brown and his men surrounded by the natives, attempts to restore peace. He misjudges Brown, who soon after murders Dain Waris. In final compensation, Lord Jim offers himself to Doramin as a sacrifice. Jim's death, Marlow concludes, represents the sailor's incontrovertible attainment of the moral integrity he earlier lost.

Throughout his career Conrad examined the impossibility of living by a traditional code of conduct; his novels demonstrate that the complexity of the human spirit does not allow absolute fidelity to any ideal, or even to one's conscience. Most of Conrad's greatest works take place on board ship or in the backwaters of civilization; a ship or a small outpost offered an isolated environment where Conrad could develop his already complex moral problems without unnecessary entanglements that might obscure the situations. In both *Lord Jim* and *Heart of Darkness,* Conrad's two greatest examples of moral tragedy, the role of the narrator, Marlow, is crucial to an understanding of Conrad's intentions. Marlow offers a tentative view of a complex and ambiguous world. The reader should not accept all of Marlow's judgments as the only interpretations of events. Marlow is the most refined example of Conrad's use of an unreliable narrator, but in all of his works Conrad relies upon time shifts, flashbacks, and multiple perspectives of several characters to portray the unreliability of human perception.

Heart of Darkness (novella, 1902)

One of Conrad's most popular and highly regarded works, *Heart of Darkness* takes place in the Belgian Congo during the late nineteenth century. On the surface it is a dreamlike tale of mystery and adventure; however, it is also the story of a man's symbolic journey into his own inner being. Conrad heightens the enigmatic tenor and mythical power of the tale through his use of dual narrators: the actual observer, **Captain Marlow,** and a shadowy listener, who recapitulates the narrative Marlow delivers one night aboard a cruising yawl in the Thames estuary. In this manner the novella details the story of the seaman Marlow who, fresh from Europe, is sent on a boat journey up the Congo River to relieve **Kurtz,** the most successful trader in ivory working for the Belgian government. Prior to their personal encounter, Marlow knows and admires Kurtz through his reputation and his writings regarding the civilizing of the African continent, and, despite portentous warnings, sets out on a journey excited at the prospect of meeting him. Marlow's difficult expedition through the hot, barbaric interior of Africa inspires revulsion at the dehumanizing effects of colonialism, a disgust that culminates when he discovers that Kurtz, who is dying, has degenerated from an enlightened civilizer into a deranged, power-hungry subjugator of the African natives. Marlow's journey forces him to confront not only Kurtz's corruption, but also those elements within himself which are subject to the same temptations that affected Kurtz.

The affinity between Marlow and Kurtz is considered the most crucial relationship between characters in the story. Two pivotal scenes hint at the source of the men's bond, but the precise intention of Conrad remains ambiguous. The first of the scenes, in which Kurtz near the end of the novella utters his famous cry, "The horror, the horror!" is regarded by many critics as Kurtz's realization of the terrifying nature of his unrestrained behavior, a realization that is transferred to Marlow, who is allied with Kurtz through a complex mixture of repugnance and fascination. Consequently, Marlow glimpses the barbarous depths to which civilized man can sink, affirming a kinship between the "cultured" Europeans and the "savage" Africans in the lawless jungle. This knowledge alters Marlow's perception of the nature of truth and humanity and leads to the development of the second pivotal scene, which occurs after Marlow returns to Brussels. There, he is asked the nature of Kurtz's final words by the dead man's innocent fiancee, and he tells her that Kurtz repeated her name. Marlow's lie is a widely discussed element of the novella and is subject to many diverse interpretations. In the end, it reflects both the act of a man creating a personal morality based on the protection of the innocent from unpalatable truth and Marlow's final acceptance of Kurtz as an apostle of truth, one who has encountered in himself the essential barbarism of humanity.

Conrad's consciously ambiguous presentation of the relative nature of truth and morality, which compels the reader to take an active part in understanding the novella, is often considered a forerunner of many modernist literary techniques. For this reason, Frederick R. Karl has called *Heart of Darkness* the work in which "the nineteenth century becomes the twentieth." The novella's artistic cohesion of image and theme, its intricately vivid evocation of colonial oppression, and its detailed portrait of psychological duplicity and decay have inspired critics to call *Heart of Darkness* the best short novel in the English language.

Nostromo (novel, 1904)

Nostromo, widely recognized as Conrad's most ambitious novel, takes place in the fictitious South American country of Costaguana during the early twentieth century. The work examines the ideals, motivations, and failures of several participants in a revolutionary conflict there. To compensate for an intentional lack of straightforward narrative development, Conrad instead emphasized the development of four major characters: **Charles Gould, Dr. Monygham, Nostromo,** and **Martin Decoud.** Gould, an English aristocrat, reopens an abandoned silver mine in the Occidental Province of Costaguana, believing that the project will benefit Sulaco, the major city of the province. The enterprise in fact works to the detriment of the people of the city and precipitates a revolt against the dictatorial government of Costaguana. Because of his material interests, Gould supports the government and obsessively tries to save the mine from disaster. As a consequence of the obsession, he neglects his wife, **Emilia,** one of the most sympathetic characters in the novel, who finally resigns herself to the effective dissolution of her marriage. As Gould's love for Emilia wanes, another man, Dr. Monygham, falls in love with her. Monygham is a cynic who loathes himself for betraying several friends while under torture, but his cynicism is softened by the influence of Emilia's compassionate nature. When the Goulds and the silver mine are threatened by revolutionary forces, Monygham risks his life to save Emilia's by pretending to betray the Goulds while actually giving the revolutionaries false information.

"Nostromo" is the nickname of **Giovanni Battista Fidanza,** an Italian boatswain who abandons his ship on the coast of Costaguana and becomes a hero to the people of Sulaco. Although the word "nostromo" is an Italian nautical term meaning boatswain, many critics consider the name a contraction of the Italian "nostro uomo," meaning "our man," for Nostromo is the only character in the novel trusted by both the government authorities and the common people. When charged during the revolution with protecting the silver from the San Tomé mine, Nostromo buries it on an uninhabited island, Great Isabel, leaving Martin Decoud to guard it. Decoud, one of Conrad's most nihilistic characters, had become one of the leaders of the revolt due to his love for the revolutionary **Antonia Avellanos,** but while on the island he gradually loses the will to live and commits suicide by rowing out into the ocean, weighing himself down with four silver ingots from the hoard, shooting himself, and falling overboard. When Nostromo returns to the island, he discovers that the ingots are missing and thus cannot return the silver without being suspected as a thief. To avoid the appearance of theft, he claims that the barge sank and the silver was lost. Now corrupted by the "incorruptible metal," he periodically steals from the cache and is mistakenly shot by the island's lighthouse keeper while returning from a nocturnal theft. Nostromo dies in the presence of Emilia, who will not allow him to reveal the location of the ingots for fear that greed will continue to plague the region. Nonetheless, the Sulaco region, having become the Occidental Republic, flourishes, largely due to Gould's successful management of the San Tomé mine.

One of the most important themes of this and many other Conrad novels is the proposition that every ideal is fallible and contains within it the seeds of its own debasement. Conrad emphasizes this theme by relating events in a chronologically disarranged order, a structure that often reveals the collapse of an endeavor before its idealistic beginning is portrayed. The effect of this presentation is to create in the reader a fatalistic sense that progress is impossible, underscoring another of the novel's major themes—that human endeavor, including political action, is ultimately ineffective. While the unity of *Nostromo* may be questioned, the novel is now more often praised for its realistic and complex characterization and honest exploration of human corruption. Conrad's most profound and intricate expression of his major themes, *Nostromo* is considered by many critics to be one of the greatest novels of the twentieth century.

FURTHER READING

Berthoud, Jacques. *Joseph Conrad: The Major Phase*. Cambridge: Cambridge University Press, 1978.

Contemporary Authors, Vol. 104. Detroit: Gale Research Co.

Curle, Richard. *Joseph Conrad and His Characters: A Study of Six Novels*. London: Heinemann, 1957.

Dictionary of Literary Biography, Vols. 10, 34. Detroit: Gale Research Co.

Guerard, Albert. *Conrad the Novelist*. Cambridge: Harvard University Press, 1958.

Hay, Eloise Knapp. *The Political Novels of Joseph Conrad: A Critical Study*. Chicago: University of Chicago Press, 1963.

Kimbrough, Robert, ed. *"Heart of Darkness": An Annotated Text, Backgrounds and Sources Criticism*. Rev. ed. New York: W. W. Norton & Co., 1971.

Land, Stephen K. *Paradox and Polarity in the Fiction of Joseph Conrad*. New York: St. Martin's Press, 1984.

Leavis, F. R. *The Great Tradition: George Eliot, Henry James, Joseph Conrad*. Cambridge: Harvard University Press, 1957.

Najder, Zdzislaw. *Joseph Conrad: A Chronicle*, translated by Halina Carroll-Najder. New Brunswick: Rutgers University Press, 1983.

Roussel, Royal. *The Metaphysics of Darkness: A Study in the Unity and Development of Conrad's Fiction*. Baltimore: Johns Hopkins Press, 1971.

Stallman, R. W. *The Art of Joseph Conrad: A Critical Symposium*. East Lansing: Michigan State University Press, 1960.

Twentieth-Century Literary Criticism, Vols. 1, 6, 13, 25. Detroit: Gale Research Co.

Verleun, J. A. *The Stone Horse: A Study of the Function of the Minor Characters in Joseph Conrad's "Nostromo."* Groningen: Bouma's Boekhuis B. V., 1978.

Julio Cortázar
1914-1984

Argentinean novelist, short story writer, and essayist.

Hopscotch (novel, 1963)

This novel, Cortázar's most celebrated work, was a hugely influential achievement that transformed the literary language of a generation of Latin American writers, liberating narrative from the confines of logical, rational style. The novel is divided into 155 chapters, and the reader may read the novel in a variety of ways: it can be apporoached as a linear narrative; the reader can follow a table of instructions prepared by the author, playing a game of "hopscotch" with the text; or the reader is free to create an independent system of reading, for Cortázar saw his text as offering a limitless number of possibilities. Cortázar called the "active reader" the main character of the work, for he or she participates in the creation of the fiction through the process of reading. The actual story, which revolves around **Horacio Oliveira** and his quest, is interspersed with what Cortázar called "dispensable chapters" devoted to commentary on the novel and on the art of writing a novel. These are often a platform for the opinions of **Morelli,** who choses Oliveira to be the keeper of his manuscript, a collection of fragments.

Duality is a constant theme in the work, evident from the two settings in which the action takes place. The novel is divided into two parts, the first taking place in Paris, where Oliveira is a member of a group of expatriates, and the second in Buenos Aires, after he has returned to his native land. In Paris, Oliveira searches for the "kibbutz of desire" through his indulgence in bizarre, absurd experiences. His journey for self-understanding and expression leads him to a relationship with **La Maga**, who is described as a representative of disorder and primitive impulses and with whom he plumbs the depths of sensuous experience. Oliveira wishes to "live absurdly to abolish the absurd," trying to purge himself of human feeling. He leaves La Maga and indulges in even more destructive behavior; he spends a night with a Parisian vagrant and lands in jail. La Maga disappears, and whether she dies, commits suicide, or just leaves the city is unclear.

The second section, set in Buenos Aires, is dominated by Oliveira's relationship with **Manuel Traveler** and his wife, **Talita.** The Traveler—ironically named, for he has never left Argentina—and Talita both function as doubles, the Traveler for Oliveira and Talita for La Maga. The Traveler is an everyman, a representative of modern man in the contemporary world, whose values are those that Oliveira has rejected and who has avoided the search that has driven his friend from Buenos Aires and back again. Talita offers a bridge between the two men and what they represent. In the conclusion, the three are working in an insane asylum, where one night Oliveira believes he sees Talita as La Maga, playing hopscotch, a game in which he had always envisioned one square as a symbol for the end of his spiritual quest. The two descend to the morgue, kiss, and emerge reborn. Cortazar offers three confusing and conflicting endings to the novel and the reader is free to choose whether Oliveira goes mad, kills himself, or simply goes to a movie.

"Blow-Up" (short story, 1956)

In this, one of the most famous of his short stores, Cortázar continues his exploration of the theme of duality. His protagonist, **Roberto Michel,** is both a translator and photographer and is of both French and Chilean descent. Michel has taken a photograph of what he believes is a woman attempting to seduce a young boy. When he enlarges the photo, he thinks he sees a more sinister force at work, for he discerns a man lurking in the background and senses that the boy is in danger. He relives and rethinks the experience to the point of madness, becoming completely obsessed by the picture. We see that Michel's interpretation of the photo may be simply the result of self-delusion, for who the people in the photograph are—mother and son, or seducer and victim—is determined solely by Michel's response. When he takes the photo of the woman and boy, he creates a story for them in his mind, and the blow-up he makes of the picture parallels his exaggeration of the incident. The photo becomes menacing, and he sees the woman and man pursuing him for foiling their planned seduction. Yet the evil he perceives in the photo is a product of his imagination; as it takes over his existence, it deprives him of identity and sanity.

The story explores the limitations of the senses as Cortázar examines the pursuit of truth and the danger of self-delusion. Both Michel's first-person monologue and an objective third-person narrator are employed as narrative voices in the work until the conclusion, when we are totally within the subjective, tortured consciousness of the protagonist, who has been driven to madness by the powers of the imagination.

FURTHER READING

Alazraki, Jaime and Ivar Ivask, eds. *The Final Island: The Fiction of Julio Cortázar.* Norman: University of Oklahoma Press, 1978.

Brody, Robert. *Julio Cortázar: "Rayuela."* London: Tamesis, 1976.

Callado, Antonio. "Stages in the Latin-American Novel." In *Censorship and Other Problems of Latin-American Writers,* pp. 34-47. Cambridge: Cambridge University Press, 1974.

Cohen, Keith. "Cortázar and the Apparatus of Writing." *Contemporary Literature* 25, No. 1 (Spring 1984): 15-27.

Contemporary Authors, Vols. 21-24, rev. ed.; *Contemporary Authors New Revision Series,* Vol. 12. Detroit: Gale Research Co.

Contemporary Literary Criticism, Vols. 2, 3, 5, 10, 13, 15, 33, 34. Detroit: Gale Research Co.

Irby, James E. "Cortázar's *Hopscotch* and Other Games." *Novel: A Forum on Fiction* 1, No. 1 (Fall 1967): 64-70.

Rabassa, Gregory. "Lying to Athena: Cortázar and the Art of Fiction." *Books Abroad* 50, No. 3 (Summer 1976): 542-47.

Stephen Crane
1871-1900
American novelist, short story writer, and poet.

The Red Badge of Courage (novel, 1895)

The novel is set during the American Civil War and recounts the experiences of **Henry Fleming** as a Union soldier. It is essentially a story of Henry's coming of age, and Crane depicts his maturation from an innocent boy, prompted by a naive sense of patriotism and heroism to enlist, his disillusionment with the life of a soldier, and his confrontation with the horrors of war. Avoiding traditional forms of narrative, Crane renders Henry's story in a series of impressionistic scenes, replicating the disorientation of his protagonist as he confronts the terrors and dangers of war.

Throughout the novel, Henry encounters a natural environment that he finds ominous and threatening. He deserts during his first battle, fleeing what he sees as "monsters" on the battlefield, frightened less by the carnage than by the natural elements he sees enlisted against him. Yet nature offers a kind of solace as well and can be both perilous and nurturing, depending on Henry's ever-changing state of mind. Crane shows how Henry's battle with the landscape mirrors his internal struggle with his vanity and immaturity. Ironically, Henry is wounded when a frightened fellow soldier accidently injures him with the butt of his rifle. This becomes Henry's "red badge of courage," which he treats as a war wound and which draws the respect of his comrades. Henry lives in fear that he will be found out, but as with his desertion, no one ever learns the truth. Yet Henry grows in self-awareness, learning the true meaning of honor and courage, and the novel records his bravery as he leads men into battle. The conclusion shows Henry as a man, aware of his maturity, his "soul changed." Nature in this last scene is benevolent, with images of clover, flowers, and the clouds parting to reveal the warmth and light of the sun.

Crane's impressionistic method reveals his concern with delineating the psychological workings of his character's mind. The novel is considered an innovative force in American letters, for in addition to its impressionistic aspects, critics have noted elements of realism, naturalism, and symbolism. Crane explores the meaning of fear, cowardice, courage, and honor, and he delineates his themes in a story which pits the reality of war against Henry's naive expectations and sentimentalized vision. *The Red Badge of Courage* is considered a masterpiece of American fiction.

FURTHER READING

Contemporary Authors, Vol. 109. Detroit: Gale Research Co.

Colvert, James B. "Structure and Theme in Stephen Crane's Fiction." *Modern Fiction Studies* 5, No. 3 (Autumn 1959): 199-208.

Dictionary of Literary Biography, Vols. 12, 54. Detroit: Gale Research Co.

Nagel, James. *Stephen Crane and Literary Impressionism.* University Park: Pennsylvania State University Press, 1980.

Solomon, Eric. *Stephen Crane: From Parody to Realism.* Cambridge, Mass.: Harvard University Press, 1966.

Twentieth-Century Literary Criticism, Vols. 11, 17. Detroit: Gale Research Co.

Walcutt, Charles Child. "Stephen Crane: Naturalist and Impressionist." In *American Literary Naturalism, a Divided Stream,* pp. 66-86. Minneapolis: University of Minnesota Press, 1956.

Robertson Davies

1913-

Canadian novelist, essayist, and dramatist.

"The Deptford Trilogy": *Fifth Business* (novel, 1970); *The Manticore* (novel, 1972); *World of Wonders* (novel, 1975)

Set variously in Canada, Switzerland, and other locales, "The Deptford Trilogy" is considered Davies's finest literary achievement and the basis for his international reputation. The three novels center on three protagonists—**Dunstan Ramsay,** whose story is related in *Fifth Business,* **David Staunton,** the central figure in *The Manticore,* and **Paul Dempster,** also known as **Magnus Eisengrim,** whose story forms the narrative of *World of Wonders.* The three characters are linked by a single incident, the throwing of a snowball, that unites their fates and gives the trilogy its focus. Throughout the work, Davies concentrates on several themes, including the search for identity, the necessity to examine one's life and to accept the consequences of one's actions, and the need to acknowledge the unconscious, irrational elements of human nature. Each of these stories is a confession of sorts, and each moves toward a moment of self-awareness, imbued with symbols and imagery from myth and invoking the importance of the integrated self. The protagonists explore three alternate means of self-knowledge, Ramsay through religion and myth, David through the myth and symbol of Jungian analysis, and Paul through magic. Davies's trilogy is a work that, for all its moral seriousness, is a lively, humorous, and fascinating tale of the eternal quest for self-awareness.

Fifth Business begins in the town of Deptford, Ontario, a setting that links all the characters. The novel is given in the first person in the form of a letter that Ramsay composes to the headmaster of the school where he has taught for forty-five years and from which he has recently retired. He wants to overcome his reputation as a colorless old scholar obsessed with hagiography, and proceeds to relate his remarkable life. His recollections begin when he is a boy of ten, as he describes life in a typical, provincial Canadian village, providing a platform for Davies's recurrent theme of the close-minded, hypocritical nature of small-town life. The incident of the snowball occurs early in the story. Ramsay's friend, **Percy Boyd Staunton,** is the fair-haired boy of Deptford, wealthy, handsome, and destined for success. He is also a bully, and he chases Ramsay home one day, throwing snowballs at him. But one, with a stone in it, misses Ramsay and hits **Mrs. Mary Dempster,** the pregnant wife of the Baptist minister, **Reverend Amasa Dempster;** she goes into labor and delivers a son, Paul, prematurely. Ramsay feels terribly guilty and blames himself for ducking the snowball meant for him. Small and sickly, Paul Dempster grows up under Ramsay's care as his mother slips into a kind of child-like dementia. Yet she becomes as a pivotal figure in Ramsay's life, for although she is ostracized by the community of Deptford, he is drawn to her particular serenity and grace.

One day Mary disappears and is found by Ramsay making love with a tramp in the local gravel pit. Though forbidden by his mother, Ramsay continues to see her, for he is certain that she displays the characteristics of a saint. He credits her with bringing his brother back to life, and later, during the war, he believes that a vision of her saves him from death.

The novel also focuses on the tremendous financial success of Percy, now called Boy Staunton, including his marriage to the town beauty. They move to Toronto and have two children, **David** and **Caroline.** Ramsay remains a close friend of the family and begins his career as a schoolmaster, continuing to pursue his interest in the lives of the saints. During a visit to Europe, he meets Paul Dempster, who had run away when he was ten to join the circus and has now become Magnus Eisengrim, one of the finest magicians of his time. When he later meets Eisengrim in Mexico, Ramsay is introduced to the remarkable **Liselotte Vitzlipützli,** called Liesl, a woman of grotesque features and exquisite sensibility who aids Eisengrim in his magic. Eisengrim and his entourage are performing in Toronto as the novel ends with the bizarre death of Boy Staunton, who is found at the bottom of a lake with a stone in his mouth.

In *The Manticore,* David Staunton, a successful criminal lawyer, arrives in Switzerland to begin analysis with **Dr. Johanna von Haller,** a Jungian psychiatrist. He is an alcoholic with his life in shambles following his father's death. He is also a man obsessed with logic and truth, but more importantly, with his father. "It is not easy to be the son of a very rich man," he tells the doctor, and relates how his father's love was based on the proof that he could "be a man." The manticore, an image that emerges from his dreams during his analysis, is a vivid symbol of the unintegrated being, with the head of a man, the body of a lion, and the tale of a serpent. David spends a year in analysis, and his recollections parallel Ramsay's and focus on his coming of age as the son of the famous and remote Boy Staunton. A large portion of the novel is presented as his journal, which he keeps for his meetings with Dr. Haller and which is presented as a kind of brief. His dreams and their interpretation are the central focus of the novel, he comes to realize the importance of recognizing and acknowledging the fragmented elements of his being. Many of the same incidents related in *Fifth Business* by Ramsay are recounted here, with different insights and emphasis. In the conclusion, his analysis is ended, and he spends a strange Christmas holiday with Ramsay, Liesl, and Eisengrim at Liesl's Swiss mansion, where he learns even more about his father and himself.

World of Wonders takes place in Switzerland as Eisengrim takes part in a movie about Houdin, a magician from nineteenth-century France. He, too, relates his life story—to Ramsay, Liesl, and the camera crew—focusing, like David before him, on the heritage of a cruel father, who had blamed his son for the madness of his mother. Eisengrim relates how he was kidnapped from his home by a carnival magician who sodomized and brutalized him. His recollections form a vivid contrast to the sweet, sentimental vision of the life of Houdin. Yet for all its cruelty, Eisengrim's life in the circus is full of wonder: the grotesquely figured dwarves and freaks who became his family, his ability to enchant his audience, and the way in which the sundered human psyche can be made whole. As Ramsay's pursuit of the meaning of saints and myth had colored the first volume, and David's quest for inner wholeness through the mythic interpretations of the human condition the second, this volume focuses on the wonder of magic, including the protagonist's miraculous transformation from Paul Dempster to Magnus Eisengrim. The novel follows him all over the world, from the Canadian carnival to the London stage to Zurich, where he tells his tale. But perhaps the most important stop of his personal and professional career occurs in Toronto, where, after a performance, he meets Boy Staunton and learns from Ramsay the story of the snowball, and Boy Staunton learns its moral legacy at the hands of a master prestidigitator.

FURTHER READING

Baltensperger, Peter. "Battles with the Trolls." *Canadian Literature,* No. 71 (Winter 1976): 59-67.

Barclay, Pat. "Noble and Confused." *Canadian Literature,* No. 56 (Spring 1973): 113-14.

Contemporary Authors, Vols. 33-36, rev. ed.; *Contemporary Authors New Revision Series,* Vol. 17. Detroit: Gale Research Co.

Contemporary Literary Criticism, Vols. 2, 7, 13, 25, 42. Detroit: Gale Research Co.

Grant, Judith Skelton. "Robertson Davies, God and the Devil." *Book Forum* 4, No. 1 (1978): 56-63.

King, Bruce. "Canada: Robertson Davies and Identity." In *The New English Literatures: Cultural Nationalism in a Changing World,* pp. 196-214. New York: St. Martin's Press, 1980.

Monk, Patricia. *The Smaller Infinity: The Jungian Self in the Novels of Robertson Davies.* Toronto: University of Toronto Press, 1982.

Moore, Brian. "There's Life in the Old Novel House." *Book World—The Washington Post* (26 November 1972): 8.

Prescott, Peter. "White Magic." *Newsweek* (22 March 1976): 80-1.

Stouck, David. "Robertson Davies." In *Major Canadian Authors: A Critical Introduction,* pp. 197-212. Lincoln: University of Nebraska Press, 1984.

James Dickey

1923-

American poet, novelist, and essayist.

Deliverance (novel, 1970)

In this award-winning poet's first novel, four friends from a large Southern town plan a canoe trip down an isolated, dangerous river which is soon to be closed off by a dam. **Ed Gentry, Drew Ballinger,** and **Bobby Trippe** are typical middle-class American males who view the outing as an escape for a short time from the dullness of their suburban lives and as a chance for some harmless adventure. Their leader, **Lewis Medlock,** is a seasoned outdoorsman and champion archer who considers the trip an opportunity to pit himself against nature. On the second day of their river journey, two of the group are viciously attacked by mountain men, one of whom Lewis kills. The other escapes and begins to follow the group down river. When Drew is wounded and Lewis's leg is broken, Ed is forced to hunt down the mountain man and kill him. Their adventure is further marred by Drews's death by drowning. When the three survivors finally reach civilization again, they invent a story about Drew's death that will appease the authorities without revealing the murders of the other two men. After returning home, Ed and Lewis contemplate their journey, chastened by the lessons learned in their encounter with the natural world.

In this novel, Dickey continues to examine themes that are prevalent in his poetry, particularly the redemptive relationship that exists between humanity and nature. Although *Deliverance* was originally considered by many critics to be a sensationalistic adventure story, later assessments acknowledge Dickey's powerful writing and skillful use of symbolism.

FURTHER READING

Christensen, Paul. "Toward the Abyss: James Dickey at Middle Age." *Parnassus: Poetry in Review* (Spring-Summer 1986): 202-19.

Contemporary Authors, Vols. 9-12, rev. ed.; *Contemporary Authors New Revision Series,* Vol. 10; *Contemporary Authors Bibliographical Series,* Vol. 2. Detroit: Gale Research Co.

Contemporary Literary Criticism, Vols. 1, 2, 4, 7, 10, 15, 47. Detroit: Gale Research Co.

Dictionary of Literary Biography, Vol. 5; *Dictionary of Literary Biography Yearbook: 1982.* Detroit: Gale Research Co.

Doughtie, Edward. "Art and Nature in *Deliverance.*" *Southwest Review* 64, No. 2 (Spring 1979): 167-80.

Stephenson, William. "*Deliverance* from What?" *The Georgia Review* (Spring 1974): 114-20.

Joan Didion
1934-

American novelist, essayist, journalist, scriptwriter, and short story writer.

Play It as It Lays (novel, 1970)

Didion's second novel is set in Hollywood and parts of the American Southwest. **Maria Wyeth,** who grew up in a dying Nevada town, leaves the West to begin a career as a model in New York and later becomes a Hollywood actress. She is married to **Carter Lang,** the director of two of her films, and has a four-year-old daughter, **Kate.** It is indicative of Maria's state of mind that her favorite of these two movies is the one in which she plays a tough member of a motorcycle gang who has complete control of her life, in vivid contrast to her own sense of helplessness. She is sickened by the second film, entitled "Maria," a collection of vignettes taken from her daily life. The novel follows her mental breakdown as she becomes overwhelmed by a world filled with chaos and nothingness. She is haunted as well by two particular events from her past: the violent death of her mother in an automobile accident and an abortion which Carter forced her to have. Her life deteriorates into a series of meaningless actions and relationships, but neither sex, drugs, nor religion help relieve her dread at facing the world each day.

Maria's existence is one of hopeless desolation, an empty place without meaning or purpose where life is a crap game. Just before he commits suicide, her friend **BZ** asks her why anyone should choose life over death; "why not?" is Maria's answer, and that is as close to a life-affirming statement as she can articulate. Her degeneration leads to her confinement in a mental institution, from which she emerges in the conclusion. She has at last gained a new determination to confront the nihilistic world and to go on living for the sake of her daughter.

Play It as It Lays was a popular success and was often viewed as an allegory for the moral decline of contemporary American society brought about by the erosion of traditional values. The novel's loose structure and detached tone serve to enhance Maria's inner turmoil.

A Book of Common Prayer (novel, 1977)

Didion's first major critical success, and her third novel, is set in the imaginary Central American country of Bocca Grande. **Grace Strasser-Mendana,** an American anthropologist who is dying of cancer, has inherited from her husband most of the arable land and political power in Bocca Grande. She narrates the story of another American, **Charlotte Douglas,** who comes to Bocca Grande in search of her daughter, **Marin,** a political activist wanted by the FBI. Charlotte has led a sheltered and self-deluded life, believing what she wants to believe and even reconstructing events in her own mind to her personal satisfaction. Charlotte still considers Marin to be her innocent child, with whom she enjoyed a close, nurturing relationship. Marin, a political revolutionary who had rejected her mother's way of life and who had disappeared months ago and severed contact with her mother, interprets their relationship quite differently. After arriving in Bocca Grande, Charlotte becomes involved with the people and politics of the country and begins administering malaria inoculations and working in a birth control clinic. When a group of revolutionaries stages a violent coup, Charlotte is killed in the crossfire. Ironically, Marin is incapable of believing in her mother's selfless aid to the people and is in fact a supporter of the revolution which killed Charlotte. In relating Charlotte's story, Grace comes to an understanding of her own delusions and life.

This work, like Didion's other novels, portrays through one individual's story the fragmentation of American society and culture. Here, the focus is on the deterioration of the parent/child relationship and the misunderstandings and misconceptions which keep them apart, as well as a commentary on the inability of political changes to speak to human needs.

FURTHER READING

Coale, Samuel. "Didion's Disorder: An American Romancer's Art." *Critique* 25 (Spring 1984): 160-70.

Contemporary Authors, Vols. 5-8, rev. ed.; *Contemporary Authors New Revision Series,* Vol. 14. Detroit: Gale Research Co.

Contemporary Literary Criticism, Vols. 1, 3, 8, 14, 32. Detroit: Gale Research Co.

Dictionary of Literary Biography, Vol. 2; *Dictionary of Literary Biography Yearbook: 1981, 1986.* Detroit: Gale Research Co.

Henderson, Katherine Usher. *Joan Didion.* New York: Ungar, 1981.

Hinchman, Sandra K. "Making Sense and Making Stories: Problems of Cognition and Narration in Joan Didion's *Play It as It Lays.*" *The Centennial Review* 29 (Fall 1985): 457-73.

Merivale, Patricia. "The Search for the Other Woman: Joan Didion and the Female Artist-Parable." In *Gender Studies: New Directions in Feminist Criticism,* pp. 133-47. Bowling Green: Popular Press, 1986.

Isak Dinesen

1885-1962

Danish short story writer, autobiographer, and novelist.

"The Dreamers" (short story, 1934)

A novella-length gothic tale, "The Dreamers" takes place in 1863 aboard a dhow en route to Zanzibar. In the imaginative storytelling spirit of the *Arabian Nights,* a rich Englishman named **Lincoln Forsner** regales the renowned, aging fable-maker **Mira Jama** with a captivating story that soon encompasses additional tellers with tales that mirror one another. Lincoln's narrative finally reveals itself as a cautionary account of thwarted ambition and nameless existence, an account intended to rouse Lincoln's brooding young companion, **Said Ben Ahamed,** an escapee whose hope of revenge upon those responsible for his unjust imprisonment "was in reality forcing the boat on." Lincoln recounts how, twenty years earlier at the age of twenty-three, he fell in love with a woman in a Roman brothel. Her name was **Olalla.** Extraordinary in every sense, she gave Lincoln a luminous accord with "all the winds and currents of life." Although the relationship blossomed, it ended suddenly with Olalla's disappearance. A single clue—the mysterious presence of an elderly Dutch Jew, **Marcus Cocoza,** Olalla's silent shadow and the one who facilitated her departure—thrust Lincoln on an arduous quest to recover his lover.

Eventually in his world travels he meets and dines with two men, **Friederich Hohenemser** and **Baron Guildenstern,** who each share a tale of an encounter with a singularly fascinating woman. Like Olalla, both women, though vastly different in occupation and personality, carry a delicate scar running from the left ear to the collarbone. When the tales have been told, the men realize that the woman of their dreams has just exited the hotel in which they are staying. They also spy the Jew of Amsterdam and, in a dangerous pursuit of the woman along a steep mountain path, attempt to solve the mystery that has enveloped them. The woman, not wishing to reveal her tragic story, jumps from a cliff, nearly killing herself. When the three rescue her, Cocoza appears. He identifies himself as the true friend of **Pellegrina Leoni,** the famed Italian opera singer, believed to have died in a Milan theater fire. Pellegrina is the woman in question, once a "divinity," a performer of uncanny power, devoted to "worshipping the sinners" and unselfishly serving the masses. When her singing voice was ruined by the fire, she faked her death with the aid of Cocoza and embarked on a series of invented, unfettered lives. In the end, Pellegrina dies, after briefly resurrecting the mammoth persona which was once hers.

"The Dreamers" concludes back on the dhow. Mira and Lincoln reveal a wisdom achieved only through experience and retrospection; Said, still unshakable, thinks only of reaching his destination at dawn. Among the finest of the stories from her best-known work, *Seven Gothic Tales,* "The Dreamers" is typical of Dinesen's narrative art in its geographical and temporal distancing and its exotic characters. Her collection is based on the classic storytelling tradition which favors action and imagination over intellectual analysis and views the telling of the story as an end in itself.

"The Monkey" (short story, 1934)

"The Monkey" is set in an unnamed Northern European country during the nineteenth century. **Cathinka,** owner of a little gray monkey, is Virgin Prioress of Cloister Seven, a nonreligious retreat for unmarried women and widows of noble birth. Fall has arrived and her monkey, as is customary, has taken a lengthy sojourn in the woods to escape and hunt berries. During her precocious pet's absence, Cathinka occupies herself with sinister matchmaking. Her favorite nephew and godson, **Boris,** has hastily arrived at the convent seeking advice. At the age of twenty-two, he has been labelled a corrupter of youth; his private thoughts dwell on orgies, and he is perhaps homosexual. Wishing to maintain his status as a lieutenant in the royal guard, he has reluctantly decided to marry. Cathinka suggests that **Athena Hopballehus,** an unusually strong and independent daughter of a neighboring nobleman, will be the perfect mate. Boris receives **Count Hopballehus**'s blessing but Athena rejects his suit outright.

Hearing of this, Cathinka, with deadly determination, plans a seductive dinner for the couple. Drunk with wine, Athena retires early. After Cathinka administers a love philter to Boris, the young couple meet and grapple in a dark, crimson room. Athena wins the battle, for she brutally repels Boris until the potion weakens. However, Boris has managed a bloody kiss that renders the innocent girl unconscious. In the morning Cathinka, fiendishly triumphant, preys upon Athena's naivete, claiming the only possible course for the girl is to marry, for she is surely pregnant with Boris's child. Athena eventually promises to do so but also promises to kill Boris after the wedding. Then, in a climactic, unearthly metamorphosis, Cathinka shrivels and panics as the monkey returns and, after several moments of furious struggle, once again becomes the true Virgin Prioress. This final event divides Boris and Athena from the rest of the world and brings them closer together.

Like much of Dinesen's short fiction, "The Monkey" is rooted in the gothic, decadent, and romantic literary traditions. This story is further distinguished for its artful fusion of classical and Wendish mythology and its underlying theme of social and psychological captivity, a predicament all the characters face in various ways. The strikingly original flavor of Dinesen's *Seven Gothic Tales,* as well as her highly acclaimed collection of reminiscences, *Out of Africa,* have earned her a reputation as one of Denmark's major modern authors.

FURTHER READING

Contemporary Authors, Vols. 25-28, rev. ed.; *Contemporary Authors Permanent Series,* Vol. 2. Detroit: Gale Research Co.

Contemporary Literary Criticism, Vols. 10, 29. Detroit: Gale Research Co.

Hannah, Donald. *"Isak Dinesen" and Karen Blixen: The Mask and the Reality.* New York: Random House, 1972.

Johannesson, Eric O. *The World of Isak Dinesen.* Seattle: University of Washington Press, 1961.

Langbaum, Robert. *Isak Dinesen's Art: The Gayety of Vision.* Chicago: University of Chicago Press, 1975.

Svendsen, Calra, ed. *The Life and Destiny of Isak Dinesen.* New York: Random House, 1970.

Thurman, Judith. *Isak Dinesen: The Life of a Storyteller.* New York: St. Martin's Press, 1982.

Whissen, Thomas R. *Isak Dinesen's Aesthetics.* Port Washington: Kennikat Press, 1973.

E. L. Doctorow
1931-
American novelist.

The Book of Daniel (novel, 1971)

Set in New York in the 1950s, the novel tells the story of **Daniel Lewin**'s upbringing and his relationship with his parents, **Paul** and **Rochelle Isaacson.** Based on the famous Julius and Ethel Rosenberg trials, *The Book of Daniel* traces the Isaacson family's involvement in politics. They are arrested for conspiring to commit espionage, convicted, and executed. Daniel struggles to support and trust his parents, but it is clear that, though they argued their innocence to their death, Daniel is unconvinced. As he reflects many years later, he is still torn, and his dilemma forms the moral crisis of his mature years. His sister is driven to the point of madness, and Daniel becomes a victim of alienation and despair. Doctorow parallels Daniel's story to the biblical Book of Daniel, juxtaposing his character's dilemma with those of the Jewish people. The novel is presented as Daniel's own narrative account of the life and death of his parents, and conveys his own moral and psychological confusion as he tries to understand their import.

Daniel is alternately objective and subjective in telling his story, and Doctorow uses first- and third-person narrative to reflect Daniel's crisis. Daniel assesses one of the major political incidents of the modern era both as a son and as a commentator. Doctorow's story abounds with detail, and shifts often in time and place, creating an elaborate, multi-leveled novel in which he examines the machinations of the political left and the Communist Party during the Rosenberg era.

Ragtime (novel, 1975)

Set in New York City at the turn of the century, *Ragtime* focuses on a representative cross-section of America in the era prior to World War I. It relates the story of **Coalhouse Walker, Jr.,** a poor black man who is determined to rise above his station in life. Intermingled with Walker's experiences are the lives of **Jateh** and **Mameh,** a Jewish family, and the prosperous **Father, Mother,** and **Younger Brother,** the family of the narrator. Doctorow also chronicles the lives of such famous historical figures of the era as **Henry Ford, Emma Goldman, J. P. Morgan,** and **Sigmund Freud.** The novel's conflict occurs when Coalhouse is racially harassed, and his car is vandalized by local firemen. Walker goes into hiding and threatens to destroy every firehouse until his car is returned to its previous condition. While he is in seclusion, his wife, **Sarah,** dies. He and Younger Brother, who embraces Walker's cause of racial justice, take over the J. P. Morgan Library, a symbol of the evils and excesses of capitalism. In the conclusion, Younger Brother escapes to Mexico, and Walker is killed by a firing line of policemen.

Doctorow's portrait of an era portrays characters who are victims of historical, social, and economic forces over which they have no control. His narrative style evokes the rhythms of ragtime music in a closely detailed series of vignettes. The novel has come under criticism for Doctorow's blending of fact and fiction, particularly in his portrayals of historical figures, but *Ragtime* remains his best-known and most popular work.

FURTHER READING

Contemporary Authors, Vols. 45-48, rev. ed.; *Contemporary Authors New Revision Series,* Vol. 2. Detroit: Gale Research Co.

Contemporary Literary Criticism, Vols. 6, 11, 15, 18, 37, 44. Detroit: Gale Research Co.

Dictionary of Literary Biography, Vols. 2, 28; *Dictionary of Literary Biography Yearbook: 1980.* Detroit: Gale Research Co.

Emblidge, David. "Marching Backward into the Future: Progress as Illusion in Doctorow's Novels." *Southwest Review* (Autumn 1977): 397-409.

Estrin, Barbara L. "Surviving McCarthyism: E. L. Doctorow's *The Book of Daniel.*" *Massachusetts Review* 16 (Summer 1975): 577-87.

Green, Martin. "Nostalgic Politics." *American Scholar* 45 (Winter 1975-1976): 841-45.

Knorr, Walter L. "Doctorow and Kleist: 'Kohlhass' in *Ragtime.*" *Modern Fiction Studies* (Summer 1976): 224-27.

Raban, Jonathan. "Easy Virtue: On Doctorow's *Ragtime.*" *Encounter* (February 1976): 71-4.

Stark, John. "Alienation and Analysis in Doctorow's *The Book of Daniel.*" *Critique* 16, No. 3 (1975): 101-10.

John Dos Passos

1896-1970

American novelist, essayist, and poet.

Three Soldiers (novel, 1921)

Set in France during World War I, the novel chronicles the effects of the war on three representative soldiers from the United States. **John Andrews** is from a wealthy Virginia family, **Dan Fuseli** is an Italian-American from San Francisco, and **Chrisfield** is from rural Indiana. The course of the novel takes us from boot camp to the French front, focussing particularly on the deadening effects of the military life: the repetition, boredom, and the senseless, demeaning labor that characterize the existence of all three soldiers. Fuseli represents the middle-class American of ambition, striving for advancement no matter what the cost. Insinuating and opportunistic, he desperately wants to become a corporal. Chrisfield is a violent and brutal man, and during the novel he murders a German officer and an American sergeant, equally without guilt. John Andrews is a Harvard student, sensitive and interested in music. One of the main sections of the novel deals with his time in Paris, where he is stationed. He becomes increasingly disaffected with army life and leaves the city without a pass; he is then put in a labor brigade, from which he deserts. In the novel's conclusion, both Chrisfield and Andrews have gone AWOL.

Dos Passos's theme in this novel is the brutality and destructive power of war. He specifically focuses on the war as a machine, a dehumanizing force that robs individuals of their freedom and their lives. The work was considered original for its focus on war rather than on the men who fight it and influenced a generation of war novels. As in other of his early works, Dos Passos here presents a harsh indictment of capitalism, seeing it as a means for American and European industrialists to become wealthy while the soldiers pay the price with their lives. The characters' speech marks an important element of his method, for each figure speaks in his own idiom, reflecting his geographic and social background, a technique Dos Passos repeated in much of his later fiction.

Manhattan Transfer (novel, 1925)

The novel takes place in New York City in the early decades of the twentieth century. Manhattan represents urban America and its dehumanizing effects on its inhabitants. The atmosphere Dos Passos creates is one of chaos and despair, with characters who are depicted as victims of societal forces beyond their control. We are first introduced to **Ellen**

Thatcher as an infant, and we follow her through a life marked by rootlessness and lack of values. She marries three men during the course of the novel: first, **Jojo Oglethorpe,** an aging homosexual whom she believes can help her career in the theater. After her divorce from Oglethorpe, she marries **Jimmy Herf,** but that marriage too ends in divorce. The only man she ever truly loved, **Stan Emery,** commits suicide, and Ellen aborts the child they had conceived together. As the novel ends, she marries **George Baldwin,** a wealthy lawyer. Ellen is depicted as a woman who uses and discards men, but she is not held up to scorn or judged by Dos Passos. Rather, she represents the soulless urbanite, searching but never finding the love she craves.

Jimmy Herf is a journalist whom we first see coming to America from Europe with his mother as a child. He is a sensitive and intuitive man, and many critics have noted that he is in some ways an alter ego for Dos Passos himself. He serves in the ambulance corps during World War I, where he meets Ellen. They marry and have a child, but the relationship disintegrates. Throughout the novel, Jimmy is juxtaposed to characters who represent the venality and corruption of the capitalist system, a structure he continues to resist. In the novel's conclusion, Jimmy is seen leaving Manhattan and its corrosive influence, without money, but with hope.

Manhattan Transfer signalled a departure from more traditionally structured novels, for it is given in a series of vignettes that are juxtaposed to produce a form that has been described as mosaic. Thus the pattern of the novel reflects the fragmented nature of the modern urban existence it depicts. The word play and vivid imagery that characterize the novel's language clearly reveal the influence of James Joyce and lend an imagistic quality to the prose. Although an impersonal narrator presents most of the story, Dos Passos also makes use of interior monologue to depict the inner workings of his characters' minds. Thematically, this novel continues Dos Passos's indictment of the capitalist system and the moral degeneracy it perpetuates.

"U.S.A.": *The 42nd Parallel* (novel, 1930); *1919* (novel, 1932); *The Big Money* (novel, 1936)

The trilogy is set in America in the first three decades of the twentieth century. As in *Manhattan Transfer,* Dos Passos here analyzes the state of the country through several representative characters. **Charley Anderson,** depicted in an early volume as a pilot during World War I, returns in the last volume of the trilogy to start an aviation company. Through him Dos Passos examines the corrupting influence of capitalism, as Charley pursues wealth at the expense of his own moral values, becoming a drunk and a womanizer. **Fenian McCreary,** known as "Mac," is a printer who loses his job and becomes a tramp. As an itinerant worker, he becomes involved in the labor movement, elucidating Dos Passos's view of workers' rights jeopardized by big business. **J. Ward Moorehouse** is a public relations man who represents the venality of a system based on words rather than work. He is a selfish man and a hypocrite: in one telling sequence, Dos Passos shows him taking part in the peace process after World War I, as he works to ensure that the interests of big business are served and will continue to maintain wealth and power in the postwar world. **Eleanor Stoddard** is an interior designer and one-time mistress of Moorehouse. She is depicted as a hard, grasping woman, who utilizes her artistic gifts to monetary ends.

Dos Passos employs four separate methods of narration in this work. In addition to the fictional narrative, he uses "Newsreel" sections made up of contemporary newspaper articles and verses of popular songs; "Camera Eye" sequences that represent his own thoughts and memories, rendered in the style of a prose poem; and "Biographies" of such famous people of the era as Eugene Debs, Thomas Edison, Isadora Duncan, and Woodrow Wilson. Through this technique, Dos Passos creates a portrait of America from a myriad of angles, using private and public lives and events to elucidate his theme. As in his earlier fiction, Dos Passos here continues his study of the moral decay of the nation. His characters are depicted as victims of the social machine, unable to control their fates. The tone of the novels is bitterly pessimistic, reflecting Dos Passos's view of a nation in the throes of moral chaos. As in his earlier fiction, the characters speak in their own idiom, reflecting their social class and education.

FURTHER READING

Beach, Joseph Warren. "Dos Passos 1947." *The Sewanee Review* 55, No. 3 (Summer 1947): 406-18.

Becker, George J. *John Dos Passos.* New York: Ungar, 1974.

Colley, Iain. *Dos Passos and the Fiction of Despair.* London: Macmillan, 1978.

Contemporary Authors, Vols. 1-4, rev. ed., 29-32, rev. ed.; *Contemporary Authors New Revision Series,* Vol. 3. Detroit: Gale Research Co.

Contemporary Literary Criticism, Vols. 1, 4, 8, 11, 15, 25, 34. Detroit: Gale Research Co.

Dictionary of Literary Biography, Vols. 4, 9; *Dictionary of Literary Biography Documentary Series,* Vol. 1. Detroit: Gale Research Co.

Hook, Andrew, ed. *Dos Passos: A Collection of Critical Essays.* Englewood Cliffs: Prentice-Hall, 1974.

Kriegel, Leonard. "Architect of History." *The Nation* 239, No. 15 (10 November 1984): 485-88.

Marz, Charles. "'U.S.A.': Chronicle and Performance." *Modern Fiction Studies* 26, No. 3 (Autumn 1980): 398-416.

Morse, Jonathan. "Dos Passos' 'U.S.A.' and the Illusions of Memory." *Modern Fiction Studies* 23, No. 4 (Winter 1977-78): 543-56.

Schwartz, Delmore. "John Dos Passos and the Whole Truth." *The Southern Review* 4, No. 2 (October 1938): 351-67.

Wagner, Linda W. *Dos Passos: Artist as American.* Austin: The University of Texas Press, 1979.

Arthur Conan Doyle
1859-1930
English short story writer, novelist, and essayist.

The Hound of the Baskervilles (novel, 1902)

This, the most famous story Doyle ever wrote concerning his world-renowned detective, **Sherlock Holmes,** is set in the Devonshire moors and involves the mystery surrounding the curse upon the Baskerville family. Narrated by Holmes's great friend and colleague, **Dr. John Watson,** the story begins as the two are visited in their flat in Baker Street by **Dr. James Mortimer,** who comes to ask their help in resolving the eerie circumstances surrounding the death of **Sir Charles Baskerville,** recently found dead on the ancestral estate in Devonshire. Through his retelling of the circumstances of Sir Charles's death, we learn the hideous legacy of the Baskerville family: a nefarious ancestor had been killed by a huge dog, a supernatural being of unearthly powers. Now, legend has it, the beast has been seen again and was somehow involved in Sir Charles's unfortunate demise. His heir, **Sir Henry Baskerville,** is due to arrive from Canada to take over the estate, and Mortimer wants Holmes's help in determining what happened to Sir Charles. Mortimer himself had been called to the scene of his death, and had seen nearby "the footprints of a gigantic hound."

Holmes dispatches Watson to Devonshire to look after Sir Henry while he presumably takes care of other business in London. Watson meets several of the local townspeople, including a naturalist, **Jack Stapleton,** and his sister, **Beryl.** Sir Henry is quite taken with Beryl, a dark beauty, but although his intentions are honorable, Stapleton opposes the match. Watson notes the strangeness of his behavior, but is perplexed by it. After days of investigation, duly reported to Holmes in London, he comes upon his colleague, who has been hiding on the moor, disguised and conducting a parallel investigation. Holmes reveals to Watson that he is sure the criminal is Stapleton, who has passed off his wife, Beryl, as his sister to use her as a decoy. He has also purchased and trained a giant hound, which he used to frighten Sir Charles to death and which, Holmes is sure, he plans to use to kill Sir Henry. Acting quickly, and accompanied by his old Scotland Yard friend, **Inspector Lestrade,** Holmes sets a trap for Stapleton. But as they wait outside his house, they encounter the beast: a huge monster of a dog, terrifying and breathing fire. It almost kills Sir Henry, but Holmes and company arrive in time to save him. Stapleton flees across the moor, and is seen no more; later Holmes assumes that he perished in the mire. He was, it is learned, a descendent of the Baskerville family who had plotted to murder the men who stood in the way of his inheritance.

This brilliantly paced narrative has long been a favorite of Sherlockians the world over. Doyle created a rich and wonderfully detailed fictional world and in Holmes developed one of most beloved and enduring fictional characters of all time. His prose is distinguished by wit, charm, and concision, and in *The Hound of the Baskervilles,* he employs a variety of narrative types, including letters, journal entries, and inquest reports. These supplement the first-person recollections of Watson, whose rather limited powers of deduction highlight Holmes's brilliance. As a character type, Holmes is a descendent of the earlier detectives of Poe and Gaboriau, yet Doyle created a character whose fascination with the reading public has transcended the genre of detective fiction. Holmes embodies a strict code of Victorian morality, motivated to use his dazzling powers in a one-man crusade against evil. His uncanny ability to discern an individual's identity from clues as seemingly trivial as a cigarette ash, a walking stick, or a mud-caked boot continually astounded Watson and delighted his many fans. He represents a world and set of values that were quickly disappearing from England, and that is perhaps one of the sources of his continuing appeal.

FURTHER READING

Contemporary Authors, Vols. 104, 122. Detroit: Gale Research Co.

Dictionary of Literary Biography, Vols. 18, 70. Detroit: Gale Research Co.

Hall, Trevor. *Sherlock Holmes: Ten Literary Studies.* New York: Duckworth, 1969.

Harrison, Michael, ed. *Beyond Baker Street: A Sherlockian Anthology.* New York: Bobbs-Merrill, 1976.

Twentieth-Century Literary Criticism, Vols. 7, 26. Detroit: Gale Research Co.

Wilson, Edmund. "'Mr. Holmes, They Were the Footprints of a Gigantic Hound!'" In *Classics and Commercials: A Literary Chronicle of the Forties,* pp. 266-74. New York: Noonday Press, 1950.

Margaret Drabble

1939-

English novelist, biographer, and critic.

The Needle's Eye (novel, 1972)

The Needle's Eye, the work that established Drabble as a major English novelist, is set in contemporary Britain. **Rose Vassiliou,** a wealthy heiress, rejects her money in favor of searching for spiritual truths. She marries a poor Greek man, **Christopher,** and chooses to live in a run-down neighborhood. But life with Christopher sours, enlivened only by her children, whom she loves deeply. In the midst of her quest for enlightenment, she meets **Simon Camish,** who narrates the novel, an attorney who is intrigued by Rose's eclectic approach to life. Simon soon takes over Rose's personal business and, by so doing, questions his own hypocritical values, particularly his own loveless marriage. He stands by her as she becomes involved in a bitter divorce and custody battle with Christopher. Trying to remain true to herself and the values she has worked so hard to forge, Rose must eventually capitulate. In the conclusion, she has given up Simon and returned to Christopher, although their relationship seems doomed.

Drabble's portrayal of her strong-willed but seemingly defeated protagonist reveals her complex concern for an individual's struggle for self-awareness. It is considered one of her finest and best-written works.

The Ice Age (novel, 1977)

Set in contemporary Britain, this novel tells the story of **Anthony Keating,** who has left a relatively secure job in television to embark on a real estate career. The main focus of the novel is the social and moral malaise of Britain in the 1970s. Drabble's wide-ranging examination of a culture in chaos and decline is reflected in her portrait of Anthony, who has recently suffered a heart attack and awaits prosecution for his alleged unscrupulous business dealings. He is involved with **Alison Murray,** who is devoted to her handicapped daughter, **Molly,** and constrained by the rebellious actions of her adolescent daughter, **Jane.** The work focuses on the frustrations and boredom of modern British life as seen in Anthony and Alison. Alison's life is portrayed as particularly hopeless: the role of mother that had provided her sense of self is ebbing as her children begin to establish their own lives, and she appears bereft of purpose or identity. Her life seems bleak and unfocussed as middle-age encroaches and she seems defeated by life. Anthony, on the other hand, is granted a sort of spiritual renewal, and after a brief imprisonment his future and state of mind provide an optimistic turn in an otherwise bleak psychological landscape.

Stylistically, the work reflects Drabble's use of an ironic, detached authorial voice that often dictates the fates of her characters and the direction of the work, a device some commentators found objectionable. For its relentless portrait of a country in decline, *The Ice Age* is admired as one of Drabble's strongest works.

FURTHER READING

Beards, Virginia K. "Margaret Drabble: Novels of a Cautious Feminist." *Critique* 15 (1973): 35-46.

Contemporary Authors, Vols. 13-16, rev. ed.; *Contemporary Authors New Revision Series,* Vol. 18. Detroit: Gale Research Co.

Contemporary Literary Criticism, Vols. 2, 3, 5, 8, 10, 22. Detroit: Gale Research Co.

Dictionary of Literary Biography, Vol. 14. Detroit: Gale Research Co.

Fox-Genovese, E. "Ambiguities of Female Identity: A Reading of the Novels of Margaret Drabble." *Partisan Review* 46 (1979): 234-48.

Libby, Marion V. "Fate and Feminism in the Novels of Margaret Drabble." *Contemporary Literature* 16 (Spring 1975): 175-92.

Manheimer, Joan. "Margaret Drabble and the Journey to the Self." *Studies in the Literary Imagination* 11 (1978): 127-43.

Myer, Valerie Grosvenor. *Margaret Drabble: Puritanism and Permissiveness*. London: Vision Press, 1974.

Rose, Ellen C. *The Novels of Margaret Drabble: Equivocal Figures*. London: Macmillan, 1980.

Theodore Dreiser

1871-1945

American novelist.

Sister Carrie (novel, 1900)

Set mainly in Chicago and New York, the novel recounts the life story of **Caroline Meeber,** called **Sister Carrie,** a young woman driven by the dream of success and wealth, an ideal that always seems to elude her grasp. Carrie is eighteen when the novel begins, having moved to Chicago from her childhood home in Wisconsin. She is eager for success and all its trappings, but because of her background she must start work in a sweatshop. She becomes the mistress of a wealthy salesman, **Charles Drouet,** seeing it as her way out of poverty. Drouet provides her with clothes and an apartment, yet she yearns for more. She finds it with **George Hurstwood,** a friend of Drouet's and the manager of a bar. Hurstwood, desperately in love with Carrie, behaves recklessly and compromises his professional and personal life for her, for both his marriage and his social position are placed in jeopardy by the affair. He ignores the implications of their romance and steals money to flee with Carrie to Montreal. They eventually settle in New York, where Hurstwood opens a bar; but when the building is sold, he loses everything. His plight is sympathetically dramatized by Dreiser as the fate of a man who challenges the conventions of a repressive society hoping for happiness, only to fail.

Carrie, oblivious to Hurstwood's personal tragedy, continues to want more and, true to her adaptable character, she finds a means of income on the stage, where her progress is steady and she becomes a star. She has abandoned Hurstwood, who, driven to despair, commits suicide. Always restless and in pursuit of what and whom she thinks is "better," Carrie meets **Robert Ames,** a man of depth and intellect who has a profound impact on her. Through him she sees the weakness and superficiality of her life and commercial success; the conclusion depicts her as a sad, vulnerable woman, continuing to be plagued by her emptiness.

With *Sister Carrie,* Dreiser presented a masterpiece of naturalistic fiction, marking a decided departure from the genteel realism that dominated American fiction at the end of the nineteenth century. Although his writing style has been faulted for its poor construction and grammar, the work has had a tremendous impact on American letters. Thematically, the novel reflects Dreiser's concept of determinism, which dictates that an individual is the victim of his or her environment. For Dreiser, social and financial situation, and even intellectual ability, decide an individual's fate, for one is not master of one's destiny. Thus, he does not condemn Carrie for her behavior; rather, he shows how she is able to adapt to her ever-changing environment and to survive no matter what the circumstances.

An American Tragedy (novel, 1925)

The novel relates the story of the life and death of **Clyde Griffiths,** another of Dreiser's deluded characters who is driven to pursue wealth and the purported happiness it brings. The early portion of the novel describes Clyde's upbringing by evangelists. Through them he learns the cruel lessons of poverty, and this drives his ambition to be a financial success, although he does not seem to know how to achieve it. At the age of sixteen, he moves to Kansas City where he works as a bellhop, still frustrated by the wealth of others and his own inability to succeed. After being involved in an accident with a stolen car, he is forced to go into hiding. Through a wealthy uncle, he finds a job in a factory in upstate New York. Still hoping for a chance to succeed, he becomes involved with a wealthy woman, **Sondra Finchley,** whom he sees as his way out of his limited circumstances. But he also begins an affair with **Roberta Alden,** a fellow factory worker, and she becomes pregnant. Clyde is desperate to silence Roberta and her demands that he marry her, wishing instead to pursue a promising future with Sondra. He plots to murder Roberta, and he takes her to the country, where she drowns in a boating accident. Dreiser is purposely unclear regarding Clyde's actual involvement in Roberta's death, for Clyde is as unable to master the circumstances surrounding Roberta's death as he is to take charge of his own life. He is tried and convicted of murder and put to death.

Clyde's fate reveals Dreiser's indictment of the corruption he saw at the heart of American values. Like Carrie, Clyde is a victim of the false dreams of prosperity and happiness that American culture fosters. Dreiser saw it as his task to illuminate the discrepancies between the spurious ideals and the reality of life in America. The work has been criticized for its weak structure and unpolished prose, but it continues to be considered an important work of American naturalism.

FURTHER READING

Contemporary Authors, Vol. 106. Detroit: Gale Research Co.

Dictionary of Literary Biography, Vols. 9, 12. *Dictionary of Literary Biography Documentary Series,* Vol. 1. Detroit: Gale Research Co.

Howe, Irving. "Dreiser and Tragedy: The Stature of Theodore Dreiser." In *Dreiser: A Collection of Critical Essays.* Englewood Cliffs: Prentice-Hall, 1971.

Kazin, Alfred. "Dreiser: The Esthetic of Realism." In *Contemporaries,* pp. 87-99. Boston: Little, Brown, 1962.

Lundquist, James. *Theodore Dreiser.* New York: Ungar, 1974.

Matthiessen, F. O. *Theodore Dreiser.* New York: William Sloan Associates, 1951.

Shapiro, Charles. *Theodore Dreiser: Our Bitter Patriot.* Carbondale: Southern Illinois University Press, 1962.

Twentieth-Century Literary Criticism, Vols. 10, 18. Detroit: Gale Research Co.

Warren, Robert Penn. *Homage to Theodore Dreiser, August 27, 1871-December 28, 1945: On the Centennial of His Birth.* New York: Random House, 1971.

Lawrence Durrell
1912-
English novelist and poet.

"The Alexandria Quartet": *Justine* (novel, 1957); *Balthazar* (novel, 1958); *Mountolive* (novel, 1959); *Clea* (novel, 1960)

"The Alexandria Quartet" is considered Durrell's masterpiece and a major work of modern fiction. Set in Alexandria in the years immediately prior to and following World War II, the work is, in the words of the author, "an investigation of modern love." The city of Alexandria is a palpable presence in the novel, richly and evocatively described as a sensuous, squalid place where the ancient and primitive collide with the modern and civilized. Durrell explores the nature of truth and reality in this work, revealed in the complex sexual relationships between his characters. Their varying perspectives are brought to bear in the first three novels, which are essentially three separate reworkings of the same events; the fourth novel is an epilogue of sorts, suggesting a culminating vantage point from which to view the previous three.

The central theme of the novel is the nature of creativity; thus, Durrell chooses as his principal figure the character **L. G. Darley,** an English novelist, and focuses on his coming of age as an artist. In the first novel, Darley, the first-person narrator, has fallen in love with **Justine Hosnani,** an enigmatic, beautiful Jewish woman, whose cruel, passionate nature obsesses him. He leaves his mistress, **Melissa Artemis,** for her, and she apparently abandons herself to Darley, with little thought for her husband, **Nessim.** Their unhappy affair ends badly, and Darley retreats to an island to sort out the relationship in prose; in fact, *Justine* is purportedly his creation.

The next installment, *Balthazar,* presents a differing perspective on the affair. Darley has sent **S. Balthazar,** his friend and a psychiatrist, the manuscript of *Justine* for his comments. Darley learns from Balthazar that Justine had not been in love with him at all, but had used him as a cover to hide from her husband her true love, **Percy Pursewarden,** an English diplomat and novelist. He had spurned her advances, however, and finally committed suicide. This volume incorporates several different styles of narrative, including excerpts from letters, Balthazar's commentary on Darley's novel, and Darley himself recounting and reconstructing the past in the first person.

The third volume, *Mountolive,* reflects yet another viewpoint on Justine. **David Mountolive** is the English ambassador in Alexandria and a friend of Justine and Nessim. He is the recipient of Pursewarden's suicide note in which it is revealed that Justine and Nessim, to support the goals of a group of radical Coptic Jews, are involved in a plot against the British in Egypt. Thus, we learn that Justine's affairs had a political motivation, and although Pursewarden did not succumb to her overtures, he did believe her intent and therefore ignored the report he had received implicating the Hosnanis in the conspiracy. When Mountolive notifies the Egyptian authorities, the Hosnanis are subjected to blackmail, and losing all their money, are socially ostracized as well.

Clea, the fourth novel, focuses on Darley, now returned to Alexandria and in love with **Clea Montis,** an artist with whom he finds a love and sexual relationship that provides the sustenance for his creativity. Throughout the novel Durrell explores the way in which sexuality provides both a means to self-awareness and an impetus to the artistic spirit. Clea is the victim of a macabre accident in which she loses her hand, but with a mechanical one she is able to paint pictures of even greater beauty and insight, and Darley, despite earlier frustrations, is able to write again. This work is interspersed with sections from Pursewarden's diary, which Darley examines for the light it throws on all the characters.

Durrell explores the extremes of sensuality in his characters, who are depicted as compulsive, lonely, frustrated people. As the characters struggle to give meaning and context to their lives, he examines the essential isolation of the human condition. For all the sexual entanglements related in his work, the characters remain alone, for Durrell posits that sex can be a means to self-knowledge, but it cannot help them to transcend the fundamental loneliness that is their fate. Through his examination of the variety of perspectives in the novel, Durrell finds that truth is a relative, personal matter, and that no ultimate reality exists, a philosophy informed by his understanding of Einstein's theory of space-time continuum. Durrell's prose is rich, and the exotic landscape of Alexandria is rendered in lush, descriptive passages.

FURTHER READING

Contemporary Authors, Vols. 9-12, rev. ed. Detroit: Gale Research Co.

Contemporary Literary Criticism, Vols. 1, 4, 6, 8, 13, 27, 41. Detroit: Gale Research Co.

Decancq, Roland. "What Lies Beyond?" *Revue des Langues Vivantes* 36, No. 2 (1968): 135-50.

Dictionary of Literary Biography, Vols. 15, 27. Detroit: Gale Research Co.

Fraser, G. S. *Lawrence Durrell.* London: British Council, 1970.

Friedman, Alan W. *Lawrence Durrell and the Alexandria Quartet.* Norman: University of Oklahoma Press, 1970.

Morris, Robert K. "Lawrence Durrell—The 'Alexandria Quartet': Art and the Changing Vision." In *Continuance and Change: The Contemporary British Novel Sequence,* pp. 51-70. Carbondale: Southern Illinois University Press, 1972.

Pinchin, Jane Lagoudis. "Durrell and a Masterpiece of Size." In *Alexandria Still: Forster, Durrell, and Cavafy,* pp. 159-207. Princeton: Princeton University Press, 1977.

Scholes, Robert. "Return to Alexandria: Lawrence Durrell and Western Narrative Tradition." *Virginia Quarterly Review* 40, No. 3 (Summer 1964): 411-20.

Steiner, George. "Lawrence Durrell and the Baroque Novel." In *Language and Silence: Essays on Language, Literature and the Inhuman,* pp. 280-87. Boston: Atheneum, 1967.

Friedrich Dürrenmatt

1921-

Swiss dramatist, novelist, short story writer, and essayist.

The Visit (drama, 1956)

Dürrenmatt's most frequently performed play takes place in the small Swiss town of Güllen, a name which in dialect means "liquid manure." Reeling from a stagnant economy that seems to affect only their town, The Gülleners desperately search for scapegoats responsible for their plight. Their posture is uniformly shallow and hypocritical. After a forty-five-year absence, **Claire Zachanassian** returns to her hometown the richest woman on earth. Although formerly despised in Güllen, she is welcomed with great, albeit awkward, fanfare, for the townspeople hope to manipulate her into giving them money. Her arrival is marked with foreboding and punctuated by a grotesque entourage, which includes two American gangsters, **Toby** and **Roby;** two blind eunuchs, **Koby** and **Loby;** a grim-faced butler, formerly a Güllen judge; a caged black panther; and an empty coffin. Crippled emotionally and physically, (her right arm and left leg are prostheses), Claire announces at the dinner in her honor that she will pay five hundred million to the town treasury and five hundred million to be distributed equally among the town's families, provided someone present kills **Alfred Ill.** Claire's former lover, whom she named her black panther, Ill long ago caused Claire's ouster from the community. When she revealed that she was pregnant with his child, he solicited two "witnesses" (Koby and Loby, whom she has tracked down, blinded, and castrated) to discredit her testimony in a paternity suit. The mayor loftily refuses the money, but Claire waits for the inevitable outcome. Though Ill was the one first designated to persuade Claire to aid her hometown, he now becomes the subject of bitter castigation and thinly veiled threats. Following a town meeting convened to decide his fate, a resolute crowd surrounds Ill and, when they part, he is dead. Labelled a heart attack, his death represents for the townspeople a just retribution for his earlier misdeed.

A black comedy about greed, *The Visit* prompted diverse critical interpretations upon its first performance; most disagreement centered on the question of whether Ill atones for his crime against Claire and attains heroic stature by accepting his sentence of death, or whether he becomes an absurd figure, since his death fails to significantly alter the inhumanity of the villagers. For Dürrenmatt, though, such dilemmas are characteristic. Unlike such contemporary playwrights as Albert Camus and Samuel Beckett, he considers the world neither absurd nor incomprehensible, but rather an alternately cruel, grotesque, or paradoxical human stage where existence may assume limited significance.

The Physicists (drama, 1962)

One of Dürrenmatt's most important dramas, *The Physicists* takes place in a private European mental asylum against the tension-laden backdrop of the Cold War. **Möbius,** a physicist whose "discovery of universal value" could possibly doom a morally irresponsible world, has voluntarily entered the institution, hoping to safeguard his research. He proclaims himself King Solomon. **Beutler** (Newton) and **Ernesti** (Einstein), physicist spies from the West and East, respectively, are also patients feigning insanity; each hopes to win Möbius to his side. During the play three murders occur, perpetrated by the three physicists in order to ensure the absolute secrecy of their goals. When the remaining attendants are replaced by bodyguards, the three inmates confess their motives to one another. Möbius convinces the two adversaries that to protect humanity they must all declare a truce and remain sequestered. Their period of relieved rejoicing is short-lived, however. The director of the asylum, **Fraulein von Zahnd,** reveals herself a madwoman who, under the influence of the historical King Solomon, has copied Möbius's work and delivered the volatile package to a power seeking world domination. The play closes with the three men submissively resuming their mad guises.

The Physicists is highly regarded for its objective presentation of the issue of scientific responsibility in the nuclear age. Typical of Dürrenmatt's work, the shocking drama takes no final social, moral, or political stance. Dürrenmatt explains the grotesque, tragicomic, ambiguous nature of his oeuvre as "a way of expressing in a tangible manner, of making us perceive physically the paradoxical, the form of the unformed, the farce of the world without a face." For him, as he expressed in his essay "Points Concerning *The Physicists*", a comic plot fulfills itself only after it has dutifully arrived at the worst imaginable conclusion. Dürrenmatt is among the most celebrated German-language dramatists to emerge after World War II.

FURTHER READING

Arnold, Armin. *Friedrich Dürrenmatt,* translated and revised by Armin Arnold with Sheila Johnson. New York: Ungar, 1972.

Contemporary Authors, Vols. 17-20, rev. ed. Detroit: Gale Research Co.

Contemporary Literary Criticism, Vols. 1, 4, 8, 11, 15, 43. Detroit: Gale Research Co.

Dictionary of Literary Biography, Vol. 69. Detroit: Gale Research Co.

Fritzen, Bodo and Heimy F. Taylor, eds. *Friedrich Dürrenmatt: A Collection of Critical Essays*. Normal: Applied Literature Press, 1979.

Ketels, Violet. "Friedrich Dürrenmatt at Temple University: Interview." *Journal of Modern Literature* 1, No. 1 (1971): 88-108.

Tiusanen, Timo. *Dürrenmatt: A Study in Plays, Prose, Theory*. Princeton: Princeton University Press, 1977.

Whitton, Kenneth S. *The Theatre of Friedrich Dürrenmatt: A Study in the Possibility of Freedom*. London: Oswald Wolff, 1980.

Umberto Eco

1932-

Italian essayist and novelist.

The Name of the Rose (novel, 1980)

In this novel the author, a leading scholar of semiotics, presents a fictional universe that can be apprehended on several levels. It is at once a murder mystery, a study of the medieval way of life, and an inquiry into philosophical, religious, and literary theory.

The work is set in Northern Italy in a Benedictine abbey in 1327 and begins with a depiction of the cloister in turmoil. The Church fathers are concerned about the followers of fra'Dolcino, a former Franciscan who had advocated total poverty and who had been burnt as a heretic twenty years earlier. His disciples, who are called the "Fraticelli," are being encouraged by secular powers who wish to diminish the authority of the Church. **William of Baskerville,** an Englishman and a Franciscan, whose name reflects his literary connection to the famous fictional sleuth Sherlock Holmes, appears at the abbey to help resolve the conflict. When a monk dies mysteriously, Baskerville is asked to use his brilliant powers of detection, which have lain dormant since his decision to become a friar, to solve the crime.

In his investigation, Baskerville is assisted by his "Watson," **Adso da Melck,** who also serves as the narrator. They discover that the secret to the criminal, who has now taken seven lives, lies somewhere in the abbey's library, described as a labyrinth and the intellectual and cultural center of the world of the religious brothers. The victims have all seen a mysterious codex, which turns out to be Aristotle's second book of poetics, long thought lost, which centers on comedy. When the murderer, **Jorges da Burgos,** is revealed, we learn his motivation: he feared that the discovery would prove to be the undoing of civilization. The monastery, and with it the enriching words of Aristotle, are lost in the fire that ends the novel.

This finely crafted work contains a number of long digressions that allow Eco, a distinguished medieval scholar, to provide an insightful view into the life and culture of the Middle Ages. Its theme of comedy and humor as profane and sacrilegious presents a brilliant defense of humor and a fascinating speculation on Aristotelian theory.

FURTHER READING

Contemporary Authors, Vol. 77-80; *Contemporary Authors New Revision Series*, Vol. 12. Detroit: Gale Research Co.

Contemporary Literary Criticism, Vol. 28. Detroit: Gale Research Co.

Dirda, Michael. "The Letter Killeth and the Spirit Giveth Life." *Book World—The Washington Post* (19 June 1983): 5, 14.

Ferrucci, Franco. "Murder in the Monastery." *The New York Times Book Review* (5 June 1983): 1, 20-1.

Schaire, Jeffrey. "*The Name of the Rose.*" *Harper's* 267, No. 1599 (August 1983): 75-6.

Ralph Ellison
1914-
American novelist, essayist, and short story writer.

Invisible Man (novel, 1952)

The unnamed narrator of Ellison's novel, known only as the **Invisible Man,** is the central character of this famous work, for which Ellison received the National Book Award.

The novel recounts the protagonist's quest for identity as a black man in a white world. The novel begins as the Invisible Man is a boy growing up in the American South. The opening scene depicts young black boys, blindfolded, forced to fight in a boxing ring, for the "entertainment" of white men. This scene of degradation points to Ellison's major theme: in a racist society, the black man is invisible, without identity. But Ellison's protagonist refuses to accept the labels that white, racist society places on him. We follow his quest as he journeys north, encountering an economic and political reality different from the South but similar in its rigid, racist policies. He is attracted to the radical politics expounded by the "Brotherhood," Ellison's depiction of the Communist party, which the protagonist rejects because of their narrow, ruthless philosophy. These events, and a cataclysmic race riot in Harlem, send the Invisible Man underground, where he lives in a cellar. Although it would appear that he is to pass his days in "darkness," Ellison uses the symbolism of light and darkness ironically here: the Invisible Man has illuminated his new home with over one thousand light bulbs, stealing the power from the electric company. The novel's conclusion is ambiguous, for the protagonist's search for self-knowledge has ended in despair and self-exile, rather than in a sense of awareness and inner peace.

Ellison's searing indictment of racism is noted for its complexity and verbal richness, incorporating narrative styles ranging from the realistic to the fantastic, and including allusions to the European and Afro-American literary traditions. The influence of blues and jazz are also evident in the language and structure of the work. For all the seriousness of its themes, the novel is ironic and often comic in tone.

FURTHER READING

Baker, Houston A., Jr. "A Forgotten Prototype: *The Autobiography of an Ex-Colored Man* and *Invisible Man.*" *Virginia Quarterly Review* 49 (Summer 1973): 433-49.

Christian, Barbara. "Ralph Ellison: A Critical Study." In *Black Expression,* edited by Addison Gayle, Jr., pp. 353-65. New York: Weybright & Talley, 1969.

Contemporary Authors, Vols. 9-12, rev. ed. Detroit: Gale Research Co.

Contemporary Literary Criticism, Vols. 1, 3, 11. Detroit: Gale Research Co.

Dictionary of Literary Biography, Vol. 2; *Concise Dictionary of American Literary Biography, 1941-1968.* Detroit: Gale Research Co.

Griffin, Edward M. "Notes from a Clean, Well-Lighted Place: Ralph Ellison's *Invisible Man.*" *Twentieth Century Literature* 15 (October 1969): 129-44.

Hersey, John, ed. *Ralph Ellison: A Collection of Critical Essays.* Englewood Cliffs: Prentice-Hall, 1974.

Langman, F. H. "Reconsidering *Invisible Man.*" *Critical Review* 18 (1976): 114-27.

Trimmer, Joseph A., ed. *A Casebook on Ralph Ellison's "Invisible Man."* New York: Crowell, 1972.

James T. Farrell
1904-1979
American novelist, short story writer, and essayist.

"Studs Lonigan: A Trilogy": *Young Lonigan* (novel, 1932); *The Young Manhood of Studs Lonigan* (novel, 1934); *Judgment Day* (novel, 1935)

Set in Chicago, the trilogy traces the life of **Studs Lonigan** from a young man growing up on the South Side after World War I until his early death during the Depression. The series chronicles the rise and fall of Studs as a victim of the American economic and political system, particularly the false dreams generated by the American myth of success and progress based on capitalism, industrialism, and class. Studs's is a story of self-destruction caused by his own weakness and the failure of his background to provide him with the positive, believable values he needs to make sense and a success of his life.

The first volume depicts Studs as a young adolescent, full of yearning for life and experience, but Farrell shows us how he makes the wrong choices that will determine his fate. He breaks off his relationship with his girlfriend, **Lucy Scanlan,** joins a gang, forgoes education, and becomes a tough. Ignoring any finer instincts in himself, Studs denies his sensitive side, a decision that will have fatal consequences. In the second part of the trilogy, Studs drops out of school, tries to enlist in the army, and does a variety of odd jobs. He becomes part of the gang that hangs around the pool hall, reveling in what he sees to be the freedom of a lifestyle devoted to having the "real stuff," and feeling that he is the envy of those men who have chosen lives of drudgery. Farrell shows him isolated in his chosen world, closed to the vitalizing forces represented by the world outside his neighborhood and his gang. Part Three outlines the destruction and death of Studs Lonigan. Not yet thirty, he has made nothing of his life: he has worked at and lost a number of nondescript jobs, has drunk and womanized too much, and returns to his parent's house to die.

Rather than creating a protagonist from a poor home facing an impossible battle against society, Farrell depicts Studs as an average young man from a middle-class family. It is both the decisions he makes as well as the falseness of the American dream he believes in that prove to be his undoing. Throughout the novels, Farrell offers a multiplicity of points of view, presenting events as seen through Studs's eyes, through objective description, and from the prespectives of Studs's friends and family. Studs's observations come in his own language, the idiom of the South Side tough, peppered with cliches. The trilogy is considered Farrell's finest literary work, and Studs is undoubtedly his best-known and most carefully drawn character.

FURTHER READING

Beach, Joseph Warren. *American Fiction, 1920-1940,* pp. 273-308. New York: Macmillan, 1941.

Branch, Edgar M. *James T. Farrell*. New York: Twayne, 1971.

Contemporary Authors, Vols. 5-8, rev. ed., 89-92; *Contemporary Authors New Revision Series,* Vol. 9. Detroit: Gale Research Co.

Contemporary Literary Criticism, Vols. 1, 4, 8, 11. Detroit: Gale Research Co.

Dictionary of Literary Biography, Vols. 4, 9; *Dictionary of Literary Biography Documentary Series,* Vol. 2. Detroit: Gale Research Co.

Douglas, Ann. "*Studs Lonigan* and the Failure of History in Mass Society." *American Quarterly* 29 (Fall 1977): 487-505.

Frohock, William M. *The Novel of Violence in America, 1920-1950,* pp. 69-85. Dallas: Southern Methodist University Press, 1958.

Herbst, Josephine. "James T. Farrell's *Judgment Day.*" *New Masses* 15 (25 May 1935): 25-6.

Kazin, Alfred. *On Native Grounds,* pp. 296-300. New York: Reynall and Hitchcock, 1942.

Wald, Alan M. *James T. Farrell: The Revolutionary Socialist Years.* New York: New York University Press, 1978.

William Faulkner
1897-1962
American novelist, short story writer, and poet.

The Sound and the Fury (novel, 1929)

Set in Faulkner's fictional Yoknapatawpha County, Mississippi, the novel deals with the decline of the Compson family and incorporates character types, themes, and stylistic techniques that resonate throughout Faulkner's fiction. The work is told in four parts, from the point of view of four figures: **Benjy, Quentin, Jason,** and **Dilsey.** Benjy, one of the four Compson children, is a severely retarded young man whose narrative is rendered in stream-of-consciousness format replicating the wanderings of the mind of an idiot. The reaction he elicits from the family around him is telling: his sister **Caddy** loves him, and he worships her; his elder brother Jason despises him: when Benjy tries to molest a young girl, Jason has him castrated; after the death of their mother, he has Benjy put away in a mental hospital. For his younger brother Quentin, Benjy is further evidence of the curse he sees upon the Compson family, and of the doom that the family is fated to suffer. Dilsey, the family's black servant and confidant of all the children except Jason, treats Benjy with the love and caring the Compson parents deny him and all their children; Benjy was initially named Maury, after his uncle, but when his idiocy was confirmed, his mother changed his name.

Quentin is a character obsessed with death and the decay of the Compson family. He harbors an incestuous desire for his sister Caddy, which Faulkner indicates is less a sexual passion than a perverted obsession with the loss of Caddy's virginity and an outdated code that equates chastity with honor. His section of the novel is a tormented sequence, covering one day in his life as he prepares to commit suicide. The narrative form is once again stream-of-consciousness as Quentin reveals his preoccupation with Caddy, with time, and with death.

Jason's section of the novel, rendered in straightforward, first-person form, reveals a man devoted to business and the acquisition of money. He is filled with anger and bitterness toward his family, particularly Caddy, whom he treats with cruelty and contempt. After the disintegration of her first marriage, Caddy returns home and leaves her daughter, **Quentin,** with Jason to raise. She sends money to Jason for her daughter's upbringing, which Jason keeps for himself. At the age of seventeen, Quentin robs Jason and runs away. The last male of the Compson line, Jason is a bachelor who is destined to die childless.

Dilsey is a character of warmth, sacrifice, and selfless love who protects Benjy, Quentin, and Caddy from Jason and the painful legacy of a loveless family. Her sequence of the novel is given through the eyes of an objective third-person narrator. She emerges as the only figure who can accept, nurture, and love the emotionally impoverished children in her care. Although Caddy does not have a narrative voice in the novel, she is its main focus, and she is revealed to the reader through the perceptions of the other central characters.

The decline and fall of the Compson family is portrayed against the backdrop of the degeneration of the Old South and the almost feudal way of life it represented. In comparison with the Compsons of the past, including Civil War heroes and men of courage and determination, the current generation seems pale and lifeless. Even the old Compson home, once called the Governor's house, is overgrown with weeds and decaying. One aspect of that tradition, and one of Faulkner's most significant themes here and throughout his work, is the importance of familial love and responsibility, which the parents in this novel have certainly evaded. The father, **Jason Compson III,** offers only drunkenness and cynicism to his children as a means of confronting and understanding the world. The mother, **Caroline Compson,** hides behind imagined ailments to distance herself from her children. Faulkner's recurrent theme of time, especially the way in which the past informs the present, is revealed here particularly through Quentin's obsession with the past. The motifs of incest, illegitimacy, and insanity that inform this work are echoed in later works as well.

The Sound and the Fury was a highly influential work, principally for its stylistic innovations. Through the use of stream-of-consciousness narrative and interior monologue, Faulkner was able to reveal the inner workings of his characters' minds, exploring conscious and unconscious motivations. Certainly one of Faulkner's greatest achievements was the creation of Yoknapatawpha County, a fictional setting that he was to use for most of his novels and short stories. He interweaves the lives of his characters through several generations, and individual figures recur throughout the oeuvre. Quentin Compson reappears as a narrator of *Absalom, Absalom!* (see below).

As I Lay Dying (novel, 1930)

Set in Yoknapatawpha County, the novel recounts the death and burial of **Addie Bundren,** specifically her wish to be buried with her relatives in Jefferson. The novel is divided into fifty-nine interior monologues which focus primarily on Addie and her family, told from the viewpoint of fifteen different characters. Addie's relationship with her husband, **Anse,** and five children forms the center of the work. **Cash,** the eldest, is a carpenter; **Darl,** next in line, is extremely sensitive and emotionally fragile; **Jewel,** Addie's favorite child, is the illegitimate son of Addie and her former lover, **Preacher Whitfield;** her only daughter, **Dewey Dell,** is pregnant and unmarried; her last child, **Vardaman,** is nine years old when his mother dies. Addie is a woman who has always distrusted words, and this suspicion of language is a major theme throughout the novel and informs her relationship with her husband. He is a man of consummate laziness, whom she thinks has tricked her through words into believing that their life together will be happy, loving, and fulfilling, when in reality he is responsible for the meaninglessness and bitterness of her life. Addie's story begins as she lays dying, watching her son Cash make her coffin. After her death, the family begins the journey to Jefferson, which proves to be treacherous: the mules and wagon are almost lost in an accident, Addie's body is almost burned in a barn fire, and vultures circle over the party, attracted by the unembalmed body. Upon reaching Jefferson, the family buries Addie, Dewey Dell seeks out a pharmacist to find abortion pills, Darl is placed in a mental institution, and Anse finds a new wife.

The novel's importance lies in the rich characterizations Faulkner is able to effect through the use of multiple narrators and the centrality of his theme of family and the way in which the various members define themselves and one another through their relationship with their mother. The tone of the work is humorous and tragic in turn, reflecting the variety of voices and scenes depicted.

Light in August (novel, 1932)

Once again, the setting is Yoknapatawpha County and the focus of the novel is **Joe Christmas**'s search for his origins and identity. The work is characterized by the use of shifting scenes and time frames as Faulkner reconstructs the story of Christmas's past. An orphan, he is raised first in an orphanage and later in a repressive foster home, where his yearning for an understanding of his parentage begins to obsess him. One aspect of his background, his race, is never clearly explained, and Faulkner uses this element to reveal certain facets of his character and to explore the racial tensions of the South. Although he appears to be white, Christmas exploits the idea that he might be black, alienating himself from the community. Caught between the white and the black world, he is an isolated figure.

He enters the small town of Jefferson and the life of another alienated character, **Joanna Burden.** The daughter of a New England abolitionist, she is also an outsider in Southern society. She takes Christmas in, and he becomes her helper as well as her lover. He brings out a passionate response in her, but also her "philanthropical" side: she feels she is burdened with guilt for the white man's treatment of blacks, and she uses her relationship with Christmas almost as a form of penitence. Thus, after the affair has gone on for three years, she tries to transform Christmas: a devotee of social causes to benefit blacks, she seeks ways to help him "better" himself as a black man. When she realizes that he will not be changed, she threatens to shoot them both, and he kills her. He flees and hides in the forest, but decides he must go back and confront his fate. He escapes from jail, but is captured, lynched, and castrated by **Percy Grimm,** whose brutality and racial hatred reflect the community's own.

Joe Christmas's tragic and violent story is framed by the narrative of **Lena Grove,** a young woman who comes to Jefferson from her home in Alabama in search of the father of her unborn child. She seeks the help of a mill hand, **Byron Bunch,** who relates her tale to **Gail Hightower,** a former minister repudiated by the community and now living in isolation. Through Bunch he also learns of the murder of Joanna Burden and the flight of Joe Christmas, whose bootlegging partner, **Lucas Burch,** is the father of Lena's child. Burch has told the police of Christmas's crime, his affair with Burden, and, most importantly, that Christmas is a "nigger," information that transforms the character in the eyes of the townsfolk, labelling him a figure of evil. Hightower is asked to provide an alibi for Christmas, which he refuses to do. However, when Christmas is cornered in Hightower's house by Grimm, he pleads for the man's life, telling the lynch mob that he was with Christmas the night of the murder. The day after Christmas's death, Hightower delivers Lena's baby, an act which seems to break his period of isolation and indicates his spiritual transformation and rebirth. In the novel's conclusion his self-realization, in which he takes responsibility for his wife's suicide and his self-imposed seclusion, is complete.

The three main characters are all isolated figures who are obsessed with their pasts and reject the community: Christmas scorns the white and the black world in his quest to understand his identity; Joanna Burden is rebuffed by the community and lives in the shadow of her reformist ancestors; Hightower, deprived of his congregation, relinquishes his interest in the present to indulge his obsession with the Civil War. Thus they reflect Faulkner's enduring interest in the themes of alienation and the preoccupation with the past.

Absalom, Absalom! (novel, 1936)

Once again, the setting for the work is Yoknapatawpha County, Mississippi. The focus of the novel is the rise and fall of the fortunes of **Thomas Sutpen** and his family. Returning to his themes of incest, miscegenation, and the obsession with the past, Faulkner chronicles one hundred years in the Sutpen family, from the early 1800s to the early 1900s. Faulkner employs four separate narrators to tell the story: **Rosa Coldfield,** sister of Sutpen's wife **Ellen,** who, after Ellen's death, is engaged and later jilted by him; **Jason Compson III,** a character who had appeared previously in *The Sound and the Fury;* **Quentin Compson,** Jason's son, also from the previous novel, and **Shreve McCannon,** Quentin's college roommate. Each of these characters is unrealiable as a narrator, and each of them relates only fragments of the narrative, leaving the reader to piece the tale together.

Thomas Sutpen, born of poor parents in West Virginia, is a man obsessed with wealth and property. He moves to Haiti where he meets and marries a Haitian woman who bears him a son, but Sutpen repudiates them both when he discovers that the woman has black blood. Moving to Yoknapatawpha, he begins to construct his own world: Sutpen's Hundred, his estate, is a testament to his monomania, built by black slaves and a French architect. He marries Ellen Coldfield, a respectable woman of the town, by whom he has two children, **Judith** and **Henry.** While at the University of Mississippi, Henry meets **Charles Bon,** who, unknown to him, is his half-brother, his father's first son by his Haitian wife. Charles and Judith later meet, fall in love, and become engaged, but Sutpen opposes the marriage. Henry repudiates his birthright, and leaves with Charles. They serve together in the Civil War, growing closer, with Henry emulating the characteristics of his friend. After the war, having learned of Bon's true identity, Henry kills him to prevent the incestuous union, after which he flees. Sutpen has another illegitimate child by **Milly Jones,** daughter of **Wash Jones,** a squatter on Sutpen's property, who kills Sutpen, Milly, and her child to avenge himself on Sutpen. In the conclusion of the family's tragedies, Henry returns to Sutpen's Hundred after years of self-imposed exile. **Clytie,** an illegitimate daughter of Sutpen by a slave, shelters Henry and, thinking that the law has come to capture Henry for the murder of Bon, sets fire to the house, killing herself and Henry.

All of the narratives are filtered through Quentin's consciousness: Rosa Coldfield tells her version of the story to him, as does his father. Quentin himself discusses the story with Shreve and the two argue over the story and embellish it with their own explanations. This method is basic to Faulkner's purpose here, for Quentin is a character obsessed by the degeneration of his own family and haunted with his incestuous feelings for his sister, even willing, like Henry, to commit murder to preserve her honor. Certain portions of the narrative are unclear or incomplete, and Faulkner allows his characters to fill in what is missing, revealing their own obsessions through their interpretations.

The Hamlet (novel, 1940)

The Hamlet is the first of three novels that chronicle the life of **Flem Snopes** and his family. The setting is Yoknapatawpha, during the early years of Frenchman's Bend. The story is told in four parts—"Flem," "Eula," "The Long Summer," and "The Peasants"—with Faulkner employing an omniscient narrator and also the narrative presence of **V. K. Ratliff,** a sewing machine salesman, through whom we learn about the early years of Flem Snopes. Flem is a man who is ruthless and unscrupulous in his purusit of wealth. He begins his career in Frenchman's Bend working for **Will Varner,** self-appointed autocrat of the village. Flem's own natural selfishness and avarice is developed under Varner's teaching, as he learns to cheat and undermine his neighbors. He maries Varner's daughter, **Eula,** even though she is preganant by another man, to get her property. Eula embodies the sensuality and fertility of a mythical goddess, in vivid contrast with her husband, who, obsessed only with money, is impotent. Throughout the novel Faukner contrasts the Snopes's avarice with the actions of natural characters like Eula, who represent the human and instinctual. The Snopes clan is dominated by men consumed with greed, who steal (**Byron**), murder (**Mink**), and burn the barns of those who oppose them (**Ab**). The only exception is **Ike,** an imbecile, who is passionately attached to his cow. Thus it would seem that the only Snopes capable of selflessness is both sexually and mentally deranged.

Faulkner's theme in this work is the rise of capitalism in the South and the decay of old southern way of life. The tone of the novel is more humorous and light than Faulkner's previous fiction, and the characters often appear as grotesque embodiments of their passions. Faulkner continued his exploration of the Snopses family in *The Town* and *The Mansion.*

The Bear (novella, 1942)

Isaac McCaslin, called Ike, is the central figure of *The Bear,* a novella drawn from the larger work *Go Down, Moses* , which deals with descendants of the McCaslin clan. The story is set in Yoknapatawpha County and focuses on Ike's coming of age. The work is divided into five sections. The first three and the last segments form a hunting narrative that relates the killing of the mythical bear, Old Ben, and Ike's initiation into the wilderness. The fourth section, equal in length to the other four together, recounts Ike's repudiation of his inheritance, the McCaslin plantation.

The first three parts of the hunting narrative describe Ike's preparation for the life of a hunter and his three his encounters with the legendary bear. He undergoes his initiation under the tutelage of **Sam Fathers,** a part-black, part-Indian guide who, as his name indicates, serves as Ike's spiritual father. Through his training, spanning the ages of ten to sixteen, Ike becomes a superb woodsman and goes in search of Old Ben alone. His first encounter with the animal is in the dead of the forest, armed only with a compass. Later, he meets the bear again, this time saving his small dog from the bear's jaws. In his third and final encounter with Old Ben, the mythic bear is slain by **Boon Hogganbeck.** Sam collapses and dies soon after, both he and Old Ben are given burials suitable to two great heroes of the forest.

The fourth section consists of a dialogue between Ike and his cousin **McCaslin Edmonds** (Cass) as they discuss Ike's repudiation of his inheritance. Ike, now twenty-one, rejects the concept of private property, believing instead that the land is no one's to buy, sell, or inherit. But more importantly, he has discovered that his grandfather, **Lucius Quintas Carothers McCaslin,** had set in motion a curse upon his land and his descendants, bequeathing a legacy of miscegenation and incest. Cass's and Ike's conversation is interwoven with sections from the McCaslin ledger in which Ike's father and uncle had described the fate of **Eunice,** a slave owned by Lucius McCaslin, by whom he had a daughter, **Tomasina,** whom he later raped and who bore him a child, driving Eunice to suicide. Thus, the McCaslin lineage is actually comprised of two families, one white, land-owning heirs, the other of mixed race and illegitimate.

Section five moves back in time and depicts Ike, eighteen, hunting again in the wilderness that had once been the home of Old Ben, but is now disappearing as man encroaches.

Faulkner here returns to his themes of miscegenation, incest, and the changing South. In Ike McCaslin he has created a character who, after his initiation into manhood, possesses the courage and sense of honor to confront the evil of his heritage.

FURTHER READING

Adams, Richard P. *Faulkner: Myth and Motion.* Princeton: Princeton University Press, 1968.

Blotner, Joseph. *Faulkner: A Biography.* New York: Random House, 1974.

Brooks, Cleanth. *William Faulkner: The Yoknapatawpha Country.* New Haven: Yale University Press, 1963.

——. *William Faulkner: Toward Yoknapatawpha and Beyond.* New Haven: Yale University Press, 1978.

Contemporary Authors, Vols. 81-84. Detroit: Gale Research Co.

Contemporary Literary Criticism, Vols. 1, 3, 6, 8, 9, 11, 14, 18, 28. Detroit: Gale Research Co.

Cowley, Malcolm. "Faulkner: The Yoknapatawpha Story." In *A Second Flowering,* pp. 130-55. New York: Viking, 1973.

Creighton, Joanne V. *William Faulkner's Craft of Revision: The Snopes Trilogy, "The Unvanquished" and "Go Down, Moses."* Detroit: Wayne State University Press, 1977.

Dictionary of Literary Biography, Vols. 9, 11, 44; *Dictionary of Literary Biography Yearbook: 1986; Dictionary of Literary Biography Documentary Series,* Vol. 2. Detroit: Gale Research Co.

Edel, Leon. "How to Read *The Sound and the Fury.*" In *Varieties of Literary Experience,* pp. 241-57. New York: New York University Press, 1962.

Guerard, Albert J. *The Triumph of the Novel: Dickens, Dostoevsky, Faulkner.* New York: Oxford University Press, 1976.

Howe, Irving. *William Faulkner: A Critical Study.* New York: Vintage, 1951.

Irwin, John T. *Doubling and Incest/Repetition and Revenge: A Speculative Reading of Faulkner.* Baltimore: Johns Hopkins University Press, 1975.

Levins, Lynn. *Faulkner's Heroic Design: The Yoknapatawpha Novels.* Athens: University of Georgia Press, 1976.

Page, Sally R. *Faulkner's Women: Characterization and Meaning.* DeLand: Everett/ Edwards, 1972.

Reed, Joseph. *Faulkner's Narrative.* New Haven: Yale University Press, 1973.

Rubin, Louis D., Jr. "Chronicles of Yoknapatawpha: The Dynasties of William Faulkner." In *Writers of the Modern South: The Faraway Country,* pp. 43-71. Seattle: University of Washington Press, 1963.

Schoenberg, Estella. *Old Tales and Talking: Quentin Compson in William Faulkner's "Absalom, Absalom!" and Related Works.* Jackson: University Press of Mississippi, 1977.

Short Story Criticism, Vol. 1. Detroit: Gale Research Co.

Thompson, Lawrance. *William Faulkner: An Introduction and Interpretation.* New York: Holt, Rinehart and Winston, 1967.

Volpe, Edmond L. *A Reader's Guide to William Faulkner.* New York: Farrar, Straus and Giroux, 1971.

Wagner, Linda W. *Hemingway and Faulkner: Inventors/Masters.* Metuchen, N.J.: Scarecrow Press, 1975.

F. Scott Fitzgerald
1896-1940
American novelist and short story writer.

"The Diamond as Big as the Ritz" (short story, 1922)

One of Fitzgerald's earliest and most widely anthologized stories, "The Diamond as Big as the Ritz" is set primarily in Montana around 1920. A sixteen-year-old prep-school boy from the Midwestern town of Hades, **John T. Unger,** befriends a reserved classmate, **Percy Washington.** Percy invites John to spend the summer at his family's chateau in Montana, boasting that his father, "by far the richest man in the world," owns a diamond bigger than the Ritz-Carlton Hotel. Charmed by Percy's sophistication and gaudy claim, John accepts. Upon his arrival in a surreal landscape in the middle of the Montana Rockies, he apprehends the incredible enormity of the Washington's wealth. In dreamy fascination, he lives opulently among Percy and his eccentric family, learning that their palatial Shangri-la rests atop a diamond mountain, the only five-square-mile expanse of land in the country yet unsurveyed. Percy's father, **Braddock,** inherited the land from his father, a direct descendant of George Washington. Following numerous covert transactions and deposits in banks around the world, actions that have ensured the longevity of the family fortune, Braddock has sealed the mountain forever and wired it for defensive purposes. His greatest fear is that his secret refuge will be accidentally discovered. Therefore, he and his family have selfishly adopted whatever measures necessary to block, capture, or kill all intruders.

John's love for Percy's sister, **Kismine,** threads through the lush narrative, providing an innocent counterpoint to the erotic madness of power and privilege that envelop the estate. Under threat of a sudden aerial attack, the two, accompanied by Kismine's older sister, **Jasmine,** escape. Percy remains with his mother, father, and the family servants, all of whom perish when the mountain is detonated. The dream thus shattered, the story closes with a somber dialogue between Jasmine and John, who muses: "His was a great sin who first invented consciousness."

Although structurally flawed, Fitzgerald's satirical fantasy is nevertheless eminently readable and provocative. As in several other stories of the period, Fitzgerald here displayed the hauntingly poetic style and acute observation of the upper class that he later united masterfully in *The Great Gatsby.*

The Great Gatsby (novel, 1925)

Fitzgerald's most famous novel is set in New York City and Long Island in 1922 and is narrated by **Nick Carraway,** a transplanted Midwesterner who sells bonds and has purchased a small house in West Egg. At a dinner party he reunites with a distant cousin, **Daisy Buchanan,** and her husband, **Tom,** and also meets an attractive, impulsive woman named **Jordan Baker.** Nick, who claims to be the only completely honest person he knows, readily succumbs to the lavish recklessness of his neighbors and the knowledge of the secret moral entanglements that comprise their essentially hollow lives. Central to the ensuing action is Tom's ongoing affair with **Myrtle Wilson,** the dowdy wife of a struggling auto repairman. The pivotal figure, however, is **Jay Gatsby,** a shadowy, extremely wealthy man prone to hosting extravagant parties. Gatsby immediately captures Nick's fascination, prompting him to uncover the man's past, which appears a dark, enchanting riddle. He learns of Gatsby's undistinguished Midwest origin and his early love for Daisy, who disobeyed her heart and married Tom to ensure her financial security rather than gamble her future on Gatsby, who was then poor. Nick also deduces that Gatsby is both a racketeer and an incurable romantic, whose ill-gotten wealth has been acquired solely to gain prominence in the sophisticated, moneyed world of Daisy's circle. Through Nick, Daisy and Gatsby become reacquainted, but the expected love affair never occurs, for Gatsby is murdered shortly afterward. The culminating moment was preceded by the partially accidental hit-and-run death of Myrtle. Only Gatsby and Daisy were in the car and, as Nick later learned, Daisy, not Gatsby, had been driving. In bitter retaliation toward his romantic rival, Tom revealed Gatsby's address to Myrtle's husband, who ironically believed Gatsby to be his wife's lover and killer. At the end of the novel Nick ponders the deaths of Myrtle and Gatsby and the culpability of himself, Tom, and Daisy in the bizarre, meaningless tragedy. He determines to return to the Midwest upon realizing the fallacy of the American Dream, concluding: "So we beat on, boats against the current, borne back ceaselessly into the past."

Considered the finest achievement of Fitzgerald's literary career, *The Great Gatsby* is widely recognized as a classic of American literature. Like most of his best-known works, Fitzgerald's masterwork examines the Jazz-Age generation's search for the elusive American Dream of wealth and happiness and scrutinizes the consequences of that generation's adherence to false values. Set amid the glamour and raucousness of the Roaring Twenties, Gatsby's tragic quest and violent end foretell the collapse of an era and the onset of disillusionment.

"Babylon Revisited" (short story, 1931)

Set during the Depression, "Babylon Revisited" is the story of businessman **Charlie Wales**'s return to Paris and attempt to regain custody of his nine-year-old daughter, **Honoria.** He finds the once wild city radically changed following the stock market crash of 1929. Sober and resolute, he has also changed during the three years following the long drunken spree that culminated in his wife's death from heart problems. **Marion Peters,** Charlie's sister-in-law, assumed guardianship of Honoria at the time, while Charlie was recovering in a sanitorium, and still blames Charlie for the death. Marion's husband, **Lincoln,** harbors no ill will but is perhaps slightly resentful of Charlie's recent successes as a Prague businessman.

During a quiet, elegant luncheon the following day, Charlie learns from Honoria that she would be delighted to stay with him permanently. His confidence thus bolstered, he discusses the issue with Marion and Lincoln, prepared to endure Marion's accusations and verbal abuse until she realizes the rightness of his request. With Lincoln's palliative influence, Charlie wins the promise of custody. However, when he later meets at the Peters home to agree on final arrangements, two heavily intoxicated friends from his dissipated past burst in. Marion cannot tolerate the rude intrusion and painful reminder of earlier, reckless times, and retires to bed. Lincoln informs Charlie the following day that, despite his innocence in the matter, he will have to wait another six months for Honoria; Marion is in a state of mental exhaustion and Lincoln wishes to prevent further psychological hardship. Charlie agrees to wait patiently: "he wanted his child, and nothing was much good now, beside that fact."

Despite his disillusionment—his broken memories of the "boom" as well as his failed visit—Charlie maintains faith in himself and cautious hope for the future. Fitzgerald's use of contrasting perspectives, characters, and settings to support this theme make "Babylon Revisited" one of the finest, most personally revealing stories of his career.

Tender Is the Night (novel, 1934)

Tender Is the Night is set in Paris and on the French Riviera during the 1920s. Through a shifting chronology, Fitzgerald details the professional, moral, and psychological dissolution of **Dick Diver,** an expatriate American psychiatrist recognized by his European colleagues as a budding genius in the field. Dick met his wife, **Nicole,** while conducting research in advanced psychology at a Zurich clinic. A beautiful patient from a wealthy Chicago family, Nicole was recovering from an emotional breakdown brought on by memories of an incestuous relationship with her father. Dick was instrumental in her cure and consequently earned Nicole's self-effacing obedience and adoration. With Nicole's health delicately intact, save for occasional, controllable schizophrenic episodes, the Divers engage in a seemingly endless stream of parties with a continually enlarging group of moneyed sophisticates.

Dick's brief enchantment with a young American actress, **Rosemary Hoyt,** endangers Nicole's health and their increasingly strained marriage. However, Nicole gains in strength and independence as she repeatedly attempts to rescue Dick from his alcoholic binges and accompanying public scenes. Her complete recovery becomes possible only with the dissolution of her marriage; she eventually leaves Dick for **Tommy Barban,** a virile professional soldier. Following further mental deterioration, the forced abandonment of his Swiss clinic, and the divorce, Dick returns to America. There he dwindles into professional obscurity and social isolation.

Tender Is the Night reflects the anxiety and disillusionment caused by the Great Depression and, for Fitzgerald personally, Zelda Fitzgerald's breakdown suffered in 1930. Through Dick's tragic fall, ironically precipitated by his social charm and concomitant lack of introspection, Fitzgerald tolls the demise of American idealism and the widespread onset of ambitionlessness and ineffectuality. A long, stylistically masterful novel, *Tender Is the Night* also represents one of the most credible and tragic love stories in modern fiction.

FURTHER READING

Bruccoli, Matthew J. *The Composition of "Tender Is the Night": A Study of the Manuscripts.* Pittsburgh: University of Pittsburgh Press, 1963.

Bryer, Jackson R., ed. *F. Scott Fitzgerald: The Critical Reception.* New York: Burt Franklin & Co., 1978.

Callahan, John F. *The Illusions of a Nation: Myth and History in the Novels of F. Scott Fitzgerald.* Urbana: University of Illinois Press, 1972.

Contemporary Authors, Vol. 110. Detroit: Gale Research Co.

Dictionary of Literary Biography, Vols. 4, 9; *Dictionary of Literary Biography Yearbook: 1981; Dictionary of Literary Biography Documentary Series,* Vol. 1. Detroit: Gale Research Co.

Fahey, William A. *F. Scott Fitzgerald and the American Dream.* New York: Thomas Y. Crowell, 1973.

Higgins, John A. *F. Scott Fitzgerald: A Study in the Stories.* Jamaica: Saint John's University Press, 1971.

Hoffman, Frederick J., ed. *"The Great Gatsby": A Study.* New York: Scribners, 1962.

Kazin, Alfred, ed. *F. Scott Fitzgerald: The Man and His Work.* New York: Collier Books, 1962.

LaHood, Marvin J., ed. *"Tender Is the Night": Essays in Criticism.* Bloomington: Indiana University Press, 1969.

Lehan, Richard D. *F. Scott Fitzgerald and the Craft of Fiction.* Carbondale: Southern Illinois University Press, 1966.

Lockridge, Ernest H., ed. *Twentieth-Century Interpretations of "The Great Gatsby": A Collection of Critical Essays.* Englewood Cliffs: Prentice-Hall, 1968.

Miller, James E., Jr. *F. Scott Fitzgerald: His Art and His Technique.* New York: New York University Press, 1964.

Mizener, Arthur. *The Far Side of Paradise: A Biography of F. Scott Fitzgerald*. Boston: Houghton Mifflin, 1949.

Piper, Henry Dan. *F. Scott Fitzgerald: A Critical Portrait*. New York: Holt, Rinehart and Winston, 1965.

Stern, Milton R., ed. *Critical Essays on F. Scott Fitzgerald's "Tender Is the Night."* Boston: G. K. Hall & Co., 1986.

Twentieth-Century Literary Criticism, Vols. 1, 6, 14. Detroit: Gale Research Co.

Ford Madox Ford

1873-1939

English novelist, poet, and critic.

The Good Soldier (novel, 1915)

The novel is set in England during the early part of the twentieth century. **John Dowell** is the narrator of the story, and it is his ambition to relate the life of **Edward Ashburnham,** the "good soldier" of the title, which, as he relates in the first line, is the "saddest story I have ever heard." Ford's choice of his narrator is an important facet of the novel: Dowell is an American among the English, and his is a tale of destructive passion, although he himself is curiously passionless. Thus he is an outsider, in both nationality and temperament. The reader is made aware of Dowell's limited consciousness, for his recount of Ashburnham's life is full of contradictions and uncertainties. The narrative moves backward and forward in time as Dowell tries to perceive and understand the man he revered above all others, but one capable of betrayal and cruelty.

In Dowell's eyes, Ashburnham was the epitome of the responsible, respected English gentleman, always doing and saying what is right. However, as Dowell discovers, Ashburnham was a sexually promiscuous man, perpetually drawn into affairs with women and needing their approval, love, and passionate response. He even seduces Dowell's wife, and their affair drives her to take her own life. Ashburnham too ends life a suicide. The central problem Dowell sets for himself—to discern what it is that drives people to such self-destructive behavior, to betrayal and intrigue—is left unanswered at the end. Dowell is ultimately sympathetic to Ashburnham's character, although baffled by it.

The novel is characterized by an ironic, ambiguous tone. Through his uncomprehending, bewildered narrator, Ford explores the nature of truth, life, and reality, and offers a variety of interpretations of the lives he illustrates.

"Parade's End": *Some Do Not . . .* (novel, 1924); *No More Parades* (novel, 1925); *A Man Could Stand Up—* (novel, 1926); *The Last Post* (novel, 1928)

The tetralogy begins with the pre-war years in England. **Christopher Tietjens** is introduced as a conservative Edwardian— respectable, proper, and dedicated to the behavior required of his class and standing. He is at odds with the world around him: his wife, **Sylvia,** is malicious and unfaithful, his friends and business acquaintances betray him, all seemly driven to destroy him because of his devotion to what is right and his predictable perfection. The world outside Tietjens's narrow sphere is crumbling, but he refuses to be destroyed along with it, despite those who seek to ruin him and to undermine his values. At the end of the novel, he has fallen in love with **Valentine Wannop,** a young feminist, but, in accordance with his moral code, he has refused to give in to his passionate impulses.

The second and third novels relate Tietjens's experiences during World War I. The demonic Sylvia again plots against him, and using her influence with a relative, causes Tietjens to lose his command. Although he is able to rise above these humiliations, he later suffers a breakdown. He is nursed back to health by Valentine, and the two at last become lovers. The third novel also deals with Tietjens's repudiation of his inheritance. The final novel is considered inferior to the others, flawed by sentimentality and a contrived happy ending. Sylvia has at last relented, even granting Tietjens a divorce. He is pictured at the conclusion happy with Valentine, and she is pregnant.

Ford's central theme here is the decline of Western culture signalled by the end of the Edwardian era, the chaos of World War I, and the emergence of the valueless, superficial modern era. Like his precursor Ashburnham of *The Good Soldier,* Tietjens is a man confronted with a changing world, seemingly out of step with his times. He is pictured by Ford as the last Tory, the final representative of the conservative political class mourned by Ford. Tietjens is depicted in both public and private life as a victim of forces and people he cannot control, refusing to save himself in the conflict of class and culture that spell the end of his world. Yet, unlike Ashburnham, Ford grants his later protagonist a good measure of happiness.

FURTHER READING

Cassell, Richard A. *Ford Madox Ford: A Study of His Novels.* Baltimore: Johns Hopkins University Press, 1961.

Contemporary Authors, Vol. 104. Detroit: Gale Research Co.b

Dictionary of Literary Biography, Vol. 34. Detroit: Gale Research Co.

Leer, Norman. *The Limited Hero in the Novels of Ford Madox Ford.* East Lansing: Michigan State University Press, 1966.

Meixner, John A. *Ford Madox Ford's Novels.* Minneapolis: University of Minnesota Press, 1962.

Mizener, Arthur. *The Saddest Story: A Biography of Ford Madox Ford.* New York & Cleveland: World, 1971.

Moser, Thomas C. *The Life in the Fiction of Ford Madox Ford.* Princeton: Princeton University Press, 1980.

Ohmann, Carol. *Ford Madox Ford: From Apprentice to Craftsman.* Middleton: Wesleyan University Press, 1964.

Poli, Bernard J. *Ford Madox Ford.* New York: Twayne, 1968.

Stang, Sondra J. *Ford Madox Ford.* New York: Ungar, 1977.

Twentieth-Century Literary Criticism, Vols. 1, 5. Detroit: Gale Research Co.

Wiley, Paul L. *Novelist of Three Worlds: Ford Madox Ford.* Syracuse: Syracuse University Press, 1962.

E. M. Forster

1879-1970

English novelist, short story writer, essayist, and critic.

The Longest Journey (novel, 1907)

Set in Cambridge and Wiltshire, the novel chronicles the lives of **Rickie Elliot** and **Stephen**

Wonham, half-brothers. Rickie is an intellectual and a cripple; Stephen is earthy and full of physical vitality. Together they represent the dichotomy of human nature that Forster was to explore so often in his fiction. After an unhappy childhood, Rickie is seen as the novel begins as an undergraduate at Cambridge, where his sensitivity and scholastic ability are encouraged and flourish. While at Cambridge, he meets and becomes engaged to **Agnes Pembroke,** a woman very unlike himself, whose vulgarity and insensitivity will ruin their relationship. This point is strengthened by the warnings of Rickie's closest friend, **Stewart Ansell,** who foresees the damage that Agnes will do. However, after Cambridge, Rickie takes a position at Sawston Public School, run by Agnes's brother. There his spirit and his marriage begin to disintegrate. Forster's title is taken from Shelley, for whom "the longest journey" is that taken with the wrong partner. While engaged to Agnes, Rickie had become aware that he and Stephen were half-brothers, a fact that had been kept from him by his family. Stephen is the illegitimate son of Rickie's mother, a secret from her past. Although Rickie has a difficult time accepting Stephen, as his marriage deteriorates, he is drawn more and more to his brother, and eventually leaves his wife, devoting most of himself to his brother. In the novel's conclusion, Rickie dies saving Stephen from an oncoming train.

Stylistically, Forster makes use of repeated images from nature to add unity to his story. As is evident in most of his works, the characters in this novel function symbolically, representing such elements as sensitivity, animal energy, and bourgeois hypocrisy. Although the novel has been seen by some critics as structurally flawed, it is considered rich in theme, imagery, and symbolism and is his first significant novel.

A Room with a View (novel, 1908)

The novel is set in Florence, Italy, where **Lucy Honeychurch** and her chaperon are staying in a pension. They complain that their room has no view, but another guest, **Mr. Emerson,** graciously gives them his. Lucy is a young woman on the verge of adulthood and self-awareness, and she responds to the warmth and physical beauty of Italy, its art, and its people. Forster here compares and contrasts the natural, human vitality of the Italian way of life with the staid and conformist culture of England, particularly in Lucy's two suitors, **Cecil Vyse** and **George Emerson.** Cecil, Lucy's fiance, is cultured and conventional. George, the son of Mr. Emerson, is unpredictable and sensual. Lucy falls in love with George, but denies it to herself and is offended when he impulsively kisses her. She flees to Rome and to Cecil, but George remains on her mind. When she returns to England she realizes, with the help of Mr. Emerson, that Cecil can never fulfill her needs, and she breaks their engagement.

Forster here continues his exploration of the many-faceted nature of human existence and the deadening aspects of English culture. As in his previous work, the characters have a symbolic importance. For Forster, the head and the heart, the intellect and the passionate side of human nature must be acknowledged and allowed expression. He satirizes the conventions of middle-class society in his depiction of Cecil and his family, focussing on the repressed and rational elements of their lives. In his heroine he stresses the significance of the discovery of the sensual, passionate, and impulsive in her nature as necessary to her self-knowledge.

Howards End (novel, 1910)

The novel is an exploration of the state of English society at the close of the Edwardian era. **Helen** and **Margaret Schlegel** are representatives of the cultured intelligentsia of the middle class who cultivate the "inner life" and prize personal relationships. They are juxtaposed to the Wilcoxes, a bourgeois family devoted to the pragmatic demands of a life of commerce. Helen—idealistic, passionate, and impulsive—shuns the Wilcoxes. Margaret—even-tempered and wise—acknowledges the need for proportion in social and human spheres and is drawn to **Henry Wilcox,** whom she marries. The book's famous epigraph, "only connect," is Margaret's phrase, and represents her efforts to unite the prose and the passion of human nature. The "Howards End" of the title is the home of the Wilcoxes, left to them by Henry's first wife, **Ruth Wilcox,** whose spirit pervades the novel, and who in temperament is much like Margaret. Helen is drawn to **Leonard Bast,** a working-class character disdained by the Wilcoxes. When Leonard is personally humiliated by them, Helen becomes his lover. Later, she learns she is pregnant. Henry feels Helen has shamed the family and refuses to allow her to live with them. Margaret rejects her husband's cruel response and leaves him to go with her sister to Germany where the baby is born. In the novel's conclusion, Henry's son **Charles Wilcox** kills Leonard Bast during a heated argument, an event that leaves Henry emotionally shattered. Yet the future appears fortunate for the Schlegel sisters, whose belief in the primacy of human relationships appears triumphant in the end: Margaret has endured much, but is at last the true mistress of Howards End; Helen returns from the Continent to raise her child, at peace with her sister and herself.

For Forster, the Schlegel sisters embody a central tenet of the moral life: the need to nurture and protect the private life, which "holds out the mirror to infinity." Particularly in the characterization of Margaret, Forster again argues for the importance of the balance of the rational and emotional in human relationships. In one of his most distinguished works, critics have applauded his luminous prose style, noting its realistic yet poetic qualities.

A Passage to India (novel, 1924)

The work takes place in the imaginary Indian city of Chandrapore and focuses on a group of Indian, English, and Anglo-Indian characters living under the British colonial system. **Dr. Aziz,** a physician, is an Indian and a Moslem. **Mrs. Moore** is an English woman who has come to India to visit her son, **Ronny Heaslop,** with Ronny's fiancee, **Adela Quested.** Aziz is introduced to Mrs. Moore through his English friend **Cecil Fielding,** an Anglo-Indian and a principal of a college in Chandrapore. Aziz arranges a picnic and a visit to Chandrapore's famous Marabar Caves for the English guests. This is the central incident of the novel. While inside the caves, Adela becomes disoriented; when she recovers, she believes she has been sexually assaulted by Aziz. She flees the caves and tells her story to the police. For Mrs. Moore, the experience is even more damaging. In the caves, she hears an echo, which resonates with the message: "nothing has value." Previously a devoted Christian, Mrs. Moore's belief is shattered by her experience. Bereft of faith, she gives up hope in life.

Accused of rape, Aziz stands trial. But on the witness stand, Adela becomes confused and can no longer remember what happened to her. Aziz is acquitted, but remains angry at the legal system that entrapped him and at his friend Fielding, who, although he had supported him in his defense, tries to effect a reconciliation between Aziz and Adela. The novel's conclusion is ambiguous: Mrs. Moore has died en route to England, her faith never restored. Aziz is free, but his friendship with Fielding has undergone tremendous strain. The two men are depicted at the end of the novel riding together, imagining India's future, which will reflect the irreconcilable differences emblemized in the cultural rift between them.

Forster uses the political, social, and religious differences represented by his characters to explore the racism, imperialism, and lack of understanding that typified the rule of the English Raj and to examine the hope of reconciliation among the Moslem, Hindu, and Christian beliefs of the people of India. In the character of Mrs. Moore, he indicates the failure of Christianity to offer answers to the eternal mysteries of life as represented in the Marabar Caves. Critics speculate that this aspect of the novel reflects Forster's own belief in the Hindu philosophy of total acceptance and his personal rejection of Christian faith. The work is characterized by a mystical tone and Forster's lustrous prose. For its thematic richness, the depth of its characterizations, and its evocative prose style, *A Passage to India* is considered one of the most significant novels of the twentieth century.

FURTHER READING

Beer, J.B. *The Achievement of E. M. Forster.* New York: Barnes & Noble, 1962.

Bradbury, Malcolm. ''E. M. Forster as Victorian and Modern: *Howards End* and *A Passage to India.*'' In *Possibilities: Essays on the State of the Novel,* pp. 91-120. London & New York: Oxford University Press, 1973.

Brower, Reuben A. ''The Twilight of the Double Vision: Symbol and Irony in *A Passage to India.*'' In *The Fields of Light: An Experiment in Critical Reading,* pp. 182-98. New York: Oxford University Press, 1951.

Burke, Kenneth. ''Social and Cosmic Mystery: *A Passage to India.*'' In *Language as Symbolic Action: Essays on Life, Literature, and Method,* pp. 223-39. Berkeley: University of California Press, 1966.

Contemporary Authors, Vols. 25-28, rev. ed.; *Contemporary Authors Permanent Series,* Vol. 1. Detroit: Gale Research Co.

Contemporary Literary Criticism, Vols. 1, 2, 3, 4, 9, 10, 13, 15, 22, 45. Detroit: Gale Research Co.

Crews, Frederick C. *E. M. Forster: The Perils of Humanism.* Princeton: Princeton University Press, 1962.

Dictionary of Literary Biography, Vol. 34. Detroit: Gale Research Co.

Gransden, K. W. *E. M. Forster.* New York: Grove, 1962.

Leavis, F. R. ''E. M. Forster.'' *Scrutiny* 7 (September 1938): 188-202.

McConkey, James. *The Novels of E. M. Forster.* Ithaca: Cornell University Press, 1957.

Pinchin, Jane Lagoudis. *Alexandria Still: Forster, Durrell and Cavafy.* Princeton: Princeton University Press, 1977.

Rosecrance, Barbara. *Forster's Narrative Vision.* Ithaca: Cornell University Press, 1982.

Stallybrass, Oliver, ed. *Aspects of E. M. Forster: Essays and Recollections Written for His Ninetieth Birthday January 1, 1969.* New York: Harcourt, Brace & World, 1969.

Trilling, Lionel. *E. M. Forster.* Norfolk: New Directions, 1943.

Woolf, Virginia. ''The Novels of E. M. Forster.'' *Atlantic Monthly* 140 (November 1927): 642-48.

John Fowles

1926-

English novelist, short story writer, poet, and essayist.

The Magus (novel, 1966; revised, 1977)

The locales of this psychological thriller and cult classic are London, the Greek island of Phraxos, and Athens. The action begins in the summer of 1952, following **Nicholas Urfe,** an egocentric Oxford graduate, from England to the Mediterranean, where he experiences a complex psychodrama which radically alters his life. Prior to his departure, Nicholas has been a seeker of swift, smoothly severed affairs, his last being that with **Alison Kelly.** A crude Australian girl dissatisfied with her country and former romantic relationships, Alison kindles in herself and Nicholas a strong yet fragile love that painfully persists despite Nicholas's willful isolation as an English teacher on Phraxos. Once on the island, Nicholas meets **Maurice Conchis,** a wealthy, highly cultured, elderly Greek man. The magus, or magician, of the story, Conchis seduces Nicholas with his enigmatic presence and provocative theories, fascinating secluded villa, and collections of books, paintings, and erotic curiosa. After many visits to Conchis's estate, Nicholas becomes enmeshed in a complex, allegoric sequence of events orchestrated by his host. Initially, Nicholas considers himself privileged to be simultaneously entertained by and actively engaged in a metadrama with a boundless stage, an invisible audience, an all but inscrutable plot, and a perpetual transformation of reality, time, and guise. Conchis spares no expense and no ingenious dark twist with his grand masque, purportedly meant for Nicholas's enlightenment but also obviously serving as an elaborate catharsis for Conchis, a man compelled to retell and reenact his past. Hired by Conchis, two beautiful twins, **Lily** and **Rose Montgomery**, lead Nicholas further into the masque's mysteries and cause him to question Conchis's motives and sanity. In a brief respite, Nicholas meets Alison in Athens for a liaison, abruptly shattered when Nicholas reveals his love for the enchanting Lily.

Back on Phraxos he learns by letter of Alison's suicide; but the letter and substantiating detail have been supplied by Conchis, who has now involved the suffering Alison in his metaphysical sorcery. Helpless to elude the increasingly dangerous masque, Nicholas becomes a tortured, constantly wary sleuth intent on liberating himself and Lily from Conchis's grip, yet it is not until the enactment of a disturbing, symbolically laden trial scene that Nicholas reaches some degree of self-knowledge. Soon after, Nicholas returns to England in search of Alison. After considerable self-deprecation, followed by signs of spiritual and psychological renewal made possible by **Lily de Seitas,** the twins' mother and Conchis's lover, Nicholas reunites with Alison. Both have acquired some portion of the mystical wisdom that envelops Conchis and the elder Lily. Yet, the couple's final movement is toward freedom, *eleuthería,* rather than each other, and so Nicholas stolidly parts from Alison beneath a gray autumn sky.

Fowles's reputation as an important contemporary author rests on novels that combine myth and mystery with realism and existentialist thought. *The Magus* epitomizes this powerful narrative blend. As in his other works, simple solutions to the protagonist's problems are never provided. In *The Aristos,* in many ways a nonfiction genesis of *The Magus,* Fowles expressed the opinion that the world needs mysteries more than solutions because curiosity about the unknown prompts active participation in the quest for answers. If there is one central meaning in this multilayered novel of multiple meanings, it is that ''questions are a form of life'' and ''and answer is always a form of death.''

The French Lieutenant's Woman (novel, 1969)

The French Lieutenant's Woman is a pseudo-Victorian novel set primarily in Wessex in 1967. **Charles Smithson,** an amateur paleontologist and privileged nobleman's nephew, is engaged to **Ernestina Freeman,** the daughter of a wealthy industrialist. But after encountering the beautiful, impoverished **Sarah Woodruff,** whom the locals refer to as ''The French Lieutenant's woman,'' Charles breaks off with Ernestina. Flouting conventional morals, Charles pursues Sarah, albeit clandestinely. After several trysts he risks his inheritance and litigation by Ernestina's family and proposes marriage to Sarah by means of a letter. Charles's valet, **Sam Farrow,** fails for his own romantic reasons to deliver it. By the time Charles has discovered Sam's duplicity, Sarah has vanished. For nearly two years Charles desperately searches for her. The novel concludes with three possible resolutions, none definitive but all consistent with what has transpired.

Called Fowles's most ambitious and innovative work, *The French Lieutenant's Woman* examines Victorian manners and morals from a present-day perspective. While Fowles's numerous time-and-space manipulations allow truths to be discovered by the characters, they also lead to further uncertainties. The final ambiguity of the multiple ending firmly underscores Fowles's ruling theses: that reality is illusory and can be altered; that conformity, limitations, and servitude are abhorrent; and that freedom, innovation, and emancipation are inestimable. For his characters and for himself, Fowles seeks self-determination and the erasure of all restrictions. His choice of a self-conscious, playfully witty, and resourcefully intrusive narrator who continually tests the bounds of the novel form represents a continual reminder of this. Fowles has delineated the restrictions of attempting to represent reality in art, but within those confines he still tries to achieve freedom and authenticity for himself, his characters, and his readers.

FURTHER READING

Bradbury, Malcolm. "The Novelist as Impresario: John Fowles and His Magus." In *Possibilities: Essays on the State of the Novel,* pp. 256-71. Oxford: Oxford University Press, 1973.

Conradi, Peter. *John Fowles.* New York: Methuen, 1982.

Contemporary Authors, Vols. 5-8, rev. ed; *Contemporary Authors New Revision Series,* Vol. 25. Detroit: Gale Research Co.

Contemporary Literary Criticism, Vols. 1, 2, 3, 4, 6, 9, 10, 15, 33. Detroit: Gale Research Co.

Dictionary of Literary Biography, Vol. 14. Detroit: Gale Research Co.

Huffaker, Robert. *John Fowles.* Boston: G. K. Hall, 1980.

Olshen, Barry N. *John Fowles.* New York: Ungar, 1978.

Palmer, William J. *The Fiction of John Fowles.* Columbia: University of Missouri Press, 1974.

Wolfe, Peter. *John Fowles, Magus and Moralist.* Lewisburg, Pa.: Bucknell University Press, 1976.

Max Frisch

1911-

Swiss novelist, dramatist, and diarist.

I'm Not Stiller (novel, 1954)

Frisch's best-known and most widely read novel incorporates his recurrent theme of the search for identity. As the novel opens, a man named **Mr. White** is apprehended at the Swiss border, accused of being the sculptor **Anatol Stiller,** who has been missing for six years. In prison, Stiller relates his life through diary entries and stories; people from his earlier life, including his estranged wife, **Julika,** also relate their interpretations of the character.

This rich and complex novel tells the story of a man eager to discard his former self and create a new one. The tone of the novel is one of irony and ambivalence, and the work is imbued with ambiguity and paradox. Stiller is obsessed with the question of identity and struggles to free himself of the false persona appended to him. The novel explores the way in which the character perceives himself as opposed to the man based on the perceptions of others. He is full of feelings of impotence and insignificance; he knows he is a failure as a sculptor and that his gifts are limited. He endeavors to destroy this aspect of his past when he demolishes all of the works in his studio. His life with Julika is also flawed, for neither of them are capable of emotional attachment and Julika binds Stiller to her through fear.

Stiller explores a new identity as a member of the Republican forces during the Spanish Civil War, learning that his conception of himself as a hero is a sham, for he acts with cowardice in facing the enemy. His marriage to Julika continues to deteriorate, and Stiller flees the country, going to the United States and Mexico and indulging in bizarre adventures. After his imprisonment, he confesses to various crimes committed during his travels, but only as Mr. White, not as Stiller. While in prison, he becomes close to the Public Prosecutor, who treats him with sympathy and understanding, in vivid contrast to Stiller's attorney, **Dr. Bohnenblust,** who badgers his client for the "truth." Stiller responds with a host of stories, with which he regales his jailer, **Knobel.** After his trial and acquittal, Stiller makes a sincere effort to reconcile with Julika, but it is not successful. After she dies, Stiller lapses into silence.

The novel has been variously interpreted as an examination of the anxiety of modern humanity, an interpretation of the artist, and an examination of marriage. Whatever the perspective, the novel remains one of Frisch's most important and challenging works.

The Firebugs (drama, 1958)

Frisch calls this work a "morality play without a moral," and in it he relates the story of **Gottlieb Biedermann,** a successful hair-oil manufacturer. He is a bourgeois everyman who embodies acquiescence, compromise, and hypocrisy, and who refuses to recognize the truth. As the play opens, two arsonists, **Schmitz** and **Eisenring,** arrive at the home of Biedermann and his wife, **Babette,** asking for shelter. From their arrival, Biedermann refuses to acknowledge their intent, even though they store gasoline in his attic and ask for matches. Biedermann cannot bear to be thought of as uncharitable and refuses to face the consequences of his bad decisions. He grows more irrational and absurd in his behavior toward the arsonists and continues to ignore his suspicions. We learn that underlying Biedermann's obsequiousness is a hidden source of guilt, of which he appears to be unaware: a former employee had committed suicide after being refused a share of the company's profits which he felt were rightfully his. Biedermann, the quintessential bourgeois, must ingratiate himself with two men who pose a violent threat to the community because he cannot view himself as other than an honest, generous man. When the accomplice of the arsonists hands Biedermann a note outlining their plans, he ignores that, too. In consequence, the entire town is burned to the ground.

In the epilogue, Biedermann and Babette are punished, in a kind of mock hell, as arsonists. They insist on their innocence and try to justify the outcome by commenting on the new architecture of the city and claiming that the fire was beneficial.

Frisch makes use of a chorus in this play, who comment on the action of the drama, yet appear as capable of self-deception as Biedermann. Many critics have noted the parallels between the complacency embodied in Biedermann and that of Europe during the rise of fascism.

FURTHER READING

Butler, Michael. *The Novels of Max Frisch.* London: Oswald Wolff, 1976.

Contemporary Authors, Vols. 85-88. Detroit: Gale Research Co.

Contemporary Literary Criticism, Vols. 3, 9, 14, 18, 32, 44. Detroit: Gale Research Co.

Dictionary of Literary Biography, Vol. 69. Detroit: Gale Research Co.

Hoffmann, Charles W. "The Search for Self, Inner Freedom, and Relatedness in the

Novels of Max Frisch." In *The Contemporary Novel in German: A Symposium,* edited by Robert R. Heitner, pp. 91-114. Austin: University of Texas Press, 1967.

Natan, Alex. "Introduction." *German Men of Letters: Twelve Literary Essays, Vol. III,* pp. 1-33. London: Oswald Wolff, 1968.

Probst, Gerhard F. and Jay F. Bodine, eds. *Perspectives on Max Frisch.* Louisville: The University Press of Kentucky, 1982.

Subiotto, Arrigo. "The Swiss Contribution." In *The German Theatre: A Symposium,* pp. 171-88. New York: Barnes & Noble, 1975.

Weisstein, Ulrich. *Max Frisch.* New York: Twayne, 1967.

Christopher Fry

1907-

English dramatist.

The Lady's Not for Burning (drama, 1948)

The play is set in the fifteenth century in the English town of Cool Clary and recounts the tale of **Thomas Mendip,** a soldier of fortune who is world-weary and longing for death. He meets **Jennet Jourdemayne,** an alchemist's daughter accused of witchcraft, while the two of them are in jail. She has been falsely accused of sorcery by **Hebble Tyson** who wishes to gain her property and who also wants to find a way to stop Mendip from confessing crimes that will lead to his death. Mendip, trying to get himself hanged, has confessed to the murder of **Old Skipps;** Jennet has been imprisoned for supposedly turning the old man into a dog. In the course of the play, Jennet infuses Mendip with the will to live through the power of love, for when he falls in love with her, he is motivated to try to save her life. As she seeks escape from captivity and death, she enchants him, drawing out his fine qualities while extinguishing his misanthropy. When Old Skipps turns up at the end of the play very much alive, the two lovers are allowed to escape.

The Lady's Not for Burning was the first of four plays Fry wrote in celebration of the seasons, and a spring-like atmosphere imbues the play with a light-hearted, life-affirming tone. The influence of the Elizabethan dramatists is evident in the bawdy tang of the humor and the elegant verse style of the play.

FURTHER READING

Collins, J. A. "Poet of Paradox: The Dramas of Christopher Fry." *Literary Half-Yearly* 12, No. 2 (July 1971): 62-75.

Contemporary Authors, Vols. 17-20, rev. ed.; *Contemporary Authors New Revision Series,* Vol. 9. Detroit: Gale Research Co.

Contemporary Literary Criticism, Vols. 2, 10, 14. Detroit: Gale Research Co.

Daiches, David. In *The Present Age in British Literature,* pp. 166-67. Bloomington: Indiana University Press, 1958.

Dictionary of Literary Biography, Vol. 13. Detroit: Gale Research Co.

Roy, Emil. *Christopher Fry.* Carbondale: Southern Illinois University Press, 1969.

Carlos Fuentes
1928-
Mexican novelist, dramatist, and essayist.

The Death of Artemio Cruz (novel, 1962)

Set in Mexico City in 1959, the novel describes the life and death of **Artemio Cruz,** a wealthy, corrupt businessman whose life mirrors the recent history of Mexico, from the early idealism inspired by the Mexican Revolution to its subsequent moral decay.

As the novel begins, Cruz is seventy-one years old and has suffered a gastric attack which confines him to bed. As he lies near death, the novel unfolds. The work is related in three narrative voices: the first-person singular "I" for the present, which focusses on Cruz as he faces death, the second-person singular "you" which relates Cruz's thoughts on the future, and an objective third-person narrator who relates the historical past. These three voices and the events they recount are interrelated throughout the novel in a series of flashbacks that create a disjointed narrative sequence.

The sections that cover the past are depicted in twelve segments that relate to twelve important days in Cruz's life. We learn through them that he is the illegitimate son of a landowner and a mulatto woman. During the early days of the Mexican Revolution of 1910-1920, Cruz joins the revolutionary cause and loses his girlfriend and his fellow comrade, **Gonzalo Bernal.** After the war, he goes to Gonzalo's home, where he convinces Bernal's reluctant sister to marry him. Cruz takes over their estate and embarks on his life as a corrupt businessman, gaining land through unscrupulous dealings. The corruption that characterizes his professional life is mirrored in his personal life as well, reflected in his loveless marriage and his hostile relationship with his daughter. Further reflections on the past lead to an investigation of the history of Mexico, seen partially through the eyes of Cruz's grandmother, born in 1810, the year of the Mexican war of independence from Spain. The adulteration of the ideals of this revolution are reflected in the election of Porfirio Diaz, dictator of Mexico from 1870 to 1910, and the subsequent power struggle during the years of the revolution as different warring factions, through brutality and murder, fought for control.

The struggle for dominance is a major theme in this novel, for as the ideals of the revolution fade, corruption seeps into all aspects of life: in the exploitation of Mexico by U.S. interests, aided and abetted by men like Cruz; and in the ever-widening gulf between rich and poor. Cruz, confronted with the reality of his way of life as he approaches death, is overcome with disgust. The conclusion offers a compassionate view of a complex man, as the three narrative voices merge into one at the moment of his death.

The Death of Artemio Cruz is considered Fuentes's greatest novel and is praised for its deft handling of narrative and its broad sweep of history.

FURTHER READING

Contemporary Authors, Vols. 69-72; *Contemporary Authors New Revision Series*, Vol. 10. Detroit: Gale Research Co.

Contemporary Literary Criticism, Vols. 3, 8, 10, 13, 22, 41. Detroit: Gale Research Co.

Moody, Michael. "Existentialism, Mexico, and Artemio Cruz." *Romance Notes* 10 (1968): 27-31.

Shaw, Donald L. "Narrative Arrangement in *La muerte de Artemio Cruz.*" In *Contemporary Latin American Fiction*, edited by Salvador Barcarisse, pp. 34-47. Edinburgh: Scottish Academic Press, 1980.

World Literature Today, Carlos Fuentes Issue, Fall, 1983.

Athol Fugard

1932-

South African dramatist.

"Master Harold" . . . *and the Boys* (drama, 1982)

The play is set in Port Elizabeth, South Africa, in 1950. In a fading tea room owned by his mother, **Hally,** a white adolescent, talks with his companions **Sam** and **Willy,** two black servants who have raised him from childhood. As in all of his drama, Fugard's theme here is the nature of racial hatred as it permeates South African life through the policies of apartheid. Hally, an idealistic young man who espouses humanitarian ideals and yearns to be a writer, seemingly rejects the politics of his country, particularly because he relates them to his father—a racist, alcoholic, cripple. Instead, he has looked to Sam all of his life as a father figure and has transferred his filial affection to him. Fugard makes the audience aware of the complexities and tensions implicit in this arrangement, and as the play builds to its explosive denouement, makes a statement on the corrosive effects of apartheid on the souls of its perpetrators and victims.

Two phone calls from his parents—his despised father and his disaffected mother—prove a catalyst to Hally's dormant aggressiveness, and he explodes in a tirade of verbal violence designed to humiliate his friends. He spits in Sam's face, demanding that he and Willy refer to him as "Master Harold" and telling an insulting racist joke. Sam responds by showing Hally how the weakness and cowardice of his nature have been revealed in his peevish outburst; Hally, embarrassed and ashamed, withdraws. No reconciliation appears to be forthcoming after the explosion, for the relationship based on trust and affection has been irrevocably damaged.

The play, considered one of Fugard's finest efforts, is praised for its simplicity and dramatic intensity. For many critics, the work's strength lies in the way Fugard makes the audience aware of the true source of hatred and cruelty: the lack of tolerance and compassion that can characterize an individual relationship or a brutal system of government.

FURTHER READING

Barnes, Clive. "*Master Harold* Is a Masterful Look at South African Life." *New York Theatre Critics' Reviews* 33, No. 6 (3-10 May 1982): 307.

Contemporary Authors, Vols. 85-88. Detroit: Gale Research Co.

Contemporary Literary Criticism, Vols. 5, 9, 14, 25, 40. Detroit: Gale Research Co.

Rich, Frank. "Stage: *Master Harold,* Fugard's Drama on the Origin of Hate." *The New York Theatre Critics' Reviews* 33, No. 6 (3-10 May 1982): 305-06.

Simon, John. "Two Harolds and No Medea." *New York Magazine* 15, No. 20 (17 May 1982): 76, 79.

William Gaddis

1922-

American novelist.

The Recognitions (novel, 1955)

The novel recounts **Wyatt Gwyon**'s quest for spiritual salvation, covering thirty years and taking place in a variety of settings. The central theme of the novel is the nature of artistic and human truth in a modern world characterized by forgery and falsehood. Wyatt is an artist, raised in New England by a Calvinist father to follow him into the ministry. Rejecting his father's vocation and his faith, Wyatt flees to Paris, where he studies to become a painter. In Paris, he meets **Esther,** a writer, whom he later marries. They move to New York where they become part of a bohemian artistic circle. Gaddis's novel is full of talk about art and artists, some of it serious and legitimate, most of it shallow and revealing the insubstantial nature of modern life and art. Much of this conversation is from the mouths of the numerous minor characters who function as caricatures defined by their spurious philosophies, who are the objects of Gaddis's parody.

Driven to be a true artist, Wyatt leaves Esther and returns to Europe, obsessed with the works of the Flemish masters and becoming a forger of their paintings. Surrounded by counterfeiters of all types, Wyatt seeks in his work and life moments of "recognition," the epiphanies that bring him personal enlightenment. Frustrated by his search, he returns to New England to seek guidance from his father, who has become a member of a cult that worships the sun. Still seeking his liberation, Wyatt murders **Recktall Brown,** the art dealer responsible for selling his forgeries, and **Basil Valentine,** a former priest and art critic, a man false to faith and art. Wyatt is last depicted in Spain, having reached the conclusion of his tortuous quest. Although the ending is ambiguous, it is clear that he has journeyed from a circumscribed love of art and a narrow concept of God to a recognition of himself as an artist, an understanding of the nature of creation, and a comprehension of the importance of love.

Gaddis's novel is a dense and allusive work, reflecting his encyclopedic knowledge of art, music, and literature. The literary allusions range from the *Recognitions* of Clementine to Goethe's *Faust,* and Dante's *Inferno,* and references to the work of the such Northern Renaissance masters as Memling and the brothers Van Eyck also inform the work. The novel contains a wide variety of elements including newspaper headlines and snippets from advertising that reveal Gaddis's central concern with the vapidity of modern life. The chaos and fragmentation that characterize contemporary society for Gaddis are reflected in the truncated narrative and abrupt changes of scene. Yet the novel is interwoven with recurrent scenes, themes, and characters that lend a unity to this vast and difficult work.

JR (novel, 1975)

Set in contemporary New York, the novel tells the story of **JR Vansant,** an eleven-year-old schoolboy who amasses a fortune in the stock market. Gaddis's chief theme in this work is the emptiness of modern American life evident in a society where the values of capitalism and corporate greed guide the lives of the people. Related to this theme is his depiction of the plight of the artist in a society perverted by the power of money. Gaddis focuses his novel on two primary settings, the Long Island School that JR attends and the apartment that houses the headquarters of his JR Family of Corporations. JR is little more than an infantile projection of the greed that dominates American life. Although he is a child, he is motivated to undermine his fellow students in his financial schemes, doing deals on field trips and during school hours. For all his ruthlessness, he is depicted as a pathetic figure, convinced that money will buy him the security and love he wants. His school reflects the values of the corporations: the teachers speak in meaningless jargon, the students are taught by television, and the atmosphere reflects the violence and corruption of the society. Gaddis portrays a world in which technology and science have triumphed; his characters behave like automatons, machine-like receptors who are fed and process data.

JR's apartment house is peopled with lonely, isolated figures, many of them artists who have put off their creative drives in the pursuit of money. **Edward Bast,** a would-be composer who has exploited his talent for commercial purposes and who acts as a front for

JR in his business dealings, is typical of the adults who live off JR's business. In the conclusion, JR's financial empire and the apartment building have collapsed, yet he appears unscathed, ready to create another empire of paper.

The tone of the novel is savagely satirical, revealing the irreversible chaos and despair that Gaddis sees at the core of contemporary life. The work is given almost entirely in dialogue, full of truncated conversations that reflect the debasement of language and the characters' futile attempts at communication. The individual speakers are often unidentified, and the reader must learn to distinguish the personal patterns of their speech. Language, according to Gaddis, has been destroyed by the jargon of corporateese and advertising. Gaddis was awarded the National Book Award for *JR* in 1975.

FURTHER READING

Benstock, Bernard. "On William Gaddis: In Recognition of James Joyce." *Wisconsin Studies in Contemporary Literature* 6 (Summer 1965): 177-89.

Contemporary Authors, Vols. 17-20, rev. ed.; *Contemporary Authors New Revision Series,* Vol. 21. Detroit: Gale Research Co.

Contemporary Literary Criticism, Vols. 1, 3, 6, 8, 10, 19, 43. Detroit: Gale Research Co.

Dictionary of Literary Biography, Vol. 2. Detroit: Gale Research Co.

Gregson, David E. *"The Recognitions."* In *Survey of Contemporary Literature,* edited by Frank N. Magill, pp. 243-47. Englewood Cliffs: Salem Press, 1972.

Klemtner, Susan Strehle. "'For a Very Small Audience': The Fiction of William Gaddis." *Critique* 19, No. 3 (1978): 61-72.

Madden, David. "William Gaddis' *Recognitions*." In *Rediscoveries,* pp. 291-304. New York: Crown, 1971.

O'Hara, J.D. "Boardwalk and Park Place vs. Chance and Peace of Mind." *Virginia Quarterly Review* 52 (Summer 1976): 523-26.

Tanner, Tony. *City of Words: American Fiction 1950-1970.* . New York: Harper & Row, 1971.

John Galsworthy
1867-1933

English novelist, essayist, critic.

"The Forsyte Saga": *A Man of Property* (novel, 1906); **"Indian Summer of a Forsyte"** (short story, 1920); *In Chancery* (novel, 1920); *To Let* (novel, 1921)

"The Forsyte Saga" is the work for which John Galsworthy is best known. Although these four pieces make up the saga, he was to continue to chronicle the lives of the fictional Forsytes in six more short novels. The initial series begins in the 1880s and continues through the turn of the century and shortly beyond.

Soames Forsyte is the character whom readers come to understand the most, and he provides a central figure around which much of the narrative evolves. He personifies those men of England who were enjoying the rise of a middle class in which men of property had begun to live lives of affluence and power based upon their land, their principal capital, and its interest.

Soames's marriage to **Irene Forsyte,** a woman of beauty but no property, is not happy despite his attempts to make it so, for propriety's sake. Irene does not love him and feels herself to be no more than one of his possessions, since most of his time is spent getting and spending. Soames's tragedy is two-fold, for his vision of himself is flawed, and this makes him unable to love or to be loved.

When Irene falls in love with **Philip Bosinney,** the fiance of **Young Jolyon Forsyte**'s daughter, **June,** and the architect whom Soames has hired to build an estate at Robin Hill, family concordance is shaken once more. In an earlier scandal, Young Jolyon had divorced June's mother and married a governess; now, Irene and Bosinney cause family tongues to wag again. When Bosinney is accidentally killed after a financial rift with Soames, Irene is devastated and leaves Soames in an attempt to rebuild her life.

''Indian Summer of a Forsyte'' provides the long interlude in the saga, and is the story of the demise of **Old Jolyon Forsyte,** Soames's uncle and one of the last of the early generation of the family. Here, there is reconciliation between Irene and the old man, who has been lonely and estranged from his son and grandchildren. Irene's decision to spend time with Old Jolyon, who had taken on the house at Robin Hill, provides tenderness and love for him in his decline. He appreciates her beauty and her comfort in his last days, and is finally and happily reconciled with his son.

The opening sentence of *In Chancery*—''The possessive instinct never stands still''—acts as metaphor for the second novel of the saga. In it, Soames acquires more property and from time to time regrets that he has no heir. His pernicious, acquisitive tendencies are further marked by his vacillation and his desultory attempts to reconcile with Irene, who represents the one property which he cannot possess. Her indifference to him and his wealth and his desire to obtain her as an object of both love and revenge show Galsworthy's remarkable ability to stylistically create tension in the dynamics of character interaction.

Irene's legacy from Old Jolyon allows her independence and a re-connection with the family in the person of Young Jolyon, who is now a respectable artist, a widower, and the legal trustee of her finances. In what seems a perplexing number of Forsyte characters who are flat at best, there is much interaction between other members of the family. Soames's sister's husband deserts her and cousins fall in love with cousins. The older generations of brothers and sisters jealously guard secrets from each other, sniff at each other's acquisitions, and generally enjoy membership in the environs of the leisure class.

When Irene and Young Jolyon become lovers, Soames goes to great lengths to prove her infidelity and divorces her in order to free himself to marry a young Frenchwoman. After the Boer War claims the life of Jolyon's son, Irene and Jolyon marry and have a son, **Jon Forsyte,** at Robin Hill, Jolyon's legacy from his father. Soames's wife provides him with a daughter, **Fleur Forsyte,** and this brings the second volume to a close.

To Let begins in 1920. World War I has come and gone, Jon and Fleur are young adults, and this tale is about their love affair. They meet for the first time by accident, in June's art gallery. They are attracted from the first and fall deeply in love. Once again, Galsworthy's adept handling of plot tension and dramatic irony are shown. The lovers are cousins, Irene and Soames have become bitter enemies, and the scenario is one of disaster. Beyond these plot elements, Jolyon is now dying of heart disease, and worry over Jon and Fleur accentuates his condition. Desperate, Irene prevails upon Jon to accompany her to Italy for a holiday, hoping that separation will end the affair, but her efforts are unsuccessful.

Just before Jolyon's death, he writes a final letter to Jon in which he reveals the unhappy background of events and his wish that Jon renounce Fleur. Jolyon is convinced that Irene will suffer deeply if Jon is in any way connected with Soames, the man she has come to despise. This influences Jon to sadly reject Fleur, in order to abide by his father's wishes. Jon sends his final message to his beloved Fleur through Soames, who has clumsily tried to make amends with Irene, and now becomes the source of Fleur's unhappiness. It is for Soames a supreme irony, since Fleur is the only possession he has whom he has truly come to love.

In the final chapter of the story, Fleur's marriage to **Michael Mont**, another man of property, and the death of **Timothy Forsyte,** the last of the older generation, provide a transition from the Edwardian age to the modern era and lays the groundwork for the continuation of the chronicles.

While Galsworthy's tone is often one of irony and subtle social criticism, and his mastery of satire is shown in his often droll characterizations of the elder Forsytes and their manipulations, it is significant that he was writing about the social class to which he himself belonged. Most critics now agree that while Galsworthy was not a writer of great stature, his capabilities lay in his talent to provide interesting insight into an era of British cultural history which was transformed after World War I, as well as to give subtle prophecy of the many social changes which were to follow.

FURTHER READING

Aiken, Conrad. "Galsworthy, John." In *Collected Criticism,* pp. 213-17. New York: Oxford University Press, 1968.

Bergonzi, Bernard. "Man as Property." In *The Turn of a Century: Essays on Victorian and Modern English Literature,* pp. 134-38. New York: Barnes & Noble, 1973.

Burgess, Anthony. "Seen Any Good Galsworthy Lately?" *The New York Times Magazine* (16 November 1969): 57-64.

Contemporary Authors, Vol. 104. Detroit: Gale Research Co.

Dictionary of Literary Biography, Vols. 10, 34. Detroit: Gale Research Co.

Ford, Ford Madox. "Galsworthy." In *Portraits from Life,* pp. 124-42. Boston: Houghton Mifflin, 1937.

Hynes, Samuel. *The Edwardian Turn of Mind.* Princeton: Princeton University Press, 1968.

Lambert, J. W. "The Galsworthy Saga." *Horizon* (Autumn 1968): 106-11.

Twentieth-Century Literary Criticism, Vol. 1. Detroit: Gale Research Co.

Gabriel García Márquez

1928-

Colombian novelist, short story writer, and essayist.

One Hundred Years of Solitude (novel, 1967)

This novel, García Márquez's undisputed masterpiece and a central work of twentieth-century fiction, is set in the fictional village of Macondo and chronicles one hundred years in the Buendía family. This vast, epic work is unified by the themes of solitude and time, and it reflects the author's rich and complex prose style in which he incorporates fantasy, realism, and social and political satire in the creation of a fictional world where the real and the surreal coexist.

The founder of Macondo and the head of the family dynasty is **José Arcadio Buendía,** who builds his village from a vision in a dream. He and his wife, **Ursula,** are cousins and fear that they will produce an heir with a pig's tail, as had an incestuous couple in their ancestry. For García Márquez, they represent Adam and Eve, and their union is emblematic of original sin. Indeed, six generations of Buendías fear a recurrence of the curse of the pig's tail, yet they appear irresistibly drawn to incestuous unions, one of which ends the dynasty.

This is linked to the theme of solitude, for they are an egocentric and isolated family, plagued with the inability to love and to communicate with those outside.

The history of Macondo is a record of the movement from paradise in the early days of the village to its ultimate corruption and destruction. In the early days, the Buendías flourish, and García Márquez records the generations of husbands, wives, and legitimate and illegitimate children. They live alone and out of touch with the real world, and their only visitors are gypsies, whose supernatural feats of magic entrance the family. One of them, **Melquíades,** a character of mythical wisdom who after his death returns to live with the family, introduces José Arcadio to the wonders of science, which absorbs the indefatigable patriarch to the exclusion of all else. He ends his life in madness, tied to a tree and babbling in Latin. Ursula, conversely, is strong and pragmatic. She is the only character who lives to see the beginning and end of the Buendía dynasty. Throughout her long life, she reinforces one of García Márquez's central themes: that time is circular, and that it is characterized by endless repetitions and recurrences. The actual events of life in Macondo are described in mythic and epic terms, lending the work an atemporal quality. The ghosts of the dead are ever-present members of the family, and they, too, seem to defy time.

Macondo only exists in isolation for a brief time, then the outside world intrudes, with the divisive elements of religion and politics. The civil strife that erupts brings to the forefront the character of **Colonel Aureliano Buendía,** the son of José Arcadio and Ursula, who becomes a leader of the rebels during the long civil wars. He begins as a heroic character and a fighter against corruption, yet falls victim to a lonely solitude and embodies the absurdity of modern life. Macondo is further corrupted by the arrival of the Americans, who plan to exploit the people and the natural resources; they are aided by government representatives who gather the workers together, ostensibly to discuss their wage demands, then assassinate them. The heavens open, and a torrential rain that lasts for five years is visited on the land, a flood that is a symbol of purification, cleansing the community that had forgotten its ties with nature and had witnessed and acquiesced to the corruption of its ideals.

In the midst of this atmosphere of decadence and disaster, the last remaining Buendía descendants, **Amaranta Ursula** and her nephew, **Aureliano Babilonia,** consummate their incestuous passion, which ends in the birth of a child with a pig's tail. Amaranta Ursula and the child die, and Aureliano Babilonia retreats into the study of Melquíades, who after his second death had left the family an indecipherable manuscript. Aureliano reads in it the history of his family and his own fate; the manuscript turns out to be the novel we are reading. The devastating hurricane that brings an end to Macondo and the Buendía dynasty that is foretold in the document rages outside as Aureliano Babilonia hears the voices of the past speaking to him.

One Hundred Years of Solitude presents a richly conceived fictional world, representing at once a microcosm of Latin America and a universe of wonder and enchantment. García Márquez's theme of the circular nature of time is reflected in the novel's structure through his use of repeated images, symbols, and character types.

Autumn of the Patriarch (novel, 1975)

Set in an unnamed Latin American country that nonetheless resembles the author's native Colombia and featuring an unnamed protagonist referred to as the **Patriarch,** this novel continues García Márquez's exploration of the theme of solitude and the nature of time. It is a study of corruption and totalitarianism and presents a profile of a man in a state of decadence and loneliness. The novel is divided into six sections, all of which begin with the death of the Patriarch and move backward in time, focusing on a central incident in his life. The work is structurally complex and innovative: each of the six sections is composed as a single paragraph, and some of the sentences continue for pages. García Márquez employs three types of narrative, using the first person, third person, and first person plural, in a style that blends all three types of narration to create, simultaneously, an internal and external portrait of the Patriarch.

The first section focuses on the Patriarch's double, **Patrico Aragonés,** who sacrifices his own identity to become the mirror image of the leader. The patriarch is a megalomaniacal character, who feeds his pride through the creation of a duplicate persona, and who fears the people he has oppressed so deeply that he uses Aragonés to shield himself from their anger and violence; it is Aragonés who takes the bullet meant for the patriarch and dies.

In the second section, we learn of the patriarch's rise to power. Like other twentieth-century tyrants, he is a man full of delusion who fashions himself a mythical persona. He believes he was born of a virgin, although his mother was a whore; he believes he is destined for greatness and has a divine purpose in ruling his country, yet he is a despised and threatened dictator. He is, however, a man of heroic physical proportions: he has lived to a great age, and is somewhere between 140 and 220 years old, continued to grow until he was 100, and possesses a legendary ability to defy death. In the third section, the power struggle that ends in the death of his devoted follower, **General Rodrigo de Aguilar** is outlined; the fourth deals with the death of the patriarch's beloved mother, whom he has declared a saint. In the fifth part, the patriarch marries **Leticia Nazareno,** who bears him a son, **Emanuel.** When they are murdered, he hires **José Ignacio Saenz de la Barra,** a man as sadistic and cruel as the patriarch himself, to find their assassins. In the sixth portion, García Márquez completes his portrait of the patriarch as he moves from decadence to death. This is the fullest examination of the theme of solitude in the novel, as the author depicts the patriarch's increasing isolation and deepening loneliness. His power and venality have corrupted him so deeply that he is totally estranged from humanity; in this deep seclusion, he dies.

While *Autumn of the Patriarch* has not received the praise accorded *One Hundred Years of Solitude,* it is still a highly regarded work admired for its complex structure and penetrating examination of the corruption of power.

FURTHER READING

Ciplijauskaité, Birute. "Foreshadowing as Technique and Theme in *One Hundred Years of Solitude.*" *Books Abroad* 47, No. 3 (1973): 479-84.

Contemporary Authors, Vols. 33-36, rev. ed.; *Contemporary Authors New Revision Series,* Vol. 10. Detroit: Gale Research Co.

Contemporary Literary Criticism, Vols. 2, 3, 8, 10, 15, 27, 47. Detroit: Gale Research Co.

De Feo, Ronald. "The Solitude of Power." *National Review* (27 May 1977): 620, 622.

Gallagher, D. P. *Modern Latin American Literature,* pp. 144-63. Oxford: Oxford University Press, 1973.

Harrs, Luis and Barbara Dohmann. "Gabriel García Márquez , or the Lost Chord." In *Into the Mainstream,* pp. 310-41. New York: Harper and Row, 1967.

Ortega, Julio. "*One Hundred Years of Solitude.*" In *Poetics of Change: The New Spanish-American Narrative,* translated by Galen D. Greaser, pp. 85-95. Austin: University of Texas Press, 1984.

Rabassa, Gregory. "Beyond Magic Realism: Thoughts on the Art of Gabriel García Márquez." *Books Abroad* 47, No. 3 (1973): 442-50.

West, Paul. "The Posthumous Present." *Review* (Fall 1976): 76-8.

John Gardner
1933-1982
American novelist, short story writer, poet, and essayist.

Grendel (novel, 1971)

The novel is a parodic reworking of the Beowulf legend, told from the point of view of the monster, **Grendel.** Grendel's character personifies darkness, nihilism, and the meaninglessness of existence. From his perspective, we witness the history of humankind. He is aware of the hollowness of all he sees: the march of history, the rise and fall of religions, political leaders, philosophies, culture, all the outward forms of human "progress." All human strivings he finds worthless, save one: poetry. He calls the poet "the Shaper," whom he feels gives form and meaning to life. The poet is the great artificer, and Grendel knows his creations are illusory, yet it is the poet who imparts purpose to the otherwise meaningless universe. The work delineates the struggle of order and chaos, a familiar theme in Gardner's work, with humankind as the proponent of order and Grendel the representative of chaos. In the conclusion, **Beowulf,** of the ethical, structured world of men, slays Grendel, creature of darkness and disorder. Although Grendel claims he dies by "chance," Gardner shows the meaning of his life, death, and the promise of rebirth. Though the monster may embody death, the regenerative life force is triumphant always.

The novel is divided into twelve chapters, each representing an astrological sign. It begins and ends in the spring, traditional time of renewal. Thematically, the work embodies Gardner's concept of the moral purpose of literature, as outlined most specifically in his controversial 1978 publication, *On Moral Fiction,* in which he posits that literature must affirm life and inspire the moral as well as the intellectual side of human life. Grendel's nihilism is challenged by his love for art, which offers the power of affirmation lacking in his existence. The work is noted for its ironic, humorous tone, its taut, controlled narrative style, and Gardner's deft handling of the form and theme of the epic.

The Sunlight Dialogues (novel, 1972)

The work is set in Batavia, New York, in 1966. The plot centers on the criminal career of **The Sunlight Man,** a vagrant who is arrested for painting LOVE across a road. After he escapes from jail, he is linked to a series of murders and kidnappings in the area. He is pursued by Police Chief **Fred Clumly.** As in *Grendel,* Gardner here explores the opposition of order and chaos, as embodied in his two protagonists: the Sunlight Man personifies absolute freedom; Clumly signifies law and order. In a work noted for its variety of subplots and eighty-plus secondary characters, we come to learn the true background of the Sunlight Man. **Taggert Hodge,** the troubled son of a local family, has been driven to the edge of insanity by his children's death and his wife's subsequent mental derangement. The impetus for his criminal life as the Sunlight Man is the cruelty of his father-in-law, who refuses to give him and his wife the help they need and who becomes the object of Hodge's revenge. As the Sunlight Man, he becomes larger than life, even god-like. Central to the novel are the "dialogues" between the Sunlight Man and Clumly, who begins to question his own rigid values under their influence. The subjects of the Sunlight Man's lectures encompass everything from the meaning of Plato to the philosophical implications of the conflict between the two men. Gardner portrays him as a mad visionary and sorcerer of sorts. The effect of his words on Clumly are evident as the novel nears its close, when Clumly, after losing his job, has captured the Sunlight Man, but sets him free. In the novel's conclusion, the Sunlight Man has been killed, by a "police action," but not by Clumly, who appears transformed by his encounter with the "criminal."

Although the work has been faulted by some critics as overly didactic, with Gardner's characters functioning as little more than mouthpieces for his ideas, it is considered by others to be a superb example of his continuing examination of the dual forces of order and disorder.

October Light (novel, 1976)

Set in Vermont, the novel tells the story of two elderly siblings, **Sally Page Abbot,** eighty-three, and **James Page,** seventy-two, who argue tenaciously about everything from current events to popular culture. One evening, in the heat of an argument, James take a gun and blows up Sally's television, after which he chases her upstairs and locks her in her room. Not to be outdone in this battle of wills, Sally decides to stay in her room, despite the entreaties of family and friends. She occupies herself with reading a "trashy" novel entitled *The Smugglers of Lost Souls' Rock,* the text of which forms one-third of Gardner's novel. Through his use of the novel within the novel structure, Gardner illuminates the story of his "real" protagonists, Sally and James, through the lives of the "fictional" characters in *The Smugglers.*

Smugglers is in fact Gardner's parody of the current literary penchant for alienation and despair in fiction, a method he derided in his critical work. The inner novel is simplistic, revealing the lack of depth in style, tone, and substance that Gardner saw in much modern fiction. As Sally reads, she notes parallels between characters in the novel and people in her own life. For example, **Captain Fist,** the central figure, is much like James, and the suicidal **Peter Wagner** bears a strong resemblance to James's son, **Richard,** also a suicide. What Gardner reveals is that bleakness and despair, a fictional pose in the inner novel, are very much evident in the "real" world of James and Sally. In the novel's conclusion, the brother and sister are reconciled, and James has gained insight into the rigidity of character that had estranged him from his son and inadvertently led to his untimely death. The ending gives resonance to the title, for James's understanding of himself comes in the autumn of his years, as he sees himself with the clarity that characterizes the light of late fall.

The work has been called Gardner's "Bicentennial novel," portraying the lives of two crusty Yankee characters in a novel interspersed with quotes from Jefferson, Washington, Adams, and other Founding Fathers. As such, it comments on both the American literary scene and the American character, which, like James and Sally, Gardner sees as divided and divisive.

FURTHER READING

Bellamy, Joe David and Pat Ensworth. "John Gardner." *Fiction International* 2, No. 3 (1974): 33-49.

Contemporary Authors, Vols. 65-68, 107. Detroit: Gale Research Co.

Contemporary Literary Criticism, Vols. 2, 3, 5, 7, 8, 10, 18, 28, 34. Detroit: Gale Research Co.

Dictionary of Literary Biography, Vol. 2; *Dictionary of Literary Biography Yearbook: 1982.* Detroit: Gale Research Co.

Edwards, Thomas. *"The Sunlight Dialogues." New York Times Book Review* (10 December 1972): 1, 14.

Hutman, Norma L. "Even Monsters Have Mothers: A Study of *Beowulf* and John Gardner's *Grendel." Mosaic* 9, No. 1 (Fall 1975): 19-31.

Milosh, Joseph. "John Gardner's *Grendel:* Sources and Analogues." *Contemporary Literature* 19, No. 1 (Winter 1978): 48-57.

Murr, Judy Smith. "John Gardner's Order and Disorder: *Grendel* and *The Sunlight Dialogues." Critique* 18, No. 2 (1977): 97-108.

Rudd, Jay. "Gardner's Grendel and *Beowulf:* Humanizing the Monster." *Toth* 14, Nos. 2-3 (1974): 3-17.

Strehle, Susan. "John Gardner's Novels: Affirmation and the Alien." *Critique* 18, No. 2 (1977): 86-96.

Hamlin Garland
1860-1940
American short story writer, autobiographer, novelist, and poet.

"The Return of a Private" (short story, 1891)

The story takes place immediately following the Civil War and focuses on the homecoming of **Private Edward Smith,** who is returning to his family and farmstead near LaCrosse, Wisconsin. War-ravaged and weak, Private Smith walks from the train station with fellow veterans **Jim Cranby** and **Saunders.** After parting from his friends, Smith continues toward home, thinking of the sudden death in battle of his closest companion, **Billy Tripp.** The scene shifts to the run-down farm and **Emma Smith,** who with scarce resources has been caring for the children; she is desperately awaiting her husband's belated return. Emma takes the children to the **Widow Gray's** home for a lavish Sunday dinner and enjoys a moment's respite from her many worries. Through a window she spots a soldier walking; she reunites with her frail husband in a painfully eloquent scene. At the close, one great battle has ceased but another, that of humanity against the indifferent forces of nature, has just begun.

"The Return of a Private" is perhaps the most famous of the six stories that comprise *Main-travelled Roads,* considered Garland's major literary effort. Collectively, the stories provide a study of the poverty faced by rural farmers in the industrial age. Garland's clear, concise style in these early stories and his rigid adherence to veritism—like realism, a conscious rejection of romance, sentimentality, and artifice—earned him a wide, admiring audience.

FURTHER READING

Contemporary Authors, Vol. 104. Detroit: Gale Research Co.

Dictionary of Literary Biography, Vol. 12. Detroit: Gale Research Co.

Gish, Robert. *Hamlin Garland: The Far West.* Boise: Boise State University, 1976.

Holloway, Jean. *Hamlin Garland: A Biography.* Austin: University of Texas Press, 1960.

Pizer, Donald. *Hamlin Garland's Early Work and Career.* Berkeley: University of California Press, 1960.

Twentieth-Century Literary Criticism, Vol. 3. Detroit: Gale Research Co.

William Gass
1924-
American novelist, short story writer, and essayist.

Omensetter's Luck (novel, 1966)

Set in the Ohio river town of Gilean in the 1890s, the novel is concerned with the reaction of the townsfolk to the arrival of **Brackett Omensetter** and his family. He is a man of utter simplicity—happy, natural, with an innate sense of oneness with nature and God. The community's reaction is divided: some are attracted to his simple goodness, others suspect him to be a figure of evil. One of Omensetter's first encounters is with **Harry Pimber,** whose house he visits looking for a place to rent. Pimber offers a complete contrast to the natural man that Omensetter represents: he is an anxious, guilt-ridden man, driven by thoughts of self-destruction. In further contrast to Omensetter, he and his wife are childless and infertile, while Omensetter, his wife, and large family, seem to be symbols of fecundity. In a central episode of the novel, Omensetter cures Pimber's lockjaw, after medicine and religion have failed. The event leads to Pimber's final act: he decides to commit suicide after realizing that Omensetter cannot save him from himself and his despair.

The narrative of **Jethro Thurber** takes up one-half of the book and is a brilliant if difficult exploration of character. Thurber is a minister who has been sent to Gilean, where he is a bitter outsider. Omensetter's close relationship with nature is threatening to him, for as a country preacher, he is supposedly endowed with a "natural" closeness to God. Thurber cannot understand how Omensetter could have escaped the knowledge of the separateness of man from God after the Fall in Eden. His uncomprehending attitude toward Omensetter leads him to be suspicious of him and to try to discredit him. Thurber himself is a man who has withdrawn into language and is seduced by his own rhetoric. He lives removed from the community in a world of words. He continually fights against his strong sexual longings, for unlike Omensetter, he can neither acknowledge nor act upon them, reverting instead to verbal games and limericks. His distrust of Omensetter leads him to suspect that Omensetter has murdered Pimber. When he confronts Omensetter, who has come to him in innocence to seek help with Pimber's corpse, Thurber realizes the falseness of his crusade. In the novel's conclusion, Gass depicts both Omensetter and Thurber transformed: Omensetter has gained self-awareness and Thurber has broken out of his isolation and learned to love.

The novel is considered a linguistic tour de force, particularly in the sections that depict the inner thoughts and motivations of Thurber in language that has been praised for its musical, sensuous, and sonorous beauty. Thematically, Gass explores the conflict between the natural and the intellectual in humanity, as well as the nature of knowledge and goodness. In Thurber Gass created a recurrent character type, a man who lives in an artificial world of language, isolated from his fellow human beings.

"The Pedersen Kid" (short story, 1968)

Jorge Segren, a young boy coming of age on his father's farm, is the story's narrator. As the work begins, he and **Big Hans,** a farm hand, find a young boy nearly dead in the snow. When they revive him, he tells them a tale of terror: his family has been attacked and murdered on their neighboring farm. Jorge, his father (**Pa**), and Hans go to the house, where Pa is shot by the murderer, Hans flees, and Jorge hides in the basement, freezing and terrified, to wait out the murderer. In his hallucinatory state, Jorge recollects events from his life, and we learn of his feelings of hatred for his father, who is a cruel, brutal man and a drunk, and his ambivalence for his mother, who appears only as a cold, shadowy figure. Jorge's interior monologues reveal a central tenet of Gass's literary philosophy, for he speaks in a language far beyond his education and background. Thus, by putting poetry in the mouth of a country boy, Gass heightens our awareness of the artificiality of the fictive world. When the murderer leaves, Jorge goes upstairs and lights a fire, feeling, as Gass tells us, "warm inside and out . . . with joy," convinced of his bravery in the face of danger.

The story begins as both a rite of initiation for Jorge and as a murder mystery, but Gass does not fulfill the reader's expectations in either mode. Jorge does not emerge at the story's conclusion as a hero, and the Pedersens' fate is never made clear. Instead, Gass tells a tale of isolation and artifice, for only in their minds are the characters free to order and understand their experience. As such, Jorge's bravery is a creation of his imagination, and like Thurber in *Omensetter's Luck,* he inhabits a lonely world of words.

FURTHER READING

Allen, Carolyn J. "Fiction and Figures of Life in *Omensetter's Luck.*" *Pacific Coast Philology* 9 (1974): 5-11.

Contemporary Authors, Vols. 17-20, rev. ed. Detroit: Gale Research Co.

Contemporary Literary Criticism, Vols. 1, 2, 8, 11, 15, 39. Detroit: Gale Research Co.

Dictionary of Literary Biography, Vol. 2. Detroit: Gale Research Co.

French, Ned. "Against the Grain: Theory and Practice in the Work of William H. Gass." *Iowa Review* 7 (Winter 1976): 96-106.

Gilman, Richard. "William H. Gass." In *The Confusion of Realms,* pp. 69-81. New York: Random House, 1969.

Kane, Patricia. "The Sun Burned on the Snow: Gass's 'The Pedersen Kid'." *Critique* 14, No. 2 (December 1972): 89-96.

Schneider, Richard J. "The Fortunate Fall in William Gass's *Omensetter's Luck.*" *Critique* 18 (Summer 1976): 5-20.

Shorris, Earl. "The Well Spoken-Passions of William H. Gass." *Harper's* 244 (May 1972): 96-100.

Jean Genet
1910-1986
French dramatist, novelist, and poet.

Our Lady of the Flowers (novel, 1942)

This novel, considered by many to be Genet's masterpiece, was written while the author was in prison and is a celebration of life in the Parisian underworld, focusing on the homosexual, **Divine.** The work presents an inversion of traditional Western values, glorifying and ritualizing the world of criminals and homosexuals.

Genet gives his own name to the narrative voice in the novel. As it opens, we are addressed by "**Jean Genet,**" a prisoner awaiting trial. His thoughts on the characters and the action are interspersed throughout. The narrative begins with Divine's death as an aging queen, then Genet provides flashbacks and flashforwards in time to relate the life of his protagonist. Divine, who was born **Louis Culafroy,** goes to Paris at the age of twenty and becomes a male prostitute. Once Culafroy has become Divine, Genet refers to the character as "she." The author charts Divine's homosexual encounters in the Parisian underworld in a language that is lush and evocative, peppered with the slang of criminals and homosexuals. Genet focuses in particular on Divine's relationships with two men, **Darling** and **Our Lady.** Darling, a thief and a pimp, becomes Divine's lover and the two live together for several years. Divine then lives with Our Lady, a teen-aged murderer, and **Seck Gorgui,** a black man. Both Darling and Our Lady represent dominant males, and Divine's role in her relationships with them is one of passivity, reflecting one of Genet's main themes of the sadomasochism that governs relationships. Darling is arrested for theft, and Our Lady is arrested, convicted and executed for the murder of a homosexual. Divine ages, becoming ugly and unwanted in the homosexual world. In the conclusion, she dies of tuberculosis.

The work has been called a masturbatory fantasy, and the homoerotic sections are rapturously detailed. Genet conceptualized the criminal as a kind of saint, and images of violence parallel those drawn from Christian ritual. He shows how the criminal world obeys a kind of hierarchal structure that parallels and parodies that of society. As he will so often in his works, Genet reveals how society depends on criminals to define itself, with the police, the courts, and religion—the entire moral order—dependent on sinners for their very existence.

The Balcony (drama, 1956)

This play, regarded as Genet's most significant work for the theater, is set in the Grand Balcony, a brothel run by **Madame Irma** devoted to illusion. Within this house, clients can fulfill their fantasies by playing out roles of religious, military, and judicial authority, performing the roles of bishops, judges, or generals. The work bears the influence of the Theater of Cruelty as defined by Antonin Artaud, for Genet stresses the primacy of ritual and imagination and of dreams and illusion. The prevailing force in the play is the power of language.

Genet states in his preface that the play is not a satire, but is instead a glorification of illusion. It is composed of nine tableaux, and as the work begins, we see the **Bishop,** in full religious vestments and standing before a sacristy, where he chastises a writhing female penitent as a prelude to sex. In the second scene, the **Judge**, with a female thief and an executioner with a whip, go through a similar scenario. Genet's indebtedness to Sartre's *No Exit* has been noted, and in this scene and all the others, the roles of sadist and masochist, of victim and judge, are played out. Their ritual ends as it begins, indicating the circular nature of their performance. In the third scene, the **General** admires himself in the mirror, a prop present throughout the play, and a constant reminder of the world of illusion. In his fantasy, the prostitute plays his horse, and they tour a battlefield. The General compares himself to Napoleon and tries to lose himself in the poetic images he creates.

But outside the world of the Balcony, a revolution is taking place, which represents a threat to the world of illusion. After the anarchists kill all the representatives of authority, the **Chief of Police** asks the General, Bishop, and Judge, in their assumed identities, to play their parts and restore order. As in *Our Lady of the Flowers,* Genet underscores the need society has for criminal activity to justify itself and its rituals. As the real world of society needs the illusory world of the Balcony, so the social order requires the criminal order. Yet whether or not the revolution is real or whether the rebels themselves are acting roles remains ambiguous. **Roger,** a leader of the revolt, persuades **Chantal,** one of Irma's prostitutes, to take part in their cause. She becomes an icon for the revolutionaries and is later shot; thus, the reality of death enters the world of illusion. The revolution fails, and Roger goes to the Balcony to play a role never yet requested: he wants to be the Chief of Police. Yet while performing his fantasy, he castrates himself, indicating the metaphorical impotence of the world of authority. In the conclusion, Irma speaks directly to the audience, telling them to go home to their own worlds, which are every bit as false as the one presented in the play.

The work is noted for its ritualized, incantatory use of language, ironically put in the mouths of prostitutes, pimps, and the clients of illusion, and for its exposition of Genet's recurrent theme of the interdependence of the worlds of reality and illusion.

The Blacks (drama, 1959)

This play is a scathing indictment of racial hatred and confronts the repression and hypocrisy of white society. Genet stipulated that all of the actors were to be black, and that those actors playing the roles of whites were to wear white face. Elements of ritual, ceremony, and the mass are used to heighten the symbolic effect of the play, as witnessed in the opening scene, where eight characters dance, to a minuet by Mozart, before a catafalque strewn with flowers. The court appears (played by blacks in whiteface), composed of the **Queen,** the **Queen's Valet,** the **General, Judge, Missionary,** and **Governor.** These figures of white authority preside over the enactment of a ritual, the murder and rape of a white woman. **Deodatus Village,** a black criminal, is charged with the murder and rape and is tried by the white Court. His crime is symbolic of the desire to annihilate all whites, and the members of the Court mouth the cliches of a dying culture about to be supplanted by one that is vital, primitive, and beautiful in its sense of evil. For Genet, blacks must purge themselves of all whiteness, including white values and emotions, and must revel in their blackness. Yet as **Archibald,** the "master of sacred ceremonies" tells us, there is a real revolution going on outside the parameters of the play, with blacks ready to destroy the white power structure. We learn through a messenger that a real black man has been tried and convicted of treason. The members of the Court follow the blacks to Africa, where the blacks are in command and where the "whites" are killed. Yet they arise, unharmed, and once again play their roles in the new regime. The play ends as it began, with the blacks reenacting the ritual, dancing before the casket to the strains of Mozart.

In this play, Genet uses the blacks as a symbol for the oppressed outcasts of society, and he links them to the criminals and homosexuals who live outside the accepted moral code in such earlier works as *Our Lady of the Flowers.* The play is noted for its powerful exploration of the political dynamics of racial conflict.

FURTHER READING

Abel, Lionel. "The Genius of Jean Genet." *The New York Review of Books* 1, No. 4 (17 October 1963): 7-8.

Brustein, Robert. "Antonin Artaud and Jean Genet." In *The Theatre of Revolt: An Approach to Modern Drama,* pp. 361-411. Boston: Little, Brown, 1964,

Coe, Richard N. *The Vision of Jean Genet.* New York: Grove Press, 1968.

Contemporary Authors, Vols. 13-16, rev. ed.; *Contemporary Authors New Revision Series,* Vol. 18. Detroit: Gale Research Co.

Contemporary Literary Criticism, Vols. 1, 2, 5, 10, 14, 44, 46. Detroit: Gale Research Co.

Dictionary of Literary Biography, Vol. 72. Detroit: Gale Research Co.

Dobrez, L. A. C. "The Image and the Revolutionary Sartrean Relationships in the Work of Jean Genet." *Southern Review* 11, No. 1 (March 1978): 57-71.

Esslin, Martin. "Jean Genet." In *The Theatre of the Absurd,* pp. 140-67. Garden City: Doubleday, 1961.

Grossvogel, David I. "Jean Genet: The Difficulty of Defining." In *Four Playwrights and a Postscript,* pp. 135-74. Ithaca: Cornell University Press, 1962.

McMahon, Joseph H. *The Imagination of Jean Genet.* New Haven: Yale University Press, 1963.

Oxenhandler, Neal. "Can Genet Be Saved? Remarks on *The Blacks.*" *Contemporary Literature* 16, No. 4 (Autumn 1975): 417-32.

Sartre, Jean-Paul. *Saint Genet: Actor and Martyr,* translated by Bernard Frechtman. New York: George Braziller, 1963.

André Gide
1869-1951
French novelist, diarist, and essayist.

The Immoralist (novel, 1902)

The novel is set in a variety of locales, including France, North Africa, and Italy. It relates the story of **Michel** and is considered Gide's self-portrait of his life as a married man. When the novel first opens, we hear Michel telling his story in the first person to a group of close friends. He begins with a harrowing tale of his near-fatal bout of tuberculosis soon after his marriage to **Marceline.** Although they did not marry for love, the two grew close during Michel's long convalescence. Yet when he recovers from his illness, he is a different man. He feels reborn, and renouncing traditional morality, sets out to explore life without the fetters of society. He and Marceline become estranged, for she cannot understand his transformation and knows that she no longer fits into his life. Michel, rebelling against the Christian dictum of self-sacrifice and the stultifying conventions of society, goes to North Africa where he can shed his former self and indulge in the sensuous delights that he had denied himself. He is truly transformed from the "learned Puritan" of his youth into the "immoralist" of the title. Marceline dies, and her death is a great shock and source of grief for Michel. Although he was searching for self-awareness, he did not realize that his quest had become selfish, with tragic consequences for his wife. As the novel ends, he calls three of his closest friends to him to tell them the story of his life. Michel is depicted as a lonely, enervated man, not knowing what to do and unable to understand the consequences of the unbridled freedom he had insisted upon.

Michel's story begins and ends as a plea to his friends to help him understand his dilemma. The narrative is prefaced with a letter, addressed "To the Prime Minister," written by one of Michel's friends to his brother and introducing Michel's story, and it concludes with the friends reacting to Michel's recounting of his life. The work of the "immoralist" is thus bracketed with the thoughts of those who represent convention and traditional morality. The novel is noted for its controlled, lyrical style and for its presentation of the themes of individual freedom that dominate Gide's fiction.

Strait Is the Gate (novel, 1909)

This novel relates the story of **Alissa** and **Jerome** and explores the sacrifice of human love and its consequences. Their story is narrated in the first section by Jerome, who tells how the two cousins fall in love and become engaged. Yet when Alissa learns that her sister **Juliette** has also fallen in love with Jerome, she is ready to sacrifice her happiness for her sister's. Moved by what she takes to be Alissa's selflessness, Juliette accepts an older suitor instead. Alissa, now free to pursue her life with Jerome, rejects him. Jerome leaves and travels to Greece, returning three years later to again propose marriage. Alissa, now ill and on the point of death, refuses him again. The situation is a bewildering one for Jerome until he discovers Alissa's diary, which forms the second part of the novel. Through it he learns that although Alissa was passionately in love with him, the puritanical religion to which she devoted her life would not allow her to express her feelings. Instead, she devotes herself to God, seeing in her actions a sacrifice for Jerome as well, for it is a means by which they can both follow the path of righteousness to which the title alludes.

Although Alissa's sacrifice is described as heartfelt, Gide also reveals how her efforts betray a distorted view of life. As he had in so many of his works, Gide here contrasts the liberating life of sensual and instinctive exploration to the self-renunciation and puritanical repression represented by Alissa. The work is praised for its narrative structure, which allows Gide to reveal the true nature of Alissa's refusal and sacrifice after Jerome has related his vision of their relationship, thereby only enhancing his recurrent themes of perception and self-deceit.

Lafcadio's Adventures (novel, 1914)

The premise of the novel is taken from an outrageous rumor that circulated in nineteenth-century France in which the Pope was purportedly kidnapped by Freemasons and held captive beneath the Vatican, making the current Pope an imposter. Posing as defenders of the faith, a group of unscrupulous confidence men conspired to take advantage of the situation, collecting money from unsuspecting Catholics for their plot to free the Pope. Gide takes this idea for the plot of a novel he called a "sotie," a work of satire in which events and characters are noted for their exagerrated, grotesque proportions. While enroute to Rome, **Lafcadio,** the novel's principal character, meets one of the hapless victims of the scheme, the foolish **Amedee Fleurissoire,** who has become involved in the plot to free the Pope. Lafcadio, the son of a courtesan, is unconventional, handsome, clever, and opportunistic; he is also recently heir to a fortune, having been recognized by his natural father at the time of his death. But most importantly, Lafcadio is the character who demonstrates one of Gide's most famous concepts, that of "gratuitous action." He is a man unfettered by the social constrictions that dictate most lives, and without allegiances to family, country, or morality. Thus, while travelling to Rome, he muses about throwing his companion Fleurissoire from the train. Such an action, committed without forethought, is, according to the concept of gratuitous action, free of the laws that presume to judge human begavior. He throws Fleurissoire to his death; the action has no further consequences. Instead, **Protos,** a con man who witnesses the murder, tries to blackmail Lafcadio and is himself arrested for the crime. In the conclusion, Lafcadio, his life still unrestricted, has taken the lovely **Genevieve** for his mistress, and, fearing yet another form of restraint, has his eye on the open window.

As suits the genre of farce, the characters are rather one-dimensional and the narrative often reads as a parody of the adventure novel. In its exuberant style and fast pace, the work is in vivid contrast to the controlled, lyrical quality that characterized Gide's earlier fictions; yet its concerns with personal freedom and its contempt for the restrictions and conventions of societal mores link it to all of Gide's work.

The Counterfeiters (novel, 1927)

In this novel, which is considered Gide's most ambitious work and his masterpiece, the author tried to capture the multifaceted nature of reality and to present a culmination of his thematic concerns. Gide's central character in this work, **Edouard,** is a novelist himself, and while the novel is taking place, Edouard is also writing a novel entitled *The Counterfeiters* and keeping a journal about his progress. Thus Gide explores the nature of novel writing and the function of the artist in this work, exploring the way in which reality is related to individual perception and the artist's rendering. Gide's central theme here is the concept of counterfeiting, or how each individual is involved in fabricating an artificial or counterfeit self, focusing in particular on the difficulties of living a life of authenticity. In the novel, a group of Parisian schoolboys is involved in the passing of counterfeit money, and that money serves as a motif for the way in which the characters falsify themselves and present counterfeit personalities in life.

Stylistically, Gide attempted to replicate the fragmented, multivalent nature of existence through incorporating several plots and stories at once in his narrative. We hear only snatches of a conversation, several stories are told simultaneously, and not all stories are told in their entirety. This method was confusing to some readers, and yet Gide was attempting to duplicate the flow of life and to reveal it in all its complexity, not to make a "well-made" novel in the nineteenth-century tradition. He offers Edouard as a unifying element in the work, for it is he who provides the thread between the diverse characters and who analyzes and observes them for us. Gide incorporated several types of narration in the work, including dramatic dialogue, third-person narrative, letters, and diary entries, sometimes offering several interpretations of one event through the eyes of different characters, and lending the work a fugal, contrapuntal quality.

FURTHER READING

Bettinson, Christopher. *Gide: A Study*. London: Rowman and Littlefield, 1977.

Brée, Germaine. *Gide*. New Brunswick: Rutgers University Press, 1963.

Ciholas, Karin Nordenhaug. *Gide's Art of the Fugue: A Thematic Study of "Les Faux-Monnayeurs."* Chapel Hill: U.N.C. Department of Romance Languages, 1974.

Contemporary Authors, Vol. 104. Detroit: Gale Research Co.

Davies, J.C. *Gide: "L'immoraliste" and "La porte étroite."* London: Edward Arnold, 1968.

Dictionary of Literary Biography, Vol. 65. Detroit: Gale Research Co.

Fowlie, Wallace. *André Gide: His Life and Art*. New York: Macmillan, 1965.

Holdheim, William W. "Gide's 'Caves du Vatican' and the Illusionism of the Novel." *MLN* 77, No. 3 (May 1962): 292-304.

Ireland, G.W. *André Gide: A Study of His Creative Writings*. London: Oxford at the Clarendon Press, 1970.

Kazin, Alfred. "The Journal Keeper." In *The Inmost Leaf: A Selection of Essays,* pp. 149-54. New York: Harcourt Brace Jovanovich, 1955.

O'Brien, Justin. "Gide's Fictional Technique." In *The French Literary Horizon,* pp. 91-102. New Brunswick: Rutgers University Press, 1967.

Peyre, Henri. "The Legacy of Proust and Gide." In *The Contemporary French Novel,* pp. 67-100. New York: Oxford University Press, 1955.

Starkie, Enid. *André Gide*. London: Bowes & Bowes, 1953.

Stock, Irvin. "A View of 'Les Faux Monnayeurs.'" *Yale French Studies* 7 (1951): 72-80.

Twentieth-Century Literary Criticism, Vols. 5, 12. Detroit: Gale Research Co.

Jean Giraudoux
1882-1944
French dramatist, novelist, and essayist.

Tiger at the Gates (drama, 1935)

This play is set in Troy just prior to the Trojan War. Several major characters of Greek myth are represented in the work, as Giraudoux examines the reasons behind man's love for war. As the play opens, **Cassandra,** gifted with foresight but condemned never to be believed, is telling **Andromache, Hector**'s wife, of the inevitability of war. She likens destiny to a "tiger at the gates," who waits for the opportunity to drive the men from their homes into the battlefields. **Paris,** Hector's brother, has abducted **Helen,** the beautiful wife of the Greek Menelaus, and **Ulysses,** as Greek ambassador to Troy, has come to the court of **Priam** to negotiate peace or to declare war. Hector, having just returned from battle, greets his wife with the promise that there will be no war, and the play follows his efforts to avert the coming debacle. But he is thwarted at every turn, as the folly and tragedy of man's belief in war are revealed. His father, Priam, and all the men of Troy seem as beguiled by Helen's beauty as they do by their love of war. Hector argues with his father and his council, who insist that the gods will be offended if there is no war. Priam also notes how war makes men brave and causes women to love them. Hector's countrymen, on the shores of Troy, see the Greek ships assembled and demand that they attack their enemy. Hector, desperate to preserve the peace, tries to convince Helen to return to her husband, but she is a vain and cynical character, devoted to her own pleasure. Yet she is also described by Ulysses as one of "the rare creatures destiny puts on earth for its own personal use."

In the play's concluding scene, Hector and Ulysses debate the issue, Hector arguing for the "joy of life, belief in life," Ulysses for the "pleasure of living, mistrust for life." Hector comes to realize that it is out of their hands, that the fates have decreed there will be war.

Tiger at the Gates, written between the two world wars, has a tragic, pessimistic tone and reflects Giraudoux's belief that war is an unrelenting force within humankind. Hector tries valiantly to prevent the inevitable, but is doomed to fail, for men's love for war will predominate.

The Madwoman of Chaillot (drama, 1945)

Set in Paris, this play has a fantastic, fairy-tale quality, characterized by clarity, simplicity, and charm of tone and message. As the drama begins, we are in the cafe Chez Francis, and we are introduced to the forces of greed: **The President, the Baron, the Broker,** and **the Prospector,** who are juxtaposed to the forces of good: **The Ragpicker, Irma,** the **Flower Girl** and the **Countess Aurelia,** called the **Madwoman of Chaillot,** who represent the community of positive influences. The President, offended by this ragged collection of humanity, wants order and discipline, envisioning "a standardized worker with inter-changeable parts," not the group that has interrupted his business dealings. The Madwom-an appears, collecting bones and leftovers to feed the stray animals of Paris. We learn that she has a mission: to search out the "evil ones"—"those who hate people, those who hate plants, those who hate animals"—and to destroy them. She learns that the Prospector and his group plan to drill for oil beneath the streets of Paris. She and her friends join forces to fight the evil ones, whom they try and convict in absentia, with the Ragpicker playing a variety of roles. The guilty are lured to the Countess's home and led into the sewers of Paris, from which they will never return; as they enter, the "good" men of Paris—those devoted to the preservation of the natural beauty of the world—are released. With humanity saved, the Countess goes about her business, saying that "nothing is ever so wrong in this world that a sensible woman can't set it right in the course of an afternoon."

This satirical comedy is praised for its exuberant, fanciful, compassionate spirit and is Giraudoux's most popular play. The dramatist employs the illusion of improvisation in the play in such scenes as the antagonists' plan to exploit the city and the trial of the evil ones, adding a spontaneity and lightness to the work.

FURTHER READING

Bree, Germaine. "*The Madwoman of Chaillot:* A Modern Masque." *The Tulane Drama Review* (May 1959): 51-6.

Chiari, Joseph. "Jean Giraudoux." In *The Contemporary French Theatre: The Flight from Naturalism,* pp. 113-40. London: Rockliff Publishing, 1958.

Cohen, Robert. *Giraudoux: Three Faces of Destiny.* Chicago: University of Chicago Press, 1968.

Contemporary Authors, Vol. 104. Detroit: Gale Research Co.

Dictionary of Literary Biography, Vol. 65. Detroit: Gale Research Co.

Falk, Eugene H. "Theme and Motif in *La Guerre de Troie n' aura pas lieu.*" *Tulane Drama Review* 3, No. 4 (May 1959): 17-30.

Ganz, Arthur. "Human and Suprahuman: Ambiguity in the Tragic World of Jean Giraudoux." *PMLA* 87 (March 1972): 284-94.

Twentieth-Century Literary Criticism, Vols. 2, 7. Detroit: Gale Research Co.

Valency, Maurice. "Giraudoux." In *The End of the World: An Introduction to Contemporary Drama,* pp. 206-309. Oxford: Oxford University Press, 1980.

William Golding
1911-
English novelist, short story writer, and essayist.

Lord of the Flies (novel, 1954)

This famous novel relates the story of a group of British school boys abandoned on a desert island during a global war. They are alone on the island, the only two adults having been killed when the plane carrying them crashed. They form a sort of government, with **Ralph** the appointed leader and the keeper of the fire. He is assisted by **Piggy,** an intelligent and myopic young boy, and by **Simon,** a youth of uncanny insight and sensitivity. **Jack** heads the hunting party. Golding's work is a parable about the inherent evil in human nature, reflected in the natural brutality of these children. Thus we see the boys become increasingly savage, as Jack and his band track down and murder other boys and worship a pig's head, the symbol of their created god, which they call "The Beast." This is the "Lord of the Flies" of the title, referring to Beelzebub, whose evil forces we see at work in the boys. In a pivotal scene, Simon, who had refused to believe in the Beast and its power, is overcome with fear when he believes it speaks to him, saying: "you and the Beast are one." This message is reinforced when a dead parachutist, a victim of the war that rages outside of their isolated island, lands, and they mistake it for a wild beast that they fear roams the island. Thus they confront the beast incarnate in humankind and the fearful message that evil and savagery is the lot of humanity. During the course of the novel both Simon and Piggy are killed, and Ralph is being pursued when a naval officer appears to rescue them, recalling the boys to the world of adulthood and war, where the savagery they had known so intimately reigns.

Golding's novel is an exploration of the nature of good and evil and an examination of innocence. Literary references play a major role in his works, and in this narrative the Victorian novel *The Coral Island* by Ballantyne, which depicts a group of boys marooned on an island and illuminates their natural goodness and honesty, proves to be an ironic point of departure. It is alluded to by the naval officer as he comes to rescue the boys and indicates his lack of understanding of the true nature of the scene he has come upon. Noted for its parabolic intent and lauded for its incisive, realistic prose, *Lord of the Flies* has become a modern classic.

The Inheritors (novel, 1955)

Set at the time of the dawn of humankind, the novel recounts the life of the last truly "primitive" being, a Neanderthal named **Lok,** and his encounter with the first "civilized" man, **Tuami,** a Homo sapiens. As in so many of his novels, Golding here chronicles humanity's fall from grace, depicted in the confrontation of Lok's and Tuami's people. The novel is divided into twelve chapters. The first ten are given from Lok's point of view. He and his people possess a kind of natural innocence and goodness, qualities that appear to be in descendence as Neanderthals give way to the first acknowledged precursors of modern humans. Lok interprets the emerging species for us, confused and overwhelmed by the brutality and savagery that characterize the Homo sapiens. He recreates reality in images, providing a provocative perspective. In Chapter Eleven, Tuami takes over the narrative. Lok is now referred to as an "it" and is described as an animal as perceived by Tuami and his group. Chapter Twelve focuses on Tuami's tribe as the "inheritors," their species triumphant over the Neanderthals.

Just as he treated Ballantyne's *The Coral Sea* with irony in *Lord of the Flies,* Golding here satirizes the view of Neanderthals as seen in H.G. Wells's *Outline of History.* Wells had characterized Neanderthals as brutal and primitive and praised Homo sapiens as a true step forward in the development of humankind, a thesis that Golding mocks in his treatment of the confrontation between the old and the new order of humanity.

Pincher Martin (novel, 1956)

As the novel opens, we see **Christopher Martin,** called "Pincher," marooned on a small island in the North Atlantic after his destroyer is torpedoed during World War II. The novel chronicles his agonizing yet heroic fight to survive, rendered as a monologue of his suffering. He struggles against the elements for seven days, his agony broken with flashbacks to his past life. He is described as a Promethean figure, but one also capable of evil. He is a selfish man, as his past life evidences, obsessed with subjecting others to his will. The "Pincher" in his name indicates that he is a thief, and the reader's feelings for the character vacillate between pity for his physical agony as well respect for his indomitable spirit, and repulsion for his self-centeredness and greed. The novel's conclusion casts an ambiguity on what we have witnessed, for the final pages indicate that Martin had died at the beginning of the narrative, and that what we have seen is his struggle with his conscience in the afterlife. Martin's heroic struggle with God, then, is his fight not to give up the known, corporal life for the unknown terrors of eternity.

The work abounds in literary allusions to Shakespeare, Milton, T. S. Eliot, and others, and critics have noted the influence of Shakespeare's language on the novel's imagery. The work is praised as a tour de force, reflecting once again Golding's treatment of his subjects for their allegorical and mythic effect.

Rites of Passage (novel, 1980)

The novel employs the motif of the journey and follows the voyage of **Edmund Talbot** from England to Australia in the early nineteenth century. He and his fellow emigrants form a microcosm of rigidly structured British society of that time, reinforced by the white line on the ship's deck that separates the "gentlemen" from the commoners aboard. Golding makes use of the literary device of the diary, and what we read is Talbot's journal, which he writes, he tells us, to amuse his godfather, the patron of his journey. As the novel begins, Talbot appears to be an aristocratic snob, evident in his views of his fellow travelers. Golding makes clear that Talbot's vision is flawed by his limitations, especially his priggishness, yet we note that as the novel progresses, his understanding deepens. This becomes particularly evident in his description of an incident involving the **Reverend Mr. Colley,** who is persecuted and humiliated by the brutal and tyrannical **Captain Anderson** and culminates in Colley's suicide. It is through Colley's letter to his sister, which later falls into Talbot's hands, that we perceive the true nature of his humiliation and Talbot's flawed perception: Colley, when drunk, had engaged in a homosexual encounter with a sailor, which Anderson had discovered and exploited and which led to Colley's public disgrace and death.

Golding probes the nature of good and evil and the problems of individual perception in this work. Colley, on the surface a man of goodness and idealism, is drawn to the darker forces within him, but cannot survive their revelation. His letter imparts to Talbot how inaccurate and flawed his vision had been and forces him to acknowledge his own culpability in Colley's death.

Stylistically, Golding utilizes and parodies the style and substance of two time-honored literary devices, the diary and the letter, in a novel that is considered his first in years to rank with his earlier masterpieces.

FURTHER READING

Babb, Howard S. *The Novels of William Golding*. Columbus: Ohio State University Press, 1970.

Baker, James R. *William Golding: A Critical Study*. New York: St. Martin's, 1965.

Biles, Jack I. and Carl R. Kropf. "The Cleft Rock of Conversion: *Robinson Crusoe* and *Pincher Martin*." *A William Golding Miscellany: Studies in the Literary Imagination* 2 (October 1969): 17-43.

Biles, Jack I. and Robert O. Evans, eds. *William Golding: Some Critical Considerations*. Lexington: University Press of Kentucky, 1979.

Contemporary Authors, Vols. 5-8, rev. ed.; *Contemporary Authors New Revision Series,* Vol. 13. Detroit: Gale Research Co.

Contemporary Literary Criticism, Vols. 1, 2, 3, 8, 10, 17, 27. Detroit: Gale Research Co.

Dick, Bernard F. *William Golding*. New York: Twayne, 1967.

Dictionary of Literary Biography, Vol. 15. Detroit: Gale Research Co.

Green, Peter. "The World of William Golding." *Review of English Literature* 1, No. 2 (1960): 62-72.

Hynes, Samuel. *William Golding*. New York: Columbia University Press, 1964.

Johnston, Arnold. *Of Earth and Darkness: The Novels of William Golding*. Columbia: University of Missouri Press, 1980.

Kermode, Frank. "Coral Islands." *Spectator* 201 (22 August 1958): 257.

——. "The Novels of William Golding." *International Literary Annual* 3 (1961): 11-29.

Niemeyer, Carl. "The Coral Island Revisited." *College English* 22 (1960): 241-45.

Oldsey, Bernard S. and Stanley Weintraub. "*Lord of the Flies:* Beelzebub Revisited." *College English* 25 (November 1963): 90-99.

Pritchett, V. S. "Secret Parables." *New Statesman* 61 (2 August 1958): 146-47.

Tiger, Virginia. *William Golding: The Dark Fields of Discovery*. London: Calder & Boyars, 1974.

Nadine Gordimer
1923-
South African novelist and short story writer.

A Guest of Honor (novel, 1970)

This novel, considered by many critics to be Gordimer's finest work, is set in an African nation shortly after independence. The protagoinst, **Colonel James Bray**, is a white African and one of the country's former District Commisoners who had been banished ten years earlier for taking part in revolutionary activites. As the novel opens, Bray has returned to the new nation as the "guest" of the title, and is feted by his hosts in a gala round of parties and receptions. He meets with several of his old friends and political allies, many of whom are now highly placed officials in the new regime, including **President Mweta,** who offers him a post in the education ministry. The country has changed, and the trappings of the modern industrial world are evident in the new factories and advertising billboards that have risen in the city.

He travels to his old village, Gala, and revels in the bucolic, slow-paced atmosphere. Here he meets with **Edward Shinza,** an old friend and hero of the revolution, now a labor organizer and seemingly forgotten by the new government. He learns that Mweta considers Shinza a threat, for he is head of a rival political faction. Shinza in turn considers Mweta a traitor to the ideals of the revolution and chides Bray for his complacency and for his suspected complicity with Mweta. Yet Bray has an ominous feeling about the true state of affairs. He had picked up a hitchhiker on his way to visit Shinza, a man who had been tortured for his political affiliations with Shinza by Mweta's men. When Bray brings the matter up with Mweta he learns that the president views Shinza as a radical malcontent; Mweta also makes it clear that he expects Bray to keep him aware of Shinza's activities, to act, in effect, as an informer. Bray must at last acknowledge that Mweta and his government are motivated by the same system of greed, corruption, and deceit that characterized the white colonial rulers.

Shinza's efforts as a union organzier continue, and he at last admits to Bray that he is plotting to take control of the government. Labor strikes are taking place all over the country, and Mweta's men enter Gala, burning buildings and beating the villagers. As Bray tries to leave, he is clubbed to death by a group of laborers who mistake him for a mercenary leader.

The novel is noted for its insightful handling of complex political issues. Critics have focused on how, through Bray, Gordimer reveals the horror and disillusionment felt by many supporters of independence for African nations when a black regime reveals the same selfishness, corruption, and inhumanity toward its people as the former white governtment. Gordimer's prose reveals her fine eye for the detail of speech and gesture that make her characters so believable.

FURTHER READING

Contemporary Authors, Vols. 5-8, rev. ed. *Contemporary Authors New Revision Series,*
   Vol. 3. Detroit: Gale Research Co.

Contemporary Literary Criticism, Vols. 3, 5, 7, 10, 18, 33, 51. Detroit: Gale Research Co.

Hope, Christopher. "Out of the Picture: The Novels of Nadine Gordimer." *London Magazine* (April/May 1975): 49-55.

May, Derwent. "*A Guest of Honor.*" *Encounter* (August 1971): 66-7.

"Scenes from African Life." *Times Literary Supplement* (14 May 1979): 555.

Maxim Gorky
1868-1936
Russian novelist, dramatist, and autobiographer.

The Lower Depths (drama, 1902)

Set in late nineteenth-century Russia, the play depicts life in the boardinghouse of **Mikhail Kostilyoff,** a man possessed by greed and scornful of the impoverished, hopeless denizens who live in his run-down hovel. His wife, **Vassilisa Karpovna,** is a cruel woman who has an affair with **Vaska Pepel** and plots with him to murder her husband. Kostilyoff's sister, **Natasha,** is a kindly, good young woman subjected to inhuman cruelty and beatings by her sister-in-law. She is drawn to Pepel and his promise of a better life for the two of them, but she hesitates to commit herself. Pepel strikes and kills Kostilyoff during an argument over Vassilisa's treatment of Natasha; when she learns that Pepel is implicated in her brother's death, Natasha has a breakdown.

The vivid drama of the Kostilyoff family is enacted against the backdrop of the colorless, depressing lives of the poor folk who inhabit the flophouse, victims of society's brutality and their own despair. They include drunks, card sharks, and prostitutes, the outcasts of society without hope or future. All of these characters are attracted to **Luka,** a wanderer who comes into their lives, listens to their tales of woe, dispenses advice and compassion, and disappears. He is a central consciousness in the novel, the outsider who embodies the wisdom and hope denied these lonely people. He is also a catalyst to their thoughts on the meaning of life and to action to regain their dignity and vigor. The authorities, in the person of Vassilisa's uncle **Abram Miedviedieff,** threaten Luka, who is travelling without a passport, and he takes his leave of the people of the ''lower depths.''

Thematically, the work reveals a division of humanity into those drawn to a life of illusion and those who view the poverty and disillusionment around them realistically and hope to better themselves and escape their lot. It is considered a parabolic piece, and the characters, portrayed with romantic exaggeration, are more symbolic than fully realized personages. Noted for its compassionate view of humanity, *The Lower Depths* is considered Gorky's finest play, despite the didacticism that, for some critics, mars his vision of the ''dregs of society.''

Mother (novel, 1907)

This novel, set in a small town in Russia in the early twentieth century, is Gorky's most famous work. Based on the political unrest in the Russian city of Sormovo in 1902, the novel relates the story of **Pelageia Vlasova,** the ''mother'' of the title, and her political coming of age. As the novel opens, we see her husband, **Mikhail,** as a victim of the brutalizing effects of a life devoted to factory labor, an existence that leads him to drink and self-destruction. He dies, and the novel focuses on Pelageia's hopes for her son, **Pavel Vlasov,** whose love for reading sets him apart from his fellow factory workers. He is a young man drawn to the insurrectionist politics that would eventually lead Russia to the revolution that liberated her people from czarist rule. Gorky's novel is a polemical protest against the brutality and insensitivity of the ruling class and a tribute to the common people and the purity of their commitment to the goals of the revolution. Through her association with Pavel and his friends, Pelageia becomes involved in the movement and devotes her life to the cause. Pavel is arrested, tried, and imprisoned for his activities. In the conclusion, Pelageia is beaten and arrested by the czarist police as she hands out pamphlets, as both mother and son become martyrs to the cause of revolution.

Although *Mother* is considered flawed by its didactic content, it was enormously influential in Russia in the early years of the twentieth century. Critics today acknowledge that the characterization is romanticized and that the idealized portraits of the revolutionaries are unconvincing. The work is dominated by dialogue, which gives the characters the necessary platform for their revolutionary passion, rendered in a rather strained, excessive rhetorical style. In Pelageia and her son, Gorky was able to personify the conversion of the simple, uneducated peasant and to champion the heroism and sacrifice of the emerging proletariat, and for this the novel is remembered.

FURTHER READING

Contemporary Authors, Vol. 105. Detroit: Gale Research Co.

Mathewson, Rufus W., Jr. "Lenin and Gorky: The Turning Point." In *The Positive Hero in Russian Literature,* pp. 156-76. Palo Alto: Stanford University Press, 1975.

Mirsky, D.S. "Gorky." In *Contemporary Russian Literature: 1881-1925,* pp. 106-20. New York: Knopf, 1926.

Muchnic, Helen. "Circe's Swine: Plays by Gorky and O'Neill." *Comparative Literature* 3, No. 2 (Spring 1951): 99-109.

Slonim, Marc. "Gorky." In *Modern Russian Literature: From Chekhov to the Present,* pp. 125-52. New York: Oxford University Press, 1953.

Twentieth-Century Literary Criticism, Vol. 8. Detroit: Gale Research Co.

Weil, Irwin. *Gorky: His Intellectual Development and Influence on Soviet Intellectual Life.* New York: Random House, 1966.

Yarmolinsky, Avrahm. "Maxim Gorky: Soviet Laureate." In *The Russian Literary Imagination,* pp. 111-29. New York: Funk & Wagnalls, 1969.

Günter Grass
1927-

German novelist, poet, and essayist.

"The Danzig Trilogy": *The Tin Drum* (novel, 1959); *Cat and Mouse* (novella, 1961); *Dog Years* (novel, 1963)

The Tin Drum is set primarily in Danzig and covers the years before, during, and after World War II. It begins in a mental hospital for the criminally insane, where **Oskar Matzerath** is an inmate and where he relates the story of his life, acting as first-person narrator as he tells his tale to his nurse, **Bruno Münsterberg.**

Oskar acts as a mirror of the times, reflecting the moral and physical degeneration of Germany under Hitler. Like Hitler, Oskar is a myth-maker who sees himself as a "savior" of the people and who is devoted to self-promotion. He is a megalomaniacal character, convinced of his predestined greatness and seeing in his rather squalid origins an illustrious ancestry. His grandfather was a fanatical arsonist, and his mother, **Agnes Matzerath,** has an active sexual relationship with her cousin, **Jan Bronski,** who is probably Oskar's true father. When he is three, Oskar throws himself down a flight of stairs so that he will remain small, and his stunted growth and grotesque form represent the effects of Nazism on a generation of German children. After his fall, he learns that he can shatter glass when he screams, accompanying himself on his toy drum. He uses this ability to break shop windows and to steal, also encouraging others to vandalism, paralleling the destruction of the homes and businesses of the innocent by the Nazis. Oskar, as the eyes and consciousness of a warped nation, is a witness to key events in the war. He is present as the Germans invade

Poland, and through a false display of outrage and innocence, brings about the death of Jan, an action that corresponds to the false innocence many Germans claimed regarding the true nature and activities of the Third Reich. Oskar joins a troupe of travelling dwarves under the direction of **Master Bebra,** who is working for Goebbels. He entertains the troops by shattering glass, and later, in Paris, destroys priceless glass objects, a parallel to the barbarism of the Nazis. Oskar's father, **Alfred Matzerath,** a loyal Nazi, dies while choking on his party pin as the Russians march into Germany, a death in which Oskar is also implicated.

In the postwar era, opportunistic Nazis now call themselves Social Democrats to evade the past. But the present is tainted with the sins and horrors of the war years. Oskar makes his living variously as a dealer in black market goods, a stone cutter, and as a model for an art academy, where he sits for a sculpture of a Madonna and Child, reflecting both his messianic impulses and the moral turpitude of postwar Germany. He murders a young nurse, an act he later vehemently denies, paralleling the postwar German consciousness which preferred to forget and to bury the past. As the novel ends, Oskar is thirty, still sees himself as a Christ-figure, and is about to be released from the mental hospital. But he fears the specter of the Black Witch, a figure of ominous evil that has haunted him since childhood. He sees this shape, previously a part of his past, coming at him from out of the future, an ominous ending indicating the omnipresence of evil.

The novel is considered a modern masterpiece. The story contains elements intended to shock the reader, with scatological and obscene images and descriptions that Grass uses to emphasize the perversion of the world under the Nazis. *The Tin Drum* is the first part of what is called Grass's "Danzig Trilogy," and Oskar and other characters reappear in the later novels, as Grass continues his exploration of the consciousness of modern Germany.

Like the other volumes of the trilogy, *Cat and Mouse* is set in Danzig during World War II. As in *The Tin Drum,* the events of the life of **Joachim Mahlke,** the protagonist, parallel political events in the history of Germany. The work is narrated by **Heini Pilenz,** a young man who is fascinated with Mahlke and describes him from a point of view of uncomprehending wonder. Pilenz sees in Mahlke's parentage, appearance, and behavior evidence of his divinity. Mahlke is a young man whose huge Adam's apple is the "mouse" of the title. This symbolizes both his inherent innocence, and like Adam, his knowledge of life. He is ashamed of his Adam's apple and tries to hide it throughout his youth. As a young man, Mahlke had been weak and unathletic, yet in 1939, simultaneously with the German state, Mahlke began to gain strength. He yearns to possess a Knight's cross, both a symbol of prowess and potency and a means for Mahlke to hide his grotesque Adam's apple. As a tank gunner, Mahlke believes the Holy Virgin guides him, and the imagery connecting his large Adam's apple, his penis, and his gun is obvious in its satiric intent. Suffering from battle fatigue, Mahlke deserts. Desperate for his Messiah, Pilenz makes sure that Mahlke, hiding in an abandoned minesweeper, cannot escape, and Mahlke drowns, but is unable to "resurrect" as Pilenz had planned. After the war, Pilenz continues to look for Mahlke, ostensibly believing in his Christ-figure, but also needing absolution for his complicity in the death of his savior.

As in *The Tin Drum,* Grass deals here with his recurrent theme of the perversion of Germany under the Nazis, examining the complicity of a people who demanded a "savior," presumed that physical prowess gave their aim of world conquest credence, and whose postwar guilt cannot be denied or absolved.

In *Dog Years,* the final volume of his Danzig trilogy, Grass continues his exploration of the meaning and legacy of the Third Reich, focussing on how the past must be understood, how it informs the future, and, in the character of **Eduard Amsel,** examining the role of the artist as seer and creator. The novel is divided into three books, each with a separate narrator.

The novel is a dense and complex work, incorporating elements of myth, legend, history, politics, fantasy, and the grotesque, and the reader only gradually becomes aware of the nature of the narrative structure. Amsel is a character of many aliases, including **Herr Brauxel** (spelled variously throughout the novel), who is the narrator of the first portion of the novel. As Brauxel, he is the owner of a potash mine and hires **Harry Liebenau,** the narrator of the second section of the novel, and **Walter Matern,** the third narrator, to write what is essentially his story. As a youth, Amsel is depicted as an artistic, intelligent type. He is half-Jewish, which marks him as a victim both literally and symbolically; his father, ashamed of his Jewishness, was killed at Verdun in World War I as he fought for the Germans, trying to erase his racial past.

As a boy, Amsel befriends Walter Matern, a young man of uncontrollable emotions and physicality, and the two form a blood brotherhood which Matern breaks whenever it is convenient to him. Amsel becomes a sculptor, using scrap he finds in the Vistula river. The Vistula functions as a symbol for time in the novel, carrying within it the remains of the past, the flotsam of history. Amsel sculpts scarecrows, which the farmers find useful. He creates legendary figures, drawn from myth and history, including a giant bird that is meant to be a scarecrow, but that turns out to be an object of fear for the people. He is forced to burn it, along with all his scraps. During the burning, Amsel has a vision in which he witnesses the coming destruction of the Nazis. Later he sculpts Nazi soldiers with pig bladders for heads and dressed in Nazi uniforms. For this, a group of Nazi thugs, led by Matern, beat Amsel, knocking out all of his teeth. He flees to Berlin, where he becomes a ballet producer and presents his work, "The Scarecrows," a visionary tale of modern Germany.

As the title would indicate, dogs are prominent in the novel. Matern's dog has a legendary ancestry, for he is descended from a she-wolf. As the dogs breed, they provide links between the various characters, including Hitler's favorite dog, Prinz, pictured as a creature of perfect evil. After Hitler loses the war, Prinz flees his master, preferring instead to pursue Matern and becoming a hound of hell. Matern, in turn a Nazi, a communist, and an antifascist, wanders Germany after the war, full of vengeance. Amsel, who has kept track of his former blood brother and persecutor, manipulates the character through his various disguises, forcing him to confront the guilt of his past. The novel concludes in Brauxel's potash mine, which has become the site of Amsel's scarecrow collection. The two descend into the cave where Matern witnesses Amsel's representation of the cruelty, barbarity, and vengefulness of men. They emerge from underground and bathe, but whether Matern is at last "cleansed" by the experience remains uncertain.

The novel focusses on the artist's responsibility to tell the truth, no matter how shocking or abhorrent. This is considered one of Grass's most polemical early works and is admired for its broad canvas, satiric insight, and vivid portrait of the German conscience.

FURTHER READING

Bruce, James C. "The Equivocating Narrator in Günter Grass's *Katz und Maus.*" *Monatshefte* 58 (1966): 139-49.

Contemporary Authors, Vols. 13-16, rev. ed.; *Contemporary Authors New Revision Series,* Vol. 20. Detroit: Gale Research Co.

Contemporary Literary Criticism, Vols. 1, 2, 4, 6, 11, 15, 22, 32, 49. Detroit: Gale Research Co.

Friedrichsmeyer, Erhard M. "Aspects of Myth, Parody and Obscenity in Günter Grass's *Die Blechtrommel* and *Katz und Maus.*" *Germanic Review* 40 (1965): 240-47.

Hatfield, Henry. "Günter Grass: The Artist as Satirist." In *The Contemporary Novel in German: A Symposium,* Robert R. Heitner, ed. Austin: University of Texas Press, 1967.

Hollington, Michael. *Günter Grass: The Writer in a Pluralist Society.* New York: Marion Boyars, 1980.

Lawson, Richard H. *Günter Grass.* New York: Ungar, 1985.

Miles, Keith. *Günter Grass.* New York: Barnes & Noble, 1975.

Ruhleder, Karl H. "A Pattern of Messianic Thought in Günter Grass's *Katz und Maus.*" *German Quarterly* 39 (1966): 599-612.

Schow, H. Wayne. "Functional Complexity of Grass's Oskar." *Critique: Studies in Modern Fiction* 19, No. 3 (1978): 5-20.

Stern, J. P. "Günter Grass's Uniqueness." *London Review of Books* (5-18 February 1981): 11-14.

Robert Graves

1895-1985

English poet, novelist, critic, and essayist.

I, Claudius (novel, 1934)

In this historical novel, Graves brilliantly recreated the era of Roman decadence under the reigns of **Augustus Caesar, Tiberius,** and **Caligula,** covering the years 10 B.C. to 41 A.D. This notorious era is seen through the eyes of **Tiberius Claudius Drusus Nero Germanicus,** called **Claudius,** the lame, stuttering son of a great Roman warrior, who, because of his physical deformity became a scholar of Roman history and who, in this semi-fictional adaptation of an infamous era in history, records the venality, unbridled lust, murder, and political treachery that was his familial legacy.

As a child, Claudius is scorned by the family, but as his knowledge and ability as a scholar grows, he catches the attention of his grandmother **Livia,** the wife of Augustus and a woman of predatory evil. Claudius believes that she had his first love poisoned, and she masterminds his first marriage, to **Urgulanilla,** whom he loathes. Yet Livia and Augustus make Claudius a priest of Mars, enhancing his status in the family. The wicked Livia also plots her own husband's death, and Claudius is quite sure that she has had Augustus poisoned when he dies and is replaced by Tiberius.

Tiberius's reign is colored with a fanatical fear of losing authority; he has his perceived enemies murdered, including Claudius's brother **Germanicus,** his friend **Sejanus,** and Augustus's son **Postumus.** Before his death, Sejanus had arranged Claudius's marriage to his sister, **Aelia,** a union that is short-lived because Tiberius forces him to divorce her. Close to death, Livia calls Claudius to her, offering to reveal the secrets of her political intrigues in exchange for his pledge that he will have her declared an immortal; the pact is sealed. Tiberius then turns against Livia's followers, executing and banishing many. He is smothered to death by his successor, Caligula, a man of inhuman cruelty and perversity. He declares himself a god and begins a reign of terror, murder, and sexual depravity. His excesses lead to his downfall, and he is replaced by the unlikely Claudius, whose reign is chronicled in the sequel to *I, Claudius, Claudius the God.*

Claudius the God and His Wife Messalina (novel, 1934)

This second volume in the history of Rome at the time of **Tiberius Claudius Drusus Nero Germanicus,** called **Claudius,** focuses on his reign, which spans the years 41 to 54 A.D. Considered a lame, stuttering fool, Claudius is at first scorned by the Romans he would rule, for they believe him to be stupid. Yet he proves himself to be an able statesman, reforming financial policies, reorganizing the Senate, and restoring a belief in government through the eradication of many of Caligula's harsh laws. His wife, **Messalina,** whom Caligula forced him to marry, is made Director of Public Morals, a position that will prove grotesquely ironic. To his childhood friend, **Herod Agrippa,** he gives Judea, Samaria, and Edom. Yet Herod has plans of his own: he wants to declare himself the Jewish Messiah and take control of the lands. His plans are vanquished when an owl appears, a figure that had been foretold in prophecy as a sign of his impending death. He dies days later.

Claudius further establishes himself as an able ruler through his armies' victories in Germany and England, where the successful campaign at Bentwood Hill leads his subjects to declare him a god. Yet at home, Messalina has made their marriage a mockery: she has moved into a separate residence and has for years indulged in outrageous sexual escapades. Claudius learns the truth about his wife from **Calpurnia,** his long-time friend and former mistress, and the Emperor seeks vengeance, having Messalina, her lover **Silius** (with whom she had plotted to murder Claudius), and many of her other paramours killed.

Claudius's fourth wife is **Agrippinilla,** who with her chancellors is allowed to run the government, as Claudius retires from public life. Agrippinilla, skilled in the ways of treachery, has her husband poisoned, assuring the ascendancy of her own son, **Lucius Domitus,** later called **Nero.**

Graves's adaptation of this turbulent, infamous period of history was enormously popular, and the two novels remain his finest works of fiction. His view of Claudius was sympathetic, an iconoclastic appraisal of a man deemed a mad autocrat by previous historians. Graves stressed the contemporaneity of the classical figures, who, in their sexual excesses, greed, and lust for power were both appealing and credible to the modern audience. His style of narration is significant: all of the events are seen through the eyes of Claudius, whose understated manner of narration heightens the reader's sense of the horrific exploits of his family.

FURTHER READING

Canary, Robert H. *Robert Graves.* New York: Twayne, 1980.

Carey, John. "Goodbye to All That." *The Sunday Times* (8 December 1985): 10.

Contemporary Authors, Vols. 5-8, rev. ed.; *Contemporary Authors New Revision Series,* Vol. 5. Detroit: Gale Research Co.

Contemporary Literary Criticism, Vols. 1, 2, 6, 11, 39, 44, 45. Detroit: Gale Research Co.

Dictionary of Literary Biography, Vol. 20; *Dictionary of Literary Biography Yearbook: 1985.* Detroit: Gale Research Co.

Quennell, Peter. "Robert Graves." In *Casanova in London,* pp. 175-86. New York: Stein and Day, 1971.

Seymour-Smith, Martin. *Robert Graves.* London: Longman, 1965.

Snipes, Katherine. *Robert Graves.* New York: Ungar, 1979.

Stade, George. *Robert Graves.* New York: Columbia University Press, 1967.

Graham Greene

1904-

British novelist, dramatist, short story writer, and essayist.

The Power and the Glory (novel, 1940)

The novel is set in Mexico during the 1930s. The work is allegorical in form and content:

Greene seeks to illuminate the meaning of faith through his examination of the **Whiskey Priest** and his juxtaposition of this character with the **Lieutenant of Police.** The two remain unnamed throughout the novel, known only to the reader by the names of their vocations, heightening their allegorical significance. The priest is the representative of the old world order of a corrupt religion. The lieutenant is symbolic of the anticlerical government that is trying to rid the country of religion. The priest has been in hiding in a village for eight years, continuing to practice his faith and to perform services for his parish.

The priest is a complex figure, a man capable of good and evil. In addition to being a priest, he is also a drunk and an adulterer; he is a man of pride, refusing to plot his escape from the country to save himself, more out of indolence than a sense of purpose. His character is contrasted to that of the lieutenant, a man of strength and conviction who exhibits many of the qualities that the priest lacks. Their allegorical confrontation takes the shape of three major encounters during the course of the novel. In the first, the priest is celebrating the forbidden mass; in the second, he is jailed for drunkenness, an experience that acquaints him with the basest in humanity. He identifies and is liberated by the episode and is filled with pity, compassion and understanding. The third covers the priest's arrest, lured by a Judas figure to administer last rites to a dying gangster. Now the priest and the lieutenant argue their points of view, as Greene reveals how the two characters are equally committed to their goals, one to the new order and to the precepts of reason and human justice, the other to his Catholic faith and to his people. The priest goes willingly to his death, choosing his martyrdom, and embracing his faith and sainthood.

Stylistically, the work is noted for its parabolic effect and for Greene's handling of the allegorical framework. The novel is imbued with an atmosphere of death, rendered in description of characters and of landscape. *The Power and the Glory* is Greene's best-known work and is considered his finest literary effort.

The Heart of the Matter (novel, 1948)

Set in colonial West Africa during World War II, the novel recounts the life and death of **Henry Scobie,** elucidating his personal struggle with his Catholic faith and with God. He is a man whose life has been marked by failure. An honest, moral man who works at his government post performing mediocre work for mediocre wages, he is overlooked for promotion. His wife, **Louise,** for whom he feels pity but not love, wants more material comforts, and it is to appease her that he becomes involved with **Yusef,** a blackmarketer. He borrows money from him and later becomes the target of blackmail; to ward off his demands, Scobie begins to smuggle diamonds. **Helen Rolt,** a widow, enters his life after being discovered in a torpedoed boat, and they begin an affair. Yet their relationship, too, is marked more by pity than love. Scobie, once a man of honesty and deep Catholic faith, is now involved in an adulterous relationship, blackmail, and smuggling. He also finds out that he is being watched by his employer because of his closeness to Yusef. He knows he is causing pain to all who are close to him: to his wife, to Helen, and most of all to God. Overwhelmed by his sense of despair, he commits suicide.

The novel's ending has made it a controversial work, for Greene's central figure takes his life out of his love for God, but condemns himself and denies himself God through his final deed. As in *The Power and the Glory,* Greene employs the motifs of death and decay and develops his characters against the background of political conflict, heightening the drama of the religious crisis suffered by his protagonist.

The End of the Affair (novel, 1951)

Set in London during World War II, the novel relates the story of the affair between **Maurice Bendrix** and **Sarah Miles.** Maurice is a novelist who through research into a work on government service meets Sarah, the wife of a bureaucrat. The two begin an affair, which Sarah ends abruptly. The remainder of the novel takes place six years after the relationship had ended and recounts Maurice's search for her and his discovery of what happened. Although Maurice is the narrator, Greene also uses Sarah's diary to offer differing points of view. It is through this device that we learn about Sarah's decision. The last time Maurice and Sarah had been together, a bomb had ripped through the room as they were making love. Although Maurice was only injured, Sarah believed him to be dead, and she began to bargain with God to allow him to live. Maurice had believed that she had fallen in love with someone else, but it is in truth God whom she grows to love. After suffering great inner turmoil as she wrestles with her decision, Sarah dedicates herself to God. She dies in the conclusion, a sainted figure.

Greene develops his themes through the opposing viewpoints of his protagonists. Maurice's account of the affair focuses on its physical aspects, and his response to Sarah's religious conversion is incomprehension. Sarah, representing the spiritual aspects of life, is portrayed as she grows to greater self-awareness and inner peace. Other perspectives are offered by the detective that Maurice hires to follow Sarah, by Sarah's husband, and by a philosopher that Sarah seeks out to discuss her faith. This multiplicity of viewpoints offers a complex setting for Greene's drama of the individual struggling with the meaning of faith.

FURTHER READING

Contemporary Authors, Vols. 13-16, rev. ed. Detroit: Gale Research Co.

Contemporary Literary Criticism, Vols. 1, 3, 6, 9, 14, 18, 27, 37. Detroit: Gale Research Co.

DeVitis, A.A. *Graham Greene.* New York: Twayne, 1964.

Dictionary of Literary Biography, Vols. 13, 15; *Dictionary of Literary Biography Yearbook, 1985.* Detroit: Gale Research Co.

Hoggart, Richard. "The Force of Caricature: Aspects of the Art of Graham Greene, with Particular Reference to *The Power and the Glory.*" *Essays in Criticism* 3 (October 1953): 447-62.

Hynes, Samuel, ed. *Graham Greene: A Collection of Critical Essays.* Englewood Cliffs: Prentice-Hall, 1973.

Lewis, R. W. B. "The Trilogy." In *The Picaresque Saint: Representative Figures in Contemporary Fiction,* pp. 239-64. New York: Lippincott, 1959.

Lewis, R. W. B. and Peter J. Conn, eds. *The Power and the Glory: Text and Criticism.* New York: Viking, 1970.

O'Faolain, Sean. "Graham Greene: I Suffer; Therefore, I Am." In *The Vanishing Hero: Studies in Novelists of the Twenties,* pp. 73-97. London: Eyre & Spottiswoode, 1956.

Orwell, George. "The Sanctified Sinner." In *The Collected Essays, Journalism and Letters of George Orwell,* Sonia Orwell and Ian Angus, eds., pp. 439-43. New York: Harcourt, Brace & World, 1968.

Traversi, Derek. "Graham Greene." *Twentieth Century* 149 (1951): 231-40, 319-28.

Knut Hamsun

1859-1952

Norwegian novelist, essayist, and dramatist.

Hunger (novel, 1890)

This semi-autobiographical novel takes place in late nineteenth-century Christiania, now

Oslo, and details the thoughts of the unnamed narrator, a starving would-be writer. Driven by a demonic "hunger" to practice his craft in spite of the niggardly, sporadic fees he receives, the protagonist frequently undergoes periods of madness and isolation amidst an overwhelmingly indifferent society. Yet he never indulges in self-pity nor attempts to counteract the forces which contribute to his unhealthy existence. Curiously, the most persistent of these forces is his unconscious mind, which often urges him to impulsive, ridiculous behavior.

Demonstrating the cyclical nature of the narrator's life, the novel is divided into four sections. Each of these begins with the narrator describing his impoverished state and ends with him the recipient of a brief stroke of good fortune. At the novel's conclusion, the writer leaves Christiania—"that strange city no one escapes from until it has left its mark on him"—aboard a steamer bound for England. With growing lucidity, he realizes he has suffered purposefully and is now irrevocably changed; however, despite this seemingly hopeful note, the final tone of the narrative is pessimistic, for the writer remains by nature tragically flawed and will presumably succumb once again to alienation and despair.

Rather than a work of social protest, *Hunger* is instead a concentrated exploration of the inner life, of a creative psyche dominated by an obsessive spiritual hunger. Using an abrupt, impressionistic style, Hamsun depicts the world of the mind with nightmarish reality. The novel successfully embodies Hamsun's recurrent themes, including the distrust of the intellect, the rejection of society, and the need to escape from the city. The story's prevailing gloom reflects Hamsun's philosophic acceptance of hardship, struggle, and despair as unavoidable complements to joy. *Hunger* is an important early psychological novel that significantly influenced the direction of subsequent European fiction.

Growth of the Soil (novel, 1917)

Set in the wilds of rural nineteenth-century Norway, Hamsun's epic narrative begins with the solitary figure of **Isak Sellanraa,** a simple undistinguished man who has left his small village to pursue the dream of carving out a homestead in the distant North. When he finds a place suitable for farming—near a stream, woods, and a stretch of grassland—he stops and builds his sod house. Soon he realizes he needs a companion, a woman to help with the field work and daily chores. **Inger,** a homely woman who has heard of Isak's wish, ventures north with her belongings. She proves herself a good worker and Isak, himself less than handsome, overlooks her obtrusive harelip. Following the birth of their first child, **Eleseus,** the two are married; the next year another son, **Sivert** is born. When Inger gives birth to a third child, a daughter with the same disfigurement that she bears, Isak is away from home. Knowing that the girl will suffer as she herself had done, Inger strangles the newborn and buries the body in the woods.

Isak discovers what has happened, but withholds blame; the authorities, however, hear rumors and investigate. Inger stands trial and is sentenced to eight years in prison. **Oline,** an ingratiating relative of Inger's, stays at the farm to care for the children and assist Isak. However, she is selfish and manipulative and causes Isak to yearn for his imprisoned wife. As new settlers arrive, the landscape begins to change. Inger returns to Isak, but he discovers that the city has altered her, for she now finds farm life harsh and desolate. Following his success as a farmer, Isak becomes a store-owner and mining speculator, but when these businesses sour, he and Inger gratefully renew their ties to the soil, understanding that the land will always survive and bring new growth.

Written in a laconic, lyrical style reminiscent of the Old Testament, *Growth of the Soil* is Hamsun's most famous novel and earned him the Nobel Prize for Literature in 1920. Hamsun reduced life to its most elemental forms and portrayed it with a delicate sensitivity that is neither romantic nor dispassionate. Key to Hamsun's achievement is his creation of Isak. Isak, and to a lesser extent Inger, epitomizes the human ideal seen in Hamsun's later works: the pioneer-farmer, who through self-reliance and hard work builds a homestead out of the wilderness, working in harmony with nature rather than despoiling it. For its epic scope and universal themes of love and suffering, nature and humanity, and death and life, the novel has assumed a prominent position in twentieth-century literature.

FURTHER READING

Bly, Robert. "The Art of Hunger." In *Hunger* by Knut Hamsun, translated by Robert Bly, pp. xiii-xxii. New York: Farrar, Straus, and Giroux, 1967.

Contemporary Authors, Vol. 119. Detroit: Gale Research Co.

Fergusson, Robert. *Enigma: The Life of Knut Hamsun.* New York: Farrar, Straus, and Giroux, 1987.

Gustafson, Alrik. "Hamsun's *Growth of the Soil." The American Scandinavian Review* 27, No. 3 (September 1939): 199-214.

Lovett, Robert Morse. *"Growth of the Soil."* In his *Preface to Fiction: A Discussion of Great Modern Novels,* pp. 41-52. Chicago: Thomas S. Rockwell Co., 1931.

Lowenthal, Leo. "Knut Hamsun." In his *Literature and the Image of Man: Sociological Studies of the European Drama and the Novel, 1600-1900,* pp. 190-200. Boston: Beacon Press, 1957.

Singer, Isaac Bashevis. "Knut Hamsun, Artist of Skepticism." In *Hunger* by Knut Hamsun, translated by Robert Bly, pp. v-xii. New York: Farrar, Straus, and Giroux, 1967.

Twentieth-Century Literary Criticism, Vols. 2, 14. Detroit: Gale Research Co.

Peter Handke

1942-

Austrian dramatist, novelist, and essayist.

Kaspar (drama, 1968)

This is Handke's most famous work and takes as its point of departure the true story of a young man named **Kaspar Hauser,** who, of unknown origin and with little knowledge of language or civilization, was discovered wandering the German city of Nuremberg in 1828. Handke's interpretation of the story of Kaspar does not make direct mention of the historical context of his protagonist. Instead, he uses the premise to present his ideas on the limiting, constricting forces of language.

Kaspar first appears on stage repeating the one single sentence he knows: "I want to be a person like somebody else was once." Several voices, called the "prompters," then seek to instruct him in traditional language and behavior. Through their tutelage, Handke reveals the negative power of language: how it is a conditioning process and how it restricts the freedom of the individual. Kaspar learns the words and structures from his tutors, who function as disembodied voices of civilization and of rational and logical behavior. In one speech, he reconstructs his life in a rather poetic language; but the effect of the prompters soon takes over, and he begins to parrot their moral platitudes, emphasizing the importance of order and "correct" behavior. When Kaspar first recognizes that he is a being separate and estranged from others, his response is confusion. He is further distraught when he perceives that his own understanding of language is unique to him and that language, despite the insistence of his prompters, is imprecise. One sentence had once served him; now, the endless variety of language, the syntax and vocabulary he so readily accepted, cannot give him what he needs. Other characters, all dressed like Kaspar, appear on stage, uttering incomprehensible phrases, their actions paralleling Kaspar's disorientation. His last line, "I am only accidentally I," reveals the collapse of the order and meaning of language.

Handke's work is informed by the linguistic theories of the philosopher Wittgenstein, and in this play, as in so many of his works, he explores the relationship between language and reality. As many critics have noted, Kaspar is depicted as a puppet-like character, and Handke shows how, through language, we are all susceptible to the manipulation of others. *Kaspar* is considered one of the most important works of the modern European stage.

FURTHER READING

Contemporary Authors, Vols. 77-80. Detroit: Gale Research Co.

Contemporary Literary Criticism, Vols. 5, 8, 10, 15, 38. Detroit: Gale Research Co.

Hern, Nicholas. *Peter Handke.* New York: Ungar, 1972.

Kauffman, Stanley. *"Kaspar and Other Plays." The New Republic* 162, No. 9 (28 February 1970): 19, 30-1.

McAuley, Gay. "The Problem of Identity: Theme, Form, and Theatrical Method in *Les Negres, Kaspar,* and *Old Times." The Southern Review* (March 1975): 51-65.

Thomas Hardy
1840-1928

English novelist, short story writer, and poet.

Far from the Madding Crowd (novel, 1874)

Set in Hardy's fictional Wessex, the novel relates the story of **Bathsheba Everdene** and the three men who love her. She is a spirited and beautiful girl who inherits a farm from her uncle. **Gabriel Oak,** whom she has refused as a husband, is also a farmer, but has lost his farm and works for Bathsheba as a shepherd. **William Boldwood** is a neighboring farmer who also loves Bathsheba and courts her before her engagement to **Francis Troy,** a reckless young soldier who is drawn to Bathsheba for her money and beauty. Their marriage is destroyed when it becomes known that Troy had seduced one of the servants, **Fanny Robin,** and that she is with child. Both Fanny and the baby die, and Troy disappears and is given up for dead. Mr. Boldwood again begins courting Bathsheba, and she appears ready to accept him when Troy reappears, demanding his wife and her money. Boldwood, obsessed with Bathsheba to the point of madness, shoots and kills Troy. In the aftermath of all of this death and despair, Hardy ends his novel on a happy note, for Bathsheba realizes her love for Gabriel and agrees to marry him.

Bathsheba has been praised as a fully realized and sympathetically rendered female portrait, a believable character who is at once independent and willful, confident yet capricious, capable of running her farm and also of dealing with the adversity of life. Although the novel ends fortunately for Bathsheba and Gabriel, Hardy introduces themes that will echo throughout his fiction: that human life is governed by forces that are beyond the individual's control, and that characters such as Troy and Boldwood are ruined by their natures, Troy by his sensuality and Boldwood by his obsessive love for Bathsheba.

One of the most remarkable aspects of Hardy's achievement is his invention of Wessex, a fictional recreation of his own home in rural Dorset. His countryside included cities and villages renamed by the author for his purposes, and he even created maps to give his tales a greater sense of place. Of particular interest to Hardy's imaginative world are his peasant characters, who are rendered naturalistically and who represent Hardy's nostalgia for a way of life that was past; he thus took great care to recreate their speech, mannerisms and way of life for posterity.

The Return of the Native (novel, 1878)

Set once again in Hardy's fictional Wessex, the work takes place in the area of Egdon Heath. Hardy's recurrent theme of the old world in collision with the new is manifest in this novel, in which the characters represent the opposing views and virtues of the traditional way of life and the lure of the world outside the heath. **Clement Yeobright,** called Clym, is the "native" of the title, returned to his home after a successful career in Paris. Drawn to the established way of life in the heath, he decides to settle there and falls in love with **Eustacia Vye,** a selfish and independent woman who yearns to leave Wessex and explore the outside world. In marrying Clym, she has broken her engagement with **Damon Wildeve,** the keeper of an inn, a character as restless and headstrong as she. When it becomes apparent that Clym will not offer her a way out of the country she loathes, Eustacia and Damon recommence their affair, even though Damon has married Clym's cousin, **Thomosin Yeobright.** Like Clym, Thomasin represents the traditional way of life and remains loyal to her unfaithful, cruel husband. Damon plans to elope with Eustacia to Paris, but their scheme ends in tragedy when she commits suicide by throwing herself into a river, and he drowns in an attempt to save her.

Hardy's deterministic view of human existence is evident in this work, as he portrays his protagonists drawn inexorably to their fates. He is concerned in this novel with the theme of time, exploring how the individual changes and evolves through time, and how the forces that govern fate remain unchanged. The setting functions symbolically in the novel, especially the heath, which represents the powers beyond human control.

The Mayor of Casterbridge (novel, 1886)

The novel is set in Hardy's Wessex, this time in the town of Casterbridge, Hardy's reconstruction of Dorchester. **Michael Henchard** is a character whose willfulness and uncompromising nature foretell his tragic end. As the novel opens we see Henchard as a young man who in a fit of drunkenness has sold his wife and child at an auction to a sailor named **Richard Newson.** His wife, **Susan,** furious and humiliated, leaves him and with her infant child goes to live with Newson. Henchard in later life becomes a successful grain merchant and eventually the mayor of Casterbridge. His friend and business rival, **Donald Farfrae,** represents the rational, scientific approach to life and business, and Hardy contrasts him to the impetuous, intuitive Henchard. Once again Hardy deals with the theme of the new world replacing the old way of life and sets the stage for Farfrae's eventual triumph over Henchard. Susan and her daughter, **Elizabeth-Jane,** return to Casterbridge, and thinking that Newson is dead, she remarries Henchard. But the story of his cruel treatment of his wife and child eventually becomes known and Henchard is ruined: he loses his position, business, and ultimately his family as Newson returns in the closing section of the novel, and Elizabeth-Jane decides to marry Farfrae. Henchard dies alone, alienated from his people, humiliated by his past.

Henchard is considered by some critics to be Hardy's finest male character. He is a man at war with himself, isolated from others by his very nature. He is a titanic creation, doomed from the outset to be destroyed by his own willful, stubborn, inflexible temperament.

Tess of the d'Urbervilles (novel, 1891)

The novel is once again placed in Wessex. The story relates the tragic life of **Tess Durbeyfield,** whom Hardy portrays as a victim of unyielding Victorian mores and whose fate he links to the end of the rural way of life in England. As the novel begins, Tess's father, a poor carter, has discovered that he is the descendent of privileged ancestry and is part of the ancient family of the d'Urbervilles. He spends his days drinking in the local pub, revelling in his new-found status and leaving his family to poverty. Tess, a beautiful, innocent, young girl, is sent by her parents, hoping to capitalize on their association, to the home of **Alec d'Urberville,** who has purchased a large estate in the area. He is a cynical, shallow man, and he and his family represent for Hardy the cruel rapaciousness of the nouveau riche, drawn by the beauty of the land, as Alec is drawn to Tess, to possess it. Attracted to Tess, Alec sets out to seduce her, and she is his hapless victim. She soon finds herself pregnant, and the child she has by Alec dies.

In humiliation and grief, she leaves her home and becomes a milkmaid on a dairy farm, where she meets **Angel Clare.** He is the son of an old and respected family but has shunned their plans for him in the clergy to become a farmer. Although he claims to be an independent, caring man, his treatment of Tess reveals that he is as much a part of the hypocritical Victorian order as Alec. He is attracted to Tess for her beauty and purity, and he asks her to marry him. She at first refuses, but at last relents and they are married. However, on finding out about her past, Angel scorns and deserts her, although he, too, had admitted to a premarital affair. Abandoned and in despair, Tess still clings to her love for Angel and is forced to find work as a farm laborer. Alec has continued to pursue her, and she at last agrees to be his mistress. When Angel suddenly returns to her, she kills Alec, out of hatred and hopelessness. She and Angel flee, and in a penultimate scene, reach Stonehenge, where Tess lays down on a stone used for ritual sacrifice. She is later caught, convicted, and hanged for her crime.

The novel is considered Hardy's masterpiece, admired for its thematic richness and evocative prose. In his handling of Tess's tragic life, Hardy revealed the hypocrisy of the Victorian code of morality that would allow Tess to be used and discarded by a man like Alec, only to become the victim of a man like Angel who despite his protestation, is a representative of the rigid morality that undermines and finally destroys Tess. As the novel makes clear, Tess is indeed a sacrificial victim of a cold, unyielding culture. The work has received much praise for its natural description, which Hardy employs as a mirror for his character's consciousness, reflecting in the landscape the interior workings of Tess's mind.

Jude the Obscure (novel, 1895)

The novel is set in the Wessex countryside as well as in "Christminster," Hardy's fictionalized depiction of Oxford. The work traces the unhappy life and early death of **Jude Fawley,** a man whom happiness and success eludes. Throughout the novel Hardy highlights Jude's isolation and the familial happiness that is denied him: he is an orphan, raised by a relative who counsels him never to marry because of the family's history of marital unhappiness. Jude's first disappointment occurs when he is unable to go to Christminster to reap the benefits of education and to realize his dream of becoming a scholar. To emphasize his point, Hardy has his character first see the city not as a student but as a stonemason, for Jude's destiny is to remain forever on the outside of the world of promise symbolized by Christminster. Instead, he realizes the family curse of unfortunate marriages as he becomes entrapped in a union with **Arabella Donn,** who tricks him into marrying her, and who, unsatisfied with their life, leaves him. Jude then rekindles his romance with his cousin, **Sue Bridehead,** who, as a student at Oxford is a representative of educated, independent women in contrast to the earthy, cunning Arabella. Although Sue is married to **Richard Phillotson,** Jude's former teacher and a man much older than she, the two decide to live together. But their happiness is short-lived and ends in tragedy when Jude's son by his first marriage murders their children and commits suicide. Sue is transformed by the catastrophe and leaves Jude to return to Phillotson. In the novel's conclusion, Jude dies a young but broken man, still alone and in despair.

For many critics, this deeply pessimistic novel, which was Hardy's last, is a portrait of marital unhappiness that took much from his own life. As he had in *Tess of the d'Urbervilles,* Hardy here examines the hypocritical moral code that disallowed the honest expression of human sexuality and condemned any union outside the bonds of marriage. The work is also noted for its rich imagery, dominated by Christian symbolism, with Jude's suffering and early death paralleled to Christ's sacrifice.

FURTHER READING

Brown, Douglas. *Thomas Hardy.* London: Longmans, Green, 1954.

Cecil, David. *Hardy the Novelist: An Essay in Criticism.* London: Constable and Co., 1943.

Cockshut, A. O. J. "The Pessimists." In *Man and Woman: A Study of Love and the Novel 1740-1940,* pp. 100-35. New York: Oxford University Press, 1978.

Contemporary Authors, Vol. 104. Detroit: Gale Research Co.

Dictionary of Literary Biography, Vols. 18, 19. Detroit: Gale Research Co.

Draper, R. P., ed. *Hardy: The Tragic Novels: "The Return of the Native," "The Mayor of Casterbridge," "Tess of the d'Urbervilles," "Jude the Obscure."* London: The Macmillan Co., 1975.

Duffin, H. C. *Thomas Hardy: A Study of the Wessex Novels, the Poems, and "The Dynasts."* Manchester: Manchester University Press, 1937.

Gregor, Ian. "The Novel as Moral Protest: *Tess of the d'Urbervilles.*" In *"Tess of the d'Urbervilles" by Thomas Hardy: An Authoritative Text, Hardy and the Novel, Criticism,* Scott Elledge, ed., pp. 450-61. New York: W. W. Norton & Company, Inc., 1965.

Guerard, Albert J. *Thomas Hardy.* New York: New Directions, 1964.

Howe, Irving. *Thomas Hardy.* New York: Macmillan, 1967.

Miller, J. Hillis. *Thomas Hardy: Distance and Desire.* Cambridge: Belknap Press, 1970.

Millgate, Michael. *Thomas Hardy: His Career as a Novelist.* London: Bodley Head, 1971.

Mizener, Arthur. "*Jude the Obscure* as a Tragedy." *The Southern Review* 6, No. 1 (Summer 1940): 193-213.

Page, Norman. *Thomas Hardy.* London: Routledge & Kegan Paul, 1977.

Pinion, F. B. *A Hardy Companion: A Guide to the Works of Thomas Hardy and Their Background.* London: Macmillan, 1968.

Sankey, Benjamin. *The Major Novels of Thomas Hardy.* Denver: Alan Swallow, 1965.

Southerington, F. R. *Hardy's Vision of Man.* New York: Barnes & Noble, 1971.

Twentieth-Century Literary Criticism, Vols. 4, 10, 18. Detroit: Gale Research Co.

Wagner, Geoffrey. "*Tess of the d'Urbervilles:* The 'Pure' Woman." In *Five For Freedom: A Study of Feminism in Fiction,* pp. 183-211. Rutherford: Fairleigh Dickinson University Press, 1972.

Winner, Anthony. "Hardy's Moderns: The Ache of Uncertain Character." In *Characters in the Twilight: Hardy, Zola, Chekov,* pp. 28-72. Charlottesville: University Press of Virginia, 1981.

Bret Harte

1836?-1902

American short story writer and novelist.

"The Luck of Roaring Camp" (short story, 1868)

Situated in a California mining camp during the Gold Rush, the story revolves around the newborn son of a prostitute named **Cherokee Sal,** who dies in labor. Save for the child, the inhabitants of Roaring Camp are largely gruff, amoral frontiersmen greedily intent on making their fortunes. They include two miners, **Kentuck** and **Stumpy,** and a gambler, **Oakhurst.** After revealing their hidden tenderness as they lavish gifts on the baby, the three of them decide to raise the child themselves. Stumpy, who once claimed to have two wives, boasts the greatest domesticity and so accepts primary responsibility as caretaker. Wishfully named by the men, **Tommy Luck** innocently exerts a profound effect on their lives. Amidst the untamed Sierra foothills "The Luck" thrives and the miners, similarly, become happy, responsible men.

Fortune arrives at Roaring Camp the following summer, when the men find rich yields of gold. They attribute their prosperity to the Luck, whom they treat with reverence, and they confidently plan for the future. However, a winter flood shatters their dreams as it causes the death of both Luck and Kentuck.

More tale than realistic story, "The Luck of Roaring Camp" adheres to the predominant formula of exposing in characters a "heart of gold" beneath a coarse or depraved exterior. While essentially true to mid-nineteenth-century American frontier life, the narrative relies on the acceptance of a remarkable occurrence: the mystical birth of Luck and the sudden reversal of the men's natures. Nevertheless, for most scholars the story rises above superficial allegorical and sentimental interpretations due to Harte's skilled employment of humor and use of a sophisticated narrator who relates the story in an ironic style. Stories such as this one by Harte were instrumental in establishing for a generation of regionalist writers a treasury of uniquely American character types.

"The Outcasts of Poker Flat" (short story, 1869)

A gambler, two prostitutes, a thief, a young man, and his girlfriend are the main figures in Harte's classic story of the Old West. The story begins in 1850 in the California mining town of Poker Flat, whose citizens have decided, in a purifying fury, to either hang or banish all undesirable persons. Sentenced to banishment, **John Oakhurst, the Duchess, Mother Shipton,** and **Uncle Billy** are forced to the outskirts of town and forbidden to return. The poorly equipped party embarks upon a narrow, mountainous trail leading toward the distant settlement of Sandy Bar. Oakhurst, a gambler of stoic coolness, assumes leadership of the group. Upon reaching the steep Sierras they make camp and, except for Oakhurst, drown their sorrows in liquor. A young man from Sandy Flat, **Tom Simson,** called the "Innocent," arrives late in the day, headed for Poker Flat to be married and make his fortune. **Piney Woods,** his girlfriend, had run away with him, against her father's wishes. Tom and Oakhurst had first met months earlier, during a poker game in which the Innocent had lost all his money to the seasoned professional. After the game, Oakhurst returned Tom's money and advised him never to gamble again. Grateful ever since, Tom enthusiastically informs the party that he has ample food and that they can take shelter at an old log house he passed on the trail.

In the early morning, Oakhurst awakes to discover that Uncle Billy has stolen the mules and that a massive storm has come upon them, leaving them snowbound. Trying to protect Tom and Piney's idealism, Oakhurst doesn't tell them about Uncle Billy, and asks the Duchess and Mother Shipton to do the same. During the days that follow, the entire group becomes touched by the gaiety of Tom and the purity of his love for Piney. The two prostitutes become particularly motherly, deeply affected by the girl's genuine perception of them as friendly, respectable women. The storm continues, and by the tenth day Mother Shipton dies; she had starved herself, saving her rations of the previous week, which she in her last words instructs Oakhurst to give to Piney. After Mother Shipton's burial, Oakhurst, fully aware of the desperate situation, advises Tom that if he wishes to save Piney he must travel to Poker Flat to seek help. The story closes when, days later, the huddled, frozen bodies of the Duchess and Piney are found inside the cabin; Oakhurst, who was to accompany Tom part-way and then return to the cabin, is found beneath the snow beside a pine tree bearing a self-inscribed epitaph. The gambler, "who struck a streak of bad luck," had shot himself.

All of the outcasts except for Uncle Billy endure their fate heroically, despite their standing in "respectable" society. The theme of the individual wronged by society—frequently addressed in fiction of the era—acquires considerable power as Harte sympathetically focuses on the small exiled community and the moral code that arises within it. Representative of Hart's best fiction, the story is entertainingly told and, though essentially tragic, contains fine examples of local-color humor and hyperbole.

FURTHER READING

Brooks, Cleanth, Jr., John Thibaut Purser, and Robert Penn Warren. Discussion of "The Luck of Roaring Camp." In *An Approach to Literature*, edited by Cleanth Brooks, Jr., et al, pp. 86-7. New York: Appleton-Century-Crofts, 1952.

Chesterton, G. K. "Bret Harte." In *Varied Types*, pp. 179-95. New York: Dodd, Mead, 1921.

Contemporary Authors, Vol. 104. Detroit: Gale Research Co.

Dictionary of Literary Biography, Vol. 12. Detroit: Gale Research Co.

Morrow, Patrick. *Bret Harte*. Boise: Boise State University Press, 1972.

O'Brien, Edward J. "Bret Harte and Mark Twain." In his *The Advance of the American Short Story*, pp. 98-116. New York: Dodd, Mead, and Co., 1923.

Pattee, Fred Lewis. "Bret Harte." In *The Development of the American Short Story: An Historical Survey*, pp. 220-41. New York: Harper, 1923.

Quinn, Arthur Hobson. "Bret Harte and the Fiction of Moral Contrast." In his *American Fiction: An Historical and Critical Survey*, pp. 232-42. New York: Appleton-Century-Crofts, 1936.

Twentieth-Century Literary Criticism, Vols. 1, 25. Detroit: Gale Research Co.

Gerhart Hauptmann

1862-1946

German dramatist and novelist.

The Weavers (drama, 1893)

This play, considered Hauptmann's finest work, is set in the Silesian cities of Kaschbach,

Peterswaldau, and Langenbielau in the 1840s. It concerns the fate of a group of weavers who, confronted with the loss of their livelihood as factories begin to dominate their craft, are driven to revolt. There are nearly forty characters in the play, each individually realized, all of whom form a collective portrait of poverty and despair.

In the first act, the weavers wait humbly in line at the home of **Dreissiger,** a cotton merchant, where their webs are inspected and their wages are determined by the manager, **Pfeifer.** The weavers are described as resembling one another, for their bodies and spirits have been broken by years of hard work and deprivation. One by one they are forced to accept the meager wages and humiliation heaped on them by Pfeifer. Dreissiger admonishes those that challenge his policies and threatens them, for a young band of weavers have passed his house in the night, singing "Bloody Justice," a song of protest that recurs throughout the play, functioning as a *leitmotiv* for the weaver's cause. **Baecker,** a young weaver still brave enough to confront Pfeifer and Dreissiger, is openly defiant of them. In the second act, **Moritz Jaeger,** a soldier, returns to the village and joins the forces of revolt. He reads the words of the song to two of the old weavers, **Old Baumert** and **Wilhelm Ansorge,** who are driven to a state of fury by the song's forceful recounting of the injustices done them.

The third act takes place in a tavern in Peterswaldau, where several of the bar's middle-class patrons relate their unsympathetic attitudes toward the impoverished weavers, depicting them as lazy and irresponsible. Their conversation is interrupted first by Ansorge and Old Baumert and then by Jaeger and Baecker, who enter with a militant group of weavers singing "Bloody Justice." Act Four takes place at the Dreissiger home, where the owner and his family are shown to be complacent, well-to-do, and disdainful of the weavers and their demands for a decent life. Again the strains of "Bloody Justice" interrupt the scene. The angry mob breaks into the house and destroys it, forcing the Dreissiger family to flee.

The final act takes place at the home of the weaver **Old Hilse,** where **Hornig,** a ragpicker, relates the tale of the weavers' destruction of Dreissiger's home. The revolt continues, as the strains of the song are heard in the distance; their target is now the merchant **Dittrich,** who uses steam-powered looms. The mob confronts the soldiers who have been called to restore order; shots ring out, and several weavers are killed. Old Hilse, who had refused to join his brothers in revolt, is killed by accident as he sits at his treadle.

Hauptmann was responsible for bringing the tenets of literary naturalism to the German theater, and in this play he portrays his characters as they struggle against the hereditary and environmental restrictions that dictate their fate. The simple, peaceful weavers become by the end of the play an angry, violent mob, yet no solution to their problem is offered in the conclusion, and the play ends on a note of tragedy and despair. The author's sympathy and pity for his characters is evident as he examines their lives of poverty and hopelessness. The work moves forward with a powerful, relentless force; when the tension ends in violence and death, the bloody justice sought by the weavers only seems to have intensified their plight.

FURTHER READING

Contemporary Authors, Vol. 104. Detroit: Gale Research Co.

Dobie, Ann B. "Riot, Revolution, and *The Weavers." Modern Drama* 12, No. 3 (September 1969): 165-72.

Garten, F. *Gerhart Hauptmann.* New Haven: Yale University Press, 1954.

Sinden, Margaret. *Gerhart Hauptmann: The Prose Plays.* Toronto: University of Toronto Press, 1957.

Twentieth-Century Literary Criticism, Vol. 4. Detroit: Gale Research Co.

John Hawkes

1925-

American novelist, short story writer, and dramatist.

The Lime Twig (novel, 1961)

The novel is set in London in the 1960s and recounts the psychic journey of **Michael Banks** as he pursues his obsessive dream of power. As the work begins, we read the first-person account of **William Hencher,** who is a boarder with Banks and his wife, **Margaret.** Hencher relates his life with his mother during World War II, when they lived in the house now occupied by the Banks. The themes, imagery, and obsessions that Hencher reveals in this opening section prefigure the fate of Banks and his wife. A recurrent theme in Hawkes's work is the artist who, obsessed with the past, finds a vehicle through which he can recreate his life. Here, Hencher appears to create and control the narrative. He passes his obsessions on to Banks, who sees in the race horse Rock Castle the embodiment of his dreams of power and potency.

The latter portion of the novel, rendered in the third-person with an objective narrator, depicts Michael and Margaret as a staid, unhappy couple whose existence is enlivened when Michael steals Rock Castle. But the destructive elements of dreams and their fulfillment become evident as Michael and Margaret come under the control of **Larry,** a gang leader, and his vicious company, who want the horse back. Hencher is kicked in the head by the horse and dies, a murder arranged by the gang, and Margaret is kidnapped and brutalized. As the dream world and reality merge, Margaret's brutal beating and rape is related in a scene that reveals how the sadistic act is weirdly consonant with her sexual fantasies. Michael's dealings with Larry and the underworld all take place in a foggy atmosphere, which enhances the uncanny mood of the work. In the conclusion, Rock Castle is entered in a race he is destined to win, but Michael throws himself under the horse, ending his life and his dream.

The novel presents a shocking, nightmarish literary landscape, and the action and imagery reveal a violent, brutal world, rendered with cold detachment through the eyes of the narrator. It is Hawkes's purpose to disturb the reader's preconceptions about fiction by revealing the power of the unconscious through his stories of dream, illusion, and the violence of the imagination.

The Blood Oranges (novel, 1970)

The novel takes place on the bleak island of Illyria and relates how **Cyril,** a self-styled "sex-singer," tries to create a terrestrial paradise based on sexual freedom. The work is divided into forty-two sections, randomly arranged, which are composed of introspective ramblings and memories. One of the controlling motifs in the book is the image of life as a tapestry. The novel is in essence Cyril's weaving, his vision of life, which unravels and is rewoven to incorporate the experiences of the characters.

Although the sections are not arranged chronologically, the plot as it emerges reveals the story of Cyril and his wife, **Fiona.** They have been married for eighteen years, are childless, and have never practiced sexual monogamy, hoping to avoid the sterility of traditional marital bonds. When **Hugh,** his wife **Catherine,** and their children come to the island for vacation, Cyril tries to engage them in a four-way relationship, or "quarternion," that will expand their sexual and spiritual senses. Catherine is willingly seduced, but Hugh revolts against the concept. He is a dark projection of sexuality and functions in the novel as Cyril's double. For Hugh, sex is a voyeuristic, solitary pursuit, and he tries as best he can to ruin Cyril's vision. In one key scene, he and the others visit an abandoned fortress, where Hugh finds a chastity belt which he forces on Catherine, symbolizing his sexual repression and his jealousy of Cyril. In this scene, Hawkes reveals how the other characters are strangely drawn to Hugh's vision of death and sex. Hugh finally agrees to make love with Fiona, but he hangs himself accidently. Catherine suffers a breakdown, and Fiona leaves the island with the children. When Catherine is released from the mental hospital, she rejoins Cyril. They recommence their relationship, but its exact nature remains unclear. Cyril seeks renewal and rebirth after their tragedy, and one final scene indicates that he and Catherine will indeed find a way to a new life together. The two of them join with the townsfolk and a goat-like man in the launching of a new boat, an event that echoes a fertility rite. The experience suggests a "marriage" of Cyril and Catherine, a blending of their pasts and an exuberant expression of sexuality.

Cyril's attempt to create a harmonious, idyllic paradise fails, and he is revealed to be a self-centered man whose need to control reality is linked to both his narcissistic nature and to his role as one of Hawkes's artists, at work on his tapestry of life. The novel is noted for its evocative prose and its exploration of sex, myth, and dream.

FURTHER READING

Busch, Frederick. *Hawkes: A Guide to His Fictions*. Syracuse: Syracuse University Press, 1973.

Contemporary Authors, Vols. 1-4, rev. ed.; *Contemporary Authors New Revision Series,* Vol. 2. Detroit: Gale Research Co.

Contemporary Literary Criticism, Vols. 1, 2, 3, 4, 7, 9, 14, 15, 27, 49. Detroit: Gale Research Co.

Dictionary of Literary Biography, Vols. 2, 7; *Dictionary of Literary Biography Yearbook, 1980*. Detroit: Gale Research Co.

Edenbaum, Robert I. "John Hawkes: *The Lime Twig* and Other Tenuous Horrors." *Massachusetts Review* 7 (Summer 1966): 462-75.

Frohock, W. M. "John Hawkes's Vision of Violence." *Southwest Review* 50 (Winter 1965): 69-79.

Greiner, Donald J. *Comic Terror: The Novels of John Hawkes*. Memphis: Memphis State University Press, 1973.

Guerard, Albert J. "The Prose Style of John Hawkes." *Critique* 6 (Fall 1963): 19-29.

Knapp, John W. "Hawkes' *The Blood Oranges:* A Sensual New Jerusalem." *Critique* 17 (Spring 1976): 5-25.

Tanner, Tony. *City of Words: American Fiction 1950-1970*. New York: Harper & Row, 1971.

Joseph Heller

1923-

American novelist and essayist.

Catch-22 (novel, 1961)

The setting for the novel is the imaginary Mediterranean island of Pianosa during World

War II. **John Yossarian** is a bombardier with the American Air Force who has come to the conclusion that he must do anything he can to save himself from death in what has become for him an absurdist conflict. Thus the novel chronicles his often hilarious attempts to outwit the Army to keep from being killed. The "Catch-22" of the title refers to the Army dictate that whatever is commanded is right, no matter how absurd, illogical, or inhumane. Throughout the novel, Heller brilliantly parodies the hopelessly convoluted bureaucratese that characterizes the written and spoken language of the Army.

Although the tone of the novel is exuberantly comic, Heller's treatment of his theme is serious. The Nazis are hardly mentioned in the novel; rather, the perpetrators of evil are the rigid, dehumanizing institutions of the military that deprive Yossarian and his friends of their freedom, and, under the name of patriotism, will deprive them of their lives. The novel abounds in memorable secondary characters, often portrayed as caricatures defined by their obsessive personality traits. One such figure is **Milo Minderbinder,** who has made it his goal to make as much money as he can off the war. He tries to involve Yossarian in his numerous absurd schemes. Perhaps his most illustrative act is bombing his own base, from which he hopes to realize a handsome profit. **Major Major Major,** whose name reflects his father's cynical idea of a practical joke, has come to the army with an attitude of unquestioned subservience to authority. His rapid advancement is due to a computer error, and his personality and position make him an object of derision. When he is named commander of the squadron, he is further vilified and retreats into a life of isolation. When Yossarian's friend **Snowden** is killed, the terror and absurdity overwhelm him and he flees to Rome. There, in a famous sequence entitled "The Eternal City," he decides to desert to Sweden.

The plot of the novel does not follow a linear, chronological format; instead, time is disordered and confused. Incidents are recalled by characters before they are related in the text, and conflicting accounts of events abound throughout the story. The disorientation this creates in the reader is adumbrated by Heller's use of flashbacks and *deja vu,* underlining the surrealism of Yossarian's experience and Heller's theme of the folly of war.

Something Happened (novel, 1974)

Set in suburban Connecticut and Manhattan, the novel is a merciless depiction of the emptiness of modern life. Unlike his predecessor Yossarian, **Bob Slocum** is an unlikable character. Vapid and selfish, he is a middle-aged businessman whose life is overwhelmed by paranoia. Both his public and private lives are shaped by anxiety: in the nameless "Company" in which he works, the hierarchy is determined by fear, and in his home life he is obsessed with dreams and visions of violence and horror. The men he works with are faceless automatons, with names like White, Black, and Grey. Slocum's family is distant from him: he and his wife communicate mainly through sex, his adolescent daughter annoys and frightens him with her insights into his unhappy life, and one of his sons is hopelessly brain-damaged. His nine-year-old son, however, is bright and affectionate, and Slocum loves him deeply. Yet in the novel's conclusion, the boy is the victim of a car accident, and, desperately trying to comfort him, Slocum smothers him.

The work is given as a monologue with Slocum as the narrator. Thus, all we know about the world of the novel is filtered through his consciousness. Heller probes the mind of his protagonist to offer a portrait of modern life that is relentless in its depiction of the sterile, dehumanizing forces at work in American society. The prose style is clear and dispassionate; Slocum's voice is flat, and his obsessive concerns are rendered through the repetition of thoughts, phrases, and memories. The tone of the novel is bitterly pessimistic, unrelieved by the humor that characterized Heller's first novel. For many critics, the work was both puzzling and disappointing. Others, however, praised Heller for his unsparing honesty in portraying the despair of modern existence.

Good as Gold (novel, 1979)

The novel takes place in Brooklyn and Washington, D.C., and Heller makes use of these two settings to explore the dilemma of his hero. **Bruce Gold** is a Jewish academic yearning for money and success, who, as the novel opens, is negotiating with publishers to write a book on the Jewish experience in America. Yet he has also caught the eye of the current administration in Washington, who offer him a position in the government. In this way, Heller sets up the dramatic battle for the heart and mind of Gold. He is a rather repellant protagonist, hypocritical, cynical, and driven by personal gain. His large Jewish family, humorously depicted as obnoxious, unloving and quarrelsome, thinks he is a failure.

Gold moves to Washington to seek a new career and to enter the world of WASPs and political power. He wants to divorce his Jewish wife and marry the tall, blonde daughter of the penultimate wealthy, WASP power-broker, **Hugh Biddle Conover,** who despises Gold because he is a Jew. This context sets the stage for Gold's diatribe on Henry Kissinger, who embodies all that Gold despises in himself: he is a hypocrite and a Jew who tries to shed his Jewishness to make it in the WASP stronghold of Washington. In the novel's conclusion, Gold receives word that his brother has died on the night he is to meet the President. Gold makes his decision: family concerns must take precedent over political ambitions. He returns to his family and leaves Washington.

As in *Catch-22,* Heller here satirizes the language of the bureaucracy, revealing its obscurity and absurdity. He also deals with the deteriorating values of Jews anxious to assimilate into the mainstream of American culture and the vapidness of the American political process, where good government is neither a goal nor a reality. As many critics have suggested, Gold's proposed book on the Jewish experience in America is perhaps Heller's book on Gold.

FURTHER READING

Aldridge, John W. "Vision of Man Raging in a Vacuum." *Saturday Review* 2 (18 October 1974): 18-21.

——. "The Deceits of Black Humor." *Harper's* 258, No. 1546 (March 1979): 115-18.

Bradbury, Malcolm. "Catch-79." *The Observer* (29 April 1979): 37.

Contemporary Authors, Vols. 5-8, rev. ed.; *Contemporary Authors New Revision Series,* Vol. 8; *Contemporary Authors Bibliographical Series,* Vol. 1. Detroit: Gale Research Co.

Contemporary Literary Criticism, Vols. 1, 3, 5, 8, 11, 36. Detroit: Gale Research Co.

DeMott, Benjamin. "Heller's Gold and a Silver Sax." *The Atlantic Monthly* 243, No. 3 (March 1979): 129-32.

Dictionary of Literary Biography, Vols. 2, 28; *Dictionary of Literary Biography Yearbook: 1980.* Detroit: Gale Research Co.

Hassan, Ihab. "Laughter in the Dark." *American Scholar* 33 (Autumn 1964): 634-39.

Pinsker, Sanford. "Heller's *Catch-22:* The Protest of a *Puer Eternis.*" *Critique* 7, No. 2 (Winter 1964-1965): 150-62.

Searles, George B. "*Something Happened:* A New Direction for Joseph Heller." *Critique* 18 (1977): 74-81.

Vonnegut, Kurt, Jr. "*Something Happened.*" *New York Times Book Review* (6 October 1974): 1-2.

Lillian Hellman
1905-1984
American dramatist and memoirist.

The Little Foxes (drama, 1939)

Set in the South at the turn of the century, this play is widely acknowledged to be Hellman's finest and presents what many critics describe as her most memorable character, **Regina Giddens,** whom one commentator called a "magnificent embodiment of evil." The play takes place at the home of Regina and her terminally ill husband, **Horace.** Regina has brought Horace home from the hospital to try to convince him to give her the money she needs to invest in a cotton mill. She and her brothers, **Benjamin** and **Oscar Hubbard,** are representations of corruption in the work: ruthless, rapacious and greedy people who will allow nothing to stand in the way of their plans. Benjamin and Oscar steal Horace's bonds when he makes it clear that he wants nothing to do with the mill project. To prevent Regina from gaining from her brothers' scheme to use the bonds, Horace alters his will, naming her as the sole inheritor of the profits. When it becomes clear that he plans to thwart her financial plans, Regina unleashes on Horace the full measure of her loathing and contempt. When he suffers an attack, she refuses to give him the medicine he needs to save his life, and he dies. Their daughter, **Alexandra,** who had stood by her father throughout his illness and the battle with her mother, now leaves her and the rest of the family in disgust.

The play has been praised for its well-paced construction, trenchant characterization, and dramatic dialogue noted for its clarity and economy. Now widely known for her memoirs, Hellman first established herself as a playwright of importance, and *The Little Foxes* is regarded as her finest dramatic achievement.

FURTHER READING

Brustein, Robert. "Epilogue to Anger." *The New Republic* 191, Nos. 7-8 (13-20 August 1984): 23-5.

Contemporary Authors, Vols. 13-16, rev. ed., 112. Detroit: Gale Research Co.

Contemporary Literary Criticism, Vols. 2, 4, 8, 14, 18, 34, 44, 52. Detroit: Gale Research Co.

Dictionary of Literary Biography, Vol. 7; *Dictionary of Literary Biography Yearbook: 1984.* Detroit: Gale Research Co.

Falk, Doris V. *Lillian Hellman.* New York: Ungar, 1978.

Moody, Richard. *Lillian Hellman: Playwright.* New York: Bobbs-Merrill-Pegasus, 1974.

Ernest Hemingway
1899-1961
American short story writer, novelist, essayist, and poet.

"Big Two-Hearted River" (short story, 1925)

Set following World War I in the deep woods of Michigan's Upper Peninsula, the story traces the solitary, curative activities of a shell-shocked young American who has just deboarded a train at Seney, an abandoned lumber town. The landscape is black and desolate from a recent fire. **Nick Adams** walks down the track to the bridge over the river and stares for a long time at the trout "Keeping themselves steady in the current." After hiking cross-country for some time, Nick reaches the edge of the fire line but continues onward, planning to camp beside the river far upstream. Finding a suitable spot, he stops, and with methodical care raises his tent and stores his belongings before building a fire and eating. As he makes coffee he remembers **Hopkins,** a good friend who deserted Nick's circle when he became wealthy. Nick wakes the following morning and is immediately excited by his surroundings. After eating and making the necessary preparations, he heads for the river to fish. The water delivers a "rising cold shock" as he wades in. Although he loses a large trout and shakily moves toward the bank to rest and wait out his disappointment, he later catches two smaller trout and recovers his earlier happy feeling. As Nick lunches, he ponders the swamp downstream, its entrance marked by a large overhanging cedar. He decides not to go there that day, for "in the fast deep water, in the half life, the fishing would be tragic." He cleans the fish and returns to camp, knowing he can visit the swamp another day.

"Big Two-Hearted River" cannot be understood satisfactorily unless its relationship to the preceding narratives and vignettes of *In Our Time*—in which Nick appears at various stages in his life—is considered, for nowhere within the culminating story does Hemingway refer to the war. Much of the story's power, consequently, lies in what is omitted, in accordance with Hemingway's "tip of the iceberg" theory of exposition. By intensively focusing on Nick's thoughts and actions, Hemingway creates an atmosphere of endlessly meaningful sensation, a captivating natural world in which both regenerative and destructive forces may prevail. The pacing is purposefully slow, painfully deliberate, for Nick knows he must not "rush . . . his sensations," for to do so would be to resurrect the memory of the war before his psychic healing is complete.

Detractors of Hemingway complain primarily of two weaknesses in his writing: his style of contrived rhythms and ostentatiously simple diction and his limited subject matter. However, Hemingway adherents assert that in the majority of his stories, particularly the apprenticeship tales of Nick Adams, his most fully drawn protagonist, Hemingway presented a rich fictional world through which he addressed life's most burdensome concerns with consummate narrative skill.

The Sun Also Rises (novel, 1926)

Told by **Jake Barnes,** an American newsman, Hemingway's first novel is a revealing portrayal of expatriate life in post-World War I Europe. The story begins in Paris's Left Bank and centers on Jake, his wealthy tennis friend, **Robert Cohn,** and their mutual love, **Lady Brett Ashley.** Brett shares Jake's love but must look toward other men for sexual fulfillment, for Jake has been emasculated during the war. She and Robert leave for San Sebastian on a brief, carefree holiday. Jake's old friend **Bill Gorton** arrives and the two plan to travel to Spain to fish trout and view the bullfights. Before their departure they arrange to meet Brett and her fiance, **Mike Campbell,** in Pampalona. Robert, just back from San Sebastian and desiring to follow Brett, convinces Jake to meet him at Bayonne before going down to the San Fermin festival. The group eventually congregates in Pampalona, where all of them drink heavily and partake in the celebrations. Robert, a frustrated writer and former boxing champ, eventually ostracizes himself when he knocks down Mike and Jake in a bar and then savagely beats **Pedro Romero,** a handsome young bullfighter whom Brett has taken to bed. To Jake especially, Pedro symbolizes a special combination of natural grace, integrity, and bravery and serves as foil to Robert's brutal selfishness and inability to accept Brett's fickle behavior. The novel closes when the party disperses and Jake and Brett reunite in Madrid. She has sent Pedro away and has decided to settle down with Mike. Yet she is still attracted to Jake and so the two tour the city by taxi, cheerlessly, aimlessly, purposelessly.

The Sun Also Rises is Hemingway's most unrelenting treatment of post-war ennui and disillusionment. The novel's title was inspired by an opening quote from Ecclesiastes, and the prevailing mood of the characters is a fulfillment of Gertrude Stein's famous comment:

"You are all a lost generation." Symbolically, Jake Barnes is both physically and psychologically wounded as the result of the war. Yet his esteem for the natural world and his knowledge that sport, friendship, and stoicism support him, mitigate his predicament. Through Jake the reader discovers what values can still be attained and held in an otherwise amoral world. These are the values embodied in Pedro Romero, who achieves them through innate athleticism, and **Count Mippipopolous,** a minor character who achieves them through wisdom and age. Despite an overriding strain of pessimism, the novel remains among Hemingway's most admired for its many memorable characters, rural scenes, and passages of vibrant description.

A Farewell to Arms (novel, 1929)

Set in northern Italy and the Swiss Alps during World War I, *A Farewell to Arms* documents a young American's growing disillusionment with the war and concurrent love affair with an English nurse. The protagonist, **Lieutenant Frederic Henry,** serves in an Italian ambulance unit on the front lines. Through his hedonistic doctor friend, **Rinaldi,** he meets **Catherine Barkley** at a British hospital station. Catherine is emotionally vulnerable, having recently lost her lover to the war. The two rapidly develop a close, confiding relationship, but it is not until Frederic returns from the front, badly wounded in the legs, that he considers himself in love. As he convalesces, Catherine cares for him constantly. By the time Frederic is ready to return to the front, Catherine informs him that she is pregnant. Amidst a massive Italian retreat, chaos breaks out. Officers are being held, tried, and executed by firing squads in the field; Frederic is among those detained. By nightfall he escapes, plunging himself into a nearby river and seizing a piece of driftwood that carries him to safety. Following a long trek to Milan, he learns that Catherine has been transferred to Stresa. When he arrives there, knowing that the authorities may soon find and arrest him, he arranges to escape by boat with Catherine to neutral Switzerland and make a separate peace there. Although upon their arrival the couple is interrogated, they are soon freed and travel to Montreux to spend the fall and winter.

Their time together is idyllic, though not without uncertainties and grave foreboding. Near the end of Catherine's pregnancy they leave the beautiful sheltering mountains for Lausanne, to be near a hospital. Catherine suffers greatly during labor and, after the doctor administers anesthetic, delivers a stillborn baby by caesarean section. Despite the doctor's assurance to Frederic, Catherine soon dies. As Frederic walks back to the hotel the sky is dark and it is raining.

Hemingway once referred to this novel as his *Romeo and Juliet*. Although there may be few parallels, the two classics are similar in that they are essentially tragic and concern fated lovers entrapped in a hostile environment. An alternating sense of dependency and detachment characterizes both Frederic and Catherine. Their closeness becomes most visible when the couple's thoughts and words become closely affined. Yet the cloud of war always prevents them from believing their love is safe or is more than a wonderful, delicate dream. For its poignant presentations of this theme and its widely praised scenes of war, *A Farewell to Arms* stands as a preeminent work of the post-war era.

"The Short Happy Life of Francis Macomber" (short story, 1936)

Situated in the African plains during the 1920s, this popular adventure story probes the coming of age of **Francis Macomber,** a wealthy American on safari with his beautiful, unloving wife, **Margot.** The plot traces the rise of Macomber from a cowering hunter and powerless husband to a courageous sportsman who eventually considers himself incapable of further fear. The initial tense scene shows the couple having a drink before lunch with **Robert Wilson,** their professional guide. The atmosphere is pervaded by Macomber's earlier display of weakness when, charged by a lion, he panicked and fled. Wilson wishes to forget the incident but Macomber, painfully aware of his wife's contempt, cannot.

Although Wilson silently deplores Macomber, particularly after Macomber beseeches him not to divulge the morning's incident to others, he agrees with Macomber that a fine kill during the next day's hunt may erase his failure. During the night, Macomber sleeps restlessly and wakes in fear of a lion roaring in the distance. At the scene of the hunt, Macomber flees again and exacerbates the already troubled expedition. Margot, who witnesses her husband's cowardice, and in fact has coldly anticipated it, impulsively kisses Wilson on the mouth, in full view of her husband. Macomber awakens that night and realizes Margot has crept out to sleep with Wilson. In the final scene the next day, Macomber faces three buffalo and shoots well, redeeming himself in his and Wilson's eyes. When a gun-bearer informs the party that one of the animals is wounded and lying in the bush, Macomber eagerly anticipates the kill. At the climactic moment, Macomber stands his ground and fires calmly as the bull charges until "he felt a sudden white-hot, blinding flash explode inside his head and that was all he ever felt." Margot, wary of her husband's newfound potency, had shot Macomber from behind.

In this story, the taut reportorial style, ironic dialogue of the characters, and understated, mildly ambiguous tone of the denouement function as ideal technical components through which Hemingway's themes attain penetrating focus. Hemingway's personally held motto of "grace under pressure" sustains the narrative and focuses attention on Macomber, who in his last mortal act internalizes the same moral code held by Wilson and, by extension, the animals. For its consummate pacing, masterful foreshadowing, and meaningfully ironic stance it remains one of Hemingway's most widely admired short stories.

"The Snows of Kilimanjaro" (short story, 1936)

The story takes place in the remote Masai country of Africa, where a middle-aged writer and his wealthy wife are on safari. **Harry** rests on a cot, suffering from gangrene, the result of a minor cut which he neglected to treat earlier. Morose and vindictive, he lashes out at **Helen** and says he has never loved her. In a flashback, Harry recalls scenes from his life, taking pleasure in their vivid recall but knowing he will never write about them. He alternates between these memories, his perceptions of his immediate surroundings, and strained dialogue with his wife. Sensing the approach of death, for which the stench of his wound, a group of onlooking vultures, and a patrolling hyena are continual reminders, Harry critically examines his life. He realizes that the comfortable existence he and his superficial wife have led has dulled his artistic powers. Thus, he dreams of his younger days when he was capable of fulfilling and remaining true to his talent. Gradually, Harry's bitterness towards his wife and himself recedes, and he finds that he can face death squarely.

When Harry sleeps deeply near the end of the story, he dreams that it is morning and a plane has landed. **Compton,** the pilot, greets the couple breezily and has Harry loaded on the plane. They take off and Harry is able to see the wildlife moving "in long fingers across the plain." Continuing its ascent, the plane turns and heads toward the top of Mt. Kilimanjaro. When Harry sees the snow-capped peak he "knew that there was where he was going." Back at camp the hyena howls, signalling death; Helen awakens and discovers Harry in still repose, his infected leg hanging down alongside the cot.

Consciously modeled after Leo Tolstoy's "The Death of Ivan Ilych," "The Snows of Kilimanjaro" is concerned with personal and professional corruption. The heroes in both stories are self-pitying and view their present diseased state as the culmination of poor choices and false, convenient values. However, through final, honest confrontation with their own mortality, both achieve self-redemption. Written near the height of his career, Hemingway's story, for many, represents his most intimate and masterfully expressed personal confession, a revelation about the course his own literary and personal life was already taking.

For Whom the Bell Tolls (novel, 1940)

For Whom the Bell Tolls is the story of the Spanish Civil War and of one American's involvement with the Loyalist cause. Behind Fascist lines **Robert Jordan** works closely with a gypsy-guerilla band led by **Pablo** and his wife, **Pilar.** Of the two, Pilar attains moral dominance, for her husband is inwardly weak as a result of witnessing the war's atrocities and is prone to boasting, drunkenness, and treachery; she, contrarily, is spiritually strong beyond her vituperative tongue, and is far more devoted to the rebellion. Jordan, an explosives expert, must coordinate plans for studying and destroying a strategically located bridge at a precisely defined time. His stiff, emotionless demeanor is softened by **Maria,** a beautiful young peasant girl who was imprisoned, brutalized, and raped by the Fascists before recently escaping. Although she is still psychologically scarred, she makes love to Jordan their first night together; during the coming days they grow increasingly close. When Jordan's preparations are nearly complete, Pablo deserts the group, stealing the explosives and detonators necessary for the mission. Although Pablo eventually returns and is forgiven, Jordan must now blow up the bridge by hand grenades, for the other explosives have been destroyed. At the arranged time Jordan and **Anselmo,** an older, honorable guerila whom Jordan can rely upon, approach the bridge. Anselmo kills the sentries; when the bombing attack at the other end commences, Jordan destroys the bridge and avoids injury. However, Anselmo dies in the blast and Jordan blames the death on Pablo, for the mission would have been far safer had the original detonator been available. Jordan reunites with the guerrillas and Maria and aids them in their flight from Fascist territory. Tragically, Jordan's horse is wounded by gunfire and collapses on him, crushing his leg and rendering him unable to continue. After affirming his love for Maria and explaining that he lives within her and will therefore travel wherever she goes, he takes his leave of the group. After Maria is forcibly led away, Jordan, machine gun in hand, prepares to meet the approaching enemy troops. He contemplates ending his pain by suicide but instead achieves a moral victory by resolving to do "one thing well done"; an enemy officer comes into view and Jordan will wait patiently for the perfect shot.

Robert Jordan is an archetypal Hemingway hero in that he consciously strives to embody physical and emotional courage in the face of overwhelming adversity. Significantly, the novel's title—taken from John Donne's meditation beginning "No Man is an Island"— underscores Jordan's and Hemingway's conviction that the Loyalist cause was ultimately humanitarian and that each fighter's death tolled a common death for all who believed in the effort. Generally regarded as Hemingway's most ambitious undertaking, *For Whom the Bell Tolls* is distinctive for its replication in English of the idiomatic grace of Spanish and for its complementary depiction of the Spanish gypsy temperament, inescapably violent and noble. Although variously received at the time of publication, the novel is now generally viewed as one of the masterpieces of modern fiction.

The Old Man and the Sea (novella, 1952)

Winner of the Pulitzer Prize and an undisputed American classic, *The Old Man and the Sea* takes place on the gulf-stream waters off the coast of Cuba. A thin, weather-beaten old man named **Santiago** has endured eighty-four days without catching a fish. Because of Santiago's poor luck, **Manolin,** a young boy who has previously assisted the veteran fisherman, no longer accompanies him, for his father has forbidden it. The boy still visits the old man, bringing food to his shack and discussing American baseball. Santiago still believes his luck will change and rows far out into the gulf the next morning. During his time at sea he reveals through his thoughts and actions that he treasures all life and senses a great kinship with the creatures of the sea. Santiago speaks aloud to himself as he fishes; after he has traveled far beyond the other boats a large fish strikes the bait on one of his lines. Without seeing the fish, Santiago knows it is the largest he has yet encountered. For three days he tries to subdue and land the fish in his small skiff. With incredible stamina and determination he succeeds, though by the time he has lashed the fish to the side of his boat the old man's strength is nearly gone. A second, more terrible, phase of Santiago's ordeal begins when sharks viciously attack the massive marlin. Santiago returns home, beaten and exhausted. Manolin weeps for him and promises that he will always accompany him from now on. The old man sleeps and dreams, as he has often done, of lions on the beach that he once saw during his youth.

The story is at once a confirmation of the naturalistic state of human existence and a celebration of the sacred interdependence between the human and the natural world. Indeed, Hemingway's epic portrayal of the marlin and Santiago suggests an empathy between the two figures that renders them inseparable. Despite his losing the marlin to sharks, Santiago maintains a purposive, peaceful resolve with his fate, a heroic dignity epitomizing the ''victory in defeat'' ideal that Hemingway recurrently addressed in his fiction. A tale of remarkable power and beauty that attains mythic proportions through its Christian symbolism, *The Old Man and the Sea* is widely considered one of the most masterfully wrought and thematically rich stories in American fiction.

FURTHER READING

Baker, Carlos. *Ernest Hemingway: A Life Story*. New York: Charles Scribner's Sons, 1969.

——. *Hemingway: The Writer as Artist*. 4th ed. Princeton: Princeton University Press, 1972.

Baker, Sheridan. *Ernest Hemingway: An Introduction and Interpretation*. New York: Holt, Rinehart and Winston, 1967.

Benson, Jackson J., ed. *The Short Stories of Ernest Hemingway: Critical Essays*. Durham, N.C.: Duke University Press, 1975.

Bloom, Harold, ed. *Hemingway: Modern Critical Views*. New York: Chelsea House Publishers, 1985.

Contemporary Authors, Vols. 77-80. Detroit: Gale Research Co.

Contemporary Literary Criticism, Vols. 1, 3, 6, 8, 10, 13, 19, 30, 34, 39, 41, 44. Detroit: Gale Research Co.

Dictionary of Literary Biography, Vols. 4, 9; *Dictionary of Literary Biography Yearbook: 1981; Dictionary of Literary Biography Documentary Series*, Vol. 1. Detroit: Gale Research Co.

Flora, Joseph M. *Hemingway's Nick Adams*. Baton Rouge: Louisiana State University Press, 1982.

Gurko, Leo. *Ernest Hemingway and the Pursuit of Heroism*. New York: Thomas Y. Crowell Co., 1968.

Howell, John M., ed. *Hemingway's African Stories: The Stories, Their Sources, Their Critics*. New York: Charles Scribner's Sons, 1969.

Jobes, Katharine T., ed. *Twentieth-Century Interpretations of "The Old Man and the Sea": A Collection of Critical Essays*. Englewood Cliffs: Prentice-Hall, 1968.

Lee, A. Robert, ed. *Ernest Hemingway: New Critical Essays*. Totowa: Barnes & Noble, 1983.

Meyers, Jeffrey, ed. *Hemingway: The Critical Heritage*. London: Routledge & Kegan Paul, 1982.

——. *Hemingway: A Biography*. New York: Harper & Row, 1985.

Oldsey, Bernard. *Hemingway's Hidden Craft: The Writing of "A Farewell to Arms."* University Park: Pennsylvania State University Press, 1979.

Rovit, Earl. *Ernest Hemingway.* New York: Twayne, 1963.

Short Story Criticism, Vol. 1. Detroit: Gale Research Co.

Wagner, Linda Welshimer, ed. *Ernest Hemingway: Five Decades of Criticism.* East Lansing: Michigan State University Press, 1974.

Waldhorn, Arthur. *A Reader's Guide to Ernest Hemingway.* New York: Farrar, Straus & Giroux, 1972.

Weeks, Robert P., ed. *Hemingway: A Collection of Critical Essays.* Englewood Cliffs: Prentice-Hall, 1962.

Young, Philip. *Ernest Hemingway: A Reconsideration.* University Park: Pennsylvania State University Press, 1966.

O. Henry
1862-1910

American short story writer, humorist, and journalist.

"The Gift of the Magi" (short story, 1906)

"The Gift of the Magi" takes place on Christmas Eve during the early 1900s in a shabby eight-dollar flat in the city. It is the story of young lovers **Della** and **James Dillingham Young,** who, though poor, are blessed in their love and regard for one another. Each character, yearning to give a worthy Christmas gift to the other, sacrifices his only possession of value to that end. Della's most outstanding trait and source of pride is her hair, a mane described as so magnificent that it would inspire envy in the Queen of Sheba. Having been unable to save enough money to buy her husband a gift, Della sells her hair for twenty dollars, which she uses to buy a beautiful platinum fob chain for her husband's most prized possession, his grandfather's gold watch. Della is unaware that the watch, described as grand enough to rival the treasures of King Solomon, had also been sold that day, enabling Jim to purchase a set of jeweled tortoiseshell combs for Della's wonderful hair.

The Youngs are typical O. Henry characters: vagabonds, shop girls, cowboys, and minor criminals who suffer poverty, hunger, and loneliness. Yet despite their circumstances, these figures tend to accept rather than bemoan their humble situations while maintaining a belief that all will be for the best. O. Henry's stories are famous for their ironic conclusions, as evidenced in "The Gift of the Magi." The allusions to the Queen of Sheba and King Solomon add to the humor of the tale, while the descriptions of the couple's meager circumstances and innocent love provide pathos. Thematically, in this story, as well as in most of his work, O. Henry demonstrates that even the most insignificant of us has a story to tell and, as spokesman for the underdog, he relates his tales with humor and compassion.

"The Last Leaf" (short story, 1907)

Set in the beginning of the twentieth century in Greenwich Village, "The Last Leaf" describes the impoverished surroundings of three unpromising artists. **Sue** and **Johnsy,** two young women, share an upper flat in a three-story brick building. On the lowest level lives **Old Behrman,** described as having the head of a satyr with the body of an imp. Past sixty and a drinker, Behrman has yet to paint his long-awaited masterpiece.

In November, Johnsy contracts pneumonia, and because she is inclined toward the melodramatic, claims that she chooses not to fight for her life. The doctor, concluding that she had lost the will to live, gives Johnsy only a one-in-ten chance for survival. She contents herself with watching the leaves fall from a dying ivy plant outside of her bedroom window and explains to Sue that she fancies her life will end as the last leaf falls from the ivy.

Concerned with the welfare of her roommate, Sue confides her troubled thoughts to Old Behrman who, that night in the icy rain, paints his masterpiece—an ivy leaf upon the wall. Unaware of his action, and after days of waiting for the last leaf to fall, Johnsy renounces her foolish attitude and takes a marked turn for the better. Ironically, Old Berhman's act of affection and artistry leads to pneumonia, and he dies.

Much of the tale's charm is due to the author's understanding and successful communication of a young girl's romantic ideas and melodramatic notions. O. Henry ironically employs art as a tool of deception, inspiring health and well-being as well as illness and death. He also shows how Old Behrman's actions are not totally selfless, for his heroic deed enabled him to realize his life's dream: the painting of his masterpiece.

FURTHER READING

Brooks, Van Wyck. "New York: O. Henry." In *The Confident Years: 1885-1952*, pp. 271-82. New York: E. P. Dutton, 1952.

Current-Garcia, Eugene. *O. Henry*. Boston: Twayne, 1965.

Forman, Henry James. "O. Henry's Short Stories." In *Waifs and Strays: Twelve Stories by O. Henry*, pp. 277-80. New York: Doubleday, Page and Co., 1917.

Leacock, Stephen. "The Amazing Genius of O. Henry." In *Essays and Literary Studies*, pp. 231-66. Toronto: McClelland and Stewart Limited, 1916.

Pattee, Fred Lewis. "O. Henry and the Handbooks." In *The Development of the American Short Story: An Historical Survey*, pp. 357-76. New York: Harper and Row, 1923.

Peel, Donald F. "A Critical Study of the Short Stories of O. Henry." *The Northwest Missouri State College Studies* 25, No. 4 (1 November 1961): 3-24.

Twentieth-Century Literary Criticism, Vols. 1, 19. Detroit: Gale Research Co.

Hermann Hesse
1877-1962

German-born Swiss novelist, poet, and short story writer.

Demian (novel, 1919)

The novel, set in Germany before World War I, is **Emil Sinclair**'s chronicle of self-exploration. The work is deeply influenced by Hesse's own experiences in psychotherapy and Carl Jung's interpretation of dreams and symbols. The work begins when Sinclair is ten years old and on the threshold of adolescence. While at school he meets **Max Demian,** a young man of uncanny insight and sensitivity to whom he is drawn. Demian is the first person who Sinclair hears questioning traditional beliefs, which sparks and develops his own doubts regarding family, society, and faith.

Demian moves away, and Sinclair is sent away to school. There, he lives a dissolute life, but is moved to reform when he sees a lovely young woman whom he never meets but who becomes a symbol of spiritual longing and purity; he names her Beatrice. Sinclair has begun to paint, and his dreams become vivid with new images, which he tries to capture in his art. One day he paints a portrait of Beatrice but realizes that the face is Demian's and that the painting also incorporates his "inner self" and his "daemon." He sends Demian a painting of a bird inspired by a dream, and Demian replies, interpreting the work and mentioning the name Abraxas, a figure representing the union of the godly and the demonic in humankind. Sinclair learns more about Abraxas through **Pistorius,** a former theology student and a musician who functions as teacher to Sinclair during the last years of his schooling and who encourages his inward quest.

Sinclair has a recurrent dream in which he embraces his mother, who is transformed into a hermaphroditic figure resembling Demian. He realizes that this figure lives within him and to understand it will lead him to greater self-knowledge. When he next meets Demian, he meets his mother as well, recognizing in her his dream image, incorporating "daemon and mother, fate and beloved." **Frau Eva,** as her name implies, is a universal mother figure; Sinclair loves her deeply, and she appears to know and understand his innermost being, desires, and dreams. Through Eva and her circle, Sinclair learns of the coming cataclysm of war. When the war begins, Demian and Sinclair enlist. Sinclair is wounded, and as he lies recovering, he sees Demian in the bed next to him. Demian dies, and Sinclair, transformed by the experience, knows that Demian is within him as "my brother, my master."

Noted for its poetic prose style, the novel also incorporates such recurrent themes in Hesse's work as the double and the spiritual quest. It is also noted for its portrait of a generation whose lives were irrevocably changed by World War I.

Siddhartha (novel, 1922)

The novel is set in India and, like much of Hesse's fiction, is autobiographical in nature, reflecting his study of Eastern religions and philosophies. The story follows the events of **Siddhartha**'s spiritual quest, taking him from youth to old age. As the novel begins, we see Siddhartha, the son of a wealthy Brahmin, disturbed at the discrepancy between the teaching of his youth and life as it exists. Siddhartha is searching for fulfillment, truth, and peace, and feeling that he cannot find them in his privileged home life, he gives up his possessions and decides to become a wandering monk. As a Samana, he learns to fast and to deny the sensual aspects of his being, but neither this, nor a meeting with the Buddha, gives him the sense of unity that he seeks. He then chooses to lead a life devoted to commerce and the sensual pleasures, which provides him with wealth and the joys of the flesh, which he learns from the beautiful courtesan, **Kamala.** Although he is a success at this worldly life, he yearns for more. He leaves, not knowing that Kamala is pregnant by him. Wandering in despair, he even contemplates suicide; but he remembers the indestructibleness of life and decides to continue on his quest for self-knowledge.

Siddhartha spends the next several years in the company of **Vasudeva,** a ferryman who teaches him the secret of the river, a symbol for the natural forces of the universe. His contemplative existence is disturbed when Kamala, accompanied by his son, reach the ferry landing one day on a religious pilgrimage. Kamala is bitten by a snake and dies, and Siddhartha is forced to confront a bitter, unloving son who resents his father and who robs him and runs away. The experience wounds Siddhartha deeply, but over time he learns, through self-renunciation, to devote himself in love and acceptance to the powers of the universe. The conclusion finds him at one with God in this understanding.

The novel is considered to be one of Hesse's best-written works, admired for the simplicity and lyricism of its prose. It was embraced by a generation of young readers in the 1960s and 1970s for its evocative portrayal of youth in quest of self-knowledge.

Steppenwolf (novel, 1927)

The novel relates the story of **Harry Haller,** a fifty-year-old writer. Harry, isolated from the bourgeois society he loathes, calls himself a ''wolf of the Steppes,'' and, like many other heroes in Hesse, is an outsider. And like other Hesse characters, he contains autobiographical elements, as evidenced in his name and the names of other central figures in the novel which begin with ''H.'' Harry is always searching for truth and longing for spiritual fulfillment, driven by his loneliness and despair to even consider suicide. But because he has devoted himself to the cerebral and spiritual, he has denied the sensuous in human experience, which he must learn and which he must integrate to find the peace he seeks.

He encounters **Hermine,** a prostitute who functions as Harry's double and who, like Demian, is a hermaphroditic character, described as boyish in appearance and reminding Harry of his childhood friend, Hermann. With Hermine, he enters the ''magic theater,'' a realm of mirrors and of fantasy. When Harry looks in the mirrors, he sees his fragmented self, which he must learn to make whole. In the company of Hermine and her friend **Pablo,** Harry explores the realms of the senses, experimenting with sexuality, alcohol, and drugs in an atmosphere imbued with jazz music. He finds Hermine and Pablo together one day in the magic theater and, furious with jealousy, stabs and kills Hermine. He is tried and convicted of bringing reality into the realm of fantasy in the magic theater, of stabbing the ''reflection'' of a girl, and of being ''devoid of humor.'' Mozart is present at the proceedings, and after denouncing Harry's actions, he is transformed into Pablo. It becomes apparent that the murder and trial have been a game, one in which Harry was an unwilling participant, but one that has shocked him into self-knowledge.

The story of the Steppenwolf is structured as the ''record'' of Harry Haller, labelled ''For Madmen Only,'' and is introduced by a preface purportedly written by the son of Harry's landlady, warning the reader of the curious life of Haller and the extent of his isolation. The novel continues Hesse's exploration of the double, the search for identity, and the isolation of the tormented individual in quest of self-knowledge and spiritual wholeness.

The Glass Bead Game (novel, 1943)

The novel takes place several centuries in the future and focuses on the life of **Joseph Knecht.** It is divided into several sections: the first describes the origins of the glass bead game, the second relates the life of Joseph Knecht, the Master of the Game, or the Magister Ludi, and the final portions contain Knecht's posthumous writings. In this work Hesse relates his despair for life and culture in the twentieth century, for from the vantage point of 2400 A.D., his narrator describes the madness and corruption of the era. Because of the disintegration of culture, the society of the future has provided a place—Castalia—for the intellectual elite to live and nurture the life of the mind. This aristocracy, sequestered from society, is the world of Knecht, and we see him grow from youth to become master of the community. The game itself is a synthesis of the function and activity of music, mathematics, philosophy, and science, and cultivates the minds of those who play it, schooling them in the cultural wealth of the ages.

As Knecht grows, he encounters a variety of teachers who influence his thought. He debates with **Plinio Designiori,** who instructs him in the worldly life, and with **Father Jacobus,** who stresses the importance of history. The greatest influence on Knecht is his music teacher, through whom he learns the serenity and inner freedom of the life devoted to music. Yet the world of Castalia, although seemingly devoted to the ideals of freedom, brotherhood, and democracy, is plagued by the lure of power and domination that has troubled humankind through the ages. That it is also a place devoted solely to the life of the mind weighs heavily on Knecht, who, like so many figures in Hesse's fiction, feels the need to integrate the intellect with the life of action. Thus, he decides to leave Castalia and to devote himself to his young pupil, **Tito.** At his death, Kencht has grown from the master of the intellect to one who embodies the ability and the will to unite the divided self in active life.

The work is considered one of Hesse's finest accomplishments and won him the Nobel Prize in Literature in 1946. For all its seriousness, the novel has a comic tone, evidenced in the narrator's pedantic manner, the linguistic jokes that abound in the work, and Hesse's thinly disguised portraits of such literary figures as Friedrich Nietszche and Thomas Mann.

FURTHER READING

Beerman, Hans. "Hermann Hesse and the 'Bhagavad-Gita.'" *The Midwest Quarterly* 1, No. 1 (October 1959): 27-40.

Contemporary Authors, Vols. 17-18; *Contemporary Authors Permanent Series,* Vol. 2. Detroit: Gale Research Co.

Contemporary Literary Criticism, Vols. 1, 2, 3, 6, 11, 17, 25. Detroit: Gale Research Co.

Fickert, Kurt J. "The Development of the Outsider Concept in Hesse's Novels." *Monatshefte* 52, No. 4 (April-May 1960): 171-78.

Flaxman, Seymour L. *"Der Steppenwolf:* Hesse's Portrait of the Intellectual." *Modern Language Quarterly* 15, No. 4 (December 1954): 349-58.

Freedman, Ralph. "Romantic Imagination: Hermann Hesse as a Lyrical Novelist." In *The Lyrical Novel: Studies in Hermann Hesse, André Gide, and Virginia Woolf,* pp. 42-118. Princeton: Princeton University Press, 1963.

Johnson, Sidney M. "The Autobiographies in Hermann Hesse's *Glasperlenspiel.*" *The German Quarterly* 29, No. 3 (May 1956): 160-71.

Mann, Thomas. "Introduction." In *Demian* by Hermann Hesse, pp. v-xi. New York: Harper & Row, 1965.

Middleton, Christopher. "Neighing in the Wind." *New York Review of Books* 26, No. 3 (8 March 1979): 31-5.

Sammons, Jeffrey L. "Hermann Hesse and the Over-Thirty Germanist." In *Hermann Hesse: A Collection of Critical Essays,* Theodore Ziolkowski, ed., pp. 112-33. Englewood Cliffs: Prentice Hall, 1973.

Schwarz, Egon. "Hermann Hesse, the American Youth Movement, and Problems of Literary Evaluation." *PMLA* 85, No. 4 (October 1970): 977-87.

Seidlin, Oskar. "Hermann Hesse: The Exorcism of The Demon." In *Hermann Hesse: A Collection of Critical Essays,* Theodore Ziolkowski, ed., pp. 51-75. Englewood Cliffs: Prentice-Hall, 1973.

Ziolkowski, Theodore. *The Novels of Hermann Hesse.* Princeton: Princeton University Press, 1965.

William Dean Howells
1837-1920
American novelist, critic, and essayist.

The Rise of Silas Lapham (novel, 1885)

Set in nineteenth-century New England, the story centers on **Silas Lapham,** a self-made paint manufacturer. His recent rise in wealth and social class have earned him an interview with **Bartley Hubbard,** a bemused, subtly mocking, Bostonian journalist to whom the uncultured Lapham proudly unravels his humble beginnings and determined pursuit of financial success. To his credit, Lapham gratefully acknowledges his wife's industry, forethought, and companionship. Yet, he avoids mention of a **Mr. Milton K. Rogers,** his early creditor and partner, whom he unscrupulously edged out of the business when huge profits were imminent. **Mrs. Persis Lapham** was always troubled by the incident; so, too, was Lapham. While never admitting to any wrongdoing or ethical misconduct, he assuages his conscience by agreeing to loan Rogers a substantial sum.

The symbol of Lapham's materialism and shallowness is the construction of a palatial home in Boston's Back Bay district. His daughters, **Irene** and **Penelope,** are apprehensive of the move, for they recognize their parents' social inadequacies and limitations. Further embarrassment occurs when **Tom Corey,** a member of the Bostonian elite, visits the Laphams, ostensibly interested in Irene. Two moral dilemmas follow. First, Corey belatedly reveals his love for Penelope rather than Irene and must choose between the two daughters. Second, Lapham—whose fortunes are crumbling and whose incomplete house has been ruined by fire—must choose to accept money under questionable pretenses or resign himself to certain loss. Both men choose properly, according to personal dictates of conscience as well as the socially responsible mandates of utilitarianism. At the novel's conclusion, **David Sewell,** the family minister, shows Lapham a changed man, now humble and honest instead of boastful and superficial. Lapham has salvaged a small portion of his once towering wealth, but, more importantly, he has saved his humanity.

Silas Lapham's rise begins with the elevation of moral character and his willingness to see his behavior as inextricably tied to the welfare of those around him. Howells, rebelling against the popular romantic fiction of the day, sought through realism, a theory central to his fiction, to disperse "the conventional acceptations by which men live on easy terms with themselves" that they might "examine the grounds of their social and moral opinions." Through presentation of detailed impressions of everyday life and the conscious absence of authorial commentary, he accomplished these ends in his best-known work.

A Hazard of New Fortunes (novel, 1890)

A semi-autobiographical novel, *A Hazard of New Fortunes* takes place in New York City in the 1880s. After eighteen undistinguished years with a Boston insurance firm, **Basil March** resigns. An acquaintance, **Mr. Fulkerson,** persuades March to move to New York and assume the editorship of a new literary magazine he is currently promoting. The enterprise seems suited to March, who once hoped for a literary career. His wife, **Isabel,** and children also become convinced, after long deliberation, of the propitiousness of the venture. From the first issue, *Every Other Week* is a huge success, thanks to the tutelage of **Henry Lindau,** a German socialist whom March had hired to handle foreign articles and reviews. Although several characters important to the magazine's operation are introduced and detailed, it is the magazine's owner, **Mr. Dryfoos,** and his son **Conrad** who emerge as most significant to the narrative development. A newly made millionaire, Dryfoos has bought the magazine to make Conrad its publisher and to dissuade him from a career in the ministry.

The scheme self-destructs after Dryfoos hosts a party to toast the magazine's success and discovers that Lindau is a socialist whose economic views vehemently oppose the capitalistic sentiments held by Dryfoos. Some time after Lindau's resignation from the staff, a streetcar strike occurs. Conrad, severely unhappy as a businessman and continually at odds with his father, joins the workers on the street. When he spies Lindau among the protesters being beaten by the police, he intervenes but dies from a stray bullet fired during the melee. Lindau dies shortly after, before Dryfoos can apologize for what he now recognizes as his own woefully misguided behavior. The shock of Conrad's death forces Dryfoos to undergo a radical transformation of character. The novel closes when the millionaire graciously sells the periodical to March and Fulkerson under terms highly favorable to them, thus enabling both men to realize secure futures.

Written at the peak of his literary powers, *A Hazard of New Fortunes* was the product of Howells's growing awareness of the hardships inflicted upon the poor and working class by the *laissez-faire* capitalist system. During this time Howells followed Leo Tolstoy's example and promoted Christian socialism as a just alternative to economic inequalities and injustices, embracing Tolstoy's theory of complicity: the doctrine that each person bears responsibility for the spiritual and physical well-being of all other persons.

FURTHER READING

Bennett, George N. *William Dean Howells: The Development of a Novelist.* Norman: University of Oklahoma Press, 1959.

Carrington, George C. *The Immense Complex Drama: The World and Art of the Howells Novel.* Syracuse: Syracuse University Press, 1958.

Contemporary Authors, Vol. 104. Detroit: Gale Research Co.

Cook, Don L., ed. *The Rise of Silas Lapham,* by William Dean Howells. Norton Critical Edition. New York: W. W. Norton & Co., 1982.

Dictionary of Literary Biography, Vol. 1. Detroit: Gale Research Co.

Ebel, Kenneth. *Howells: A Century of Criticism.* Dallas: Southern Methodist University Press, 1962.

Kirk, Clara M. and Rudolf Kirk. *William Dean Howells.* New York: Twayne, 1962.

McMurray, William. *The Literary Realism of William Dean Howells.* Carbondale: Southern Illinois University Press, 1967.

Twentieth-Century Literary Criticism, Vols. 7, 17. Detroit: Gale Research Co.

Vanderbilt, Kermit. *The Achievement of William Dean Howells: A Reinterpretation.* Princeton: Princeton University Press, 1969.

Zora Neale Hurston
1891-1960
American novelist, short story writer, and critic.

Their Eyes Were Watching God (novel, 1937)

Hurston's best-known novel is set in Florida in the 1920s and 1930s. Its heroine is **Janie Crawford,** a young woman of intelligence, energy, and spunk who spends nearly the first four decades of her life tied to two mundane, materialistic husbands. She has married them largely to please her grandmother, who constantly urged her beloved granddaughter to find someone to provide well for her so that she wouldn't suffer the black woman's burdened and broken fate. But Janie realizes gradually what has been in her heart all along: that the genuine fulfillment she has always craved requires far more than material objects and leisure. **Vergible "Tea Cakes" Woods** is the vital spirited man who comes along and urges Janie to truly pursue life. Although he is several years younger than she and their liaison considered scandalous, the two marry and together exist in almost Edenic happiness, equally giving and taking and living without regard to societal expectations or restrictions. Their blissful life ends abruptly when Janie is forced to shoot Tea Cake to death after he is bitten by a rabid dog. But Janie, feeling that her third husband has given her the resources to remain happy and whole, accepts his death, joyful for the time the two shared. As she tells her best friend, **Phoeby,** ''if yuh kin see de light at daybreak, you don't keer if you die at dusk. It's so many people never seen de light at all. Ah wuz fumblin' round and God opened de door.''

The novel, considered an early, powerful affirmation of black womanhood, is praised for its quick, idiomatic dialogue and vivid depiction of life in rural Florida, Hurston's native milieu. Rediscovered during the 1960s, *Their Eyes Were Watching God* is now regarded as a classic of black American feminist fiction. Similarly, Janie Crawford is revered and acknowledged as a foremother of the many powerful black female characters created by such writers as Toni Morrison and Alice Walker.

FURTHER READING

Contemporary Authors, Vols. 85-88. Detroit: Gale Research Co.

Contemporary Literary Criticism, Vols. 7, 30. Detroit: Gale Research Co.

Dictionary of Literary Biography, Vol. 51. Detroit: Gale Research Co.

Hemenway, Robert. *Zora Neale Hurston: A Literary Biography.* Champaign: University of Illinois Press, 1977.

Howard, Lillie P. *Zora Neale Hurston.* Boston: Twayne, 1980.

Turner, Darwin T. *In a Minor Chord.* Carbondale: Southern Illinois University Press, 1971.

Aldous Huxley
1894-1963

English novelist, essayist, and poet.

Point Counter Point (novel, 1928)

The novel is a complex and difficult work, made up of a series of short scenes covering a wide range of characters. The music of Bach and the harmonic method of counterpoint are central to the work: as in musical counterpoint, the lives of the characters are juxtaposed as competing themes to reveal the fragmented nature of human existence and the essential isolation of humanity. **Philip Quarles** is a novelist who keeps journals for his ruminations on the nature of life. As an artist, he wants to capture the multiplicity of points of view that he notes in the world about him. He wishes to be a novelist of ideas, and there is the sense in his work that he does indeed live his life through ideas and through fiction, alienated and separate from others. Juxtaposed to him are two characters, **Mark Rampion** and **Maurice Spandrell,** who offer opposing views of life. Rampion is an artist whose paintings focus on the fragmented life he sees around him. A realist, he finds the vapidness of modern life reprehensible and preaches a wholeness of vision in art and in life. Just as he represents the belief in the unity of life, Spandrell embodies negativity. He is governed by the belief that all action is preordained by God, and he lives a life of amorality and nihilism, punctuated with acts of violence and cruelty, as if to question and challenge an unknowable God; he ends his life a suicide.

Huxley's use of counterpoint is both a stylistic and thematic tool, for he is able, through the juxtaposition of character and scene, to illustrate the fragmented reality of the modern world, showing how the separate lives are interwoven, like the individual voices in a piece of music, creating little harmony but much dissonance.

Brave New World (novel, 1932)

Huxley's famous dystopian novel is set in a future society in which the horrors of modern technology have created a static human order. It is a world free of war and disease in which a set number of classes of people (Alphas, Betas, etc.) are bred in test tubes for specific levels of intelligence and suitablity to types of work. All diversity and creativity has been ''bred'' out of them, and they are conditioned, through ''sleep teaching,'' to conform to a society that rejects individuality and personal freedom. A drug, ''soma,'' dulls the senses to feelings of loneliness or sadness; sex is for recreation only, free of moral strictures or emotional ties. Marriage, family, and child rearing are replaced by state-run child production and education. Henry Ford, creator of the assembly line, is the godhead of the culture, and the opening sequence depicts fetuses in test tubes on conveyor belts, going through their process of maturation.

But a dissenter against the order exists: **John the Savage,** born ''naturally'' of a mother who forgot to take her birth control pills while visiting an Indian reservation, is a young man who has been raised outside the utopian society. He knows about humans through the Indians and through a copy of Shakespeare he found on the reservation.

He is discovered and taken back to the civilized world by **Bernard Marx** and **Lenina Crowne,** who have come to the reservation for a vacation. Bernard is considered something of a misfit himself, because he wants to commit to a monogamous relationship with Lenina, who finds his emotions alarming. In fact, there are rumors that Bernard received an imbalance of chemicals during his incubation, resulting in his often strange thoughts and behavior. John is taken to London and displayed as a kind of freak. He weeps at his mother's death, refuses to have casual sex with Lenina, and commits similar offenses and challenges to the society in which he is a Savage. He meets **Sir Mustafa Mond,** a World Controller and the only other human who knows Shakespeare, who lectures him on the dangers of the writer. Mond's society denies the brilliant variety of humanity that abounds in Shakespeare's work—the joy and tragedy, the knowledge of self and death—and that has formed the character of the Savage. John is especially torn by his attraction to Lenina, drawn to her sexually, yet tormented by his strong emotional needs. Out of rage and frustration, he kills her, after which, in an act of penitence, he commits suicide.

Huxley's satiric masterpiece depicts the destruction of the individual, whose will and sense of personal purpose he saw threatened by the values of modern culture. He also cautions against the view that history is linear and charts the inevitable progress of humanity. Instead, he posits that history is the story of individuals of diverse backgrounds, thoughts, and achievements. In a work noted for its brilliant parody and chilling insight, Huxley created a novel that stands with George Orwell's *1984* as the major dystopian literature of the century.

FURTHER READING

Beach, Joseph Warren. ''Counterpoint: Aldous Huxley.'' In *The Twentieth Century Novel: Studies in Technique,* pp. 458-69. New York: Century, 1932.

Bowering, Peter. *Aldous Huxley: A Study of the Major Novels.* New York: Oxford University Press, 1969.

Contemporary Authors, Vols. 85-88. Detroit: Gale Research Co.

Contemporary Literary Criticism, Vols. 1, 3, 4, 5, 8, 11, 18, 35. Detroit: Gale Research Co.

Daiches, David. *The Novel and the Modern World.* Chicago: University of Chicago Press, 1939.

Dictionary of Literary Biography, Vol. 36. Detroit: Gale Research Co.

Firchow, Peter E. *Aldous Huxley, Satirist and Novelist.* Minneapolis: University of Minnesota Press, 1972.

Maurois, André. *Prophets and Poets,* translated by Hamish Miles. New York: Harper, 1935.

May, Keith M. *Aldous Huxley.* London: Elek, 1972.

Joris-Karl Huysmans
1848-1907
French novelist and critic.

Against the Grain (novel, 1884)

This novel, considered Huysmans's most important work, is best known for its presentation of the character of **Jean Floressas des Esseintes,** whose story forms "the history of a decadent soul in search of an earthly paradise," according to one critic.

Duke des Esseintes, a wealthy aristocrat, is a man devoted to pleasure and the life of the senses. He prizes the realm of the imagination and rejects the world of reality, abandoning himself to the sensual. Tiring of the world of Parisian society, he retreats to the seclusion of his house at Fontenay, where he surrounds himself with a collection of art and literature notable for its exoticism, perversity, and beauty. The work is essentially plotless, and the major portion of the novel is devoted to des Esseintes's thoughts on art and literature, which have been studied as Huysmans's own aesthetic philosophy.

As indicated in the title, des Esseintes is a representative of the cult of artificiality: he is "against the grain," against nature, and his rejection of the natural order is revealed in his perverse, exotic tastes. Solitary and removed from society, he tries to stimulate his senses through his indulgence in aberrant and self-destructive behavior, pursuing pleasure to the point of exhaustion and boredom. His artistic credo, embraced by the decadent movement, is art for art's sake, and this sensibility governs his thought. The elaborate, tortured literary language that characterizes the work reveals des Esseintes's inner turmoil, and his religious conflict in particular is revealed in his thoughts on spiritual and sensual desire, a central concern throughout Huysmans's work.

For its distillation of the philosophy of decadence, *Against the Grain* influenced such later writers as Oscar Wilde, George Moore, and Aubrey Beardsley, and Huysmans himself said that it contained all of the themes he was to elaborate in his later works. Stylistically, the novel is characterized by a complex, exotic prose and reflects Huysmans's revolt against the precepts of naturalism that he had embraced earlier in his career. The novel is also noted for its detailed, often grotesque description, which Huysmans claimed was a result of his Dutch ancestry and which reflects the influence of the Dutch school of still-life painting on the work.

FURTHER READING

Contemporary Authors, Vol. 104. Detroit: Gale Research Co.

Ellis, Havelock. "Huysmans." In *Affirmations,* pp. 158-211. New York: Houghton Mifflin, 1922.

Ridge, George Ross. *Joris-Karl Huysmans.* New York: Twayne, 1968.

Praz, Mario. "Byzantium." In *The Romantic Agony,* pp. 301-403. Oxford: Oxford University Press, 1951.

Twentieth-Century Literary Criticism, Vol. 7. Detroit: Gale Research Co.

Henrik Ibsen
1828-1906
Norwegian dramatist.

A Doll's House (drama, 1879)

The play is Ibsen's most famous work, well-known throughout the world for its handling of the theme of the oppression of women in society. As the play begins, we see **Nora,** the wife of **Torvald Helmer,** depicted as a manipulative, frivolous woman, obsessed with money and condescendingly referred to by her husband as a "lark," a "squirrel," and a "featherhead." But as the play develops, we learn that Nora's frivolity is a mask. Several years earlier, to raise money when Torvald was ill, she had forged her father's signature on a bond to borrow from an unscrupulous money-lender named **Nils Krogstad.** Nora presents herself as she does because she desperately needs the money her husband dangles before her, forcing her to perform like a "doll" for him.

Krogstad, a lawyer with a low-ranking position in her husband's bank, has lost the respect of the community because he, too, forged a document. He threatens Nora with exposure to her husband if she does anything to deprive him of his position and has written Torvald a letter outlining Nora's actions. She desperately tries to prevent her husband from receiving the letter, but her efforts are in vain. When he has read it, Torvald's attitude changes from that of an indulgent, patronizing husband to a scorned and shamed man, and he threatens to throw Nora out of the house, telling her she is unfit to raise their children. At that moment, a letter from Krogstad arrives, returning Nora's bond and releasing her from her debt. Torvald's manner towards Nora changes immediately, and he is full of love and forgiveness; but the experience has profoundly affected Nora. Her actions had been motivated by love for him, and yet he was able to renounce his love for her, to deprive her of the home and family she had worked so boldly to save. Now, although he reminds her that her duties are to him and her children, she can claim that "I believe that before all else, I am a human being . . . or at least I should try to become one." She wants a real marriage, based on mutual respect, which she knows is impossible with Torvald. She leaves her stammering and bewildered husband, slamming the door behind her.

A Doll's House reflects Ibsen's passionate commitment to presenting social concerns within a realistic format. Thus the work centers on the legal and social plight of women in nineteenth-century society, particularly on their subjection to men. Stylistically, the play represents a departure from Ibsen's earlier verse dramas, written in prose and similar in structure to other "well-made" plays of the late nineteenth century.

Ghosts (drama, 1882)

The play is set on a mist-obscured fjord in western Norway in the home of **Helen Alving.** She is a widow about to open an orphanage in honor of her late husband. Her son, **Oswald,** an artist who lives in Paris, has returned home for the event. As the play begins, we see Mrs. Alving talking with **Manders,** the parish pastor. He is depicted as a narrow-minded, hypocritical prig, upbraiding Mrs. Alving for her "modern ideas" and trying to shame her with remembrances of her youth, when she had left her husband. Mrs. Alving, a woman of strength and independence, tells Manders that her husband was an alcoholic and a profligate, and that their life together was misery. She had also left her husband hoping to be welcomed by Manders, whom she truly loved; he seems as unable to acknowledge this as he is to accept the truth about her life with her husband. She had sent Oswald away as a young boy to spare him from his father, and yet has spent the years since her husband's death creating an image of a great man for her son; now they are preparing to commemorate his life with an orphanage. Yet the truth will emerge, and the "ghosts" of the title, both the presence of the dead among the living and the "dead ideas" that haunt the characters, begin to appear.

Two recurrent themes in Ibsen's work are evidenced in this drama. His condemnation of the hypocrisy of society is evident in his mocking portrayal of Manders, the representative of staid, middle-class morality. Ibsen often explored the factor of heredity in determining the personality and fate of the individual. Here, we get a glimpse of the presence of these "ghosts" when Mrs. Alving sees Oswald making sexual advances to the maid, **Regina.** Years before, she had caught her husband and the maid **Joanna** in the same situation, and the union had resulted in Regina. Mrs. Alving had quickly found a husband for Joanna and had raised Regina as a servant. When Oswald makes it clear that he wishes to marry Regina, Mrs. Alving is forced to reveal the truth to them. But Oswald's "inheritance" from his father goes farther: he is going mad, a congenital condition acquired through his father. He entreats his mother to help him to commit suicide when his next attack comes; she is horrified at the prospect. As the play closes, the sun has at last broken through the mist, yet the light has come into Oswald's life too late, and he appears lost to the darkness of his mental state. The play is noted for its harsh social criticism and its straight-forward presentation of such controversial topics as adultery, syphilis, and incest, which created a storm of protest when the play first appeared. The symbolism which later dominated Ibsen's work is evident here in the recurrent images of light and darkness.

Brand (drama, 1885)

The play takes place in a coastal village in Norway in the mid-nineteenth century. Although the play was first performed in 1885, it was written in 1865 and represents Ibsen's exploration of the hero.

Brand, a mission preacher who sees his calling as "the salvation of Man," is an uncompromising man, as is evident in his "all or nothing" philosophy. Early in the play, he meets his old school friend **Enjar** and his betrothed, **Agnes.** Their light-hearted gaiety offends Brand, who speaks of the sickness of the modern era and chides his friend for his life of compromise. As he journeys in the mountains he meets **Gerd,** whom the villagers call a witch. She tells Brand she has been attacked by a hawk and invites him to go with her to the Ice Church. Later, Brand enters a village where the people are starving and where a woman appears looking for a priest to shrive her husband, who has killed one of their children in desperation. Brand willingly goes despite great danger and is accompanied by Agnes, who leaves Enjar. We are also introduced to Brand's mother, who is presented as a cold woman, caring for little but money and encouraging her son to live a more conventional life, stressing the importance of the sacrifice she has made for him and his inheritance.

Three years elapse before the next act begins. Brand and Agnes are married with a young son, **Ulf.** Brand's mother is dying, and she sends for her son, who refuses to go to her until she agrees to renounce all of her wealth; the mother dies without seeing her son. His friend the doctor urges him to change, to "be humane," but he cannot. Ulf is ill, and the doctor tells Brand that they must move to another climate to save the boy's life. But Brand is reminded that his leaving would constitute a compromise in his mission. Once again tormented by the demands of his God and the inability to betray his faith, Brand remains in the village; his beloved child dies. Brand decides that he must build a new church; by the time it is complete, Agnes is dead. As his final act, Brand leads his followers into the mountains, yet they turn on him and stone him. When he reaches the summit, the figure of Agnes appears, telling him that his previous life was a dream and urging him to renounce his philosophy. He dismisses the figure as the hawk, "the spirit of compromise." He then sees Gerd, who mistakes him for Christ, and the two perish in an avalanche.

Written as a verse drama, *Brand* was intended by Ibsen to be considered a dramatic poem and not a work for the stage. He wanted to create a work unfettered by the limitations of the theater and the intellectual and aesthetic close-mindedness of his audience. In Ibsen's depiction of a hero driven by an uncompromising philosophy who ultimately learns the necessity and the consequences of fidelity to one's convictions, *Brand* evinces the influence of Kierkegaard's theories, particularly as revealed in his *Either-Or* and *Fear and Trembling*.

The Wild Duck (drama, 1885)

The play begins at the home of **Haakon Werle;** the occasion is a dinner party to which **Hjalmar Ekdal,** a boyhood friend of Werle's son **Gregers,** has been invited. The gaiety of the evening is momentarily broken when **Old Ekdal,** Hjalmar's father, appears. After being imprisoned for his involvement in a land scandal, Old Ekdal, formerly Werle's business associate, has been reduced to copying documents, and it is this that has brought him to Werle's house. Gregers, a disillusioned young man with a misplaced passion for honesty, is curious about his old friend's fate. Hjalmar is now a photographer, having been set up in business by Werle after his father's imprisonment. Hjalmar had also married **Gina,** a former maid in the Werle house, and the two have a daughter, **Hedvig,** who is fourteen. Hedvig is the keeper of the wild duck of the title, an animal that Werle had once wounded and given to the Ekdals. The duck lives in the attic of the Ekdal's home, among rabbits and fowl that Hjalmar and his father raise and shoot. Hedvig is a loving, innocent girl, devoted to her parents and her pet. Their domestic life is revealed as warm and affectionate, uniting the rather eccentric characters.

Gregers, still angry at his callous father's treatment of his late mother, sees in his handling of the Ekdals the need to make reparations for Werle's misdeeds. He knows that Gina had been his father's mistress, and the fact that Hedvig has weak eyes, like Werle, suggests that Hjalmar is not her real father. Driven by an idealism that convinces him that truth is always the best course, Gregers reveals what he knows to Ekdal. But his message shatters the family's happiness and ends in tragedy. When Hjalmar learns of Gina's past, he rejects both her and Hedvig. Gina is able to face his accusations, but Hedvig is bewildered and humiliated at her father's rejection. Gregers, always ready to idealize and symbolize a situation, convinces Hedvig that if she could make a sacrifice to her father in killing the wild duck, she could regain his love. Hedvig disappears into the attic and shoots herself.

The Wild Duck is one of Ibsen's best-known and most frequently performed plays. Although the work was written at the climax of Ibsen's period of social realism, it contains the emphasis on symbolism that marked his final phase. The wild duck as a symbol has been explored by numerous critics, who find parallels between the animal and Hedvig, Hjalmar, and other characters. In addition to his recurrent theme of the inescapable bonds of heredity, Ibsen also deals with falsehood and self-deception in this work.

Hedda Gabler (drama, 1891)

The drama is set in a villa in Christiana (now Oslo). It relates the story of **Hedda Tesman,** (née **Hedda Gabler**), the aristocratic daughter of a general, now married to **George Tesman,** a young scholar, and bored with the prospects her new life offers. As the play begins, the Tesmans have just returned from their wedding trip. Her character as it is revealed in the course of the play appears complex, ambiguous, and contradictory: she is at once materialistic and idealistic, yearning for honesty and beauty yet cruel and deceptive. As we learn in a scene in which Hedda and **Eilert Loevborg** talk, when Hedda was a young girl, he would amuse her with stories of his dissolute life. Hedda's curious voyeuristic nature is revealed in this relationship, for she was content to listen to Eilert's tales, but when he suggested that they might become involved, she threatened to shoot him. Now a respected historian whose brilliance threatens the appointment promised to the prosaic George, Eilert has begun an attachment with a married woman, **Thea Elvsted,** who is devoted to him and aids him in his work. Hedda is outraged at their happiness and plots to ruin them. She is obsessed with the idea of molding another's destiny and wants Eilert to be the object of her passion. She forces him to go a party with George, a situation she knows will drive him to old habits. As she had hoped, Eilert ends the evening in a dissolute state, but more importantly, he has lost his manuscript, which George has found and wishes to return to him, but which Hedda burns.

Eilert returns to the Tesman home looking for his manuscript, but Hedda calmly tells him it is not there. He knows he is a ruined man, and Hedda takes the opportunity to suggest that he end his life "beautifully," using one of her treasured pistols. Eilert takes the pistol and goes. Later we learn that he is dead, but not in the idealized way Hedda had imagined. Meanwhile, George and Mrs. Elvsted have decided to devote themselves to the recreation of Eilert's lost manuscript. Hedda's friend **Judge Brack** has discovered that her pistol has been involved in Eilert's death, and he plans to use the information to his own benefit. Hedda, who has tried and failed to control the lives of others, defiantly takes her own life.

Hedda is a destructive, vindictive, and dangerous woman, self-centered and rejecting all that represents warmth and compassion. Her hatred of physical and personal intimacy is stressed throughout the play, as in the vague references to her possible pregnancy, an idea she finds as revolting as Judge Brack's suggestion that she loves her husband. Praised for its finely delineated heroine and its taut construction, *Hedda Gabler* is one of Ibsen's finest dramatic works.

The Master Builder (drama, 1893)

The drama is set in the home of **Halvard Solness** in Norway. An architect, Solness is a man obsessed with youth and the threat of the younger generation. In his firm he employs **Knut Brovik,** an old man in failing health who was formerly head of the business, and Brovik's son, **Ragnar.** Threatened by the son, Solness endeavors to keep Ragnar in doubt about his own ability. He also employs **Kaia Fosli,** Ragnar's fiancee, whom he has convinced of his undying devotion. Solness and his wife **Aline** have a loveless marriage, due in large part to the deaths of their infant twin sons, who died when their mother, out of the overwhelming sense of "duty" that guides her life, nursed the children when she was ill, following a fire that ruined their home. The fire and the death of his sons transformed Halvard, for from that day he built no churches and devoted himself instead to designing "homes for human beings." He has become well-known and successful in this endeavor, outstripping his former master, Brovik, in the pursuit of the emblem of what is denied to him: a house full of love and children. Into this unhappy arrangement comes **Hilda Wangle,** a young woman in her twenties who had fallen in love with Solness years before, when he had dedicated a church in her town. He had teased her, calling her a princess and promising her a "kingdom"; now she has come to collect on the promise.

Hilda represents the youth that Solness fears and yet longs for, and she will prove to be his destruction. He is drawn to her and is carried away by her dreams of "castles in the air," yet there is an ominous presaging of events as Solness talks of his wife's fear that he is mad. In the conclusion, Solness, who has always been afraid of heights, is encouraged by Hilda to climb to the top of his own new home to hang a ceremonial wreath; all watch in horror as he falls to his death.

Acclaimed for its richly symbolic texture, *The Master Builder* is a major work of Ibsen's last period, when symbol and metaphor dominated his dramatic language. Solness is a man isolated by his art, his despair, and his madness, and is representative of the tormented protagonists who people Ibsen's final works.

FURTHER READING

Bentley, Eric. *The Playwright as Thinker: A Study of Drama in Modern Times.* London: Reynal & Hitchcock, 1946.

Bradbrook, M. C. *Ibsen the Norwegian: A Revaluation.* London: Chatto & Windus, 1948.

Brandes, Georg. "Henrik Ibsen." In *Eminent Authors of the Nineteenth Century: Literary Portraits,* translated by Rasmus B. Anderson, pp. 405-60. New York: Thomas Y. Crowell, 1886.

Brustein, Robert. "Ibsen and Revolt." In *The Theatre of Revolt: An Approach to the Modern Drama,* pp. 37-83. Boston: Atlantic-Little, Brown, 1964.

Clurman, Harold. *Ibsen.* New York: Macmillan, 1977.

Downs, Brian W. *A Study of Six Plays by Ibsen.* Cambridge: Cambridge University Press, 1950.

——. *Ibsen: The Intellectual Background.* Cambridge: Cambridge University Press, 1946.

Durbach, Errol. *"Ibsen the Romantic": Analogues of Paradise in the Later Plays.* London: The Macmillan Press Ltd., 1982.

Esslin, Martin. "Ibsen: *An Enemy of the People, Hedda Gabler, The Master Builder.*" In *Reflections: Essays on Modern Theatre,* pp. 29-48. Garden City: Doubleday, 1969.

Gilman, Richard. *The Confusion of Realms.* New York: Random House, 1969.

Gray, Ronald. *Ibsen—A Dissenting View: A Study of the Last Twelve Plays.* Cambridge: Cambridge University Press, 1977.

Hardwick, Elizabeth. "Ibsen's Women." In *Seduction and Betrayal: Women and Literature,* pp. 31-83. New York: Random House, 1974.

Harmer, Ruth. "Character, Conflict, and Meaning in *The Wild Duck.*" *Modern Drama* 12, No. 4 (February 1970): 419-27.

Knight, G. Wilson. *Henrik Ibsen.* New York: Grove Press, 1962.

Nicoll, Allardyce. "The Triumph of Realism: Ibsen." In *World Drama: From Aeschylus to Anouilh,* pp. 524-46. New York: Harcourt, 1950.

Steiner, George. *The Death of Tragedy.* New York: Alfred A. Knopf, 1961.

Twentieth-Century Literary Criticism, Vols. 2, 8, 16. Detroit: Gale Research Co.

Weigand, Hermann J. *The Modern Ibsen: A Reconsideration.* New York: Holt, Rinehart and Winston, 1925.

Eugène Ionesco

1912-

Rumanian-born French dramatist.

The Bald Soprano (drama, 1950)

This drama, which Ionesco calls an "anti-play," is an important contribution to modern theater and embodies many of Ionesco's most important themes, such as the debasement of language in modern culture and the impossibility of communication.

The piece is set in the interior of a bourgeois English home. The illogical, absurd tone of the play is evident in the conversation between the Smiths as the play begins, characterized by banalities, platitudes, and sheer nonsense. As **Mr. Smith** reads the paper to **Mrs. Smith,** he notes that "Bobby Watson" is dead. But who is Bobby Watson? It turns out that everyone else in the news story is also named Bobby Watson. Modern humans have no identity, and therefore their names are meaningless. For all the seriousness of its themes, the play is funny, and as the absurdities mount, the audience responds with laughter. **Mr. and Mrs. Martin,** the Smith's dinner guests, arrive. Surprisingly, as they begin to talk, it appears that they don't know one another. In an absurd conversation, they realize that they live in the same place, sleep in the same bed, have the same child. Again Ionesco points to the lack of communication between two supposedly "intimate" people, also offering a parody of love and romance. Later, the four characters sit and talk, their speech nothing more than cliches, platitudes, and non sequiturs. Their conversation disintegrates into senseless babbling, followed by a dimming of the lights. When the lights go up again, the Martins have taken the place of the Smiths, and the play begins again, with the Martins repeating the senseless lines of the Smiths.

Ionesco seeks to expose the alienation and isolation of modern life and the emptiness of existence as revealed in meaningless and fragmented language. Parodying traditional theatrical conventions, he creates a dramatic world without regard to plot, character development, or unities of time. *The Bald Soprano* is considered a major work of modern drama and one of the central pieces of the Theater of the Absurd.

The Chairs (drama, 1952)

This play, which Ionesco termed a "tragic-farce," is concerned with the themes of emptiness and death. The **Old Man** is ninety-five, the **Old Woman** is ninety-four; together, they live in a tower surrounded by fetid water, isolated from humankind. As the play begins, they reflect on their lives, discussing their childhoods and their life together. The setting and the images that characterize their conversation create a picture of death and decay, describing their marriage, world, and world vision. The Old Man is rocked like a child in the lap of the Old Woman, who consoles him. He knows his life is near its end, and he is filled with emptiness and anguish for his meaningless existence. As the play progresses, they ready their home for the arrival of the **Orator** who is to speak that day, and they busy themselves arranging rows of chairs for the guests. The Old Man has created an imaginary setting, with speaker and guests, to confront his consciousness before his death. The visitors, invisible to us, arrive and crowd the room. The Orator represents the Old Man's intelligence, his elevated self, with his message for the world. The guests have assembled for the Old Man's testimony, for the revelation of the meaning of his life. Yet before the Orator begins to speak, the Old Man and Woman leap to their deaths. When the Orator finally speaks, only incoherent noise comes from his mouth; he writes a word on the blackboard that is at first unintelligible, but is finally discerned as goodbye.

As in his previous works, Ionesco here shows the inefficacy of language to communicate meaning. The Old Man's message to the world is rendered into nothingness by the Orator—a deaf mute—and the Old Man himself commits suicide before his message can be given. Once again Ionesco stresses the failure of language and the meaningless of existence.

Rhinoceros (drama, 1960)

Bérenger, the central character of several of Ionesco's plays, is the hero of this work, which many critics consider to be his most political piece. As the play begins, Bérenger and his friend **Jean** are sitting in a cafe, and Jean, a representative of social and political respectability, is upbraiding his friend for his appearance and lack of conformity. Suddenly a rhinoceros charges through the streets. Bérenger is much disturbed by the event, but the other inhabitants are indifferent. When another rhino is seen, the people become absorbed in discussing what type of rhino it is, but not what its appearance means. A **Logician** discusses the rhino in meaningless syllogisms; Jean lectures Berenger on moral behavior, revealing once again Ionesco's concern for the debasement of language. Gradually all the city's inhabitants are becoming rhinos, including Jean, who rationalizes his transformation as he becomes more animal-like, finally threatening to trample his former friend. Even Bérenger's girlfriend deserts him to become part of the "herd." The rhinos spout the same language, characterized by slogans and cliches, adapting their speech to the new norm. Bérenger, isolated and alone as the world is taken over by rhinos, resists, offering a message of hope for those who refuse to conform.

Ionesco here examines the force of conformity, seeing in the epidemic of "rhinoceritis" the acceptance and acquiescence of people to prevailing political ideologies. Ionesco was prompted to write the play in response to the threat of Hitler and his totalitarian regime, which appealed to the prejudice and irrational emotionalism of individuals. Bérenger, who functions as a sort of Everyman in Ionesco's plays, has the will to resist conformity, even when he is the last human, isolated by his very humanity from those who comply rather than challenge authority, and who give up their freedom to choose.

FURTHER READING

Bermel, Albert. "Ionesco: Anything but Absurd." *Twentieth Century Literature* 21, No. 4 (December 1975): 411-20.

Bradby, David. "The Parisian Theatre II: The New Theatre." In *Modern French Drama: 1940-1980,* pp. 53-86. Cambridge: Cambridge University Press, 1984.

Clurman, Harold. "Eugène Ionesco: *Rhinoceros.*" In *The Naked Image: Observations on the Modern Theatre,* pp. 85-7. New York: Macmillan, 1966.

Contemporary Authors, Vols. 9-12, rev. ed. Detroit: Gale Research Co.

Contemporary Literary Criticism, Vols. 1, 4, 6, 9, 11, 15, 41. Detroit: Gale Research Co.

Danner, G. Richard. "Bérenger's Dubious Defense of Humanity in *Rhinocéros.*" *The French Review* 53, No. 2 (December 1979): 207-14.

Esslin, Martin. "Ionesco and the Creative Dilemma." In *Reflections: Essays on Modern Theatre,* pp. 115-26. Garden City: Doubleday, 1969.

Glicksberg, Charles I. "Ionesco and the Comedy of the Absurd." In *The Literature of Nihilism,* pp. 222-33. Lewisburg: Bucknell University Press, 1975.

———. "The Politics of the Absurd." In *The Literature of Commitment,* pp. 186-93. New York: Associated University Presses, 1976.

Knowles, Dorothy. "Eugène Ionesco's Rhinoceroses: Their Origins and Western Fortunes." *French Studies* (July 1974): 294-307.

Schwarz, Alfred. "Condemned to Exist." In *From Büchner to Beckett: Dramatic Theory and the Modes of Tragic Drama,* pp. 334-56. Athens, Ohio: Ohio University Press, 1978.

John Irving

1942-

American novelist, short story writer, and essayist.

The World According to Garp (novel, 1978)

This darkly comic novel, which catapulted Irving to international prominence, begins in Boston in 1942. **Jenny Fields,** an unmarried nurse with unconventional ideas, decides to become a mother. While on duty she sexually arouses a severely brain-damaged but otherwise normal Air Force technical sergeant named **Garp,** with whom she conceives a child. Not knowing the gunner's first name, she whimsically christens the boy **T. S. Garp,** echoing with the initials the father's official rank. A double entendre, the name also reveals the influence of Laurence Sterne's eighteenth-century novel *Tristram Shandy.* The action moves from a New Hampshire preparatory school to Vienna to New York City and back to New Hampshire as Garp matures, marries **Helen Holms,** a strikingly attractive English professor, becomes a successful writer, and ominously struggles with artistic and moral values amidst palpable symbols of violent loss, isolation, severance, and death. Jenny also becomes famous as an outspoken feminist and author of the sensational autobiography *The Sexual Suspect.* The novel culminates in the sudden heroic deaths of Jenny and Garp. Jenny's innate ability to assimilate and overcome tragedies as they occur has afforded her a stoical happiness throughout life. Contrarily, Garp has continually wrestled with personal tragedy: his marital infidelities, Helen's retaliatory love affair, and the bizarre, punitive death of his son **Walt.** In his final moments, however, Garp triumphs over the destructive forces that have surrounded him.

The World According to Garp is an alternately endearing and shocking story of one of the more memorable protagonists in recent American fiction. Irving's work as a whole, while not difficult to read, is structurally complex and reveals itself on several levels. Among his recurring themes are the values of the family, the inexorability of fate, the helplessness that often accompanies misfortune, and the relationship between art and life. Despite its several overtly grotesque episodes, a host of absurd characters, and a decidedly nineteenth-century narrative bent—representative elements of Irving's writing which have provoked critical denigration—*Garp* is widely regarded as Irving's finest work for its masterful integration of the themes and motifs explored in his first three novels.

The Hotel New Hampshire (novel, 1981)

More psychosexual fairy tale than novel, *The Hotel New Hampshire* begins in the 1940s at a summer resort hotel in Maine. The narrator, **John Berry,** imaginatively describes the first meeting of his parents, **Winslow** and **Mary,** coworkers at the resort. They befriend **Freud,** a Viennese Jew, and his performing bear. After their marriage they settle in Dairy, New Hampshire, and, in pursuit of Winslow's idealistic vision, purchase an old girl's school which they convert into the first Hotel New Hampshire. Amidst a backdrop of alternating joy and sorrow (the latter symbolized by the family dog, Sorrow), they raise their children: John, **Franny, Frank, Lilly,** and **Egg.** During adolescence, Franny is raped by a prep-school quarterback; the event leaves an indelible impression on both Franny and John, who believes he should have been able to save his closest sister. The first part of the novel concludes when the family is invited by Freud to manage a hotel in Vienna.

Mrs. Berry and Egg, flying separately from the rest of the family, die in a plane crash. The remaining family members receive their initiation into a yet more brutal, tragic world. The second hotel is a haven for prostitutes and terrorists and a place in which John, Franny, and Frank explore and assess their variously troubled sexual natures. A primary tension emerges between John, who confesses his illicit love for Franny, and Franny, who gradually heals herself through impassioned heterosexual and lesbian encounters. After sabotaging a terrorist plot to explode the opera house, a dangerous plan in which Freud bravely sacrificed himself and Mr. Berry was accidentally blinded, the Berrys settle for a time in New York City. The trip is funded by the physically stunted Lilly, who has become a successful novelist. Although Lilly eventually kills herself following the failure of her second novel and her inability to effectively deal with her mother's death, John, Franny, Frank, and Mr. Berry eventually achieve happiness. His consciousness cleared following a painful, but cathartic, incestuous union with Franny, John recognizes his love for **Susie,** a rape victim and Franny's earlier lover. Together they convert the third Hotel New Hampshire, the former Maine summer resort, into a rape crisis center.

The Hotel New Hampshire represents a departure from Irving's previous fictional methods. Less emphasis is placed on character and setting development so that the narrative structure, recurrent motifs, and symbols can assume primary focus. Consequently, the novel becomes both a creative casebook of Freudian psychology and a cautionary tale of maturation, the search for identity, and the inherent dangers of following illusions. Much of the controversy surrounding Irving's fiction centers on his graphic depiction of violence. Some critics find these incidents sensational and gratuitous, while others argue that they are necessary to underscore the irony of his novels. Despite his portrayal of bizarre and morbid events, Irving's novel has a life-affirming quality evident in the resiliency of his characters, particularly those of John and Franny Berry.

FURTHER READING

Contemporary Authors, Vols. 25-28, rev. ed. Detroit: Gale Research Co.

Contemporary Literary Criticism, Vols. 13, 23, 38. Detroit: Gale Research Co.

Davies, Robertson. "John Irving and His Travelling Menagerie." *Book World—The Washington Post* (6 September 1981): 1-2.

Dictionary of Literary Biography, Vol. 6; *Dictionary of Literary Biography Yearbook: 1982.* Detroit: Gale Research Co.

Harter, Carol, C. *John Irving.* New York: Twayne, 1986.

Hill, Jane Bowers. "John Irving's Aesthetics of Accessibility: Setting Free the Novel." *The South Carolina Review* 16, No. 1 (Fall 1983): 38-44.

Irving, John. Interview by Ron Hansen. In *Writers at Work*, eighth series, pp. 413-44. New York: Penguin Books, 1988.

Miller, Gabriel. *John Irving.* New York: Ungar, 1982.

Priestley, Michael. "Structure in the Worlds of John Irving." *Critique: Studies in Modern Fiction* 23, No. 1 (1981): 82-96.

Christopher Isherwood

1904-1986

English novelist and autobiographer.

Mr. Norris Changes Trains (novel, 1935)

Set in Germany in the 1930s, this novel is the first installment of what have come to be called Isherwood's "Berlin stories," the work for which he is best known. The scene is Berlin at the end of the Weimar Republic, and although the work is comic in tone, a sense of decadence and despair permeate the book, with the ominous presence of the Nazis felt throughout. **William Bradshaw** is the first-person narrator and is presented as a passive character of limited judgment and perception. **Arthur Norris** is a dazzling figure who introduces Bradshaw to the underworld of Berlin, with its illicit sex, drugs, and atmosphere of corruption. Norris is involved in political intrigues as well, and Isherwood reveals the flaws in his narrator's perspective when Bradshaw fails to realize the evil inherent in Norris's way of life. Norris seems to weave a spell on Bradshaw, who finds him at once intriguing and menacing, but who remains in awe of him. As critics observe, Isherwood draws parallels between Norris and Hitler, for Norris is ruthless in his destruction of such characters as **Baron von Pregnitz** and **Ludwig Bayer,** revealing his cruelty and sadism. As

Norris becomes ever more absorbed in his decadent lifestyle, Germany is falling into the hands of the fascists, but Bradshaw is unable to see the moral turpitude of his friend or its consequences.

In allowing the reader to know more and see more than his narrator, Isherwood presents a perspective that enables one to judge and comprehend the impending disaster. Isherwood has acknowledged the influence of German film on his literary technique, which is reflected in the episodic nature of the novel.

Goodbye to Berlin (novel, 1939)

Like *Mr. Norris Changes Trains,* this novel is also set in Berlin during the 1930s and constitutes the latter half of Isherwood's famous "Berlin stories." Divided into six sections, the novel is framed by Isherwood's Berlin diaries and includes sketches of the people encountered by the first-person narrator, "**Christopher Isherwood.**" Once again, the story is played out against the overwhelming sense of doom that unites all of the seemingly disparate characters, who are caught in the cataclysmic chaos of the last days before Hitler's rise to power. Isherwood focuses on the seductive nature of the city: it is a seemingly lively, vital place, home to sexual and romantic adventures, but only in appearance. Berlin is truly in a state of sickness and decay, and Isherwood's characters, mirroring this passivity and decadence, appear to be weary with pleasure, isolated, and unable to act or to stop the inevitable destruction of their way of life.

Unlike William Bradshaw, Christopher is never intimately involved with the characters whose portraits he depicts; he remains detached, and his famous line: "I am a camera, quite passive, recording, not thinking," indicates his narrative stance. Of all the characters he portrays, **Sally Bowles** is perhaps the best known. She is a young British woman rebelling against her repressive, domineering heritage, who claims to have taken many lovers and is constantly relating her adventures to Christopher. The two live together in the rooming house of **Frau Lina Schroeder,** who spies on her lodgers, but appears tolerant of their various sexual exploits. Other acquaintances include **Natalia Landauer**—rich, Jewish, and sexually repressed—and her cousin **Bernhard Landauer,** whose passivity and sense of the absurdity of life lead him to a feeling of indifference even as the Nazis come to power and threaten his very existence.

In the conclusion, Christopher is leaving Berlin. The portrait he has drawn is one of a series of isolated figures, an alienation he himself shares. Alone in their helplessness and despair, the characters inhabit a world stripped of the comic sense of *Mr. Norris Changes Trains* and replaced with a nameless, ill-defined dread. Throughout this novel Isherwood parallels the decay of the German political system with the personal chaos of his characters' lives. His vivid portrait of Germany on the edge of the abyss is studied and admired as both a literary and historical document.

FURTHER READING

Contemporary Authors, Vols. 13-16, rev. ed., 117. Detroit: Gale Research Co.

Contemporary Literary Criticism, Vols. 1, 9, 11, 14, 44. Detroit: Gale Research Co.

Dictionary of Literary Biography, Vol. 15; *Dictionary of Literary Biography Yearbook: 1986.* Detroit: Gale Research Co.

King, Francis. *Christopher Isherwood.* Harlow, Essex: Longman, 1976.

Mayne, Richard. "The Novel and Mr. Norris." *Cambridge Journal* 6 (June 1953): 561-70.

Piazza, Paul. *Christopher Isherwood: Myth and Anti-Myth.* New York: Columbia University Press, 1978.

Rosenfeld, Isaac. "Isherwood's Master Theme." *Kenyon Review* 8 (Summer 1946): 488-92.

Summers, Claude J. *Christopher Isherwood.* New York: Ungar, 1980.

Shirley Jackson
1919-1965
American short story writer and novelist.

"The Lottery" (short story, 1948)

The story is set in a New England village in contemporary times. As it begins, the village is preparing for the annual lottery, the nature of which is kept from the reader until the conclusion. The atmosphere is festive, and as the men and women chat about their farms, homes, and families, the children gather stones. The families then gather together, and an air of excitement comes over the crowd. **Joe Summers,** a revered member of the community and the administrator of the lottery, calls the town to order. He draws a slip of paper from a black box, and announces the name of **Tessie Hutchinson.** Led by Summers, the townsfolk proceed to stone Tessie to death

The work is considered one of the most haunting, enigmatic short stories of modern American fiction. In her allegorical tale, Jackson revealed the evil that is inherent in human nature in an objective, detached manner of narration that heightens the reader's surprise and horror at the story's conclusion. She recreated the ancient ritual of the scapegoat sacrificed for the betterment of the community, exposing the violence, brutality, and mindless vengeance that is still part of "civilized" people. Joe Summers represents tradition, for as some skeptical townspeople talk about villages that have done away with their "lotteries," he stresses the importance of the ritual, reflecting the ease with which the community takes part in the act of barbarity. When Tessie's name is chosen, she protests the method used to pick her; she is revealed as a hypocrite, for she is happy to take part in the lottery until she is chosen as its victim. Although some townsfolk question the lottery, most hold firmly to the belief that the ritual is necessary to insure a bountiful harvest, and all take part in the stoning with unquestioning fidelity. "The Lottery" has become one of the most famous and frequently anthologized short stories of the modern era.

FURTHER READING

Brooks, Cleanth and Robert Penn Warren. "Interpretation." In *Understanding Fiction,* pp. 72-6. New York: Appleton-Century-Crofts, 1959.

Contemporary Authors, Vols. 1-4, rev. ed.; *Contemporary Authors New Revision Series,* Vol. 4. Detroit: Gale Research Co.

Contemporary Literary Criticism, Vol. 11. Detroit: Gale Research Co.

Dictionary of Literary Biography, Vol. 6. *Concise Dictionary of American Literary Biography, 1941-1968.* Detroit: Gale Research Co.

Friedman, Lenemaja. *Shirley Jackson.* Boston: Twayne, 1975.

Nebeker, H. E. "'The Lottery': Symbolic Tour de Force." *American Literature* 46 (March 1974): 100-07.

Henry James
1843-1916

American novelist, short story writer, critic, and essayist.

The American (novel, 1877)

The novel is set in late nineteenth century America, France, and England. The wealthy American commercialist, **Christopher Newman,** visits Europe in search of aesthetic pleasure and an aristocratic wife. Visiting the Louvre, he meets **Mademoiselle Nioche,** a copyist, and is introduced to her shopkeeper father who offers him French lessons. Further, he is reunited with a Civil War comrade, **Tristram**, whose wife introduces him to **Clare de Cintre,** widowed daughter of **Mme. de Bellegarde.** Clare's husband had been a rich but insufferable bore. Newman sees in Clare the ideal wife but is hampered in his suit by her arrogant brother, the **Marquis de Bellegarde.**

Newman then becomes more involved with the Nioches when he offers the father dowry money for his daughter to prevent her from prostituting herself for wealth. Upon his return to Paris after a summer of travel, Newman learns that the de Bellegardes will receive him and Newman finds **Valentin de Bellegarde** to be a true friend who will help him with his marriage plans, with positive results. Meanwhile, Newman has introduced Valentin to Mlle. Nioche and they become lovers, after which Valentin challenges her former lover to a duel and leaves for Switzerland. When Newman next visits Clare to formalize their marriage plans, he is informed that the de Bellegardes have reconsidered and cannot accept a merchant in their family; to his bewilderment, Clare refuses him.

Events move swiftly: Newman receives word that Valentin is dying and wants to see him. In Switzerland, Valentin confides that the servant, **Mrs. Bread,** has a letter with evidence implicating his mother and brother in the death of his father. This document, in Newman's hands, will force the de Bellegardes to accept Newman's proposal to Clare. A visit in Paris to Mrs. Bread provides the letter, written by the old Marquis who was convinced before his death that his wife and son would kill him, in revenge for his objection to Clare's earlier marriage of convenience. But when Newman confronts Mme. de Bellegarde and the marquis with a copy of evidence, they reject him again, saying that no one in their social class would believe Newman or his letter.

Bitter and frustrated, Newman leaves for America where revenge becomes his sole motivation; neither business nor pleasure interest him. He returns to Paris to recover his perspective and decides that revenge for its own sake is worthless. In a final visit to Mrs. Tristram, he burns the incriminating letter. The aristocrats had counted on his naive, puritanical morality and they had been right.

In retrospect, James was to call *The American* a romance, representative of that genre's "disconnected, uncontrolled" experiences. He presents his familiar themes of revenge and moral certitude, and once again he dramatizes the confrontation between the innocent American and the corruption of the *ancien regime.*

Daisy Miller (novel, 1879)

The novel is set in Switzerland and Italy in the late 1800s. **Daisy Miller,** an American tourist, **Frederick Winterbourne,** an American expatriate, and **Giovanelli,** Daisy's American companion are the main characters in this early and successful novel. Daisy is travelling in Europe with her mother and younger brother when she meets Winterbourne. Attracted by her youth and beauty, and although he considers her to be "completely uncultivated," he agrees to take her on a tour of a famous castle. He is surprised that she does not want a chaperon; his aunt, **Mrs. Costello** considers the Millers "common," and will not meet Daisy. Daisy is disappointingly circumspect during the tour, but is flirtatiously angry when Winterbourne announces his departure for Geneva, and promises that they will meet in Rome for the winter season.

In Rome, Winterbourne finds that Daisy has been escorted, again without chaperon, by Giovanelli. This has so shocked her American compatriots that her social acceptability is diminishing. When Winterbourne suggests that she conform more to conventional behavior, she laughs at his appeal and teases him when she says she might or might not consider engagement to the Italian. Within a week, Winterbourne is shocked to find Daisy and Giovanelli in intimate conversation while viewing the Colosseum at midnight. Although now convinced that Daisy's reputation is ruined, and even relieved to have done with her, Winterbourne cautions her about the danger of contracting malaria from the ruins in the night air. She is deaf to his solicitude, but surprisingly asks if he cares if she is engaged to Giovanelli; he assures he does not, and Daisy is chagrined at his rejection. When Daisy becomes dangerously ill with malaria, Winterbourne visits, but she is unable to see him. Her mother does tell him, however, that Daisy wants him to know that she is not engaged.

Daisy dies; at her funeral, Giovanelli convinces Winterbourne of Daisy's innocence and admits that their relationship had been superficial. Winterbourne is saddened, realizing that he had misjudged Daisy and regretful that he no longer understands the ways of young American women.

Daisy Miller presents a relatively uncomplicated use of the theme of innocent Americans who are baffled by the European experience, and is the last work of James's early period. James called this work a ''study,'' since he felt his story to have a ''flatness of denomination with little hope of stirring scenes.'' What is successfully presented is simply an impressionistic glimpse of his main character's American audacity and her naivete. Later heroines would be more fully developed through James's desire to present not only a character but the very consciousness of that character at work.

The Portrait of a Lady (novel, 1881)

Isabel Archer, an American, is invited by her aunt, **Mrs. Touchett,** to Gardenwood, her estate in England. There she meets her ailing and charming uncle, her cousin **Ralph Touchett** and **Lord Warburton,** an English aristocrat, who is at once attracted by her beauty and independent spirit. He soon asks her to be his wife, but his offer is refused. When **Henrietta Stackpole,** Isabel's American friend, arrives in London, she is invited to Gardenwood and announces that Isabel's American suitor, **Caspar Goodwood,** has come with her from America to ask Isabel to reconsider his previous offer of marriage. In London, Isabel remains firm in her desire to remain free of any ties and asks Goodwood to wait two years for her decision about marriage. A report from Gardenwood brings news that Mr. Touchett is dying and sends Isabel and Ralph to a death vigil at Gardenwood. There, Mrs. Touchett has been joined by her friend **Madame Merle,** whom Isabel comes to admire for her sophistication and friendly manner.

Earlier, Ralph, in growing admiration for his cousin, had convinced his dying father to provide Isabel with a generous inheritance and had offered to share his own bequest to this end, since he had discovered himself to be dying. This allotment has allowed Isabel to later accompany the widowed Mrs. Touchett to Paris. When she and Mrs. Touchett decide to reside in Italy, they are reunited with Mme. Merle. She introduces Isabel to **Gilbert Osmond,** having secretly encouraged him to consider Isabel as a prospective wife. Now, Isabel's betrayal begins, as Osmond charms her with his cultivated ways and Isabel falls deeply in love.

In spite of the opposing views of her relatives, Isabel marries Osmond and becomes the stepmother of his daughter **Pansy.** Ralph is dismayed and angers Isabel with his criticism of her husband; their relationship as loving cousins becomes strained.

Four years elapse, during which time Isabel becomes more and more perplexed by

Osmond's selfish and domineering ways. In spite of this, she still manages to conduct herself with decorum in Roman society, as the "portrait" of a lady. A telegram brings news that Ralph Touchett is dying, and Isabel's plans to visit him are delayed by Osmond's implication that her motives are suspect and would embarrass him socially; she is further shocked to discover that Pansy is the daughter of Madame Merle and Osmond, this the result of an earlier and secret extra-marital affair for both of them.

In spite of her unhappiness Isabel resolves to keep her marriage vows, taking the only course which she considers to be ethical. Her high sense of duty and morality, even in the face of adversity, will not allow her to do less. She will not succumb to the corruption of her European counterparts. She is James's most fully developed American heroine, thus far. Seeking neither martyrdom nor revenge, her moral stance provides both strength and reward. James's dynamic use of his characters' interior monologues give this first novel of his second period extraordinary textual depth.

The Turn of The Screw (novella, 1897)

This story is set in England, in London and at Bly, a country estate. There are two narrative voices. One, in a short prologue, is in the first-person and introduces the tale; the other recounts the story and is in the first-person voice of the governess. **The Governess** is the main character and it is from her perspective alone that the story unfolds; her internal monologues are dramatic and her reactions to the novel's events combine to give the narrative its impact.

She takes her first position as a governess in Bly, for the children of the **Master,** whose terms are that she will be in complete charge of **Flora** and **Miles,** the pre-adolescent children of a deceased brother; she must not trouble the absent master for advice in their care. With **Mrs. Grose,** the housekeeper, and other servants to help, the Governess is happy, since Miles and Flora seem to be perfect, beautiful charges. But when she notices what appears to be the figure of a strange man, at first at a distance and later at a window, she is disturbed upon describing him to Mrs. Grose to find that he resembles **Mr. Quint,** a former valet at Bly, but now known to be dead. The next apparition is that of a lady whom Mrs. Grose feels must be like **Miss Jessel,** the former governess and also deceased. When Mrs. Grose further implies that a strange intimacy existed between Quint and Jessel while alive, the Governess suspects that these ghosts might corrupt the children, who must be protected at all costs. Soon after, both the Governess and Mrs. Grose notice that the children are developing subtle but negative personality changes. Moreover, the Governess is convinced that, despite their denial of seeing Quint and Jessel, the children are deliberately plotting with each other, as well as the phantoms, against her. In a frenzied state of interrogation, she pleads with Miles for explanation of his association with Quint. When she sees, horrified, Quint's appearance at the window and points him out to Miles, Miles gives no evidence of being able to see what she vainly describes. In a paroxysm of terror, Miles dies in her arms.

Questions of textual ambiguity, narrative authority, authorial intent, and "real" or hallucinatory ghosts have been argued by critics for nearly a century. What is generally agreed upon is that the novella is a brilliant *tour de force* which can be apprehended in two ways: as the vivid and morbid recounting of a pathological governess, or from the perspective, as one critic maintains, of the reader who sees the ghosts as representative of evil, the children corrupted by them, and the Governess as representative of "good". Whatever the final opinion, the meticulous craftsmanship so characteristic of James's narrative technique is what gives this work its stunning impact. In response to criticism of too few specifics in the plot about how, exactly, the children had been corrupted by Quint and Jessel, James's reply was that a writer's presentation of "a general vision of evil" in the mind of the Governess would, as it merged with a perceptive reader's sensibility, provide the particulars needed for individual dimension of horror. Such effective combination, he felt, would embody the true artistic creativity of the novelist, which is to bring his reader's imagination into full play so as to provide the ultimate in felt experience.

The Wings of the Dove (novel, 1902)

Kate Croy is a young English girl who is being urged by her aunt, **Mrs. Lowder,** to marry **Lord Mark,** a wealthy man of good social standing. But Kate is in love with the journalist **Martin Densher,** a fact which is unknown to her ambitious aunt. When Densher is sent on assignment to America, he and Kate decide to become secretly engaged and to keep their romance alive. While in New York, Densher meets the affluent American **Milly Theale.** Densher casually suggests that she call him, if she should decide to travel abroad.

When advised by her physician to travel, Milly invites her friend, **Mrs. Stringham** to accompany her to Europe. There is a pleasant reunion in London between old friends and new. Moreover, Kate and Milly become confidants and Milly meets Lord Mark, who is immediately attracted to her and to her money. But the ailing Milly soon finds it necessary to consult a London doctor, and his advice is that she should enjoy life to its fullest. The narrative implication that she will soon die is ambiguous and unclear in her dialogue with the doctor, but is reinforced in Milly's long, interior monologue which occurs during her walk in the London streets after leaving his office. Here, mastery of the technique which James had worked so long to perfect is obvious. Readers are vividly aware of the mental suffering of the character, as Milly struggles to come to terms with her fear and sadness, and of her conclusion to gracefully accept the "gift" of a shortened life since it will, she feels, have an intensity of experience perceived only by one who is aware that death is close.

While Kate admires Milly for her spirit and independence, she also calculates that Milly's demise can be useful. Thus, she convinces Densher to feign love for Milly and propose marriage, so that at her death he will inherit the money to satisfy Mrs. Lowder's requirements as a suitable match for her niece. He agrees, and once again, the difference in value systems between Americans and Europeans as one of James's most important themes is reinforced; what will later be seen as a cruel and devious plot by Milly is rationalized by her two new friends as an expediency to provide her a final, loving relationship and themselves financial security, at her expense.

Milly is pleasantly compliant to Densher's advances, but reserved about making a commitment; her decency and good nature make him subtly aware that she has an integrity which he and Kate lack. He is puzzled, one day, to find that she will not receive him, and later disturbed to learn that Lord Mark has visited her, proposed marriage and been rejected, and has angrily divulged the fact of Kate and Densher's long-time love affair. With the news of Milly's death comes word that Milly has left Densher a generous inheritance, but in his final meeting with Kate, he confesses that he cannot in conscience accept it. Kate, unable to cope with Densher's guilt and his memory of Milly, renounces him and they part. Milly Theale, like her predecessor, Daisy Miller, has left her companions the legacy of her virtue, along with a new and uneasy self-realization of their own and questionable morality.

James's use of myth and symbol underscores his desire to present a tale which is ambiguous and lacking in specific details of narrative clarity. His title has biblical reference, as it comes from Psalm 55. The image of Milly as benevolent "dove," as Leon Edel points out, "summons out the full orchestra of [James's] symbolic imagination."

The Ambassadors (novel, 1903)

New England born, middle-aged **Lambert Strether** is commissioned by his fiancee to return her expatriate son **Chad Newsome** home to his familial duties in America. She is concerned that his long stay abroad and a love affair are destroying his Puritan sense of values. Strether is soon pleasantly surprised to find in Chad a sophisticated, intelligent young man who is completely in command of his own situation. Among Chad's friends are the **Comtesse de Vionnet,** her daughter, and **John Bilham,** an American artist. They are attractive, friendly, and seem to provide a good influence on Chad rather than a negative one.

After Bilham's remark that Mme. de Vionnet is quite above reproach, Strether relaxes and begins to enjoy Paris and its environs. He soon reverses his opinion that Chad should return home and begins to doubt that it would be best to deny himself the pleasure of Chad's company, of his friends, and the European experience. His feelings are evident in his dispatches to Massachusetts, and **Mrs. Newsome** sends **Mamie Pocock,** her choice as Chad's future wife, as well as Chad's sister and her husband in righteous pursuit.

The trio's intent is to appraise both Chad and Strether of their previous responsibilities, but the newcomers are soon caught up in the excitement of travel abroad. Strether, having immersed himself in the beauty of the countryside as well as the intellectual and aesthetic excitement of his new view of the world, advises Chad to remain in Europe. He argues that the absorption of what Europe offers will be more rewarding than a return to the constraints of puritanical Massachusetts; Chad is easily convinced, but later has his own doubts about staying in Europe.

However, in the end, Strether cannot take his own advice. Despite the inevitable break with Mrs. Newsome, he feels bound to return to America. While his sojourn in France has provided new self-knowledge, the conflict between his new and venturesome sensibility and his innate value system of responsibility and duty is a painful reminder that his experience of freedom has come too late, and is only an illusion.

The Ambassadors has in it what was the beginning of a new movement in fiction called the psychological novel. The innovative narrative technique which allows the reader to share in the emotions of the characters, in their mental conflicts, and in feelings of regret as well as joy is one which would be emulated by such later writers as Virginia Woolf and James Joyce.

The Golden Bowl (novel, 1904)

This novel is set in England and Italy at the beginning of the twentieth century. **Maggie** and **Adam Verver, Prince Amerigo** and **Charlotte Stant** are the characters around which the intricate plot revolves; **Fanny** and **Robert Assingham** provide information about both past and present which helps to move the story to its conclusion. The narrative point of view is omniscient, but in his preface to the novel, James admitted to a deliberate desire for the presented action to be "indirect and oblique." Thus it is through the consciousness of the Prince, in volume one, that events are given form, while in volume two, the narrative is presented from Maggie's point of view. Allowing readers into the minds and emotions of these two would provide, James felt, "compositional resource of the highest order."

Maggie and Adam Verver have a singular relationship; as father and daughter they are completely compatible as they travel in Europe searching for artifacts for themselves and for a museum which Adam hopes to found on their return home to America. In Italy, they are introduced to the Prince by the Londoner, **Mrs. Assingham,** who has become Maggie's only close friend in Europe. The charming, seemingly passive nobleman is, however, realistic enough to propose to Maggie as resolution to his financial problems. Maggie, innocent of his motives, happily accepts and plans a London wedding. She is unaware that earlier, and before her arrival in Italy, the Prince had had a love affair with her old school friend, Charlotte. This had been dissolved, since neither had had the freedom nor the resources to marry. The unhappy Charlotte had returned to America but is now in London, at Maggie's invitation to the wedding.

Charlotte's first move is to invite the Prince to shop with her for Maggie's wedding present, a pretense, since she is frank to admit her admiration for him. The present she selects is a glass gilded bowl. It is flawed with a tiny crack, only perceptible to an expert, and it is thus affordable. Since it is not perfect, she rejects it on the advice of the Prince. It will become James's symbol of the imperfections which exist in a seemingly perfect society, and in certain relationships where hidden flaws in character and personality disguise appearance from reality.

Charlotte's plan is now to remain in Europe, at the mercy of hospitable friends, among whom is the sympathetic Mrs. Assingham. There follows for Maggie what appears to be a happy marriage, the birth of a son, and uninterrupted proximity to her father in the continued search for art treasures. But Maggie soon sees herself as having abandoned Adam, and sets the stage for his marriage to Charlotte. Thus, thrown together by Maggie's naive design, Charlotte and the Prince become re-involved.

Maggie's naivete ends and her rite of passage from innocence to experience begins when she discovers, accidentally, that Charlotte and the Prince have been, and are still, lovers. Shopping for a present for her father, she happens upon the golden bowl and buys it. The shopkeeper reveals that Charlotte and Prince had seemed intimate friends before the wedding day. Once again, through James's relentless use of internal monologue, we see and feel Maggie's anguish at what has happened to her most carefully planned existence and her decision to act in accordance with her rigorous beliefs.

It is her friend Mrs. Assingham who convinces her that it will be Adam and his happiness with Charlotte which will suffer if she does not come to terms with her knowledge of the betrayal by her husband and her friend, and, that if the bowl is a symbol of one circumstance, the flaw in the bowl invalidates the reality of the circumstance. Mrs. Assingham destroys the bowl, and it is over its fragments that Maggie and the Prince have a frank discussion about themselves and their marriage. Maggie's further decision to remain silent about Charlotte's infidelity to Adam, to preserve his illusion about his marriage, and to remain the wife in a marriage from which earlier enchantment has been lost completes her transition from an innocent girl to a mature woman. Her action has been resolute; in saving her father, she has lost him, but has found in herself a well-spring of American virtue and strength, not unlike the characters of Isabel Archer and Milly Theale.

James's final masterpiece provides the culmination of his efforts to create the novel as an art form, and his notion that the goal of the novelist, as artist, is to attempt to represent life as it is, with its rhythmic irregularities of pain and pleasure. Winning the battle of moral propriety in conflict with evil, said Schiller, is the penultimate life experience; Henry James devoted his life as a novelist to remind readers of the fact.

FURTHER READING

Beach, Joseph Warren. *The Method of Henry James*. Philadelphia: Albert Saifer, 1954.

Brooks, Cleanth. "The American 'Innocence' in James, Fitzgerald, and Faulkner." In *A Shaping Joy: Studies in the Writer's Craft*, pp. 181-97. London: Methuen & Co., 1971.

Brooks, Van Wyck. *The Pilgrimage of Henry James*. New York: Dutton, 1925.

Brownell, W. C. "Henry James." In *American Prose Masters: Cooper, Hawthorne, Emerson, Poe, Lowell, Henry James*, pp. 280-332. New York: Charles Scribner's Sons, 1923.

Canby, Henry Seidel. *Turn West, Turn East: Mark Twain and Henry James*. Boston: Houghton Mifflin, 1951.

Contemporary Authors, Vol. 104. Detroit: Gale Research Co.

Crews, Frederick C. *The Tragedy of Manner: Moral Drama in the Later Novels of Henry James*. New Haven: Yale University Press, 1957.

Dictionary of Literary Biography, Vols. 12, 71; *Concise Dictionary of American Literary Biography, 1865-1917.* Detroit: Gale Research Co.

Dupee, F. W. *Henry James.* New York: William Morrow, 1974.

Edel, Leon. *Henry James.* 5 Vols. Philadelphia: J. B. Lippincott, 1953-1972.

Edgar, Pelham. *Henry James: Man and Author.* Boston: Houghton Mifflin, 1927.

Geismar, Maxwell. *Henry James and the Jacobites.* Boston: Houghton Mifflin, 1963.

Leavis, F. R. "Henry James." In *The Great Tradition: George Eliot, Henry James, Joseph Conrad,* pp. 126-72. London: George W. Stewart, 1948.

Lubbock, Percy. *The Craft of Fiction.* New York: Charles Scribner's Sons, 1955.

Matthiessen, F. O. *Henry James: The Major Phase.* New York: Oxford University Press, 1944.

Poirier, Richard. *The Comic Sense of Henry James.* New York: Columbia University Press, 1960.

Schneider, Daniel J. *The Crystal Cage: Adventures of the Imagination in the Fiction of Henry James.* Lawrence: Regents Press of Kansas, 1978.

Stewart, J.I.M. *Eight Modern Writers.* Oxford: Clarenden Press, 1963.

Twentieth-Century Literary Criticism, Vols. 2, 11, 24. Detroit: Gale Research Co.

Van Ghent, Dorothy. "On *The Portrait of a Lady.*" In *The English Novel: Form and Function,* pp. 211-28. New York: Harper & Row, 1961.

Wagenknecht, Edward. *The Novels of Henry James.* New York: Ungar, 1983.

Winters, Yvor. "Maule's Well, or Henry James and the Relation of Morals to Manners." In *In Defense of Reason,* pp. 300-43. Chicago: Swallow, 1947.

Alfred Jarry

1873-1907

French dramatist.

Ubu Roi (drama, 1896)

This famous scatological farce is a pivotal work of modern drama and was a major influence on the Theater of the Absurd. The character of **Pere Ubu** is a grotesque embodiment of brutal, destructive impulses, and he is set in a drama in which Jarry declared his rebellion against the tenets of theatrical realism and the complacent bourgeois audience. Ubu's first word is "merdre," an opening that resulted in a riot at the first performance of the play, rallying those forces who saw Jarry's piece as a work of liberation, and those that condemned him and his work as obscene and monstrous.

The play is purposely simplistic in plot and character. It begins as Ubu is urged by his wife, **Mere Ubu,** to attempt to overthrow the King of Poland. Ubu follows her wishes, killing the king and usurping his throne. Thereafter, he gives rein to his perversely evil yet comically absurd nature, killing the king's son and nobles, and planning a system of taxation in which he will drain the people of their money and then kill them all. At one point, he distributes money to the poor, who trample one another in their greed, an indication that humankind is motivated by the same impulses that drive Ubu. The play ends with Ubu removed from power, on his way back to France.

The story of *Ubu Roi* is simple on the surface, but its true meaning is not revealed in a plot synopsis. Ubu is a greedy, cruel, barbaric character, a figure of stupidity, but not an innocent: he is frightening because he is so human. That early audiences took him for a comic character was opposed to Jarry's purpose, for Ubu is a symbol of the evil in ourselves, and Jarry wanted to hold a mirror up to the audience in which they could recognize their own vices. The language of the piece is intentionally vulgar and employed to shock. Ubu was first presented as a figure in a puppet play, and Jarry intended that the actors should be masked, incorporate the stylized movement of marionettes, and speak their lines in a monotone to heighten the absurdity of the realism that dominated the French stage of that time.

Thematically, the work reveals Jarry's deep revulsion for all aspects of life and is his statement of open rebellion and defiance of all authority, reflecting his philosophy of "Pataphysics," a nihilistic rejection of all systems of thought. Jarry was an avowed influence on Antonin Artaud, Eugene Ionesco, and other proponents of the Theater of the Absurd.

FURTHER READING

Contemporary Authors, Vol. 104. Detroit: Gale Research Co.

Grossman, Manuel L. "Alfred Jarry and the Theater of the Absurd." *Educational Theatre Journal* 19, No. 4 (December 1967): 473-77.

Grossvogel, David I. "Les enfants terribles: Jarry, Apollinaire, Cocteau." In *The Self-Conscious Stage in Modern French Drama,* pp. 19-67. New York: Columbia University Press, 1958.

Hassan, Ihab. "Interlude: From 'Pataphysics' to Surrealism." In *The Dismemberment of Orpheus: Toward a Postmodern Literature,* pp. 48-79. Madison: The University of Wisconsin Press, 1982.

Innes, Christopher. "Dreams, Archetypes, and the Irrational." In *Holy Theater: Ritual and the Avant Garde,* pp. 18-58. Cambridge: Cambridge University Press, 1981.

Shattuck, Roger. "Suicide by Hallucination" and "Poet and 'Pataphysician.'" In *The Banquet Years: The Arts in France, 1885-1918: Alfred Jarry, Henri Rousseau, Erik Satie, Guillaume Apollinaire.* New York: Harcourt, 1959.

Sarah Orne Jewett
1849-1909
American short story writer, novelist, and poet.

The Country of the Pointed Firs (short stories, 1896)

This work is considered to be Jewett's masterpiece. A series of sketches about a fictional town called Dunnet Landing and its adjacent islands on the upper coastline of Maine, it firmly established its author, with Mark Twain and others, as one of the finest of the American school of rural local colorists.

A first-person narrator and **Almira Todd** are the two characters around which the sketches revolve. It is through the narrator's eyes and her conversations with Mrs. Todd that the other characters are given life. The narrator/writer arrives at the small village to spend the summer in the company of Almira, an herbalist, healer, and confidante of the community who knows all, sees all, and tells what she believes should be heard, with judiciousness. The widow Todd is connected, in one way or another, to most of the inhabitants of the area and the surrounding islands and villages. The time is at the turn of the century and the characters, isolated and simplistic in nature, cling to a subtly changing value system which combines a hearty skepticism with good will and joy in the simple pleasures, as well as an acceptance and endurance of the pain which nature provides. Each sketch presents a character who evokes a particular aspect of these sturdy, indomitable people. There is **Captain Littlepage,** a retired, reclusive seaman whose tale is of a sea voyage, a shipwreck, and a strange, surrealistic island which is uncharted and lies farther north than ships have ever sailed. The Captain surprises the narrator as well with his quotes from *Paradise Lost,* his knowledge of Milton's work, and his preference for that writer over Shakespeare.

On Green Island, the narrator is introduced to Almira's brother, **William Blackett,** and the octogenarian mother of the two, **Mrs. Blackett.** She is charmed by the grace and hospitality of this lady and her bashful and kind son and touched when Almira reveals her sadness at the death of her own husband in an earlier shipwreck, a common occurrence for families of seafaring men, but always accepted with stoicism. The family also relates the tale of "poor **Joanna,**" who lived out her life in seclusion on Shell Island, in a kind of medieval penance for the sake of unrequited love. Fascinated by the tale, the narrator later visits the island and Joanna's grave. Jewett's mastery of delicate style and her awareness of the inherent loneliness in each of us are evident in her description of Joanna's island as "a place remote and given to endless regret or secret happiness [where we can] understand our fellows . . . to whatever age of history they may belong."

There is a journey by wagon, up-country, to a family reunion, where the narrator participates in a celebration of Mrs. Blackett as the oldest and most revered guest of honor. The procession to a picnic grove reminds the narrator of ancient and ritualistic gatherings of thanksgiving, as it culminates in a noble feast, with speeches and anecdotes reminiscent of times long past.

Up to this point, the narrator has felt like a welcome observer. But when a weathered and taciturn old fisherman, **Mr. Tilley,** shares with her his grief over the loss of his wife in a charmingly sentimental way, and when the silent William permits her knowledge of his patient courtship of a shepherdess who will not be free to marry until the death of her mother, the narrator is again moved by the simple and extraordinary trust in her that these people reveal and feels that she is now an accepted insider. Jewett's skill in the presentation of the opposing sides of the human personality and of what lies beneath what is at first observed in people is clearly demonstrated in her straightforward and penetrating style.

Her real *tour de force* is her description of the narrator's introduction to **Abby Martin,** who is known and accepted by the community as the "Queen's Twin." Born on the same day as Queen Victoria and also the widow of a man named Albert, Abby has had a similar number of children, all named for the royal family. Her one brief glimpse of her heroine came when both were young women and Abby had accompanied her seafaring husband on a voyage to England. Now, as they have both become old women, Abby's strong identification with the monarch is both humorous and beautifully poignant. But it is in Jewett's description of the acceptance of her fantasy and the gentle encouragement by Almira that the reader is moved, because Almira, like Jewett, understands that even simple folk need the play of the imagination to "buoy them . . . over the shoals of life."

Returning to the village after a winter's hiatus in the city, the narrator learns of William's impending marriage. The tender, curious, and loving attention given to this event by friends is rendered in Jewett's beautiful, heartening description; here, the writer has shown her ability to capture the essence of the people, the sea, and a way of life which disappeared and would never be recovered.

Willa Cather has observed that Sarah Orne Jewett's eye for description and her ear for the language of a people in their native idiom made her the epitome of a "living simplicity and directness of style," and one of the best American writers.

FURTHER READING

Contemporary Authors, Vol. 108. Detroit: Gale Research Co.

Cross, Olive. "From *Deephaven* to *The Country of the Pointed Firs.*" *Florida State University Studies* 5 (1952): 113-21.

Dictionary of Literary Biography, Vol. 12. Detroit. Gale Research Co.

Matthiessen, Francis Otto. *Sarah Orne Jewett.* Boston: Houghton Mifflin, 1929.

More, Paul Elmer. "A Writer of New England." *The Nation* 91, No. 2365 (27 October 1910): 386-87.

Thorp, Margaret Farrand. *Sarah Orne Jewett.* Minneapolis: University of Minnesota Press, 1966.

Twentieth-Century Literary Criticism, Vols. 1, 22. Detroit: Gale Research Co.

Waggoner, Hyatt H. "The Unity of *The Country of the Pointed Firs.*" *Twentieth Century Literature* 5, No. 2 (July 1959): 67-73.

James Jones
1921-1977
American novelist.

From Here to Eternity (novel, 1951)

The story of life in the armed forces, *From Here to Eternity* is set in Hawaii just prior to the Japanese attack on Pearl Harbor. **Robert E. Lee Prewitt,** a private, is a gifted, highly moral man who is locked in a conflict with his superiors because he will not exercise his considerable boxing talent. Prewitt once injured an opponent in a match, and swore never to fight again. **Milton Warden,** his sergeant, pressures Prewitt to change his mind, but as the two become closer, Warden finds it difficult persuade his friend. Prewitt and Warden both fall in love with young women who abandon them in search of more socially acceptable men. Jones depicts men torn by their opposing natures: Warden believes he must follow orders and uphold the prerogatives of the military but is in conflict over how he should deal with Prewitt, whose integrity he respects, and Prewitt is shown to be an idealistic man who is nonetheless drawn to violence, which punctuates the entire novel. When **Fatso Judson** beats his friend **Blues Berry,** Prewitt finally agrees to fight again, and in a rage he murders the attacker. Ironically, Prewitt is never punished for the killing, but his life ends tragically: he is killed by the military police after going AWOL.

In this and many of his later works Jones detailed a particularly masculine world in which the characters are in search of the meaning of existence, often depicted in an atmosphere of ominous violence. The author received the National Book Award for *From Here to Eternity* in 1951, and it continues to be considered one of his finest efforts.

FURTHER READING

Aldridge, John W. *The Devil in the Fire*, pp. 241-48. New York: Harper's Magazine Press, 1972.

Contemporary Authors, Vols. 1-4, rev. ed., 69-72; *Contemporary Authors New Revision Series*, Vol. 6. Detroit: Gale Research Co.

Contemporary Literary Criticism, Vols. 1, 3, 10, 39. Detroit: Gale Research Co.

Dictionary of Literary Biography, Vol. 2. Detroit: Gale Research Co.

Lardner, John. "Anatomy of the Regular Army." *New Yorker* (10 March 1951): 117.

Viorst, Milton. "James Jones and the Phoney Intellectuals." *Esquire* 69 (February 1969): 131-32.

Erica Jong
1942-
American novelist, short story writer, and poet.

Fear of Flying (novel, 1973)

Isadora Wing, the protagonist of this popular and controversial work, is a woman in search of self and satisfaction. As a writer, she grapples with the problems of creativity; as a woman, she finds herself restless in a conventional marriage and longing to explore the radical possibilities outlined in her fantasies. The novel opens in Vienna, where she leaves her psychiatrist husband in search of liberation. She meets the free-wheeling **Adrian Goodlove**, who preaches about the joys of open relationships and encourages Isadora to divorce her husband. However, after several weeks, she realizes that Adrian's concepts of love are no more open than the restrictions of marriage. She has a number of ultimately meaningless sexual relationships and feels stymied in her search for both sexual freedom and direction as an artist. At the novel's end, Isadora is offered the guilt-free physical encounter that she had once dreamed of. Repelled, she rebuffs the man, and contemplates her disillusionment.

The novel shocked readers upon its publication, for Jong employed vivid, often graphic language in chronicling her heroine's sexual escapades. Yet for all its bawdy humor, the novel contains a serious exploration of the dilemma of a modern woman who, dissatisfied with the traditional path for her as artist or lover, longs and reaches for more.

FURTHER READING

Contemporary Authors, Vols. 73-76. Detroit: Gale Research Co.

Contemporary Literary Criticism, Vols. 4, 6, 8, 18. Detroit: Gale Research Co.

Dictionary of Literary Biography, Vols. 2, 5, 28. Detroit: Gale Research Co.

Theroux, Paul. "Hapless Organ." *New Statesman* 87 (19 April 1974): 554.

Updike, John. "Jong Love." *New Yorker* 49 (17 December 1973): 149-53.

Vendler, Helen. "Do Women Have Distinctive Subjects, Roles, and Styles?" *New York Times Book Review* (12 August 1973): 6-7.

James Joyce
1882-1941
Irish novelist, short story writer, poet, and dramatist.

"The Dead" (short story, 1914)

"The Dead" is the longest piece in *Dubliners,* Joyce's unified short story collection. Set in

Dublin around the turn of the century, the story centers on **Gabriel Conroy,** a quasi-intellectual Irish teacher and literary critic, who with his wife **Gretta** attends the annual post-Christmas party given by his aunts, **Julia** and **Kate Morkan.** The body of the story is a rich accumulation of revealing, sometimes comic detail, depicting the party's guests, conversation, musical entertainment, and climactic holiday supper, at which Gabriel delivers a self-conscious and somewhat pompous little speech. This and other aspects of Gabriel's behavior during the course of the festive evening reveal sides of the dutiful nephew and loving husband that are intellectually snobbish and smugly self-satisfied. The impression is conveyed that Gretta, a beauty from the wild west of Ireland, is one of the attributes of which he is most satisfied and that, though married ten years, he still considers himself a passionate lover. These revelations prepare the reader for Gabriel's awakening, or epiphany, which occurs at the end of the story when Gretta is visibly moved by a singer's ballad of tragic love.

As the couple settles into a Dublin hotel room for the night, Gretta quietly tells her disturbed husband that the ballad had summoned the memory of a boy, **Michael Furey,** who had died very young of love for her. Realizing painfully that he neither has nor ever will feel such passion, Gabriel suddenly feels himself exposed in all his petty airs and self-delusion. Standing at the window watching snow fall, he broods on the past, the inevitable death that awaits his aunt, all his loved ones, and himself. The story's famous, final passage comments movingly—in what may or may not be Gabriel's voice—on the snow falling throughout Ireland, on Michael Furey's grave, on "all the living and the dead."

This early, masterful work is praised as one of Joyce's finest achievements in the short story and is noted for its revelation of the harsh, restrictive world of Ireland, a theme that Joyce returned to throughout his fiction. The story is related in the spare prose style characteristic of his early fiction, and his central concept of epiphany—of the painful moment when one of life's truths is revealed—is hauntingly and beautifully evoked.

A Portrait of the Artist as a Young Man (novel, 1916)

Set in Dublin in the late nineteenth century, Joyce's first novel is considered an important artistic recreation of the author's youth and young manhood, as well as an early formulation of the revolutionary technique and language that distinguished his later works. The novel centers on **Stephen Dedalus,** Joyce's fictional alter-ego whose story is continued in *Ulysses;* it depicts the formation of his artist's consciousness from childhood, the awakening of his senses, and his decision to depart the stultifying atmosphere of Ireland for an artist's life in Paris. Although the narrative is largely in the third-person, the reader is often privy to Stephen's acute consciousness and sensations. The reader follows him through the first two chapters from the spiritual torments and emotional rigors of Jesuit schooling to his precocious adolescent "fall" into the arms of a prostitute. In chapter three the boy is reconverted to feverish Catholic piety as a result of violent guilt over his sexual transgressions. The fourth chapter, however, finds him confronted ultimately with his muse—the simple, religious, yet erotic image of a young girl wading—and he determines finally to forsake the Catholic priesthood he had considered for the vocation of artist, or what he terms "the priest of the eternal imagination." The book's fifth and final chapter depicts Stephen leaving behind family, friends, religion, and nation "to forge in the smithy of my soul the uncreated conscience of my race."

Throughout *A Portrait of the Artist as a Young Man,* the often rarefied vision of Stephen's evolving consciousness is underscored by the banality and strife of Irish life and of relationships with such characters as his increasingly drunken, embittered father, **Simon Dedalus;** his loving but overburdened mother, **Mrs. Dedalus; Father Dolan,** one of his Jesuit teachers; and his classmates and nemeses **Davin, Lynch,** and **Heron.** Also depicted are his relationships with his two young loves, **Eileen** and **Emma.** The final section of chapter five presents entries from Stephen's diary, so that the artistic soul which has been chronicled throughout the book fittingly, at the book's conclusion, assumes his artistic role and speaks for himself.

Ulysses (novel, 1922)

In style, structure, theme and nearly every element, *Ulysses* is considered a major landmark in modern literature. Set in Dublin entirely on 16 June 1904, the novel is Joyce's attempt to recreate, in all its drabness and heroism, a single day in the life of its principal character, **Leopold Bloom,** an Irish-Jewish advertising salesman. The narrative also highlights **Stephen Dedalus,** a writer and teacher who was the protagonist of Joyce's first novel, *A Portrait of the Artist as a Young Man,* and **Marion Tweedy Bloom,** called **Molly,** a second-rate singer and Leopold's unfaithful wife. Partly to underscore the ironic contrast between the exhausted modern world and the glorious epoch of ancient Greece, Joyce structured his masterpiece after the books of the Odyssey of Homer, and each of the characters corresponds with a character in that epic. For example, Leopold, the questing adventurer in Dublin, is Ulysses; Stephen, Leopold's spiritual son, is linked to Ulysses's son, Telemachus; and Molly represents Ulysses's wife, Penelope. In addition, Joyce assigned various other meanings to each of the book's eighteen episodes, including a dominant color, a time of day, central symbols and disciplines (such as literature, philosophy, or history) and a part of the body. Because many of the episodes incorporate linguistic flights that involve dense literary allusion and parody, puns, and free-ranging interior monologue, the style of the books is radically experimental, although the actual action is straightforward enough and has been classified by some as psychological realism.

Ulysses' first three chapters focus on the morning activities of Stephen, Joyce's autobiographical artist depicted in *A Portrait of the Artist as a Young Man,* who has returned home from a brief sojourn in Paris in order to attend to his dying mother. Living with **Malachi Mulligan,** called **Buck,** a dissolute medical student, in a medieval tower on the outskirts of Dublin and dissatisfied with his teaching job at a boy's school, Stephen is also guilt-ridden for refusing the request of his mother, a devout Catholic, to pray at her deathbed. In chapter four attention turns to Bloom, whose morning is also recounted. He eats breakfast, musing on his sixteen-year marriage to Molly, whom he suspects of having an affair with her manager, **Blazes Boylan,** and on his daughter **Milly,** a fifteen-year-old working away from home as a photographer's apprentice. He also thinks about his son **Rudy,** who had died as an infant. Eventually Bloom ventures into the streets of Dublin, stopping first at the post office to fetch a letter from the woman with whom he has begun an epistolary romance. He also enters a Catholic church, where he listens desultorily to mass being said, then joins a party of mourners at the funeral of **Paddy Dignan,** in a death-centered episode corresponding to Ulysses's descent into Hades. Later he sees but does not speak to Stephen in the office of a newspaper that is printing one of his advertisements, then stops for a snack at Davy Byrne's pub. At his next stop, the National Library, he again sees Stephen, who is pontificating to his friends on the works of Shakespeare. At the Ormond Hotel for supper, Bloom glimpses Blazes Boylan, on his way to Bloom's own home and the waiting Molly. After a near-brawl at a pub, Leopold walks along the Sandymount beach at twilight, lost in his own amorous reveries, realizing later that at that very time he was being cuckolded by Molly.

Bloom encounters Stephen for the third time at the refectory of a maternity hospital where he has stopped to inquire about a neighbor. Concerned about the seriously intoxicated young man, Bloom accompanies him and his friends to a pub, then quietly watchful, follows him to a brothel. He finally brings Stephen home to recover from his drunken disorientation, and speaks to him about science and art. Refusing Bloom's invitation to give up his hard-drinking medical student friends and come to live at the Bloom's house, Stephen leaves for his tower. Leopold gets into bed beside his wife. In the final chapter, the reader enters Molly's mind for a stream-of-consciousness interior monologue that embraces her rushing thoughts on such subjects as her girlhood, her courtship with Bloom, Stephen Dedalus, Blazes Boylan, and most rhapsodically, the mysteries and pleasures of sexuality.

No summation of events can adequately communicate the essence of *Ulysses* and its characters. Joyce's rich narrative draws on myriad details and allusions to create through accumulated detail the sense of the flux of personal consciousness, history, and life itself. Within the narrative, the central characters, too, are revealed gradually through snatches of conversation, stretches of thought, as well as the behavior and reactions of the Dubliners around them. The novel is widely considered the most innovative and influential in the twentieth century, and Leopold Bloom in particular is acknowledged as one of literature's most distinguished characters, vividly revealed by Joyce as simultaneously comic, mundane, and ultimately heroic in his very humanity.

Finnegans Wake (novel, 1936)

The time and setting for Joyce's final and most challenging novel is difficult to state, because here Joyce endeavored to encompass in a literary work all time and space. Little or nothing in the novel is concrete: time, narrative voices, styles, and language are all constantly shifting, changing, subsuming one another, or reappearing in different forms. Jungian and Freudian theories of psychology, wordplay, literary allusions, myth, legend, history, and Joyce's own personal history are combined here in what is considered a masterful modernist novel.

The characters who loosely populate this flight into time and space are somewhat elusive, with some characters often taking on different personas. What plot exists revolves around **Humphrey Chimpden Earwicker,** a pubkeeper in Chapelizod, Dublin. An Irishman of Danish descent, he still suffers guilt about a transgression he committed—which is never fully explained—against two young women in Dublin's Phoenix Park. The second of the novel's four "books" depicts the Earwicker family on a quiet evening: **Ann Earwicker,** Humphrey's wife, **Isobel,** their daughter, and their twin sons, **Kevin** and **Jerry.** Humphrey is at the pub with his patrons, and he drinks to extreme excess before going to bed. Book three comprises Earwicker's dream, floated along apparently on alcohol and guilt in which he and his family are transformed, either explicitly or tacitly, into figures from history and myth. Earwicker becomes a character called **Here Comes Everybody** and **Haveth Childer Everywhere,** and is linked with such figures as the Biblical Adam, Tristram, Jonathan Swift, Jesus Christ, and Napoleon. His daughter Isobel becomes Tristram's lover, **Iseult,** while his twin sons signify **Shaun the Postman** and **Shem the Penman,** the postman being the pragmatic man who bears messages without grasping their meaning; and the Penman representing the noble writer, or creator of culture and tradition. Humphrey's wife Ann, for her part, is **Anna Livia Pluralulle,** the Dublin's River Liffey, representing the woman as the stream of life that flows ceaselessly to the sea. Book three's intricate, dense reverie ends with Humphrey and Ann in younger days, being awakened at first light by a disturbed child, and book four revolves around the idea of a true dawn coming over Dublin, and of the flowing river that is time, history, and consciousness, ultimately referring back to the first passage of the novel, linking all the books' narrative into an unbroken circle.

Critics note that while Joyce in *Ulysses* projected experimental passages on a base of relatively straightforward fictional action, in *Finnegans Wake* the author abandons such a base for a pure flight of language, ideas, and allusion. Joyce is credited with inventing a language in the book with which to relate a vision of humankind unbounded by space or time. For this bold and revolutionary conception, unmatched before or since, as well as his other immeasurable contributions, Joyce is acclaimed by many as the central figure of twentieth-century literature.

FURTHER READING

Bengal, Michael H. and Fritz Senn. *A Conceptual Guide to "Finnegans Wake."* University Park: Pennsylvania State University Press, 1974.

Benstock, Bernard. *James Joyce: The Undiscover'd Country.* Dublin: Gill & Macmillan, 1977.

Benstock, Shari and Bernard Benstock. *Who's He When He's at Home: A James Joyce Directory.* Urbana: University of Illinois Press, 1980.

Boyle, Robert R. *James Joyce's Pauline Vision.* Carbondale: Southern Illinois University Press, 1978.

Campbell, Joseph and Henry Morton Robinson. *A Skeleton Key to "Finnegans Wake."* New York: Viking, 1944.

Contemporary Authors, Vol. 104. Detroit: Gale Research Co.

Dictionary of Literary Biography, Vols. 10, 19, 36. Detroit: Gale Research Co.

Ellmann, Richard. *James Joyce.* New York: Oxford University Press, 1959, rev. ed., 1982.

——. *Ulysses on the Liffey.* New York: Oxford University Press, 1972.

Gilbert, Stuart. *James Joyce's "Ulysses."* London: Faber & Faber, 1930.

Gottfried, Roy K. *The Art of Joyce's Syntax in "Ulysses."* Athens: University of Georgia Press, 1980.

——. *Structure and Motif in "Finnegans Wake."* Evanston: Northwestern University Press, 1963.

Hart, Clive, ed. *James Joyce's "Dubliners."* London: Faber & Faber, 1969.

Hart, Clive and David Hayman, eds. *James Joyce's "Ulysses."* Berkeley: University of California Press, 1974.

Kain, Richard M. *Fabulous Voyager: James Joyce's "Ulysses."* Chicago: University of Chicago Press, 1947.

Kenner, Hugh. *Dublin's Joyce.* Berkeley: University of California Press, 1978.

Levin, Harry. *James Joyce.* New York: New Directions, 1941.

Litz, A. Walton. *The Art of James Joyce.* New York: Oxford University Press, 1961.

Riqueline, John Paul. *Teller and Tale in Joyce's Fiction.* Baltimore: Johns Hopkins University Press, 1983.

Twentieth-Century Literary Criticism, Vols. 3, 8, 16, 26. Detroit: Gale Research Co.

Franz Kafka

1883-1924

Austro-Czech novelist, short story writer, and diarist.

The Metamorphosis (novella, 1915)

The finest among the small number of works Kafka published during his lifetime, *The Metamorphosis* takes place in early twentieth-century Prague. With this arresting opening: "When **Gregor Samsa** woke up one morning from unsettling dreams, he found himself changed in his bed into a monstrous vermin," Kafka set his elusive psychological fantasy in motion. A traveling fabric salesman, Gregor must now deal with the vivid perception that he is indeed a giant, beetle-like insect. Surprisingly, he accepts his metamorphosis matter-of-factly, though he finds difficulty moving, as he is lying on his heavy, thick-shelled back while his many tiny legs flail helplessly in the air. After countless attempts to right himself, he falls to ruminating on the difficulties of his job, at which he cheerlessly toils to repay a huge debt incurred by his father. Gregor lives in an apartment with his father, mother, and sister, **Grete.** In rapid procession the three interrupt his thoughts with queries from behind the three doors to his bedroom. When his office manager arrives and inquires why he has missed the early train, Gregor responds confusedly, quickly losing the ability to communicate with the outside world. With painful difficulty, Gregor opens his door with his toothless mouth but succeeds only in frightening his manager, who flees.

This first emergence from isolation, followed by a brutal shove from his father that forces Gregor back inside his room, marks the climax of the work's first section. In the two remaining sections, which encompass Gregor's ruminations upon his family and himself, Gregor again emerges briefly, each time accentuating the horrible chasm that separates him from his family. Finally, Grete, who has been the source of greatest sympathy and service for Gregor, convinces her parents that "it has to go." She no longer believes that the abhorrent presence behind the door is her brother. Gregor thinks back on his family with deep emotion and love and, locked inside his room, quietly ends his life by ceasing to breathe. The family begins life anew. **Mr.** and **Mrs. Samsa** watch their daughter "getting livelier and livelier" and consider that it will soon be time to find her a good husband.

The Metamorphosis is one of the most frequently analyzed works in literature. While it is not uncommon for criticism of similar insight and conviction to reach dissimilar conclusions on the meaning of a given work, Kafka's narrative has been the focus of a particularly varied body of discussion and judgments. Three frequent critical interpretations of Gregor's transformation are that it serves either as retribution, as wish-fulfillment, or as an extended metaphor, carried from abstract concept to concrete reality. For its technical excellence, as well as for the nightmarish and fascinating nature of the metamorphosis, Kafka's story has come to be considered one of the central enigmas not only of modern literature but of the literary imagination itself.

The Trial (novel, 1925)

The Trial, the first of Kafka's three major posthumously published, unfinished novels, takes place in a surrealistic twentieth-century Germany. The narrative begins with the sentence: "Someone must have traduced **Joseph K.,** for without having done anything wrong he was arrested one fine morning." K., a bank employee, is arrested on his thirtieth birthday by two "warders" named **Franz** and **Willem,** and neither they nor the inspector who questions K. are able to inform him of the crime of which he has been accused. They do not take him into custody, stating that the arrest is merely to inform K. of his status as an accused man and to record his reaction, nor do they provide evidence that they have the authority to arrest him, treating the justice of his arrest as self-evident and his objections as incomprehensible and irrelevant. The Court that arrests K. is unrelated to the ordinary criminal court system: the offices are located in the attics of slums, the actions of Court officials and employees toward K. are bizarre and impenetrable, and the information offered to K. by those from whom he solicits help is contradictory. After his arrest, K. attempts to ignore his trial, refusing to recognize the Court's authority over him; as the trial advances, however, he is forced into progressively greater involvement with his defense, hiring a lawyer at the insistence of his uncle, neglecting his office duties even though the advancement of his career had formerly been his most important goal, and finally becoming so obsessed with the trial that he regards his work as an impediment to his defense.

As K. becomes frustrated by the apparent lack of progress effected by his lawyer, he begins to search for other avenues of assistance. One who offers a lucid but despairing picture of the Court is the painter **Titorelli,** who claims to have important connections with many Court judges. Titorelli outlines for K. three avenues of defense corresponding to three desired outcomes: definite acquittal, ostensible acquittal, and indefinite postponement. Upon further explanation the options appear absurdly improbable. In the final chapter, K. is broken in spirit and compliant in his execution, for without having determined the crime of which he is accused he has been unable to build a successful defense. He finds himself waiting for the executioners on the evening before his thirty-first birthday and leads them to the place of execution. Unable to bring himself to obey the executioners' implied demand that he himself carry out the sentence through suicide, he reaches out toward an illusory hope just before the end and dies in shame, "like a dog."

The Trial is considered one of the most brilliant and enigmatic novels in modern literature. Through its nightmarish juxtaposition of realistic and fantastic elements, it is often considered to presage the breakdown of traditional beliefs and values in the twentieth century. Today most scholars consider the novel a profound work that supports various and even mutually exclusive interpretations. Such divergent assessments suggest that the story of Joseph K.'s persecution, a powerful study of human guilt unique in world literature, conveys truths that defy rational analysis.

The Castle (novel, 1926)

The Castle, a timeless philosophical and religious allegory, begins in the town below the castle of **Count Westwest. K.,** a seeker, arrives when "the Castle hill [is] hidden, veiled in mist and darkness." After a long walk through deep snow he enters an inn and falls asleep beside the fire. He is rudely awakened by a man requesting to see his permit to stay in the town. K. declares that he is the Land Surveyor, there on official business for the castle. In the first of numerous hauntingly remote and convoluted communications with the castle, K.'s claim is verified. This announcement prickles K.'s senses for it is either a good omen that he is acknowledged at the castle and will be admitted or a portentous sign that he is being watched and will be challenged. The next day K. sees two men leaving the castle and attempts to speak with them; they refuse flatly. That evening, however, the same inescapably comic and mischievous pair introduce themselves as **Arthur** and **Jeremiah,** K.'s assistants. Their help to K. in his quest to visit the castle and meet the authorities there is minimal at best. A young man named **Barnabas** proves somewhat more useful. He serves as messenger between **Klamm,** a castle chief, and K. To K.'s utter frustration, Klamm himself, a mysterious figure revered by the villagers, is completely unapproachable. K. persists in determining why he was summoned as Land Surveyor, but discovers from the town superintendent that the paperwork has been hopelessly confused and that his presence is apparently unnecessary. K. decides to marry **Frieda,** a barmaid and former consort of Klamm, hoping by virtue of Frieda's elect status to eventually penetrate the as yet impervious castle. He accepts a menial job as janitor of the school. Following many more ambiguous leads and ineffectual attempts to become both an accepted citizen and a trusted recipient of the castle's confidence, K. loses Frieda forever. Kafka planned to bring the novel to conclusion with K., on his deathbed, receiving a message from the castle allowing him to live in the town in peace.

In a dreamworld that operates according to cryptic and indecipherable laws, K. finds himself, like many Kafka protagonists, on a quest consisting of a series of dehumanizing defeats without ultimate resolution. Yet, despite the implicitly hostile and profoundly enigmatic atmosphere of *The Castle,* Kafka's work is uncommonly rich in humor that meaningfully complements its theme of spiritual doubt and uncertainty.

Amerika (novel, 1927)

Amerika traces the adventures of an adolescent immigrant who, dispossessed by his family after having impregnated a seductive maidservant, travels to New York City. Diffident, gullible, and limited in intelligence, **Karl Rossmann** lucklessly shifts from one guide and resource to another. The first of these is the **Stoker,** whom he meets during his passage to America. Like Karl, the Stoker is a perpetual sufferer. Through absurd coincidence, the Stoker leads Karl to **Uncle Jacob,** a wealthy businessman who believes Karl to be his nephew. Under Jacob's shield Karl is rescued from indigence and harsh experience in a country where people and customs will remain forever foreign to him. However, Uncle Jacob exacts total submission from Karl. Eventually, he is driven from Uncle Jacob's house for an action which he discovers to have been subversive. Directionless and ill-prepared, he takes to the road. Two immigrant tramps, an Irishman called **Robinson** and a Frenchman called **Delamarche,** ostensible befriend him. Yet, they prey upon the unwitting Karl repeatedly. Eventually Karl takes refuge at the Hotel Occidental, run by **Grete Mitzelbach.** She, like Karl, is a native of Prague. Through her he secures a job as lift boy but, true to his nature, becomes rapidly enmeshed and enslaved by the complex machinations that sustain the hotel. When dismissed from his position for unspecified reasons, Karl resumes his purposeless peripatetic wandering. Although unfinished, Kafka's novel closes somewhat optimistically: Karl is headed toward Oklahoma where he will join the Nature Theatre as a "technical worker." The company has attracted him with its recruitment placard, which reads, "Employment for everyone, a place for everyone."

Like the protagonist of *The Castle,* Karl seeks meaning through a sense of belonging. Kafka's controlled presentation of scenes that reflect psychological, social, political, and metaphysical instability and confusion has been recognized as a product of the author's own life. During Kafka's childhood his personality was eclipsed by that of his extrovert father, causing self-doubt and feelings of inadequacy that were to haunt him throughout his short, troubled life. This autobiographical theme recurs in Kafka's greatest works and forms the basis for his philosophical approach to the dilemma of the individual's relationship to an incomprehensible world.

FURTHER READING

Beck, Evelyn Torton. "Kafka's Traffic in Women: Gender, Power, and Sexuality." *The Literary Review* 26, No. 4 (Summer 1983): 565-76.

Cantrell, Carol Helmsetter. "*The Metamorphosis:* Kafka's Study of a Family." *Modern Fiction Studies* 23, No. 4 (Winter 1977-78): 578-86.

Contemporary Authors, Vols. 105, 126. Detroit: Gale Research Co.

Emrich, Wilhelm. "The World as Court of Justice: The Novel *The Trial.*" In *Franz Kafka: A Critical Study of His Writings,* pp. 316-64. New York: Ungar, 1968.

Flores, Angel, ed. *The Kafka Debate: New Perspectives for Our Time.* New York: Gordonian Press, 1977.

Gray, Ronald. *Franz Kafka.* Cambridge: Cambridge University Press, 1973.

Hayman, Ronald. *Kafka: A Biography.* New York: Oxford University Press, 1982.

Jaffe, Adrian. *The Process of Kafka's "Trial."* Lansing: Michigan State University Press, 1967.

Kuna, Franz. *Franz Kafka: Literature as Corrective Punishment.* Bloomington: Indiana University Press, 1974.

Pascal, Roy. *Kafka's Narrators: A Study of His Stories and Sketches.* London: Cambridge University Press, 1982.

Pawel, Ernst. *The Nightmare of Reason: A Life of Franz Kafka.* New York: Farrar, Straus, and Giroux, 1984.

Politzer, Heinz. *Franz Kafka: Parable and Paradox*. Ithaca: Cornell University Press, 1966.

Sokel, Walter H. *Franz Kafka*. New York: Columbia University Press, 1966.

Spann, Meno. *Franz Kafka*. Boston: Twayne, 1976.

Tauber, Herbert. *Franz Kafka: An Interpretation of His Works*. New Haven: Yale University Press, 1948.

Twentieth-Century Literary Criticism, Vols. 2, 6, 13, 29. Detroit: Gale Research Co.

Yasunari Kawabata

1899-1972

Japanese novelist, short story writer, and critic.

Snow Country (novel, 1947)

Snow Country, the novel for which Kawabata is best known, takes place at a popular hot-spring resort amidst the snow-covered mountains of Niigata Prefecture. In early December **Shimamura,** a rich Tokyo dilettante, travels by train to the resort. He is intent on reuniting with **Komako,** a modest young music student and party hostess with whom he had become sexually intimate the previous May. During the train ride, Shimamura watches the reflection of a young woman, **Yoko,** nursing a slightly older man, **Yukio,** who is dying from tuberculosis. The "inexpressible beauty" of the innocent girl's mirrored face strongly accords with Shimamura's sense of the aesthetic. He prefers, in his own writing, to describe what he has never witnessed in order to preserve the ideal in his mind. Consequently, he has specialized as a scholar of Western ballet, avoiding actual performances. Upon his arrival at the resort, Shimamura learns that Komako has become a professional geisha. Ironically, she has done so to raise money to nurse Yukio, whom she once loved deeply. By the end of his stay, Shimamura, realizing this, nevertheless senses her continuing love for him. The following autumn Shimamura returns to the snow country and discovers that Yukio has died. This time Komako shatters Shimamura's illusions about her while telling a story of exploitation parallelling her own fate. Shimamura's affections gravitate to Yoko, who haunts the burial ground of Yukio. Komako's enmity toward Yoko, though initially great, gradually recedes; however, she does not fully forgive Shimamura for selfishly using and then abandoning her. Near the end of the novel, as Shimamura watches Komako rescue Yoko from a burning building, he comes to a sudden painful realization of the anguish he has caused Komako.

With its oblique narrative movement and ending, *Snow Country* functions more as an extended poetic metaphor of spiritual journey than a conventional novel of interpersonal conflict. Some critics have suggested the work's structural similarity to Japanese Noh drama. When it is examined in that context, the enigmatic character of Komako assumes primary focus. Through his aesthetic devotion, Shimamura represents a priest seeking enlightenment. He undertakes the task of penetrating to the core of Komako's personality, which is inextricably linked in his mind to the beautiful and tragic setting of the snow country. Kawabata's highly revered style—lyrical, gracefully precise, and symbolically potent—brilliantly conveys the poignancy of the novel's underlying meaning: Kawabata's conviction that life at its core is hollow and the search for ideal beauty is consequently futile.

The Sound of the Mountain (novel, 1954)

Often regarded as Kawabata's most important work, *The Sound of the Mountain* is set in

Japan during the early 1950s. Near senility, a businessman named **Shingo** desires to spend his time in quiet contemplation, sustaining himself with his still vivid memories of the past. Instead, he finds that he must deal with a growing family problem: the troubled marriage of his son and daughter-in-law, who reside in his Kamakura home outside Tokyo. Shingo's son, **Shuichi,** has been neglecting **Kikuko** for the affections of a war widow. Despite his own unhappy marriage, Shingo advocates traditional morality—responsibility to family and devotion to the institution of marriage—over personal fulfillment. Consequently, he is appalled by his son's behavior, especially his open mistreatment of Kikuko, whom Shingo cares for deeply. Despairing of ever reconciling with Shuichi, Kikuko decides to have an abortion when she learns she is pregnant. Shingo is shocked by her action, but welling with love and sympathy, forgives her and gravely accepts a share of responsibility for the child's death. After Shuichi's affair dissolves, his mistress, also pregnant, wants to have the child. For a time Shingo had encouraged her to have an abortion, but had later changed his mind, not wishing to have two deaths on his conscience. The novel closes with an uncomfortable, if poetically serene, sense of irresolution. Shuichi and Kikuko have tentatively reconciled, but **Fusako,** Shingo's daughter, remains estranged from her violent, suicidal husband. Able to look beyond the problems of his household, Shingo suggests the family take a trip to the country soon, to view the maple trees.

In *The Sound of the Mountain,* Kawabata demonstrates, to a degree not found in his other works, an extreme sensitivity toward his characters. In Shingo Kawabata presented his most fully drawn protagonist. Like his creator, Shingo is attracted to the beautiful, whether found in art or nature. His prescient awareness of death and the end of beauty elevates his story to tragedy. He continually dreams of the dead and, during his waking moments, imagines he hears the eerie, death-tolling sound of the mountain. For Shingo, life and death intertwine in complex, painful harmony. Kawabata's lyrical evocation of such timeless themes, and his pioneering, episodic construction of the modern Japanese novel, earned him the Nobel Prize for Literature in 1968.

FURTHER READING

Araki, James T. "Kawabata and His Snow Country." *The Centennial Review* 13 (1969): 331-49.

Contemporary Authors, Vols. 33-36, rev. ed., 93-96. Detroit: Gale Research Co.

Contemporary Literary Criticism, Vols. 2, 5, 9, 18. Detroit: Gale Research Co.

Keene, Donald. "Kawabata Yasunari." In *Dawn to the West: Japanese Literature in the Modern Era,* Vol. 1, pp. 786-845. New York: Holt, Rinehart and Winston, 1984.

Miyoshi, Masao. "The Margins of Life." In *Accomplices of Silence: The Modern Japanese Novel,* pp. 95-121. Berkeley: University of California Press, 1974.

Rimer, Jo. Thomas. "Kawabata Yasunari, Eastern Approaches: *Snow Country.*" In *Modern Japanese Fiction and its Traditions,* pp. 162-81. Princeton: Princeton University Press, 1978.

Yamanouchi, Hisaaki. "The Eternal Womanhood: Tanizaki Jun'ichiro and Kawabata Yasunari." In *The Search for Authenticity in Modern Japanese Literature,* pp. 107-36. New York: Cambridge University Press, 1978.

Nikos Kazantzakis

1883-1957

Greek novelist, poet, and dramatist.

Zorba the Greek (novel, 1946)

This novel, considered Kazantzakis's finest, is set on the island of Crete, where the protagonist, an unnamed narrator known only as "**The Boss,**" has come to reopen his lignite mine. He is a scholar and writer who has decided to abandon the contemplative life, and as he waits to board a boat to take him to the island, he meets **Alexis Zorba,** who will become his foreman and cook, but most importantly, will reacquaint him with the passionate aspects of life.

The novel embodies Kazantzakis's recurrent theme of the duality of human nature, of the war between the spirit and the flesh. For Kazantzakis, this aspect was most vividly presented in Nietzsche's concept of the Apollonian and Dionysian elements in humankind, also exemplified in the difference between Western and Eastern culture. Apollonian societies value order, rationalism, and pragmatism; the Dionysian represents the primitive, passionate, and illogical in humankind. These two opposing philosophies are embodied in the "boss" and Zorba. Much of the novel is taken up with their arguments regarding the two forces they represent. Zorba is Dionysian man at his most elemental: he is cunning, funny, exuberant, irrepressible, and passionate in all realms: emotionally, sexually, in eating or drinking. His ties to Dionysus are reinforced in his love of music and dance, through which he abandons himself to the primal rhythms of the unfettered human spirit. The "boss," by contrast, even though he claims to seek the active life, is depicted with his copy of Dante or his manuscript on Buddha in hand. His is a journey of synthesis, in which he learns, through confrontation and reconciliation, the ways of Zorba.

In the conclusion, the "boss" has absorbed the message of his teacher: he will take what he has learned of the passional, illogical, primal forces and, applying the Apollonian order of art, create again. This novel is noted for its brilliant portrayal of Zorba, a character who has been embraced by readers all over the world. Whether or not one accepts or understands the philosophical background of Kazantzakis's work, Zorba's immortality seems assured.

The Last Temptation of Christ (novel, 1955)

In this, one of his most famous and controversial works, Kazantzakis explores the figure of **Jesus Christ** as a man torn between the opposing forces of the spirit and the flesh. In his prologue, the author reveals that what drew him to Christ was his own, similar turmoil. His Christ is a man tempted by the ordinary, and he is drawn to the fulfillment of a particularly human destiny: to love, marry, to have a family. His is a journey of rebellion, reconciliation, and finally, submission. In Kazantzakis's hands, Christ is shown to embody the conflict between the very human desire for communion with his fellow beings and the yearning to be one with God.

The novel is set in biblical times in Palestine, where we first see Jesus as he is tormented by dreams in which his disciples, reduced to disfigured grotesques, search for him, to force him to his destiny as the savior of humankind. He is a poor carpenter, who is fashioning a large wooden cross when we first come upon him. His vivid dream foreshadows the central focus of the novel, revealed in the final portion dealing with Christ's last temptation. As he hangs on the cross near death, Jesus faints. When he revives, he is in the company of a guardian angel who takes him first to **Mary Magdalene,** the former prostitute who had chosen the path of Jesus, but who now becomes his lover. Jesus now appears to have become very much a mortal man. In later scenes, her death by stoning is related. Next the angel takes Jesus to the home of **Mary** and **Martha,** the sisters of **Lazarus,** whom Jesus had risen from the dead. He becomes husband to both, and revels in the joys of the flesh: of fatherhood and of life lived within the human sphere. As an old man, he is visited by his disciples, who rebuke him for turning away from the path of crucifixion and eternal life. **Judas Iscariot** calls Jesus a traitor, telling him his place was on the cross. **Matthew** laments that all of his hard work on the gospel had been for nothing, noting how he had struggled to dramatize Jesus's life and how his fame is in jeopardy because of Christ's refusal to be a savior. Suddenly, they vanish. Jesus regains consciousness on the cross, and realizes that the vision that has occurred is the work of the devil, who had saved this for his last temptation. As he utters his final words, he dies in triumph.

This portrait of Jesus focuses, in the words of the author, on the part of him that was "profoundly human." But for the representatives of organized religion, Kazantzakis's portrait was blasphemous. Still, in the opinion of many critics, the public is misled if they accept the work as a heretical tract. It is perhaps better understood as the culmination of Kazantzakis's thoughts on the human condition, of modern humankind torn between the demands of the spirit and the flesh, revealed in a tribute to the struggle and triumph over those forces.

FURTHER READING

Bien, Peter. *Nikos Kazantzakis.* New York: Columbia University Press, 1972.

Contemporary Authors, Vol. 105. Detroit: Gale Research Co.

Doulis, Tom. "Kazantzakis and the Meaning of Suffering." *Northwest Review* 6, No. 1 (Winter 1963): 33-57.

Karnezis, George T. *"Zorba the Greek:* The Artist and Experience." *Carnegie Series in English* 9 (1970). 43-52.

Levitt, Morton P. *The Cretan Glance: The World and Art of Nikos Kazantzakis.* Columbus: Ohio State University Press, 1980.

Stavrou, C. N. "Some Notes on Nikos Kazantzakis." *The Colorado Quarterly* 12, No. 4 (Spring 1964): 317-34.

Twentieth-Century Literary Criticism, Vols. 2, 5, 33. Detroit: Gale Research Co.

Ziolkowski, Theodore. "The Christomaniacs." In *Fictional Transfigurations of Jesus,* pp. 98-141. Princeton: Princeton University Press, 1972.

Thomas Keneally
1935-

Australian novelist and essayist.

The Chant of Jimmie Blacksmith (novel, 1972)

The novel takes place in the New South Wales territory of Australia at the turn of the century. It centers on the fate of **Jimmie Blacksmith,** half-white and half-Aborigine, and is based on a true story in which a half-caste went on a murderous rampage, killing several white women. Keneally depicts Jimmie as an outcast, a victim of two cultures, both of which reject him. He is portrayed as a sensitive and ultimately self-destructive young man, driven by a lifetime of indignities to revenge himself on the white culture. The world of the whites—Christian, Western, and racist—has taught Jimmie to yearn for the material well-being that marks success and acceptance in that culture. Yet it is clear from his treatment at the hands of that society that he will never be accepted within it. His background as an aborigine he also shuns, for their way of life has been debased and deprived of its meaning at

215

the hands of the white culture, who represent the emerging victors in the battle for control over Australia's destiny. Rootless, and with his hope for a better life denied him, Jimmie is driven to madness, and he and his brother **Mort** begin their killing spree, which is related in all its savage brutality. Now outlaws, they flee across New South Wales, with Jimmie described in a desperate attempt to elude his past, tormented by the ghosts of his primitive, aboriginal ancestry and the vestiges of his Christian beliefs. He is finally apprehended and killed.

The novel is noted for its fast-paced, compelling narrative, finely etched characterizations, and revealing treatment of the racial tensions of Australia. It is widely regarded as one of Keneally's finest works.

FURTHER READING

Brady, Veronica. "The Most Frightening Rebellion: The Recent Novels of Thomas Keneally." *Meanjin* 38, No. 1 (April 1979): 74-86.

Contemporary Authors, Vols. 85-88. Detroit: Gale Research Co.

Contemporary Literary Criticism, Vols. 5, 8, 10, 14, 19, 27, 43. Detroit: Gale Research Co.

Tiffin, Chris. "Victims Black and White: Thomas Keneally's *The Chant of Jimmie Blacksmith.*" In *Studies in the Recent Australian Novel,* edited by K.G. Hamilton, pp. 121-40. Brisbane: University of Queensland Press, 1978.

"Over the Fence." *Times Literary Supplement,* No. 3680 (15 September 1972): 1041.

Jack Kerouac
1922-1969
Canadian-born American novelist and poet.

On the Road (novel, 1957)

Sal Paradise is the narrator of Kerouac's most popular novel, which focuses on his relationship and travels with **Dean Moriarty.**

Much of Kerouac's writings are fictionalized autobiography, collectively known as "The Legend of Kerouac" or "The Legend of Dulouz." His most popular novels revolve around a loosely knit group of friends who came to be known as "The Beat Generation." The Beats—a term coined by Kerouac—dabbled in drugs, alcohol, religion, sex, poetry, prose, and art. This experimentation was never an end in itself, but a means of challenging and expanding what they perceived to be a restrictive society.

The characters in Kerouac's works are usually ascribed to real-life counterparts. For example, Dean Moriarty is based on Kerouac's friend Neal Cassady. Likewise, **Old Bull Lee** is William Burroughs, and **Carlo Marx** is Allen Ginsberg. Sal Paradise is the persona of Kerouac himself. Originally written in what Kerouac labeled "spontaneous prose," *On the Road* abandons the formal structure of the novel in order to convey the forward rush of events as they occur.

The book depicts the first meeting of Sal and Dean, and Sal's first cross-country journey alone. To Sal, Dean embodies the essence of "Beat—the social root, the soul of Beatific." Born in a jalopy in 1926, Dean has already spent much of his life on the road when he encounters Sal at the beginning of the novel. Dean's rejection of traditional values and unabashed enthusiasm for adventure provide the impetus for the pair's travels and untempered forays into drinking and sex. The book also details Sal and Dean's quest for "IT," a form of agape in which the essence of all things becomes clear. Their quest leads them across the United States and into Mexico City, where Sal realizes that "IT" and death are closely intertwined. Pure knowledge and understanding, then, come at too great a cost.

The novel is praised for its loose, episodic structure and for its celebration of an unorthodox life and approach to art that influenced a generation of writers. Widely acknowledged as Kerouac's finest novel, *On the Road* continues to be read and is considered a major work of American literature of the mid-twentieth century.

FURTHER READING

Charters, Ann. *Kerouac, A Biography*. San Francisco: Straight Arrow, 1973.

Contemporary Authors, Vols. 5-8, rev. ed., 25-28, rev. ed. Detroit: Gale Research Co.

Contemporary Literary Criticism, Vols. 1, 2, 3, 5, 14, 29. Detroit: Gale Research Co.

Dictionary of Literary Biography, Vols. 2, 16; *Dictionary of Literary Biography Documentary Series*, Vol. 3; *Concise Dictionary of American Literary Biography, 1941-1968*. Detroit: Gale Research Co.

Hipkiss, Robert A. *Jack Kerouac: Prophet of the New Romanticism*. Lawrence: University of Kansas Press, 1977.

Jarvis, Charles E. *Visions of Kerouac*. Lowell: Ithaca Press, 1973.

Ken Kesey

1935-

American novelist, essayist, and short story writer.

One Flew Over the Cuckoo's Nest (novel, 1962)

One Flew Over the Cuckoo's Nest, Kesey's first novel, is set in the contemporary United States in a ward of a mental hospital. The rigidly regimented order enforced there by the ruthless **Nurse Ratched,** or **Big Nurse,** is thrown into upheaval by the appearance of an ebullient, energetic, fast-mouthed hustler, **Randle Patrick McMurphy.** Transferred from a prison work farm, McMurphy arrives expecting a jovial time, and proceeds to produce one in spite of the forbidding Big Nurse. The story is related by **Bromden,** an enormous, schizophrenic American Indian who long ago shut out the alien American society by faking muteness. He describes how he and the other inmates, wearied into submission by the cold, calculating routines and regulations of Big Nurse, come alive under the tutelage of the irrepressible McMurphy and acquire the courage and spirit to rebel against her. McMurphy taught them, Bromden says, that "you have to laugh at the things that hurt you just to keep yourself in balance, just to keep the world from running you plumb crazy." The lesson is invaluable to the inmates, who respond vividly to the McMurphy treatment. But Big Nurse, shaken to the core by McMurphy's usurpation of her omnipotence, takes matters into her own hands, effectively removing McMurphy's disruptive personality by arranging for his lobotomy.

The novel, a wide critical and popular success, is praised for its dramatization of the conflict between the vitality, humor, and humanity of McMurphy and the authoritarian, bureaucratic repressiveness of Big Nurse, who stands as a chillingly effective symbol of the impersonal modern world. Commentators also acknowledge Kesey's tight, fast-paced writing style, and his use of allusions ranging from the Bible to comic books, which provide the novel with a serio-comic, mythic dimension.

FURTHER READING

Contemporary Authors, Vols. 1-4, rev. ed.; *Contemporary Authors New Revision Series,* Vol. 22. Detroit: Gale Research Co.

Contemporary Literary Criticism, Vols. 1, 3, 6, 11, 46. Detroit: Gale Research Co.

Dictionary of Literary Biography, Vols. 2, 16. Detroit: Gale Research Co.

Foster, John Wilson. "Hustling to Some Purpose: Kesey's *One Flew Over the Cuckoo's Nest.*" *Western American Literature* 9 (August 1974): 115-29.

Leeds, Barry H. "Theme and Technique in *One Flew Over the Cuckoo's Nest.*" *Connecticut Review* 7 (April 1974): 35-50.

Pratt, John Clark, ed. *"One Flew Over the Cuckoo's Nest": Text and Criticism.* New York: Viking, 1973.

Rudyard Kipling

1865-1936

English short story writer, poet, novelist, essayist, and autobiographer.

"The Strange Ride of Morrowbie Jukes" (short story, 1885)

The supernatural tale is set in the Indian desert in the 1880s. **Morrowbie Jukes,** a British civil engineer suffering from fever, is trying to sleep. The baying camp dogs disturb him and so he kills one of them, displaying its fresh corpse to silence the others. Instead of humbly retreating the remaining dogs greedily devour the body and renew their disquieting howls. Enraged, Morrowbie attempts to shoot the loudest dog but his weakened senses prevent him. A nightmarish scene ensues as Morrowbie, spear in had, saddles his pony and charges the menacing dog. Strangely unable to stop, the pony gallops for several miles before stumbling down a deep ravine. When Morrowbie regains consciousness he finds himself inside a large horseshoe-shaped crater, the far side bounded by the river Sutlej. In dreamlike motion, some sixty-five Indians of various castes slowly emerge from holes in the ground. One of them is **Gunga Dass,** a Brahman and former telegraph master whom Morrowbie recognizes. From Gunga Dass, Morrowbie learns that he is amidst a city of the living dead, whose inhabitants are the victims of cholera and the ghostly fugitives of premature cremations. Gunga Dass also reveals that a gunboat patrols the Sutlej to ensure that no one flees.

Morrowbie realizes that his whiteness, which commands immediate respect in civilized India, no longer matters within the crater's confines. Formerly his lesser, Gunga Dass assumes control of Morrowbie. The residents kill Morrowbie's pony and distribute the meat equally as Gunga Dass justifies the action with the words: "greatest good of greatest number." Morrowbie secretly plans to leave the crater, stiffened in his resolve by the knowledge that Gunga Dass has once before killed a Briton who stumbled down the crater. In the climactic scene Gunga Dass strikes Morrowbie in the head for attempting to escape. Morrowbie slowly awakens to the calls of his servant boy, **Dunnoo.** Dunnoo rescues Morrowbie from the vacant crater, explaining that he arrived after tracking the pony's hoofprints for fourteen miles.

A story abounding in verbal parallels and character reversals, ''The Strange Ride of Morrowbie Jukes'' chillingly explores, through the vehicle of nightmare, the themes of equality vs. social stratification, cooperation vs. survival, and choice vs. predestination. For its biting social commentary and stunningly vivid depiction of an illusory setting, the tale ranks as one of Kipling's finest stories.

''The Man Who Would Be King'' (short story, 1888)

Narrated by a young reporter for the *Backwoodsman* in late-nineteenth-century India, the story begins on a train. The narrator is joined by a vagabond and the two discuss a wanderer's life. The narrator discovers that his railway companion has often impersonated a newsman but only mentions that he should not do so now because there is a real one in the vicinity. The two part with the understanding that the narrator will perform a favor by delivering a message at a specified time and place to the vagabond's friend, a large red-bearded man. Long after the favor is satisfied and the narrator reports the two men as impersonators to the authorities, **Peachey Carnehan** and **Daniel Dravot** startle the newsman in his office during the middle of the night. With comic flair, Kipling pits the two coarse vagabond adventurers against the tired, irritated reporter. Dravot, the red-haired man, takes control of the discussion, asserting that the reporter owes him and his partner a favor to make amends for their recent capture by the authorities. Assuring the newsman that they are neither drunk nor sunstruck, Dravot and Carnehan unveil an elaborate plan to make themselves kings of Kafiristan, a distant unsettled region in northeastern Afghanistan. Bemused by his colorful guests' earnestness, the narrator assists them with various maps and resources. Before day breaks he witnesses the contract between the two, which prohibits liquor and women during their quest for a kingdom.

The next afternoon Dravot and Carnehan begin their trek disguised as a mad priest and his servant and riding camels loaded with charms to sell. Hidden among the camel bags are twenty rifles and ammunition sufficient for fomenting revolution and establishing power. Three years pass before Carnehan returns, horribly maimed and virtually unrecognizable, to describe with mystical fervor the glorious, tragic events in Kafiristan. Through fighting and self-promotion as prophesied gods, Dravot and Carnehan had elevated themselves to ruling status. Dravot became crowned king of Kafiristan and Carnehan chief of the country's rapidly enlarging army, Dravot's brutal demise directly followed his taking a native wife and the natives discovering that he bled like an ordinary mortal. Once omnipotent and entertaining grand schemes of expanding his dominions, he was forced to walk upon a high rope bridge and fall to his death. Carnehan, crucified for a day and then freed, is given his friend's severed, still-crowned head, which he carries with him on his painful journey back to India. The story closes after Carnehan is admitted to an asylum and dies of sunstroke.

Kipling structured ''The Man Who Would Be King'' around two different views of reality: the narrator's objective, but mundane, perceptions and Peachey's grandiose, but symbolically true, account. Beyond these two is a third reality, which manifests itself in Kafiristan during Peachey and Daniel's reign; the two men have led the natives to believe that they are gods and that they will bring power and prosperity to their lands. Beneath this narrative framework rests Kipling's reactions to British imperialism, for him a system as great and tenuous as that devised by his English wayfarers. An entertaining fable, a parody of biblical history, and a shocking tragedy, this story is among Kipling's most popular and seriously examined works.

Kim (novel, 1901)

Situated in late nineteenth-century British India, the novel traces the adventures of a clever Lahore beggar boy, an orphan cared for by a half-caste woman. Born of Irish parents, the birthright of **Kimball O'Hara,** called Kim, goes unnoticed due to his dark-tanned skin. An itinerant Tibetan lama, **Teshoo Lama,** in search of the Master's holy River of the Arrow, enters the city and encounters Kim. Thirsting for adventure and willing to accompany and aid the elderly lama, Kim becomes his *chela,* or apprentice. Kim travels to Umballa with the lama and delivers a coded message written by **Mahbub Ali,** a supposed horse-trader who has frequently employed Kim for such duties. After Kim delivers the message—a favor to the British Secret Service—he naturally listens and watches for information which later proves useful to him. He becomes separated from the lama, for whom his devotion is steadily increasing, when he sees an Irish regiment. The regiment carries a flag displaying a red bull against a green background and this symbol accords perfectly with a prophecy that Kim has heard and believed in since he was abandoned, that when such a symbol appears to him his luck will increase greatly. Two regimental chaplains discover and question Kim and eventually learn, through the contents of an amulet Kim wears, that he is the son of a former, undistinguished Irish soldier. The lama tearfully takes his leave of Kim, promising to pay for his schooling, which the chaplain's agree he will receive at St. Xavier's in Partibus.

As Kim studies and matures, he is indoctrinated into the Secret Service through a network that includes Mahbub Ali, **Colonel William Creighton, Mr. Lurgan,** and a friendly babu named **Hurree Chunder Mookerjee.** After three years of schooling, Kim resumes his travels about India with the lama. Near the foothills of the Himalayas Kim meets Hurree, working undercover, and assists him in sabotaging the efforts of Russian and French spies. The novel closes after Kim has descended from the mountains and recuperated from a long fever. For his heroic actions, he is commended by Mahbub Ali and Hurree. The lama, who believes he has finally found his river and that Kim has been the divine agent, thanks him deeply. Kim is left to ponder what form of man he has become, for in his young life he has lived by cunning and deception, not by honesty and humility.

Called "the finest story about India in English," *Kim* is also considered a revealing self-portrait about its author. Through his young protagonist, Kipling explored the duality of his emotional commitment to both British imperialism and Eastern philosophy and values. While some critics contend that a lack of introspection on the part of the protagonist forms the primary fault in a potentially great work, others hold that Kipling's penetrating scrutiny of his dual attachments, as well as his sympathetic depiction of the Indian people, place this novel among the masterpieces of English literature.

"The Gardener" (short story, 1926)

The story begins during the 1890s in Hampshire, England. Described as open and self-sacrificing, **Helen Turrell** publicly claims to have assumed the upbringing of her late brother's illegitimate offspring, a baby boy named **Michael.** At six Michael asks why he cannot call Helen "Mummy." Helen allows that he may do so, but only at bedtime; when Michael discovers that she has spoiled this mutual secret by mentioning it to her friends he vows that he will hurt her, that he will die soon, and that he will hurt her more after his death. As Michael matures he remains close to Helen. Eventually, despite winning a scholarship to Oxford, Michael enlists in the army. After several uneventful maneuvers with a battalion, he is killed in France by a shell splinter. Helen travels to France to visit Michael's gravesite. There she encounters **Mrs. Scarsworth,** an Englishwoman who frequents the cemeteries on the continent, locating and photographing the graves of acquaintances' loved ones. Ostensibly doing so as favors, Mrs. Scarsworth reveals to Helen, in a passage of high emotion, that she is living a lie, that she in fact continually returns not so much for her friends as for herself, to mourn the death of her secret lover. This encounter, along with events immediately preceding, greatly unsettles Helen. The next day she visits the cemetery, where twenty-one thousand are buried. Overwhelmed by "a merciless sea of black crosses," she solicits the help of a man "firming a young plant in the soft earth.'' Although she requests the grave of Lieutenant Michael Turrell, her nephew, the knowing man says, ''Come with me, and I will show you where your son lies.''

Through an opening epigraph from his companion poem ''The Burden,'' and through biblical allusion to the story of Mary Magdalene, who mistakes the resurrected Jesus for a gardener, Kipling presents a cautionary tale focusing on one woman's gradually rising guilt and need for forgiveness. Helen Turrell, much more so than Mrs. Scarsworth, has founded her life on a lie for appearance's sake. She has never acknowledged Michael as her actual son and never allowed a deep, abiding love for him to overtake her. The story's subtle, elliptical style and heavily ironic tone epitomize the finest elements of Kipling's later fiction.

FURTHER READING

Amis, Kingsley. *Rudyard Kipling and His World*. New York: Charles Scribner's Sons, 1975.

Birkenhead, Lord. *Rudyard Kipling*. New York: Random House, 1978.

Brooks, Cleanth, Jr. and Robert Penn Warren. ''''The Man Who Would Be King,' Rudyard Kipling.'' In *Understanding Fiction*, pp. 28-64. New York: F.S. Crofts & Co., 1943.

Contemporary Authors, Vols. 105, 120. Detroit: Gale Research Co.

Dictionary of Literary Biography, Vols. 19, 34. Detroit: Gale Research Co.

Dobrée, Bonamy. *Rudyard Kipling: Realist and Fabulist*. London: Oxford University Press, 1967.

Gilbert, Eliot L. *The Good Kipling: Studies in the Short Story*. Oberlin: Ohio University Press, 1970.

Green, Roger Lancelyn, ed. *Kipling: The Critical Heritage*. New York: Harper & Row, 1971.

Gross, John, ed. *The Age of Kipling*. New York: Simon and Schuster, 1972.

Hart, Walter Morris. *Kipling: The Story-Writer*. Berkeley: University of California Press, 1918.

Henn, T. R. *Kipling*. London: Oliver and Boyd, 1967.

Rutherford, Andrew, ed. *Kipling's Mind and Art: Selected Critical Essays*. Stanford: Stanford University Press, 1964.

Tompkins, J. M. S. *The Art of Rudyard Kipling*. London: Methuen & Co., 1959.

Twentieth-Century Literary Criticism, Vols. 8, 17. Detroit: Gale Research Co.

Wilson, Angus. *The Strange Ride of Rudyard Kipling: His Life and Work*. New York: Viking Press, 1978.

John Knowles

1926-

American novelist.

A Separate Peace (novel, 1960)

The novel is set at a New Hampshire prep school during the first years of America's involvement in World War II. **Gene Forrester** narrates the story as an older man looking back fifteen years to his school days. The young Gene is portrayed as a conservative, conscientious student intent on his studies and fearful of his future. Despite his reserved nature, Gene is drawn to his roommate **Phineas**'s wild and irreverent love of life and physical play. The two become hard and fast friends despite their disparate personalities and viewpoints. Against the backdrop of the war in Europe, Phineas and Gene individually battle the "enemy within" as their friendship grows in complexity. Although they have many differences, the crux of their problem lies in one hapless action: while daring each other to jump from a tree into the cold Devon river, Gene impulsively jounces the limb Phineas is balanced on. Phineas's resulting injury and inability to face his friend's malicious intent is contrasted to Gene's feeling of guilt and slow recognition of something spiteful and instinctive inside himself.

During Phineas's recuperative absence, Gene is increasingly influenced by **Brinker Hadley,** the purer embodiment of Gene's own conservative nature. Together they plan to enlist. However, Gene soon gravitates back to Phineas after his return. Permanently unable to enlist because of his crippling injury, Phineas adamantly denies the reality of the war, calling it a fiction made up by Roosevelt and Churchill. At the same time, Finny transfers his athletic aspirations to Gene, training him for the next Olympics. Although Gene is attracted to his friend's illusions, he is quickly brought back to reality by the reappearance of **Elwin Lepellier,** the "leper, a schoolmate who enlisted and was discharged for psychological reasons. Just as the distant horror of war appears in the form of a now deranged Lepellier, the inner horror of Gene's own guilt resurfaces in the form of a mock trial, which Brinker stages to publicize Gene's true responsibility for Phineas's fall. In the dark and hollowed halls of the First Academy Building, Brinker forces Gene and Phineas to face reality. Finny, however, is no more prepared than ever. He runs out of the trial, tripping down the stairs and causing a second and ultimately fatal leg injury. Reviewing the events as an adult, Gene is calm and reflective, but the issues seem to live inside of him. His understanding of his original spiteful impulse and of "something ignorant in the human heart" seems to bind the world of Devon to the world at war and to human nature in general.

In this complex psychological exploration of adolescent friendship and self-understanding, Knowles achieved his most critically acclaimed success. The work has been praised for its artful combination of symbolism and verisimilitude and for its consistent and penetrating characterization. Critics have also cited Knowles's calculated narrative technique, arguing that he simultaneously creates empathy, a dispassionate distance, and understanding in the reader.

FURTHER READING

Contemporary Authors, Vols. 17-20, rev. ed. Detroit: Gale Research Co.

Contemporary Literary Criticism, Vols. 1, 4, 10, 26. Detroit: Gale Research Co.

Dictionary of Literary Biography, Vol. 6. Detroit: Gale Research Co.

Ellis, James. *"A Separate Peace:* The Fall from Innocence." *English Journal* 53, No. 5 (May 1964): 313-18.

Weber, Ronald. "Narrative Method in *A Separate Peace." Studies in Short Fiction* 3, No. 1 (Fall 1965): 63-72.

Wolfe, Peter. "The Impact of Knowles's *A Separate Peace." University Review* 36, No. 3 (March 1970): 189-98.

Arthur Koestler
1905-1983
Hungarian-born English novelist and essayist.

Darkness at Noon (novel, 1941)

Koestler's famous political novel is set in Moscow during Stalin's infamous purge trials of the 1930s. It concerns the fate of **Nicholas Salmanovitch Rubashov,** an Old Bolshevik and ex-Commissar of the People, who has been falsely accused of plotting against the State. A loyal Communist, he has fallen victim to his own methods. As he awaits trial, he reflects on his life, thinking of the individuals he had ruined in the name of the system which now seeks to destroy him. He remembers in particular his former secretary and lover, **Arlova,** who had been executed after he had denounced her for objectionable activities. Rubashov must now confront his conscience as well as the pressures of his two interrogators, **Ivanov** and **Gletkin.** Ivanov is an old friend of Rubashov's from school and the military, and he tries to persuade Rubashov to admit his errors and confess to the false charges, seeing in his admission the last thing he can do for his party. These two old Bolsheviks are vividly contrasted to Gletkin, the representative of the new Russia under Stalin, a man characterized by ruthless brutality and pitiless certainty in his devotion to the State.

Rubashov's fall from power, imprisonment, and humiliation draw out his humanistic impulses that had lain dormant for so long, as witnessed in his memories of Arlova and his "conversations" with No. 402, an anonymous prisoner with whom he communicates through tapping messages on their adjoining cell wall. He sees the folly and barbarity of a system supposedly based on reason and logic but now dedicated to dehumanizing and destroying its people. Midway through his trial, Ivanov is taken away and executed, supposedly for mishandling Rubashov's case. In the conclusion, Rubashov confesses, renouncing his "oppositional attitude" and denouncing his "error" publicly; he is then put to death.

Koestler's novel is a searing indictment of totalitarianism under Stalin, which he witnessed first-hand as an attendant at the Moscow Trials in the 1930s. Rubashov represents a composite of the many people whom Koestler knew who suffered and died under Stalin's regime, and his book is dedicated to their memory.

FURTHER READING

Contemporary Authors, Vols. 1-4, rev. ed., 109; *Contemporary Authors New Revision Series,* Vol. 1. Detroit: Gale Research Co.

Contemporary Literary Criticism, Vols. 1, 3, 6, 8, 15, 33. Detroit: Gale Research Co.

Dictionary of Literary Biography Yearbook: 1983. Detroit: Gale Research Co.

Glicksberg, Charles I. "Arthur Koestler and the Revolution Betrayed." In *The Literature of Commitment,* pp. 277-88. Lewisburg: Bucknell University Press, 1976.

Howe, Irving. "Malraux, Silone, and Koestler: The Twentieth Century." In *Politics and the Novel,* pp. 203-34. New York: Horizon, 1957.

Levene, Mark. "Arthur Koestler: On Messiahs and Mutations." *Modernist Studies: Literature & Culture, 1920-1940* 2, No. 2 (1977): 37-48.

Jerzy Kosinski

1933-

Polish-born American novelist.

The Painted Bird (novel, 1965)

The Painted Bird is a novel concerned with the inherent, fundamental depravity of human nature. The story takes place in various villages in Eastern Europe during World War II. The main character is an anonymous young boy of Jewish or Gypsy descent who, for his safety and well-being, is sent by his parents to a distant village where he is to remain for the duration of the war.

The boy is initially placed with **Marta,** an old woman who is nearly blind. Here, he learns some of the local superstitions, and is told not to look directly into the eyes of another person or animal, that frequent bathing is undesirable, and that one could fall prey to an early death if he should display his teeth. It is in this setting that the boy also gets his first taste of violence, as he witnesses a group of village boys torturing and finally setting fire to a small squirrel. When Marta dies and her cabin burns to the ground, the boy finds himself on his own. He wanders from village to village, where each new encounter with humankind proves more barbaric than the last: he witnesses a farmer tearing out the eyes of another man, and sees the gang rape and murder of a woman. He suffers torture, beatings, and sexual abuse, and comes to despise his own dark coloring while admiring the physique and uniform of a German officer. His experiences in a joyless, hopeless world result in his muteness and his belief in violence and dominance as the traits most necessary to existence.

After the war, he is reunited with his parents, who are horrified at the transformation of their son. Sent to the mountains for his health, he has a skiing accident and is hospitalized. The novel ends as he is convalescing and regains his ability to speak.

The novel's theme—the human capacity for violence and depravity—is underscored by the author's use of a detached narrative stance. The young protagonist, deprived of home, family, and any coherent social system with which to confront and understand his experience, comes to understand that to survive in a depraved world, one must also become base. Although the novel's unremitting depiction of brutality and horror have made it a controversial piece, it is Kosinski's best-known work.

FURTHER READING

Cahill, Daniel J. "Jerzy Kosinski: Retreat From Violence." *Twentieth Century Literature* 18 (April 1972): 121-36.

Contemporary Authors, Vols. 17-20, rev. ed.; *Contemporary Authors New Revision Series,* Vol. 9. Detroit: Gale Research Co.

Contemporary Literary Criticism, Vols. 1, 2, 3, 6, 10, 15. Detroit: Gale Research Co.

Dictionary of Literary Biography, Vol. 2; *Dictionary of Literary Biography Yearbook: 1982.* Detroit: Gale Research Co.

Howe, Irving. "From the Other Side of the Moon." *Harper's* 238 (March 1969): 102-05.

Prendowska, Krystyna. "Jerzy Kosinski: A Literature of Contortions." *The Journal of Narrative Technique* 8, No. 1 (Winter 1978): 11-25.

Milan Kundera

1929-

Czechoslovakian novelist, dramatist, and poet.

The Book of Laughter and Forgetting (novel, 1979)

Like nearly all of Kundera's novels, *The Book of Laughter and Forgetting* is divided into several distinct sections that find their unity not in a linear plot but in a common theme. In this work, focused upon modern life in Czechoslovakia under totalitarian rule, recurring images of laughter and forgetting become symbolic reminders of moral, intellectual, and spiritual vacuity. Though present in only two sections, **Tamina,** a Czech widow living in exile in Western Europe, functions as the unifying force, through whom the remaining characters and events attain significant meaning. Tamina leads a hollow life as a waitress. When her husband, **Mirek,** died shortly after their emigration, she attempted suicide; now, realizing that the memory of her life with Mirek is quickly deteriorating, Tamina solicits friends traveling to Prague to recover her letters and journals, kept by her mother-in-law. She allows **Hugo,** a writer and café patron, to make love to her in gratitude for his anticipated offer to retrieve the papers. However, he chooses not to endanger his political freedom and so avoids the trip. Tamina abandons all further contact with her native country. She meets **Raphael,** a young man who promises to relieve her sadness in a place where things "weigh nothing at all." A laughing boy guides them by rowboat to a magical island of children. There, for a time, she acquiesces to the seductive sensuality and unconcern of the islanders. Eventually, desperately attempting to reassert her memory and humanness, she swims away from the island but fails to spot the mainland. She drowns as a group of eager children in a nearby boat look on.

Tamina differs from the characters in the other sections—men and women who seek escape from memory and history through meaningless sexual encounters—in her pursuit of truth, value, and personal integrity. Her husband once declared that "the struggle of man against power is the struggle of memory against forgetting." Such was Tamina's struggle, valiant despite her defeat by the offspring of totalitarian power, Kundera's haunting "nation of children."

A symphonic blend of autobiography, philosophy, political commentary, fairy tale, literary criticism, and psychological narrative, *The Book of Laughter and Forgetting* is perhaps Kundera's most profound fictional treatise of totalitarianism and all its attendant dangers. Indeed, the thematic scope of his work touches the all of the contemporary world, continually questioning the survival of the fully human individual amidst all forms of repression.

The Unbearable Lightness of Being (novel, 1984)

The Unbearable Lightness of Being is set in Czechoslovakia before, during, and after, the 1968 Soviet invasion and follows two couples as they define and redefine their romantic relationships and personal ideologies. **Tomas,** a successful surgeon and inveterate womanizer meets **Tereza,** a waitress. Following their marriage, Tomas continues his compulsive pursuit of women. Although hurt by Tomas's infidelities, Tereza accepts them as a burden she must bear. **Sabina,** Tomas's regular mistress, befriends Tereza and helps launch her in a photography career. Tereza finds purpose, beyond her sacrificial love for Tomas, in her documentation of the invasion. When Tomas receives an offer to direct a hospital in Zurich, the couple emigrate to preserve their liberty, as does Sabina, who meets **Franz,** a Swiss professor, and becomes his illicit lover. When Tereza discovers she is incapable of abandoning her language, culture, and friends, she returns to Prague, leaving an explanatory note for her husband. Tomas cannot bear life without Tereza; he returns to his shattered homeland, knowing that in a police state he can no longer control the course of his career. He and Tereza eventually manage a small dairy cooperative and later die together in a preventable auto accident. Franz dies in Bangkok, away from Sabina, participating in a peace march. Sabina, meanwhile, has become a famous artist; she resides in America and has exchanged responsibility for superficiality.

A complexly layered, circular work, Kundera's most esteemed novel addresses a number of human contrarieties: fidelity and betrayal, strength and weakness, masculinity and femininity, spirituality and vulgarity, joy and sorrow. Each pertains to the dominant themes of lightness and weight, and the myth of the eternal return. Lightness may be understood as the absence of earthly burden, weight the opposite. Eternal return may be defined as the reality in which all events and all lives recur ad infinitum. As the intrusive, philosophic narrator, Kundera thus posits a difficult dilemma: "In the world of eternal return the weight of unbearable responsibility lies heavy on every move we make . . . If eternal return is the heaviest of burdens, then our lives can stand out against it in all their splendid lightness. But is heaviness truly deplorable and lightness splendid?" Judging from his title and the varying degrees of sympathy he demonstrates for his characters, Kundera's answer is that moral and emotionally honest life is always preferable, whatever burdens it may bring.

FURTHER READING

Bell, Pearl K. "The Real Avant-Garde." *Commentary* 70, No. 6 (December 1980): 66-9.

Contemporary Authors, Vols. 85-88; *Contemporary Authors New Revision Series,* Vol. 19. Detroit: Gale Research Co.

Contemporary Literary Criticism, Vols. 4, 9, 19, 34. Detroit: Gale Research Co.

Lodge, David. "Milan Kundera and the Idea of the Author in Modern Criticism." *Critical Quarterly* 26 (Spring-Summer 1984): 105-21.

Podhoretz, Norman. "An Open Letter to Milan Kundera." *Commentary* 78 (October 1984): 34-9.

Porter, Robert. *Milan Kundera: A Voice from Central Europe.* Aarhus, Denmark: Arkona, 1981.

Roth, Philip. "Afterword: A Talk with the Author." In *The Book of Laughter and Forgetting* by Milan Kundera, translated by Michael Henry Heim, pp. 229-37. New York: Penguin, 1981.

Updike, John. "The Most Original Book of the Season." *The New York Times Book Review* (30 November 1980): 7, 74, 76, 78.

Pär Lagerkvist
1891-1974
Swedish novelist, dramatist, and poet.

Barabbas (novel, 1949)

Barabbas is set in Palestine, the Near East, and Rome at the time of **Jesus Christ**'s crucifixion and resurrection. Despite its simple, documentary-like narration, the novel is a symbolic account of one man's dark, lonely struggle with the issues of faith, guilt, betrayal, and salvation. A condemned thief whose place Christ took on the cross, **Barabbas** witnesses the crucifixion at Golgotha and hears Christ's dying words: "My God, my God, why hast thou forsaken me?" Disturbed by the staggering gloom which surrounds the event, Barabbas returns to Jerusalem and resumes his life of debauchery and drunkenness. He wishes to solve the mystery of Christ's life, death, and teachings and discusses his uncertainties with various friends. An unnamed woman with whom he has consorted considers Christ a miracle-worker, a Savior who has been resurrected but will return to build a new kingdom on earth. Barabbas visits Christ's opened tomb but refuses to believe his body has risen. As Barabbas continues his questioning, never satisfied with the answers he receives, even from Christ's followers, he disentangles himself from the sordid crowd he once followed. Despite his distrust of emotional religiosity, Barabbas attempts to defend a young woman as she is being stoned for espousing her Christian faith. He knifes one of the throwers and later claims the woman's martyred body.

After indeterminate wandering, Barabbas is seized by Romans and sent to the mines. **Sahak,** a fellow slave to whom Barabbas is chained, delights in Barabbas's knowledge of Christ. An ardent Christian, Sahak listens attentively while Barabbas utters half-truths and lies which further his belief. When the two men are identified by another slave as Christians, Barabbas readily renounces his tentative faith. Sahak refuses to do so and is crucified before Barabbas. When he is freed from the mines, Barabbas visits the catacombs near Rome, where the Christians worship. Upon leaving the desolate gathering places he senses fire around him and begins burning everything in sight, believing he is contributing to Christ's triumphal, purifying return. The fires, he later discovers, were begun by Caesar's soldiers to discredit the Christians. At the moment of his own crucifixion for his supposed membership among a group of imprisoned believers, Barabbas seems to reveal a faint glimmer of final faith. Yet, the conclusion is ambiguous, for there is no indication that Barabbas's final words are inspired by true faith.

Barabbas derives its unusual power from its hauntingly realistic scenes and language, enigmatic message, and compelling, deeply etched portrait of an overlooked biblical character. For his achievement in this and other works of the period, Lagerkvist was awarded the Nobel Prize for Literature in 1951 and won world renown.

The Sibyl (novel, 1956)

The Sibyl is a timeless philosophical fable set in Delphi, Greece. A former priestess and lover of Apollo, the elderly **Sibyl** resides atop a mountain overlooking the Delphic temple and her native village. She lives in quiet contemplation with her middle-aged idiot son. An itinerant foreigner—recognizable, though never identified, as Ahaseurus, the Wandering Jew—seeks the Sibyl as his last untried source of solace and enlightenment. As the two figures meet on the mountain they exchange life stories, one stemming from Christian tradition, the other from Greek mythology. Ahaseurus explains that he once lived with his wife and son beside the road to Calvary. There he frequently watched criminals pass by, condemned to crucifixion. One day **Jesus Christ,** whom Ahaseurus did not know, came near the house to rest. Ahaseurus showed no sympathy for the cross-bearing prisoner and chased him away. In so doing, he elicited his curse: to wander the earth endlessly, never finding rest. Ahaseurus later hears of Jesus's message of love, but rejects it.

In contrast, the Sibyl has been condemned to a lonely existence not for her unkindness but for her charity. Chosen by the village priests as a suitable virgin and acquiescent human vessel for the god Apollo, the Sibyl once derived fulfillment from their ecstatic unions. Only gradually did she perceive that her necessary isolation from humanity was undesirable and that Apollo's needs were strictly lustful. She sought and found happiness in a relationship with a mortal man, but Apollo soon took revenge, drowning the Sibyl's lover while ravishing his unfaithful consort. When the Sibyl realized she was pregnant she fled the town for the mountain summit and eventually gave birth. At the close of her tale the Sibyl wonders whether her son is Apollo's cruel joke or is in fact fully human. Suddenly aware that her son has disappeared, she and Ahaseurus follow his eerily ascending footprints, which finally seem to vanish into the heavens. Ahaseurus interprets the event as further evidence of divine malevolence. The Sibyl simply accepts the departure of her son, asserting that God's ways are unfathomable to humans. Consequently, she offers Ahasuerus no prophecy, instead confiding her belief that all lives, no matter how different or how desolate, are forever bound with God.

In this tale the Christian and pagan deities are commingled to stress the importance of both the biblical and mythic traditions to humanity. Furthermore, both are depicted as inscrutable, emphasizing the individual's most burdensome limitation, the utter alienation from divine truth and meaning. The fable's message, found in the Sibyl's final stance of peaceful acceptance, is that the search for absolute meaning is vain and that only lives founded on love are valuable.

FURTHER READING

Contemporary Authors, Vols. 49-52, 85-88. Detroit: Gale Research Co.

Contemporary Literary Criticism, Vols. 7, 10, 13, 54. Detroit: Gale Research Co.

Gide, André. Letter to Lucien Maury. In *Barabbas* by Pär Lagerkvist, translated by Alan Blair, pp. viii-ix. London: Chatto & Windus, 1974.

Scandinavica 10, No. 1 (1971). Special Lagerkvist issue.

Sjoberg, Leif. *Pär Lagerkvist.* New York: Columbia University Press, 1976.

Swanson, Roy Arthur. "Evil and Love in Lagerkvist's Crucifixion Cycle." *Scandinavian Studies* 38, No. 4 (November 1966): 302-17.

Weathers, Winston. *Pär Lagerkvist: A Critical Essay.* Ann Arbor, Mich.: Books on Demand, University Microfilms International.

Giuseppe Tomasi di Lampedusa
1896-1957
Italian novelist.

The Leopard (novel, 1958)

The novel is set in Sicily in the middle of the nineteenth century and relates the story of **Don Fabrizio di Salina,** a representative of the dying nobility in Italy that gave way before the forces of unification led by Garibaldi in the 1860s. The work chronicles the way in which Fabrizio deals with the rise of the nouveau riche following the collapse of the Bourbon state and the decline of the power and efficacy of the aristocracy.

As the novel begins, Fabrizio's son has left Sicily to pursue a career as a businessman in London, and his heir and favorite nephew, **Tancredi Falconeri,** has taken the part of the Garibaldians and fallen in love with **Angelica Sedara,** the beautiful daughter of a middle-class family. Tancredi asks his uncle to plead his case with Angelica's father, **Don Calogero,** the mayor of the town, who embodies all the vulgarity, selfishness, and materialism that Fabrizio despises in the middle classes. Although Fabrizio's daughter **Concetta** had been in love with Tancredi, he follows Tancredi's wishes and the marriage is arranged.

Fabrizio, the "Leopard" of the title, is the last symbol of the feudal lords of Sicily, and he embodies a natural nobility, integrity, and elegance. He is ambivalent toward the encroaching change and toward his own class and its values, for while he exemplifies the nobleness of the aristocratic spirit, he is aware of the dangers of hubris and complacency to which his class has succumbed. The work is imbued with images and reminders of death and change, and the Prince himself has an obsession with decay and death as he watches his way of life give way to the social and economic realities of the new Italian state. He knows that Tancredi's decision to marry Angelica is motivated by his love for her as well as by her large dowry, and he admires the vitality and shrewdness of his nephew. In their youthful, playful sensuality the young lovers are juxtaposed to the old Leopard, now in a state of decline. The conclusion of the novel recounts the death of Fabrizio, and in the final pages Concetta discards a final remnant of her father's memory, Bendico, the Prince's faithful hunting dog, who had lain for years, stuffed, in a corner. Yet, as he is being tossed out, the old dog seems to come to life again, embodying the Leopard for an instant, then coming to rest as a "little heap of livid dust."

The Leopard, Lampedusa's only novel and based in part on his own family's history, is the most popular Italian novel of the twentieth century. The ironic, detached narrative voice of the novel parallels the ambivalent, disinterested character of Don Fabrizio, reflecting the point of view of the vanquished upper classes.

FURTHER READING

Contemporary Authors, Vol. 111. Detroit: Gale Research Co.

Gomme, Andor. "Irony and *The Leopard.*" *The Oxford Review,* No. 6 (29 September 1967): 23-35.

Kuhns, Richard F. "Modernity and Death: *The Leopard.*" *Contemporary Psychoanalysis* 5, No. 2 (Spring 1969): 95-119.

Meyers, Jeffrey. "Symbol and Structure in *The Leopard.*" *Italian Quarterly* 9, Nos. 34-35 (Summer-Fall 1965): 50-70.

Twentieth-Century Literary Criticism, Vol. 13. Detroit: Gale Research Co.

D. H. Lawrence
1885-1930

English novelist, short story writer, poet, and essayist.

Sons and Lovers (novel, 1913)

Set in a mining community in the English Midlands during the early twentieth century, the novel relates the first twenty-five years in the life of **Paul Morel.** The son of an uneducated coal miner and a domineering mother, Paul is seen by most critics as an autobiographical figure and his portrait is part of a revealing depiction of lower-class life. *Sons and Lovers* was Lawrence's first major novel, containing themes and character types that resonate throughout his fiction.

The first portion of the novel deals with the early married life of Paul's parents, **Gertrude** and **Walter Morel.** Whatever happiness their early life together contained gives way to a frustrated, loveless relationship, with Gertrude displacing her fervent affection and ambition from her husband to her sons. Walter is a crude man, given to drinking and beating his wife. Lawrence stresses that the father, dominated by the mother, is an outsider in his own family. When the eldest son, **William,** dies in his twenties, the mother's full attention is focused on Paul, who echoes her disdain for life in a mining town and the lot of a miner's son. The relationship between Paul and his mother is the central focus of the book; it reveals Lawrence's recurrent theme of the struggle for dominance that characterizes all relationships in his works, developed here as the Oedipal conflict between Paul and Gertrude.

Although Paul accepts his mother's thinking on the limitations of his origins, he cannot acquiesce to her faith, for he sees in her Protestant religion a stultifying, life-denying force. His feelings about religion further influence his relationship with **Miriam Leivers,** the daughter of a local farmer and Paul's first girlfriend. She, too, in her emphasis on Christian faith, represents repression, especially sexual repression. Paul leaves her, and becomes involved with **Clara Dawes,** an older woman separated from her husband. Their sexual experiences awaken Paul to the power of passion, making him aware of the regenerative force of sex, a theme that echoes throughout Lawrence's work. Paul eventually breaks off the affair, for he is unable to give Clara the emotional commitment she demands; instead, he befriends her estranged husband and forces Clara to return to him. In the conclusion, Paul's mother dies of cancer, her painful end eased by Paul, who administers an overdose of barbiturates to her. The final chapter finds Paul in despair over his mother's death, and haunted with the desire to die. Yet Lawrence depicts him finally walking toward the "city's gold phosphorescence," and toward life.

The novel is regarded as a fully realized portrait of provincial life, incorporating such themes as dominance in human relationships, the need for the open expression of sexuality, and the dehumanizing aspects of industrialization, all of which recur in Lawrence's later work.

The Rainbow (novel, 1915)

The novel is set in the late nineteenth and early twentieth centuries in England and covers three generations of the Brangwen family. The first generation is represented by **Tom Brangwen,** a farmer and a passionate man who seeks to break the traditional bonds of sexual repression through his marriage to **Lydia,** an aristocratic Polish widow. Their life together is at first full of passion, but their happiness is threatened by the struggle of dominance that later ensues, a recurring motif in Lawrence's depiction of relationships. The pivotal character representing the second generation is **Anna,** Lydia's child from her first marriage, who marries her cousin, **Will.** Their life together is also plagued by the inevitable waning of passion and the rise of conflict. Anna becomes obsessed with motherhood, focusing her life on her children and shutting Will out. Their daughter **Ursula** becomes the chief character of the third generation of Brangwens to be analyzed.

Ursula's story forms a major part of the novel and relates her coming of age. As a young girl she becomes involved with **Anton Skrebensky,** a cousin, through whom she learns about sex. Yet he is a stolid, conventional type, and Ursula realizes that he cannot fulfill all of her needs. While he is away at war, she becomes a schoolteacher and discovers the stultifying way of life in an educational institution. She then goes to university, only to learn that it is a place devoted to turning out graduates obsessed with making money. While a student, she becomes involved with a woman, **Winifred Inger,** and they begin a lesbian affair. Winifred goes on to marry Ursula's **Uncle Tom,** an industrialist and a representative of the repressed, money-obsessed class that Lawrence despised. Anton and Ursula recommence their affair on his return, but it is unhappy for both. Ursula still strives for a sense of spiritual and sexual fulfillment and for a sensuous experience that will provide her with a sense of the infinite in existence. These longings dominate nearly all of Lawrence's characters, and as with most of them Ursula remains unfulfilled. The final section of the novel depicts Ursula, pregnant and alone, in a field of wild horses. Frightened and disoriented, she suffers a miscarriage. A rainbow appears, a traditional symbol of hope, but its meaning for Ursula—isolated and out of place in the modern world—is ambiguous.

Ursula and her sister, **Gudrun,** are the principal characters of Lawrence's next major work, *Women in Love,* where he continues his exploration of the deadening aspects of modern existence, the need for free sexual expression, and the inescapable struggle for dominance that dictates human relationships. Because of Lawrence's provocative sexual themes and descriptions, *The Rainbow* was suppressed upon publication, and the notoriety this cast on his work dominated its reception throughout his life.

Women in Love (novel, 1920)

Set in the English Midland town of Beldover, the novel continues the exploration of the life of **Ursula** and **Gudrun Brangwen** begun in *The Rainbow,* focusing on the love affairs between Ursula and **Rupert Birkin** and Gudrun and **Gerald Crich.** Lawrence's theme in this novel is the importance of desire and its fulfillment. This is the issue which consumes Birkin, whom Lawrence modelled on himself. His darkly pessimistic vision of human nature incorporates many of Lawrence's previous themes, for he is concerned with the degrading effects of modern technology on humankind and with the primacy of sensuality as a key to self-knowledge. His relationship with Ursula involves the inevitable struggle for dominance; although Rupert wants their relationship to be based on equality, she interprets his actions differently and finds him domineering. He believes that passion should be unsullied by personal and sentimental feeling, but she longs for "a close and abiding connection" and for his submission to her will. Throughout the novel their relationship is characterized by contention and confrontation, and yet Lawrence depicts theirs as a successful alliance, and their love—in contrast to that of Gerald and Gudrun—as a triumph against the forces of nihilism in the modern world.

The affair of Gudrun and Gerald is a ceaseless struggle for domination ending in death, for Gerald commits suicide in the novel's conclusion. Birkin and Gerald, although friends, represent opposite poles of humanity for Lawrence, with Birkin as the dissenter from the ways of the modern world, searching for a new life, and Gerald, the son of an industrialist, the representative of the technological malaise that Rupert resists. Their friendship has homoerotic overtones as well, as is evidenced in the novel's conclusion, when Rupert, thinking of his dead friend, tells Ursula that he had wished for "an eternal union with a man" as well as with her. Gerald's death convinces Rupert of the futility of modern life, for neither heterosexual nor homosexual eroticism provide a satisfactory defense against the inevitable nihilism of existence.

Lawrence noted in his introduction to *Women in Love* that the novel bore the influence of a world in the throes of war, and his pessimistic view of humankind is brought to life in a fictional world in which the irrational, fragmented nature of society is reflected in the instability and unhappiness of his characters.

Lady Chatterley's Lover (novel, 1928)

Lawrence's most notorious work, *Lady Chatterley's Lover* was censored for years in England and the United States and was the subject of a landmark obscenity trial in 1960. The novel is set in the English town of Tevershall and depicts the love affair between **Lady Constance Chatterley** and her gamekeeper, **Oliver Mellors.** Once again Lawrence focuses on the effects of industrialism on modern humanity and the regenerative power of passion. As the novel begins, Constance is portrayed as the victim of a loveless marriage. Her husband, **Sir Clifford,** is a representative of the established order, a cold and insensitive man whom Lawrence described as "the death of the great humanity of the world." He is impotent, snobbish, and withdrawn; thus his wife seeks comfort first through an affair with a writer and later with Mellors. More than a simple gamekeeper, Mellors is a disenchanted intellectual from the lower classes. He has been a miner and a soldier, and has been subjected to a cruel and unloving marriage to a wife from whom he is now separated. He is a misogynist, and like Birkin in *Woman in Love,* sees the modern world as decadent and hostile.

The sexual relationship between Constance and Mellors is explicitly described, with Lawrence employing terms considered obscene by the novel's first audience. Their relationship is characterized by the same struggle for dominance described in Lawrence's earlier works. Constance is depicted in conflict with her rational self, which argues against her submission to Mellors, and her primitive desires, which incline her to yield to him. Yet through her compliance she is able to achieve passionate release and is awakened to the beauty of the physical world. At last able to denounce her husband and the social order he represents, she decides to leave him. In the conclusion, she is pregnant with Mellor's child, and the two plan to begin a new life together in rural Scotland.

Constance and Mellor's retreat to the country represents the longing for a utopia and the disgust with contemporary society shared by earlier Lawrencean characters. Whether or not they will achieve their goal and happiness is uncertain at the novel's close, but it is a definitive statement on Lawrence's part that life cannot be lived within the confines of society.

FURTHER READING

Contemporary Authors, Vol. 104. Detroit: Gale Research Co.

Dictionary of Literary Biography, Vols. 10, 19, 36. Detroit: Gale Research Co.

Draper, Ronald P. *D. H. Lawrence.* Boston: Twayne, 1964.

Freeman, Mary. *D. H. Lawrence, A Basic Study of His Ideas.* Gainesville: University of Florida Press, 1955.

Green, Martin B. *The von Richthofen Sisters: The Triumphant and the Tragic Modes of Love.* New York: Basic Books, 1974.

Leavis, F. R. *D. H. Lawrence, Novelist.* New York: Knopf, 1955.

Meyers, Jeffrey, ed. *D. H. Lawrence and Tradition.* Amherst: University of Massachusetts Press, 1985.

Moore, Harry T. *The Life and Works of D. H. Lawrence.* New York: Twayne, 1951.

Moynahan, Julian. *The Deed of Life: The Novels and Tales of D. H. Lawrence.* Princeton: Princeton University Press, 1963.

Pritchard, Ronald E. *D. H. Lawrence: Body of Darkness.* London: Hutchinson, 1971.

Sanders, Scott. *D. H. Lawrence: The World of the Major Novels.* New York: Viking Press, 1974.

Stoll, John E. *The Novels of D. H. Lawrence: A Search for Integration.* Columbia: University of Missouri Press, 1971.

Tedlock, Ernest W. *D. H. Lawrence, Artist and Rebel.* Albuquerque: University of New Mexico Press, 1963.

Twentieth-Century Literary Criticism, Vols. 2, 9, 16. Detroit: Gale Research Co.

Voelker, Joseph C. "The Spirit of No-Place: Elements of the Classical Ironic Utopia in D. H. Lawrence's *Lady Chatterley's Lover." Modern Fiction Studies* 25, No. 2 (Summer 1979): 223-39.

Ursula K. Le Guin
1929-

American novelist, short story writer, poet, and editor.

The Left Hand of Darkness (novel, 1969)

This novel is a part of what has become known as Le Guin's Hainish Cycle and is considered her first major work. In Le Guin's imagined universe, the people of the planet Hain were the first to explore and colonize other worlds in the galaxy, including the planet Earth.

Genly Ai, the central character of *The Left Hand of Darkness,* is an inhabitant of Earth sent to the planet Gethen, or Winter, bearing a message of peace. He is the representative of an organization called the Ekumen, whose members promote free trade and communication between distant worlds. Although Gethen's cultural development is similar to Earth's, the planet's extreme cold influences many of the Getheneans' customs and traditions. The most distinctive feature of the planet, however, is the fact that its inhabitants are androgynes, neither male nor female. They remain sexually dormant except during kemmer, periods of sexual fertility when they can take on the characteristics of either male or female for the purpose of reproduction. Genly Ai's main contact on Gethen is with **Therem Harth rem ir Estraven,** prime minister of the Karhide region of Gethen. The two characters form an uneasy alliance when Estraven realizes that the Ekumen represents the same values and ideals which he has advocated throughout his political career. Their relationship grows into one of mutual love when they must cross the great ice field after Estraven rescues Genly Ai from an Orgota prison. Although Estraven eventually assumes the feminine role during kemmer, they do not physically consummate their love, but come together mentally as they accept each other's culture, signifying the harmony which can evolve between dissimilar peoples after shared hardships.

Genly Ai tells his story in the first person as well as through the use of earlier Ekumenical reports from Gethen, myths and legends from that planet, and Estraven's diaries. The novel raises questions about the ways in which biology, geology, and sociology shape our perceptions of the world. Le Guin employs the journey of discovery, a familiar motif in her works, to explore some possible answers.

"The Earthsea Trilogy": *A Wizard of Earthsea* (novel, 1968); *The Tombs of Atuan* (novel, 1971); *The Farthest Shore* (novel, 1972)

Le Guin's Earthsea Trilogy follows the youth, young adulthood, and old age of **Ged,** who rises from goatherd to great wizard during the course of the novels.

In *A Wizard of Earthsea* Ged is a student of the master wizard **Ogion.** Before Ged's powers are fully developed and he is able to understand them, he attempts a spell beyond his abilities and must be saved by Ogion's intervention. Refusing further instruction from Ogion, Ged goes to the school of wizardry on Roke Island where he again attempts magic beyond his control. This time Ged glimpses death and his own shadow, which represents the dark side of his personality. Unable to accept what he has seen, Ged seeks refuge with Ogion. Eventually, at Ogion's prompting, Ged sets out in search of his shadow. When he finally meets it face to face on the high seas, Ged recognizes and acknowledges that it is a part of himself, thus fulfilling the purpose of his journey and becoming a fully integrated human being.

The Tombs of Atuan focuses on the coming of age of **Tenar,** a young woman who at birth was renamed Arha, or the Eaten One, and taken to the temple of the Nameless Ones to be trained as a priestess. The temple is consecrated to the worship of death and evil, and no men are allowed inside. Ged comes to the tombs beneath the temple to search for the missing half of the ring of Erreth-Akbe, which will restore peace and unity to all of Earthsea. Ged is discovered and imprisoned by Tenar, who is intrigued by his masculinity. Ged gives the restored ring into her safekeeping, signifying the male/female relationship which is forbidden to her. He also tells Tenar her true name and eventually leads her out of the darkness of the tombs to be reborn as a whole human being.

In *The Farthest Shore,* Ged is an old man who has come to terms with his mortality and wishes to pass on his hard-earned wisdom to the next generation. Great troubles have descended upon Earthsea, and Ged takes the young **Prince Arren,** a self-centered youth interested only in his own immortality, with him to seek out the source of the problems. After many dangerous encounters, during which Prince Arren develops into a mature and caring person, they discover that the renegade wizard **Cob** has opened the gate separating the world of the living from the dead, dangerously unbalancing the equilibrium of the universe. Although now it is possible for everyone to live forever, life has been robbed of its joy. Ged and Arren must descend into the kingdom of the dead, where Ged again closes the door between life and death. Arren helps the exhausted Ged over the Mountains of Pain into renewed life, and on to the Island of Roke where Ged disappears on the back of a dragon. Arren is crowned King of all Earthsea, having fulfilled the prophecy that a great ruler would journey to the land of the dead and back. *The Farthest Shore* received the National Book Award for children's literature.

In her Earthsea Trilogy, Le Guin creates a humanistic universe in which each person must act wisely in order to maintain the equilibrium of the world. Each novel is a coming of age story symbolizing the journey all individuals must make to achieve psychic wholeness and to accept their own mortality. The style of these works is reminiscent of Le Guin's other fictions where she fuses fantasy and magic with commonplace concerns, and which make her work accessible and interesting to a wide audience of readers.

FURTHER READING

Bittner, James W. *Approaches to the Fiction of Ursula K. Le Guin.* Ann Arbor: The University of Michigan Press, 1984.

Bucknall, Barbara J. *Ursula K. Le Guin.* New York: Ungar, 1981.

Contemporary Authors, Vols. 21-24, rev. ed.; *Contemporary Authors New Revision Series,* Vol. 9. Detroit: Gale Research Co.

Contemporary Literary Criticism, Vols. 8, 13, 22, 45. Detroit: Gale Research Co.

Dictionary of Literary Biography, Vols. 8, 52. Detroit: Gale Research Co.

Esmonde, Margaret P. "The Psychological Journey in the Earthsea Trilogy." In *Ursula K. LeGuin,* edited by Joseph D. Olander and Martin Harry Greenberg, pp. 15-35. New York: Taplinger, 1979.

Hull, Keith N. "What Is Human? Ursula Le Guin and Science Fiction's Great Theme." *Modern Fiction Studies* 32 (Spring 1986): 65-74.

Maddern, Philippa. "True Stories: Women's Writing in Science Fiction." *Meanjin* 44, No. 1 (March 1985): 110-23.

Spivack, Charlotte. *Ursula K. Le Guin.* Boston: Twayne, 1984.

Doris Lessing
1919-
Persian-Born English novelist.

"Children of Violence": *Martha Quest* (novel, 1952); *A Proper Marriage* (novel, 1954); *A Ripple from the Storm* (novel, 1958); *Landlocked* (novel, 1965); *The Four-Gated City* (novel, 1969)

Lessing's "Children of Violence" series comprises five novels that appeared over a period of seventeen years. Paralleling Lessing's life, the series follows the English heroine

Martha Quest from age fifteen in Rhodesia through various political affiliations, two marriages, children, and immigration to England. In a departure from the psychological realism of the preceding four novels, the final book in the series culminates in an apocalyptic vision of the near future in which first Britain and then the entire world are destroyed by humanity's own violence.

The first novel, *Martha Quest,* introduces the young Martha, an intelligent and idealistic girl seeking to escape the confines of her provincial, bigoted hometown and a possessive, narrow-minded mother. She moves to the city of Zambesia, where she finds a job, joins a leftist political group, and becomes sexually involved with a Jewish intellectual, **Solly Cohen.** At the novel's end, she has met and married **Douglas Knowell,** a young bureaucrat.

Set during World War II, *A Proper Marriage* depicts Martha as constantly unsatisfied and restless in her married state. Douglas departs for military duty, leaving Martha pregnant and increasingly concerned with social and racial justice, a persistent obsession. Following the baby's birth, Martha gets involved once again in leftist politics and, after Douglas's return, finds their comfortable bourgeois life ever more repugnant to her sense of self and freedom. She decides, over the objections of many, particularly her parents, to leave Douglas.

In *A Ripple from the Storm,* Martha has become involved working with European war refugees, and meets through her work **Anton Hesse,** a German Jew who escaped Hitler's horror. When he is faced with deportation, Martha marries him, and while the liaison is not happy, they are united by work with their Communist political group, which Anton leads. Some of their fellow members, however, find Anton and Martha too militant, and the group breaks into radical, moderate, and labor factions.

In *Landlocked,* Martha and Anton are leading essentially separate lives. The war is nearly over, and the book is populated with numerous refugees, including **Thomas Stern,** a Polish man with whom Martha has a fulfilling love affair. Thomas emigrates from Africa to Israel, returns, then dies from fever when he moves to the bush to work with native Africans. Faced with other losses, including her father's death, a divorce form Anton, and increasing alienation from the younger political radicals, Martha determines to move to England.

The Four-Gated City, the fifth and final novel, finds Martha in postwar London, where she is the secretary and mistress of a well-known author, **Mark Coldridge.** The city, depressing and half destroyed, stands in ironic contrast to the place young Martha envisioned in the series' first novel as "four-gated, dignified . . . when black and white and brown lived as equals and there was no hatred or violence." Martha, now middle-aged, is disillusioned and unsure of her identity or her ability to attain the sense of freedom for which she has quested so long. As if the world reflects the chaos of Martha's mind, we are told at the end of the book that Britain is destroyed in the 1970s and the entire world decimated in the 1990s.

While some critics note a lack of continuity and unity among the novels in the "Children of Violence" series, the work is considered a major achievement in the detailed depiction of an independent, uncompromising woman attempting to move through the forces of history toward freedom, both personal and universal.

The Golden Notebook (novel, 1962)

Lessing's profound and detailed examination of a woman's psyche, *The Golden Notebook* is widely regarded as her masterpiece. The novel is set is London in the 1950s, but contains reminiscences about colonial Africa and earlier times in the life of its heroine, **Anna Freeman Wulf,** a writer. Lessing has said that the novel's "meaning is in the shape," and indeed the novel's innovative and complex form perfectly reflects the heroine's sense of fragmentation. The novel comprises four parts, with each part containing the following: a section of a formal, third-person novel by Anna Wulf about a "character" named Anna Wulf, followed by one section each from four notebooks written by Anna in the first person. The black notebook deals with her youth in Africa; the red explores her experiences as a member of the Communist Party; the yellow presents a narrative about **Ella,** Anna's fictionalized alter ego; and the blue is a more traditional, straightforward account of Anna's daily life. A brief section of Anna's novel, also titled "The Golden Notebook," is presented at the end of the four parts, and the novel concludes with a section titled "Free Women."

As may be gleaned from the novel's form, Anna Wulf is regarded as one of the most introspective, exhaustively self-examining characters in literature. In seeking relief from her sense of restlessness and shattered identity, she devises the notebook scheme to explore herself from several different aspects, and it is this very intimate self-analysis that readers share. Anna is an immigrant to London from Africa, where her acute sense of social injustice was nurtured by the racial inequality and hypocrisy she observed around her. This social awareness led her into activism in the Communist Party, ultimately a bitterly disillusioning experience. Now living in London with her daughter, Anna is deeply aware of the dilemma of women attempting to balance emotional and sexual fulfillment while retaining personal autonomy. Indeed, the treatment in the book of women's issues is acknowledged to be remarkably ahead of its time. In addition to her inner thoughts, Anna describes her "outer" life; her relationships with **Molly Jacobs,** her supportive friend; **Saul Green,** an American Jew with whom she has a love affair; and **Mrs. Marks,** or "Mother Sugar," the Jungian psychoanalyst who encouraged her to allay her anxiety by writing down her experiences. While the black, red and blue notebooks provide Anna's intensely subjective observations, the sections devoted to "Ella" and the fictional Anna furnish a valuable counterpoint in Anna's attempt to objectify her life and experiences. The concluding "Golden Notebook" and "Free Women" sections represent an affirmative vision of the possibilities of wholeness and self-actualization toward which Anna is steadily moving. For its ingenious form and generous exploration of a modern woman, *The Golden Notebook* is widely acknowledged as a twentieth-century classic.

FURTHER READING

Contemporary Authors, Vols. 9-12, rev. ed. Detroit: Gale Research Co.

Contemporary Literary Criticism, Vols. 1, 2, 3, 6, 10, 15, 22, 40. Detroit: Gale Research Co.

Dictionary of Literary Biography, Vol. 15; *Dictionary of Literary Biography Yearbook: 1985.* Detroit: Gale Research Co.

Draine, Betsy. "Nostalgia and Irony: The Postmodern Order of *The Golden Notebook.*" *Modern Fiction Studies* 26 (Spring 1980): 31-48.

Fishburn, Katherine. "The Nightmare Repetition: The Mother-Daughter Conflict in Doris Lessing's 'Children of Violence.'" In *The Lost Tradition: Mothers and Daughters in Literature,* edited by Cathy N. Dandson and E. M. Brown, pp. 207-16. New York: Ungar, 1980.

Gindin, James. *Postwar British Fiction,* pp. 65-86. Berkeley: University of California Press, 1962.

Hinz, Evelyn and John J. Teonissen. "The Pieta as Icon in *The Golden Notebook.*" *Contemporary Literature* 14 (Autumn 1973): 457-70.

Holmquist, Ingrid. *From Society to Nature: A Study of Doris Lessing's "Children of Violence."* Gothenburg: Gothenburg Studies in English, 1980.

Hynes, Joseph. "The Construction of *The Golden Notebook.*" *Iowa Review* 4 (Summer 1973): 100-13.

Libby, Marian V. "Sex and the New Women in *The Golden Notebook.*" *Iowa Review* 5 (Fall 1974): 106-20.

C. S. Lewis
1898-1963

English novelist, essayist, and critic.

Out of the Silent Planet (novel, 1938); *Perelandra* (novel, 1943); *That Hideous Strength* (novel, 1945)

Out of the Silent Planet is Lewis's first novel and the first in a trilogy of science fiction adventures. In this novel, the hero of the trilogy, **Elwin Ransom,** an English philologist at Cambridge, is abducted to Malacandra (representing Mars) by **Dr. Weston** and **Dick Devine,** two characters representative of the forces of evil on Thulcundra (representing Earth). Weston, a renowned physicist, hopes to spread human civilization throughout the universe while Devine, a former classmate of Ransom, is interested in exploiting the resources and inhabitants of outer space in order to increase his already excessive wealth.

While on Malacandra, Weston escapes from his captors and becomes acquainted with its inhabitants, discovering that they are both wise and peaceful. He learns, moreover, that every planet in the universe is governed by an Oyarsa, an angel-like creature who serves the Lord of the universe, except in the case of Thulcundra, which is called the Silent Planet because it is under the control of an Oyarsa who is "bent." Ransom finds that the Oyarsa of Malacandra actually arranged for him to be kidnapped by Devine and Weston so as to enlist Ransom's help in the struggle against evil on Thulcundra.

Devine and Weston, having killed one of the inhabitants of Malacandra, are tried, found guilty, and sentenced to return to Thulcundra. Ransom goes with them and the novel closes with a narration by "**Lewis,**" a friend of Ransom, who explains his purpose in recording Ransom's story: to support the battle against Weston and Devine and the forces they represent, and to stop them before they corrupt the entire planet and spread their plague to other planets as well.

In *Perelandra,* the second novel in Lewis's science fiction trilogy, Ransom is sent to prevent the equivalent of the Fall of Adam and Eve from taking place on Perelandra (Venus), a planet as pristine and unmarred as the Garden of Eden. The tempter, in this case, is **Dr. Weston,** the evil scientist from Lewis's first novel, who has now come completely under the power of the "bent" Oyarsa who holds planet Earth under his influence. Ransom's task is to persuade the Perelandran Eve, the **Green Lady,** to resist Weston. The Green Lady is the **Queen of Perelandra,** her husband the **King of Perelandra** and she has a special relationship with **Maleldil,** the Lord of the Universe, and can communicate with him directly in a way that Ransom, being from a fallen race, cannot completely understand. Weston attempts to weaken her faith in Maleldil and persuade her to violate the one "commandment" she has been given, the counterpart to God's injunction not to eat of the Tree of Knowledge of good and evil. She begins to falter under Weston's arguments that she must establish her independence from her husband and Maleldil, but Ransom takes on the task of struggling against Weston, first through verbal debate—a lengthy portion of the novel—and finally through actual physical struggle. Ransom ultimately triumphs, and Perelandra and its Eve are saved from a fall which would have allowed evil to enter that world. To celebrate the glorious victory, the leaders of the various planets come together to join in a dance of rejoicing.

That Hideous Strength, the third novel in Lewis's space trilogy, tells of the hero Ransom's struggle against evil forces as they are manifested on Earth. The focus of evil here is a scientific organization, N.I.C.E., the National Institute of Coordinated Experiments, which plans to take over the planet. Hoping to revive the magician Merlin of Arthurian legend in order to employ his powers in the accomplishment of their goals, N.I.C.E. approaches the young sociologist **Mark Studdock** with an offer to work with them to save humanity and bring about a better world. Mark's new wife, **Jane,** is the ultimate object of N.I.C.E.'s interest, as she has been having dreams in which she can locate Merlin's grave. Jane, however, discovers that N.I.C.E. is involved with demonic forces and comes into contact with Ransom, now called **Fisher King,** who works together with her in the struggle against N.I.C.E. The Oyarsas, or angelic guides, of all the planets come together and summon Merlin to use his power against N.I.C.E. and they, together with Jane and Ransom, ultimately triumph over the forces of evil.

The science fiction genre was, for Lewis, not merely a means for exercising his powers of imagination, but was also a vehicle for translating the eternal truths of Christianity into refreshing forms that the modern mind would find attractive, both morally and aesthetically. For Lewis, to regard science and technology as the source and instrument of the salvation of mankind is not merely naive, but plays into the hands of the dark spiritual forces, the "principalities and powers." Lewis does not condemn science and technology per se, but warns against regarding scientific advances as synonymous with true human development. Lewis upholds and points to the underlying spiritual realities which, he stresses, must remain central to the Christian vision, and invites his readers to listen to the resonances between the ancient, eternal wisdom of the Bible and the circumstances of the modern world.

FURTHER READING

Contemporary Authors, Vols. 81-84. Detroit: Gale Research Co.

Contemporary Literary Criticism, Vols. 1, 3, 6, 14, 27. Detroit: Gale Research Co.

Cooke, Alistair. "Mr. Anthony at Oxford." *The New Republic* 110, No. 17 (24 April 1944): 578-80.

Dictionary of Literary Biography, Vol. 15. Detroit: Gale Research Co.

Edwards, Bruce L., ed. *The Taste of the Pineapple: Essays on C. S. Lewis as Reader, Critic, and Imaginative Writer.* Bowling Green: Bowling Green State University Popular Press, 1988.

Hannay, Margaret Patterson. *C. S. Lewis.* New York: Ungar, 1981.

Houand, Thomas. *The Achievement of C. S. Lewis: A Reading of His Fiction.* Wheaton: H. Shaw Publishers, 1980.

Purtill, Richard. *Lord of the Elves and Eldils: Fantasy and Philosophy in C. S. Lewis and J. R. R. Tolkien.* Grand Rapids: Zondervan Publishing House, 1974.

Ribe, Neil. "That Glorious Strength: Lewis on Male and Female." *Bulletin of the New York C. S. Lewis Society* 14, No. 1 (November 1982): 1-9.

Schakel, Peter J., ed. *The Longing for a Form: Essays on the Fiction of C. S. Lewis.* Kent: Kent State University Press, 1977.

Tolkien, J. R. R. Letter to Stanley Unwin on March 4, 1938. In *The Letters of J. R. R. Tolkien,* edited by Humphrey Carpenter with Christopher Tolkien, pp. 32-5. Boston: Houghton Mifflin, 1981.

Walsh, Chad. *The Literary Legacy of C. S. Lewis.* New York: Harcourt Brace Jovanovich, 1979.

Sinclair Lewis
1885-1951
American novelist, short story writer, and essayist.

Main Street (novel, 1920)

Main Street is set in the fictitious small town of Gopher Prairie, Minnesota, an ugly little settlement populated by an appalling collection of blustering, inarticulate oafs and prying, vicious shrews, in the years surrounding World War I. An unmarried, idealistic college graduate, **Carol Milford,** assumes the role of social and cultural crusader in this highly satiric novel. She meets **Will Kennicott,** a Gopher Prairie doctor infatuated with his home town, and agrees to marry him. Even before arriving in Gopher Prairie, Carol suspects that her life there will be difficult, for her ideas for social change and personal betterment are at drastic odds with Midwestern mundaneness and small-minded complacency. Her fears are confirmed when the two women's clubs she joins stifle her progressive views and humanistic zeal. Because Will does not share Carol's sympathies and sophisticated tastes, the Kennicott marriage gradually sours. After giving birth to a boy, **Hugh,** Carol regains a sense of community belonging but resolves that her son's life, through a privileged education, will transcend the bounds of the town, filled as it is with gossip, prejudice, triviality, and hypocrisy. Continually searching for a kindred soul to whom she might confess her dissatisfactions and dreams, she discovers an effete young tailor, **Erik Valborg,** and begins talking regularly with him. Town gossip, however, quells the platonic friendship. Desperately needing to escape from her husband and Gopher Prairie, Carol flees with Hugh to Washington D. C., to participate in the war effort. After a year away she returns home to Will, now fully able to appreciate his good qualities and also willing to contribute, without further forward-thinking antagonism, to the Gopher Prairie community.

While Carol serves as critic of the small town—articulating Lewis's own views based on his provincial upbringing in Sauk Centre, Minnesota—Will represents, at times, the finest aspects of American village life: quiet determination, charity, and humility. Consequently, Lewis's final social stance is ambivalent and in keeping with his acknowledged love/hate attitude toward small-town America. *Main Street* has nevertheless been credited with helping to deflate sentimental myths of the ideal community.

Babbitt (novel, 1922)

Babbitt is set during the prohibition era in the fictional Midwestern town of Zenith. **George F. Babbitt,** the protagonist, is a middle-aged real estate broker motivated by the pursuit of money, respectability, and power. During the first half of the story his daily routines and relationships are depicted in detail. Blindly self-satisfied, Babbitt is a man with "zip and zowie," proud of his business acumen but oblivious to his hypocrisy, flexible morality, and rat-race existence. His rise in social stature is marked by a successful cocktail party (planned and hosted by his wife, **Myra**), unexpected triumph as a political orator, and his election to the Booster Club vice-presidency. His closest relationship is not with his wife, but his friend **Paul Riesling,** a tar-roofer married to a shrewish wife named **Zilla.** To escape their wives, Paul and Babbitt vacation together in Maine; there Babbitt reevaluates his frenzied lifestyle and vows to modify it. However, the trappings of the business life prove inescapable and so Babbitt continues in his usual routines until he receives a call from Myra one day. She informs him that Paul has shot his wife and is now in custody. His life rendered meaningless by the actions of his friend, Babbitt finds renewal after a pretty widowed client named **Mrs. Tanis Judique** visits him one day. He soon joins her circle of Bohemian friends and lives recklessly and lavishly. Liberal ideas now seem agreeable to him and he begins to spurn his community duties. After his former friends fall away and Myra becomes ill, Babbitt reaffirms his love for his wife and his commitment to the community. His conservatism and boosterism return. The only sign that he has changed inwardly is his private endorsement of his son's elopement.

In *Babbitt,* Lewis skewered the loud, hypocritical American businessman as well as members of America's public service organizations, focussing especially on their endless, vapid speeches and inane rituals. In the character of George F. Babbitt, Lewis created an Amerian literary archetype and the novel stands as one of the most effective and memorable satires in American literature.

Arrowsmith (novel, 1925)

Arrowsmith begins in the fictional prairie town of Elk Mills, in the state of Winnemac. As a boy, **Martin Arrowsmith** spends his spare time with **Doc Vickerson,** who encourages Martin's interest in medicine. Later, at the University of Winnemac's medical school, he studies bacteriology under the noted German scientist **Professor Max Gottlieb.** There he also falls in love with two women, **Madeline Fox** and **Leora Tozer**, and impossibly engages himself to both. Martin eventually marries Leora, an attractive nurse, and establishes a family practice in his wife's hometown, Wheatsylvania, North Dakota. Thereafter, Martin continually struggles with contravening interests and questions of medical ethics, particularly the personal dilemma of whether he can best serve society as a physician or a research scientist.

A venture into public health medicine leads Martin to Nautilus, Iowa, where he serves as Assistant Director to **Dr. Almus Pickerbaugh.** To Martin's disappointment, Pickerbaugh acts more as a preening orator than a conscientious, scientifically oriented health official. Following Pickerbaugh's election to Congress, Martin becomes Acting Director of Public Health. Although his research and actions are impeccable, he is forced to resign after inadvertently undermining certain business interests. Martin reunites with Gottlieb in New York and devotes himself entirely to research. Following experimentation with a new antitoxin, Martin travels with Leora and the Swedish scientist **Gustave Sondelius** to St. Hubert, West Indies, to fight an epidemic. Tragically, Leora and Sondelius die. Martin suffers greatly, even more so because he realizes that in his unhesitant, compassionate treatment of the islanders he has jeopardized the validity of his ongoing research. Following a second marriage, Martin moves to rural Vermont, where with his old friend **Terry Wickett** he begins seeking a cure for pneumonia.

Arrowsmith tells of the battles of a humanitarian scientist to conduct medical research against the beckoning forces of fame, commercialism, and material comforts. Widely acclaimed as one of America's most significant voices of the postwar era, Lewis won the 1926 Pulitzer Prize in fiction for *Arrowsmith,* but refused to accept the award, claiming that it was intended only for champions of American wholesomeness. Evidence from Lewis's letters suggests that another, less idealistic reason for his refusal was his anger that Edith Wharton's *The Age of Innocence* had been chosen over *Main Street* as winner of the 1921 Pulitzer Prize. In any event, *Arrowsmith* represents Lewis's most ambitious undertaking and perhaps his most successful attempt to present, through the travails of its protagonist, a representative metaphor of American life.

FURTHER READING

Contemporary Authors, Vol. 104. Detroit: Gale Research Co.

Dictionary of Literary Biography, Vol. 9; *Dictionary of Literary Biography Documentary Series,* Vol. 1. Detroit: Gale Research Co.

Dooley, D. J. *The Art of Sinclair Lewis.* Lincoln: University of Nebraska Press, 1967.

Douglas, George H. "*Main Street* after Fifty Years." *Prairie Schooner* 44, No. 4 (Winter 1970-71): 338-48.

Grebstein, Sheldon N. *Sinclair Lewis.* New York: Twayne, 1962.

Griffin, Robert J., ed. *Twentieth-Century Interpretations of "Arrowsmith."* Englewood Cliffs: Prentice-Hall, 1968.

Light, Martin, ed. *The Merrill Studies in "Babbitt."* Columbus: Charles E. Merrill, 1971.

———. *The Quixotic Vision of Sinclair Lewis.* West Lafayette: Purdue University Press, 1975.

Lundquist, James. *Sinclair Lewis.* New York: Ungar, 1973.

O'Connor, Richard. *Sinclair Lewis.* New York: McGraw-Hill, 1971.

Schorer, Mark. *Sinclair Lewis: An American Life.* New York: McGraw-Hill, 1961.

Schorer, Mark, ed. *Sinclair Lewis: A Collection of Critical Essays.* Englewood Cliffs: Prentice-Hall, 1962.

Sherman, Stuart P. *The Significance of Sinclair Lewis*, 1922. Reprint. Freeport: Books for Libraries Press, 1971.

Twentieth-Century Literary Criticism, Vols. 4, 13, 23. Detroit: Gale Research Co.

Wyndham Lewis
1882-1957
Canadian born English novelist, essayist, and critic.

Tarr (novel, 1918)

The novel is set in Paris in 1910 and follows several members of the artist community, including **Frederick Tarr** and his fellow protagonist, **Otto Kreisler**. Tarr is an English art student, devoted only to his craft. He is tiring of his mistress, **Bertha Lunken,** a German art student with romantic notions of a happy marriage with Tarr that end when he breaks their engagement. He is seen by most critics as Lewis's spokesman in the novel and is a representative of the intellectual side of man, as opposed to the emotional aspects represented in the brooding, impoverished Kreisler, a young German artist alienated from the society in which he desperately wants to be accepted. Kreisler is in love with the beautiful Russian **Anastasya Vasek,** who for the moment has become Tarr's mistress, although Tarr, unfettered by social convention, prefers a string of mistresses to commitment. Bertha, trying to arouse Tarr's jealousy, excites Kreisler, and he rapes her. When she becomes pregnant as a result of this assault, Tarr does agree to marry Bertha, although he continues to live with Anastasya. Always a slave to his passionate nature, Kreisler, still wanting Anastasya, fights a duel with **Louis Soltyk,** whom he considers a rival for her affections, and kills him. He flees the country and is arrested; while in jail, he commits suicide.

As in much of his work, Lewis focuses on the plight of the artist in modern society through his two protagonists. Tarr remains aloof from emotional involvement in the world and thereby can focus his life on his art; Kreisler, a man of uncontrolled emotions who is shown to be of limited artistic and intellectual gifts, is doomed to a life of poverty and failure. Critics have noted the misogynist theme of the work, which is informed by Lewis's understanding of Nietzsche's concept of the male artist's need to dominate the female sex. The work is recognized for its combination of a variety of prose styles and its vivid rendering of the artist's milieu in Paris before the First World War.

The Apes of God (novel, 1930)

In this, his best-known work, Lewis presented a satire on the artistic world of his time, a roman à clef in which many members of the English literary and artistic elite were savagely ridiculed. The novel centers on the picaresque adventures of **Dan Boleyn,** a character modelled on the English poet Stephen Spender, as he explores the world of literary London in the 1920s. He is led on his search by **Horace Zagreus,** who tries to alert his protege to the hypocrisy and fakery of the modern art world. In particular, he wants to inculcate Boleyn with the philosophy of **Pierpoint,** who had been his teacher in the realms of art and who represents the opinions of Lewis in the novel. Although Pierpoint never appears in the work, he offers, through objective, narrative statements called "broadcasts," the defining consciousness to the novel.

On Boleyn's tour, we are introduced to caricatures of such well-known artists of the day as T. S. Eliot, James Joyce, Aldous Huxley, and members of the Bloomsbury group, and Lewis savagely attacks their prose, poetry, paintings, and way of life, including their sexuality. The "apes" of the title refers to these would-be artists who, according to Lewis, are mere imitators of the god of creativity. They represent conformity, lack of originality, and are described as artistically and politically ignorant, unaware of the world around them and mindless in the pursuit of their "art." In the opinion of many critics, the satire is so cruel that the characters are diminished to grotesques—even Boleyn is shown to be moronic—and the reader can neither identify with them nor understand Lewis's invective. The novel gained Lewis a reputation and notoriety that was to color responses to many of his later works.

FURTHER READING

Contemporary Authors, Vol. 104. Detroit: Gale Research Co.

Dictionary of Literary Biography, Vol. 15. Detroit: Gale Research Co.

Henkle, Roger B. "The 'Advertised' Self: Wyndham Lewis's Satire." *Novel: A Forum on Fiction* 13, No. 1 (Fall 1979): 95-108.

Jameson, Frederic. *Fables of Aggression: Wyndham Lewis, the Modernist as Fascist.* Berkeley: University of California Press, 1979.

Kenner, Hugh. *Wyndham Lewis.* Norfolk: New Directions, 1954.

Materer, Timothy. *Wyndham Lewis the Novelist.* Detroit: Wayne State University Press, 1976.

Pritchard, William. *Wyndham Lewis.* New York: Twayne, 1968.

Twentieth-Century Literary Criticism, Vols. 2, 9. Detroit: Gale Research Co.

Wagner, Geoffrey. *Wyndham Lewis: A Portrait of the Artist as Enemy.* London: Routledge & Kegan Paul, 1957.

Jack London
1876-1916
American novelist, short story writer, and essayist.

"To Build a Fire" (short story, 1902)

An unnamed tenderfoot is the main figure of this classic short story, a widely anthologized work that is often termed London's masterpiece. The story takes place deep within the Yukon territory during the dead of winter. The overconfident man is attempting to travel on foot through several miles of frigid, snow-ridden wilderness with only the aid of a wolf-dog and a few simple supplies. In contrast to the man, the husky is fully aware of the severe, potentially deadly cold from the beginning: the temperature is seventy-five below zero. The man frequently reflects on how cold it is and on the advice of an old-timer, who once warned him that no man should travel alone in the Klondike when temperatures exceed fifty below. He doesn't perceive the danger of his journey, but only its resultant discomfort, which he willingly endures. Hours pass and the man stops for lunch; unable to eat because his fingers are numb, he carefully builds a fire. Once warmed he decides it is time to continue. The degree to which he has underestimated his predicament and overvalued his intelligence and skill soon surface. Lulled by false security, he falls into a hidden spring, drenching the lower half of his body.

Now he must quickly build another fire or face certain death, for he is still several miles from camp. He succeeds and believes himself saved until the fire is suddenly dowsed from snow that has fallen from an overhanging tree. Growing worried, he tries to build a third fire and rapidly loses the use of his hands. Increasingly frantic, he tries to warm himself through a series of last desperate acts, including the hopeless attempt to kill his dog to warm himself on the carcass. Finally the man acknowledges his foolhardy quest and dreamily, powerlessly accepts his inevitable death. Once the husky is certain of his master's decease he instinctively heads for camp, where he knows he will find warmth and food.

"To Build a Fire" epitomizes the brisk story of individual struggle against natural forces of which London is an undisputed master. Through the detached voice of an omniscient narrator, London portrays the idiocy and ineptitude of one man, who represents the antithesis of the elemental world that faithfully rewards native instinct but is indifferent to human inadequacies. Sharp imagery and ironic verbal repetition contribute to the story's relentlessly pessimistic tone and carefully wrought progression. Here, as in much of London's work, the raw power of nature underscores the relative insignificance of humanity.

The Call of the Wild (novel, 1903)

Buck, a crossbreed of Scottish shepherd and St. Bernard, is the central figure of London's most famous and widely read work. Set in Alaska during the gold rush of the 1890s, this naturalistic adventure story documents Buck's initial enslavement and harsh journey from a California estate to the unsettled and unforgiving environment of the Klondike. As a sled-dog, Buck quickly learns to aggressively defend himself against his rival dogs. A calculated, fatal attack on his first team's lead dog signals his rise to power. Soon the driving force of a team known for record-breaking runs, he becomes prized and famous. However, his French-Canadian drivers are forced to sell him; eventually, during a long, hazardous journey under incompetent, ruthless masters, Buck tires near a cabin and refuses to move. Threatened with death, Buck is saved by the cabin owner, **Jack Thornton.** Love and admiration develop between dog and man as Buck regains his health. Following further adventures, which lead to a gold-hunting expedition, the novel closes with Buck's return to camp to discover the slaughtered bodies of dogs and men. Finding his friend dead, Buck takes vengeance on a fleeing band of Indians. Afterwards, he resides with a wolf pack, returning yearly to the scene of the massacre to mourn his friend's death.

Epitomizing London's vigorous, compact style, *The Call of the Wild* exposes the brute realities of human and animal life. It is based in part on London's own experiences, and takes its dominant themes—survival of the fittest and the rise to power—from the theories of Charles Darwin and Friedrich Nietzsche. Also present throughout the work is a Marxian interest in social cooperation and action for mutual benefit. A briskly paced narrative that powerfully conveys London's greatest artistic concerns, the novel endures as an American classic.

The Sea-Wolf (novel, 1904)

Set at sea aboard a schooner named the *Ghost,* the story begins in San Francisco Bay. **Wolf Larsen,** the ship's captain, rescues **Humphrey Van Weyden,** the apparent victim of a ferry collision. The gruff, sadistic Wolf forces Humphrey to work as his cabin boy as the *Ghost* embarks on a long, treacherous seal-hunting expedition to the Bering Sea and the coast of Japan. Often compared to Satan, Faust, Caliban, and Captain Ahab, Wolf impresses upon Humphrey his absolute repudiation of God, morality, and the civilized world. However, as Humphrey discovers, the captain is not simply an unreasoning, indomitable sadist, for he reads the works of Spencer, Browning, and Shakespeare.

Following an attempted mutiny—in which Humphrey, despite barbarous treatment by Wolf, did not participate—Wolf promotes Humphrey to mate. Humphrey grows to love sailing and the open sea, but finds Wolf's animalistic mania increasingly intolerable, and finds himself at a loss to solve the paradox of the captain's dual nature.

Maud Brewster, the survivor of a shipwreck, enters the story when she is found in an open boat. A poet and essayist whose ethereal beauty attracts both men, she represents the antipode of Wolf, whose brutal lust for her soon erupts. Saved from rape by Humphrey, the two escape the *Ghost* and land on an uninhabited island. The novel resolves when Wolf, now blind but still intent on harm, lands alone on the island, suffers a seizure, and is buried at sea by the couple, who are eventually rescued.

Suffused with the Nietzschean doctrine of the superman, the novel contains some of London's most evocative naturalistic writing. However, the facile storybook ending and the cloudy matter of London's final philosophic stance—whether or not he advocated Larson's views—have detracted from the work's critical stature. Still, the novel is recognized for its unforgettable portrayal of Larsen and for its brilliant exploration and refutation of the extreme possibilities inherent in Nietzsche's doctrine.

White Fang (novel, 1906)

White Fang, a wolf dog, is the main figure in one of London's most artistically successful longer works, conceived as a "complete antithesis" to *The Call of the Wild.* Set initially in the Alaskan wilderness, the novel details White Fang's birth in the wild and steady progression from a young, predatory member of a primitive wolf pack to a mature, devoted house pet. After learning the prime edict of the natural world—eat or be eaten—the obedient wolf dog is led by his uncaring mother back to her former master, **Gray Beaver.** There at his camp the dog is mistreated, particularly by the ruling dog, Lip-Lip. Consequently, the abandoned White Fang develops into a powerful and deadly creature, suspicious of all who approach him. Later he is sold to a new master for a bottle of liquor. Under **Beauty Smith**'s sadistic dominion, White Fang's strength and savagery grow as he is trained to become a lethal dog-fighter.

The course of White Fang's life is altered when **Weedon Scott,** a wealthy California landowner, rescues the dog from his bloody existence. Gradually converted to a life based on kindness and trust, White Fang returns with Weedon to his Santa Clara valley ranch. In this new environment he becomes further domesticated and thrives. Near the end of the novel he is renamed Blessed Wolf in gratitude for a heroic attack on an escaped convict who was trying to kill Weedon's father.

Both sociological fable and graphic adventure story, *White Fang* is primarily concerned with exploring the theory of environmental determinism. London, an outspoken critic of the social injustices of his time, considered physical, social, and environmental factors crucially important to the development of behavior and personality. Through the archetypal character of White Fang, he intended to demonstrate that behavior can be continually reshaped and, further, that social reform can be successfully applied to effect both individual and societal improvement.

FURTHER READING

Baltrop, Robert. *Jack London: The Man, the Writer, the Rebel.* London: Pluto Press, 1976.

Dickey, James. Introduction to *The Call of the Wild, White Fang, and Other Stories,* edited by Andrew Sinclair, pp. 7-16. New York: Penguin Books, 1981.

Dictionary of Literary Biography, Vols. 8, 12. Detroit: Gale Research Co.

Hedrick, Joan D. *Solitary Comrade: Jack London and His Work.* Chapel Hill: University of North Carolina Press, 1982.

Hendricks, King. *Jack London: Master Craftsman of the Short Story.* Logan: Utah State University Press, 1966.

Labor, Earle. *Jack London.* New York: Twayne Publishers, 1974.

Lundquist, James. *Jack London: Adventures, Ideas, and Fiction.* New York: Ungar, 1987.

Ownbey, Ray Wilson, ed. *Jack London: Essays in Criticism.* Santa Barbara: Peregrine Smith, 1978.

Tavernier-Courbin, Jacqueline. *Critical Essays on Jack London.* Boston: G. K. Hall, 1983.

Twentieth-Century Literary Criticism, Vols. 9, 15. Detroit: Gale Research Co.

Walker, Franklin. *Jack London and the Klondike: The Genesis of an American Writer.* San Marino: Huntington Library, 1966.

Watson, Charles N., Jr. *The Novels of Jack London: A Reappraisal.* Madison: University of Wisconsin Press, 1983.

Wilson, Ray, ed. *Jack London: Essays in Criticism.* Santa Barbara: Peregrine Smith, 1978.

H. P. Lovecraft
1890-1937

American short story writer, novelist, and essayist.

"The Call of Cthulhu" (short story, 1928)

"The Call of Cthulhu" was the first of several fictional works written by Lovecraft which together form what is known as his Cthulhu Mythos. These are considered Lovecraft's most pertinent works, for they reveal his eminence as the foremost writer of supernatural fantasy in the twentieth century.

The story's basic concept is that fearful and powerful alien beings who had reigned on Earth prior to the advent of man are, even now, slumbering beneath the Pacific Ocean, waiting for the time when their dominance will be reestablished. Set in 1926 and 1927 in Rhode Island, the story begins as a young man describes the mysterious death of his grand-uncle, **George Gammell Angell,** a professor of Semitic Languages at Brown University and an international authority on ancient inscriptions. The young man, the professor's heir and executor, stumbles upon a curious collection of notes and artifacts among his uncle's possessions. Upon further investigation, he learns of the existence of cults devoted to the alien **Cthulhu** in Greenland, Louisiana, and China. He also discovers that the aliens have the ability to transmit messages that have been picked up by certain gifted artists and writers in the form of dreams. After chancing upon an old newspaper clipping, the young man travels to Australia and then to Norway, hoping to locate a sailor whom he suspects has actually seen the alien. The sailor, although dead, has left a diary which describes the monster and his habitat. The mysterious nature of his uncle's death, coupled with the equally disturbing details of the sailor's demise, convince the young man that, in all likelihood, he too would meet an untimely end, for he has learned too much.

Lovecraft's prose in the Cthulhu Mythos has been described as ornate and extravagant, which many critics find a suitable style for his bizarre and fascinating tales. These works are noted for their blending of myth, mysticism, and elements of the occult, through which Lovecraft created what are considered masterpieces of supernatural fantasy.

FURTHER READING

Contemporary Authors, Vol. 104. Detroit: Gale Research Co.

Joshi, S. T., ed. *H. P. Lovecraft: Four Decades of Criticism.* Athens: Ohio University Press, 1980.

Schweitzer, Darrell. *The Dream Quest of H. P. Lovecraft.* San Bernardino: Borgo Press, 1978.

Shreffler, Philip A. "Lovecraft's Literary Theory." In *The H. P. Lovecraft Companion,* pp. 3-38. Westport: Greenwood Press, 1977.

Twentieth-Century Literary Criticism, Vols. 4, 22. Detroit: Gale Research Co.

Wilson, Edmund. "Tales of the Marvelous and the Ridiculous." In *Classics and Commercials: A Literary Chronicle of the Forties,* pp. 286-90. New York: Farrar, Straus & Giroux, 1950.

Malcolm Lowry

1909-1957

English novelist and short story writer.

Under the Volcano (novel, 1947)

The novel, set in the fictional Mexican town of Quauhnahuac, takes place on November 2, 1938, and covers the tortuous last day in the life of **Geoffrey Firmin.** An alcoholic Englishman, Firmin is the former British Consul to Quauhnahuac who has lost his job in the wake of a political crisis between England and Mexico. A cultivated, sensitive man, he is depicted as a soul on the edge of the abyss, sinking deeper into alcoholism and spiritual disintegration. His wife, **Yvonne,** who had earlier left him in despair and disgust over his drinking, returns to try to effect a reconciliation. Their efforts to repair their marriage are futile in the face of the chaos that surrounds them and the internal strife of their past life together, brought into focus by the presence by two of her former lovers, a shallow,

pleasure-seeking film director named **Jacques Laruelle,** and Firmin's brother, **Hugh.**
Firmin's last hours are spent in a hallucinatory state of drunkenness and turmoil, and
Lowry's tragic story ends in catastrophe, with Firmin the victim of a fascist assassin and
Yvonne trampled by a horse.

The novel is considered a major work of modern fiction and Lowry's masterpiece. It has
been explicated on a variety of levels: as a political allegory, an apocalyptic vision of the
twentieth century, and as an examination of the fallen state of man. On the political and
historical level, Firmin's last hours in Mexico reflect the instability of a world on the verge
of war. On another plane, Firmin has been interpreted as Adam, driven from Eden and
condemned to the horrors of hell. Indeed, Lowry had originally conceived *Under the
Volcano* as the first part of a trilogy that would parallel Dante's *Divine Comedy,* with the
first volume as a representation of the *Inferno.* Lowry's treatment of the Mexican landscape
perhaps links these interpretations, for he depicts it as a lush, exotic land of ancient
civilizations in prose infused with references to archetypal myth and ritual, which he
juxtaposes to the squalid chaos of contemporary life. The work has been noted for its
autobiographical elements, and Lowry, himself an alcoholic, renders with vivid intensity
the self-destructive horror that is the life of his protagonist. Noted for its philosophic depth
and symbolic richness, *Under the Volcano* is considered a landmark work of twentieth-
century fiction.

FURTHER READING

Bradbury, Malcolm. "Malcolm Lowry as Modernist." In *Possibilities: Essays on the State
of the Novel,* pp. 181-91. London: Oxford University Press, 1973.

Contemporary Authors, Vol. 105. Detroit: Gale Research Co.

Cross, Richard K. *Malcolm Lowry: A Preface to His Fiction.* Chicago: The University of
Chicago Press, 1980.

Dictionary of Literary Biography, Vol. 15. Detroit: Gale Research Co.

Epstein, Perle S. *The Private Labyrinth of Malcolm Lowry: "Under the Volcano" and the
Cabbala.* New York: Holt, Rinehart and Winston, 1969.

Twentieth-Century Literary Criticism, Vol. 6. Detroit: Gale Research Co.

Naguib Mahfouz
1911-
Egyptian novelist, short story writer, dramatist, and essayist.

Miramar (novel, 1967)

This novel, set in Alexandria in the 1960s, focuses on the life of a young peasant woman,
Zohra, who has fled her traditional background and come to the city to express her
independence and explore a new way of life. She becomes a chambermaid at the Pension
Miramar, where the novel takes place. The theme of the novel, a recurrent one for Mahfouz,
is the changing social and political life in modern Egypt, and in this work his heroine
functions as a symbol for that country. She immediately draws the attention of several of the
male boarders at the pension, and their reaction to her as they are attracted to her beauty and
simple goodness and try to exploit her innocence reflects the plight of Egypt in the
contemporary world.

Four of these boarders serve as the novel's narrators, and together they form a microcosm of

Egyptian society. **Amer Wagdy** at the age of eighty is a representative of the aging, liberal middle-class. A supporter of the early insurrectionist activities that led to Egypt's revolution in 1952, he has lived to see the country's dreams evaporate. Indeed, the novel's tone is one of despair, as the characters talk over the way in which the social, political, and agricultural policies of Nasser have failed to bring the country forward and has left each of them in a state of hopelessness. **Mansour Bahy,** depicted as a dreamy, sentimental former leftist, is another of the novel's narrators, and with the three young men in the house, is a rival for Zohra's affections. **Hosni Allam** is a member of a formerly wealthy and influential family who is full of contempt for the current regime. **Serhan El-Beheiry,** although he speaks favorably of the revolution, is shown to be an amoral hypocrite. He is also a heartless rake, and he tries to seduce the naive Zohra, who mistakes his overtures as a prelude to marriage. His attempted seduction and eventual rejection of her as beneath him fills her with rage and yet teaches her many of the truths of life in the modern world.

In her rejection of the traditional way of life, Zohra symbolizes Egypt, which, after the abolishment of the monarchy and parliamentary government in the wake of the 1952 revolution, embarked on what many hoped would be a path to freedom and self-fulfillment as a nation. The city of Alexandria is also a symbol, for its state of physical decay parallels the moral decay of Egypt. Considered one of the author's finest efforts, it is an outstanding example of the compassionate, committed work of Mahfouz, the first Arabic-language author to win the Nobel Prize in Literature.

FURTHER READING

Contemporary Literary Criticism, Vols. 52, 55. Detroit: Gale Research Co.

Dictionary of Literary Biography Yearbook: 1988. Detroit: Gale Research Co.

Fowles, John. "Introduction." In *Miramar* by Naguib Mahfouz, edited by Maged el Kommos and John Rodenbeck, translated by Fatma Moussa-Mahmoud, pp. vii-xv. London: Heinemann, 1978.

Peled, Mattityahu. *Religion My Own: The Literary Works of Naguib Mahfouz*. New Brunswick: Transaction Books, 1984.

Somekh, Sasson. *The Changing Rhythm: A Study of Naguib Mahfouz's Novels*. Leiden: E. J. Brill, 1973.

Norman Mailer

1923-

American novelist and essayist.

The Naked and the Dead (novel, 1948)

This novel explores the limits of individual integrity when confronted with overpowering impersonal mechanisms generated by contemporary society as represented by the war machine. The story takes place during World War II on Anopopei, a fictitious Pacific island controlled by the Japanese, and concerns the personal development of the men in a single platoon.

One of the main characters is **Major General Edward Cummings,** the personification of the war machine. Cummings is a brilliant reactionary who has an inflated vision of the importance of his own destiny. He has little regard for the men under his command and wields his power ruthlessly when encountering resistance of any kind. Cummings's aide, **Lieutenant Robert Hearn,** both admires and fears him. He is, or wants to be, a liberal, but he is a snob and is drawn to power. When he does exercise his will against the General, he is personally humiliated and sent to lead a platoon on a dangerous mission behind Japanese lines.

A parallel conflict occurs within the platoon between its leader, **Sergeant Sam Croft,** and one of his men, **Private Red Valsen.** Like the General, Croft is ruthless. He is also sadistic and violent, capable of crushing an injured bird in his hand while the horrified platoon looks on. He resents Hearn's authority in the platoon and coldly arranges his death. Croft's only real opponent, Valsen, finds himself unable to act upon his convictions because, like Hearn, he lacks the commitment and courage necessary.

Although Croft and Cummings prove victorious in their personal battles, they both face defeat in their ambitions. After the death of Hearn, Croft seeks to complete his mission by climbing Mount Anaka with his platoon. The mountain proves deadly and invincible; the mission, a terrible waste of life, proves totally unnecessary. Similarly, Cummings, whose major concern is a successful campaign against the Japanese, was absent from his post during the important battle; **Major Dalleson,** the ineffectual second-in-command, bungles his way to a brilliant victory.

Mailer emphasizes the horrors of war through his portrayal of human waste and suffering, creating characters that are realistic and credible. *The Naked and the Dead* is considered one of the most important and influential novels about World War II.

An American Dream (novel, 1965)

The novel concerns the spiritual evolution of one man living in contemporary urban society who attempts to realize salvation through the acknowledgement of his most primitive instincts. **Stephen Rojack** is a former war hero, congressman, and writer who is currently working as a talk-show host and professor. As the story opens, Rojack is contemplating suicide. He is despondent over what he perceives to be his failure in life and is particularly unhappy about his deteriorating marriage. He visits his wife, **Deborah,** and during a turbulent fight, kills her. After engaging in violent sex with his wife's maid, Rojack returns to his wife's room and attempts to make her death appear to be a suicide. Rojack is then interrogated by the police who, based on evidence of strangulation gained during the autopsy, are clearly convinced of his guilt. He is eventually cleared, however, due to the enormous influence of his father-in-law, **Barney Kelly.** After his initial interrogation, Rojack meets and falls in love with **Cherry,** a mediocre nightclub singer and former mistress of Kelly. Rojack is summoned to Kelly's hotel room, admits his guilt to him, and learns of Kelly's incestuous feelings toward Deborah. On Kelly's terrace, Rojack walks a parapet thirty stories high as a kind of mystical absolution. Upon returning to Cherry, he finds her dying. Rojack then flees to Las Vegas. The novel ends with Rojack still in flight, traveling to Central America.

Stephen Rojack is a man driven by an inner voice, witnessing events that seem to be the result of supernatural forces. His walk on the parapet is described by Mailer as symbolic of man's tenuous balance between good and evil, sanity and madness, and creation and destruction. The novel is considered one of his finest literary efforts.

FURTHER READING

Alvarez, A. ''Norman Mailer's *An American Dream.*'' In *Beyond All This Fiddle*, pp. 213-17. New York: Random House, 1969.

Braudy, Leo, ed. *Norman Mailer: A Collection of Critical Essays.* Englewood Cliffs: Prentice-Hall, 1972.

Contemporary Authors, Vols. 9-12, rev. ed.; *Contemporary Authors Bibliographical Series,* Vol. 1. Detroit: Gale Research Co.

Contemporary Literary Criticism, Vols. 1, 2, 3, 4, 5, 8, 11, 14, 28, 39. Detroit: Gale Research Co.

*Dictionary of Literary Biography,*Vols. 2, 16, 28; *Dictionary of Literary Biography Yearbook: 1980, 1983; Dictionary of Literary Biography Documentary Series,* Vol. 3. Detroit: Gale Research Co.

Merrill, Robert. *Norman Mailer.* Boston: Twayne, 1978.

Poirier, Richard. *Norman Mailer.* New York: Viking, 1972.

Schroth, Raymond A. "Mailer and His Gods: Norman Mailer Goes to War." *Commonweal* (9 May 1969): 226-29.

Waldron, Randall H. "The Naked, the Dead, and the Machine: A New Look at Norman Mailer's First Novel." *PMLA* 87 (March 1972): 271-77.

Bernard Malamud

1914-1986

American novelist and short story writer.

The Natural (novel, 1952)

Roy Hobbs, the "natural" of the title, is a baseball player whose story is told by Malamud as a variation of the Grail legend. A young player with great "natural" talent, Hobbs is on his way to a tryout for the major leagues when he is shot by a young woman. His career recommences at the age of thirty-three, when he returns to the game and leads his team, the Knights, towards the top of the league. However, at the height of his career, Hobbs sells out to gamblers and the team and Hobbs are defeated.

In his use of the myth of the Grail in *The Natural,* Malamud employs structure and imagery for their symbolic rather than naturalistic effects. He parallels the ritualistic aspects of baseball with the quest for the Holy Grail. Roy is the "savior" of the team, the "Knights," who are coached by "Pop Fisher," who represents the wounded Fisher King who must be healed to restore the team, that is, to lead it to a winning season. Hobbs is drawn to two different women, one who represents the power of evil and who introduces him to the gambler who will prove to be his undoing; the other a symbol of selfless love and the power of life. Thus, Malamud, infuses his novel with an allegorical framework and characterization.

Although Malamud is known as a Jewish novelist, *The Natural* contains no Jewish characters. And yet in its themes of suffering and redemption and its blend of realism and fantasy, it foreshadows many of Malamud's later works.

The Assistant (novel, 1957)

Morris Bober is a poor Jewish grocer in Depression-era New York during the 1930s. He is a man shaped by poverty and suffering. His store is depicted as dark and prison-like, an image that will recur throughout Malamud's fiction. The store is a source of despair for Morris: he negotiates to sell it, but can't bring himself to inflict his burden on another; he talks to an arsonist willing to burn it for the insurance money, but Morris is unable to go ahead with it. Instead he tries to set a fire himself, nearly destroying himself and his livelihood.

Frank Alpine, the "assistant" of the title, enters the life of Morris and is transformed by it. A petty thief, he helps to rob Morris early in the novel, but returns to help the old man, eventually becoming his shop assistant. Originally arrogant and anti-semitic, Frank learns to respect Morris and his way of life. Of Italian-American descent and an orphan, Frank seeks his identity in a world of Jews. His relationship with Morris is central to the story, for it is through him that he learns the values of Jewishness as Malamud presents them: honesty, integrity, and the redemptive power of suffering. Indeed, in the course of the novel, Morris becomes Frank's spiritual father.

Frank has also fallen in love with Morris's daughter, **Helen,** yet their affair, kept secret from Morris, ends horribly when Frank, after rescuing Helen from a sexual assault, rapes her himself, an act that seems to set in motion again the cycle of victimizer and victim. Morris dies suddenly from a heart attack suffered while shoveling snow in front of his store. His Jewishness is summarized by the rabbi presiding over his funeral. Admitting that he had not known him in life, he says: "When a Jew dies, who asks if he is a Jew? . . . Yes, Morris Bober was to me a true Jew because he lived in the Jewish experience and with the Jewish heart." After his death, Frank takes over the store, yet his process of atonement is not complete. In the novel's conclusion, the assistant is finally transformed, as Frank has himself circumcised and becomes a Jew.

Malamud in this novel explores what it means to be a Jew. Morris does not attend services, keep kosher, or follow any specific strictures. Instead, he is a man of integrity, who works hard and suffers. Rather than depicting a religious man who follows the dictates of his faith, Malamud portrays a man whose life and death become an allegory for goodness. The novel is rendered in a somber tone, with a realistic prose style in sharp contrast with the highly symbolic elements of *The Natural*. Yet Malamud blends realism with fantasy, as the narrative moves from a depiction of Morris's dreary, prison-like existence to Frank's dream-like visions of the life of St. Francis of Assisi.

The Assistant has been critically popular since its publication. The first of Malamud's works to focus on Jewish characters and themes, it is still studied for an understanding of his concept of faith and Jewishness. The novel is also greatly admired for its powerful characterization, taut structure, and fine use of Yiddish dialect.

The Fixer (novel, 1966)

The character of **Yakov Bok** is based loosely on the life of Mendel Beiliss, a turn-of-the-century Russian Jew accused of the ritual murder of a Christian boy. Bok is interned for over two years and subjected to physical and spiritual deprivation and humiliation as he is coerced to confess to the crime. Refusing to be the scapegoat for the authorities—his name means "goat" in Yiddish—Bok endures his suffering. His Jewishness had had little meaning for him prior to his arrest, in fact, he had left the ghetto for Kiev, and was able to pass as a Gentile. His incarceration brings home to him the fact that he cannot escape his ethnic heritage or the fate of his people. It is through his suffering that he learns the meaning of his Jewishness, and though the exact nature of his faith is still in doubt at the novel's end, he is committed to understanding himself as a Jew and enduring his torment heroically. The novel ends with Bok's fate still in question: unlike his real-life model, who was acquitted of murder, we last see Bok leaving prison for the court, before his trial begins.

The story of Yakov Bok is rendered in powerful, controlled prose. Of particular importance are the dream sequences which take place during Yakov's internment in which he confronts and challenges the Czar for his treatment of the Jewish people. The themes of Jewishness and suffering central to *The Assistant* and many of Malamud's works are also developed here. Many critics consider *The Fixer* Malamud's finest novel, praising the work's psychological, emotional, and intellectual depth; the work won the author both the Pulitzer Prize and the National Book Award.

FURTHER READING

Aldridge, John W. *Time to Murder and Create: The Contemporary Novel in Crisis*, pp. 52-94. New York: McKay, 1966.

Alter, Robert. "Malamud as Jewish Writer." *Commentary* 42, No. 2 (September 1966): 71-6.

Baumbach, Jonathan. "The Economy of Love: The Novels of Bernard Malamud." *Kenyon Review* 25 (Summer 1963): 438-57.

Contemporary Authors, Vols. 5-8, rev. ed., 118; *Contemporary Authors Bibliographical Series,* Vol. 1. Detroit: Gale Research Co.

Contemporary Literary Criticism, Vols. 1, 2, 3, 5, 8, 9, 11, 18, 27, 44. Detroit: Gale Research Co.

Dictionary of Literary Biography, Vols. 2, 28; *Dictionary of Literary Biography Yearbook: 1980, 1986; Concise Dictionary of American Literary Biography, 1941-1968.* Detroit: Gale Research Co.

Fiedler, Leslie. "Jewish-Americans, Go Home!" In *Waiting for the End,* pp. 89-104. New York: Stein and Day, 1964.

Hicks, Granville. "Bernard Malamud." *Literary Horizons,* pp. 65-83. New York: New York University Press, 1970.

Kazin, Alfred. "Bernard Malamud: The Magic and the Dread." In *Contemporaries,* pp. 202-07. Boston: Little, Brown, 1962.

Pinsker, Sanford. "The Achievement of Bernard Malamud." *Midwest Quarterly* 10 (July 1969): 379-89.

Richman, Sidney. *Bernard Malamud.* New York: Twayne, 1966.

Roth, Philip. "Writing American Fiction." *Commentary* 31 (March 1961): 223-33.

Tanner, Tony. "Bernard Malamud and the New Life." *Critical Quarterly* 10 (Spring-Summer 1968): 151-68.

André Malraux

1901-1976

French novelist and essayist.

Man's Fate (novel, 1933)

Based on the Shanghai insurrection of 1927, the novel takes place in China and follows a group of revolutionaries as they plot to control the city. Malraux's theme in this work is the solitude that distinguishes the human condition, and he draws his characters from a variety of national backgrounds and examines the political and personal differences which mark them as isolated, alienated beings. For them, revolution is a means by which they can transcend their lives and their feelings of despair.

As the novel opens, **Ch'en Ta Erh,** a Chinese terrorist, commits his first murder, a politically motivated act that he performs in order to seize the arms aboard the ship *Shantung* for the Communist forces. He is later congratulated by his fellow revolutionaries, **Kyo Gisors,** a man of French and Japanese descent, and **Katov,** a Russian insurrectionist. Kyo is married to a German doctor, **May,** and Kyo is tormented by May's confession of a love affair. In his depiction of their marriage Malraux focuses on the irreconcilable differences between lovers, as he does throughout the novel in the disparity between political comrades and enemies.

Kyo, Katov, and Ch'en are involved with various acts of sabotage that they hope will allow their forces to gain control over the city. Although there had initially been an alliance formed between the Communists and the forces of Chiang Kai-shek, plans change, and the revolutionaries are now engaged in an uprising from which they hope to emerge in power. When Chiang's forces reach the city, they take control; the Communists are ordered to surrender their weapons to Chiang, but many of them refuse and decide to fight on their own. Ch'en determines that he must kill Chiang, and he loses his own life as he throws himself under the general's car with a bomb. Chiang is not in the car and survives, ordering his police to capture and execute the revolutionaries. In prison, Katov gives Kyo his final capsule of cyanide, and as his friend dies, he knows he must face execution. *Man's Fate* is notable for its terse, reportorial style and for its finely delineated portraits of a group of committed revolutionaries who elucidate Malraux's theme of human solitude in the midst of political solidarity.

FURTHER READING

Boak, Denis. *André Malraux*. Oxford: Oxford University Press, 1968.

Contemporary Authors, Vols. 21-24, rev. ed., 69-72. *Contemporary Authors Permanent Series,* Vol. 2. Detroit: Gale Research Co.

Contemporary Literary Criticism, Vols. 1, 4, 9, 13, 15. Detroit: Gale Research Co.

Dictionary of Literary Biography, Vol. 72. Detroit: Gale Research Co.

Frank, Joseph. "André Malraux: The Image of Man." In *The Widening Gyre: Crisis and Mastery in Modern Literature,* pp. 105-30. New Brunswick: Rutgers University Press, 1963.

Gannon, Edward, S. J. *The Honor of Being a Man: The World of André Malraux.* Chicago: Loyola University Press, 1957.

David Mamet

1947-

American dramatist.

American Buffalo (drama, 1975)

American Buffalo, which is set in contemporary Chicago, explores the predatory and unethical nature of business in the United States and the deterioration of the American myth. **Donny Dubrow,** a small-time junk dealer, becomes convinced that one of his customers has cheated him out of a valuable Buffalo-head nickel. Enraged, he determines to recover his loss by stealing the man's coin collection, and enlists **Bobby,** a teenager who views him as a mentor, to spy on the customer's apartment. When **Walter Cole,** called **Teach,** a volatile crony, moves in on the break-in plan, he convinces Donny that Bobby can't be trusted to take part in the scheme. Donny concedes, but counters that Teach himself is ineffectual and brings in the street-smart **Fletcher** to serve as hit-man.

In Act II, tensions and ironies mount, as does mistrust and jealousy between Don, Bobby, and Teach, and in a series of mishaps and reversals the robbery plan unravels. Teach subsequently injures Bobby, while Don, blaming Teach for the robbery's failure, lashes out physically at him. Teach retaliates by destroying the junk-shop, and the play ends with him edgily and pitifully trying to secure Donny's forgiveness and approval.

Much of the structure and meaning of the play lie in Teach's vivid dialogue, in both its nervous, peculiarly American energy and the ironic contrast between his cliches about honor, friendship, and free enterprise, and his ruthless determination to get as big a cut as possible from the heist, and also to wrest from Bobby Don's undivided respect and loyalty. Critics note the irony of the American buffalo—reminiscent of the proud tradition of the American pioneering life and its inherent honor—as a central symbol in a play about petty greed and betrayal, which Mamet strongly implies is America's lot in contemporary life.

Glengarry Glen Ross (drama, 1984)

Like Mamet's earlier *American Buffalo,* this Pulitzer-Prize-winning play is set in contemporary Chicago and explores themes of American business and male relationships, featuring a plot that revolves around a robbery. Act I, which takes place in a Chinese restaurant, reveals a group of men who sell dubious undeveloped Florida real estate bearing such bucolic names as "Glengarry Highlands" and "Glen Ross Farms." They are upset by a recent office sales competition which will single out one winner and one runner-up—with the rest to be fired. **Shelley Levene,** untalented, over fifty, and desperate, unsuccessfully begs the office manager, **John Williamson,** for a better list of customer leads in order to save his job. **Dave Moss,** the contest runner-up, challenges another loser, **George Aaronow,** to steal the offices's bank of leads and sell them to a rival business, a suggestion Aaronow neither accepts nor rejects. The first act also introduces **Ricky Roma,** the top salesman, who in a virtual monologue reveals his business philosophy of doing "those things which seem correct to one *today.*" The play's second act occurs in the disheveled real-estate office, where the robbery has in fact occurred. It seems clear that Moss is behind it, but it is uncertain whether Aaronow did the breaking-in. To underscore the tension, a police detective, **Baylen,** is leading each man individually off-stage to interrogate him. Throughout the unbroken act, the bonds of friendship or mistrust between the various men are sharply focused; prominently revealed is the warm and admiring relationship between the sales star Roma and the hapless Levene. After a number of complex reversals among various salesmen, Levene misspeaks when defending Roma and unwittingly reveals himself as the robber. He thus is ruined professionally and personally, thrust forever both from the circle of his cronies and from his profession of salesman, which constitutes his principal source of identity.

As in *American Buffalo* and other Mamet plays, the dialogue in *Glengarry Glen Ross* creates the pace of the play and holds its meaning. In the salesmen's salty, rapid-fire discourses, particularly in their colorful ruminations on the soul and shady technique of American salesmanship, Mamet has been credited with creating a new language for the American theater.

FURTHER READING

Brustein, Robert. "Show and Tell." *The New Republic* 190, No. 18 (7 May 1984): 27-9.

Contemporary Authors, Vols. 81-84; *Contemporary Authors New Revision Series,* Vol. 15. Detroit: Gale Research Co.

Contemporary Literary Criticism, Vols. 9, 15, 34, 46. Detroit: Gale Research Co.

Dictionary of Literary Biography, Vol. 7. Detroit: Gale Research Co.

Eder, Richard. "David Mamet's New Realism." *New York Times* (12 March 1978): 40, 42, 45, 47.

Harvey, Stephen. "*Glengarry Glen Ross.*" *The Nation* 238, No. 16 (28 April 1984): 522-23.

Rich, Frank. "A Mamet Play: *Glengarry Glen Ross.*" *The New York Times* (26 March 1984): C17.

Storey, Robert. "The Making of David Mamet." *The Hollins Critic* 16, No. 4 (October 1979): 1-11.

Wetzsteon, Ross. *Village Voice* (5 July 1976): 101, 103-04.

Thomas Mann
1875-1955

German novelist, short story and novella writer, essayist, and critic.

Buddenbrooks (novel, 1901)

Set in the German town of Lübeck, this novel, published when Mann was only twenty-six, immediately established him as a major author. It is the story of four generations of the Buddenbrook family, spanning the years 1835 to 1877 and depicting the decline and fall of a prosperous bourgeois family. The novel contains the themes that were to resonate throughout Mann's fiction, including his concern with the forces of decadence, illness, and death and the isolation of the artist in modern culture.

The novel begins with the history of the successful patriarch of the family, **Johann Buddenbrook,** who has left his prosperous grain business to his son **Johann Buddenbrook, Jr.,** called Jean, a sensitive, religious, and family-oriented man. His half-brother, **Gotthold Buddenbrook,** the son of his father's first wife, lacks Jean's ambition and, ostracized from the family, becomes a shop owner and makes a poor marriage. But Jean has married the lively and beautiful **Elizabeth Kröger,** and their rich family life includes four children, **Antonie,** called Tony, **Thomas, Christian,** and **Clara.** Tony is an impetuous and high-spirited girl, given to childlike self-indulgence. She marries and divorces twice in her life, once to **Bendix Grunlich,** and once to **Alois Permaneder,** both of whom are more drawn to her money than to her. She is a rather shallow woman, very much concerned with the status of the Buddenbrook family.

Mann's theme of decay is evident in this generation, especially in the characters of Thomas and Christian. Thomas is clever and shrewd and takes over the family firm at his father's death. But he is depicted as detached and isolated from life. He is neither the practical businessman his grandfather was, nor is he an artistic dreamer, although he loves music and literature. Caught between two worlds, he begins to show signs of premature aging and to hate life. When he dies at the age of forty-nine, the firm, which had been losing money under his direction, is liquidated. Thomas's brother Christian is the first true embodiment of decadence presented in the novel. Dissolute and hypochondriacal, he avoids all business responsibilities, devoting himself instead to women and the theater. He is institutionalized by his wife, a former prostitute, when Thomas dies. Clara, quiet and deeply religious, dies of tuberculosis as a young woman.

Thomas had married the wealthy and talented **Gerda,** and with her had had a son, **Hanno,** who is the last and most stunning portrait of the family decadence. He is a fragile child from birth and is drawn, like his mother, to music, particularly the work of Wagner. Remote and isolated, dreamy and musical, Hanno exudes an air of self-destruction and longs for death. He dies at sixteen of typhoid fever, ending the dynasty.

This brilliant novel is noted for its atmosphere of life closely observed, presented with Mann's characteristic blend of irony, humor, and compassion. Long narrative passages are devoted to realistic description of people, their actions, and thoughts, rendered with precision and detachment. Mann's treatment of his recurrent subject of decadence is perhaps his greatest thematic achievement here, as he shows the emergence of the heightened, artistic sensibility that marks the decline of the family, beginning with Jean's religiosity, carried on in Christian's decadent lifestyle and Thomas's longing for death, then coming to full bloom and dying with Hanno.

Death in Venice (novella, 1913)

Considered Mann's finest achievement in the novella form, this work incorporates his familiar themes of decadence and the position of the artist in society. The work centers on the life of **Gustave von Aschenbach,** a German writer of great distinction whose life reflects the austere coldness of his prose. His work exemplifies the rigorous devotion to form and intellect and the willed neglect of the spontaneous and sensual, a fateful denial of the duality of human nature that leads to his self-destruction.

A widower living an isolated existence in Munich, Aschenbach is the child of two disparate parents, a motif that recurs in such later pieces as *Tonio Kröger;* his mother is the descendent of a musician and his father is from a distinguished line of judges. Thus, the dichotomy of discipline and licence that reverberates throughout this work and much of Mann's fiction is evident in Aschenbach's heritage. The detached, third-person narrator tells us that Aschenbach's typical hero is a figure of "intellectual and virginal manliness," whose decadence is shrouded in "aristocratic self-command," a description of Aschenbach himself and evidence of a narcissistic bent in his art that will have ramifications later.

Deciding to take a holiday in Venice, Aschenbach settles at the Hotel des Bains where he encounters **Tadzio,** a youth of fourteen who embodies for Aschenbach all the attributes of physical beauty found in Greek sculpture. Indeed, his skin is described as being marble-like and he is compared to Narcissus, yet he also appears to be fragile and sickly, one doomed to die young. Aschenbach falls in love with Tadzio, and although he at first plans to leave Venice for a healthier climate, he changes his mind, relinquishing control over his life and abandoning himself to his passion and to death. Throughout the novel, imagery of decadence portends the conclusion and reinforces the novel's themes: fruits are eaten in a state of "dead-ripeness," and stagnation and unclean air and water characterize the declining city of Venice. Aschenbach notes how this city had been an inspiration to painters and musicians, who responded with works marked by their "lusty" and "lascivious" qualities. Yet this same city harbors corruption in government as well, for we learn that cholera has been discovered and quietly covered up. Although Aschenbach sees signs of the pestilence in the declining number of tourists and has his fears confirmed, he prefers to stay in Venice. Nor does he take the chance to regain his self-respect by warning Tadzio and his family. He dyes his hair and wears makeup to attract the attentions of young Tadzio, whom he never touches and to whom he never speaks, preferring to follow him silently through the streets of Venice. Just before his death, Aschenbach has a vivid and horrifying dream in which men and women indulge in a Dionysian revel of lust, an orgy of excess that he knows is emblematic of his fall. On Tadzio's last day at the resort, Aschenbach watches him lovingly as he bathes in the sea, and from this vantage point the great author dies.

Death in Venice is one of the masterpieces of modern literature, and the work's richly suggestive themes, mythic symbolism, and elegant, controlled language have captivated readers for generations. An enigmatic work, it has elicited numerous interpretations and remains one of Mann's most allusive, eternally evocative fictions.

The Magic Mountain (novel, 1924)

Set in the International Sanatorium Berghof in Davos, Germany, the novel focuses on the life of **Hans Castorp.** A *bildungsroman* of sorts, the novel witnesses his coming of age, as he enters the institution a young, unformed man and emerges after seven years deeply changed. It is placed in a sanitorium for tuberculosis patients, reflecting Mann's recurring

256

themes of sickness and disease, this time presented as a metaphor for the decadence and isolation of Europe on the eve of the First World War.

Castorp goes to the sanitorium to visit his cousin, **Joachim Ziemssen** who is confined there, and plans to visit for only three weeks. But his stay turns into seven years; he learns that he has tuberculosis and must stay for treatment, but he is also lured to the "magic" of the sanitorium, a setting where time appears to stand still. His is a journey of the spirit, and in the company of several patients from the institute, he explores the various and conflicting aspects of human knowledge and experience that play such an important part in Mann's fiction.

One of his first acquaintances is **Ludovico Settembrini,** an Italian scholar who represents rationality, democracy, and humanistic philosophy. An encyclopedist, he embodies the spirit of reason that motivated the philosophers of the Enlightenment. He is Castorp's first teacher and is often depicted in verbal battle with **Leo Naphta,** who exemplifies antithesis and paradox. Born a Jew and a convert to Catholicism, he represents the mystical and irrational in life, continually at odds with Settembrini and with himself. Castorp's inauguration into the life of the senses comes through **Clavdia Chauchat,** a Russian woman who symbolizes sensual desire. She is a woman of intelligence and depth and remains distant from the protagonist after their one night of passion. Clavdia comes and goes from the sanitorium regularly and returns at one point with **Mynheer Peeperkorn,** a man once vital and representative of physical strength who has now succumbed to disease. He ends his life a suicide.

The novel is replete with the presence of death. After a quarrel which Naphta had provoked, Settembrini challenges him to a duel; instead of firing on his opponent, Naphta kills himself. Castorp's cousin Joachim also dies during the course of the novel, a victim of disease. Castorp himself manifests a strong fascination with death, as evidenced in his love of Schubert's well-known Romantic lieder "Der Lindenbaum," which contains a clear if understated death wish. Yet in the climax of the novel, in a section called "Snow," Castorp undergoes a transformation. Becoming lost in a snowstorm, he experiences a vision of "paradise and blood sacrifice," representing the Apollonian and Dionysian elements that figured so prominently in *Death in Venice* and illustrating the duality of human nature that need to be recognized and acknowledged, and which in his vision are reconciled. In this divination of the integrated life, Castorp is able to overcome his obsession with disease and death and to embrace life. It is a celebration of human love in which the dialectical positions of Settembrini and Naphta are rejected, the power of death over thought and action is abolished, and life is reaffirmed. But when he returns to the sanitorium, he has no memory of the dream; it is beyond his comprehension. We last see Castorp on the battlefield during World War I. His vision, unaccepted and unassimilated by a decadent world, cannot prevent the cataclysm of war.

This richly symbolic and powerful work was cited by the Nobel committee when Mann received the prize in literature in 1929. A profound presentation of the themes of the duality of human nature and the antithetical philosophies of humankind in which they are perpetuated, the novel ends with a world at war, but only after Mann has presented a vision of affirmation. He presents the novel through the voice of an ironic, third-person narrator, and his realistic prose portrays a fictional life closely observed.

Doctor Faustus (novel, 1947)

This dark and pessimistic novel relates Mann's tortured statement on the fate of his nation during World War II. It recounts the story of **Adrian Leverkühn,** a composer who believes he has sold his soul to the devil in return for the gift of creativity. Narrated by his friend **Serenus Zeitblom** after his death, the work evokes three levels of time: the time in which Zeitblom composes the biography (1943-1945) while the war in Europe rages on; the life span of the protagonist (1885-1940); and the sixteenth century, the era which produced the first known source of the Faust legend. These layers of time merge in the present, in the barbarity, anti-intellectualism, and anti-cultural stance professed by the Nazis and their followers.

Adrian is born in Buchel and is described as a cold, proud young man. He first studies theology, then is drawn to music, particularly through the influence of **Wendell Kretschmar,** his music teacher. Kretschmar exercises a great authority over his pupil and introduces him to the theories of Schönberg, whose twelve-tone scale is adopted by the aspiring young composer. Yet Adrian is also shown to be thwarted by the rich musical tradition of Germany, and, cowed by the past and afraid of losing his artistic creativity, he sells his soul to the devil. His actual meeting with Satan is clouded with ambiguity: it takes place in Palestrina, Italy, and appears to be a hallucination. Yet Adrian is convinced of its existence and efficacy. Like the legendary Faust, with whom he identifies strongly, the pact is to last for twenty-four years. In a work that unifies the themes of music, decadence, and death, Mann has his protagonist encounter a prostitute, **Esmeralda,** with whom he spends one night, even though he knows she is infected with syphilis. Through his contact with contagion, Adrian's creative powers are further engendered.

Adrian's music is admired and praised by a select group of musicians and critics, but the public finds his work to be cold and inaccessible, reflecting the character of its creator. Indeed, his detachment and isolation colors all of his contact with others. His friendship with **Rudolf Schwerdtfeger,** a violinist for whom he writes a violin concerto, has distinctly homoerotic overtones, and Adrian is responsible for sending Rudi to his death at the hands of a jealous woman. The only person for whom he feels deep affection is his young nephew **Nepo.** Nepo's death at the age of five deprives Adrian of the last vestige of human love.

Adrian gathers his friends for the performance of his final and greatest work, an oratorio entitled "The Lamentation of Dr. Faustus." Here, he relates to them his pact with the devil, which he believes inspired the work. As the piece begins, he suffers a stroke from which he never recovers.

The decline and fall of Leverkühn is paralleled to that of Nazi Germany. The novel's tragic tone reflects the author's own horror and despair at the destruction of his country, and is an indictment of the German people, who allowed the perversion and evil of the Nazis to flourish, and who, in a sense, made a pact with the forces of evil and paid for it with their souls. Adrian's madness spans ten years, an analogy to the years in which Germany was in the grip of the Third Reich. The novel contains many digressive sections, where Mann discusses music theory and the works of great composers at length. *Dr. Faustus,* Mann's last major novel, is considered one of his most complex and somber works.

FURTHER READING

Apter, T. E. *Thomas Mann: The Devil's Advocate.* London: Macmillan, 1978.

Contemporary Authors, Vol. 104. Detroit: Gale Research Co.

Dyson, A. E. "The Stranger God: Mann's *Death in Venice.*" In *Between Two Worlds: Aspects of Literary Form,* pp. 81-99. London: Macmillan, 1972.

Hatfield, Henry. *Thomas Mann.* Norfolk: New Directions, 1962.

Hatfield, Henry, ed. *Thomas Mann: A Collection of Critical Essays.* Englewood Cliffs: Prentice-Hall, 1964.

Heller, Erich. *The Ironic German: A Study of Thomas Mann.* London: Secker and Warburg, 1958.

Hollingdale, R. J. *Thomas Mann: A Critical Study.* Lewisburg: Bucknell University Press, 1971.

Kaufmann, Fritz. *Thomas Mann: The World as Will and Representation.* Boston: Beacon Press, 1957.

Lovett, Robert Morss. *"Buddenbrooks."* In *Preface to Fiction: A Discussion of Great Modern Novels,* pp. 81-96. Chicago: Thomas S. Rockwell, 1931.

Mann, Thomas. "The Making of *The Magic Mountain."* In *The Magic Mountain,* translated by H. T. Lowe-Porter, pp. 710-29. New York: Knopf, 1958.

Nemerov, Howard. "Thomas Mann's Faust Novel." In *Poetry and Fiction: Essays,* pp. 303-15. New Brunswick: Rutgers University Press, 1963.

Reed, T. J. *Thomas Mann: The Uses of Tradition.* Oxford: Oxford at the Clarendon Press, 1974.

Swales, Martin. *Thomas Mann: A Study.* Totowa: Rowman and Littlefield, 1980.

Thomas, R. Hinton. *Thomas Mann: The Mediation of Art.* Oxford: Oxford at the Clarendon Press, 1963.

Twentieth-Century Literary Criticism, Vols. 2, 8, 14, 21. Detroit: Gale Research Co.

Peter Matthiessen

1927-

American novelist and essayist.

Far Tortuga (novel, 1975)

This novel, hailed as Matthiessen's most impressive work of fiction, takes place aboard the decrepit schooner *Lillias Eden* and details her final voyage. The nine crew members, headed by **Captain Raib Avers,** includes Avers son, **Jim Eden Avers, William Parchment, Byrum Watler, Wodie Greaves, Vemon Evers, Athens Ebanks, Junior Bodden,** and **Miguel Moreno Smith.** They come from various places in the Caribbean and are an assortment of petty thieves and drunks, semi-literate and rough-hewn. These men become known to us not through their thoughts, but through their speech, for Matthiessen presents the book almost completely as dialogue between the crew members, with occasional third-person narration. The speakers are not identified, and the reader learns to distinguish each man by the cadences of his individual speech. The work presents a unique typographic design, for Matthiessen incorporates large amounts of white space between descriptions or conversations, creating large intervals between blocks of text.

The voyage of the *Lillias Eden* begins in the Cayman Islands, one of the last remaining unspoiled areas of the Caribbean. In this setting, Matthiessen explores the end of a way of life threatened by the world of progress that has irrevocably changed the West Indies. The ship is bound for the turtle fishing areas of the Caribbean, and the narrative follows the men in their daily lives, invoking the boredom and repetition of their tasks, occasionally enlivened by outbursts of anger or a sea of turtles. As they speak, we learn about their lives and about the primitive brotherhood that binds these men to the sea. Their conversations are imbued with the legends of the sea—shipwrecks, sea lore, and the tales of the Far Tortuga, an uncharted cay in the Misteriosa Reefs from which ships and men never return. Through their dialogue we also learn about the captain, an uncompromising individualist, quick to anger and driven by a complex mixture of greed and indomitable will. In the novel's climax, the ship hits an uncharted rock. One by one the men die off, each death marked by a black blotch on the page, as the narrative trails off into a fragment of description.

The novel is noted for its stylistic innovation and for the poetic quality of its descriptive passages. Unlike many tales of the sea, it does not bear a heavy allegorical message, for Matthiessen does not try to portray a ''ship of fools,'' or to give the lives of the men an epic quality. His intent is perhaps best understood by the epigraph of the book, ascribed to Everyman, which speaks of death come too soon, for this story tells of a group of ordinary men and the universal forces that lead them to their deaths.

FURTHER READING

Contemporary Authors, Vols. 9-12, rev. ed.; *Contemporary Authors New Revision Series,* Vol. 21. Detroit: Gale Research Co.

Contemporary Literary Criticism, Vols. 5, 7, 11, 32. Detroit: Gale Research Co.

Dictionary of Literary Biography, Vol. 6. Detroit: Gale Research Co.

Edwards, Thomas R. *''Far Tortuga.''* The New York Review of Books (7 August 1975): 34-5.

Kennedy, William. ''Sea Spun Tale.'' *The New Republic* (7 June 1975): 28-30.

Styron, William. ''Portraits and Farewells: Peter Matthiessen.'' In *This Quiet Dust and Other Writings,* pp. 249-52. New York: Random House, 1982.

W. Somerset Maugham
1874-1965
English novelist, dramatist, and short story writer.

Of Human Bondage (novel, 1915)

The novel, considered Maugham's finest work, takes place in the early twentieth century and focuses on the life of **Philip Carey.** As the novel opens, his mother dies and he is left an orphan. He is a lonely, sensitive child, whose club foot symbolizes both his isolation and the impediment that keeps him from truly loving and being loved. He is raised by relatives, whose stupidity and hypocrisy he links to their narrow-minded, Puritanical values. As a young man, Philip is consumed with learning about life; he studies medicine and art and engages in endless conversations with his friends on philosophical issues. His relationships with women are all characterized by a lack of reciprocity: he loves women who are unable to return his feelings and is loved by those whose devotion he can never reciprocate. Of these tortuous relationships, perhaps the most important is with **Mildred Rogers,** who cruelly exploits Philip's obsession for her, draining him emotionally and financially.

The ''bondage'' of the title is a recurrent theme in Maugham's work, and here it represents the bonds that love relationships as well as societal convention and morality place on the individual. In the novel's conclusion, Philip has learned that his mistress, **Sally Athelney,** is going to have a child, and he feels his life of freedom threatened. Faced with her pregnancy, he is forced to reevaluate his life. He had always been concerned with ''the figure in the carpet,'' to create ''a design, intricate and beautiful, out of the myriad, meaningless facts of life.'' Yet with Sally, he is at last willing to accept a more simple pattern of marriage, children, the course of life and death. Although it turns out that Sally is not pregnant, Philip asks her to marry him anyway, for through her he has learned to ''surrender to happiness''; no longer obsessed with the future, he is at last content to live in the present, free of bondage.

An avowedly autobiographical work, the novel is noted for its straightforward, realistic prose style and its depiction of the alienation, isolation, and final transformation of the central character.

FURTHER READING

Brander, Laurence. *Somerset Maugham: A Guide*. Edinburgh: Oliver & Boyd, 1963.

Brown, Ivor W. *Somerset Maugham*. London: International Textbook, 1970.

Contemporary Authors, Vols. 5-8, rev. ed., 25-28, rev. ed. Detroit: Gale Research Co.

Contemporary Literary Criticism, Vols. 1, 11, 15. Detroit: Gale Research Co.

Curtis, Anthony. *The Pattern of Maugham: A Critical Portrait*. New York: Taplinger, 1974.

Dictionary of Literary Biography, Vols. 10, 36. Detroit: Gale Research Co.

Mary McCarthy
1912-
American novelist, short story writer, and essayist.

The Group (novel, 1963)

The novel takes place largely in New York City and covers the years 1933 to 1940. **Kay Strong Petersen,** the protagonist, is a member of a "group" of Vassar graduates that includes **Elinor Eastlake, Libby MacAusland, Mary Prothero, Dottie Renfrew, Helena Davison, Polly Andrews,** and **Priss Hartshorn.** McCarthy chronicles their lives, with Kay at the center, from their graduation to Kay's death. One week after graduating, Kay marries **Harold Petersen,** a melancholy and egotistical man and an unsuccessful playwright. Their marriage seems doomed from the start: neither of them profess to love the other, for they are too modern and "progressive" for that. Throughout the novel, McCarthy parodies the belief in progress shared by all the characters. Whether discussing marriage, child-rearing or sex, the characters recite the findings of the modern experts and fashion their attitudes accordingly. They also believe in the importance of material well-being, and the work sometimes reads like a catalog of upper-class materialism, focussing on clothes, food, luggage, all the trappings of financial success. The work has gained a certain notoriety for its handling of sexuality, but here, too, McCarthy satirizes the then-current attitudes toward sex, particularly in her depiction of Dottie Renfrew's first sexual encounter. McCarthy's penchant for detailed description—used throughout the novel in describing such things as furniture, recipes, and kitchen gadgetry—is here used to comically describe the liaison and later the birth-control paraphernalia Dottie purchases.

As Kay's marriage deteriorates, she suffers a nervous breakdown, divorces Harold, and leaves New York. After a year's convalescence, she returns, and, while leaning out of a window trying to identify an airplane, she falls to her death. The nature of Kay's death remains a mystery, and whether it was accidental or intentional is never established. The novel's conclusion reunites the group for Kay's funeral.

McCarthy's novel has often been misread as a realistic depiction of a representative group of women from a specific era and class, and yet she herself has stressed that the work is a satire and the characters are comic. As such, there is little of the character development that one would associate with more traditionally written novels. Instead, McCarthy uses the work to expose the folly of the belief in progress: in technology, reason, and the faith in material well-being that dominate her characters.

FURTHER READING

Contemporary Authors, Vols. 5-8, rev. ed.; *Contemporary Authors New Revision Series,* Vol. 16. Detroit: Gale Research Co.

Contemporary Literary Criticism, Vols. 1, 3, 5, 14, 24, 39. Detroit: Gale Research Co.

Dictionary of Literary Biography, Vol. 2; *Dictionary of Literary Biography Yearbook: 1981.* Detroit: Gale Research Co.

Niebuhr, Elizabeth. "The Art of Fiction XXVII: Mary McCarthy." *Paris Review* 27 (Winter-Spring 1962): 58-94.

Showalter, Elaine. "Killing the Angel in the House: The Autonomy of Women Writers." *Antioch Review* 32 (Fall 1973): 339-53.

Stock, Irvin. *Mary McCarthy.* Minneapolis: University of Minnesota Press, 1968.

Carson McCullers

1917-1967

American novelist, short story writer, poet, and playwright.

The Heart Is a Lonely Hunter (novel, 1943)

The setting for the novel is a small Southern town in the late 1930s. **John Singer** is a deaf-mute who is the confidant of a group of lonely and unhappy denizens of the town. Elucidating McCullers's recurrent theme of isolation, these characters—**Biff Branner,** a restaurant owner, **Jack Blount,** a political radical, **Benedict Mady Copeland,** a black doctor, and **Mick Kelly,** a young adolescent girl—seek out a man who can neither hear nor respond to their individual pain. Singer's closest companion is another mute, **Antonapoulos,** who is slowly losing his wits, and whom he loves with unrequited passion. When Antonapoulos dies, Singer commits suicide, left alone and without love. The characters who depended on him as an outlet for their despair are bereft of their solace.

Mick Kelly is one of McCullers's finest portraits of an adolescent enduring the traumas of maturity and closely resembles Frankie Addams of *Member of the Wedding.* She is a twelve-year-old tomboy, and like the other characters of the novel is isolated by her yearning and lonely nature. The novel chronicles her initiation into the world of adulthood. Her first sexual experience is with the boy next door, and this event creates more confusion, for Mick is ambivalent about the experience and not sure that she wants to accept the female role. As her boy's name indicates, she symbolizes the sexual ambiguity that characterizes so many McCullers figures. Her adolescent isolation gives way to the knowledge that adulthood promises only more of the same: the human condition is the condition of loneliness.

As in so much of her work, McCullers here uses grotesque figures, the mute and the mad, whose outward deformities symbolize the agonizing isolation of human beings. John Singer embodies her recurrent theme of the yearning for love, and the pain of loving another incapable of reciprocating. Similarly, the characters who surround Singer pour out their hearts, seeking love and understanding, yet incapable of giving and receiving love. Stylistically, the work is characterized by McCullers's simple, unadorned prose style. The motif of music resonates throughout the novel, and the characters unburden themselves to Singer in a series of monologues that McCullers presents in a fugal, contrapuntal fashion, revealing again the isolation and lack of communication between her characters.

The Ballad of the Sad Café (novella, 1943)

The work is set in a remote Southern town and tells the story of an unusual love triangle . **Miss Amelia Evans** is a cold and lonely woman whose estranged husband, **Marvin Macy,** is in prison. **Cousin Lymon,** a hunchbacked dwarf, befriends her, pretending to be her cousin. Amelia is drawn to Lymon, whom she grows to love. In turn, he brings out in her the warmth and affection so contrary to her former nature. At his urging, she opens the café of the title, which becomes a warm, congenial gathering place for the local townspeople. Macy returns from prison, full of anger and contempt for his unloving wife. Lymon falls passionately in love with Macy, and a battle ensues between husband and wife for the affection of the dwarf. Amelia and Macy engage in a grotesque arm wrestling match, which Amelia loses. In response, Macy and Lymon revenge Macy's hatred for Amelia by destroying the café. Amelia closes the café, and we see her in the novel's conclusion sitting behind closed blinds, with her eyes crossing.

Once again, McCullers creates a group of grotesque figures to symbolize her major theme of the isolation of the individual and the inability of human beings to give and receive love. The work takes its shape from the ballad of the title: imbued with elements of fairy tale and folklore, the novella reveals a world of exaggerated characters and action. The town is depicted as an isoalted outpost, estranged form the real world. Of critical importance to McCullers's design is her use of an objective narrator, who is a realistic yet compassionate onlooker and whose impressions are rendered in McCullers's lyrical prose.

Member of the Wedding (novel, 1946)

Frankie Addams is the main character of McCullers's second novel, a work considered one of her finest efforts and which she adapted as a successful stage play.

Set in a small Southern town, the novel chronicles Frankie's painful adolescence and entry into adulthood. Like Mick Kelly of *The Heart Is a Lonely Hunter,* Frankie is a twelve-year-old tomboy suffering from the pain and loneliness of adolescence. The two friends who share the burden of her isolation are **Berenice Sadie Brown,** the family's black cook who acts as both mother and confessor to Frankie, and **John Henry,** Frankie's six-year-old cousin. Much of the novel takes place in the kitchen of Frankie's home, where the three are constantly engaged in conversation. Frankie wants desperately to belong and to lose her sense of loneliness, so she decides to become a member of her brother Jarvis's wedding to Janice Williams. So intent is she on becoming one with the couple that she changes her name to "F. Jasmine" so that her name will more closely match theirs and also insists that she will accompany them on their honeymoon. Berenice tries to convince Frankie that she must learn to be herself, to which Frankie responds that she wants to be "the we of me." However, over the course of the novel Frankie does indeed mature, facing the death of her beloved young cousin and finally becoming "Frances" by the novel's conclusion, indicative of her acceptance of her role as a young woman.

Frankie is considered one of McCullers's most charming and likeable characters, although some critics find her more believable before her transformation in the conclusion. Although the novel harkens back to McCullers's earlier works in its treatment of the essential loneliness of human beings, it reveals a greater warmth of tone and a more hopeful approach to character and theme.

FURTHER READING

Carr, Virginia Spencer. *The Lonely Hunter: A Biography of Carson McCullers.* Garden City: Doubleday, 1975.

Contemporary Authors, Vols. 5-8, rev. ed., 25-28, rev. ed.; *Contemporary Authors New Revision Series,* Vol. 18; *Contemporary Authors Bibliographical Series,* Vol. 1. Detroit: Gale Research Co.

Contemporary Literary Criticism, Vols. 1, 4, 10, 12. Detroit: Gale Research Co.

Dictionary of Literary Biography, Vols. 2, 7. *Concise Dictionary of American Literary Biography, 1941-1968.* Detroit: Gale Research Co.

Durham, Frank. "God and No God in *The Heart Is a Lonely Hunter.*" *South Atlantic Quarterly* 56 (Autumn 1957): 494-99.

Evans, Oliver. *The Ballad of Carson McCullers.* New York: Coward-McCann, 1966.

Gossett, Louise Y. "Dispossessed Love: Carson McCullers." In *Violence in Recent Southern Fiction,* pp. 159-77. Durham: Duke University Press, 1965.

Griffith, Albert J. "Carson McCullers's Myth of the Sad Café." *Georgia Review* 21 (Spring 1967): 46-56.

Hamilton, Alice. "Loneliness and Alienation: The Life and Work of Carson McCullers." *Dalhousie Review* 50 (Summer 1970): 215-29.

Hassan, Ihab. "Carson McCullers: The Alchemy of Love and Aesthetics of Pain." *Modern Fiction Studies* 5 (Winter 1959-1960): 311-26.

McNally, John. "The Introspective Narrator in *The Ballad of the Sad Café.*" *South Atlantic Bulletin* 38 (November 1973): 40-4.

Rubin, Louis D., Jr. "Carson McCullers: The Aesthetic of Pain." *Virginia Quarterly Review* 53 (Spring 1977): 265-83.

Wikborg, Eleanor. *The Member of the Wedding: Aspects of Structure and Style.* Atlantic Highlands: Humanities Press, 1975.

Thomas McGuane

1939-

American novelist.

Ninety-Two in the Shade (novel, 1973)

"Nobody knows, from sea to shining sea, why we are having all this trouble with our republic." Thus begins McGuane's novel, set in the Florida Keys and relating the story of **Thomas Skelton,** a disillusioned young man who becomes a fishing guide to escape the banality and ruin of modern life. He is weary of "Hotcakesland," McGuane's metaphor for modern America, a place where life has lost its meaning and values have been replaced by a constant yearning for material goods. In the Keys, Skelton meets **Nichol Dance,** also a guide, but a representative of the natural man, unspoiled by contact with the corruption of American culture. When Dance plays a practical joke on Skelton, Skelton responds by blowing up his boat. Furious, Dance warns Skelton that he will kill him if he ever tries to guide a fishing tour again. Skelton confronts him, and in the melee that ensues, loses his life in a battle described with ritualistic overtones.

As in much of his fiction, McGuane explores the ethos behind modern man in this novel, examining male relationships, aggression, and competitiveness with humor and satire. Critics have noted how, in his bleak parody of modern life, McGuane mocks the Hemingway code of machismo, of men remaking themselves through the challenge of the wilderness. Skelton is a young man on a journey of self-knowledge, looking for meaning in his life and trying to find something to do with himself; why he chooses to become a fishing guide rather than to channel his energies and talents in a more traditional way is central to McGuane's purpose, for his protagonist rejects an America riddled with hypocrisy and a faded sense of self-worth. The novel is noted for its satirical tone and detailed description, both of the lush beauty of the Keys and the outward trappings of the good life in materialistic America.

FURTHER READING

Carter, Albert Howard III. "Thomas McGuane's First Three Novels: Games, Fun, Nemesis." *Critique* 17, No. 1 (August 1975): 91-104.

Contemporary Authors, Vol. 49-52; *Contemporary Authors New Revision Series,* Vol. 5. Detroit: Gale Research Co.

Contemporary Literary Criticism, Vols. 3, 7, 18. Detroit: Gale Research Co.

Dictionary of Literary Biography, Vol. 2; *Dictionary of Literary Biography Yearbook: 1980.* Detroit: Gale Research Co.

Katz, Donald R. "Thomas McGuane: Heroes in 'Hotcakesland.'" *The New Republic* 181, No. 7 (18 August 1970): 38-9.

Sissman, L. E. "Living by the Sword." *The New Yorker* (23 June 1973): 88-9.

Larry McMurtry

1936-

American novelist and essayist.

The Last Picture Show (novel, 1966)

The novel is set in the fictional town of Thalia, Texas, and relates the story of **Sonny Crawford** coming of age in a small town. Through Sonny's adolescent yearnings, we see the suffocating loneliness that characterizes life in Thalia. A central focus for the town's teenagers is the movie theater, which is the source for their conceptions of sex, love, and beauty, and which offers a brief respite from the stultifying atmosphere of small-town life.

Sonny and his friend **Duane Jackson** share a passion for a young woman named **Jacy Farrow,** and the novel chronicles their awkwardness in dealing with their first feelings of love and sexual awareness. The sense of anxiety and alienation inherent in this experience is revealed in such scenes as Duane's and Jacy's evening in a motel and the visit Sonny and Duane pay to a Mexican bordello. The bittersweet wisdom gained by sexual experience is also revealed in Sonny's brief affairs with two older woman, Jacy's mother and **Ruth Popper,** the wife of the school coach. McMurtry notes how even the adults are so oppressed with the feeling of alienation and boredom that permeates the town that they, too, seek escape through sex. Jacy's mother had once had an affair with a legendary figure in the community, **Sam the Lion,** who is a paternal presence for both Sonny and Duane. In the conclusion, several events point to the death of the decaying town: Sam dies, the movie theater is closed, and Duane leaves his childhood behind as he goes to Korea and the world of war.

The novel is rendered through an omniscient narrator, who reveals the varying points of view given by the main characters. The novel is noted for its vivid recreation of adolescence and compassionate portrayal of the deadening effects of small-town life on the sensitive psyche of its protagonist.

Terms of Endearment (novel, 1975)

The novel is set in Houston, Texas, and focuses on the life of **Aurora Greenway,** a lively, garrulous, and often over-bearing woman. She can be rude, affectionate, or funny, overwhelming the defenses of friends, lovers, and family. A widow in her late forties without any intention of marrying again, she entertains a group of aging, rather sad suitors who seem both captivated and puzzled at her character.

The novel centers on the relationship between Aurora and her daughter, **Emma Horton.** Emma is married to a pedestrian English professor with a penchant for young students. When she becomes pregnant and relates the news to her mother, Aurora is horrified. Vain and fearful of aging, Aurora feels her youth is in jeopardy at the thought of becoming a grandmother. During the novel's second half, Emma bears three more children, including a daughter, **Melanie,** who appears to have inherited her grandmother's spirit. When Melanie is three, Emma learns she has cancer. She faces death with strength and resignation and attempts to come to terms with her mother, husband, and each of her children as the end nears. A Renoir painting that Aurora had inherited from her mother becomes a symbol for the illusion of youth in the book. Aurora had used it to escape the reality of her own aging at the time of Emma's first pregnancy, and the painting now hangs in Emma's hospital room, where it serves as a release from the world of death and provides an escape to a world of timeless youth, beauty, and ease.

The novel is noted for the sensitive, effective portrayals of mother and daughter and for its portrait of strength in confronting and accepting loss.

Lonesome Dove (novel, 1985)

This novel, for which McMurtry was awarded the Pulitzer Prize, begins in the 1870s in the town of Lonesome Dove, Texas, where two retired Texas Rangers, **Augustus McCrae** and **Woodrow Call,** are the owners of a livery stable and ranch. Gus is portrayed as a lazy, loveable man, a nonstop talker given to whiskey and reminiscence. Call, stiff and taciturn, is a withdrawn and unhappy personality. Together they embody the mythic characteristics of the American cowboy, and their story is an epic saga of the West. **Jake Spoon,** an old friend and fellow Ranger who is on the run from the law, appears at the ranch and talks the two into taking part in a cattle drive to Montana. With their days as Rangers, Indian fighters and cattle rustlers behind them, Call and Gus decide to take part in the new adventure.

The epic sweep of the narrative carries the reader across the American West, where the characters encounter experiences seemingly drawn from myth and folklore, battling natural and human elements including snowstorms, sandstorms, locust swarms, an attack of water moccasins, hostile Indians, and gunfighters. McMurtry employs a number of subplots with characters drawn from the Old West: cowboys, Indians, settlers, gamblers, U.S. Cavalry troops, and backwoodsmen people the broad canvas of the novel. Danger and violence prevail in the West, as is evident in the brutal deaths and atrocities chronicled in the novel. While the narrative and the characterization sometimes threaten to collapse into the cliches familiar to the Western, McMurtry imbues his material with a freshness and reality that defies the narrow scope of stereotype.

McMurtry is admired for his handling of female characters, and in this book **Lorena Wood** and **Clara Allen,** the two women in Gus's life, have been singled out for praise. Lorena is another character with seemingly stereotypical origins, for she is the whore with a heart of gold. She travels with the cattle drive in hopes of reaching San Francisco, an emblem to her of happiness. Her relationship with Gus is deeply and warmly evoked. Clara's independence is in vivid contrast to Lorena's sensuality. Like Gus, she is a character molded by the land, and she is a settler of the wilderness, fiercely independent.

The novel traces the transformation of Gus and Call into heroic figures, for as they are confronted with adversity, hardship, and death, they act with the dignity and strength that distinguish them as heroes. The work is noted for its laconic prose style and vivid dialogue.

FURTHER READING

Contemporary Authors, Vols. 5-8, rev. ed.; *Contemporary Authors New Revision Series,* Vol. 19. Detroit: Gale Research Co.

Contemporary Literary Criticism, Vols. 2, 3, 7, 11, 27, 44. Detroit: Gale Research Co.

Dictionary of Literary Biography, Vol. 2; *Dictionary of Literary Biography Yearbook: 1980.* Detroit: Gale Research Co.

Goodwyn, Larry. "The Frontier Myth and Southwestern Literature." In *Regional Perspectives: An Examination of America's Literary Heritage,* edited by John Gordon Burke, pp. 175-207. Chicago: American Library Association, 1973.

Landess, Thomas. *Larry McMurtry.* Austin: Steck-Vaughn, 1969.

Lemann, Nicholas. "Tall in the Saddle." *The New York Times Book Review* (9 June 1985): 7.

Peavy, Charles D. "Coming of Age in Texas: The Novels of Larry McMurtry." *Western American Literature* 4 (Fall 1969): 171-88.

Perrin, Noel. "Larry McMurtry's Western Epic." *Book World—The Washington Post* (9 June 1985): 1, 13.

Phillips, Raymond C., Jr. "The Ranch as Place and Symbol in the Novels of Larry McMurtry." *South Dakota Review* 13, No. 2 (1975): 27-47.

Reynolds, R. C. "Trilogy-Adventures Rounded Out." *Southwest Review* (Winter 1976): 102-05.

Sewell, Ernestine P. "McMurtry's Cowboy-God in *Lonesome Dove.*" *Western American Literature* 21, No. 3 (November 1986): 219-25.

Towers, Robert. *"Terms of Endearment." The New York Times Book Review* (19 October 1975): 4.

George Meredith
1828-1908
English novelist and essayist.

The Egoist (novel, 1879)

In this novel, widely considered Meredith's finest work, he humorously conveys the dangers of excessive egoism as revealed in the fate of his protagonist, **Sir Willoughby Patterne.** Meredith believed that comedy had a positive effect on the social good, for it allowed readers to identify with and laugh at a character's folly as if it were their own. The work is in part a satire on the philosophy of John Stuart Mill, who posited that an individual's actions should be unfettered as long as they did no harm to others. Through Sir Willoughby's despotic dominance of the other characters, we see how he has been allowed—through the self-delusion, distortion, and isolation of his egoism—to deprive them of their individuality and their freedom. The novel portrays the growing vanity of Sir Willoughby and the joining of forces among the other characters to thwart his tyrannical authority.

The novel takes place on Sir Willoughby's estate, where he is shown to control the fate of all the characters. Slowly we see his true character revealed. He is first jilted by **Constantia Durham,** who abandons him to marry another shortly before their wedding. He next becomes betrothed to **Clara Middleton,** whose father, **The Reverend Dr. Middleton,** encourages the match, although whether for Clara's benefit or for his proximity to Patterne's fine wine cellar and book collection we are not sure. Clara gains insight into the man she would marry, discovering that behind the forceful personality she is attracted to is a pompous, duplicitous man whose snobbery, pretense, and manipulative qualities begin to repel her. Deciding she must break the engagement, she enlists the help of **Vernon Whitford,** who is willing to assist not only because he loves Clara but also because he sees in Patterne's treatment of his impoverished relation **Crossjay Patterne** the machinations of an aggressive, tyrannical force. Crossjay is also the concern of **Laetitia Dale,** who has been in love with Patterne for years. She is also poor, eking out a living as a writer on the Patterne estate where she cares for her aging father and teaches young Crossjay. She is a kind and long-suffering soul who eventually wearies of her continual support for the monstrous Patterne; indeed, when Clara finally rejects him, it is Laetitia he turns to, but he no longer holds her in his sway. She now knows him for what he is, and she despises him. She will agree to be his wife, but only on her own terms. Chastened, Patterne agrees; under Laetitia's hand, we imagine that the reformation of the egoist is underway in the conclusion.

The novel is noted for its fine dialogue, well-paced plot, and ironic, third-person narrator. In addition to revealing the dangers of egoism, Meredith turned in this work to a theme that resonates throughout his fiction, the constricted role of women in Victorian society.

FURTHER READING

Contemporary Authors, Vol. 117. Detroit: Gale Research Co.

Dictionary of Literary Biography, Vols. 18, 35, 37. Detroit: Gale Research Co.

Handwerk, Gary J. "Linguistic Blindness and Ironic Vision in *The Egoist.*" *Nineteenth-Century Fiction* 39, No. 2 (September 1984): 163-85.

Twentieth-Century Literary Criticism, Vol. 17. Detroit: Gale Research Co.

Wilt, Judith. *The Readable People of George Meredith.* Princeton: Princeton University Press, 1975.

Wright, Walter F. *Art and Substance in George Meredith: A Study in Narrative.* Lincoln: University of Nebraska Press, 1953.

Arthur Miller

1915-

American dramatist, essayist, and short story writer.

All My Sons (drama, 1947)

The drama is set in America in World War II. **Joe Keller** is an airplane component manufacturer whose company has sold defective parts to the Air Force, resulting in the deaths of American pilots. Keller is a man whose greed and pride overwhelm his sense of social responsibility, and he lets his business partner go to jail for the crime and takes the company over himself. **Chris,** one of his two sons, is an idealistic young man and a war hero. He is convinced that one must adhere to the truth at all costs; however, his own hypocrisy will allow him to work for his father, even though he knows his father is responsible for the deaths of innocent men. The family is shattered by the news that Joe's other son, **Larry,** is missing in action. The full horror of the situation is revealed in a letter Larry has written to his former girlfriend, now Chris's fiance: he tells her that because of his father's complicity in the deaths of his fellow soldiers, he plans to take his own life. Joe is destroyed by the revelation, and he, too, commits suicide.

This drama presages many of Miller's later works, both thematically and stylistically. The theme of social responsibility and the importance of the individual's moral stance recurs in such later works as *The Crucible* . The often tortured nature of relationships between fathers and sons is explored in several of Miller's works, most notably *Death of a Salesman*. The play's language is simple and naturalistic, a style of dialogue that Miller was also to use to great effect in several subsequent works.

Death of a Salesman (drama, 1949)

The play is set in Brooklyn, New York. **Willy Loman** is a salesman whose career is nearly over. The play is given in a combination of flashbacks, dream sequences, and contemporary action as Willy reviews his life. He is a man whose life has been devoted to the dream of success. His boys, **Biff** and **Happy,** are the objects of his unbridled adoration, and it had always been his intent to leave them with enough money to begin their own business. Yet Willy's dreams and his life itself are based on self-deception. Despite the flamboyant, exaggerated stories of his successes, his career as a salesman has been mediocre, and he is fired from his position early in the play.

His sons have never fulfilled their father's dreams of achievement. Biff, who had been a high school athlete, cheated on exams to get through school and is refused admission to a good college for failing a math class. Happy is a salesman like his father, and, like his father, a failure and a womanizer. Both of the boys engage in petty thefts in their jobs, furthering the undercurrent of deception in the play. In a pivotal scene, the boys have planned to meet their father in a restaurant, which was to have been the scene of triumph, with Biff announcing that he had found a financial backer for a sporting goods business. However, there is no backer, and the two sons desert their father and leave with two women. This brings about a final, tortuous argument between Biff and Willy, in which Biff confronts his father with his failure as a salesman and as a husband, for Biff has seen through his father's masks and has accidently witnessed one of his father's extramarital affairs, all of which bring home to him the atmosphere of lies and self deception that mark the family. Yet Biff and Willy eventually reconcile. Willy is determined to go ahead with his plan to commit suicide, providing Biff with the money from a life insurance policy to start the store. In the conclusion, Willy has killed himself in a car accident, and his funeral, unlike the lavish, well-attended affair he had dreamed of, consists of his family and one neighbor, a man he had always treated with contempt and condescension.

As in *All My Sons,* Miller here continues his examination of the father/son relationship in a play whose language reflects the cadences of simple, natural speech. Many critics have interpreted the play as an indictment of an American Dream that is based on materialism and a lack of moral values. For others, Willy Loman is a modern tragic hero. What ever their critical perspective, most commentators consider the play to be one of the finest of the modern era; it won Miller the Pulitzer Prize.

The Crucible (drama, 1953)

The play is set in Salem, Massachusetts, in 1692. The setting and characters are based on the infamous witch trials of the late seventeenth century. The work also implicitly parallels the anti-communist hearings conducted by Senator Joseph McCarthy carried on by the House Committee on Un-American Activities that took place in the early 1950s. The play is a study in mass hysteria and guilt by association as the community turns against itself. As the play begins, a group of young girls has begun to accuse local townspeople of witchcraft. **John Proctor,** a farmer, has been accused by a young woman named **Abigail.** Far from being a witch, Proctor is indeed a sinner: he has committed adultery with Abigail, and she

269

now uses the mounting hysteria of the community to her own ends to ruin Proctor and his wife, **Elizabeth.** Miller reveals the way in which other characters also make use of the current mood to gain property and prestige through their false accusations, as innocent people go to their deaths. In the play's conclusion, Proctor lies to save himself: he confesses to the false charge of witchcraft, but refuses to implicate others. When he realizes that his confession will be used to ruin others, however, he destroys the confession, condemning himself death.

In this play Miller examines the theme of the rights of the individual and the crowd's urge to suppress their expression. Although the parallels to the McCarthy hearings are inescapable, most critics consider Miller's point to be more universal than topical, for his concern with the issues of social responsibility and the moral prerogative of the individual is a recurrent one. The language of this play differs from the naturalistic dialogue that characterizes his other works, for here he tried to replicate the pattern of seventeenth-century speech.

A View from the Bridge (drama, 1956)

The drama is set in Brooklyn, New York. **Eddie Carbone** is a longshoreman, who with his wife, **Beatrice,** has raised his niece **Catherine** since she was a child. As the story begins, two of Beatrice's relatives, Italian-immigrant brothers named **Rodolpho** and **Marco,** are hiding from the immigration authorities in their home. Catherine and Rodolpho fall in love and plan to marry. Eddie's reaction is immediate and negative. He has unconsciously harbored an incestuous passion for Catherine for years and now does everything in his power to ruin the relationship. Eddie falsely accuses Rodolpho of being a homosexual and of seeking to marry Catherine simply to gain citizenship in the United States. In two pivotal scenes, he tries to humiliate Rodolpho: he challenges him to a boxing match, hoping to enhance his masculinity in Catherine's eyes and undermine Rodolpho's manhood, an event that brings out Marco's anger and sets the stage for the violent conclusion. In a later scene, he kisses Rodolpho, hoping again to expose his effeminacy and to regain Catherine's affection and, like Judas, presaging his final betrayal. When his wife confronts him with the true motive behind his actions, Eddie refuses to believe her, so bent is he on destroying Rodolpho and denying his own feelings. In the play's conclusion, Eddie betrays Rodolpho and Marco to the immigration authorities, an action that at once violates the code of honor among the immigrant community and that leads to his death at the hands of Marco.

Miller had previously dealt with the theme of self-deception in his plays, but in *A View from the Bridge* he elevates his subject to tragic proportions. Eddie's lawyer, **Alfieri,** is the narrator of the work, and functions like a Greek chorus in his objective retelling of the story. Like a character out of ancient myth, Eddie is unable to face the truth about the nature of his feelings for Catherine and brings down ruin on himself and his family.

FURTHER READING

Barclay, Bates. "The Lost Past in *Death of a Salesman." Modern Drama* 11 (1968): 124-36.

Barksdale, Richard. "Social Background in the Plays of Miller and Williams." *College Language Association Journal* 6 (March 1963): 161-69.

Blumberg, Paul. "Sociology and Social Literature: Work Alienation in the Plays of Arthur Miller." *American Quarterly* 21 (1969): 291-310.

Contemporary Authors, Vols. 1-4, rev. ed.; *Contemporary Authors New Revision Series,* Vol. 2. Detroit: Gale Research Co.

Contemporary Literary Criticism, Vols. 1, 2, 6, 10, 15, 26, 47. Detroit: Gale Research Co.

Corrigan, Robert. "The Achievement of Arthur Miller." *Comparative Drama* 2 (1968): 141-60.

Dictionary of Literary Biography, Vol. 7; *Concise Dictionary of American Literary Biography, 1941-1968.* Detroit: Gale Research Co.

Douglass, James. "Miller's *The Crucible:* Which Witch is Which?" *Renascence* 15 (1963): 145-51.

Driver, Tom. "Strength and Weakness in Arthur Miller." *Tulane Drama Review* 4 (May 1960): 45-52.

Ferguson, Alfred. "The Tragedy of the American Dream in *Death of a Salesman.*" *Thought* 53 (1978): 89-98.

Gross, Barry. "*All My Sons* and the Larger Context." *Modern Drama* 18 (1976): 15-27.

Hill, Philip. "*The Crucible:* A Structural View." *Modern Drama* 10 (1967): 312-17.

Jacobson, Irving. "Family Dreams in *Death of a Salesman.*" *American Literature* 47 (1975): 247-58.

Martin Robert. "Arthur Miller's *The Crucible:* Background and Sources." *Modern Drama* 20 (1977): 279-92.

Moss, Leonard. *Arthur Miller.* New York: Twayne, 1967.

Oberg, Arthur. "*Death of a Salesman* and Arthur Miller's Search for Style." *Criticism* 9 (1967): 303-11.

Parker, Brian. "Point of View in Arthur Miller's *Death of a Salesman.*" *University of Toronto Quarterly* 35 (January 1966): 144-57.

Popkin, Henry. "Arthur Miller's *The Crucible.*" *College English* 26 (1964): 354-67.

Henry Miller

1891-1980

American novelist and essayist.

The Tropic of Cancer (novel, 1934)

Miller described much of his writing as "autobiographical romances," of which *Tropic of Cancer* is perhaps the most accomplished and certainly the most famous. This notorious work, which like most of Miller's work met with censorship problems upon publication, relates the quest of his liberated persona, unfettered by the moral and religious codes that condemn humankind to a banal existence.

The book chronicles the adventures of an American expatriate named **Henry Miller** during his first year in Paris. Through the use of interior monologue, Miller relates his experiences in the poorer sections of Paris where he lives a life of indigence. The author renders the decadent side of the city in order to portray the whole of society on the brink of self-destruction, but also to allow his protagonist the opportunity to plumb the depths of the dark forces at work in the human personality. Henry has numerous sexual encounters with women, and later falls in love with and marries **Mona,** a young American woman who remains a shadowy presence. The treatment of sexual and bodily functions is frank and coarse, displaying Miller's attempt to celebrate all aspects of life, especially those previously considered too base for fictional treatment. Two friends of Miller, **Van Norden** and **Carl,** represent varying approaches to women and sexuality. Van Norden views sex as a mechanical act, performing with a starving prostitute in front of Miller; Carl is involved in an affair with a wealthy woman. Miller observes these characters with an air of detachment, realizing that it is money rather than passion that dominates them, and endeavoring in his own life to remain liberated from the constraints of wealth and class.

The city of Paris is beautifully and evocatively presented in this work, which also reveals Miller's attempt to blend elements of surrealist and naturalist narrative style. *Tropic of Cancer* is considered by many critics to be Miller's finest achievement, and it was a profound influence on a number of later writers for whom Miller's experiments in style and subject proved to be a liberating force.

FURTHER READING

Contemporary Authors, Vols. 9-12, rev. ed., 97-100. Detroit: Gale Research Co.

Contemporary Literary Criticism, Vols. 1, 2, 4, 9, 14, 43. Detroit: Gale Research Co.

Dictionary of Literary Biography, Vols. 4, 9; *Dictionary of Literary Biography Yearbook: 1980.* Detroit: Gale Research Co.

Gordon, William A. *The Mind and Art of Henry Miller.* Baton Rouge: Louisiana State University Press, 1967.

Hassan, Ihab Habib. *The Literature of Silence: Henry Miller and Samuel Beckett.* New York: Knopf, 1967.

Mitchell, Edward B., ed. *Henry Miller: Three Decades of Criticism.* New York: New York University Press, 1971.

Yukio Mishima

1925-1970

Japanese novelist, short story writer, and dramatist.

The Sailor Who Fell from Grace with the Sea (novel, 1963)

Set in Yokohama years after World War II, this short novel revolves around **Noboru Kuroda,** a thirteen-year-old boy, and **Ryuji Tsukazaki,** a passionate sailor. Noboru's thirty-three-year-old widowed mother, **Fusako Kuroda,** has taken Ryuji as her lover. Witnessing the couple's first liaison through a tiny bedroom peephole, Noboru experiences a "universal order," "an ineluctable circle of life," in which his mother, the sailor, himself, and the sea coalesce as the distant scream of a ship's horn sounds. "If this is ever destroyed," Noboru murmurs, "it'll mean the end of the world." Ryuji, who believes himself destined for glory, experiences a similar oneness that same instant. For him, Fusako, the sea, glory, and death mingle in awesome harmony. Ryuji's inability to reconcile his unbridled passion for the sea and his increasingly domestic love for Fusako foreshadows his fall. Noboru, who initially regarded Ryuji as a proud, flawless, mythological hero, soon recognizes the sailor's commonness, artificiality, and overall weakness. Through secret meetings with his fellow gang members, all self-proclaimed geniuses who adhere to a nihilistic philosophy loosely based on samurai tradition, Noboru steels himself against the corrupt world, which encompasses all adults, particularly fathers. After documenting Ryuji's "crimes" against internal and universal order, Noboru agrees with the gang's leader that the sailor's heroism must be restored. The boys invite Ryuji—who has now decided to abandon the sea, marry Fusako, and help manage her clothing business—to meet and regale them with sea stories. As Ryuji sits on a quiet hill, captivated by his own romantic dreams, the boys serve him poison tea. They thus ensure his eternal glory while offering a blood sacrifice to the dying world, for they will disembowel him as the traditional *seppuku* ritual prescribes.

One of Mishima's most superbly fashioned tales, *The Sailor Who Fell from Grace with the Sea* addresses the author's foremost, composite theme: the dichotomy of the spirit and the flesh, adolescence and adulthood, and traditional and modern values. Youth, beauty, nihilism, and death emerge as the only conceivable venues that can counteract the forces contributing to the decay of the modern world.

"The Sea of Fertility": *Spring Snow* (novel, 1969); *Runaway Horses* (novel, 1970); *The Temple of Dawn* (novel, 1971); *The Decay of the Angel* (novel, 1971)

Spanning several decades of the twentieth century, "The Sea of Fertility" consists of four novels that trace the sexual and psychological development, early death, and successive reincarnations of **Matsugae Kiyoaki.** An extraordinarily handsome upper-class Tokyo boy, Kiyoaki acquires a privileged education at the aristocratic household of **Count Ayakura.** Ayakura's beautiful daughter, **Satoko,** becomes Kiyoaki's closest childhood friend and, though she is two years his senior, she falls deeply in love with him. Kiyoaki is greatly attracted to Satoko but reveals through diary entries the reason for his cold hostility toward her: he perceives her as haughty and condescending and is gravely disillusioned in his love; therefore he has ceased to pursue her. As plans for Satoko's marriage to an imperial prince unveil, she sinks into a deep depression. Only when the union is imminent does Kiyoaki profess his love; soon he and Satoko meet clandestinely and consummate their tragic passion. They continue their dangerous rendezvous despite the inevitability of the wedding. However, when Satoko becomes pregnant, her parents—in order to preserve their stature—arrange for an abortion in Osaka, followed by Satoko's stay in a remote convent. To everyone's distress, Satoko renounces the world. She refuses to see Kiyoaki despite his repeated journeys through the snow to her. The novel closes when **Shigekuni Honda,** Kiyoaki's academy classmate, takes the delirious, dying Kiyoaki home.

The second volume focuses on Honda, now thirty-eight and a prominent judge. At a *kendū* match he is curiously drawn to a young player named **Isao Iinuma.** Later Honda spies Isao playing beneath a waterfall and notices three moles underneath the youth's left arm. With difficulty Honda becomes convinced that Isao, who bears the same distinctive birthmarks as Kiyoaki and has fulfilled Kiyoaki's dying prophecy by his appearance at the falls, is indeed the reincarnation of Kiyoaki. After a brief, dangerous career of right-wing political activism, Isao assassinates one of Japan's most important business leaders and then commits ritual suicide at the age of twenty.

The third novel records Honda's encounter with Isao's reincarnation, a Thai princess named **Ying Chan.** This volume focuses even more closely on Honda, now a wealthy forty-six-year-old international lawyer. Depicted as a pitiful voyeur whose marriage has become passionless, Honda travels to India after having seen the intriguing young Ying Chan. He studies Buddhism and contemplates reincarnation on the banks of the Ganges. Late, after Ying Chan has matured and come to Japan to study, Honda unmistakably ascertains her identity. After Ying Chan returns to Thailand, Honda eventually learns of her sudden death by snakebite at the age of twenty.

In the final novel, Honda adopts **Tūru Yasunaga,** a sixteen-year-old lower-class orphan, upon discovering the boy's three moles. Throughout the work, the question of whether Tūru represents a true reincarnation of Kiyoaki is omnipresent, for Honda has neglected to verify the date of Ying Chan's death. Domineering and merciless, Tūru learns of his possible former lives and probable fate from **Keiko Hisamatsu,** Honda's lesbian companion. Tūru attempts suicide by poison but only blinds himself. At the close of the novel he is pictured married to a madwoman and exhibiting all the outward signs of a decaying angel. Honda, now eighty-one and seriously ill, travels to Nara to see Satoko. She denies ever knowing Kiyoaki and suggests that such a person never existed. The two walk to the empty convent garden, a place with no memories, where they gaze at nothingness.

Mishima was obsessed both in his life and his art with what he called "my heart's leaning toward Death and Night and Blood." He created a literature, often autobiographical and darkly sensual, in which he attempted to deal with the meaninglessness of life; he was especially distressed by the materialism of post-war Japan. He completed *The Sea of Fertility,* widely considered his masterpiece, only months prior to his ritual suicide. Through the work's pervasive fire and sea imagery, preoccupation with youth and beauty, exploration and seeming rejection of reincarnation, and glorification of *seppuku,* Mishima united his lifelong concerns in a hauntingly lyrical, singularly brilliant sequence of novels. The tetralogy's title, also the ironic name for a barren moon crater, underscores Mishima's conviction that modern life is inescapably desolate, particularly so when youth and beauty inevitably subside.

FURTHER READING

Contemporary Authors, Vols. 29-32, rev. ed., 97-100. Detroit: Gale Research Co.

Contemporary Literary Criticism, Vols. 2, 4, 6, 9, 27. Detroit: Gale Research Co.

Hisaaki, Yamanouchi. "A Phantasy World: Mishima Yukio." In *The Search for Authenticity in Modern Japanese Literature,* pp. 137-52. New York: Cambridge University Press, 1978.

Keene, Donald. "Mishima Yukio." In *Dawn to the West: Japanese Literature of the Modern Era, Vol. 1,* pp. 1167-1224. New York: Holt, Rinehart and Winston, 1984.

Nathan, John. *Mishima.* Boston: Little, Brown & Co., 1974.

Petersen, Gwenn Boardman. "Mishima Yukio." In *The Moon in the Water: Understanding Tanizaki, Kawabata, and Mishima,* pp. 201-319. Honolulu: University Press of Hawaii, 1979.

Scott-Stokes, Henry. *The Life and Death of Yukio Mishima.* New York: Farrar, Straus and Giroux, 1974.

Wagner, Dick and Yoshio Iwamoto. "Yukio Mishima: Dialectics of Mind and Body." *Contemporary Literature* 16, No. 1 (Winter 1975): 41-60.

Yourcenar, Marguerite. *Mishima: A Vision of the Void.* New York: Farrar, Straus and Giroux, 1986.

Brian Moore

1921-

Irish-born Canadian novelist, short story writer, and essayist.

The Lonely Passion of Judith Hearne (novel, 1955)

Moore's first and best-known novel is set in Belfast, Ireland, during the 1950s. **Judith Hearne** is a middle-aged spinster and devout Catholic who finds solace in alcohol after bitterly assessing her life as a failure. Desperately wanting a husband and family of her own, she instead spends the best years of her adult life as companion and nurse to her **Aunt D'Arcy,** the relative who took care of her when both of her parents died. After the death of Aunt D'Arcy, she is left with few financial resources and is forced to live in a number of run-down boarding houses, all of which she is eventually asked to vacate because of her alcoholic behavior. She continues to pray for a husband and as her prayers go unanswered, she drinks even more and begins to lose her faith in God. When a series of humiliating incidents culminates in her drunken assault of the altar in the parish church, she is taken to a nursing home to recover. There, under the supervision of nuns, her faith seems to be returning. The novel ends ambiguously however, for she shows no signs of wanting to return to the outside world.

This novel received widespread acclaim for Moore's depiction of Judith's spiritual dissolution and for his spare, lucid writing style. In theme and characterization, *The Lonely Passion of Judith Hearne* prefigures many of Moore's later works which focus on protagonists who are searching for self-definition amid social, spiritual, and physical turmoil.

FURTHER READING

Ably, Mark. "Beyond Belief." *Books in Canada* 12 (November 1983): 15-16.

Contemporary Authors, Vols. 1-4, rev. ed.; *Contemporary Authors New Revision Series,* Vol. 1. Detroit: Gale Research Co.

Contemporary Literary Criticism, Vols. 1, 3, 5, 7, 8, 19, 32. Detroit: Gale Research Co.

Flood, Jeanne. *Brian Moore.* Lewisburg: Bucknell University Press, 1975.

McSweeney, Kerry. "Brian Moore: Past and Present." *Critical Quarterly* 18 (Summer 1976): 53 66.

Alberto Moravia

1907-

Italian novelist, short story writer, and essayist.

The Time of Indifference (novel, 1929)

Set in Rome, the novel recounts the hopeless, frustrating lives of **Carla,** twenty-four, and her younger brother, **Michele,** as they confront their loveless, meaningless lives. Indifference governs their actions, the only response of which they are capable in the decadent, hypocritical world in which they live. Their mother, **Mariagrazia,** is obsessed with her lost youth and beauty and the unfaithfulness of her lover, **Leo Mermucci.** Leo, unthinking, unfeeling, and unconstrained by the indifference that immobilizes the other characters, is motivated by money and sex. He has transferred his lust from mother to daughter, and in an atmosphere in which each person is viewed as a commodity, he conspires to "buy" Carla through marriage, which will get him the object of his sexual desires and Mariagrazia's property. **Lisa,** Mariagrazia's friend, wants Michele, whom she sees as her means to recapturing her lost youth and attractiveness. Carla and Michele are depicted as the victims of the materialist and sexual desires of the older generation, and both are consumed with thoughts of rage and frustration. Yet they are incapable of action: for all their dreams of liberation from the monotony and repetition of their lives, they are unable to break free. In the conclusion, Carla has succumbed to Leo's desires and has agreed to marry him, deceiving herself with dreams of her life with him, and viewing it not for the sordid reality it will be, but as her entree into society and a life filled with glamour. Michele, filled with impotent rage, also seems to be falling into Lisa's hands and is immobilized by his indifference.

Moravia's literary technique has been called cinematic, for he reveals each of his characters first from the outside, through physical description, and then from within, through the use of interior monologue. In a world where the banality of existence is echoed in the cliches that pass for conversation, it is only through their inner thoughts that the characters are able to express themselves. The dominant imagery in the novel is of masks and other symbols of deceit, and the characters are often described as marionettes, incapable of controlling their own destinies. *The Time of Indifference* is considered a precursor to the later works of such existential writers as Sartre and Camus for its examination of lives of alienation and despair.

FURTHER READING

Contemporary Authors, Vols. 25-28, rev. ed. Detroit: Gale Research Co.

Contemporary Literary Criticism, Vols. 2, 7, 11, 18, 27, 46. Detroit: Gale Research Co.

Heiney, Donald. *Three Italian Novelists: Moravia, Pavese, Vittorini,* pp. 1-82. Ann Arbor: University of Michigan Press, 1968.

Kibler, Louis. "Imagery as Expression in *Gli indifferenti.*" *Italica* 49, No. 3 (Autumn 1972): 315-34.

Radcliffe-Umstead, Douglas. "Moravia's Indifferent Puppets." *Symposium* 24 (1970): 44-54.

Toni Morrison

1931-

American novelist, essayist, and editor.

Song of Solomon (novel, 1977)

The story begins in Michigan, the home of the protagonist, **Milkman Dead,** and proceeds to various settings in the South. The narrative chronicles Milkman's search for himself, focusing on his black heritage and how he learns to understand and accept the meaning of his ancestry. Milkman's father, **Macon Dead,** is a wealthy black businessman who has paid the price of success in the white man's world with his own humanity. As his name indicates, he is truly "dead" to human feeling, favoring instead money and material success and trying to imbue his son with these values. Milkman instead follows those offered by his **Aunt Pilate,** who represents family feeling and the importance of self-understanding through self-exploration. In his quest, Milkman journeys southward, where he traces members of his family in Pennsylvania and Virginia. His most important discovery is of his great-grandfather, **Solomon**, a character of mythic strength and knowledge who fled his captors and who, legend said, knew how to fly. In the novel's conclusion, Milkman is reunited with his friend **Guitar,** who has become a bitter, hateful member of a group of black vigilantes that murders whites, and who now attacks his former friend. Milkman has moved from selfishness to self-knowledge: armed with his heritage and the certainty it offers, he faces death, knowing he will survive. In the final scene, he takes flight, imbued with the courage and supernatural ability of his great-grandfather.

Morrison employs elements of myth, fairy tale, and folktale in this work, which she combines with a naturalistic narrative style. This blend of the fantastic and the realistic is a hallmark of her technique. Thematically, *Song of Solomon* is a precursor of her later work in its concern for the importance of family and the legacy of black folk culture for Afro-Americans.

Tar Baby (novel, 1981)

The novel, an allegorical fable based on the legend of the Rabbit and the Tar Baby, is also an exploration of the effects of colonial rule on blacks. The work is set on the imaginary island of Isle des Chevaliers in the French West Indies, where, according to legend, the ghosts of African horsemen who refused to be slaves roam the hills. **William Green,** known as Son, who is on the run after murdering his unfaithful wife, is the "Rabbit" of the tale, and represents the natural, instinctive element in the black experience. **Jadine,** the "Tar Baby," is a black model who was educated in Europe at the expense of **Valerian Street,** a wealthy white landowner and the employer of her **Uncle Sydney** and **Aunt Ondine.** She embodies the black spirit that denies its origins and embraces those of white, Western culture. The two main characters meet and fall in love on Street's estate, a setting that throws into relief the two opposing viewpoints they represent, for their sense of individual identity and ability of love centers on their understanding of their racial heritage. Son finds Jadine's acceptance of Street's money to be a form of slavery; she considers it her only path to freedom. However, the power of the Streets over the other characters—Jadine's aunt and uncle and the other servants—disintegrates through the unnaturalness of the colonizers: when it is revealed that his wife had abused their children, Street collapses, and the servants take over the mansion. On this imaginary island, the plants and animals are endowed with speech and emotions, and Morrison shows the wild growth of the jungle eagerly taking back the land from the usurper. In the novel's conclusion, Son and Jadine have ended their affair, each of them returning to their former selves and natural environments: Son into the jungle, and Jadine enroute to Europe to the life of a white man's mistress.

As she had in her earlier works, Morrison here focuses on the search for black identity and explores the meaning of individual freedom as opposed to the demands of family and community. The work is noted for its lush natural description and for Morrison's deft handling of the fabulist elements of her story.

Beloved (novel, 1987)

Set in Cincinnati in 1873, the narrative moves back and forth in time, depicting events in the life of **Sethe** and focusing on the theme of slavery and its devastating legacy. In a flashback, we see Sethe as a member of a group of slaves in pre-Civil War Kentucky, working on a farm ironically called Sweet Home. The slaves are owned by a man named **Garner,** who treats them with comparative dignity. **Halle Suggs,** one of the slaves and the future husband of Sethe, makes a bargain with Garner to buy his mother's freedom. **Baby Suggs,** Halle's mother and the spiritual center of the novel, moves to Cincinnati and the first freedom she has ever known. When Garner dies, the farm is taken over by a cruel, sadistic man whom the slaves call "**Schoolteacher,**" a man whose brutality forces them to plot their escape. During their flight, all of the men, including Halle, are killed or disappear; Sethe and her three children reach Cincinnati and safety, with Sethe bearing her fourth child on the way. Sethe's life in Cincinnati is a barren and isolated one. She is a cook in a restaurant and lives a lonely existence in Baby Suggs's house with her only remaining daughter, **Denver,** and the two of them are ostracized from the community. Her two sons have left her, and her other child, a daughter, is dead. The lives of Sethe and Denver are filled with grief, seclusion, and despair, and they are haunted by the ghost of Sethe's dead daughter. The spirit is seemingly exorcised by the appearance of **Paul D.,** a fellow fugitive from Sweet Home. Yet the ghost returns, this time in bodily form, calling herself **Beloved.** Morrison's story is indeed a ghost story of sorts, and the spirit here is a palpable, frightening presence. She possesses a memory that includes her ancestor's history, with knowledge of what it was like to come to America in chains; she is also a voracious being obsessed with food and with her mother's love. It is not until halfway through the novel that the cause of Sethe's overwhelming grief and Beloved's consuming passion for her mother is made clear: after Sethe and her family had fled, Schoolteacher had appeared to claim them and return them to slavery. Rather than subject her children to that life, Sethe had tried to kill them, but had succeeded in murdering only one, Beloved. The revelation shocks and overwhelms Paul D., who leaves her. Yet

Sethe learns that she must not be overcome by the past, and that she must confront it, forgive herself, and learn to live again. Through the power of self-acceptance and self-love, Sethe also learns to live as a member of the community. In the novel's conclusion, Beloved disappears, and Sethe and Paul D. are reunited.

In her exploration of slavery, Morrison deals with her recurrent theme of family. The characters are deprived of all aspects of ancestry—mates, children, forebears and the sense of self-hood and dignity that they hold, and, most importantly, the ability to love. Also of central purpose to her theme is the importance of memory: the past is revealed in fragments, as if Sethe's memories were too overwhelming to be presented at one time. Yet once she confronts her grief and guilt, the projection of that hideous memory, Beloved, vanishes. The elements of the mythical and supernatural that have marked all of Morrison's works are prominent here, particularly in her characterization of Beloved. Morrison received the Pulitzer Prize for *Beloved,* and it is considered her finest work of fiction.

FURTHER READING

Atwood, Margaret. "Haunted by Their Nightmares." *The New York Times Book Review* (13 September 1987): 1, 49-50.

Bischoff, Joan. "The Novels of Toni Morrison: Studies in Thwarted Sensitivity." *Studies in Black Literature* 6 (1976): 21-3.

Brown, Rosellen. "The Pleasures of Enchantment." *The Nation* 245, No. 12 (17 October 1987): 418-21.

Contemporary Authors, Vols. 29-32, rev. ed. Detroit: Gale Research Co.

Contemporary Literary Criticism, Vols. 4, 10, 22, 55. Detroit: Gale Research Co.

Crouch, Stanley. "Aunt Medea." *The New Republic* 197, No. 16 (19 October 1987): 38-43.

Dictionary of Literary Biography, Vols. 6, 33; *Dictionary of Literary Biography Yearbook: 1981.* Detroit: Gale Research Co.

Dowling, Colette. "The Song of Toni Morrison." *New York Times Magazine* (20 May 1979): 40-42, 48, 52, 54, 56, 58.

Harris, A. Leslie. "Myth as Structure in Toni Morrison's *Song of Solomon.*" *MELUS* 7 (Fall 1980): 69-76.

O'Meally, Robert G. "Tar Baby, She Don' Say Nothin'." *Callaloo* 4, Nos. 1-3 (October-February 1981).

Royster, Philip M. "Milkman's Flying: The Scapegoat Transcended in Toni Morrison's *Song of Solomon.*" *CLA Journal* 24 (June 1981): 419-40.

Sheed, Wilfrid. "Improbable Assignment." *Atlantic* 247 (April 1981): 119-20.

Iris Murdoch

1919-

Irish-born English novelist, dramatist, poet, and essayist.

The Black Prince (novel, 1973)

Murdoch's sixteenth novel, arguably her finest, is set in London during the 1960s. A retired tax inspector and now a writer, **Bradley Pearson** narrates his retrospective story of doomed love, hatred, madness, flight, and destruction with erudite eccentricity. Intent upon creating a literary masterpiece, Pearson adopts the role of ascetic artist and attempts to shun all outside contact. He is continually thwarted by several secondary characters, among them his newly widowed former wife, **Christian Evandale;** his suicidal sister, **Priscilla Saxe;** friends **Arnold** and **Rachel Baffin;** and their twenty-year-old daughter, **Julian.** Especially distressing to him are Rachel's calculating advances, stimulated by her intolerably mundane marriage to Arnold, and Arnold's effortless success and annoying contentment as a best-selling author of middlebrow fiction. Pearson placates himself with the belief in his moral superiority to those around him and the expectation that his muse will soon arrive. The action, dialogue, and philosophy of Shakespeare's *Hamlet*—a primary inspiration for the character of Pearson, the novel's black prince—continually recur in his thought and writing. Suddenly and momentously, he falls in love with Julian Baffin, thirty-eight years his junior. Like Vladimir Nabokov's Lolita Haze, Julian is a silly, unsophisticated girl incapable of understanding or fully reciprocating her admirer's complex mixture of passion, idealism, and literary contemplation. Tensions rise rapidly when Julian's parents learn of Pearson's unbridled affection for their daughter and impose strict isolation between the two.

Following flight to the country and a desperate, forceful consummation of his love for Julian, the affair ends abruptly, and Pearson returns to London. The narrative closes after a tumultuous series of events that have led Rachel to murder Arnold and then coerce Pearson into incriminating himself. Pearson's prison manuscript is edited by a fellow inmate **P. Loxias,** who includes along with his own postscript critiques of the account by Christian, Julian, Rachel, and **Francis Marloe.** As Pearson's personal messenger and the story's most disinterested witness, Marloe offers perhaps the deepest insights into the validity of the manuscript's details and the nature of Pearson's unusual mind. Nevertheless, the reader is left with multiple interpretations and little dependable evidence. Murdoch offers the following words as the novel's summation: ''Art tells the only truth that ultimately matters. It is the light by which human things can be mended. And after art there is, let me assure you all, nothing.''

A superbly crafted novel of intrigue, *The Black Prince* is also esteemed for its serious exposition of life's greatest paradoxes: art vs. reality, love vs. hatred, suffering vs. redemption. Through numerous allusions and thematic similarities, Murdoch aligns her novel with several great works of literature, including Dostoevski's *The Brothers Karamazov*. *The Black Prince* won the James Tait Black Memorial Prize in fiction.

The Sea, the Sea (novel, 1978)

A massive novel and one of Murdoch's foremost fictional achievements, *The Sea, the Sea* takes place near the small English seaside village of Narrowdean. The narrator, a retired theater director named **Charles Arrowby,** records his solitary delight living in his newly purchased cottage, Shruff End. Perched upon a small promontory, the cottage affords him a breathtaking view of the rocky coastline and endlessly changing sea. For a time Charles, an egotistical sensualist, is content to ruminate about his past and assess the content of his diary-in-progress. However, an obsessive love overtakes him, ruling his directorial, dictatorial mind. Once Charles's adolescent girlfriend, **Hartley Fitch** is now a sixty-year-old, happily married woman. Oblivious of all evidence that her love for him has long ago vanished, Charles pursues Hartley like a mad magician, powerfully disrupting, complicating, and endangering the lives of all those involved. Because of Charles's disastrous meddling, Hartley's young adopted son, **Titus,** whom Charles dreamed of raising himself, senselessly drowns. Sick with remorse, Charles begins an awkward reevaluation of himself and those who figure in the dark drama he has set in motion. His moral regeneration is made possible by his cousin, **James Arrowby,** who miraculously saves him from drowning, and by **Angela Godwin,** a virginal figure who promises to conceive a son to replace Titus. By the end of his narrative Charles comes to several realizations about "the demon-ridden pilgrimage of human life," and acknowledges the vanity of his former actions. He has shed his illusions and gained the comforting, simple love of his longtime admirer, **Lizzie Scherer.**

A parodic counterpart of *The Tempest*'s Prospero, Charles represents the lowest form of creative artist, one whom Murdoch in her *The Fire and the Sun: Why Plato Banished the Artists* describes as perpetuating an "irrational kind of awareness." However, as Charles ascends through moral and aesthetic planes he acquires both real and artistic goodness. The motif of the sea flows through the entire work, a force which, though potentially deadly, imparts its curative powers and brings renewal. For her distinguished novel, Murdoch was awarded the Booker McConnell Prize in 1978.

The Good Apprentice (novel, 1985)

Considered by some Murdoch's most thematically and stylistically brilliant novel, *The Good Apprentice* is situated in and around contemporary London. The work relates the search of **Edward Baltram** for redemption following the death of his close friend, **Mark Wilsden.** Convinced that Mark's experience will be mystical and life-altering, Edward gives a hallucinogenic drug to his unknowing companion. Mark, "transfigured by luminous ecstasy," sees a glorious, sustained vision of God, and Edward departs to visit a friend. Left sleeping peacefully, Mark inexplicably jumps through a window to his death before Edward returns. After ineffectual psychiatric treatment by **Thomas McCaskerville,** Edward accepts an invitation to visit his estranged, eccentric father, **Jesse,** at Seegard, an elaborate estate in the English wilderness. Burdened with guilt and self-loathing, Edward struggles to discover meaning and purpose in his life. He is aided by his contact with his two virginal half-sisters, **Ilona** and **Bettina,** and **May,** the girls' mother and Jesse's second wife. The Baltram women, through their nun-like daily rituals and natural reverence for Seegard, impart a spiritual power and wisdom that enlivens and intrigues Edward. Yet the three women thwart his efforts to meet with Jesse, an artist gone mad who is kept cloistered from public view. Eventually father and son meet. The saintly Jesse, upon hearing of Edward's misdeed, offers his forgiveness, which Edward receives with overwhelming gratitude. The spiritual bond between them, symbolized by a ring, continues even after Jesse's mysterious death.

Edward's painful pursuit of the good contrasts with the publicly proclaimed, ascetic apprenticeship of his half-brother, **Stuart Cuno.** To the consternation of his family, particularly his father, **Harry,** Stuart abandons his rising academic career in mathematics, renounces sex, and pledges to throw himself fully into some socially useful work. As various subplots involving characters in emotional, spiritual, sexual, and intellectual entanglements intertwine, Stuart and Edward progress toward increasingly clearer views of reality. At the close Stuart decides to become a teacher of small children, hoping to "give them an idea of what goodness is, and how to love it." Edward, though still searching for answers and possibilities, has been able to help others while healing himself; he can finally affirm that "there are good things in the world."

As A. N. Wilson has written, "Any attempt to summarise the story of Iris Murdoch's novels conveys nothing of the way they feel when you are inside them." Murdoch's art—reliant upon a typically large *dramatis personae*, complex interrelationships, fusion of the fantastic and ordinary, numerous symbolic overtones, and a continually twisting plot—is that of a virtuosic conjurer. She weaves novels that are both inordinately enchanting and philosophically profound.

FURTHER READING

Baldanza, Frank. *Iris Murdoch*. New York: Twayne, 1974.

Byatt, A. S. *Degrees of Freedom: The Novels of Iris Murdoch.* London: Chatto & Windus, 1965.

Contemporary Authors, Vols. 13-16, rev. ed.; *Contemporary Authors New Revision Series,* Vol. 8. Detroit: Gale Research Co.

Contemporary Literary Criticism, Vols. 1, 2, 3, 4, 6, 8, 11, 15, 22, 31, 51. Detroit: Gale Research Co.

Dictionary of Literary Biography, Vol. 14. Detroit: Gale Research Co.

Dipple, Elizabeth. *Iris Murdoch: Work for the Spirit.* Chicago: University of Chicago Press, 1982.

Gerstenberger, Donna. *Iris Murdoch.* Lewisburg: Bucknell University Press, 1975.

Rabinovitz, Rubin. "Iris Murdoch." In *Six Contemporary British Novelists,* edited by George Stade, pp. 271-332. New York: Columbia University Press, 1976.

Todd, Richard. *Iris Murdoch: The Shakespearean Interest.* New York: Barnes & Noble, 1979.

Wolfe, Peter. *The Disciplined Heart: Iris Murdoch and Her Novels.* Columbia: University of Missouri Press, 1966.

Vladimir Nabokov

1899-1977

Russian-born American novelist, poet, essayist, short story writer, critic, and translator.

Lolita (novel, 1955)

Centered in contemporary New England, *Lolita* is the tragic-erotic memoir of its pseudonymous protagonist, **Humbert Humbert.** A European emigré scholar with an illicit passion for young nymphets, Humbert marries **Charlotte Haze,** an unappealing middle-aged widow, so that he might satisfy his pedophiliac yearnings for Charlotte's physically precocious twelve-year-old daughter, **Dolores,** whom he usually refers to as **Lolita.** Humbert vacillates between an idealistic, aesthetically sophisticated love for Lolita and a self-debasing enactment of and uncertain reflection upon his sexual deviancy. To Humbert's absolute delight, Charlotte is accidentally run over by a car only a month into their marriage. Diabolically intent on severing all contact with Charlotte's friends and relatives, Humbert retrieves Lolita from summer camp and with her commences a year-long odyssey across the United States. Lolita astonishes Humbert with her vulgarity and sexual experience acquired while at Camp Climax, and her willful seduction of him at The Enchanted Hunters Inn. Despite his obsession with Lolita—who is capable only of reciprocating his lust, not his intellectual synthesis of art, history and romance—Humbert develops a semi-rational, enduring love that at once recognizes and transcends Lolita's pettiness and materialism.

Returning east after the long cross-country escapade, Humbert enrolls his step-daughter in a girls' prep school. While there, Lolita succumbs to the dark influence of **Clare Quilty,** who enlists her in the play *The Enchanted Hunters,* written and directed by him. When Quilty, generally understood as Humbert carried to a sinister extreme—absconds with Lolita, Humbert commences a futile two-year search for the couple. After unhappily settling down with a pathetically immature woman, Humbert hears from Lolita, who is now sixteen, newly married, and in need of money. Upon meeting her again, Humbert perceives her precocity and charm have given way to mediocrity; he insists, however, upon having his revenge and gains enough information from his former love to locate Quilty. In a climactic scene of grotesque comedy, Humbert manically spars with and then murders his rival. In prison he composes his memoir, which is published following both his death by heart attack and Lolita's brought on by childbirth.

Nabokov became a literary celebrity with this notorious novel. Rejected by four American publishers due to its subject matter, the book attracted a wide underground readership upon its publication in France and became a bestseller when published in the United States in 1958. Any serious analysis of the novel must recognize that ultimate meanings cannot be found within the plot itself. For Nabokov, Lolita represented all that is superficial and earthy in American culture. Humbert, despite his sexual deviancy, lives life from a sophisticated European perspective. Beyond the satire of American values, the novel explores the relationship between fiction, reality, and irrationality. Regardless of what Humbert signifies on the surface, his effort to impose aesthetic order on a severely troubled life and to reconcile his idealistic view of youth with the vulgar mediocrity of adulthood is both heroically comic and excruciatingly tragic, the essence of all great fiction.

Pnin (novel, 1957)

One of Nabokov's most complex yet accessible works, *Pnin* centers on the bumbling attempts of a Russian emigré scholar to adapt to life at an American college during the 1950s. **Timofey Pavlovich Pnin**'s story is sympathetically, if selectively, told by an unnamed professor who eventually replaces Pnin at Waindell, a diploma-mill college in upstate New York. After nine years of capable teaching but ineffectual politicking, Pnin has failed to earn tenure. His Old World sensibility, meek disposition, unintentional, comedic misuse of the English language, and preposterously silly silhouette have made him the brunt of endless mimicry and ridicule by the students and other faculty. Self-confidence and mastery infuse Pnin only when he is away from Waindell. On a retreat with fellow Russian immigrants to a mountain resort, Pnin's timidity vanishes and he conquers the croquet course with deadly proficiency.

Pnin's former wife, psychologist **Liza Wind,** visits Pnin at Waindell. Although cruelly used years earlier by Liza—who, pregnant, sought passage to America only to divorce Pnin and marry the child's father—Pnin hopes for a reconciliation. Liza, however, wishes only for Pnin to contribute to her son's education. Pnin consents but pitifully bemoans his fate: "I haf nofing lift, nofing, nofing!" Near the end of the novel, the narrator reveals himself as one who knew Pnin long ago in St. Petersburg, who later managed a brief affair with Liza while in Paris, and who will replace Pnin at the college. From **Dr. Herman Hagen,** Pnin's sole, steadfast supporter, Pnin learns that his Russian chair will be eliminated at the end of the year. The novel closes with the narrator rushing to catch a glimpse of Pnin departing. He records that Pnin's "little sedan boldly . . . spurted up the shining road, which one could make out narrowing to a thread of gold in the soft mist where hill after hill made beauty of distance, and where there was simply no saying what miracle might happen."

An often overlooked work in Nabokov's canon, *Pnin* is nonetheless considered a stunning technical achievement, a novel of both stylistic and structural innovation. Guided by a string of anecdotes, an etymological mind, and his own, occasionally unreliable point of view, the narrator pieces together the essence of one of the most endearing characters in modern fiction. The novel's concern with factuality and misunderstanding undergird Pnin's own dilemma: his inability, despite his most heartfelt actions, to escape social isolation. Yet, Pnin ultimately prevails, for Nabokov resurrects him in his succeeding novel, *Pale Fire.*

Pale Fire (novel, 1962)

Set on a small college campus in New Wye, Appalachia (Ithaca, New York), *Pale Fire* contains a complex 999-line poem about death, immortality, and art written in rhymed couplets and attributed to **John Shade,** whom Nabokov called "the greatest of *invented* poets." The author of the accompanying exegesis is **Charles Kinbote,** in actuality **V. Botkin,** an emigré colleague of Shade who imagines himself the exiled king (Charles the Beloved) of Zembla, a remote Soviet satellite nation. Thus, two stories intermingle with tragicomic drama: the poetic retelling of the late Shade's deeply lived life and the delusionary transformation of this masterpiece by Kinbote, in every sense the antithesis of Shade. A grotesque representative of the type of pedantic scholar Nabokov despised, Professor Kinbote throughout his long commentary persists in the view that Shade's autobiographical poem is really a disguised historical account of the Kingdom of Zembla. Consequently, Shade's accidental death at the hands of **Jack Grey,** a madman who mistakes Shade for the judge who sentenced him, becomes in Kinbote's commentary the work of **Jacob Gradus,** a Zemblan assassin who had as his target Kinbote. Kinbote's psychosis emerges fully when he treats the forty-year love affair of John and **Sybil Shade;** here his commentary deteriorates into a prolonged, loathsome confessional of his pederastic urges and homosexuality.

The novel purposefully closes without a clear resolution of either Kinbote or Shade's life. Such is characteristic of Nabokov, who through his intricate, self-conscious fiction investigated the illusory nature of reality and the artist's relationship to his craft. Nabokov maintained that "art at its greatest is fantastically deceitful and complex." Hence through his two characters Nabokov reiterated his artistic ideals, plumbing both the depths and heights of the creative mind, while composing one of the most innovative works of the twentieth century. The final power of *Pale Fire* resides in Shade's poem itself, one of the greatest testaments to Nabokov's literary genius. Many critics regard *Pale Fire* as among the most brilliant, thoughtful, and original poems in contemporary literature.

Ada; or, Ardor: A Family Chronicle (novel, 1969)

Nabokov's longest and most difficult novel, *Ada,* is both a romance and literary parody which takes place in Amerussia an the planet Antiterra, also called Demonia. Divided into five successively smaller sections, the narrative, a clumsily edited, relentlessly erudite philosophical memoir, traces the life of its aristocratic author, **Ivan Demonovlich Veen (Van).** As a teenager Van falls in love with his twelve-year-old cousin, **Adelaida Veen (Ada).** Their love, unrestrained and furiously erotic, is symptomatic of that found on Antiterra, where incest, pedophilia, nymphomania, and other forms of aberrant or socially unacceptable sexuality reign. By the end of the novel, Ada and Van, now ninety-five and ninety-seven, respectively, have lived together as ardent lovers for forty-five years. Yet, even in old age they are despicable characters who continue to prey upon a host of victims in order to satisfy their boundless, primitive appetites. Their fellow inhabitants, both victims and victimizers, long for a different world, a Utopian Terra, or Earth, in which an abiding morality quells all cruelty and misguided passion. Van's consistently repellent memoir, however, provides no indication that the attainment of this ideal is possible.

Nabokov scholars differ over the merits of *Ada;* some have termed it a culminating work and his masterpiece, while others regard it as preposterous intellectual exhibitionism. The difficulty in reading and assessing *Ada* lies in its purposeful absence of authorial viewpoint and its myriad literary allusions and linguistic games. Here as nowhere else in his canon, Nabokov marshalled in extreme form all the elements of his highly imaginative art. Consequently, his meaning-laden novel of anti-values continues to engage as well as confound the reader. Despite various excesses and a profound textual complexity, *Ada* conveys, like the best of Nabokov's fiction, a poignant regard for human feelings and morality and an unusually incisive, cleverly evolved criticism of modern society.

FURTHER READING

Appel, Alfred, Jr., ed. *The Annotated Lolita.* New York: McGraw-Hill, 1970.

———. *Nabokov's Dark Cinema.* New York: Oxford University Press, 1972.

Bader, Julia. *Crystal Land: Artifice in Nabokov's English Novels.* Berkeley: University of California Press, 1972.

Contemporary Authors, Vols. 5-8, rev. ed., 69-72; *Contemporary Authors New Revision Series,* Vol. 20. Detroit: Gale Research Co.

Contemporary Literary Criticism, Vols. 1, 2, 3, 6, 8, 11, 15, 23, 44, 46. Detroit: Gale Research Co.

Dembo, L. S., ed. *Nabokov: The Man and His Work.* Madison: University of Wisconsin Press, 1967.

Dictionary of Literary Biography, Vol. 2; *Dictionary of Literary Biography Yearbook: 1980; Dictionary of Literary Biography Documentary Series,* Vol. 3; *Concise Dictionary of American Literary Biography, 1941-1968.* Detroit: Gale Research Co.

Field, Andrew. *Nabokov: His Life in Part.* Boston: Little, Brown and Co., 1967.

Fowler, Douglas. *Reading Nabokov.* Ithaca, N. Y.: Cornell University Press, 1974.

Lee, L. L. *Vladimir Nabokov.* Boston: Twayne, 1976.

Mason, Bobbie Ann. *Nabokov's Garden: A Guide to Ada.* Ann Arbor: Ardis Press, 1974.

Proffer, Carl. *Keys to Lolita.* Bloomington: Indiana University Press, 1968.

Roth, Phyllis A., ed. *Critical Essays on Vladimir Nabokov.* Boston: G. K. Hall, 1984.

Rowe, William W. *Nabokov's Deceptive World.* New York: New York University Press, 1971.

Stegner, Page. *Escape Into Aesthetics: The Art of Vladimir Nabokov.* New York: William Morrow, 1966.

V. S. Naipaul

1932-

Trinidadian-born English novelist and essayist.

A House for Mr. Biswas (novel, 1961)

Set in Trinidad, the novel is considered Naipaul's finest literary effort. It traces the life of **Mohoun Biswas,** an East Indian from an impoverished Hindu family, from birth through maturity to death. The novel is prefaced with a prologue in which the key events of the story are related: we learn that Mr. Biswas, forty-six, ill and waiting to die, has struggled and achieved the symbol of success he dreams of—a house of his own. He has faced almost insurmountable odds, including poverty and the tyranny of of his wife's demanding and overwhelming family, to achieve his modicum of independence, represented in his heavily mortgaged, ramshackle house. It is clear from his introduction that Naipaul sees his character as a heroic figure despite his lowly birth, for he ends the prologue referring to him as an "unnecessary and unaccommodated" man, an allusion to Shakespeare's Lear.

As the novel begins, we are introduced to the facts surrounding the childhood of Mr. Biswas. His family is described as poor and superstitious: after his birth, a pundit is called who reads Mr. Biswas's horoscope and predicts a bad life. The colonialism that exploited the people of the West Indies is revealed in the situation of his family, for his father is a laborer on a sugar plantation and his two young brothers, despite the laws against child labor, work for the sugar estate as well. Throughout the novel, Naipaul shows the deadening effects of the poverty that was the legacy of this inhuman exploitation through the experience of his protagonist.

After his father's death the family breaks up, and Mr. Biswas is sent to school, studies to be a pundit, and eventually becomes a sign painter. In this capacity, he meets his future bride, **Shama,** as he works for her family, the Tulsis. This large, chaotic, and tyrannical clan becomes the force against which Mr. Biswas's rebellion is waged. He becomes a journalist for the Trinidad Sentinel, and through his success he glimpses the first fruits of freedom and sense of achievement. He finally attains his dream of a house of his own, a symbol of his liberation. Yet happiness eludes him, and his struggles with his own children are a continual source of pain to him. The estrangement that separates him from his beloved son **Anand,** who is away from home on scholarship, and who is a bit embarrassed of his father and his origins, is poignantly described. In the concluding chapters, Mr. Biswas lays close to death, and his letters to Anand go unanswered. Still in debt, still struggling to hold on to his house and his freedom, Mr. Biswas dies.

The novel is related in the third person, but it is through the consciousness of Mr. Biswas that we interpret this fictional world. We share his sense of impotence, alienation, and isolation, yet the darkness is relieved by the comic current that runs throughout the novel. Naipaul's portrait of Mr. Biswas has been praised as affectionate, ironic, and believable, and the work has been compared to the works of Charles Dickens for its breadth and depth.

FURTHER READING

Blodgett, Harriet. "Beyond Trinidad: Five Novels by V. S. Naipaul." *South Atlantic Quarterly* (Summer 1974): 388-403.

Contemporary Authors, Vols. 1-4, rev. ed.; *Contemporary Authors New Revision Series,* Vol. 1. Detroit: Gale Research Co.

Contemporary Literary Criticism, Vols. 4, 7, 9, 13, 18, 37. Detroit: Gale Research Co.

Dictionary of Literary Biography Yearbook. 1985. Detroit: Gale Research Co.

Hamner, Robert D. *V. S. Naipaul.* Boston: Twayne, 1973.

Thorpe, Michael. *V. S. Naipaul.* Essex: Longman Group, 1976.

Sōseki Natsume
1867-1916
Japanese novelist, essayist, poet, and critic.

Kokoro (novel, 1914)

This novel is divided into three parts. The first two sections are narrated by a young man whose name is not given, the last consists of a letter written to him by **Sensei.** Far apart in age and experience, Sensei and the narrator nevertheless develop a close relationship. In the beginning portion of the novel, Sensei is seen through the eyes of the narrator, who senses some tragedy in his mentor's life. The second part of the book concerns the narrator's familial situation and his growing alienation from parents and siblings. His friendship with Sensei has so affected the younger man that he leaves his father's death bed and returns to Tokyo after receiving Sensei's letter in the third section of the novel. In his missive, Sensei explains that many years earlier he and his best friend, identified only as **K,** were in love with the same woman. Sensei married her, and K, unable to bear his sadness, killed himself. Sensei never forgave himself for K's death and indicated in his letter that he also intends to commit suicide.

Isolation from other human beings is the main theme of most of Natsume's works. In *Kokoro,* he shows that death is the only escape from individual loneliness and that no matter how close two people may be, they cannot share each other's most profound experiences. On another level, this book, like many of Natsume's novels, functions as an indictment of modern Japanese society. In Natsume's eyes, the Japanese people have so intensified their efforts to escape from their feudal past and to catch up with the achievements of the Western world that they have left themselves no time for interaction with other individuals.

Light and Darkness (novel, 1917)

There is very little external action in this story; the focus is instead on the inner lives of the characters. **Isuda Yoshio,** the central character, is an egotistical young man who must undergo minor surgery. During the course of his recovery, the psychological makeup of each of the other main characters is compared and contrasted with that of Isuda. As the title suggests, these personalities range from darkness, indicating egocentrism, to light, representing concern for humanity in general over concern for self. The first character to be examined in this way is **O-Nobu,** Isuda's wife. Although her selfishness equals her husband's, she is closer to the light of self-abnegation than Isuda, for she is willing to admit her weaknesses and ask for help in attaining her goal, which is to have Isuda love only her. **Mrs. Yoshikawa,** the wife of Isuda's employer, delights in her acts of generosity toward her husband's underlings and forces Isuda to confront his depression and unhappiness. Although jealous of O-Nobu's freedoms as a married woman, **O-Hide,** Isuda's sister, is a young woman of insight, and her assessment of her brother's character as one of supreme selfishness is accurate. **Kobayashi,** Isuda's friend from university, is a penniless journalist. He is a nonconformist who cares more for the lot of humanity than for himself. He berates Isuda for his lack of concern for others and urges him to change his ways in a sincere effort to make his friend a better person. At the opposite end of the spectrum from Isuda is **Kiyoko.** She is Isuda's former lover who rejected him for another man. Her section of the novel is unfinished, as is the ending of the book, but some critics feel that enough is learned about Kiyoko throughout the earlier portions of the novel to know that she represents the full light of self-denial and complete happiness, the goal toward which Isuda must travel.

Light and Darkness is considered Natsume's most ambitious work and although incomplete at the time of his death, represents the successful culmination of his major themes. It evidences his progression from a state of cynicism toward Japanese society to a philosophy based on the importance of charity and humanity.

FURTHER READING

Contemporary Authors, Vol. 104. Detroit: Gale Research Co.

Higaya, Mihoko. "'Sandra Belloni' to Sūseki." *Eigo Seinen* 132 (1987): 535-36, 598-99.

Rubin, Jay. "The Evil and the Ordinary in Sūseki's Fiction." *Harvard Journal of Asiatic Studies* 46 (December 1986): 333-52.

Twentieth-Century Literary Criticism, Vols. 2, 10. Detroit: Gale Research Co.

Ueda, Makoto. "Sūseki Natsume." In *Modern Japanese Writers and the Nature of Literature,* pp. 1-25. Palo Alto: Stanford University Press, 1976.

Viglielmo, V. H. "Afterword." In *Light and Darkness: An Unfinished Novel* by Natsume Sūseki, translated by V. H. Viglielmo, pp. 376-97. London: Owen, 1971.

Yamanouchi, Hisaaki. "The Agonies of Individualism: Natsume Sūseki." In *The Search for Authenticity in Modern Japanese Literature,* pp. 40-81. Cambridge: Cambridge University Press.

Yan, Ansheng. "Natsume Sūseki's View of the Modern Japanese Society." *Foreign Literatures* 9 (1986): 70-3.

Yu, Beongcheon. *Natsume Sūseki.* Boston: Twayne, 1969.

Ngugi wa Thiong'o
1938-
Kenyan novelist, dramatist, and essayist.

A Grain of Wheat (novel, 1967)

Set in Kenya on the eve of that nation's independence, the novel centers on four characters—**Mugo, Gikonyo, Mumbi, and Karanja**—and their individual reactions to the political changes of their time. The novel takes place on the four days before the independence celebrations, but through the use of flashbacks, Ngugi establishes the interior lives of his characters, particularly their relationships to **Kihika,** a freedom fighter who has lost his life to the cause. Ngugi presents the origins of the Kenyan struggle for independence, focussing on the exploitive, paternalistic approach of the British to the nation and its people. On both the personal and national level, he explores the themes of betrayal and guilt and of sacrifice and suffering.

Mugo, an orphan raised in poverty, is an outsider to the village where the action of the novel takes place. He finds Kihika to be arrogant and naive; his natural pragmatism cannot accept the idealism embodied in the hero. Kihika tries to force him out of his isolation, to make him recognize his allegiance to his fellow human beings. Yet it is Mugo who betrays Kihika to the British authorities, resulting in Kihika's execution. Mugo becomes obsessed with his guilt, which he keeps to himself until the day of celebration, when he reveals his crime to the assembled village. Gikonyo, the husband of Mumbi, is a revolutionary who is imprisoned for his efforts. Nearly driven mad during his confinement, he renounces his involvement and betrays his fellow insurrectionists. He returns to Mumbi, who now has a child by Karanja, his old rival for her affections. He shuns his wife and tries to bury himself in his work. In the hospital after an accident, he hears of Mugo's confession, which acts as a catalyst to his own self-examination, after which he forgives his wife. Mumbi, too, is guilty of betrayal. Yet Ngugi implies that Gikonyo's demands for strict fidelity are too harsh, evident in the resolution of their relationship and Gikonyo's acceptance of the child. Karanja represents the black African stripped of his integrity who seeks the approval of the white man and pays obeisance to the colonial rule. A betrayer of his own people, he becomes a home guard, allied with the British forces. He acts as an informer against his fellow countrymen and takes part in their execution. He remains an outsider and an individual isolated by his remorse, for unlike the other characters, his guilt is never expiated.

Ngugi employs a variety of narrative styles in this work, including interior monologue through which he reveals the innermost thoughts of his characters. Considered one of Ngugi's finest achievements, *A Grain of Wheat* is noted for its compassionate, humanistic perspective, penetrating analysis of the theme of betrayal, and rich characterizations.

FURTHER READING

Contemporary Authors, Vols. 81-84. Detroit: Gale Research Co.

Contemporary Literary Criticism, Vols. 3, 7, 13, 36. Detroit: Gale Research Co.

Cook, David and Michael Okenimkpe. *Ngugi wa Thiong'o: An Exploration of His Writings.* London: Heinemann, 1983.

Obumselu, Ben. *"A Grain of Wheat:* Ngugi's Debt to Conrad.*" Benin Review* 1 (1974): 1-35.

Roscoe, Adrian. "Prose." In *Uhuru's Fire: African Literature,* pp. 168-214. Cambridge: Cambridge University Press, 1977.

Frank Norris

1870-1902

American novelist and short story writer.

McTeague (novel, 1899)

This novel, set in San Francisco at the turn of the century, is considered one of the foremost works of American naturalism. **McTeague,** the novel's hero, is described as a "young giant," a huge young man with hairy, muscular arms and body, compared to a "draught horse," and repeatedly described as stupid. He is a dentist who practices without a license, relying on his brute strength. His simple life is related with grim realism, depicting a limited, unthinking man, who works during the week and sleeps and dreams in his dentist chair on Sundays. His friend **Marcus Schouler** introduces McTeague to his fiancée, **Trina,** who soon falls in love with McTeague and becomes his wife. Schouler's revenge is to turn McTeague into the authorities, after which he loses his practice.

In McTeague, Norris depicted man as a victim of his environment, with his character and fate determined by his origins and external forces beyond his control. Thus, as McTeague's fortunes change, he becomes prey to alcoholism and to the evil which Norris describes as a hereditary force within him that he is powerless to stop. Out of brutishness and greed, McTeague goes after Trina's money. When she won't part with it willingly, he kills her. Schouler is part of the posse that goes in search of McTeague, and he finds him in the desert. The two fight, and McTeague kills his former friend, but not before Schouler has handcuffed the two of them together. Thus, McTeague is depicted at the novel's conclusion looking "stupidly" around him, attached to a corpse and facing his own death.

The novel, which profoundly influenced American fiction, bears the influence of Emile Zola's concept of literary naturalism, reflected in Norris's attempt to show how an individual is formed by heredity and external forces. Stylistically, the work moves from the realism of the early chapters to a more satiric mode in the center of the book, where McTeague and the other characters are often reduced to caricatures or grotesques. The final scene is notably melodramatic. Norris's blending of these various styles has been criticized by some, but the work is considered a landmark of American fiction.

The Octopus (novel, 1901)

The novel, set in California's San Joaquin Valley, was originally conceived as the first volume of Norris's proposed "Trilogy of Wheat," which he did not live to complete. In this work he hoped to focus on wheat as a life-force, showing how it is grown, distributed, and used by the consumer, and how its production reflected the injustices of the economic system in the United States.

As the work begins, **Presley,** a young poet, has come to the Valley to spend the summer on the wheat ranch of **Magnus Derrick.** The "Octopus" of the title is the Pacific and

Southwestern Railroad, which owns vast tracts of farmland, including part of the Derrick property. Their interests are represented in the novel by the figure of **Shelgrim,** the railroad president, who embodies the greed and selfishness of the owners. Although he claims that he is helpless to change the ways of the wheat and the railroad business, calling them forces beyond the control of man, Norris shows how he is motivated by self-interest. The railroads, after promising to sell the land to the ranchers reasonably, revoke their commitment and demand outrageous prices for the land, threatening to throw the ranchers off their own property unless they agree. A fight ensues between the ranchers and Federal agents sent by the railroad to quell the uprising, and several men are killed. Others die as the forces of industry take precedence over human life. After witnessing the waste of human life, Presley leaves the Valley, feeling himself unable to change the course of events or to achieve success as a poet. Yet the conclusion is not a pessimistic one, for the character of **Vanamee** and the mystical philosophy he expounds appears in ascendence in the final section of the novel. Vanamee is depicted as somehow above the struggle for power and money. He had become a shepherd and a recluse after the death of his girlfriend, and in the novel he schools Presley in the lesson that one man is powerless against the natural forces of the world. This philosophy, which many critics claim reflects Norris's understanding of transcendentalism, posits that good will always triumph over evil, and that all forces "work together for the good."

As in *McTeague,* Norris here explores the powers that are beyond individual control and that determine fate. In this work, Norris widens his scope to examine the relevant social issues of his day. Whether Shelgrim, Presley, or Vanamee is the hero of the novel is debated by critics, but it is clear that the philosophy of the shepherd, who preaches acceptance and optimism, provides Norris's ultimate statement on the human condition.

FURTHER READING

Contemporary Authors, Vol. 110. Detroit: Gale Research Co.

Dictionary of Literary Biography, Vol. 10; *Concise Dictionary of American Literary Biography, 1865-1917.* Detroit: Gale Research Co.

Dillingham, William B. *Frank Norris: Instinct and Art* Lincoln. University of Nebraska Press, 1969.

French, Warren. *Frank Norris.* New York: Twayne, 1962.

Frohock, W. M. *Frank Norris.* Minneapolis: University of Minnesota Press, 1969.

Graham, Don. *The Fiction of Frank Norris: The Aesthetic Context.* Columbia: University of Missouri Press, 1978.

Marchand, Ernest. *Frank Norris: A Study.* Stanford: Stanford University Press, 1942.

Pizer, Donald. *The Novels of Frank Norris.* Bloomington: Indiana University Press, 1966.

Twentieth-Century Literary Criticism, Vol. 24. Detroit: Gale Research Co.

Joyce Carol Oates
1938-

American novelist, dramatist, short story writer, poet, critic, and essayist.

Expensive People (novel, 1968)

Set in suburban Detroit, *Expensive People* is the story of **Richard Everett,** a miserably obese teenager. His father is a prosperous businessman and his mother is a Russian writer. Richard is desperately in love with his mother, but she has little interest in him; rather, her sole concern is impressing others with wealth and prestige. Richard's mental health suffers and eventually he becomes insane. Finally, Richard plans to kill his mother using an idea from one of her own stories. When she is murdered, Richard believes that he has killed his mother, but his doctors disagree and say that he only thinks he did; instead somebody else actually murdered her. Disappointed that he has failed, Richard kills himself by overeating.

A novel whose atmosphere is at once strange and unsettling, *Expensive People* is a cutting indictment of the people of the upper social strata and their values. Oates structures her novel as a satire, exaggerating the goals and desires of these "expensive people." Richard is indicative of the American youth who is victimized by the vapidity of his existence and the increasingly fast pace of contemporary American life. Though he comes from a wealthy family, he is emotionally destitute and finds solace—and, ultimately death—in food.

them (novel, 1969)

Set in Detroit, *them* is a novel of violence and despair, focussing on the Wendall family and chronicling their lives from 1937 to 1967. The novel opens with a murder. **Loretta Wendall,** a young woman, wakes to discover that her brother has killed her first lover, asleep in her bed, in cold blood. The policeman who investigates the crime, **Howard Wendall,** assaults Loretta and rapes her. This is the man she marries. Together they have two children, **Jules** and **Maureen.** Loretta's life is colored with the violence and hopelessness that characterize all the lives in this novel, yet, unlike her children, she never succumbs to the desperation that haunts their lives. Maureen is a withdrawn, sensitive young girl, who escapes into the world of literature to avoid contact with life. Like all the members of her family, she is drawn to wealth, and when as a young teenager she begins to seduce men for money, she is discovered by her stepfather, who almost beats her to death. Jules dreams of wealth and prosperity, and works for an underworld boss. The boss's daughter, **Nadine Geffen,** embodies the unattainable world of wealth and upper-class life that Jules dreams of. But when he is finally able to realize his fantasy and bed the girl of his dreams, she commits suicide.

The novel concludes in 1967, the year of the racial riots that devastated the city. Jules becomes involved with the rioting and kills a policeman. Yet he escapes prosecution and is last seen moving west for a better life. Maureen is finally able to leave behind her poor, unhappy origins by marrying a teacher, with whom she moves to the suburbs.

The novel, a literary and critical success, won for its author the National Book Award. It is noted for its unflinching examination of the world of the lower class, where violence and poverty are a way of life. It is considered by many to be her finest work.

A Bloodsmoor Romance (novel, 1982)

Set in Bloodsmoor, Pennsylvania, in the 1870s, this novel reflects a recent point of departure for the prolific Oates. Like its predecessor, *Bellefleur,* it is patterned on the Gothic romance, a form which it employs and parodies. The heroine is **Deirdre Zinn,** the adopted daughter of **John Quincy Zinn,** an inventor and educator. Together with her four sisters, Deirdre exemplifies the status of women in the nineteenth century, and Oates explores how each of them contends with, and in some cases flees from, the constrictions of their traditional roles.

Called a "feminist romance" by one critic, the novel is related in the voice of a spinster narrator, who is firmly allied with the traditional roles for women and who looks askance at the activities of the Zinn girls. As the novel begins, Deirdre is abducted in a balloon, the first of the girls to take flight. Later chapters reveal the escape of **Constance Phillipa,** who abandons her husband on her wedding night. **Malvinia** chooses the stage as her means of deliverance, and as a highly successful actress, enjoys the favors of one **Mark Twain.** **Samantha,** the intellectual of the group, follows in her father's footsteps and joins him in his scientific experiments, where she meets and falls in love with one of his assistants. Only

Octavia seems to fall prey to the conventional role of woman, marrying an older man who insists on a traditional wife. Deirdre becomes a medium, and through her we learn about the various spiritualist movements popular in the nineteenth century, for Oates weaves a complex tale incorporating the historical, political, and philosophical milieu of the era.

The novel has been praised for its fine handling of the Gothic mode, witty, satirical tone, close attention to the detail of nineteenth-century life, and its insight into the sexual, intellectual, and political repression of women of the last century.

FURTHER READING

Adams, Alice. *"A Bloodsmoor Romance." Los Angeles Times Book Review* (19 September 1982): 1, 4.

Contemporary Authors, Vols. 5-8, rev. ed. Detroit: Gale Research Co.

Contemporary Literary Criticism, Vols. 1, 2, 3, 6, 9, 11, 15, 19, 33, 52. Detroit: Gale Research Co.

Curran, Ronald. *"A Bloodsmoor Romance." World Literature Today* 57, No. 2 (Spring 1983): 290.

Dictionary of Literary Biography, Vols. 2, 5; *Dictionary of Literary Biography Yearbook: 1981.* Detroit: Gale Research Co.

Donoghue, Denis. "Wonder Woman." *The New York Review of Books* (21 October 1982): 12, 14, 16-17.

Fossum, Robert H. "Only Control: The Novels of Joyce Carol Oates." *Studies in the Novel* 7 (Summer 1975): 285-97.

Harper, Howard M. "Trends in Recent American Literature." *Contemporary Literature* 12 (Spring 1971): 204-29.

Philips, Robert. "Overview of an Extraordinary Mind." *Commonweal* (28 August 1981): 475-76.

Sullivan, Walter. "The Artificial Demon: Joyce Carol Oates and the Dimension of the Real." *Hollins Critic* 9, No. 4 (December 1972): 1-12.

Walker, Carolyn. "Fear, Love, and Art in Oates' Plot." *Critique* 15, No. 1 (1973): 59-70.

Edna O'Brien
1932-

Irish novelist, short story writer, and dramatist.

"The Country Girls Trilogy": *The Country Girls* (novel, 1960); *The Lonely Girl* (novel, 1962); *Girls in Their Married Bliss* (novel, 1964)

"The Country Girls Trilogy" comprises three novels tracing the lives of two Irish girls during the mid-twentieth century from their childhood in a village in the West of Ireland through the disillusionments and difficulties of adulthood. **Caithleen Brady,** called Kate, and **Bridget Brennan,** called Baba, are opposites: Kate the naive, introspective, and vulnerable product of a violently unhappy, alcoholic family, and Baba bold, breezy, and precociously bawdy. She is the self-confident daughter of the relatively well-to-do town veterinarian, who takes in Kate permanently after her mother drowns. In the trilogy's acclaimed first novel, which recounts these events, the girls are tossed out of convent school in their village, where Kate has become attached to a wealthy Dublin lawyer, **Mr. Gentleman,** whose country home is nearby. The two girls move to Dublin in search of worldly adventure and exciting husbands. They move into a boarding house and, largely at

Baba's instigation, plunge into drinking, dancing, smoking, and essentially running wild, often in the company of middle-aged men. ("Young men have no bloody money," Baba observes.) Their escapades and the novel end painfully when Baba contracts tuberculosis and Kate realizes, when Mr. Gentleman jilts her, that she has in the midst of selfish pursuits forgotten the anniversary of her mother's death.

The trilogy's second novel, *The Lonely Girl,* is narrated by Kate and centers largely on her ill-fated romance with **Eugene Gaillard,** a filmmaker who conceals from the lovestruck girl the fact that he has a wife and child. In spite of this, and the attempted interference of Kate's alcoholic father, the lovers stay together. Kate gradually realizes, however, Eugene's insensitivity and inability to love her as she deeply desires. Kate finally moves back in with the indomitable, always resourceful Baba, who declares that London is the place to fulfill their romantic dreams. The book's end finds them working in London at menial jobs and waiting for the excitement to happen.

Girls in Their Married Bliss details the undoing of the country girls' dreams, for which the previous novels, in their themes of loss and disappointment, had prepared us. Both "girls" have entered unsatisfactory marriages, Kate to her lover, Eugene, who leaves her after their child is born for another woman, and Baba to **Frank Durack,** whom she unapologetically scorns. Equally dissatisfying circumstances result from the women's inevitable liaisons with other men: Baba is left pregnant by **Harvey,** a drummer, and Kate comes close to a nervous breakdown when she loses her child to Eugene, who takes him away to Fiji. At the end of the book and the trilogy, the country girls are living together once again, Kate all but defeated and Baba still spirited in spite of disillusionment.

Commentators assessing the work often note the autobiographical parallels to O'Brien's own life, particularly in the first novel of the trilogy, and many attribute to this the immediacy, vividness, and credibility of its heroines. Indeed, *The Country Girls* is widely considered to be O'Brien's best novel, and Kate and Baba are regarded as a remarkable duo in contemporary literature.

FURTHER READING

Anderson, Susan Heller. "Writing: A Kind of Illness for Edna O'Brien." *The New York Times* (11 October 1977): 33.

Bannon, Barbara. "Authors and Editors." *Publishers Weekly* 197 (25 May 1970): 21-2.

Contemporary Authors, Vols. 1-4, rev. ed.; *Contemporary Authors New Revision Series,* Vol. 6. Detroit: Gale Research Co.

Contemporary Literary Criticism, Vols. 3, 5, 8, 13, 36. Detroit: Gale Research Co.

Dictionary of Literary Biography, Vol. 14. Detroit: Gale Research Co.

Eckley, Grace. *Edna O'Brien.* Lewisburg: Bucknell University Press, 1964.

McMahon, Sean. "A Sex by Themselves: An Interim Report on the Novels of Edna O'Brien." *Eire-Ireland* 2 (Spring 1977): 79-87.

Snow, Lotus. "'That Trenchant Childhood Route': Quest in Edna O'Brien's Novels." *Eire-Ireland* 14 (Spring 1979): 79-83.

Sean O'Casey
1880-1964
Irish dramatist, autobiographer, and poet.

Juno and the Paycock (drama, 1924)

In this, the second play of his "Dublin trilogy," O'Casey presents the impoverished people of the Dublin slums, and in the struggles of the Boyle family represents the conflict and eventual disintegration of Ireland.

The play is set in Dublin in 1922, when civil war had broken out between factions disputing the British division of the country. **Juno Boyle,** the matriarch and heroine, is a woman of selfless devotion to her family; their self-centeredness is in vivid contrast to her giving nature. Her husband, **Captain Jack,** is irresponsible and indolent; he drinks and dreams with his friends all day, while Juno works to support the family. He regales his drinking companion, **Joxer Daly,** with tales of his days as a seaman, and the two spin endless dreams, oblivious to the pain of the lives around them, seeking solace in reverie and alcohol as the family and their world deteriorate.

Word comes through **Charlie Bentham** that Captain Jack has inherited 2,000 pounds, and the family seems at last to have been given the chance to leave their indigence behind them. Juno's daughter, **Mary,** is drawn to Charlie, whose love of books and learning parallel her own. She also sees him as a means out of the poverty and despair she perceives in her parents' lives. She enters into an affair with him, but when she becomes pregnant, he deserts her. Charlie has also misread the will, and the legacy longed for disappears, along with Mary's hopes for a husband. Juno's son, **Johnny,** is attracted to the radical movement and has lost an arm in a political fight. But he is a young man lacking in strong moral values and informs on a friend. His cowardice proves to be his undoing, as towards the end of the play he is taken away by rebel soldiers and shot. This violent conclusion finds Juno confronted with the disintegration of the family she has fought so desperately to save. But she remains resolute, and taking Mary with her, moves to a new apartment and vows to go on.

The play is one of O'Casey's most popular, for its treatment of the political upheaval that tore Ireland apart in the early decades of this century. Stylistically, the work is noted for O'Casey's fine ear for dialect in his rendering of the idiomatic patterns of the language of his characters and for his powerful characterization in the figure of Juno.

The Plough and the Stars (drama, 1926)

Set in Dublin in 1916 at the time of the Easter Uprising, this play continues O'Casey's examination of the lives of the tenement dwellers of Dublin at the time of the "troubles." It is a portrait of a group of people who are determined to struggle and survive in their fight against the forces of death and destruction.

The play focuses on several characters who are shown in their attempt to keep the war from destroying their lives. In the first act we are introduced to **Nora Clitheroe,** a beautiful, spirited girl who attempts to convince her husband, **Jack,** to stay with her and abandon his post as a Commandant in the Citizen's Army. A nationalist and idealist, Jack is shown to be one who can forsake his pregnant wife and the life-affirming forces she represents to die for an ideal. He rejects her attempts to contain him and goes off to the conflict and his death. Nora gives birth to a stillborn child, and the effect of Jack's and the baby's death drive her to madness.

The second act takes place in a pub, which O'Casey uses to display the misplaced nationalism and ideological fervor that divides his characters. When in the ensuing acts the forces of war invade their homes, their need for one another and their humane instincts predominate, and their previous hostilities dissolve in the wake of the senseless violence that threatens them. The character of **Bessie Burgess** becomes particularly illuminated in this context. An Irish-Protestant and a supporter of England, she moves from a position of outsider in the community to become the caretaker of the mad Nora. When Nora stands in a window looking for her dead husband in the final act, Bessie pushes her out of the way and is shot by a British soldier.

Widely considered his most powerful drama, *The Plough and the Stars* reflects O'Casey's use of the expressionistic techniques that were to dominate his later plays. The final segment of his "Dublin Trilogy," it is praised for its taut construction, fine use of dialect, and complex, dramatic tension.

FURTHER READING

Armstrong, William A. *Sean O'Casey*. London: Longmans, 1967.

Ayling, Ronald, ed. *Sean O'Casey: Modern Judgments*. London: Macmillan, 1969.

Contemporary Authors, Vols. 89-92. Detroit: Gale Research Co.

Contemporary Literary Criticism, Vols. 1, 5, 9, 11, 15. Detroit: Gale Research Co.

Desmond Greaves, C. *Sean O'Casey: Politics and Art*. London: Lawrence & Wishart, 1979.

Dictionary of Literary Biography, Vol. 10. Detroit: Gale Research Co.

Krause, David and Robert Lowery, eds. *Sean O'Casey: Centenary Essays*. Gerrards Cross: Smythe, 1980.

Mitchell, Jack. *The Essential O'Casey: A Study of the Twelve Major Plays of Sean O'Casey*. New York: International Publishers, 1981.

Flannery O'Connor
1925-1964

American novelist, short story writer, and essayist.

Wise Blood (novel, 1952)

The story is set in an unspecified time in the mid-twentieth century. It takes place in Taulkinham, Tennessee, where **Hazel Motes,** newly released from the Army, has fled after finding his family home abandoned. Tormented by spiritual unrest, he decides to make a career of preaching, as did his grandfather, a fiercely religious man. But Haze, with the flawed vision that his name suggests, determines to spread the doctrines of nihilism and anti-religion rather than the Christian love and faith stressed in his fundamentalist upbringing. The action of this highly symbolic, comic, and ironic novel centers on Motes's unsuccessful attempt to deny sin, and thus God, through sin's very pursuit.

Setting up his soapbox, Motes proclaims the Church of Christ without Christ, attracting a number of grotesque figures whom he plans to lure into sin in order to prove that virtue holds no claim upon him. The cast includes the perversely seductive **Sabbath Lily Hawks;** her father, **Asa Hawks,** a phony preacher and false believer who pretends to have blinded himself as an act of faith; and **Hoover Shoats,** a smarmy radio evangelist. In his naivete, Motes fails initially to realize that these characters are thoroughly corrupt, and they leave him feeling unsatisfied, disillusioned, and still plagued by the "wild and ragged figure" of Christ, who "darts from tree to tree in the back of his mind," urging him into the world of faith.

Equally disturbing to Motes are his encounters with such true believers as the idiot boy **Enoch Emery,** who enacts his own grotesque religious rites, and the fervently religious **Solace Layfield,** who physically resembles Motes to the extent that Motes is driven to murder this embodiment of his religious "other." Haze retreats in a state of great agitation to a rooming house, where he blinds himself in one of a series of self-mortifying acts, and eventually dies. In the final scene, O'Connor implies that the light of faith, which burned ceaselessly in Motes, is transmitted at his death to his avaricious landlady, **Mrs. Flood,** who will presumably reform herself according to Christian ideals.

Wise Blood is noted for displaying characteristics that were to become the hallmark of O'Connor's work: expert depiction of the southern milieu and dialect, an artfully compressed and vivid narrative style, grotesque characters involved in intensely ironic situations, and, overriding it all, a stern sense that Christian faith offers the only possibility for meaning in the modern world.

"A Good Man Is Hard to Find" (short story, 1953)

Grandmother and **The Misfit** are the central figures of the title story of O'Connor's first short story collection, *A Good Man Is Hard to Find, and Other Stories* (1955). This, and all her short stories, also appeared in *Flannery O'Connor: The Complete Stories* (1971), which won the National Book Award in 1972.

The story begins as a southern American family—husband, wife, children, and the children's grandmother—set out on a driving vacation from their home in Georgia to Florida. The entire family is portrayed as comically vapid, ill-tempered, and self-centered, but Grandmother, with her smug pretensions about "breeding," her racial prejudice, and unceasing chatter is singled out as a particularly hollow, if harmless, personality. Grandmother has insisted that the family visit relatives in East Tennessee rather than go to Florida, making the excuse that a notorious escaped murderer, The Misfit, is believed to be headed south. When her son ignores her urging, Grandmother manipulates him to turn off the highway onto a desolate dirt road to visit a mansion she remembers from her girlhood. When she realizes that the house is in Tennessee, not Georgia, Grandmother inadvertently causes an accident that lands the car, overturned, in a ditch. The family emerges to find themselves confronted by three men, and Grandmother carelessly blurts the name of one she recognizes from a newspaper photograph: The Misfit.

Commentators often note that the automobile accident divides the story into two sections. Up to this point, the tone has been comic, although somewhat satirical and sinister; now the story becomes horrific and violent. Having been recognized, The Misfit acts swiftly to murder the family, sending all but Grandmother into the woods to be shot by his accomplices. The remaining dialogue between The Misfit and Grandmother reveals his character and unlocks the meaning of the story. While Grandmother, half mad with fear, tries to appeal to The Misfit's middle-class values and Christianity ("'You're not a bit common!'"; "'If you would pray . . . Jesus would help you'"), he rebukes her: "'Jesus was the only One that ever raised the dead . . . and he shouldn't have done it. He thrown everything off balance. . . . [It's] nothing for you to do but enjoy the few minutes you got left the best way you can—by killing somebody or burning down his house. . . . No pleasure but meanness.'" The Grandmother becomes more frenzied in her appeals until her hysteria subsides to a moment of calmness and clear vision. Reaching out to touch him she murmurs: "Why you're one of my babies. . . . one of my own children," at which point he kills her. "'It's no real pleasure in life'," comments The Misfit drily in the story's blackly comic conclusion. Critics note that The Misfit is, like Hazel Motes in *Wise Blood,* an inverted prophet who through his violence shocks Grandmother from her complacency to a moment of true grace in death.

"A Good Man Is Hard to Find" is noted for its extreme authorial detachment, which allows O'Connor to balance the comic and horrible, and for its fresh and authentic detail of local color and dialect, which is a trademark of O'Connor's fiction. For the brutality and artistry with which it conveys O'Connor's central message of Christian redemption, "A Good Man Is Hard to Find" is one of her most-often discussed and frequently anthologized stories.

"The Displaced Person" (short story, 1954)

Mrs. Shortley, Mrs. McIntyre, and **Mr. Guizac,** referred to as the **Displaced Person,** are the main characters of "The Displaced Person," which appeared as a three-part story in O'Connor's collection, *A Good Man Is Hard to Find* (1955). In its initial 1954 publication in the journal *Sewanee Review,* O'Connor included only the first section; the concluding two were added at book publication.

"The Displaced Person" is set after World War II on the Tennessee dairy farm of Mrs. McIntyre, a proud and pragmatic manager who has run the operation single-handedly since the death of her elderly husband many years before. The charitable **Father Flynn** convinces her to hire Mr. Guizac, a Polish war refugee, to work with his family on the farm. The Displaced Person proves himself an industrious and indefatigable worker, but his peaceful, unassuming presence sets off a series of crises in the farm's closed and small-minded society. The story's first section reflects the viewpoint of Mrs. Shortley, the dairyman's wife, who has an exaggerated sense of proprietorship over the farm, although she and her ineffectual husband are merely tenants. Her monumental self-confidence is shaken as it becomes clear that competent Mr. Guizac poses a threat to her husband's job. She conceives a self-righteous aversion to Guizac and his family, who in their mysterious Roman Catholicism and European foreignness represent the blight of evil manifested in the remote war overseas. When Mrs. Shortley overhears Mrs. McIntyre's declared intention to indeed fire Mr. Shortley, she plans the family's abrupt departure. In the midst of flight, however, she is stricken with a heart attack, which, leaving her body distorted and twisted in the crowded car, aligns her with the Holocaust victims whose jumbled corpses she has seen in newsreel photographs. Thus violently transported from self-complacency and joined with human suffering, Mrs. Shortley at death sees "the tremendous frontiers of her true country," a spiritual kingdom she had ignored for material concerns.

Parts two and three detail the similar transformation of Mrs. McIntyre, whose joy in the hardworking Displaced Person turns to dismay when she learns his plan to bring his Polish cousin to Tennessee to marry **Sulk,** a black farmhand. Mr. Guizac's guileless violation of the southern social order and of racial segregation drives Mrs. McIntyre to become a passive accomplice to Mr. Guizac's murder in a tractor "accident" also witnessed by Mr. Shortley and Sulk. This event precipitates the dissolution of the farm and deterioration of Mrs. McIntyre's health. Stripped of her life-defining sense of control, she learns, like Mrs. Shortley, what it is to suffer, and she is steeped in spiritual teachings by Father Flynn, her only visitor. The Displaced Person, who has remained a vague presence throughout the story, is twice explicitly identified with Christ, who is called "just another D.P." While O'Connor's characters are often brought to grace by such distorted Christ figures as Hazel Motes of *Wise Blood* and The Misfit of "A Good Man Is Hard to Find," the Displaced Person signifies Christ himself. By "displacing" Mrs. Shortley and Mrs. McIntyre from their graceless worlds, Mr. Guizac demonstrates that all human beings are displaced until they reach God's spiritual kingdom.

The Violent Bear It Away (novel, 1960)

The novel is set in mid-twentieth century Tennessee, where a fierce backwoods prophet, **Mason Tarwater,** has just died at his home, Powderhead. He leaves his grandnephew, 14-year-old **Francis Marion Tarwater,** charged with these tasks: to give his granduncle a Christian burial; to baptize **Bishop Rayber,** the idiot son of his unbelieving uncle, **George Rayber;** and thereby to assume the role of prophet for which he has been raised. Young Tarwater is soon distracted from his grave-digging, however, by the disembodied voice of a friendly "stranger," who is clearly the devil. Tarwater gets drunk, sets fire to his granduncle's house where (the boy believes) the old man's body still lies, and goes to his uncle Rayber in the city. The subsequent action of this novel, like O'Connor's *Wise Blood,* centers on the struggle of a soul against religious faith.

As old Tarwater represents fervent religious belief, George Rayber, a teacher-psychologist, stands for its opposite: secular rationalism. In a series of interwoven flashbacks, O'Connor reveals that old Tarwater had kidnapped young Tarwater from Rayber (the boy was the son of Rayber's dead sister) in order to give him religious training. Furthermore, old Tarwater had kidnapped Rayber himself from his faithless parents when *he* was a boy. Although old Tarwater succeeded in converting Rayber, his father fetched him back, and he ultimately embraced non-belief, even writing a pyschological article reducing old Tarwater's prophetic calling to "neurotic delusion." Young Tarwater is as unwilling to be initiated into his uncle's secular rationalism as into Christian faith, and his growing inner conflict drives him to drown Bishop in order to remove the constant impulse to follow his granduncle's orders to baptize him. While committing the act, young Tarwater involuntarily utters the words of baptism, but he hopes that his nihilistic deed will supersede the words of faith. For his part, Rayber is determinedly emotionless at the death of his beloved son, and thus, O'Connor implies, hopelessly dehumanized by his rationalism.

Confident that he has destroyed the possibility for his religious vocation, Tarwater starts back to Powderhead. But a slick young man who offers him a lift for the last leg of his journey embodies the demonic friendly "stranger," and he drugs Tarwater, rapes, and abandons him. Setting fire to the tainted woods where this occurred, Tarwater returns to Powderhead to find that his black neighbor, **Buford Munson,** had buried old Tarwater before the boy had burned the house down. Standing before his uncle's crucifix-marked grave, Tarwater has a transforming vision which ignites irrevocably his prophetic vocation. Smearing his forehead with earth from the grave, he turns back toward the city "where the children of God lay sleeping."

Essentially the chronicle of a soul's struggle for faith, the meaning of *The Violent Bear It Away* relies largely upon O'Connor's rich and complex system of Christian symbolism and imagery, including water, fire, hunger, the bread of life, earth, and rock. Similar in subject matter and theme to *Wise Blood, The Violent Bear It Away* is often noted for its greater symbolic density, more serious tone, and resonant prose style.

"Everything That Rises Must Converge" (short story, 1961)

The story takes place in an unnamed southern American city at the time of the Civil Rights Movement. Fearful of traveling alone on the newly integrated buses, **Mrs. Chestny** asks her son, **Julian,** to accompany her downtown to the YWCA, where she is taking a reducing class to help control her high blood pressure. Julian, a would-be writer and self-styled southern liberal, is disdainful of his mother's old southern attitudes, which lead her to cherish her faded genteel background and fear blacks, who, she maintains,"'should rise, yes, but on their own side of the fence.'" Julian's smug disdain for his mother leads him to goad her, once on the bus, by trying to befriend a black man. Thwarted in this attempt, he is delighted when a large black woman boards wearing a hideous green and purple hat identical to the one his mother has on, a recent purchase of which she is very proud. In a display of her superior breeding, Mrs. Chestny smiles away the coincidence "as if the woman were a monkey that had stolen her hat" and concentrates on admiring the woman's little boy. As the four leave the bus together, Mrs. Chestny offers the child a "shiny new penny," a transparently condescending act that causes the woman to strike Mrs. Chestny with her large handbag, knocking her to the ground. Initially exhilarated that his mother has received her comeuppance, Julian's malicious glee turns to panic when he realizes that his mother is suffering a stroke. As she, senseless, calls ironically for the beloved Negro nanny of her childhood, Julian too reverts, crying "'Mother! . . . Darling, sweetheart, wait!'" before he runs down the street for help, postponing momentarily "his entry into the world of guilt and sorrow."

In its depiction of racial integration, "Everything That Rises Must Converge" is noted as one of O'Connor's few overt treatments of social issues. But many critics point out that closer to the heart of the piece lies an examination of human pride, a favorite subject for O'Connor. In the economically drawn portraits of Julian and Mrs. Chestny, O'Connor demonstrates that the smug pride of the "liberal intellectual" can be as offensive, and perhaps more so, than the bland, offhand racism and classism of the old southerner. Both of the prideful Chestnys are deflated, horribly: Mrs. Chestny by the killing blow of the offended black woman and Julian through the imminent loss of his mother. It is clear at the end of the story that Julian realizes all at once his dependence on Mrs. Chestny and her old order, no matter what pains he took to despise them.

FURTHER READING

Asals, Frederick. *Flannery O'Connor: The Imagination of Extremity*. Athens: University of Georgia Press, 1982.

Browning, Preston M. *Flannery O'Connor*. Carbondale: Southern Illinois University Press, 1974.

Burns, Stuart L. "Structural Patterns in *Wise Blood.*" *Xavier University Studies* 8 (Summer 1969): 32-43.

Contemporary Authors, Vols. 1-4, rev. ed.; *Contemporary Authors New Revision Series*, Vol. 3. Detroit: Gale Research Co.

Contemporary Literary Criticism, Vols. 1, 2, 3, 6, 10, 13, 15, 21. Detroit: Gale Research Co.

Detweiler, Robert. "The Curse of Christ in Flannery O'Connor's Fiction." *Comparative Literature Studies* 3 (1966): 235-45.

Dictionary of Literary Biography, Vol. 2; *Dictionary of Literary Biography Yearbook: 1980; Concise Dictionary of American Literary Biography, 1941-1968*. Detroit: Gale Research Co.

Driskell, Leon V. and Joan T. Brittain. *The Eternal Crossroads: The Art of Flannery O'Connor*. Lexington: University of Kentucky Press, 1971.

Feeley, Kathleen. *Flannery O'Connor: Voice of the Peacock*, 1972. Reprint. New York: Fordham University Press, 1982.

Fitzgerald, Robert. Introduction to *Everything That Rises Must Converge*, by Flannery O'Connor, pp. 5-30. New York: Farrar, Straus, and Giroux, 1965.

Friedman, Melvin J. and Lewis A. Lawson, eds. *The Added Dimension: The Art and Mind of Flannery O'Connor*. New York: Fordham University Press, 1977.

Hawkes, John. "Flannery O'Connor's Devil." *Sewanee Review* 70 (Summer 1962): 395-407.

Hyman, Stanley Edgar. *Flannery O'Connor*. Minneapolis: University of Minnesota Press, 1966.

Martin, Carter W. *The True Country: Themes in the Fiction of Flannery O'Connor*. Nashville: Vanderbilt University Press, 1969.

Mayer, David R. "*The Violent Bear It Away:* Flannery O'Connor's Shaman." *Southern Literary Journal* 4 (Spring 1972): 41-54.

Montgomery, Marion. "Beyond Symbol and Surface: The Fiction of Flannery O'Connor."
   Georgia Review 22 (Summer 1968): 188-93.

Oates, Joyce Carol. "Ritual Violence in Flannery O'Connor." *Thought* 41 (Winter 1966):
   545-60.

Short Story Criticism, Vol. 1. Detroit: Gale Research Co.

Walters, Dorothy. *Flannery O'Connor.* New York: Twayne, 1973.

Sean O'Faolain

1900-

Irish novelist, short story writer, essayist, and critic.

A Nest of Simple Folk (novel, 1933)

This novel, which like many of O'Faolain's works centers on the Fenian struggle for Irish independence, is set in Ireland between 1854 and 1916. The central character is **Leo Foxe-Donnell,** who through his doting mother is related to an aristocratic, but now poverty-stricken, landed family. Despite these ties, however, Leo is a fervent Fenian; personally he is a wild seducer and irresponsible ne'er-do-well, but his patriotic allegiance frequently inspires him to self-sacrificing acts, for which he is twice imprisoned. After his first imprisonment, Leo impregnates **Julie Keene,** who goes to Dublin to bear and to give away their son. Eventually Leo is persuaded by the parish priest to marry Julie, and they establish a stationery store. Julie's sister, **Bid Keene,** who lives with them, marries **Johnny Hussey,** a local policeman and British sympathizer, who monitors Leo for illicit Fenian activity and helps imprison him for a second time.

After his release from prison, Leo and Julie, now elderly, live with Johnny and Bid. Johnny and Bid's eldest son, **Denis,** always quiet and watchful, is groomed by his parents for education, gentility, and a life of civil service. But at novel's end, when the Easter Uprising occurs in Dublin, Denis first helps Leo escape, and then runs off to take up the cause himself.

A Nest of Simple Folk, one of O'Faolain's most acclaimed works, is praised for its dramatic presentation of the dominant dilemma of Irish life: like Leo and Johnny, the republican and anti-republican must coexist in forced and pretended harmony. In his depiction of Johnny Hussey, O'Faolain represents what he sees as the generation of Irish who put their petty material comforts and bourgeois values above the urgent needs of their country. In the novel's conclusion, when Denis Hussey rejects his father's values for the urgency of revolution, O'Faolain expresses hope that the young Irish will continue to replace empty middle-class values with revolutionary idealism.

FURTHER READING

Contemporary Authors, Vols. 61-64; *Contemporary Authors New Revision Series,* Vol.
   12. Detroit: Gale Research Co.

Contemporary Literary Criticism, Vols. 1, 7, 14, 32. Detroit: Gale Research Co.

Davenport, Gary T. "Sean O'Faolain's Troubles: Revolution and Provincialism in Modern
   Ireland." *South Atlantic Quarterly* 75 (Summer 1976): 312-22.

Dictionary of Literary Biography, Vol. 15. Detroit: Gale Research Co.

Doyle, Paul A. *Sean O'Faolain.* New York: Twayne, 1968.

Harmon, Maurice. *Sean O'Faolain: A Critical Introduction.* Notre Dame: University of Notre Dame Press, 1966.

John O'Hara
1905-1970
American novelist and short story writer.

Appointment in Samarra (novel, 1934)

O'Hara's most popular novel, *Appointment in Samarra* incorporates the setting and themes that recur throughout his work. It takes place in the fictional town of Gibbsville, the counterpart to O'Hara's own home town of Pottsville, Pennsylvania, and concerns the jealousy and hostility between the WASP elite and the ethnic American groups struggling for social ascendancy in the America of the late 1920s and early 1930s.

The novel's protagonist is **Julian English,** the scion of a wealthy family and a member of the social elite. Yet despite his status and comfortable life as the owner of a Cadillac dealership, he is plagued by insecurities. His father, a successful physician, is a cold, critical presence who sees in his son the same failings that led to his own father's suicide. Julian's wife is vapid and manipulative, using sex as a means to control and demean her husband. Julian is seen as a victim, too, of the hypocritical, superficial society of which he is a part, and he takes a modicum of revenge on them all through his drinking, the source of his release from the inhibiting powers of Gibbsville.

The story focuses on the final three days in Julian's life, beginning with the novel's pivotal scene in a roadhouse where he throws a drink in the face of **Harry Reilly,** a wealthy, successful, Irish Catholic who has lent Julian money to keep his dealership afloat. Julian's snobbish contempt for the Irish Catholics of Gibbsville as well as his wilful self-destructiveness are centered in this action, which brings down the wrath of the Irish community. In a further act of defiance, he takes up with **Helene Holman,** the girlfriend of a bootlegger. But Julian's acts of rebellion end in his own suicide, as he asphyxiates himself in his car.

The novel is noted for its realistic prose style and close examination of the codified class system in the America of the late 1920s. O'Hara observes each of the classes in Gibbsville—the rich, the middle class, and the criminal underworld—chronicling the material trappings of success in each group and revealing his fine ear for dialect by using characters' speech to reflect social origins.

FURTHER READING

Bier, Jesse. "O'Hara's *Appointment in Samarra:* His First and Only Real Novel." *College English* 25 (November 1963): 135-41.

Carson, E. Russell. *The Fiction of John O'Hara.* Pittsburgh: University of Pittsburgh Press, 1961.

Contemporary Authors, Vols. 5-8, rev. ed., 25-28, rev. ed. Detroit: Gale Research Co.

Contemporary Literary Criticism, Vols. 1, 2, 3, 6, 11, 42. Detroit: Gale Research Co.

Dictionary of Literary Biography, Vol. 9; *Dictionary of Literary Biography Documentary Series,* Vol. 2. Detroit: Gale Research Co.

Walcutt, Charles. *John O'Hara.* Minneapolis: University of Minnesota Press, 1969.

Eugene O'Neill
1888-1953

American dramatist.

The Emperor Jones (drama, 1920)

The play is set on an island in the West Indies. **Brutus Jones,** a black American, has set himself up as tyrant and emperor of the island. As the trader **Henry Smithers** warns him, the natives are about to rebel, and he urges Jones to step down. In defiance, he refuses and flees into the woods. The rest of the play recounts his journey into the forest. This drama reflects O'Neill's use of expressionistic techniques, and as Jones goes into the forest, the natives' drums are heard, beating at seventy-two beats per minute, mimicking the human heart. They echo throughout the play, dramatically increasing as Jones encounters a variety of ghostly specters in successive, dream-like vignettes. These scenes represent unconscious memories, terrors, and remnants of his racial past, including "Little Formless Fears"; the ghost of a man he had killed; a white guard leading a group of black convicts, of which he is a part; a slave auctioneer and a planter who attempt to buy and sell him as a slave; and a witch-doctor. In each scene, Jones dispels the ghosts with a bullet from his revolver. He has kept the natives at bay by telling them that he can only be killed by a silver bullet; the last bullet he uses, on the witch-doctor, is a silver bullet, which he had saved for himself. In the final scene, **Lem,** the leader of the natives, sends his rebel forces into the forest armed with silver bullets, which he had made from money. With these, the natives shoot and kill Jones.

Considered to be O'Neill's first major dramatic effort, the work is noted for its intense, nightmarish effects, and for its portrayal of Jones's growing madness as he is pursued by the demons of his past.

The Hairy Ape (drama, 1922)

Set in and around New York City, the play tells the story of **Robert Smith,** known as **Yank,** a stoker on a ship whose fate represents for O'Neill the inherent isolation of modern man. There are several recurrent motifs in the drama, including images of cages and humans described as ape-like or bestial. When we first see Yank, he is in the cage-like forecastle of the ship. He and his fellow workers are described as Neanderthal men, with long arms and hairy chests. Despite his brutal appearance, Yank is a sympathetically drawn character, whose sense of belonging is threatened when he encounters **Mildred Douglas,** the daughter of a wealthy industrialist, who while touring the ship sees Yank and calls him a "filthy beast." The remainder of the play depicts Yank's attempts to restore his dignity and sense of self, especially his sense of "belonging," another of O'Neill's repeated themes. Yank goes to Fifth Avenue, where he is arrested for assaulting a man. He lands in jail, described as another cage, where he talks to the other prisoners, represented as nameless voices in the dark void. As he raves about revenge, he learns from the others that Mildred's father is a millionaire steel industrialist, the maker of "cages." His jail mates encourage Yank to join the Wobblies—the IWW—to revenge himself on Mildred and her father. When he is released, he joins the union, but is treated as an inferior by the men. He offers to blow up Douglas's steel factory, but they take him to be a spy. Calling him a "brainless ape," they throw him out. Yank's final scene takes place in the monkey house in the zoo. He confides in the gorilla, as if the animal understands and sympathizes with him. Again, Yank talks about his desire to belong and how out of place he feels everywhere. Yank lets the gorilla out of its cage; the gorilla crushes him, then puts Yank in its cage, where he dies.

The work is noted for its powerful, passionate evocation of a lonely, alienated man. Written in O'Neill's expressionistic mode, the action and character types are symbolic rather than realistic, as O'Neill states in his stage directions.

Desire under the Elms (drama, 1924)

The play is set on the Cabot farm in rural New England in 1850. **Ephraim Cabot** is a greedy, cold man who has buried two wives, the second of whom he worked to death to gain control of her farm. He has fathered three sons, all of whom hate him. The eldest two have left home; only the third, **Eben Cabot,** remains. His contempt for his father is so great that he has secretly bought off his two brothers so that he alone can claim the farm as his after his father's death. Ephraim has married **Abbie Putnam,** a woman half his age, to deny his sons their inheritance. But Abbie has plans of her own for the farm: she has seduced Eben and is now pregnant by him, thus insuring that her child will inherit the farm. Ephraim is proud enough to believe that the child is his, but complications arise when Abbie falls in love with Eben, and to prove her love, she murders the child when it is born, leaving Eben the sole heir. She tells Ephraim what she has done, and Eben, in shock and horror, goes for the sheriff. Yet he acknowledges that he loves Abbie, and when she is arrested, Eben goes with her to share her guilt and punishment.

The elms of the title function as a dominating presence in the lives of the characters, reflecting the cruelty of the people who inhabit the Cabot farm. In one scene, they are described as possessing a "sinister maternity," foreshadowing Abbie's brutal smothering of her baby. O'Neill's repeated themes of betrayal and loveless families are expressed in this work, which is considered the most naturalistic of his major plays.

Mourning Becomes Electra (drama, 1931)

This work, modelled on the *Oresteia* of Euripides, is divided into three parts—*Homecoming, The Hunted,* and *The Haunted.* It focuses on the fate of the Mannon family. **Lavinia Mannon,** rejected by her mother, develops a passionate attachment for her father, **Ezra Mannon,** a character who embodies O'Neill's concept of the cold, detached New Englander. **Christine,** Lavinia's mother and Ezra's wife, is involved in an affair with **Adam Brant,** who is related to the family. He is the son of **David Mannon,** who had married a servant and was rejected by the family. Adam's plot for revenge is to seduce Christine and hurt Ezra, but he falls in love with her. When Ezra returns from the war, Christine tells him of the affair, and he suffers a heart attack. Christine poisons him, and his death ends the first part of the trilogy.

In *The Hunted,* Lavinia tells her brother, **Orin,** just returned from the war, the fate of their father, and together they plot Adam's murder. Orin shoots and kills him, an act that drives Christine to suicide. The last section of the play, *The Haunted,* depicts Lavinia and Orin trying to escape the shame and guilt of their past on a South Seas Island. The journey has a transforming effect on Lavinia, who begins to look and act like her mother and is drawn to the sensuous in life. Orin, however, is unable to elude the fate he feels to be so compelling. He reminds Lavinia of their destiny: to live out the family curse of self-destruction. Although Lavinia has a lover and wishes to marry, Orin makes her return to the Mannon mansion with him, which she does out of a sense of their inescapable fate. Upon their return, Orin commits suicide; Lavinia retreats into the mansion, closing the shutters forever.

The play is considered by many critics to be O'Neill's greatest achievement. In his use of a Greek model, he gave his drama a classical theme and tension, depicting the inexorable movement toward catastrophe that marks his characters. Although some commentators feel that the language is weak in sections, the structure of the work is universally praised.

The Iceman Cometh (drama, 1946)

The play is set in New York City in 1912 and chronicles the lives of a group of lonely denizens who live, drink, and dream at **Harry Hope**'s boarding house and bar, each lost in a separate world of illusion. As the play opens, they are eagerly awaiting the annual visit of **Hickey**, a traveling salesman who always attends Harry's birthday party, bringing jokes and ribald stories about his wife and the iceman. But this year is different: Hickey has sworn off drink, and tells the others that he is now free of illusions and is at last at peace. He proceeds to destroy the dreams of the boarders, to force them to see reality. Hounded by Hickey, they leave the house the next day to try to realize the pipe dreams they have talked about and gotten drunk over for years; they return, each devastated in defeat. The final act contains Hickey's surprising confession: he says he has killed his wife, out of love for her endlessly forgiving nature. Yet he at last admits that it was hatred rather than love that motivated the murder. His actions are mirrored in those of another member of the group, **Don Parrit,** who had supposedly come to the boarding house to hide out from the police because he and his mother were involved in political activities. He now admits that he had turned his mother in for a reward. When these men admit that they, too, are still governed by illusion and self-deception, the group uses the occasion to return to their drink and their dreams.

In this play, O'Neill explores the nature of truth and illusion, focussing on the importance of delusion in human life. The "iceman" of the title represents death, and O'Neill shows how each character uses his dreams to avoid the reality of responsibility and mortality. Many critics note the influence of Maxim Gorky's *Lower Depths* on the content of the play.

Long Day's Journey into Night (drama, 1956)

Perhaps O'Neill's most acclaimed work, the play is noted for its strongly autobiographical content. It is set in Connecticut in 1912 and depicts the tortuous relationships within the Tyrone family. **James Tyrone,** the father, is a successful actor and a cold and cruel man who has succeeded in his career at the expense of his family. His elder son, **Jamie,** is also an actor and a member of his father's company. His response to his father's coldness and the family's deep problems is a mask of cynicism. **Edmund Tyrone,** who is the O'Neill figure, is a sickly young man and an aspiring writer. Their mother, **Mary,** is a drug addict who spends the play trying to convince her family that she has overcome her dependence. The play revolves around one day in the life of the Tyrones, in which we learn, through dialogue and monologue, the unhappy history of a family.

O'Neill's themes are betrayal, lack of trust, accusation, and illusion. Mary sees herself as a victim and blames her drug addiction on James's indifference and neglect; Jamie treats Edmund's artistic aspirations with a cynicism that barely cloaks his jealousy; Edmund's "cold" is really tuberculosis, but the family chooses to ignore the seriousness of his condition. Their lives of self-delusion are symbolized by the fog, which grows thicker throughout the play, first noticed outside, and in the final scene permeating the interior of the Tyrone house. The family has been destroyed by years of deceit, yet they cling to their illusory sense of unity until the end. In their tormented dialogues, they seek to tear away each other's masks to reveal the painful truth.

The journey that O'Neill depicts in this work is one into the self and the past. Yet the efforts to pierce the illusion are in vain, for in the concluding scene, Mary, drugged, descends the stairs in her wedding dress and immerses herself in the fog, indicating that these lives will remain unilluminated, and that the drama we have witnessed will be repeated endlessly.

Long Day's Journey into Night won O'Neill the Pulitzer Prize and is widely acknowledged as his masterpiece. It is considered one of his finest plays structurally and is also praised for the universality of its themes.

FURTHER READING

Alexander, Doris M. "Eugene O'Neill as Social Critic." *American Quarterly* 6 (Winter 1954): 349-63.

Andreach, Robert J. "O'Neill's Women in *The Iceman Cometh.*" *Renascence* 18 (Winter 1966): 89-98.

Blackburn, Clara. "Continental Influences on Eugene O'Neill's Expressionistic Dramas." *American Literature* 13 (May 1941): 109-33.

Clark, Barrett H. *Eugene O'Neill: The Man and His Plays.* New York: McBride, 1929.

Clark, Marden J. "Tragic Effect in *The Hairy Ape.*" *Modern Drama* 10 (February 1968): 372-78.

Contemporary Authors, Vol. 110. Detroit: Gale Research Co.

Dictionary of Literary Biography, Vol. 7. Detroit: Gale Research Co.

Engel, Edwin A. *The Haunted Heroes of Eugene O'Neill.* Cambridge: Harvard University Press, 1953.

Falk, Doris V. *Eugene O'Neill and the Tragic Tension.* New Brunswick: Rutgers University Press, 1958.

Frazer, Winifred L. *Love as Death in "The Iceman Cometh."* Gainesville: University of Florida Press, 1967.

Frenz, Horst. *Eugene O'Neill.* New York: Ungar, 1971.

Gassner, John. *Eugene O'Neill.* Minneapolis: University of Minnesota Press, 1965.

Hays, Peter, L. "Biblical Perversions in *Desire under the Elms.*" *Modern Drama* 11 (February 1969): 423-28.

Helburn, Theresa. *A Wayward Quest.* Boston: Little, Brown, 1960.

Hopkins, Vivian C. "*The Iceman Cometh* Seen Through *The Lower Depths.*" *College English* 11 (November 1949): 81-7.

Langer, Lawrence. *The Magic Curtain.* New York: Dutton, 1951.

Miller, Jordan Y. "The Georgia Plays of Eugene O'Neill." *Georgia Review* 12 (1958): 278-90.

Raleigh, John Henry. "O'Neill's *Long Day's Journey into Night* and New England Irish-Catholicism." *Partisan Review* 26 (Fall 1959): 573-92.

———. *The Plays of Eugene O'Neill.* Carbondale: Southern Illinois University Press, 1965.

Törnqvist, Egil. *A Drama of Souls.* New Haven: Yale University Press, 1969.

Twentieth-Century Literary Criticism, Vols. 1, 6, 27. Detroit: Gale Research Co.

Joe Orton

1933-1965

English dramatist and novelist.

Loot (drama, 1965)

Orton's second full-length play displays his contempt for the arbitrary and hypocritical nature of British morality. **McLeavy** is grieving the death of his wife, who has been killed by nurse **Phyllis McMahon,** called Fay, a serial murderer who hopes to marry the bereft McLeavy for his money. His son, **Harold,** called Hal, has conspired in a bank robbery with his undertaker friend—and Fay's sometime lover—**Dennis.** When police detective **Jim Truscott** comes to the McLeavy household to investigate the robbery, Dennis and Hal hide the money in Hal's mother's casket and remove the body to a locked cupboard. The body and its various removable components, including glass eyes and false teeth, become comic properties reflecting Orton's attempt to shock the audience as well as to ridicule social propriety. McLeavy's absolute belief in authority, Truscott's unorthodox and corrupt demeanor, and Dennis and Fay's morally bankrupt characters further reveal Orton's scorn for the British status quo. McLeavy, the only honest character in the play, is also the only individual arrested, and later dies under mysterious circumstances, action that further conveys Orton's ironic, darkly comic sensibility.

In this work, Orton presents a parody of the fictional detective in the character of Truscott, an unscrupulous, dishonest man and a symbol of the moral malaise that, for Orton, permeates British culture. The play is praised as a well-done farce, which savagely reveals and reviles British hypocrisy and middle-class venality. The language of the play is noted for the comic juxtaposition of formal and informal language. *Loot* is considered Orton's first major dramatic piece and is well-regarded among critics who see in the work evidence of the black comedy that Orton was to display so brilliantly in his final play, *What the Butler Saw.*

What the Butler Saw (drama, 1969)

Orton's last play is an unfinished farce that was published and produced posthumously. In this work, he both adopts and parodies the schematics of farce as outlined by French dramatist Georges Feydeau.

Dr. Prentice is the head psychiatrist of a mental hospital. While interviewing **Geraldine Barclay** for a secretarial position, Prentice attempts a seduction. Interrupted by **Mrs. Prentice,** the doctor fabricates a story to protect himself, telling his wife and **Dr. Rance,** a psychiatrist who inspects mental hospitals for the government, that Barclay is one of his patients. Mrs. Prentice, meanwhile, is being blackmailed by **Nicholas Beckett,** who demands that she find him employment. **Sergeant Match** arrives looking for Beckett, who had engaged in sexual activities with a group of juvenile women the night before. Beckett disguises himself as a woman in order to escape detection, only to be mistaken for Geraldine, whom Rance is convinced is insane. Geraldine turns out to be Prentice's long-lost daughter, and Beckett turns out to be her twin brother, a conclusion that mocks the conventional recognition scene of classical comedy. The characters are by necessity one-dimensional and are employed by Orton to lampoon the play's authority figures. Rance and Match are portrayed as hapless buffoons, and Dr. Prentice as a lecherous opportunist; Mrs. Prentice, the good middle-class wife, is revealed to be a nymphomaniac. Thus Orton continues his satire on the duplicity of the British social system, where appearance and illusion mask the underlying reality of corruption and selfishness.

Although left incomplete and unrevised at his death, *What the Butler Saw* is considered Orton's masterpiece, a perfect vehicle for his great satiric gifts. He showed himself a master at handling such stock comic devices as mistaken identity and comic reversal and revealed his keen insight into the darker aspects of human nature.

FURTHER READING

Bigsby, C. W. E. *Joe Orton.* London: Methuen, 1982.

Contemporary Authors, Vols. 85-88. Detroit: Gale Research Co.

Contemporary Literary Criticism, Vols. 4, 13, 43. Detroit: Gale Research Co.

Dictionary of Literary Biography, Vol. 13. Detroit: Gale Research Co.

Draudt, Manfred. "Comic, Tragic, or Absurd? On Some Parallels Between the Farces of Joe Orton and Seventeenth-Century Tragedy." *English Studies* 59 (1978): 202-17.

Esslin, Martin. "Joe Orton: The Comedy of (Ill) Manners." In *Contemporary English Drama,* edited by C. W. E. Bigsby, pp. 95-107. New York: Holmes & Meier, 1981.

Fraser, Keath. "Joe Orton: His Brief Career." *Modern Drama* 14 (1971): 414-19.

Nightingale, Benedict. "The Detached Anarchist: On Joe Orton." *Encounter* 52, No. 3 (March 1979): 55-61.

Smith, Leslie. "Democratic Lunacy: The Comedies of Joe Orton." *Adam: International Review* 394-396 (1976): 73-92.

George Orwell
1903-1950
English novelist, essayist, and critic.

Animal Farm (novel, 1945)

Set on a British farm during the 1940s, this classic political allegory traces the revolt of the Manor Farm animals against their oppressor, **Mr. Jones,** an inconsiderate, mean-spirited farmer. Prior to the revolt, the oldest pig, **Major,** gathers the animals together and expounds his dream of revolution. He points to humans as the source of evil and of the animals' unjust misery. After establishing rules for the new order of life he envisions, Major dies peacefully. From Major's teaching a social system called Animalism develops, formulated by the most intelligent barnyard animals, the pigs. After Jones and his wife are driven from the land, Animal Farm is founded and a list of Seven Commandments is established. The Commandments unite all animals in comradeship and mutual equality while identifying the human race as the enemy. Significantly, the pigs establish themselves as leaders over their more docile and brutish counterparts, the sheep, horses, and dogs. These masses are cleverly subjugated through **Squealer's** doubletalk and kept content, initially, by their share in the benefits that follow from increased labor. **Snowball** assumes primary control of the collective and institutes various organizational and educational reforms. However, when he presents an impressive plan for the construction of a windmill to provide electrical power, **Napoleon,** with the aid of dogs he has secretly trained, overthrows his fellow pig and assumes absolute dictatorship. He rewrites the history of the animals so that Snowball is made a traitor and he also revises the Commandments to support greater privileges for the pigs. Gradually the pigs come to resemble the humans whom they once despised. By the close of the fable, the Seven Commandments have been reduced to the single maxim: "All animals are equal, but some animals are more equal than others."

Although Orwell intended *Animal Farm* to depict the inevitable course of all revolutions, the Soviet Union was the primary target of the novel's pointed, underlying commentary. Critics hostile to Orwell's political position have endeavored to demonstrate that the novel is an inadequate treatment of extremely complicated issues, or that *Animal Farm* does not contain exact parallels to the historical events being satirized and is therefore invalid. Nevertheless, most critics concur that the basic plot of the novel closely parallels events in the Soviet Union. Snowball and Napoleon represent Leon Trotsky and Josef Stalin, even to Snowball's eventual ouster of Napoleon. The Squealer represents the official Soviet news agency *Pravda.* The simple and hardworking cart-horses and the anonymous sheep stand for whole classes of people whose uncomprehending complicity aids the tyrants who pervert the revolutionary ideal of equality to establish themselves as the ruling elite. Only the Major, who represents Karl Marx and his original doctrine of socialism, escapes Orwell's satirical indictment. In the final analysis, *Animal Farm* is the first and arguably the finest example of the fusion of artistic and political purpose in his writing and stands as a masterpiece of English prose.

Nineteen Eighty-Four (novel, 1949)

Orwell's classic dystopian novel is set in Oceania, a totalitarian state controlled by a mysterious Inner Party that exacts blind devotion to the Party and to its leader, **Big Brother.** Devotion is reinforced through constantly rewritten history (which retrospectively proves the Party infallible), two-way telescreens monitored by Thought Police, Big Brother's omnipresence, frenzied group hate sessions, and frequent public executions. The novel recounts the brief revolt of one man, thirty-nine-year-old **Winston Smith,** a writer of newspeak for the Ministry of Truth who is privy to the deliberate revision of historical records. One day Winston begins keeping a private journal, in which he pens statements antithetical to Big Brother and the Party. Soon after he begins a furtive romantic alliance with **Julia,** a member of the Anti-Sex League. Initially characterized by physical need, their relationship develops into one of close affection and understanding. An acquaintance of Winston, **Mr. Charrington,** rents them a small bedroom above his antique shop. At work Winston discovers his colleague **O'Brien** shares his subversive views and so he and Julia visit O'Brien's apartment and discuss an underground conspiracy, led by **Emmanuel Goldstein,** that plans to overthrow the Party. After O'Brien has admitted them to the conspiracy and given them Goldstein's tract to read, the two are later besieged in their flat by a voice from a hidden telescreen and then stormed by guards who arrest them. Winston and Julia are separated; Winston eventually finds that Charrington is a member of the Thought Police and O'Brien a member of the Inner Party. After undergoing days of excruciating torture and brainwashing Winston, brutalized and dispirited, is finally released. O'Brien, his interrogator, has revealed that the Party itself fashioned the Goldstein ruse, that the Party seeks power for its own sake, with no moral justification, and that it dislikes martyrs, who might breed opposition, hence Winston's fate. Although Julia and Winston meet again they are irrevocably changed, physically and mentally, and have little to say. The novel closes when Winston realizes, during a war celebration, that he truly loves Big Brother.

When *Nineteen Eighty-Four* first appeared at the height of the Cold War, it was perhaps natural to interpret the novel, as many did, as a denunciation of the Soviets. Popular perception of the novel has shifted, however, to a more generalized understanding of it as a horrific warning against all intrusive, freedom-denying governments. As testament to the novel's immense influence, the society of Big Brother has become a universal archetype for modern political oppression. *Nineteen Eighty-Four* remains Orwell's best-known and most widely read work, and is regarded as a masterpiece of twentieth-century fiction.

FURTHER READING

Dictionary of Literary Biography, Vol. 15. Detroit: Gale Research Co.

Gross, Miriam, ed. *The World of George Orwell.* New York: Simon and Schuster, 1972.

Hammond, J.R. *George Orwell Companion: A Guide to the Novels, Documentaries, and Essays,* pp. 158-68. New York: St. Martin's Press, 1982.

Howe, Irving, ed. *Orwell's Nineteen Eighty-Four: Text, Sources, Criticism.* New York: Harcourt Brace Jovanovich, 1982.

——, ed. *1984 Revisited: Totalitarianism in Our Century.* New York: Harper & Row, 1983.

Jensen, Ejner J., ed. *The Future of Nineteen Eighty-Four.* Ann Arbor: University of Michigan Press, 1983.

Kalechofsky, Roberta. *George Orwell.* New York: Ungar, 1973.

Kubal, David L. *Outside the Whale: George Orwell's Art and Politics.* Notre Dame: University of Notre Dame Press, 1972.

Meyers, Jeffrey, ed. *George Orwell: The Critical Heritage.* London: Routledge & Kegan Paul, 1975.

Twentieth-Century Literary Criticism, Vols. 2, 6, 15, 31. Detroit: Gale Research Co.

John Osborne

1929-

English dramatist.

Look Back in Anger (drama, 1956)

Alison and **Jimmy Porter** are the central figures in Osborne's first dramatic success, a work that established him as one of the "Angry Young Men" of the British theater in the 1950s. Set in the Porter's one-room apartment in a large Midland town during the 1950s, the play focuses on Jimmy in a state of rage. The objects of his anger are several: Alison, his wife, is from an upper-class family and is a representative of the rigid English class system he despises. Her cold detachment, which is truly her only defense against Jimmy, reflects for him the dishonesty that characterizes human relationships and makes their marriage a lie. Jimmy, from a working-class background and a university graduate, runs a sweetshop with his friend **Cliff Lewis,** a job that is a constant reminder of his inability to break free from the limitations of his origins. Both his professional and his personal life are full of the futility that mark the lives of so many Osborne protagonists, and his response, like all of Osborne's primary spokesmen, is a series of tirades that reveal his hatred and despair at a system that represses the lower classes and disallows the expression of true human feeling. As the recipient of his verbal abuse, Alison grows more and more withdrawn. When her friend **Helena Charles** comes for a visit, she is appalled at the marital situation and contacts Alison's father, **Colonel Redfern.** At his insistence, Alison, pregnant, returns home. During her absence, Helena is attracted to Jimmy, and they begin an affair. Alison returns home, having lost the baby, and Helena leaves. Alison and Jimmy are seen in the play's conclusion, alone together with their anger, despair, and disappointment.

Osborne's play was an immediate and controversial success. As one of the first plays in England to attack the class system, to use characters drawn from the lower classes, and to delineate their anger and frustrations, the work was groundbreaking. Stylistically, the play is traditionally plotted and characterized by brilliant, vital dialogue. Although the work was initially thought to be a socio-political attack, it has subsequently been evaluated as an insightful look at the problems of human relationships, specifically the ability to give and receive love. In his impotent ravings, Jimmy represents the powerless, alienated character who recurs throughout Osborne's dramas.

Luther (drama, 1961)

Set in Germany during the 1500s, the work covers twenty years in the life of **Martin Luther,** the sixteenth-century religious reformer and founder of the Lutheran faith. It is a study of a man in conflict and depicts his years as a monk and later as the leader of the Reformation, focusing on his public actions and their effect on the private man.

Luther's forceful invectives against the Pope and the Catholic Church are reminiscent of the powerful tirades of Jimmy Porter. The work bears the influence of Osborne's major source, Erik Erikson's landmark psychobiography, *Young Man Luther*. As such, it is an in-depth psychological study, centering on Luther's search for identity, his conflict with his father, his decision to become a man of faith, and his troubled conscience. As in such works as *Look Back in Anger,* Osborne again profiles the individual in conflict with authority, this time the Catholic Church. The work is divided into twelve scenes and encompasses a variety of settings, reflecting the span of Luther's experience and including his life in the monastery, his battle over the practice of indulgences, his debate at the Diet of Worms, and his involvement in the Peasants' Rebellion. The Luther that Osborne portrays is a man struggling with his estrangement from his family, his faith, even from his God.

Stylistically, the work owes much to the influence of Bertolt Brecht's theory of epic theater, particularly in Osborne's use of an episodic structure and a narrator who both sets the scene and comments on the action. The dialogue is a blend of elements: Luther's own words, taken from historical documents, quotations from Erikson, and Osborne's dramatic language.

Inadmissible Evidence (drama, 1957)

Set in contemporary London, the work follows the decline and fall of **Bill Maitland,** an unscrupulous solicitor. The opening scene is a dream sequence, in which Maitland is on trial before his conscience for his failure as a man and as a lawyer. He is shown to be pedestrian, hypocritical, venal, and corrupt, and the portrait he sees of himself overwhelms him and sets him off balance. Later scenes in the play take place in his law office as he becomes more and more distraught and disengaged from those around him. He can't concentrate during his conversation with three divorce clients, and his interaction with his office staff is at once bullying and vague. He also seems unreachable to his family, for during his daughter's visit to his office, she doesn't utter a word. Osborne employs the technique of telephone monologues to further indicate his character's descent into isolation as he depicts Maitland talking to first to his wife and later to his mistress, yet appearing to talk only to himself. His feverish attempts to make contact all fail. He is depicted in the play's conclusion broken and alone, sinking into alienation and despair.

As he has so often in his work, Osborne here delineates the decay and corruption of English society. In his protagonist, he has created a representative of that decay, rather than a rebel against it, as he had in such earlier works as *Look Back in Anger* and *Luther.* The play's tone is nightmarish in its evocation of Maitland's decline, and his verbal tirades are noted for their anguished brilliance and painful insight.

FURTHER READING

Banham, Martin. *Osborne.* Edinburgh: Oliver & Boyd, 1969.

Bierhaus, E. G., Jr. "No World of Its Own: *Look Back in Anger* Twenty Years Later." *Modern Drama* (March 1976): 47-55.

Carter, Alan. *John Osborne.* Edinburgh: Oliver & Boyd, 1969.

Contemporary Authors, Vols. 13-16, rev. ed. Detroit: Gale Research Co.

Contemporary Literary Criticism, Vols. 1, 2, 5, 11, 45. Detroit: Gale Research Co.

Dictionary of Literary Biography, Vol. 13. Detroit: Gale Research Co.

Elsom, John. "Breaking Out: The Angry Plays." In *Post-War British Theatre,* pp. 72-87. London: Routledge & Kegan Paul, 1976.

Rupp, Gordon. "Luther and Mr. Osborne." *Cambridge Quarterly* 1 (Winter 1965-1966): 28-42.

Simon, John. *"Luther."* In *Uneasy Stages: A Chronicle of the New York Theater, 1963-1973,* pp. 21-2. New York: Random House, 1976.

Taylor, John Russell, ed. *John Osborne: Look Back in Anger, A Casebook.* London: Macmillan, 1968.

Trussler, Simon. *John Osborne.* London: Longman, 1969.

——. *The Plays of John Osborne: An Assessment.* London: Victor Gollancz Ltd., 1969.

Amos Oz
1939-
Israeli novelist and short story writer.

My Michael (novel, 1968)

Set in Jerusalem in the 1950s, the novel relates the story of **Hannah Gonen,** the first-person narrator whose fantasy life provides a metaphor for the tensions between the Arab and Israeli communities in the Middle East. Hannah is a young woman recently married to **Michael,** a young geologist, for whom she has abandoned her studies in literature. Soon their marriage falters as Hannah comes to see her husband as cold and withdrawn, obsessed with his work and advancement in the academic world. She too withdraws, into a world of fantasy, which provides an outlet for her deep sexual yearnings and frustrated life. Often she dreams of a violent erotic encounter with two Arab men, twins whom she had grown up with in the days before the War of Independence. In her neurotic fantasies, these two men have taken on the roles of terrorists, and she is their victim. She is depicted as a woman lost and alone in the vast world of religious and political conflict.

Oz concentrates on setting in this novel, noting the way in which the city of Jerusalem, with its divided sectors, is a constant reminder of the enmity that separates its people. The hills surrounding the city are palpable symbols for Hannah of the "other" that lurks outside the Jewish homeland, ever-present and threatening. Yet in the figure of Hannah, Oz suggested that the hostile feelings that separate Jews and Arabs in the Middle East are characterized by an ambivalent, often contradictory quality, a point of view that made the novel a raging controversy in the author's homeland. The work is noted for its fine evocation of landscape and for Oz's superb handling of the first-person narrative voice of Hannah.

FURTHER READING

Alter, Robert. *"My Michael."* *New York Times Book Review* (21 May 1972): 5, 18.

Aschkenasy, Nehama. "On Jackals, Nomads, and the Human Condition." *Midstream* 29, No. 1 (January 1983): 58-60.

Contemporary Authors, Vols. 53-56. Detroit: Gale Research Co.

Contemporary Literary Criticism, Vols. 5, 8, 11, 27, 33. Detroit: Gale Research Co.

Wirth-Nesher, Hana. "Amos Oz." *Modern Fiction Studies* (Spring 1978): 91-104.

Alan Paton
1903-1988
South African novelist, short story writer, and essayist.

Cry, the Beloved Country (novel, 1948)
Paton's best-known work takes place during the 1940s in a Zulu village and in Johannesburg, South Africa.

Stephen Kumalo, a Zulu clergyman, receives a letter telling him that his sister, **Gertrude,** is ill in Johannesburg and needs his help. Although it will be a costly trip for Kumalo, he decides to go and to look for his son **Absalom** while he is there. With the help of his friend **Msimangu,** Kumalo finds his sister, a prostitute who has fallen upon hard times, and her daughter and sets them up in a boarding house while he and Msimangu try to locate Absalom. They hear many stories about all the trouble that the boy has gotten into, including getting a young girl pregnant. When they do find him, Absalom is in prison accused of murdering **Arthur Jarvis,** a white man who had given aid to the blacks. The son of Kumalo's brother has also been charged with the murder, but because of his father's influence, he is allowed to go free. Absalom is found guilty and sentenced to death. He marries the mother of his unborn child and she returns to the village with Kumalo. That year, the harvests are poor and the people are in great need. **Mr. Jarvis,** the father of the murdered man, continues the work of his son and sends aid to the villagers in the form of milk for the young children and men who will show them how to work the land to make it more productive. When the day for Absalom's execution arrives, Kumalo goes into the mountains to weep and pray for his son and for all of his people.

This novel is credited with setting in motion a new awareness of the oppression of blacks in South Africa by the white, elite ruling class. Although the story is of personal tragedy, it represents on a larger scale the tragedy of an entire nation in which the ruling minority ruthlessly suppresses the black majority. Paton writes in parable-like, biblical prose, emphasizing theme over characterization.

FURTHER READING

Contemporary Authors, Vols. 15-16; *Contemporary Authors New Revision Series,* Vol. 22; *Contemporary Authors Permanent Series,* Vol. 1. Detroit: Gale Research Co.

Contemporary Literary Criticism, Vols. 4, 10, 25. Detroit: Gale Research Co.

Linneman, Russell J. "Anachronism or Visionary." *Commonwealth Novel in English* 3 (Spring-Summer 1984): 88-100.

Monye, A. A. "*Cry, the Beloved Country:* Should We Merely Cry?" *Nigeria Magazine* 144 (1983): 74-83.

Rive, Richard. "The Liberal Tradition in South African Literature." *Contrast* 14 (July 1983): 19-31.

Cesare Pavese
1908-1950
Italian novelist, poet, essayist, translator, and critic.

The Moon and the Bonfires (novel, 1952)
The central character of this, Pavese's last and most accomplished work, is the unnamed

narrator, who observes and reports on the immediate action of the novel as well as relates past events which are relevant to the current happenings. The narrator has returned to his adopted family in the Piedmont region of northwestern Italy after an extensive world tour during which he spent a lengthy period of time in the United States. Orphaned as a child, the narrator was reared with the daughters of a wealthy Piedmontese family. The main conflict in the current story concerns the youngest daughter and her problems with both Fascist and partisan elements in her rural community. When she is discovered helping the Nazis, the girl is burned to death in accordance with an ancient agricultural myth which links the female body to the fertility of the land. As an adult, the narrator has buried his belief in such superstitions beneath a veneer of worldly sophistication. Through conversations with his childhood friend **Nuto,** however, and after witnessing the events which he relates in the book, the narrator's belief reemerges. His acknowledgement of the reality of these folk rites in the twentieth century leads to an inner reconciliation with his past and his homeland.

As in many of his previous works, Pavese's narrator in *The Moon and the Bonfires* is something of an outsider, but one who nevertheless is deeply affected by events in his homeland. This novel is generally viewed as a symbolic treatment of Italy under the Fascist regime in the 1930s and 1940s. It is also notable for Pavese's examination of human destiny as an uncontrollable element which individuals must learn to accept and of the bond between nature and humanity which, in its purest form, can lead to harmony between disparate peoples.

FURTHER READING

Contemporary Authors, Vol. 104. Detroit: Gale Research Co.

Davis, Harry. *"La luna e i faló:* What Kind of Ripeness?" *Italian Studies* 39 (1984): 79-90.

Fiedler, Leslie A. "Introducing Cesare Pavese." *Kenyon Review* 16, No. 4 (Autumn 1954): 536-53.

Heiney, Donald. "Cesare Pavese." In *Three Italian Novelists: Moravia, Pavese, Vittorini,* pp. 85-146. Ann Arbor: University of Michigan Press, 1968.

Twentieth-Century Literary Criticism, Vol. 3. Detroit: Gale Research Co.

Walker Percy

1916-

American novelist and essayist.

The Moviegoer (novel, 1961)

Binx Bolling is the hero of Percy's first novel, a work which won him the National Book Award. Set in New Orleans during the 1950s, the novel depicts Binx's spiritual quest. Reasonably affluent and educated, Binx is the manager of a brokerage firm. Outwardly happy and successful, Binx is inwardly seeking the meaning and value of life. Like all of Percy's protagonists, Binx feels the need to escape the "everydayness" of existence, the paralysing effects of the usual in life. To escape from the monotony and sterility of his life, he goes to the movies, where he finds the meaning and concreteness his life lacks; he even models his behavior on the actions of film stars. The action of the novel takes place during Mardi Gras week, and Binx's moment of self-awareness takes place on Ash Wednesday. He comes to an understanding of who he is and what is missing from his life. Like other Percy heroes, Binx is alienated from himself and from others. Crucial to his quest is his relationship with his half-brother, **Lonnie,** who is dying. His death in the novel's conclusion parallels Binx's understanding of the meaning of life and is a moment of spiritual transcendence for all the characters. As the novel ends, Binx has decided to give up the brokerage and the yearning life of the moviegoer to attend medical school.

Percy is a novelist of ideas, and his first novel is imbued with the philosophies of Kierkegaard, especially in his depiction of Binx as an alienated character overwhelmed with the banality of everyday existence. Binx is a " wayfarer," a character type that will recur throughout Percy's fiction, symbolizing the wanderer who seeks his way back from alienation to self-awareness. Yet for all its philosophical depth, the work is often humorous in tone. Binx is the first-person narrator of the work, and his musings are wry in self-analysis and compassionate in delineating the despair of others.

Love in the Ruins (novel, 1971)

This novel, which has been called a futuristic satire, is set in the South in the year 1983, recalling George Orwell's dystopian novel, *1984*. As the story begins, **Dr. Tom More** is a man down on his luck: he is an alcoholic, a lapsed Catholic, a psychiatrist whose practice has dwindled, and a cuckold. The America Percy depicts in this work is one fragmented beyond repair: political, racial, and religious differences between people have resulted in a divided, polarized country. More sees the world falling apart and wonders "why does humanism lead to beastliness?" In his effort to save humanity, he begins his quest. He invents the MOQUOL: More's Qualitative Ontological Lapsometer, a device that is designed to measure "the perturbations of the soul" and to reunite the fragmented psyche of humankind. More's efforts to save America from apocalypse are foiled by **Art Immelmann,** a Mephistophelian character who tempts Tom with visions of commercial success. Their struggle is the central action of the novel. In the conclusion, More has successfully defeated his nemesis and is shown, five years after the action of the novel takes place, remarried and happy.

Percy satirizes the divisiveness of a polarized culture in a work that is considered his lightest and most humorous. Yet while the tone is sardonic, Percy remains compassionate. He uses his protagonist, a scientist, to probe another of his recurrent themes: the problem of a world dominated by science and technology, which offer no answers to the human dilemma. For Percy, that is achieved only through love for one another and through faith in God.

Lancelot (novel, 1977)

The novel opens in a prison mental hospital, to which **Lancelot Andrewes Lamar** has been confined. The work takes the shape of a monologue as Lancelot tells his story to **Percival,** an old friend and now a priest. As the names indicate, Percy here continues his novels of quest, this time for what Lancelot calls "the unholy Grail." He tells Percival the story of his wife's infidelity and his discovery that his daughter is not his own. The awareness of her betrayal forces Lancelot to examine his wife's action philosophically, questioning the nature of good and evil. Thus, his quest as a "knight" is to examine human existence. All around him he sees the destruction of moral values, of which his wife's adultery is a part. With the help of a servant, he gathers evidence of his wife's betrayal, then murders her and burns their home. As Lancelot relates his tale to Percival, he digresses into rambling philosophical ravings, describing such things as his plans for a Third Revolution in Virginia, with a new culture based on chivalric values.

Once again in this work Percy examines and satirizes the dilemma of modern life. Unlike his earlier work, however, *Lancelot*'s tone is grim and pessimistic. The conclusion offers little hope or affirmation, and Lancelot's plans for his Virginia utopia are an ironic attempt at escaping rather than confronting the world.

FURTHER READING

Blouin, Michel T. "The Novels of Walker Percy: An Attempt at Synthesis." *Xavier University Studies* 6 (1968): 29-42.

Chesnick, Eugene. "Novel's Ending and World's End: The Fiction of Walker Percy." *Hollins Critic* 10 (October 1973): 1-11.

Coles, Robert. *Walker Percy: An American Search*. Boston: Atlantic-Little, Brown, 1978.

Contemporary Authors, Vols. 1-4, rev. ed.; *Contemporary Authors New Revision Series,* Vol. 1. Detroit: Gale Research Co.

Contemporary Literary Criticism, Vols. 2, 3, 6, 8, 14, 18, 47. Detroit: Gale Research Co.

Dictionary of Literary Biography, Vol. 2; *Dictionary of Literary Biography Yearbook: 1980.* Detroit: Gale Research Co.

Hyman, Stanley Edgar. "Moviegoing and Other Intimacies." In *Standards: A Chronicle of Books for Our Time,* pp. 63-7. New York: Horizon, 1966.

Johnson, Mark. "The Search for Place in Walker Percy's Novels." *Southern Literary Journal* 8, No. 1 (Fall 1975): 55-81.

Kazin, Alfred. "The Pilgrimage of Walker Percy." *Harper's Magazine* 242 (June 1971): 81-6.

LeClair, Thomas. "The Eschatological Vision of Walker Percy." *Renascence* 26 (Spring 1974): 115-22.

Lehan, Richard. "The Way Back: Redemption in the Novels of Walker Percy." *Southern Review* 4 (April 1968): 306-19.

Luschei, Martin. *The Sovereign Wayfarer: Walker Percy's Diagnosis of the Malaise.* Baton Rouge: Louisiana State University Press, 1972.

Marge Piercy

1936-

American novelist and poet.

Woman on the Edge of Time (novel, 1976)

Set in both a ghetto and a mental institution in New York City, this novel follows the life of **Consuelo Ramos,** a widowed Chicana woman. Lonely and destitute, Connie lives a meager existence with only **Dolly,** her niece, to brighten her days. Following a brutal scene with Dolly's boyfriend and pimp, Connie is committed to a mental hospital, where she is forced to live out her days. An uncanny ability of perception allows Connie to "travel" to the future where she visits a utopian society—one in which people exist for the welfare of all, and a true spirit of community prevails. Connie's logic and thought processes reveal her to be more sane than a good majority of the "normal" free population. Her insights into human nature and her understanding of the political and social inequities with which she is faced show a strength that can't be undermined or diminished by "the system." A gentle and loving woman, Connie becomes a victim of bureaucracy and ends up a case number in the State of New York.

This novel is written with insight and sensitivity and features a strong woman as the principal character, typical of several of Piercy's novels. Some critics include it in the science-fiction genre because of Connie's journeys to the future. Through Connie and her travels, the reader is asked to examine the societal institutions of marriage, sex roles, and medical authority. The author's concern for human existence is evident and her vision of a different society is daring and fascinating.

Vida (novel, 1979)

Alternating between the anti-war actions of the 1960s and the underground movement of the 1970s this novel follows **Davida Asch** (Vida) from city to city across the United States as she seeks to evade the authorities, who pursue her for her political activities. Through rapidly alternating scenes, Piercy gives the reader a clear picture of Vida's increasing involvement in and dedication to the morals and values of the radical left political persuasion. A woman of infinite energy, Vida begins her commitment to the cause by participating in local demonstrations. Proving herself to be a skillful organizer and an articulate speaker, she soon becomes a leader. While outwardly Vida appears to be totally committed to changing and challenging the structure and social consciousness of America at this time, she has two significant heterosexual relationships during the story that show the reader another side of her. **Leigh** is the husband who allows Vida her domesticity; she enjoys cooking and keeping house and revels in the warmth and caring of a one-to-one conventional marriage. Further on in the story, when her underground status has forced a divorce, Vida becomes involved with **Joel,** a fellow fugitive, also a sensitive, gentle, loving man. Contrasted with her half-sister **Natalie,** Vida thrives on action and instigates it when she feels the movement is losing momentum. By the end of the novel, virtually all of Vida's counterparts and acquaintances have been apprehended by local police or the FBI. She, however, continues with her unrelenting passion and commitment to changing the bourgeois hierarchy of the Establishment.

Piercy writes in an eloquent tone; many phrases and paragraphs give vivid visual images and remind the reader she is also a skillful poet. The characters in this novel act not only to move the action of the story, they are also expressions of the social sentiment during the Vietnam era. Criticized by some commentators as little more than a vehicle for Piercy's political views, *Vida* is also considered a deeply moving novel which gives a clear and accurate political and social history.

FURTHER READING

Bell, Pearl K. "Marge Piercy and Ann Beattie." *Commentary* (July 1980): 59.

Betsky, Celia. "*Woman on the Edge of Time.*" *New Republic* (9 October 1976): 38.

Contemporary Authors, Vols. 21-24, rev. ed.; *Contemporary Authors New Revision Series,* Vol. 13; *Contemporary Authors Autobiography Series,* Vol. 1. Detroit: Gale Research Co.

Contemporary Literary Criticism, Vols. 3, 6, 14, 18, 27. Detroit: Gale Research Co.

Jefferson, Margo. "Future vs. Present: *Woman on the Edge of Time.*" *Newsweek* (7 June 1976): 94.

Langer, Elinor. "After the Movement." *New York Times Book Review* (24 February 1980): 1.

Piercy, Marge. *Parti Colored Blocks for a Quilt.* Ann Arbor: University of Michigan Press, 1982.

Sale, Roger. "*Woman on the Edge of Time.*" *New York Times Book Review* (20 June 1976): 6.

Harold Pinter

1930-

English dramatist, novelist, and short story writer.

The Caretaker (drama, 1960)

The work takes place in a room cluttered with furniture and odds and ends in the house of **Aston** and **Mick,** who are brothers. As the action commences, Aston has brought **Davies,** a tramp, home after a bar fight. Aston, quiet and kindly, has offered Davies a place to spend the night. Davies is a quarrelsome man, full of racial prejudice and living off the world's good will. The next morning, Davies encounters Mick, who first throws him to the floor, then talks to him in a friendly fashion about his plans for the building, which he claims to own. He questions Davies about his past, and is by turns menacing and kind. Aston has offered Davies the job as caretaker of the house, a proposal which Mick repeats. Mick begins to confide in Davies, telling him of his decorating ideas. Aston, too confides in Davies: in a revealing conversation, he tells him that he has been subjected to shock therapy, and that things that were once clear are no longer understandable to him. He works with his hands and collects junk, the central piece of which is a statue of Buddha in the cluttered room. Davies, emboldened by the brothers' confidences, decides to make demands of Mick regarding his position as caretaker. That evening, Aston is disturbed by Davies's nocturnal ramblings and noise, and tells him so. Davies turns on Aston, deriding his mental condition. Aston quietly turns him out. In the next scene, Davies pleads with Mick about his job, and refers to Aston as "nutty." This enrages Mick, who tells him to leave. He smashes the Buddha as Aston enters; they smile at each other, and Mick leaves. In the final scene, Davies is vainly trying to effect a reconciliation with Aston.

Pinter's recurrent themes of the problems of communication and language, as well as those of domination and power, are voiced here. The tone of the drama is by turns comic, absurd, malevolent, and pathetic. The dialogue is at times naturalistic, at times fantastic, and is characterized by the repetition of words and phrases, a technique that has become part of Pinter's distinctive style. Audiences and critics were at first baffled and contemptuous of the work, but *The Caretaker* is now considered a central work of modern drama. It is one of Pinter's best known and most difficult works, and the variety and complexity of critical interpretations attest to its power.

The Homecoming (drama, 1965)

Set in a London home, the work centers on the "homecoming" of **Teddy** and his wife, **Ruth**. Teddy is a professor of philosophy at an American university and is returning after an absence of six years to the home of his father, **Max.** The opening scene sets the tone for the play. Max, his son **Lenny,** and his brother **Sam** are engaged in a verbal battle characterized by its brutality. The key to the play seems to be the characters' ambivalence towards one another, for the temper of their interactions changes suddenly from savagery to sentimentality throughout the work. When Teddy and Ruth enter the house early in the morning, he tells her how pleased he is that she will finally meet his warm and wonderful family, a description that proves false on Ruth's first encounter with Lenny, who appears strange and unpredictable. The nature of the family is further revealed at breakfast, where Max, upon meeting Ruth, calls her a whore, and compares her to **Jessie,** his dead wife. Sam defends Jessie as a fine woman, although he later reveals that she was unfaithful to Max. When Max's third son, **Joey,** intervenes, a physical altercation ensues between Max, Sam and Joey. This violent scene is followed by a maudlin attempt on Max's part to welcome his son and his wife. Teddy, disturbed by his family's behavior, decides that he and Ruth will leave for America. However, Ruth has strangely acclimated herself to the situation, and is shown in various erotic poses with Joey and Lenny, telling them of her past as an artist's model and making reference to her physical attractiveness. The men decide that she can stay and become a prostitute to support them. When Teddy leaves, she tells him she is staying, admonishing him not to become a ''stranger.'' In the play's conclusion, Ruth cradles Joey's head in her lap with Max at her feet. Sam appears to have had a stroke and lies on the floor.

In a work that appears to be more fabulist than realistic in representation, Pinter explores his themes of the nature of familial relationships, sexuality, and dominance. The tone is at once ironic and savage, and the menacing atmosphere that characterizes so much of Pinter's work is evident here. The dialogue reveals an ambiguous element in the play, for the meaning of the character's speeches is intentionally obscure, reflecting Pinter's recurrent concern with the failings of language.

Betrayal (drama, 1978)

The central focus of the play is the affair between **Emma** and **Jerry.** Emma, a gallery owner, is married to **Robert,** a publisher; Jerry, a literary agent, is Robert's best friend. The play's action spans nine years, and, in an interesting twist in his use of time and chronological sequence, Pinter begins the play at the end of the affair, in 1977, and moves the action backward in succeeding scenes, ending the play at the beginning of the relationship, in 1968. The subject of the play is taken from the title: it is about various forms of betrayal—of friends, lovers, spouses, and oneself. As the play opens, Emma and Jerry have met for a drink. She tells him that her marriage to Robert is over; she has just told him of their affair, and he has revealed to her that he, too, has engaged in many affairs. Jerry is deeply disturbed at this news. In the next scene, he meets with Robert, and learns that Robert had known about their affair for years. Thus, Jerry is betrayed by Emma, who has lied to him about Robert's knowledge, and by Robert, who had never acknowledged what he knew. Succeeding scenes reveal a similar deceit lying at the basis of all relationships. As the betrayals mount, Pinter seems to indicate that duplicity informs all aspects of life. Both Robert and Jerry are in publishing and both make money off of authors, such as the much-discussed ''Casey,'' who have little talent or literary purpose, but who provide them financial success; thus the lack of professional and personal integrity is part of the pattern of betrayal.

Although the work was a popular success, some Pinter adherents found both the characters—upper-middle-class Londoners involved in the arts—and the subject—adultery—to be too conventional to rank among the best of the Pinter canon. However, other interpreters noted the thematic concerns the work shares with other Pinter pieces, such as the problem with language and communication, that mark it as a major accomplishment. The work includes two stylistic elements distinct to this play: it reflects Pinter's work in film (he had written several major screenplays before this drama, and also adapted *Betrayal* for film) in its use of flashback sequences and the rapid juxtaposition of scenes; and Pinter here gives his audience an omniscient viewpoint, a perspective through which they know the consequences of the narrative action before it takes place. This provides insight into character and motivation and also enhances Pinter's theme of betrayal, as one observes the characters weaving their webs of deceit.

FURTHER READING

Brater, Enoch. ''Cinematic Fidelity and the Forms of Pinter's *Betrayal.*'' *Modern Drama* 24, No. 4 (December 1981): 503-13.

Brustein, Robert. ''Journeys to the End of the World.'' *The New Republic* 182, No. 6 (9 February 1980): 26-7.

Burkman, Katherine H. *The Dramatic World of Harold Pinter: Its Basis in Ritual.* Columbus: Ohio State University Press, 1971.

Clurman, Harold. ''Theater: *Betrayal.*'' *The Nation* 230, No. 3 (26 January 1980): 92-3.

Contemporary Authors, Vols. 5-8, rev. ed. Detroit: Gale Research Co.

Contemporary Literary Criticism, Vols. 1, 3, 6, 9, 11, 15, 27. Detroit: Gale Research Co.

Davies, Russell. "Pinter Land." *The New York Review of Books* 25, Nos. 21-22 (25 January 1979): 22-4.

Dictionary of Literary Biography, Vol. 13. Detroit: Gale Research Co.

Dukore, Bernard F. *Harold Pinter*. New York: Macmillan, 1982.

Esslin, Martin. *The Peopled Wound: The Works of Harold Pinter*. Garden City: Doubleday, 1970.

Hinchliffe, Arnold P. *Harold Pinter*. New York: Twayne, 1967.

Thomson, Peter. "Harold Pinter: A Retrospect." *Critical Quarterly* 20, No. 4 (Winter 1978): 21-8.

Luigi Pirandello

1867-1936

Italian dramatist and novelist.

Six Characters in Search of an Author (drama, 1921)

As the play begins, six characters, the product of an artist's imagination now abandoned by him, appear on a stage being used for the rehearsal of a play, Pirandello's own *Rules of the Game*. They are in search of an author to put them in a play and approach the **Stage Manager** to help them. The plot of their story, told by the individual characters, makes up the first act. The **Father** had discarded the **Mother** years ago, after she had given birth to the **Son,** who has grown up without maternal love and is a disillusioned, scornful young man. The Father had arranged for the Mother to have a lover, by whom she had three illegitimate children, the **Stepdaughter,** the **Boy,** and the **Child.** After the death of her lover, the Mother was left penniless, and she takes a job with **Madame Pace,** a brothel owner, as a seamstress. Madame Pace has plans for the Stepdaughter, whom she lures into prostitution. The Stepdaughter is playing the role of whore when she nearly takes the Father as her customer before the Mother rushes in and stops the scene.

During the second act, the disparity between the artifice of the theater and the "reality" of the characters' existence becomes even more evident. First the characters, then a group of actors who are to play their roles, try to act out the seduction scene between the Father and the Stepdaughter. The characters, who see their lives—their shame, guilt, and retribution—in this scene, argue with the actors and the Manager about how it should be played. The Manager and the actors represent traditional theatrical values and find the material too sordid, worrying about the response of the critics and patrons. The characters want to live through the actors, but they find them incompetent.

In the third act, the Father argues for the permanency of a character's identity over that of a human being, for the character's persona is fixed and immutable, while the human is capable of change. In the conclusion, the Son still sits sullenly, refusing to play his role. But the play continues, with melodramatic consequences: the Child is discovered drowned in a fountain, and the Boy commits suicide. This throws the play into chaos, for no one knows whether he is dead, or if this is another example of the artifice of the stage. The Manager, disgusted and confused, throws up his hands, and the curtain falls.

Six Characters in Search of an Author is Pirandello's most famous play and a major work of twentieth-century theater. Pirandello's theme concerns the artificiality of the theater and the inability of the artist's true vision to be realized. He uses the device of the play-within-a-play to heighten our awareness of the distortion of the truth—the vision of the artist and the needs of the characters—and the relativity of individual perception. Pirandello's emphasis on the artificial aspects of conventional theater has made an irrevocable impact on modern drama.

Henry IV (drama, 1922)

The play relates the story of a man, known as **Henry IV** throughout the work, who years ago had suffered a fall from a horse during a pageant in which he was playing the role of Henry IV, the eleventh-century emperor. For years he had been under the delusion that he was the historical monarch and had surrounded himself with a royal entourage content to help him live his mad fantasy. As the play begins, twenty years have passed since the accident. Unknown to his followers, Henry had regained his sanity eight years earlier, but overcome by the horrible trick fate had played on him, he had decided to retain the mask of his insanity. Deprived of his youth, the woman he loved, and his future, he revenges himself against time and fate by playing the role of a historical figure, fixed permanently in the past.

Henry's retinue includes **Doctor Dionysius Genoni,** a buffoon who receives the full butt of Pirandello's satire, for he believes he can ''cure'' his patient of his madness. He arranges the visit of Henry's former lover, playing the part of **Donna Matilda Spina,** who was the mistress of the historical Henry IV, her daughter, **Frida,** and the **Baron Tito Belcredi,** who was responsible for Henry's fall and his ensuing madness. Although they are costumed and play the roles of their eleventh-century counterparts, Henry sees through their masquerade. In the final act, Dr. Genoni has Frida, who bears a striking resemblance to her mother when young, dress like the historical Matilda. Henry is visible shaken, and the Doctor thinks he has at last cured his patient, but Henry then explodes in anger at them all. He tells them that he has been sane for years, although their cruel trick had almost taken him back to the realms of madness. He is fully aware that he has masked himself and that he forces masks on others, making them take part in his eternal deception. Yet the shock of seeing Frida makes him yearn for all that he has lost, for she represents the timelessness of beauty, love, and hope, and he rushes to embrace her. A struggle ensues, in which Henry stabs and kills Belcredi. Now reality has pierced the illusion, and Henry confronts the fact that he must preserve the pretense of his insanity in order to keep his life; his mask must now become his permanent face.

In this play, widely acknowledged as his masterpiece, Pirandello explores his recurrent themes of the duality of the human character, examining as well the nature of madness and sanity, illusion and reality, and the revolt against time. In the person of his protagonist, who takes on the persona of another to avoid the flux and change of life, Pirandello asks: who is sane—those who live in the world unaware of the masks they wear in daily life, or the one who consciously lives a life of feigned madness?

FURTHER READING

Bentley, Eric. ''Varieties of Comic Experience.'' In *The Playwright as Thinker: A Study of Drama in Modern Times,* pp. 159-90. New York: Reynall and Hitchcock, 1946.

Brustein, Robert. ''Luigi Pirandello.'' In *The Theatre of Revolt: An Approach to the Modern Drama,* pp. 281-317. Boston: Atlantic-Little, Brown, 1964.

Contemporary Authors, Vol. 104. Detroit: Gale Research Co.

Esslin, Martin. ''Pirandello: Master of the Naked Masks.'' In *Reflections: Essays on Modern Theatre,* pp. 49-55. New York: Doubleday, 1969.

Fergusson, Francis. "Action as Theatrical: *Six Characters in Search of an Author*." In *The Idea of a Theater,* pp. 35-50. Princeton: Princeton University Press, 1949.

Gilman, Richard. "Pirandello." *Yale/Theater* 5, No. 2 (Spring 1974): 94-117.

Paolucci, Anne. "Pirandello: Experience as the Expression of Will." *Forum Italicum* 7, No. 3 (September 1973): 404-14.

Twentieth-Century Literary Criticism, Vols. 4, 29. Detroit: Gale Research Co.

Sylvia Plath

1932-1963

American poet and novelist.

The Bell Jar (novel, 1963)

This is the only novel of the well-known poet Sylvia Plath, and like her poetry, the novel is noted for its vivid imagery and autobiographical content. The novel relates the coming of age of **Esther Greenwood,** a brilliant young woman and aspiring poet, and chronicles her tortured late adolescence, descent into madness, and recovery.

The novel opens with an evocative and chilling image of the electrocution of the Rosenbergs, and the themes of death, incarceration, and physical pain that this image invokes recur throughout the novel. Esther spends the summer following her junior year of college in New York City. She has been selected to work on a special issue of a women's magazine, an opportunity that gives her an insight into the choices and limitations of the adult world, particularly the realm of jobs and relationships with men. Esther is a woman of uncompromising values and wants desperately to achieve success and make use of her many talents, yet she is unable to decide how to channel her energies. She has several disappointing encounters with men, including her college boyfriend, **Buddy Willard,** a conventional young man who wants to tie Esther down to a traditional marriage. Throughout the novel, the male characters symbolize the limiting, constricted world of male dominance—sexual and physical—that Esther flees.

Frustrated and disillusioned, Esther returns home. Her mental instability had been evident in the early section of the novel, and in this portion she suffers a mental breakdown, culminating in an attempted suicide. Under the treatment of an insensitive male psychiatrist, she continues to decline. When she is placed in a private hospital under the care of the sympathetic and nurturing **Dr. Nolan,** a female psychiatrist, she is able to recover. Her return to sanity is described as tenuous, however, for the madness symbolized by the descending bell jar is an ominous, ever-present force.

The Bell Jar is noted for its striking imagery and simple prose style, which Plath varied to parallel Esther's mental state: as she descends into madness, the syntax becomes fragmented, and during her recovery, the prose, too, becomes more lucid. The novel also voices Plath's feminist concerns, evident in Esther's personal and professional dilemma. Many critics have recognized the distinct parallels between Plath and her protagonist, for both are women of great artistic gifts and ambitions, and both are driven to madness and self-destruction by their sensitivity and sense of isolation.

FURTHER READING

Barnard, Caroline King. *Sylvia Plath*. Boston: Twayne, 1978.

Butscher, Edward. *Sylvia Plath: Method and Madness*. New York: Seabury Press, 1975.

Contemporary Authors, Vols. 19-20; *Contemporary Authors Permanent Series,* Vol. 2. Detroit: Gale Research Co.

Contemporary Literary Criticism, Vols. 1, 2, 3, 5, 9, 11, 14, 17, 50, 51. Detroit: Gale Research Co.

Dictionary of Literary Biography, Vols. 5, 6. *Concise Dictionary of American Literary Biography, 1941-1968.* Detroit: Gale Research Co.

Gilbert, Sandra M. "'A Fine, White Flying Myth': Confessions of a Plath Addict." *The Massachusetts Review* 19, No. 3 (Autumn 1978): 585-603.

Katherine Anne Porter
1890-1980
American short story writer and novelist.

Noon Wine (novella, 1937)

The novella takes place on a farm in Texas and depicts one of Porter's most important themes: the way in which forces beyond human control destroy the individual. As the story begins, **Mr. Helton** has come to **Mr. Thompson's** farm looking for a job. Thompson hires him, and the farm prospers for many years. **Homer T. Hatch,** a horrifying figure of evil, comes to the farm after nine years have passed, looking for Helton. He tells Thompson that Helton is a "loonatic," and that he has taken it upon himself, in the spirit of "law and order," to capture and return men like him. Thompson refuses to believe him, and the two argue. Helton enters the room, and seeing Hatch, is overcome with fear. Hatch stabs Helton with a knife, but Thompson strikes Hatch on the head with an axe and kills him. Thompson is tried and acquitted of Hatch's death, yet the experience haunts him, especially when he learns that Helton was found uninjured after the fight. Thompson is now unsure of what really happened and is tormented by the thought that he might be a murderer. He tries incessantly to vindicate himself to his family and neighbors, but he sees that his family is unable to believe him. He writes a final note, claiming his innocence and still trying to make sense of what happened, then kills himself.

Porter explores the nature of evil in this story, a force embodied in Hatch and a power that overcomes Thompson and determines his fate. The story is noted for its dramatic power and vivid yet objective narrative tone, and is regarded as one of Porter's finest efforts.

Pale Horse, Pale Rider (novella, 1939)

Set in the American Southwest in 1918, the novella centers on **Miranda,** a character who appears in several of Porter's works, now a young journalist who has recently fallen in love with **Adam Barclay,** a young soldier. As the story begins, she awakens from an ominous dream foreboding death. The era is rife with the symbols of death and destruction: it is the fourth year of World War I and the influenza epidemic is sweeping the country. Miranda goes to work that morning feeling ill, and by that evening she has contracted influenza. She is taken to a hospital, where she is able to communicate with Adam only by note. Her delirium and especially her descent toward death are vividly evoked for the reader. As she confronts death, she recognizes the bleak void that is the end of life, feeling herself sinking deeper and deeper into the darkness. Miranda recovers from her illness, yet is somehow changed, less happy to be once again in the world of the living, disillusioned, and, in her own words, "condemned" to life. During her convalescence, she learns that Adam had fallen ill and had died while she was in the hospital. The close of the story reveals Miranda a tragic figure, marked with the knowledge of anguish and unhappiness.

The novella is noted for its haunting, evocative description, particularly in the scenes depicting Miranda's encounter with death. The work deals with Porter's recurrent theme of the ominous forces beyond individual control that so often determine the fate and destroy the happiness of her characters.

Ship of Fools (novel, 1962)

Porter's only novel and her most famous work is set on a German passenger ship bound for Bremerhaven in 1931. The passengers—Germans, Americans, and Spaniards—make up a microcosm of the world, and the specter of Hitler's Germany, readying for war, haunts the atmosphere. Porter's theme here is the illusion and self-deception that govern life, and her characters are examined in great detail. With penetrating insight, she reveals them to be self-obsessed and compulsive figures, distorted by prejudice and hatred, with none of the heroism or tragic proportions that imbue the characters of her previous works.

The journey sets the framework for the story, and several key incidents illuminate the characters. **Mrs. Treadwell** is an American divorcee in her forties, capable of cruelty, but in one important episode, inadvertently harming others. Many of the characters on board are German, most of whom share the Fascists' hatred of Jews and notions of a master race. When Mrs. Treadwell unknowingly reveals that **Herr Freytag**, a fanatical believer in Aryan supremacy, is married to a Jew, he is sent from the captain's table in shame and disgrace. **Dr. Schumann** is a distinguished physician who knows he is going home to Germany to die. He risks his reputation and all he has worked for to court the **Condesa,** a drug-addicted woman with an obsession for young men. Also on board is a travelling zarzuela troupe, including two evil children, the twins **Ric** and **Rac,** who terrorize the other passengers and who throw the dog of one of the Germans overboard. In an attempt to save the dog's life, a poor Spaniard who was travelling in steerage and who was known for his beautiful woodcarvings, is drowned, his life snuffed out for nothing.

Porter offers no happy resolution to the lives she depicts. The other Americans on board, including **William Denny,** a bigoted, narrow-minded man who becomes the victim of Mrs. Treadwell's one violent outburst, and the lovers **Jenny Brown** and **David Scott,** whose relationship is characterized by jealousy and cruelty, reflect the self-centered isolation that dictates the bleak lives of all on the ship. The work is noted for its objective, sustained narrative and bitter view of humanity. This long-awaited novel by a highly respected writer of short fiction disappointed many who felt that the novel's didactic and harsh tone marred the work; however, it remains Porter's best-known work, and for many it is a pointed indictment of the self-delusion that led the world into war in 1939.

FURTHER READING

Contemporary Authors, Vols. 1-4, rev. ed., 101; *Contemporary Authors New Revision Series,* Vol. 1. Detroit: Gale Research Co.

Contemporary Literary Criticism, Vols. 1, 3, 7, 10, 13, 15, 27. Detroit: Gale Research Co.

Dictionary of Literary Biography, Vols. 4, 9; *Dictionary of Literary Biography Yearbook: 1980.* Detroit: Gale Research Co.

Hardy, John Edward. *Katherine Anne Porter.* New York: Ungar, 1973.

Hendrick, George. *Katherine Anne Porter.* New York: Twayne, 1965.

Johnson, James William. ''Another Look at Katherine Anne Porter.'' *Virginia Quarterly Review* 36 (Autumn 1960): 598-613.

Liberman, M. M. *Katherine Anne Porter's Fiction.* Detroit: Wayne State University Press, 1971.

Solotaroff, Theodore. "*Ship of Fools* and the Critics." *Commentary* 34 (October 1962): 277-86.

Stanford, Donald E. "Katherine Anne Porter." *The Southern Review* 17, No. 1 (January 1981): 1-2.

Warren, Robert Penn. "Katherine Anne Porter (Irony with a Center)." *Kenyon Review* 4 (Winter 1942): 29-42.

Welty, Eudora. "Katherine Anne Porter: The Eye of the Story." In *The Eye of the Story,* pp. 30-40. New York: Random House, 1978.

Chaim Potok

1929-

American novelist and short story writer.

The Chosen (novel, 1967)

Set in Brooklyn, New York, near the close of World War II, the novel tells the story of two Jewish boys—one Hasid and one Orthodox—who become best friends despite their distinct brands of Judaism. The American setting for this cultural exploration is immediately evident at the boy's first meeting: an emotional baseball game between their two sects. **Reuven Malter,** the Orthodox Jew, is seriously injured in the eye by a line drive off **Danny Saunders** bat. When he visits Reuven in the hospital, Danny admits that he had wanted to hurt Reuven and tries to explain why he was feeling so angry and hateful. Not without effort, Reuven excepts Danny's apology as his father suggests and the two boys become friends. Before they can spend more time together, however, Reuven must pass the inspection of Danny's father **Reb Saunders.** Mr. Saunders is the intensely devout spiritual leader of his community and is also an extremely determined father who is raising Danny to take over his influential religious position. He is wary of outside influences on his son, particularly the liberal teachings and writing of Reuven's father, **David Malter.**

Despite their conflicting views, Reb approves of the friendship, inviting Reuven to experience the Hasidic way of life with Danny and his family. During this time, Reuven learns about several unique aspects of Hasidic culture, including their arranged marriages, inherited leadership, and the self-imposed silence between Danny and his father. The most difficult challenge to the growing friendship of Danny and Reuven occurs when Reuven's father and other Jews work for the creation of Israel, a new Jewish homeland, while Danny's father and other Hasids protest against it. Because of this conflict, Reb forbids Danny to speak with Reuven. He lifts the restriction only when Israel becomes a reality. Throughout this trial and the suffering of both sects during the horrifying revelations about the holocaust, Potok illuminates the unyielding faith and patience of his characters that buoys them above all adverse events. Near the close of the novel Danny reveals that he does not want to inherit his father's religious vocation. At this point, Reb Saunders displays a wisdom, love, and rationality very similar to Mr. Malter's and submits to his son's will.

The basis of Potok's fictional as well as scholarly works is Jewish culture and history. He was inspired to teach others about Jewish life through fiction by the works of Evelyn Waugh, who, like Potok, explores a unique cultural environment while stressing the relation of God and man in contemporary society. Many critics have admired the subtlety and grace with which Potok conveys his sincere and powerful messages about faith and human relations to the reader.

FURTHER READING

Abramson, Edward A. *Chaim Potok*. Boston: Twayne, 1986.

Bluefarb, Sam. "The Head, the Heart, and the Conflict of Generations in Chaim Potok's *The Chosen.*" *College Language Association Journal* 14 (June 1971): 402-09.

Contemporary Authors, Vols. 17-20, rev. ed.; *Contemporary Authors New Revision Series,* Vol. 19. Detroit: Gale Research Co.

Contemporary Literary Criticism, Vols. 2, 7, 14, 26. Detroit: Gale Research Co.

Dictionary of Literary Biography, Vol. 28. Detroit: Gale Research Co.

Grebstein, Norman Sheldon. "Phenomenon of the Really Jewish Best-Seller: Potok's *The Chosen.*" *Studies in American Jewish Literature* 1 (1975): 23-31.

Anthony Powell

1905-

British novelist and dramatist.

"A Dance to the Music of Time": *A Question of Upbringing* (novel, 1951); *A Buyer's Market* (novel, 1952); *The Acceptance World* (novel, 1955); *At Lady Molly's* (novel, 1957); *Casanova's Chinese Restaurant* (novel, 1960); *The Kindly Ones* (novel, 1962); *The Valley of Bones* (novel, 1964); *The Soldier's Art* (novel, 1966); *The Military Philosophers* (novel, 1968); *Books Do Furnish a Room* (novel, 1971); *Temporary Kings* (novel, 1973); *Hearing Secret Harmonies* (novel, 1975)

Set in Britain and spanning the years 1914 to 1975, "A Dance to the Music of Time" is a chronicle of upper-class England. The twelve novels are grouped into four "movements" corresponding to the seasons. The famous painting by Poussin from which the cycle takes its name is a controlling motif throughout the novels. In the painting, the four seasons, as four dancers, move to the music played by time; in the novel, the characters interact, separate, and meet again, their lives interwoven by chance, fate, and time.

As the first novel begins, we meet **Nicholas Jenkins,** the first-person narrator, who is reflecting on his life from the vantage point of age. He is a noticeably detached narrator, an observer who lets the actions of the other characters dominate as he plays the role of the ironic interpreter. We see Jenkins and his school friends, **Charles Stringham** and **Peter Templer,** first in public school and later in college, presented as children of the aristocracy and privilege and destined, it would seem, for success and greatness in later life. Set in opposition to them now and throughout the narrative is the character of **Kenneth Widmerpool,** a boy whose persona encompasses the antithesis of Jenkins and his friends: he is coarse, brutal, arrogant, and ruthless in his pursuit of money and social privilege. Even his father's occupation—a manure merchant—indicates his inherent inferiority and baseness. Yet, in keeping with Powell's central thesis that time brings about change both unexpected and incomprehensible, it is Widmerpool who rapidly advances in business and social status. Jenkins, in his ironic self-effacement, compares himself to Widmerpool at certain points in his life, both amused and perplexed at the rise of his former schoolmate. Yet Powell stresses that Jenkins is a man who is steadfast in his values and loyalties, as opposed to Widmerpool, whose lust for power and prestige warp his character.

Subsequent early volumes deal with Jenkins's career in publishing and as a budding novelist, but focus especially on the social behavior of his class, a group devoted to parties and the good life, with Powell noting a sense of the absurdity of a life devoted to pleasure. Nick becomes involved with a married woman, but later marries **Lady Isobel Tolland.** Their marriage remains miraculously free of the infidelities and anguish that mark the relationships of their friends. Widmerpool's career continues its ascendance, yet his personal life is plagued with sexual and emotional problems.

The Valley of Bones, The Soldier's Art, and *The Military Philosophers* comprise what is known as the "war trilogy," depicting the fates of the characters during World War II. Ironically, Jenkins, Stringham, and Templer all come under the command of Widmerpool, and tragically and ominously, Widmerpool is implicated in the deaths of Stringham and Templer. Stringham, portrayed in his youth as disillusioned by life, largely the result of the petty cruelty of his family, is a young man of wit and charm, yet with a strange, brooding melancholy that presages his tragic end. Now an alcoholic, he is reduced to performing the duties of a waiter in a mess hall before he is killed. Templer, who had been forced to leave school early, was involved in finance and the business world and quite a womanizer. His attitude toward Widmerpool undergoes a change during the course of the novel, and it is suggested that Widmerpool knowingly sends him on the secret operation that leads to his death. A character of minor significance early in the narrative, **Pamela Flitton,** becomes a major focus now. Depicted as a woman defined by her enormous sexual appetites, she is the lover of many of the male characters, eventually marrying Widmerpool. She is considered the most fully developed female character in the series, and Powell treats her with a certain amount of compassion, indicating that her endless sexual liaisons mark her as a desperate rather than a shallow figure. Towards the end of the cycle she dies of a drug overdose.

In the concluding volume, Jenkins is shown in his country home, still a happy man, with many successful books to his credit. As the novel concludes, he is described watching a fire, an image which began the work and which proves to be a catalyst to his thoughts on the past and the future. Widmerpool has renounced his former wealth and become a member of a cult, and we last view him naked, running with members of his group. Always the competitive over-achiever, he tries to outdistance his fellow runners and dies of a heart attack.

Powell's concept of time is vital to an understanding of the work. Although he portrays his characters as their lives are effected by the social, political and moral changes of their culture, it is the human sense of time rather than the chronological that dominates. Thus, the story goes back and forth in time, focussing on the patterns created by the interweaving of the characters' lives. As narrator, Jenkins offers commentary that is insightful, humorous, but objective; he never judges Widmerpool outright, but lets the character's actions speak for themselves, allowing the reader to judge. Although it would seem that using one narrator for twelve novels would prove repetitive and limiting, Powell allows other characters to "see" for Jenkins, so that not all we know is necessarily filtered through his consciousness. The work is noted for its elegance, charm, and understated humor and is considered one of the most important literary achievements of the mid-twentieth century.

FURTHER READING

Bergonzi, Bernard. *Anthony Powell.* London: Longmans, Green, 1962.

Contemporary Authors, Vols. 1-4, rev. ed.; *Contemporary Authors New Revision Series,* Vol. 1. Detroit: Gale Research Co.

Contemporary Literary Criticism, Vols. 1, 3, 7, 9, 10, 31. Detroit: Gale Research Co.

Dictionary of Literary Biography, Vol. 15. Detroit: Gale Research Co.

Egremont, Max. "After the Dance." *Books and Bookmen* (January 1977): 44-5.

McSweeney, Kerry. "The End of *A Dance to the Music of Time*." *South Atlantic Quarterly* (Winter 1977): 44-57.

Mizener, Arthur. *The Sense of Life in the Modern Novel*, pp. 80-102. New York: Houghton Mifflin Company, 1964.

Morris, Robert K. *The Novels of Anthony Powell*. Pittsburgh: University of Pittsburgh Press, 1968.

Russell, John. *Anthony Powell, A Quintet, Sextet and War*. Bloomington: Indiana University Press, 1970.

Spurling, Hilary. *Invitation to the Dance: A Guide to Anthony Powell's "Dance to the Music of Time."* Boston: Little, Brown, 1978.

Tucker, James. *The Novels of Anthony Powell*. New York: Columbia University Press, 1976.

Marcel Proust

1871-1922

French novelist, critic, and essayist.

"Remembrance of Things Past": *Swann's Way* (novel, 1913): *Within a Budding Grove* (novel, 1919); *The Guermantes Way* (novel, 1920); *Cities of the Plain* (novel, 1922); *The Captive* (novel, 1923); *The Sweet Cheat Gone* (novel, 1925); *The Past Recaptured* (1927)

Remembrance of Things Past ranks as one of the greatest literary achievements of all time. In this multivolume series of novels, Proust explored the nature of time, memory, and art and created a work whose profound influence is still felt on twentieth-century letters. Through the life of his narrator-protagonist, **Marcel,** Proust examines a group of bourgeois and upper-class Parisians in turn-of-the-century France, focussing on the narrator's explorations of love, society, and the realization of his artistic aspirations.

The first novel, *Swann's Way,* is divided into three sections. In the first, "Combray," the narrator relates the story of his youth at his family's home in the French countryside. He is introduced to **Charles Swann,** a neighbor, who is a mysterious, enigmatic character for him. Ostensibly the son of a Jewish stockbroker and solidly middle-class, Swann is also a part of the aristocratic circles that include the Prince of Wales and high-ranking members of the French government. Swann and the aristocratic Guermantes, who also have a country home in Combray, become in Marcel's mind representatives of two different ways of life, and it is through his association with them that the narrative takes its form. Swann represents the young narrator's initiation into the bitter, disillusioning experiences of love, and the Guermantes embody the rituals of society, which Marcel ultimately sees in all its cruelty and meaninglessness. It is also in the early section of this first novel that the narrator relates his first experience of involuntary memory, which occurs when he dips a piece of *madeleine* in a cup of tea and in its taste is transported back to a previous time. It is his first experience of his ability to recapture the past and of defeating the annihilation of time and decay, a theme that will resonate throughout the novels.

The second section of the first novel, "Swann in Love," relates the story of Swann's ill-fated passion for **Odette de Crecy,** a courtesan and a woman of faithlessness. He is a man of culture, charm, and intellect, used to travelling in the highest social circles, who, because of his marriage to Odette, is shunned by many of his former friends and is forced to attend the bourgeois salons of people like **Madame Verdurin,** whom Proust ridicules as a savage beast of cruelty and vanity. Swann's feelings of passionate jealousy serve to presage Marcel's later relationships with women, particularly **Albertine Simonet,** reflecting Proust's theme of the discrepancy between the lover's conception of the beloved and that individual's true nature. The novel chronicles Swann's early love, marriage, and the fading of his passion. In a state of disillusion and despair, Swann hears the strains of a sonata by the composer **Vinteuil,** which he had always associated with Odette and his love for her. Like Marcel, he experiences a moment in time when memory links past and present with clarity and insight, and he once again feels his early passion. In the final section of the first novel, Marcel, now in Paris, is growing up and has become infatuated with **Gilberte,** Swann's daughter; yet she remains a cipher to him, an object of his imagination and an idealized figure of innocent love.

The second novel introduces the figure of Albertine, a young woman who captivates Marcel. Their affair spans five of the novels and is characterized by pain, jealousy and disillusion. Another major character appears for the first time in this novel, the **Baron Palamede de Charlus,** a member of the Guermantes family and a figure who, in his moral depravity and life of sexual inversion represents the aristocracy in a state of decadence. In the third novel, the realm of the Guermantes and their influence supercedes that of Swann, as Marcel enters Paris society. The focus of this novel is the structures and mores of aristocratic society, represented particularly by the character of **Duchess Oriane de Guermantes,** for whom Marcel harbors an infatuated attachment. This closely observed view of society is divided into two parts, one relating the world of the salon of **Marquise Madeleine de Villeparisis,** the other devoted to a dinner party at the Guermantes. Marcel is preoccupied with disease, decay, and death, and many of his observations on the characters of society involve the physical transformation wrought by the passing years and encroaching old age. This is linked to Proust's theme of how the individual is altered by time and by Marcel's quest to determine the effect of time on personal identity. It is within this circle that Marcel, in a salon attended by the emerging artists of the day, first finds the encouragement he needs to explore his own vocation as a writer.

In *Cities of the Plain,* Proust explores the world of sexual inversion, which he employs as a metaphor for the evil in society and the perversion of the social and moral order. He focusses especially on Charlus, who, as a Guermantes, embodies the culture, taste, and knowledge of his class, but whose homosexuality reveals the depravity and self-destruction of his nature. Marcel's relationship with Albertine is also colored by rumors of her lesbian affairs. Their relationship continues to be a tortured one, intensified by Marcel's inability to break through the illusory conception he has of her and to know her for what she is.

This novel is also of importance for the section entitled "Intermittences of the Heart." Here Proust outlines his concept of memory, which he divides into "voluntary memory," the result of a conscious effort to recapture the past, which he finds false and limited, and the involuntary memory evoked in his earlier experience with the *madeleine,* in which the memory is freed of its context and becomes extra temporal. It is by these means that one is able to unlock the past and to link it with the present.

In the fifth novel, Albertine lives with Marcel in Paris. Their relationship is still plagued by agony, jealousy, and disenchantment. Amid continued hints at her life as a lesbian, Albertine leaves Marcel. The true nature of her sexuality is revealed in the sixth novel, when, after her death, Marcel learns that she had had affairs with many women and had also worked with **Charles Morel,** one of Charlus's lovers, seducing young girls and introducing them to lives of depravity. In this novel Marcel sees Gilberte again. Swann is now dead, Odette has remarried, and Gilberte marries **Robert de Saint-Loup,** a Guermantes and a close friend of Marcel.

The final volume contains Marcel's final revelation on the meaning of time, memory, and art. He is a middle-aged man now, witnessing the effects of World War I and the changes wrought by time on friends and society. The seemingly disparate paths represented by the Swanns and the Guermantes have been merged in the marriage of Gilberte and Saint-Loup and the birth of their daughter; Odette, once a social outcast, is now the mistress of the **Duke Basin de Guermantes.** While walking in Paris, Marcel has another astonishing experience with involuntary memory, as he steps on two uneven paving stones. The incident inspires him to devote his life to art, to remember and recover the past through his writing, for art is revealed as the force that liberates the individual from the constraints of time, through which the fruits of memory are preserved forever.

Proust intended *Remembrance of Things Past* to be read as a whole, for only in that context could its thematic resonances be comprehended. The work contains structural elements similar to a musical composition, with leitmotives, themes, and character types repeated and given greater depth and meaning as the work develops. Widely regarded as a masterpiece of world fiction, Proust's classic work is a testament to his literary genius.

FURTHER READING

Beckett, Samuel. *Proust*. London: Chatto and Windus, 1931.

Bell, Clive. *Proust*. London: The Hogarth Press, 1928.

Bersani, Leo. *Marcel Proust: The Fictions of Life and Art*. New York: Oxford University Press, 1965.

Bree, Germaine. *Marcel Proust and Deliverance from Time*. New Brunswick: Rutgers University Press, 1969.

Contemporary Authors, Vols. 104, 120. Detroit: Gale Research Co.

Fowlie, Wallace. *A Reading of Proust*. New York: Anchor Books, 1964.

Green, F.C. *The Mind of Proust: A Detailed Interpretation of "A la recherche du temps perdu."* Cambridge: Cambridge University Press, 1949.

Krutch, Joseph Wood. "Marcel Proust." In *Five Masters: A Study in the Mutations of the Novel*, pp. 251-328. London: Jonathan Cape, 1930.

Levin, Harry. "Proust." In *The Gates of Horn*, pp. 372-444. New York: Oxford University Press, 1963.

Maurois, Andre. *Proust: Portrait of a Genius*. New York: Harper and Brothers, 1950.

Peyre, Henri. *Marcel Proust*. New York: Columbia University Press, 1970.

Poulet, Georges. *Proustian Space*. Baltimore: Johns Hopkins University Press, 1977.

Twentieth-Century Literary Criticism, Vols. 7, 13. Detroit: Gale Research Co.

Manuel Puig

1932-

Argentinean novelist.

Kiss of the Spider Woman (novel, 1976)

Set in a Buenos Aires prison, this novel describes the story of two cell mates, **Luis Molina,** an aging homosexual, and **Valentin Arregui,** a political activist. The novel is composed almost completely of dialogue, with footnotes that form a lengthy exposition on the politics of homosexuality. Puig shows how the relationship of these two ideologically disparate men changes and develops over the course of their time together. The retelling of old movie plots creates an inventive fantasy world they share, a means of escape into the world of glamour and dreams, with Molina in particular recounting in lavish detail the sets, costumes, and inner tension in the lives of the characters. The relating of these stories becomes the focal point of their relationship and the novel itself, as Molina lulls Arregui to sleep with his narratives of love, betrayal, and sexuality, the themes that also characterize their lives in prison. One film in particular, about the Nazis and a French chanteuse, deals with the nature of politics, propaganda, and sexuality and forms a vivid parallel to the lives of the two men.

As a political prisoner, Arregui is a target of the authorities who are trying to poison him, with Molina ostensibly as their accomplice. Yet their shared lives have transformed the two men, with Arregui accepting and affectionate—obviously absorbing the "female" traits of his cell mate—and Molina capable of self-sacrifice and bravery. In the conclusion Molina has fallen in love with Arregui, and upon his release is killed when he tries to make contact with Arregui's friends.

The work is noted for its finely modulated dialogue and for Pruig's presentation of two distinct and finely differentiated voices. *Kiss of the Spider Woman* also reveals Puig's own fascination with old films, a recurring motif in his novels.

FURTHER READING

Contemporary Authors, Vols. 45-48; *Contemporary Authors New Revision Series,* Vol. 2. Detroit: Gale Research Co.

Contemporary Literary Criticism, Vols. 3, 5, 10, 28. Detroit: Gale Research Co.

Coover, Robert. "Old, New, Borrowed, Blue." *The New York Times Book Review* (22 April 1979): 15, 31.

Park, Clara Claiborne. "*Kiss of the Spider Woman.*" *The Hudson Review* 32, No. 4 (Winter 1979-80): 575-77.

Wood, Michael. "The Claims of Mischief." *The New York Review of Books* 26, Nos. 21-22 (24 January 1980): 43-7.

Barbara Pym
1913-1980
English novelist.

Some Tame Gazelle (novel, 1950)

Belinda and **Harriet Bede,** like most of Pym's heroines, are middle-aged spinsters who live quietly in a small English village. They occupy themselves by falling in love with men who have no intention of returning their affections. The novel is the story of their ultimate acceptance of their situation, and their realization that the enduring relationship in their lives is with each other. As in Pym's subsequent works, *Some Tame Gazelle* wryly depicts the world of English clergymen, anthropologists, and librarians. The focus of *Some Tame Gazelle* is the local vicarage; Belinda pines for a vain, petty archdeacon who snubs her in favor of a shallow woman, while Harriet fawns over young curates who consider her interest to be purely maternal. Despite the disappointment and solitude in their lives, the Bedes are happy with their lot in life. Though both profess to search for love, any potential suitors are instantly rejected as unsuitable. Pym stresses the dignity of their situation and the possibility of happiness in an unconventional arrangement.

In *Some Tame Gazelle,* Pym examines a recurrent theme in all her works—that romantic notions are often at odds with reality. Pym depicts her protagonists with sympathy and economy, in a work that is episodic in format and moves from comic vignette to comic vignette. Pym's writing here, and in subsequent works, is often compared to that of Jane Austen for its subtle psychological insights and subdued, genteel tone.

Excellent Women (novel, 1952)

Set in London in the 1950s, the novel follows the life of **Mildred Lathbury,** a spinster in her thirties and the daughter of a clergyman. Her life revolves around the local church. Her solitary existence is shaken when **Helena** and **Rockingham Napier,** an anthropologist and a naval officer, move into the flat above her. The Napiers see Mildred alternately as a mediator, a messenger, and a general helper—in short, as an "excellent woman" who is reliable in an emergency, but not suitable as a daily companion. Through the Napiers, Mildred meets **Everard Bone,** a shallow anthropologist. They begin to court and as the novel ends, it appears that Mildred's spinsterhood is over, only to be replaced by the role of a subservient wife. Pym does not indicate that Mildred's acquisition of a husband will lead to an idyllic existence: in inimitable Pym fashion, Mildred leaves the role of spinster to become wife and typist for Everard.

In *Excellent Women* Pym views marriage ironically. Rather than overtly criticizing the traditional feminine ideal of looking after a man, Pym mildly pokes fun at the ways of society. The men in *Excellent Women* are superficial and self-centered; not one is presented as an appealing prospect as a mate. As told in Mildred's voice, the novel also depicts her displeasure with her exposure to the rather unpleasant aspects of reality. Her life, cloistered in her flat and the vicarage, may have been dull, but she will surely miss its comfort and calm.

Quartet in Autumn (novel, 1977)

Set in a London office in the 1970s, the novel tells the story of four elderly people who must confront the meaning of old age and death. The four work together in jobs of a vague, clerical nature, which provide their only link with each other and society in general. When **Letty Crowe** and **Marcia Ivory** retire, the lives of all four are transformed. **Norman** and **Edwin Braithwaite** sense their circle growing smaller, while Marcia and Letty are unsure how to spend their abundant free time. Letty is a controlled, organized woman whose days are carefully scheduled, but retirement forces Marcia to the brink of madness. She is a nightmare of old age, hoarding newspapers and refusing to eat. When Marcia dies, she bequeaths her house to Norman, who is now in the surprising position of being a homeowner. Letty's life changes when several people appear eager for her to share living quarters; she is at once baffled and pleased by the attention of the outside world. Edwin, too, notices that his life has opened up. Pym stresses the dignity of old age; she argues that life, at any point, possesses countless opportunities for change. She shows how the absence of work that first provided a terrifying abyss is ultimately liberating.

Pym's straightforward narrative incorporates the thoughts and insights of each of her four main characters. As in most of her works, Pym's focus is on the world of solitary women, and she concentrates more on Letty and Marcia than on Edwin and Norman, evoking their different responses to solitude.

FURTHER READING

Brother, Barbara. "Women Victimized by Fiction: Living and Loving in the Novels of Barbara Pym." In *Twentieth-Century Women Novelists,* edited by Thomas F. Staley, pp. 61-80. New York: Barnes and Noble Books, 1982.

Butler, Marilyn. "Keeping Up with Jane Austen." *London Review of Books* (6 May 1982): 16-17.

Contemporary Authors, Vols. 13-14, 97-100; *Contemporary Authors New Revision Series,* Vol. 13; *Contemporary Authors Permanent Series,* Vol. 1. Detroit: Gale Research Co.

Contemporary Literary Criticism, Vols. 13, 19, 37. Detroit: Gale Research Co.

Dictionary of Literary Biography, Vol. 14. Detroit: Gale Research Co.

Glendinning, Victoria. "The Best High Comedy." *The New York Times Book Review* (24 December 1978): 8.

Gorra, Michael. "Restraint Is the Point." *The New York Times Book Review* (31 July 1983): 12, 18.

Iyer, Pico. "Tricks of Self-Consciousness." *Partisan Review* 52, No. 3 (1985): 286-91.

Kapp, Isa. "Out of the Swim with Barbara Pym." *The American Scholar* 52, No. 2 (Spring 1983): 237-42.

Larkin, Philip. "The World of Barbara Pym." *The Times Literary Supplement,* No. 3913 (11 March 1977): 260.

Rowse, A. L. "Austen Mini?" In *Punch* (19 October 1977): 732-34.

Taliaferro, Frances. "*Some Tame Gazelle.*" *Harper's* 267, No. 1599 (August 1983): 74-5.

Vogel, Christine B. "A Sip of Pym's Number One." *Book World—The Washington Post* (21 August 1983): 1, 14.

Thomas Pynchon

1937-

American novelist and short story writer.

The Crying of Lot 49 (novel, 1966)

This novel is set in contemporary Southern California and depicts a society that is nearly exhausted and apparently reaching the end of its cycle of history: total entropy is about to occur. The plot revolves around the efforts of **Oedipa Maas,** the book's principal character, to verify the existence of Tristero, an alternative postal system which she hopes can provide the foundation for a new society. Her attempt, however, is frustrated, because any clues she receives are inextricably bound up in the lives of various bizarre characters who may be distorting information. In addition, the majority of clues involve **Pierce Inverarity,** a wealthy mogul for whose estate Oedipa is co-executor, and it is likely that he would deliberately have established false leads to thwart her. Throughout the narrative Pynchon comments trenchantly on the vacuous and mechanistic nature of the society and people who live in it, pointed up notably by the long plot of a Jacobean drama that is interspersed in the novel. By this device, the sheer decadence of the two eras are underscored—and implicitly scorned. Also dealt with within the complex, ironic, and erudite narrative are such questions as the nature of communication and literature, and whether such efforts as novel-writing are at all effective in criticizing and changing society.

Ultimately, the question at the novel's center—does Tristero exist—may be answered by the sale of some postage stamps that the system allegedly issued. However, the sale, which is the "crying of lot 49," happens too late, in the book's final sentence. The reader is left, like Oedipa, with no solutions. Pynchon's second novel, *The Crying of Lot 49* is praised for its acute depiction of a society on the verge of entropy, and the accompanying sense of ambiguity and senselessness experienced by its characters.

Gravity's Rainbow (novel, 1973)

Set during and immediately after World War II, *Gravity's Rainbow* draws upon myriad historical, scientific, and cultural sources to dramatize the idea that ours is a culture of death. A dense and demanding work, it won the National Book Award and is generally regarded as a masterpiece of modern fiction.

The plot of the novel is propelled largely by the attempts of **Tyrone Slothrop** to discover why he has an erection each time a military rocket approaches him. That Slothrop is, as one character proposes, "in sexual love, with his, and the other's death," is characteristic, Pynchon implies, of our moribund culture. The author also sets forth several additional theories regarding society's preoccupation with death, implicitly indicting German thinkers in many cases, seeing them as intellectual enemies as well as political ones. Germans, he notes, were the first who learned to operate rockets at a speed faster than sound; the rocket hits before one can hear it, thus disturbing the concept of time. Even two hundred years earlier, Pynchon points out, a German philosopher and mathematician employed the same method "to break up the trajectories of cannonballs in the air." Similarly Pynchon says, film counterfeits movement, creating a force that he terms "reminders of impotence and abstraction."

Numerous allusions to cinema and filmmakers in the novel, including both real figures such as Fritz Lang, and imagined ones, serve to reinforce the notion that film contributes to the death culture. Finally, acting as a counterpoint to Pynchon's detailed and convincing portrayals of the waning culture is the theme of love as a means of conquering the obsession with death. Part of the development of the love motif is present in Pynchon's various graphic descriptions of sexual positionings.

Pynchon has been praised by critics for presenting in *Gravity's Rainbow* a rich and provocative exploration of both cultural and artistic issues through an erudite amalgam that draws upon subjects from science and mathematics as well as such popular art forms as film. Although the society he presents is a grim one, in his underlying celebration of human love, Pynchon presents at least some hope for humanity.

FURTHER READING

Abernethy, Peter. "Entropy in Pynchon's *The Crying of Lot 49.*" *Critique* 14, No. 2 (1972): 18-33.

Contemporary Authors, Vols. 17-20, rev. ed.; *Contemporary Authors New Revision Series,* Vol. 22. Detroit: Gale Research Co.

Contemporary Literary Criticism, Vols. 2, 3, 6, 9, 11, 18, 33. Detroit: Gale Research Co.

Dictionary of Literary Biography, Vol. 2. Detroit: Gale Research Co.

Friedman, Alan J. and Manfred Puetz. "Science as Metaphor: Thomas Pynchon and *Gravity's Rainbow.*" *Contemporary Literature* 15, No. 3 (Summer 1974): 345-59.

Helterman, Jeffrey. *Thomas Pynchon's "Gravity's Rainbow": A Critical Commentary.* New York: Monarch, 1976.

Leland, John P. "Pynchon's Linguistic Demon: *The Crying of Lot 49.*" *Critique* 16, No. 2 (1974): 45-53.

Levine, George and David Leverenz, eds. *Mindful Pleasures: Essays on Thomas Pynchon.* Boston: Little, Brown, 1976.

Raymond Queneau
1903-1976
French novelist, poet, and essayist.

Zazie (novel, 1959)

The novel, a surrealistic farce and Queneau's best-known work, is set in Paris. It concerns the wild adventures of **Zazie,** eleven years old, who has been sent to Paris to be cared for by her uncle **Gabriel** and aunt **Marceline,** while her mother vacations with her boyfriend. Zazie, on the threshold of adolescence, straddling childhood and adulthood, is Queneau's vehicle to reveal his unstable, unpredictable, anarchic fictional world. The novel reconstructs Zazie's hilarious and surreal adventures with her uncle, whose friend **Charles,** a taxi driver, offers to take young Zazie on a tour of Paris. But Zazie only wants to visit the *metro,* the Paris subway, which is closed because of a strike. So they visit all the tourist attractions anyway, with Zazie giving her commentary in a vulgar torrent that mystifies and disturbs her adult relatives. Yet these adults are anything but commonplace, for Uncle Gabriel makes his living as Gabriella, a dancer in a gay night club, and Marceline also switches sex roles, appearing as Marcel. Other characters also change into a series of different personas throughout the narrative. The narrative follows Zazie and her hapless uncle on a series of escapades, accompanying a group of tourists to the Eiffel Tower and witnessing a harassed bus driver who tells his group of travellers that a train station is a famous church, to which they respond with cheers.

Zazie is a satire on conventions, on sexual and social identity, and on language, for through his foul-mouthed protagonist, Queneau reveals the outmoded trappings of conventional literary language. The work is considered a linguistic *tour de force,* reflected especially in the Paris street slang, phonetically produced, that his characters use. The novel is also noted for its parody of conventional literary styles, including the epic, myth, and the psychological novel, which, through parody, are revealed in all their aridity.

FURTHER READING

Barthes, Roland. "Zazie and Literature." In *Critical Essays,* translated by Richard Howard, pp. 117-23. Evanston: Northwestern University Press, 1972.

Contemporary Authors, Vols. 69-72, 77-80. Detroit: Gale Research Co.

Contemporary Literary Criticism, Vols. 2, 5, 10, 42. Detroit: Gale Research Co.

Dictionary of Literary Biography, Vol. 72. Detroit: Gale Research Co.

Shorley, Christopher. *Queneau's Fiction: An Introductory Study.* Cambridge: Cambridge University Press, 1985.

Thiher, Allen. *Raymond Queneau.* Boston: Twayne, 1985.

Ayn Rand
1905-1982
Russian-born American novelist.

The Fountainhead (novel, 1943)

The Fountainhead is set mainly in New York in the world of architecture. The novel tells the story of one man's struggle to maintain his personal freedom and integrity in a society ruled by individuals bent on impeding human progress through the promotion of mediocrity. The central character is **Howard Roark,** a talented and creative individual who works for his own self-gratification rather than for the benefit of others. All of the characters are at once drawn to his greatness and also seek to destroy him. As the story begins, Roark has just been expelled from the Stanton Institute of Technology at the end of his junior year because he refused to comply with the school's mediocre standards. Afterwards, he travels to New York to work under the direction of **Henry Cameron,** who, though once successful, has been shunned by others in his profession because of his refusal to compromise. Following Cameron's death, Roark works temporarily doing manual labor at a quarry. Here, he meets and falls in love with **Dominique Francon.**

Peter Keating, Roark's roommate at the Institute, is graduated as valedictorian of his class and goes to New York to join the firm of Francon and Heyer. Rather than concentrate on the development of his talent, Keating builds his career upon manipulation, treachery, and compromise. He rises to the head of his firm and marries Dominique. In the end, he finds his life empty and meaningless and, true to his character, he agrees to divorce Dominique in exchange for a commission. **Gail Wynand,** the man to whom Keating sold his wife, is the book's most tragic figure. He is a self-made man and newspaper magnate, whose disillusionment and lust for power result in his ultimate downfall. When his newspaper is threatened by malevolent forces, originating from **Ellsworth Toohey,** Wynand betrays Roark and loses Dominique.

Ellsworth Toohey, a diabolical character and the true villain of the story, corrupts others by feeding upon their guilt and vanity. As Roark stands for the forces of integrity and individuality, Toohey represents the evils of "Collectivism" and compromise. Through devious means, Toohey sets himself up as an expert on architecture and becomes an influential critic, intending to amass power for himself. Although he is the primary force behind Keating's career and Wynand's ruin, he fails to defeat Roark.

Rand's idea of "objectivism," an extreme form of individualism, is demonstrated through the heroic character of Howard Roark, who struggles to maintain his integrity in a world of mediocrity. The novel was a great popular success and is noted today for its didactic exposition of Rand's political convictions.

Atlas Shrugged (novel, 1957)

Atlas Shrugged tells the story of five heroic figures who fight to save America from the destructive forces of socialism, forced upon the nation through the efforts of weak, small-minded, parasitic men. Rand divides humankind into "looters" and "non-looters," those that seek to bring all production under the aegis of the government and those that strive for independence and free enterprise. The protagonist, **Dagny Taggart,** is an intelligent, self-reliant railroad executive. She does her job well in spite of her brother, **James,** and others like him, whose altruistic rhetoric and policies are designed to handicap the nation's large industrialists and drive the country to the brink of ruin. While battling incompetent bureaucrats who view her and other industrialists as a threat to the common good, Dagny is also intent upon finding and defeating the person or entity responsible for the disappearance of the country's most talented and productive men. She calls this force "the Destroyer."

The remaining primary characters, all men, are exceptionally talented, honest and courageous individuals. **Hank Rearden** is an industrialist and inventor of Rearden Metal, an alloy that is superior to steel. The government tries to prevent the success of Rearden's venture through unfavorable press releases, legislation, and blackmail. Dagny is the first to use the metal and, shortly afterward, becomes Rearden's lover. **Francisco d'Alconia,** Dagny's childhood friend and first lover, was born to wealth and nobility and is the world's foremost copper magnate. While in college, Francisco forms a close relationship with two gifted classmates and, together they conspire to take action against the users of society.

Francisco appears to become an international playboy who, by squandering his talents and systematically wasting his fortune, drags society's "looters" into bankruptcy with him. **Ragnar Danneskjold,** one of d'Anconia's college friends, is an internationally known pirate whose self-appointed mission involves taking from the undeserving and giving back to those of worth. **John Galt,** another of d'Anconia's classmates, is the leader of the movement to "stop the motor of the world." He is Dagny's Destroyer and, with d'Anconia and Danneskjold, calls for a strike of all men of ability. Galt is an inventor who tries to persuade those creative individuals like him who refuse to bend to the pressures of modern politics and the forces of mediocrity. He builds a community in Colorado where, hidden from the rest of non-productive humanity, those of creative intelligence can be free to work and produce.

The novel is a political parable, offering a warning of the evils of socialism. Like *The Fountainhead,* critics found that the work suffers under the weight of Rand's polemical purpose, but it was a great popular success.

FURTHER READING

Baker, James T. *Ayn Rand.* Boston: Twayne, 1987.

Branden, Nathaniel. *Who Is Ayn Rand? An Analysis of the Novels of Ayn Rand.* New York: Random House, 1962.

Contemporary Authors, Vols. 13-16, rev. ed., 105. Detroit: Gale Research Co.

Contemporary Literary Criticism, Vols. 3, 30, 44. Detroit: Gale Research Co.

Gilder, George. "Ayn Rand: Sex, Money, and Philosophy." *Book World, Chicago Tribune* (29 June 1986): 1, 10.

Gladstein, Mimi Reisel. *The Ayn Rand Companion.* Westport: Greenwood Press, 1984.

Gordon, Philip. "Extroflective Hero: A Look at Ayn Rand." *Journal of Popular Culture* X, No. 4 (Spring 1977): 701-10.

Guerard, Albert. "Novel on Architectural Genius." *The New York Herald Tribune Weekly Book Review* (30 May 1943): 2.

McGann, Kevin. "Ayn Rand in the Stockyard of the Spirit." In *The Modern American Novel and the Movies,* pp. 325-35. New York: Ungar, 1978.

Pruette, Lorine. "Battle Against Evil." *The New York Times Book Review* (16 May 1943): 7, 18.

Marjorie Kinnan Rawlings
1896-1953

American novelist.

The Yearling (novel, 1938)

This novel, which won Rawlings the Pulitzer Prize, is set in the Florida backwoods during the post-Civil War period. It describes a year in the life of **Jody Baxter,** a twelve-year-old boy, and his passage to manhood.

Jody lives with his parents in a remote section of the Florida scrub. His father, **Penny Baxter,** is a farmer. He is a small but wiry man who indulges his son's boyhood's whimsies largely because of his own harsh childhood. **Ora,** Jody's mother, is a stern and humorless woman, twice the size of her husband. Although she had seven pregnancies, Jody is the only surviving child.

The beginning of the novel highlights Jody's idleness and his lack of commitment to his chores on the farm. He is a lonely little boy who idolizes his father and loves to hunt with him, but who also yearns for a playmate. The nearest neighbors are the Forresters who live four miles away. They are a large, wild brood with a boy Jody's age, a cripple named **Fodder-wing** who keeps a variety of wild animals as pets. Jody is not permitted to have a pet because of the Baxter's meager means. One day, however, while hunting for their hogs, Penny is bitten by a rattlesnake and must kill a doe in order to use its organs to draw out the poison. The doe had a very young fawn that Penny allows Jody to keep. Named Flag by Fodder-wing shortly before his death, the fawn becomes Jody's playmate and confidant.

The Baxter family is beset with many problems, including attacks by a legendary bear, Old Slewfoot, who eats the Baxter's livestock and manages to elude capture until the end of the novel. A terrible flood wipes out most of the farms' crops and is responsible for a disease that decimates the forest game animals. The Baxters are also caught in a confrontation between the Forrester men and other town friends, causing strained relations between the two families. Although Penny was in his prime at the beginning of the novel, his health begins to rapidly deteriorate, forcing Jody to take on most of the farm work himself. Flag has become a nuisance, eating or trampling a good portion of the crops. After several attempts to keep his pet out of mischief, Jody is forced to kill his beloved yearling, and with it his youth.

Rawlings uses regional dialect and her knowledge of backwoods customs to realistically portray Jody's story. She parallels Jody's growth into manhood with Flag's development into a yearling, Penny's decline into old age, and Old Slewfoot's death, reinforcing the theme of the cyclical element of nature.

FURTHER READING

Bigelow, Gordon E. *Frontier Eden*. Gainesville: University of Florida Press, 1966.

Contemporary Authors, Vol. 104. Detroit: Gale Research Co.

Dictionary of Literary Biography, Vols. 9, 22. Detroit: Gale Research Co.

Morris, Lloyd. "New Classicist." *North American Review* 246 (Autumn 1983): 179-84.

Soskin, William. "A Tom Sawyer of the Florida Scrub Lands." *New York Herald Tribune Book Review* 14 (3 April 1938): 1-2.

Twentieth-Century Literary Criticism, Vol. 4. Detroit: Gale Research Co.

Ishmael Reed

1938-

American novelist, poet, and critic.

Mumbo Jumbo (novel, 1972)

Set in New Orleans and New York City during the 1920s, *Mumbo Jumbo* is on the surface a mystery story featuring the neo-hoodoo detective **PaPa LaBas.** As Reed explained in his "Neo-Hoodoo Manifesto," neo-hoodooism is the resurgence of the Osirian animistic religion that had been suppressed by Judeo-Christian principles. PaPa LaBas sets out to find the original Hoodoo text which will liberate its ancient mysteries and allow its followers, known as the Jes Grew, to openly practice its tenets. Enemies of the Jes Grew are the Atonists, mostly people in authority who are dedicated to the preservation of Western civilization and consider the Jes Grew a danger to society. PaPa LaBas's main antagonist is **Hinckle Von Vampton,** who has taken it upon himself to locate and possess the Hoodoo text in order to keep it out of the hands of the Jes Grew. PaPa LaBas eventually traces the text to a nightclub in New York City. When he opens the box where it has been stored, however, the work is gone. He later learns that **Abdul Hamid,** a black Muslim magazine editor, had translated the text and then destroyed both copies after deciding that the content was obscene. PaPa LaBas does not despair, however; he realizes that Jes Grew is a spiritual part of all Afro-Americans and will manifest itself again and again in their art.

In *Mumbo Jumbo,* as in many of his works, Reed has used a historical perspective to depict the suppression of Afro-Americans' natural instincts by Western Culture. Reed rejects the novels of such writers as Ralph Ellison and James Baldwin for their pessimistic portrayals of black characters and advocates pride in a heritage that is essentially joyful. Reed further enhances his theme by using authentic Afro-American dialect throughout the novel.

Flight to Canada (novel, 1976)

The novel takes place during the early 1860s, with events alternating between Virginia and Canada. **Raven Quickskill** is an escaped slave and the author of the story who makes his way to Canada to enlist others in his fight against slavery. **Arthur Swille,** Raven's owner, hires trackers to find and return him, even after the Emancipation Proclamation has been issued. While Raven is dodging the slave-hunters and becoming involved with his former mistress, the Native American **Princess Quaw Quaw,** Swille is overtaken by his decadent past when the ghost of his sister returns to announce to the world their incestuous relationship, the shock of which causes him to fall into the fireplace and burn to death. Meanwhile, the slave **Uncle Robin,** an Uncle Tom-type character, has written himself into Swille's will as sole beneficiary and inherits his dead master's plantation. Uncle Robin sends for Raven to write his story, which becomes *Flight to Canada,* instead of Harriet Beecher Stowe, whom he had considered earlier.

The novel is noted for its detailed description of time and place, lending the work a vibrant authenticity. Reed's main theme is the necessity for Afro Americans to liberate themselves from Western myths which have kept them enslaved even into the twentieth century. *Flight to Canada* is also the story of how a fictional text is created, with Raven representing Reed, who learns to embrace his black heritage and to incorporate it into the art of writing.

FURTHER READING

Contemporary Authors, Vols. 21-24, rev. ed. Detroit: Gale Research Co.

Contemporary Literary Criticism, Vols. 2, 3, 5, 6, 13, 32. Detroit: Gale Research Co.

Dictionary of Literary Biography, Vols. 2, 5, 33. Detroit: Gale Research Co.

Ford, Nick Aaron. "A Note on Ishmael Reed: Revolutionary Novelist." *Studies in the Novel* 3 (1971): 216-18.

Martin, Reginald. "Reed's *Mumbo Jumbo.*" *Explicator* 44 (Winter 1986): 55-6.

Nazareth, Peter. "Heading Them Off at the Pass: Ishmael Reed and His Fiction." *The Review of Contemporary Fiction* 4 (Summer 1984): 208-26.

O'Brien, John. "Ishmael Reed." In *The New Fiction,* edited by Joe David Bellamy, pp. 130-42. Urbana: University of Illinois, 1974.

Parairsini, Lizabeth. "*Mumbo Jumbo* and the Uses of Parody." *Obsidian II* 1 (Spring-Summer 1986): 113-27.

Schmitz, Neil. "Neo-HooDoo: The Experimental Fiction of Ishmael Reed." *Twentieth Century Literature* 20 (April 1974): 126-40.

Erich Maria Remarque
1891-1970

German-born novelist.

All Quiet on the Western Front (novel, 1928)

This famous novel, set in the German trenches during World War I, relates the experiences of **Paul Bäumer,** a young German soldier. He is the narrator of the novel, and it is through his eyes and thoughts that we gain a sense of the war. Paul functions in the novel as an everyman, a common foot-soldier whose experience of war as a brutal, dehumanizing force reflects Remarque's avowed purpose in writing the novel: "to report on a generation that was destroyed by the War—even when it escaped the shells."

As the novel begins, we see Paul as a nineteen-year-old recruit. After his training, he is sent to the front, where, among his comrades, he witnesses the horrors of war. The age of Paul and his fellow soldiers is significant, for it is Remarque's intention to relate how these young men, deprived of their youth, are further stripped of their humanity and identity as they suffer the degradation of war. The novel focuses on the physical horrors of war and the way it effects their daily lives. Thus periods of boredom and fatigue are punctuated with shelling and hand-to-hand combat; scenes relating warm, loving encounters with friends, family, and lovers are juxtaposed to the hideous realities of battle. Their suffering and endurance are depicted not as a national, but as a universal response to the atrocity they confront. One by one, Paul sees his comrades die, and in one cataclysmic encounter, he stabs a French soldier. The death torments Paul, who tries to enter the dead man's consciousness to share his pain. In the conclusion, he is shot and killed by a stray bullet shortly before the declaration of the armistice.

The work is narrated in the present tense, in a simple prose style punctuated with fragmented narrative passages that mirror Paul's often disoriented state of mind. One of the most popular antiwar novel's ever written, *All Quiet on the Western Front* continues to be appreciated for its portrayal of the anguish and futility of war.

FURTHER READING

Contemporary Authors, Vols. 29-32, rev. ed., 77-80. Detroit: Gale Research Co.

Contemporary Literary Criticism, Vol. 21. Detroit: Gale Research Co.

Eksteins, Modris. *"All Quiet on the Western Front* and the Fate of a War." *The Journal of Contemporary History* 15, No. 2 (April 1980): 345-65.

Krutch, Joseph Wood. "Glorious War." *The Nation* 129, No. 3340 (10 July 1929): 43.

Rowley, Brian A. "Journalism into Fiction: *Im Westen nichts Neues." In The First World War in Fiction: A Collection of Critical Essays,* edited by Holger Klein, pp. 101-12. New York: Barnes and Noble, 1977.

Jean Rhys
1894-1979

West Indian-born English novelist and short story writer.

Wide Sargasso Sea (novel, 1966)

This novel, set in the West Indies during the nineteenth century, takes as its point of departure the early life of **Edward Rochester,** the famous character from Charlotte

Brontë's *Jane Eyre,* and his first wife, **Antoinette Rochester,** whose madness and death lead to the dramatic conclusion of Brontë's tale. Divided into three sections, the work first relates the story of Antoinette's childhood, focussing particularly on the isolation of her life and the hereditary madness to which her mother succumbs and which also claims her. Set in the era immediately following the emancipation of the slaves, the atmosphere is one of social upheaval as Antoinette and her family are forced to flee their home in the wake of increasing racial violence. Throughout the novel Antoinette is characterized as a victim: of her own culture at war with itself, of the clash between her world and the world of Rochester, and of her mind, divided against itself, as she slips into madness.

In the novel's second section, related through the character of Rochester, we learn of the early days of their marriage. Theirs is an arranged union, based on money rather than love. Their honeymoon indicates the personal abyss that separates them: she wishes to lose herself in her love for Rochester, while he draws away from her, afraid of her and the natural sensuousness and lushness of the environment. Through **Daniel Cosway,** a mulatto who claims to be Antoinette's half-brother, Rochester learns of her mother's madness and also, according to Cosway, that Antoinette had had other lovers before her marriage. Rochester responds with a sense of moral outrage. Antoinette, bewildered and desperate to win him back, tries first with a love potion and then with voodoo to entice him. Frightened by her sexuality and his own fears of losing control, he rejects her. To prove his masculinity and assuage his pride, Rochester takes a servant girl to bed, aware that it will hurt and humiliate his wife. In Part Three, Antoinette's madness emerges, precipitated by Rochester's cruelty and exacerbated by her growing sense of isolation.

The work is admired for its evocative handling of character and use of Gothic motifs. Rhys used her great descriptive powers to recreate the West Indies of her own childhood, and also displayed her keen insight into the relations between the sexes, which is a recurrent motif in her work.

FURTHER READING

Contemporary Authors, Vols. 25-28, rev. ed., 85-88. Detroit: Gale Research Co.

Contemporary Literary Criticism, Vols ?, 4, 6, 14, 19, 51. Detroit: Gale Research Co.

Dictionary of Literary Biography, Vol. 36. Detroit: Gale Research Co.

Fromm, Gloria G. "Making Up Jean Rhys." *The New Criterion* 4, No. 4 (December 1985): 47-50.

Kubitschek, Missy Dehn. "Charting the Empty Spaces of Jean Rhys's *Wide Sargasso Sea.*" *Frontiers: A Journal of Women's Studies* 9, No. 2 (1987): 23-8.

Staley, Thomas F. *Jean Rhys: A Critical Study.* London: Macmillan, 1979.

Mordecai Richler

1931-

Canadian novelist and essayist.

The Apprenticeship of Duddy Kravitz (novel, 1959)

The novel, Richler's best-known work, is set in the Jewish section of Montreal and tells the story of **Duddy Kravitz**'s coming of age. Raised in a slum, Duddy is a young Jewish man obsessed with materialism and is ruthless in his desire to achieve his goal of owning land. Richler's novel offers a satiric look at society's evils, and Duddy's greed is shown to mirror the corrupt drive for wealth that consumes society as a whole. Richler also deals with racial prejudice, exposing the ways in which people refuse to act with compassion and honesty, relying instead on the stereotypes—whether Jew, gentile, or black—that perpetuate the hatred between people. Duddy is a relentless exploiter of all he encounters, even taking advantage of his girlfriend, **Yvette,** a gentile, and his friend **Virgil Roseboro,** an epileptic. Devoid of morality or compassion, he is unable to return Yvette's selfless love or to understand it. Duddy idolizes **Jerry Dingleman,** called the Boy Wonder, a mythic figure who embodies the success Duddy craves, but who in reality is a small-time gangster. One of Richler's central themes is the importance of self-awareness, and Duddy is a character incapable of understanding himself or his life; he is depicted as a young man driven by forces he doesn't understand and is the product of a home devoid of love and nurturing. His mother died when Duddy was a boy, and his father, a pimp and a failure, is a cold, wasted man who appears to be the real cause of Duddy's moral emptiness and obsession with material things. When his **Uncle Benjy** sends him a letter entreating him to be a mensch, not a behemoth, the message is lost on Duddy. His grandfather had told Duddy that ''a man without land is nothing,'' and he took this theme literally. Duddy finally achieves his goal of ownership when he buys a tract of land in the Laurentians, which he plans to turn into a resort that will be as tasteless and money-conscious as the clientele he hopes to attract.

Richler's first major novel is highly regarded for its blend of satire and realism and for its richly comic tone. In his main character he created a figure who, for all his crass materialism, gains the reader's sympathy and pity.

St. Urbain's Horseman (novel, 1971)

The novel is set in London, the home of thirty-seven year old **Jacob Hersh,** a playwright and screenwriter who lives happily with his wife and children but who is plagued with guilt. Jake feels alone and alienated in the modern world, trying to hold on to his ideals in the wake of the despair he feels at his success. He senses that his affluence and achievement are undeserved, and he is obsessed with the fate of his fellow Jews who died in the Nazi death camps and with the millions of starving and suffering people all over the world. To compensate for this anxiety, Jake has created a fantasy avenger, the Horseman of the title, whom he sees as his cousin **Joey Hersh,** hero of the downtrodden. Joey's true nature remains obscure and mysterious throughout the novel, and whether he is a two-bit hood or an angel of mercy is left for the reader to decide. Jake also falls prey to the schemes of **Harry Stein,** a blackmailer and a pervert, a man who is obsessed with his self-image as society's victim. He is a cold, cruel man consumed with envy and plans for revenge, and he involves the curiously passive Jake in his schemes, which leads them to court and the travesty of justice that concludes the novel.

The work is noted for its successful blend of satire, farce, and fantasy, particularly in Jake's interior monologues, which are full of sexual fantasies and which reveal Richler's parody of pornography and the voyeuristic public. The novel is interspersed with advertisements, clips from newspapers, and snippets from film scripts, reflecting the vacuous nature of Hollywood and the entertainment industry and intensifying Jake's sense of uneasiness at his success. Once again in this novel Richler satirizes the vapidness of modern society, particularly in his depiction of middle-aged, middle-class Jews who have betrayed their ideals in pursuit of wealth and comfort. Many critics consider *St. Urbain's Horseman* to be Richler's finest novel.

FURTHER READING

Birbalsingh, F. M. ''Mordecai Richler and the Jewish-Canadian Novel.'' *Journal of Commonwealth Literature* 7 (June 1972): 72-82.

Contemporary Authors, Vols. 65-68. Detroit: Gale Research Co.

Contemporary Literary Criticism, Vols. 3, 5, 9, 13, 18, 46. Detroit: Gale Research Co.

Cude, Wilfred. "The Golem as Metaphor for Art: The Monster Takes Meaning in *St. Urbain's Horseman.*" *Journal of Canadian Studies* 12 (Spring 1977): 50-69.

Dictionary of Literary Biography, Vol. 53. Detroit: Gale Research Co.

Ferns, John. "Sympathy and Judgment in Mordecai Richler's *The Apprenticeship of Duddy Kravitz.*" *Journal of Canadian Fiction* 3 (Winter 1974): 77-82.

Meyers, David. "Mordecai Richler as Satirist." *Ariel* 4 (January 1973): 47-61.

Ramraj, Victor J. *Mordecai Richler.* Boston: Twayne, 1983.

Sheps, David G. "Introduction." In *Mordecai Richler,* edited by G. David Sheps, pp. ix-xxvi. Toronto: Ryerson Press, 1971.

Alain Robbe-Grillet

1922-

French novelist and essayist.

The Voyeur (novel, 1955)

This, Robbe-Grillet's best-known novel, is one of the most celebrated and controversial works connected with the "New Novel" movement in French letters. It takes place on an island where **Mathias,** the protagonist, has gone to sell watches. It is the island of his birth and early youth, and he hopes to capitalize on his connections to sell a good quantity of watches on his trip. The narrative begins on a ferry, and as Mathias approaches his destination, we notice the first mention of several objects and sensations—a child with large eyes who observes Mathias, a piece of string in the shape of a figure-eight, a cigarette pack, the rhythmic beating of the waves—that, through repetition and suggestion, will accrue the additional connotations of violence, violation, and murder in the mind of the reader.

He begins his journey, which takes the shape of a figure-eight, on bicycle. He visits **Madame Leduc,** who complains about her daughter **Jacqueline,** a sexually precocious, rebellious thirteen-year-old, whom she describes as a "wild animal," with the "devil" in her. He learns that she is tending the family sheep near a cliff overlooking the sea. The first section of the novel ends with a blank page. In Part Two, Mathias meets **Madame Marek,** an old acquaintance, on the road and claims to have tried to visit her at her farm. He journeys into town, where he learns that Jacqueline is missing. He lunches with a young man, named either **Pierre** or **Jean Robin,** who claims they are old friends, although Mathias cannot remember him, and his girlfriend, who is a friend of Jacqueline's. Mathias misses his ferry boat and remains on the island. In Part Three, the death of Jacqueline is announced in the newspaper, and several scenes depict various islanders being accused of her murder, including Jean Robin and **Julien Marek,** the son of Madame Marek. Mathias visits the site of Jacqueline's fall to her death, where he tries to dispose of evidence—cigarette butts, candy wrappers—that could incriminate him; he is discovered by Julien, who insinuates that Mathias is the murderer. Back in town, surrounded by the villagers talking about Jacqueline, Mathias faints. Visions of Jacqueline as the victim of a sadistic murder and rape repeat in his mind. In the conclusion, he leaves the island.

Whether Mathias commits the murder or whether the murder even takes place remains unclear. According to some critics, the blank page is the place in the text where the murder takes place, for it is never described in the novel. The work is deliberately ambiguous: we are within Mathias's obsessive, tortured psyche, and as he constantly imagines, invents, and interprets erotic and sadistic scenarios, we are drawn into what may only be his wild dreams. There is no final, logical interpretation, and Robbe-Grillet relies on the complicity of the reader to read, assimilate, and order this fictional reality and determine its meaning.

FURTHER READING

Baum, Alwin L. "The Metanovel: Robbe-Grillet's Phenomenal 'Nouveau Roman.'" *Boundary 2* 6, No. 2 (Winter 1978): 557-75.

Contemporary Authors, Vols. 9-12, rev. ed. Detroit: Gale Research Co.

Contemporary Literary Criticism, Vols. 1, 2, 4, 6, 8, 10, 14, 43. Detroit: Gale Research Co.

Morrissette, Bruce. *The Novels of Robbe-Grillet.* Ithaca: Cornell University Press, 1975.

Stoltzfus, Ben F. *Alain Robbe-Grillet and the New French Novel.* Carbondale: Southern Illinois University Press, 1964.

Edmond Rostand

1868-1918

French dramatist.

Cyrano de Bergerac (drama, 1897)

This famous heroic comedy, set in seventeenth-century France, is a work of international popularity. **Cyrano de Bergerac**—poet, philosopher, and soldier—is a world-renowned character, and he was inspired by the historical Cyrano, a poet and soldier of the seventeenth century. The play tells the story of a man of wit, integrity, honesty, and loyalty, whose fate is to have the soul of a poet and the face of a clown. His huge nose makes him laughable in the role of lover, a part for which his eloquence and depth of sensitivity mark him. He is a man of fierce independence and integrity, as symbolized in his white plume. The work covers a broad canvas and is filled with swashbuckling sword fights, designed to display Cyrano's verbal and physical expertise. Boastful among his fellow soldiers, he is capable of composing a ballad while fighting a duel.

Cyrano plays the part of mentor for a fellow soldier, **Christian de Neuvillette,** a handsome young man deeply in love with the beautiful **Roxanne Robin.** Handicapped by his shyness and lacking the persuasiveness and style of his teacher, Christian is unable to tell her of his love. This Cyrano does for him, composing love letters in which he speaks eloquently for his young friend, while he too falls in love with the enchanting Roxanne. In the most famous scene in the play, which takes place beneath Roxanne's balcony, he coaches his young friend, but suddenly forgets himself; he no longer speaks for Christian, but addresses himself directly to Roxanne, cloaked in darkness while revealing the depth of his ardent affection for her. After Christian and Roxanne marry, the young soldier is sent into battle and to his death by the **Comte de Guiche,** Roxanne's jealous former suitor. In her grief, Roxanne retreats to a convent, where Cyrano is her faithful visitor. In the final scene, Cyrano dies by the side of his cherished Roxanne, never having openly expressed his love for her.

The play is praised for its vivid recreation of an historical epoch as well as its vibrant language and lyrical verse. In distinct contrast to the realistic drama of turn-of-the-century France, *Cyrano de Bergerac* harkens back to the early nineteenth century and the romantic era. The character of Cyrano embodies the ideals of self-sacrifice, honor, and courage; as in his credo, he is "admirable in all," qualities that have made him a favorite figure of drama.

FURTHER READING

Amoia, Alba della Fazia. *Edmond Rostand.* Boston: Twayne, 1978.

Chiari, Joseph. "Edmond Rostand." In *The Contemporary French Theatre: The Flight from Naturalism,* pp. 32-46. London: Rockliff, 1958.

Contemporary Authors, Vol. 104. Detroit: Gale Research Co.

Smith, Hugh Allison. "Edmond Rostand." In *Main Currents of Modern French Drama,* pp. 76-106. New York: Holt, 1925.

Twentieth-Century Literary Criticism, Vol. 6. Detroit: Gale Research Co.

Philip Roth

1933-

American novelist and short story writer.

Goodbye, Columbus (novella, 1959)

The story takes place in post-war New Jersey and deals with a young Jewish man's search for identity. His quest is complicated by a doomed love affair and encompasses religious, moral, and cultural issues.

Neil Klugman, the principal character, is in his mid-twenties and works in a public library. He lives in Newark with his somewhat eccentric aunt and her family in a lower-class neighborhood. Neil is treated to a day at Green Lane, a posh country club, by one of his cousins. Here, he meets **Brenda Patimkin,** a rich Jewish girl, and the two begin a love affair. Brenda is a Radcliffe student, home for the summer, and lives with her family in the wealthy suburb of Short Hills.

The Patimkins have managed to escape their humble Newark origins and have realized the American Dream through the success of Mr. Patimkin's kitchen and bathroom sink business. At Brenda's urging, Neil is invited to stay with the Patimkin family for two weeks at the end of the summer. Here, Neil is awed by the bourgeois bounty he finds: the Patimkin backyard is littered with all manner of sporting equipment, and their basement refrigerator is full of an abundance of fresh fruit.

Neil acknowledges that Brenda is spoiled and her family coarse and shallow. He continues his amorous pursuit, however, because, although he doesn't like Brenda, he is in love with the idea of her and all that she represents. By the same token, Brenda, who is singularly insensitive in regard to Neil, continues the affair because it irritates her mother.

Neil is compassionate toward a young black boy who visits the library frequently to gaze with rapture at a book of Gauguin paintings. The little boy is taken with the book much the same way that Neil is taken with the Patimkin lifestyle, for both he and Neil attempt to insinuate themselves into dream worlds. In *Goodbye, Columbus* Roth portrays his idea of American values as they relate to Jewish life today. He mocks both the newly rich and the traditional middle-class through irony, characterization, and his use of the Jewish-American idiom, humorously disclosing the true nature of both his characters and their values. Roth won the National Book Award in 1960 for this work.

Portnoy's Complaint (novel, 1969)

Portnoy's Complaint is a satiric novel which describes a Jewish man's futile struggle for freedom from his past, specifically the guilt, restrictions, and taboos imposed upon him by his parents and religion during childhood, and his sense of alienation in the present. The story is told in monologue form by the main character, **Alexander Portnoy,** who is relating the personal details of his life to his psychiatrist, **Dr. Spielvogel.**

Portnoy, in his early thirties, presents a highly moral exterior, displayed in his job as Assistant Commissioner of the New York Commission on Human Opportunity. In his private life, however, he uses obscenity and promiscuous sexual behavior in order to rebel against his upbringing and the unsympathetic and predominately gentile society in which he lives. We learn that as a child, when frustrated by his ineffectual father, **Jake,** and his smothering, melodramatic, and domineering mother, **Sophie,** Portnoy released his anger and frustration in excessive masturbation. Outwardly an obedient child and outstanding student, his childhood sexual fantasies always involved gentile girls whose homes he envied because he perceived them to be serene and normal, much like that depicted in the popular 1950s television show, *Ozzie and Harriet.* As an adult, Portnoy acts out his fantasies with gentile girls of various origins, acknowledging that his actions are directed less against the women themselves than their backgrounds.

Portnoy, recognizing that his rebellious behavior is destructive and only leads to more feelings of guilt and frustration, makes a trip to Israel where, because everyone there is Jewish, he hopes to feel a sense of belonging. Here he meets **Naomi,** a woman in the Israeli army who reminds him of his mother. While attempting to rape her, Portnoy finds himself impotent. His flight to Israel demonstrates that he is as alienated there as at home. More to the point, the values and taboos that Portnoy ran away from and rebelled against were so ingrained within him that his hopes for escape are futile.

As in most of his fiction Roth explores the effect of culture on an individual's search for identity with humor and satire. The use of the monologue technique enables Roth to present his protagonist—confessing, exaggerating and accusing others—in a disjointed, fragmented narrative style.

Zuckerman Unbound (novel, 1981)

Zuckerman Unbound is a satirical account of one man's graceless struggle with the heterogeneous effects of sudden fame and fortune. The main character, **Nathan Zuckerman,** has just completed his fourth and most successful book, *Carnovsky.* It is a fictional narration of the sexual exploits of a Jewish boy from Newark, Gilbert Carnovsky. Unhappily, even those closest to Zuckerman believe that his book is autobiographical. They not only confuse the author with the Carnovsky character, but also take exception to the way that they perceive themselves to be portrayed. Consequently, Zuckerman is alienated from his saintly wife, his family, old friends, and others who believe that he has betrayed them.

Normally reclusive, Zuckerman finds that he has been cast to the forefront of the public eye. He is unprepared for both his new-found wealth—he keeps his money in his shoe and continues to ride the bus—and with the reaction of those around him. He is the recipient of adulation, hate mail and threatening calls; strangers feel free to approach him to comment upon his work and personal life. One such hanger-on, **Alvin Pepler,** attaches himself to Zuckerman and becomes both his most loyal fan and the object of the writer's most intense dread. Pepler, also Jewish and from Newark, was once a contestant on a popular game show in the fifties. He possessed a photographic memory and was particularly well-versed in Americana. He was, however, ousted from the program after only three weeks in favor of another contestant, a WASP, who in order to win had to be spoon-fed the answers. Pepler's chances for fame were crushed in the ensuing scandal, which left him a bitter man.

Zuckerman finds that Pepler's adulation quickly turns to vicious jealousy, and that his detailed knowledge of Zuckerman's daily life feeds his already active paranoia. By the end of the novel, Zuckerman likens Pepler to Lee Harvey Oswald and, frightened for his life, hires an armed driver.

Near the end of the book, Zuckerman is summoned to his father's death bed in Miami.

Nathan's book had apparently caused his father's final stroke. **Dr. Zuckerman**'s parting comment, directed at Nathan, is: "Bastard." Although Nathan's brother, **Henry,** was crushed by the death of his father, Nathan, who had always felt suffocated in the confines of his father's morality, feels liberated.

Zuckerman Unbound is one of a trilogy in which the character of Nathan Zuckerman appears. The character is a self-mocking autobiographical figure, as Roth suggests in the publication history of his character, whose novel *Carnovsky* is published about the same time as Roth's *Portnoy's Complaint.*

FURTHER READING

Bellman, Samuel I. "Irony: Sweet and Sour." *National Jewish Monthly* (December 1959): 39-40.

Broyard, Anatole. *"Zuckerman Unbound." The New York Times* (9 May 1981): 13.

Contemporary Authors, Vols. 1-4, rev. ed.; *Contemporary Authors New Revision Series,* Vols. 1, 22. Detroit: Gale Research Co.

Contemporary Literary Criticism, Vols. 1, 2, 3, 4, 6, 9, 15, 22, 31, 47. Detroit: Gale Research Co.

Dictionary of Literary Biography, Vol. 2, 28; *Dictionary of Literary Biography Yearbook: 1982.* Detroit: Gale Research Co.

Epstein, Joseph. "What Does Philip Roth Want?" *Commentary* 77, No. 1 (January 1984): 62-7.

Grossman, Joel. "'Happy as Kings': Philip Roth's Men and Women." *Judaism* (Winter 1977): 7-17.

Jones, Judith Patterson and Guinevera Nance. *Philip Roth.* New York: Ungar, 1981.

Kiely, Robert. "Roth's Writer and His Stumbling Block." *The New York Times Book Review* (30 October 1983): 1, 23.

Pinoker, Sanford. "Zuckerman's Success." *Midstream* 27, No. 10 (December 1981): 53-4.

Rodgers, Bernard F. *Philip Roth.* Boston: Twayne, 1978.

Rothstein, Edward. "The Revenge of the Vrai." *The New York Review of Books* (25 June 1981): 13.

Tanner, Tony. "The Gripes of Roth." *Book World: The Washington Post* (31 May 1981): 3, 6.

Salman Rushdie

1947-

Indian-born English novelist and essayist.

The Satanic Verses (novel, 1988)

Set in England and India, this complex novel is a wide-ranging examination of the struggle of good and evil. As the novel begins, the two protagonists, **Gibreel Farishta** and **Saladin Chamcha,** are falling to earth, the only two survivors of a jet that has exploded over the English Channel. As they tumble through the air, Gibreel, an Indian film star, and Chamcha, an Indian living in London whose voice has made him a fixture of English advertising and film, cling to each other, singing and screaming. When they land, they are miraculously unhurt, but that is not the only "miracle" to occur: Gibreel now possesses a halo-like glow around his head; Chamcha is growing horns and hooves. They appear to have been mysteriously chosen as embodiments of good and evil, and their struggle with these identities and with each other forms the frame story of the novel.

Discovered by an old English woman, they are taken to her home, where Gibreel is treated with warmth and hospitality, and Saladin is taken into police custody. Gibreel finds himself having vivid dreams, interwoven throughout the work, in which he appears to have taken the form of the Archangel Gabriel. He is transported back to the time of the great prophet **Mahound,** a figure representing Mohammed, who is engaged in the founding a religion, referred to here as the faith of "Submission." Within these dreams, Mahound changes from the zealous man of God to an egotistical, power-hungry man, anxious for all to be under his sway. Gibreel appears to merely confirm Mahound's pronouncements, rather than acting as the messenger of God to his servant. These visions alternate with the story of **Ayesha,** a young girl who claims to have been called by God to lead a march to the sea. Surrounded by butterflies, which provide her only clothing and sustenance, she leads her disciples on a journey that ends in death for her faithful followers.

In London, Gibreel has recommenced his affair with **Alleluia Cone,** a beautiful English moutain climber. He begins to make films again, using his visions as his screen vehicles. Chamcha, who has lost his wife to a friend, is possessed with revenge against his apparently "blessed" friend. He begins to stalk Gibreel, using his trained voice to imitate a variety of imaginary lovers who claim to have betrayed Gibreel with Allie. Driven to madness by jealousy and the demons that possess him, Gibreel kills Allie, and he commits suicide.

Rushdie's theme is the ambivalent, illusory, and interdependent nature of good and evil, which is underscored by the motif of metamorphosis. His exploration of the duality of human nature is further enhanced by the conflict within Gibreel and Chamcha over their own identities: as expatriate Indians in England, as actors, and as helpless puppets in their final roles. The novel is rich in word play, with allusions drawn from Indian, English, and American literature and dialect.

The work has been the center of a raging controversy since its publication, and several Islamic countries have banned the book on the grounds of blasphemy. After it appeared, the late Ayatollah Khomeni called for Rushdie's murder. As of this writing, the author remains in hiding.

FURTHER READING

Contemporary Authors, Vols. 108, 111. Detroit: Gale Research Co.

Contemporary Literary Criticism, Vols. 23, 31. Detroit: Gale Research Co.

Irwin, Robert. "Original Parables." *Times Literary Supplement* (6 October 1988): 1067.

King, Francis. "Perplexing in the Extreme." *The Spectator* (1 October 1988): 31.

Sinclair, Iain. "Imaginary Football Teams." *The Listener* (30 September 1988): 40-1.

J. D. Salinger

1919-

American novelist and short story writer.

"For Esme—With Love and Squalor" (short story, 1950)

The story is told in the first person in 1950 by an American writer and former soldier. He recalls an afternoon in Devon, England in April 1944 and then, switching to third person, describes a scene in Bavaria, Germany in May 1945.

The narrator begins with the information that he has been invited to a wedding in England. Going back six years, he recounts his first and apparently only meeting with the bride-to-be, who was then thirteen. The narrator-soldier, bored by a three-week army training course in Devon, wanders in the rain into town where he stops into a church and comes upon a children's choir rehearsal, which he quietly observes. Stopping afterward at a tearoom, he is joined by **Esme,** a radiant and self-possessed young girl who had captured his attention at the rehearsal. Precocious and pseudo-sophisticated, she converses brightly with the soldier, revealing that both her parents had been killed in the war, orphaning her and her 5-year-old brother, **Charles,** who presently leaves his governess at a nearby table to assail them with riddles. Esme proudly shows the narrator her prize possession, her dead father's chronographic wristwatch, and, when she learns that he is a writer, requests that he write her a story about "squalor." In the story's ensuing second section, the narrative voice switches to third person, describing **Sergeant X,** clearly the narrator himself, who is now stationed in Bavaria and on the verge of a nervous breakdown. His fatigue and despair are set against the callous comments and behavior of his jeep-mate, **Corporal Clay,** and the insensitive letters from his family back home, asking, for example, for macabre war relics for the kids. As he sifts uncomprehendingly through a stack of mail, he comes upon a small package from England, mailed almost a year before. Inside is a letter from Esme and Charles along with their father's wristwatch, the crystal broken, but otherwise intact. Seeing it, the Sergeant, who has not slept for many nights, feels a sudden sense of tranquility and ease, and a great drowsiness overcoming him; he is clearly saved by Esme's guileless gesture of love and hope.

Many critics name "For Esme—with Love and Squalor" one of Salinger's most skillful renderings of the theme of the "squalid" world versus the pure one and a fine depiction of the redemptive power of love. They also consider Esme—along with Charles—among the finest of his many memorable child characters.

The Catcher in the Rye (novel, 1951)

Sixteen-year-old **Holden Caulfield** and his sister **Phoebe,** age ten, are the main characters of Salinger's only published novel, a perennial favorite of young readers. Set in the late 1940s, the novel takes place over three days in December, chiefly in New York City. Holden, who narrates the story in a distinctively humorous, idiomatic voice, has flunked out of Pencey Prep in Agerstown, Pennsylvania, where the story's first scenes are set. This academic failure, which is sure to infuriate his parents (he was expelled from two previous schools), caps Holden's growing disgust and sense of alienation. He is fed up with such classmates as pesky **Ackley** and his slick, insincere roommate, **Stradlater,** and is impatient even with a favorite history teacher, **Mr. Spencer.** Holden decides to take the train to New York, where he will use his savings to hide out until the trouble with his parents blows over. The action of this loosely structured, episodic novel centers on several ensuing encounters that intensify Holden's despair at the "phoniness" of the world, bring him to a crisis point, and to the beginning of a resolution.

Holing up first in a seedy Manhattan hotel, Holden is punched out by a bellboy and small-time pimp, **Maurice,** after a misunderstanding with a prostitute. The next afternoon he makes a theater date with **Sally Hayes,** an old girlfriend. When she disappoints him with her self-conscious pseudo-sophistication and refuses to run away with him, Holden insults her and drives her away. Arranging next to meet an older ex-classmate at an expensive bar, Holden soon alienates him, too, with his excessive drinking and mocking comments. Drunk, low on money, and wandering in the rain, Holden decides to sneak into his parents' apartment to visit his precocious sister, Phoebe. She is clearly the only person Holden feels close to since the loss of their beloved brother **Allie,** a poetry-lover who covered his baseball mitt with verse, who died of leukemia at age ten. Trying to explain his agitation, Holden tells Phoebe he wants to be a "catcher in the rye" (an idea he got from an overheard misquote of a Robert Burns poem) who would stand in a field and keep children from going over the edge of "some crazy cliff." When the elder Caulfields arrive home, Holden sneaks out and seeks refuge with **Mr. Antolini,** a former English teacher who welcomes him despite the late hour. Drunken and garrulous, Mr. Antolini lectures Holden on the necessity of living humbly for a cause rather than seeking to die for one. Holden goes to sleep on the couch, but leaves abruptly after wakening to find Mr. Antolini stroking his hair in the darkness. Convinced of the older man's perverse intentions, Holden is now determined to flee society, to head "West," but first he must say good-bye to Phoebe. When she arrives at the Natural History Museum, their appointed meeting site, determined to go with him, he realizes he cannot take her away from society. Holden reaches a kind of resolution in a final scene as he watches Phoebe joyfully riding a children's carousel. Putting aside his initial worry that Phoebe will fall while trying to grasp the golden ring, he remarks: "The thing with kids is, if they want to grab for the golden ring, you have to let them do it. . . . " In contrast with his former desire to "catch" children before they fall, Holden is now willing to trust enough to let them risk tumbling. An epilogue reveals that Holden was sent to a California sanitarium, where part of his treatment was to write this account of his days in New York. While Holden is not yet entirely recovered, the carousel scene implies that he has been restored to the possibilities of life and is now willing to risk the pitfalls involved in leading a sincere life in an inherently "phony" world.

The Catcher in the Rye was so influential in the 1950s that the decade has been called "the age of Holden Caulfield." Many critics believe that in sensitive, alienated Holden, Salinger created a sympathetic figure comparable to such characters as Mark Twain's Huck Finn and F. Scott Fitzgerald's Gatsby in his struggle to overcome disillusionment in a flawed world. Particularly praised in the novel is the perfectly rendered idiomatic language of Holden and the other characters.

"Teddy" (short story, 1953)

The story is set in the 1950s on a transatlantic ship. The McArdle family are returning from Great Britain, where ten-year-old **Teddy,** an extraordinarily gifted child, was interviewed and observed by scientists. The first scene takes place in the family's cabin, where the reader briefly meets **Mr. McArdle,** a loutish, egocentric radio actor, and **Mrs. McArdle,** who is depicted as shallow and overly indulgent to her son. In spite of his parents' failings and his sister **Booper**'s cruel nature, Teddy is a magnanimous soul who rises above human pettiness and tries to please his family. The body of the story consists of an on-deck conversation between Teddy and an inquisitive professor of education, **Bob Nichols.** We learn through Teddy's precocious remarks that he believes in the Vedantic theory of reincarnation; that he was, in a previous life, a holy man in India; and that his soul is apparently so highly evolved that he is able to predict the future. Just before leaving Nichols to attend his swimming lesson, Teddy stresses that life is unknowable. He remarks that, for example, the swimming pool may have no water, his sister may push him, and he could die from the injuries. It was also revealed earlier in the story that Teddy had written in his diary for the day: "It will happen either today or on February 14, 1958." As the story ends, Nichols hears an "all-piercing, sustained scream—clearly coming from a small, female child. It was highly acoustical, as though it were reverberating within four tiled walls."

Critics have puzzled over the ambiguity of the story's ending: did Teddy commit suicide by jumping into the pool, or did Booper push him? While they disagree on the story's overall success, commentators generally agree that in this story of a genius and genuine holy man, Salinger gives the most explicit expression to the Zen-Buddhist ideals that inform his later fiction.

Franny and Zooey (short stories, 1961)

Franny Glass and her brother **Zooey** (born Zachary) are the main characters of this work. The book comprises two related, lengthy short stories, both of which first appeared in the *New Yorker,* in 1955 and 1957 respectively.

Franny and Zooey takes place over one long weekend in the fall of 1954 at an eastern Ivy League college and in New York City. In the book's first section, Franny arrives to attend the Yale football game at the college of her boyfriend, **Lane Coutell.**

During their pregame lunch, Lane is revealed as a self-centered snob who dominates the conversation describing his recent paper on Flaubert. Franny, who has been quiet to this point, sees that Lane epitomizes the phoniness in people that has been disturbing her greatly, and she and Lane get into an agitated discussion about poetry. Excusing herself, she goes to the lavatory and begins to cry. When she takes a small green book from her purse and presses it to her chest, she is at once soothed. She rejoins Lane and tries to explain to him how disturbed she has become with the pettiness of college life and the egocentricity she observes around her: "I'm just sick of ego, ego, ego," she exclaims. "My own and everybody else's." She reluctantly speaks then of the green book, *The Way of the Pilgrim,* which instructs one how to pray until the prayer eventually becomes self-active. Lane, intent on consuming his frogs' legs, is obviously unmoved by Franny's fervor. More disturbed than ever, Franny attempts to return to the ladies' room but faints on the way. She is revived, and as section one ends her lips are silently moving, presumably forming the words to the Jesus Prayer.

"Zooey," the book's second section, recounts the attempts of Zooey, an actor, to soothe his sister's malaise. The action takes place on the following Monday in the Glass family apartment in Manhattan, where Franny is recuperating. Unlike "Franny," which is narrated in the third person, "Zooey" is narrated by **Buddy Glass,** the protagonists' older brother and the central figure in "Raise High the Roofbeam, Carpenters." After a general, somewhat discursive introduction, Buddy leads the reader into the family bathroom, at which point he announces that he is switching to the third-person point of view. Zooey is in the bathtub, reading a four-year-old letter from **Seymour Glass,** the deceased elder brother who figures importantly in Salinger's other works. The letter, reproduced entirely for the reader, outlines the rigorous education in religion, especially Eastern religion, that Seymour and Buddy provided for their younger siblings, Zooey and Franny. Emerging from the tub after a conversation (from behind the curtain) with his mother, **Bessie,** Zooey confronts Franny in the living room. He tries to impress upon her that her withdrawal into the Jesus Prayer is in itself egocentric, and that only by acting, her chosen vocation, will she make the contribution she was meant to. Failing to reach her, he retreats to Seymour's old bedroom, where he eventually telephones Franny from Seymour's still-functioning separate line. Zooey evokes their childhood days as radio quiz kids, when Seymour instructed them always to shine their shoes and to do their best for the Fat Lady in the listening audience. "Don't you know who that Fat Lady really is?" Zooey asks. "Ah buddy. It's Christ himself, Christ himself, buddy." By summoning this image of universal human love, Zooey at last reaches Franny, who falls into a deep, restorative sleep.

Franny and Zooey features Salinger's two predominant concerns: the sensitive adolescent confronted with the ego and the unfeeling world, and a keen interest in religion and spirituality. While "Franny" is praised by some for its structure and expert depiction of the college milieu and language, "Zooey" is often regarded as diffuse. Franny and Zooey remain two of Salinger's most important and sensitively drawn characters.

Raise High the Roofbeam, Carpenters and Seymour: An Introduction (short stories, 1963)

Brothers **Buddy** and **Seymour Glass** are the central characters of *Raise High the Roofbeam,*

Carpenters and Seymour: An Introduction. Seymour Glass was first introduced in "A Perfect Day for Bananafish," which recounts Seymour's suicide. Both Buddy and Seymour are referred to in *Franny and Zooey.* Like that book, *Raise High the Roofbeam, Carpenters and Seymour: An Introduction* comprises two lengthy short stories that were first published in the *New Yorker,* in 1955 and 1959, respectively.

The book's first section takes place in New York City in late May, 1942, and the second chiefly in Buddy's mind about fifteen years later. Buddy Glass narrates the first story, which recalls Seymour's failure to show up for his scheduled wedding to **Muriel Fedder.** In the confusion following the non-ceremony, Buddy, the only Glass family member in attendance, is thrust into a hot, crowded car to drive to the non-wedding reception. His car-mates include Muriel's aunt, her tiny deaf-mute uncle, a **Lt. Burwick,** and his wife, **Edie Burwick,** the matron of honor. Not realizing that Buddy is related to the errant groom, Edie exclaims angrily that Muriel's mother must be right about Seymour, that he does indeed suffer from aberrant behavior and is clearly a schizophrenic and latent homosexual. Stalled in traffic by a parade, the group walks to the nearby apartment which Buddy and Seymour share. Eager to escape the ferocious matron of honor, Buddy slips into the bathroom with Seymour's diary, which is filled with loving sentiments about Muriel. These back up the claim Seymour made earlier that day that he was "too happy to be married." When news arrives that Muriel and Seymour have eloped, everyone leaves except for the uncle, who stays to share a toast with Buddy. Already inebriated, Buddy passes out and upon waking finds the uncle's empty glass and cigar end, which he regards as apparently sacred relics of the day.

"Seymour: An Introduction" is often considered more a reflection upon the first story than a continuation of it, and its form is regarded as closer to the form of the essay rather than fiction. Now forty years old, Buddy attempts to explain and describe the great poet and holy man who was his brother Seymour. After a general introduction, he describes and characterizes Seymour's poetry (without examples), then his prose, his physical appearance, and finally a series of anecdotes intended to reveal Seymour's purely spiritual state of being. Along the way Buddy, a writer of fiction, ruminates on the writer's debt to his readers, his characters, and himself, and he contrasts his own career with that of Seymour, who eliminated a lot of these concerns by choosing never to publish. This line of thought is believed to reflect Salinger's own thoughts about being a writer; he once referred to Buddy Glass as his own "alter ego."

While some critics view *Raise High the Roofbeam, Carpenters and Seymour: An Introduction* as overly garrulous and unstructured, others believe they are merely comic commentaries on language itself, or daring experiments in form. The immediacy and charm of the Glass family have made them among the most popular characters in American literature of the mid-twentieth century.

FURTHER READING

Baumbach, Jonathan. "The Saint as a Young Man: A Reappraisal of *The Catcher in the Rye.*" *Modern Language Quarterly* 25 (December 1964): 461-72.

Bryan, James E. "A Reading of 'For Esme—With Love and Squalor.'" *Criticism* 9 (Summer 1967): 275-88.

Contemporary Authors, Vols. 5-8, rev. ed. Detroit: Gale Research Co.

Contemporary Literary Criticism, Vols. 1, 3, 8, 12. Detroit: Gale Research Co.

Dictionary of Literary Biography, Vol. 2; *Concise Dictionary of American Literary Biography, 1941-1968.* Detroit: Gale Research Co.

French, Warren G. *J.D. Salinger.* New York: Twayne, 1963.

Glazier, Lyle. "The Glass Family Saga: Argument and Epiphany." *College English* 27 (December 1965): 248-51.

Goldstein, Bernice and Sanford Goldstein. "Zen and *Nine Stories.*" *Renascence* 22 (Summer 1970): 171-82.

Grunwald, Henry Anatole. *Salinger: A Critical and Personal Portrait.* New York: Harper, 1962.

Gwynn, Frederick L. and Joseph L. Blotner. *The Fiction of J. D. Salinger.* Pittsburgh: University of Pittsburgh Press, 1958.

Hassan, Ihab. "J.D. Salinger: Rare Quixotic Gestures." In his *Radical Innocence: Studies in the Contemporary American Novel,* pp. 259-88. Princeton: Princeton University Press, 1961.

Laser, Marvin and Norman Fruman, eds. *Studies in J.D. Salinger: Reviews, Essays, and Critiques of "Catcher in the Rye" and Other Fiction.* New York: Odyssey Press, 1963.

Levine, Paul. "J. D. Salinger: The Development of the Misfit Hero." *Twentieth Century Literature* 4 (October 1958): 92-9.

McCarthy, Mary. "J. D. Salinger's Closed Circuit." *Harper's* (October 1962): 46-8.

Seitzman, Daniel. "Therapy and Antitherapy in Salinger's 'Zooey.'" *American Imago* 25 (Summer 1968): 140-62.

Seng, Peter J. "The Fallen Idol: The Immature World of Holden Caulfield." *College English* 23 (December 1961): 203-09.

Short Story Criticism, Vol. 2. Detroit: Gale Research Co.

Slabey, Robert M. "*The Catcher in the Rye:* Christian Theme and Symbol." *College Language Association Journal* 6 (March 1963): 170-83.

Slethaug, Gordon E. "Seymour: A Clarification." *Renascence* 23 (Spring 1971): 115-28.

Stein, William Bysshe. "Salinger's 'Teddy': *Tat Tvam Asi* or That Thou Art." *Arizona Quarterly* 29 (Autumn 1973): 253-65.

Strauch, Carl F. "'Kings in the Back Row': Meaning through Structure—A Reading of Salinger's *The Catcher in the Rye.*" *Wisconsin Studies in Contemporary Literature* 2 (Winter 1961): 5-30.

William Saroyan
1908-1981

American dramatist and short story writer.

My Heart's in the Highlands (drama, 1939)

This play, adapted from Saroyan's short story, "The Man with the Heart in the Highlands," is set in 1914 in a house and grocery store in Fresno, California. The story focuses on a poor Armenian-American family trying to live life based on pure, simple values, untarnished by the greed prevalent in the outside world. **Johnny Alexander** is a nine-year-old boy who lives with his father, **Ben,** and his grandmother. Johnny is an innocent boy, sweet and perceptive. His father is a poet who, though he works very hard, makes little money. For a time, he strives for recognition of his work by sending his poems to *The Atlantic Monthly* for publication, but is constantly faced with rejection.

Jasper MacGregor, an old man who was once a talented musician, drifts into Johnny's neighborhood and takes refuge with the family for nearly three weeks. Here, he plays the bugle for the neighbors and, in appreciation, they bring the family food. Jasper, although content with the Alexander family, still lusts after greatness and is tricked into returning to the Old People's Home by a young man who offers him the role of King Lear in the Home's annual production. Jasper later reappears at the Alexander household, but dies shortly afterward.

In the conclusion, the family is evicted for failing to pay the rent. Before leaving, Mr. Alexander visits **Mr. Kosack,** the local grocer, and gives him some of his best poems in appreciation for the grocer's kindness. Kosack and his daughter, **Esther,** are both deeply moved by the gesture, and in gratitude Esther gives Johnny her meager savings. In anger and humiliation, Johnny throws the money away. He later retrieves it, having gained insight into his father, his poetry, and the true gentility of his neighbors.

My Heart's in the Highlands is typical of Saroyan's work, presenting a sentimental, compassionate view of American immigrant life. Regarded as one of his finest plays, it reflects his celebration of the integrity of the human soul, rendered in a simple, dramatic style.

The Time of Your Life (drama, 1939)

The play is set in Nick's Pacific Street Saloon, Restaurant and Entertainment Palace in San Francisco in 1939. The story centers around several lonely and somewhat eccentric characters who, through their individual efforts, triumph over loneliness and evil to become part of a mutually supportive community.

The central character is **Joe,** who has been frequenting the honky-tonk for the past three years. He is an intelligent man who drinks most of the time and claims to be striving for a civilized life, but he has been corrupted by a society that values money over human compassion. He now does small kindnesses for strangers in order to atone for his past. Prior to the action of the play, Joe had befriended **Tom,** who throughout the play acts as Joe's errand boy. Joe also befriended **Kitty Duval,** a former prostitute who, with Joe's help, regained some measure of self-respect. Eventually, Joe finds a job for Tom and gives him money so that Tom and Kitty can get married and begin life anew. Other denizens of the saloon represent different aspects of humanity: **Dudley** is a lover who can't love, **Harry** is a comedian who isn't very funny, and **Kit Carson,** a total fraud and teller of tall tales, is responsible for helping Joe see the way to a meaningful existence.

Nick, the proprietor of the saloon, tries to provide his customers with a sense of personal freedom and privacy, which is often difficult due to the visits of **Blick,** the head of the Vice Squad. He is a bully, happy only when tormenting others who are weaker than himself.

While Joe is out of the bar, Blick enters and begins to harass Kitty. When Carson comes to Kitty's aid, Blick beats him up and then attacks the young black piano player. Carson kills Blick, and through his action demonstrates his innate sense of bravery and decency.

In his recreation of a community of seemingly disparate but essentially unified souls who find meaning and happiness through sharing love and understanding, Saroyan created what many consider his finest work of literature. He was awarded, but refused, the Pulitzer Prize for *The Time of Your Life,* for the acceptance of financial rewards ran counter to his beliefs.

FURTHER READING

Bedrosian, Margaret. "William Saroyan and the Family Matter." *MELUS* 9, No. 4 (Winter 1982): 13-24.

Contemporary Authors, Vols. 5-8, rev. ed., 103. Detroit: Gale Research Co.

Contemporary Literary Criticism, Vols. 1, 8, 10, 29, 34. Detroit: Gale Research Co.

Dictionary of Literary Biography, Vol. 7; *Dictionary of Literary Biography Yearbook: 1981.* Detroit: Gale Research Co.

Dusenbury, Winifred L. "Conflict between the Spiritual and the Material" and "Conclusion." In *The Time of Loneliness in Modern American Drama,* pp. 155-78, 197-212. Gainesville: University of Florida Press, 1960.

Floan, Howard R. *William Saroyan.* Boston: Twayne, 1966.

Krickel, Edward. "Cozzens and Saroyan: A Look at Two Reputations." In *Georgia Review* (Fall 1970): 281-96.

Nathalie Sarraute

1902-

French novelist and essayist.

Portrait of a Man Unknown (novel, 1948)

This novel, Sarraute's first, reflects her philosophy of "tropisms," her term for what lies beneath the superficial gestures of communication, the realm of the unconscious where the true self, constantly in flux, is characterized by a flow of images, sensations, and visions. She is often associated with the "New Novel" movement in French letters for her avoidance of traditional narrative techniques, as is evident in *Portrait of a Man Unknown.*

The work is presented in the first-person, and the protagonist is an unnamed narrator, whose anxious, indecisive nature is immediately evident. The reader is soon aware that the narrator's perspective is subjective and unreliable. Like many of Sarraute's protagonists, he is a sensitive man in search of the meaning of existence and authenticity. His obsessive inquiry focuses on two people who live in his apartment building, an old man and his daughter, who also are unnamed. He meets and talks with them, but, more importantly, he imagines them. He seeks to know what they really are, to identify what lies behind the facade of personality. He travels to another town where he visits the portrait of the title, an anonymous work of an unknown man. This unfinished, unidentified work arrests the narrator, for in it he finds the reassurance he needs to face the incongruous, uncertain, variable nature of reality as he sees it.

The narrator returns his attention to the old man and his daughter and imagines or witnesses (we are not sure) an argument between them in which the daughter announces that she is engaged. She leaves the apartment, and the narrator follows her to an art exhibit, where he tries to communicate to her his impassioned feeling for the portrait of the unknown man. She rebuffs him. The next time he watches the two, he finds them altered, and he feels his interest in them waning. This precipitates an intense self-analysis in the narrator, for he wonders whether the change is within him or the objects of his obsession. In the conclusion, he meets the fiancé of the daughter, the only character who is given a name: **Louis Dumontet.** The narrator has thus far avoided using names, which for him represent the superficial, illusive limitations of personality. He is last seen with the old man, exchanging pleasantries and talking of death. For many critics, this indicates the failure of his search and the ultimate disintegration of the narrative persona.

This difficult novel is unified through the consciousness of the narrator, whose hesitant, unassured steps toward self-understanding take place in an indefinite fictional world where language and its meaning are tentative and the fluid nature of experience and the human personality are emphasized.

FURTHER READING

Besser, Gretchen Rous. *Nathalie Sarraute*. Boston: Twayne, 1979.

Cohn, Ruby. "Nathalie Sarraute's Subconversations." *Modern Language Notes* 79, No. 3 (May 1963): 49-62.

Contemporary Authors, Vols. 9-12, rev. ed. Detroit: Gale Research Co.

Contemporary Literary Criticism, Vols. 1, 2, 4, 8, 10, 31. Detroit: Gale Research Co.

Kostelanetz, Anne. "Manifesto for a New New French Novel." In *On Contemporary Literature,* edited by Richard Kostelanetz, pp. 544-54. New York: Avon Books, 1969.

Jean-Paul Sartre

1905-1980

French philosopher, critic, novelist, and dramatist.

Nausea (novel, 1938)

This novel, one of the most important documents of the existentialist movement in philosophy, is considered Sartre's masterpiece in fiction. It is set in the imaginary city of Bouville, where **Antoine Roquentin,** a historian, is researching the life of the Marquis de Rollebon, an eighteenth-century figure. The work is presented in the form of a diary. "Something has happened to me," it begins, for Roquentin feels that something, like an illness, has come over him. He outlines the boring, repetitive routine of his life, and relates his visits to the library, where he has met an individual whom he calls the Self-taught Man, who is trying to read all the books in the library in alphabetical order. An emblematic figure who represents the failure of the humanist tradition, his desire for knowledge is shown to be as meaningless and ludicrous as his claim that he loves all of mankind when in reality he is as lonely and isolated as Roquentin. The religion and social order represented by the bourgeoisie of Bouville are also the objects of Roquentin's contempt, and he is repulsed by their narrow-minded, self-satisfied stupidity.

Roquentin's thoughts culminate in a feeling of nausea, a revulsion from the meaninglessness of life. He abandons his research, for he sees only the absurdity and vanity of his endeavor and realizes that there is no way of truly knowing the past. As the spokesman for Sartre's philosophy of existentialism, Roquentin discerns the limitations of rationalism and knows that reality is based on individual perception only. He is aware of the nothingness that is the basis of existence, and that nothing exists within the self. Yet this revelation is both the source of his despair and the root of the possibilities for his existence, for, according to Sartre, the existentialist creates himself out of this sense of nothingness, and is free to choose what he will become. Roquentin examines and rejects all the traditional arguments that would sway him from his nausea.

The key episode in the novel revolves around Roquentin's attempt to understand the meaning of existence. As he sits in the park and examines the roots of a chestnut tree, existence unveils itself to him as he becomes fully conscious of the object. But what he comprehends is a fearful picture, for he is overwhelmed by the disorder of what he sees, and he describes the tree as "naked, in a frightful, obscene nakedness."

He suffers, trying to find a way out of his despair. In the conclusion, he listens to the strains of a jazz song as he waits for the train that will take him from Bouville. The music prompts him to find himself in art; like the musicians, he will seek, through his writing, to capture the meaning of existence that he hears in the music. Yet the end is purposely ambiguous, for what Roquentin has experienced—the nausea—is not to be overcome or dismissed; it is the fate of humankind to live with it: "I no longer have to bear it, it is no longer an illness or a passing fit: it is I."

The intense, almost claustrophobic atmosphere of the novel is heightened by Sartre's use of the first-person, diary format, which presents a vivid platform for the protagonist's torment. As a document of the then-emerging philosophy of existentialism and an influence on later European literature, *Nausea* is a work of fiction without parallel.

No Exit (drama, 1944)

The premise of Sartre's most famous play is that "Hell is others." The play is set in Hell, which is figured here as a hotel where people are punished after death and where human relations are the source of torment. The cycles of sadism and masochism that formed the lives of the play's three characters in life is also the pattern of their eternal punishment. **Inez** was involved in a sadistic relationship in which she forced her lesbian lover to torment her husband to death. Unlike **Estelle** and **Garcin**, who are occasionally allowed to see events taking place among the living, Inez is denied any view of the living world, for no one remembers her or thinks of her. She tries to enlist Estelle in a sadistic relationship, but Estelle, a child murderer, is drawn to Garcin. Garcin treated his wife with great cruelty, and his sadistic tendencies parallel Inez's. But the true source of his torment now is the lack of courage he displayed in his political convictions when he was alive. He and Estelle try to establish an erotic relationship, but it is false, based on untrue images of one another. Estelle cannot convince Garcin that he is not a coward, and he cannot convince her that she is an innocent, especially with Inez present to shatter their mutual illusions. Sartre says that "the other holds a secret—the secret of what I am," and in *No Exit,* the characters are not free to be what they see themselves to be, but must submit to the eternal judgment of others. Thus their roles of torturer and victim, based on mutual dependency, are fixed and immutable.

In the early portion of the play, the characters try to avoid the realization that they have condemned themselves through their actions on earth and that their punishment is to torture one another for eternity. They explore every chance for hope and to escape their fate, but they come to understand that their hell is self-created and eternal. The play closes with Garcin's words: "Let's get on with it," for time in Hell is circular, without beginning or end. The play is noted for its terse dialogue and inner tension. It is considered one of the major works of existentialist theater.

FURTHER READING

Bree, Germaine and Margaret Otis Guiton. "Jean-Paul Sartre: The Search for Identity." In *An Age of Fiction: The French Novel from Gide to Camus,* pp. 203-18. New Brunswick: Rutgers University Press, 1957.

Brosman, Catherine Savage. "Sartre's Nature: Animal Images in *La Nausée.*" *Symposium* (Summer 1977): 107-25.

Contemporary Authors, Vols. 9-12, rev. ed., 97-100. *Contemporary Authors New Revision Series,* Vol. 21. Detroit: Gale Research Co.

Contemporary Literary Criticism, Vols. 1, 4, 7, 9, 13, 18, 24, 44, 50. Detroit: Gale Research Co.

Dictionary of Literary Biography, Vol. 72. Detroit: Gale Research Co.

McCall, Dorothy. *The Theatre of Jean-Paul Sartre.* New York: Columbia University Press, 1969.

Peyre, Henri. "Existentialism and French Literature: Jean-Paul Sartre's Novels." In *French Novelists of Today,* pp. 244-74. New York: Oxford University Press, 1967.

Spanos, William V. "The Un-naming of the Beasts: The Postmodernity of Sartre's *La Nausée.*" *Criticism* 20, No. 3 (Summer 1978): 223-80.

Zivanovic, Judith. "Sartre's Drama: Key to Understanding his Concept of Freedom." *Modern Drama* (September 1971): 144-54.

Delmore Schwartz
1913-1966
American poet, short story writer, and essayist.

"In Dreams Begin Responsibilities" (short story, 1937)

The story is rendered as a dream in which the unnamed narrator is sitting in a movie theater viewing a film that depicts the courtship of his parents. It is June, 1909, and the couple is depicted as they visit Coney Island, have dinner, and the narrator's father proposes. The work, considered Schwartz's masterpiece, is highly autobiographical and contains themes that inform most of Schwartz's work. Like the protagonist, Schwartz was the product of an unhappy marriage, and he shows the narrator in despair as he helplessly watches his parents, moved to tears at the unhappiness the future holds for them. "There, there," an old woman says to him, it's "only a movie." He watches as his parents, even in the thrall of young love, show the vanity, selfishness, and stubbornness that will destroy their marriage and make their children miserable. The narrator is unable to contain himself, and he leaps out of his seat, shouting: "Don't do it. It's not too late to change your minds, both of you. Nothing will come of it, only remorse, hatred, scandal, and two children whose characters are monstrous." His fellow moviegoers try to get him to quiet down, but his anxiety overwhelms him, and he again jumps to his feat, shouting "What are they doing?" This time he is thrown out of the theater by an usher who lectures him about life and his own responsibilities, saying "What are *you* doing? Don't you know that you can't do whatever you want to do?" The narrator wakes up; it is the morning of his twenty-first birthday.

Considered Schwartz's finest piece of fiction, "In Dreams Begin Responsibilities" contains his recurrent themes of alienation and the deterministic nature of fate. The narrator, in despair over the unhappy yet inevitable glimpse of history he has been given, has also been given insight into the muddled matters of the world of maturity. The work is noted for its lyrical, evocative description.

FURTHER READING

Blackmur, R. P. "Commentary by Ghosts." *Kenyon Review* 5 (Summer 1934): 467-71.

Contemporary Authors, Vols. 17-18, 25-28, rev. ed.; *Contemporary Authors Permanent Series,* Vol. 2. Detroit: Gale Research Co.

Contemporary Literary Criticism, Vols. 2, 4, 10, 45. Detroit: Gale Research Co.

Dictionary of Literary Biography, Vols. 28, 48. Detroit: Gale Research Co.

McDougal, Richard. *Delmore Schwartz.* Boston: Twayne, 1979.

Rahv, Philip. "Delmore Schwartz: The Paradox of Precocity." In *Essays on Literature and Politics, 1932-1972,* pp. 85-92. Boston: Houghton Mifflin, 1978.

Peter Shaffer

1926-

English dramatist and novelist.

Equus (drama, 1973)

Set in Rokeby Psychiatric Hospital in the south of England, the play tells the story of **Alan Strang,** a seventeen-year-old stableboy who has blinded six horses. The court handling his case has ruled that he is insane, and he is sent to Rokeby and the care of psychiatrist **Martin Dysart.** During Dysart's analysis of Strang, the boy begins to reveal his past. He is the product of an unhappy home, of a mother and father who have created a religious and sexual ambivalence in their son which results in his unusual attitude toward the horses in his care. Strang sees the horses as gods, and his relationship to them is at once mythic and erotic, expressing itself in midnight rides filled with ritualistic and sexual meaning for the boy. When a stable girl tries to seduce him, the encounter confuses and humiliates Strang, who, in a horrifying scene, blinds the horses to prevent them seeing and knowing his shame. As their analysis progresses, Dysart is drawn to the elemental, passionate expression of his patient, and his own life seems to pale in comparison. Shaffer makes his character ask himself if, in "curing" the boy, he will be robbing Strang of his primitive self. As he agonizes over how to proceed, Dysart asks himself whether he too will be deprived—of the insight into the human psyche offered by so rare a patient.

Shaffer makes use of alternating scenes to depict the drama of the doctor's office and that of Strang's memory, some rendered in narration and some acted. Shaffer stresses the similarities his protagonists share, particularly their isolation and their myth-making ability, in his exploration of the effect of civilization in separating the rational self from the primal.

Amadeus (drama, 1979)

Set in Vienna in the 1780s, the drama is a fictitious reworking of the life of **Antonio Salieri,** Court Composer for **Emperor Joseph II,** paralleled with that of **Wolfgang Amadeus Mozart,** the acknowledged genius of classical music. The play begins in 1823, as Salieri, near death, confesses that he had murdered Mozart years before. Given in flashback, the play depicts scenes in the life of Salieri that he claims drove him to murder his rival.

As a young man, Salieri had made a pact with God: he would pledge lifelong fidelity and virtue if God would make him a great composer. He is a successful and well-regarded composer when he first encounters Mozart, whose music in its sublimity and profundity makes his seem mediocre. It is, for Salieri, the music of God, and Mozart is His vessel. What outrages Salieri is not only the clear superiority of Mozart's music over his, but that God has chosen such a vessel; in Shaffer's hands, Mozart is a childish, scatological, and capricious boy, foolish and obscene. It is Salieri's curse that he alone truly understands Mozart's genius, and he plots his revenge accordingly, using his influence to deprive Mozart of the commissions and students he needs to live, all the while pretending to be his truest friend. As the play nears its close, Salieri deals Mozart the cruelest blow: he sends a servant in the guise of a haunting specter to visit Mozart, now destitute and ill, to commission his final work, the Requiem Mass. Salieri then makes a final visit. Mozart, confused and overwhelmed, listens as Salieri claims that he has paid for his perfidy toward Mozart with his soul. After Mozart dies, Salieri becomes obsessed with the thought that he had poisoned him, which he is still claiming as we last see him, old, disoriented, and tormented by his treachery.

Thematically, Shaffer has presented an inversion of the Faust legend, depicting a man who makes a bargain with God instead of the devil, and whose obsession with pride and revenge prove to be his own undoing. The play is presented in dialogue and monologue, with Salieri addressing the audience directly on occasion, a device which Shaffer utilizes to reveal the inner thoughts and motivations of the character. *Amadeus* is Shaffer's most successful work for the theater to date.

FURTHER READING

Contemporary Authors, Vols. 110, 116. Detroit: Gale Research Co.

Contemporary Literary Criticism, Vols. 5, 14, 18, 37. Detroit: Gale Research Co.

Dictionary of Literary Biography, Vol. 13. Detroit: Gale Research Co.

Esslin, Martin. "*Amadeus.*" *Plays and Players* 27 (November 1979): 20.

Grusky, Oscar. "Equestrian Follies." *Psychology Today* 11 (October 1977): 21-2.

Kerr, Walter. "Waiting for an Ingenious Twist that Never Comes." *New York Times* (4 January 1981): 3.

Taylor, John Russell. "Peter Shaffer." In *Anger and After,* pp. 227-30. London: Eyre Methuen, 1962.

———. *Peter Shaffer.* Harlow: Longman, 1974.

Trewin, J. C. "In the Grand Manner." *London Illustrated News* 268 (January 1980): 73.

Ntozake Shange
1948-
American dramatist, poet, and novelist.

for colored girls who have considered suicide/when the rainbow is enuf (drama, 1975)

Shange's celebrated play, which she describes as a "choreopoem," is a cycle of poems accompanied by music and dance. It tells the story of modern black women in America, recounting their joy, sorrow, suffering, and triumph over despair. The work has a strong feminist tone, and Shange explores black women as victims of oppression in a racist, sexist society that has denied them a voice. The work has no formal structure, but is instead a loosely arranged series of vignettes, spoken, sung and witnessed by the seven "ladies,"— **lady in blue, lady in brown, lady in green, lady in orange, lady in purple, lady in red,** and **lady in yellow.**

The lady in brown is the first to speak, and she focuses on the importance of celebrating the voice and vision of black women. The early poems in the cycle relate the youthful experience of these women, as in the poem "now I love somebody more than," in which the lady in blue sings of her love for a Caribbean musician. Later poems grapple with the violence of black women's experience, relating the horrors of rape and abortion. A central focus of Shange's work is the oppression of black woman by black men, which some critics have seen as a limitation of the work. She stresses throughout the play that black men have too often abandoned their women and have negated their natural responsibilities as fathers, husbands, and helpmates by not supporting their women emotionally or financially. In one vignette, the lady in red sings with humor and despair of how she was abandoned by the man she loved. Shange also examines whether or not black women, through their passivity, have helped to perpetuate their own oppression, and she explores how through sisterhood and self-respect black women can overcome their plight and can be born again in triumph. The final lines are sung by the lady in red, while the others join in and speak of finding God within, of finding the power to survive and to flourish, ending the play on a note of joy and promise.

The work is noted for its fine rendering of black dialect, richly and realistically presented. Shange avoids the "proper" English spoken and written by whites, as is reflected in her refusal to capitalize her title or character's names. The play has been a popular if controversial success since its first appearance, and Shange is considered an important new voice in American theater.

FURTHER READING

Bambara, Toni Cade. "'For Colored Girls'—And White Girls Too." *Ms.* 5, No. 3 (September 1976): 36, 38.

Christ, Carol P. "'I Found God in Myself . . . & I Loved Her Fiercely': Ntozake Shange." In *Diving Deep and Surfacing: Women Writers on Spiritual Quest*, pp. 97-118. Boston: Beacon Press, 1980.

Contemporary Authors, Vol. 85-88. Detroit: Gale Research Co.

Contemporary Literary Criticism, Vols. 8, 25, 38. Detroit: Gale Research Co.

Dictionary of Literary Biography, Vol. 38. Detroit: Gale Research Co.

Flowers, Sandra Hollin. "'Colored Girls': Textbook for the Eighties." *Black American Literature Forum* 15, No. 2 (Summer 1981): 51-4.

Bernard Shaw

1856-1950

Irish dramatist, essayist, and critic.

Major Barbara (drama, 1905)

The play, set in London in 1906, is considered Shaw's first major work, providing a vehicle for his political and theatrical philosophies and rendered with wit and humor. **Barbara Undershaft,** the daughter of an arms manufacturer, is a major in the Salvation Army; her suitor, **Adolphus Cusins,** is a professor of Greek; Barbara's father, **Sir Andrew Undershaft,** is a man who has made millions in the production of weapons. Together they represent Shaw's theory of the Life Force: the creative evolution through which humankind advances from one age to another. Shaw demonstrates how Barbara's efforts on behalf of the poor are motivated by an honest desire to shun her upper-class background and help others. Cusins, although skeptical of Barbara's religion, believes in her honesty and integrity, and participates in her activities out of love. Undershaft confronts Barbara with the sobering truth about the relationship between poverty and religion when he gives a donation to the Salvation Army that is eagerly accepted, for he shows her the hypocrisy of a religious institution that not only takes his money yet condemns war, but that seeks to help the poor not through eradicating poverty but by offering them "salvation." According to Undershaft, there are two things necessary for salvation: "money and gunpowder." He is a millionaire of poor origins, one who knows about poverty first-hand. He challenges Barbara and Cusins with the fact that the poor cannot be forced to accept religion when they're hungry and argues that through what he represents—capitalism—poverty can be overcome through decent jobs and wages.

As a munitions manufacturer, Undershaft represents the destructive power of capitalism. In Shaw's eyes, capitalism cannot destroy poverty because it is itself a devastating force. Yet Undershaft also represents the Life Force, because destruction is part of life and leads to change and to reconstruction based on better models. Thus Barbara and Cusins inherit from Undershaft the munitions plant and the Life Force. They learn that their philosophies of religion and humanism are inadequate to meet the needs of the world; they want to use the business they inherit to become agents of revolution, giving weapons to the poor and trying to feed the minds of the workers whose bellies are full but whose hearts are empty.

In his concept of theater, Shaw rebelled against the melodramatic, well-made plays that had dominated the English stage during the nineteenth century. Instead, he used drama as a vehicle for the exposition of serious ideas based on his political beliefs. Thus the play is noted for its vivid characters, satiric brilliance, and trenchant philosophical themes.

Man and Superman (drama, 1905)

Shaw's second major work is a satiric look at the relationship between the sexes, incorporating his concept of the Life Force. **Ann Whitefield** is an aggressive, tenacious, and domineering woman, relentless in her pursuit of a husband. The object of her quest is **John Tanner,** a wealthy intellectual, revolutionary, and propagandist who is convinced that he will remain a bachelor and is unaffected by women. The play is full of debate, as the characters discuss all the major social, political, and philosophical issues of the day. The subplot of the play centers on **Violet Robinson** and **Hector Malone,** who are secretly married. After Violet becomes pregnant, Tanner uses the situation to expound on her courage in intending to raise the child alone and the foolishness of society to insist that she marry. The debate on societal pressures, love, and marriage continues, with Tanner as oblivious to Ann's designs as he is to the true nature of Violet's and Hector's relationship.

The third act of the play is a dream sequence, called "Don Juan in Hell," based on Mozart's handling of the story in *Don Giovanni* as well as other renderings of the legend. The main characters of this vignette—**Don Juan Tenorio, Dona Ana de Ulloa,** and the **Devil**—have parallels to characters in the play, especially John and Ann, and Shaw makes this point more explicit by making Tanner a descendent of the infamous figure and the scene ostensibly his dream. Don Juan, less a libertine than a philosopher, is the spokesman for the Life Force, and although these ideas have been introduced earlier in the play, notably by Tanner, here they are represented in a different context, out of place and time, providing commentary on the action of the surrounding play.

Ann pursues and finally wins Tanner in the final act, and Shaw shows how the two of them, responding to their mutual attraction for one another, have accepted the Life Force. For Shaw, it is a power capable of transforming humanity, but it must be acknowledged and followed. His characters in this play are noted for their wit and verve, and their continuous conversation on a wide variety of social and political topics reflects the breadth of Shaw's knowledge and intellect.

Pygmalion (drama, 1913)

The play is set in London during the early twentieth century and is based on the Greek myth of the sculptor Pygmalion who entreated the gods to transform his beautiful sculpture, Galatea, into a mortal. **Eliza Doolittle,** a Cockney flower girl, approaches **Henry Higgins,** a phonteticist, to teach her to speak well enough to own her own shop. Higgins takes her on, and she becomes the center of a bet between Higgins and his friend **Colonel Pickering,** also a linguist, when Higgins claims that he can transform Eliza into a lady, and "pass her off as a duchess." Shaw here focuses on the theme of speech as a determinant of class, exploring the snobbery of Higgins, a member of the upper class, and his treatment of Eliza. She works hard, trying to please him, and he in turn, seeing himself as a humane scientist, treats her like an object in an experiment. Eliza's father, **Alfred Doolittle,** enters the play. He is convinced that Higgins has taken his daughter as his mistress and blackmails him, not out of concern for Eliza's honor, but for his own profit. Higgins and Pickering are amused by his actions and give him money. Through Higgins's machinations, Alf is left a huge inheritance from an American philanthropist, which makes him miserable, for he must accept the moribund concepts of middle-class morality. Higgins triumphs when he takes Eliza to a party dressed and behaving like a member of the aristocracy. But Eliza is angry and humiliated by her treatment at Higgins's hands, and defying him, tells him she will become a teacher of phonetics herself. Higgins is impressed by her will, and considers her at last to be his equal.

In the concluding scene, Higgins sends Eliza out to buy him several items; she leaves angrily, but he assumes she will return. The more romantically inclined in Shaw's first audience were convinced that the two would marry, which was far from his conception of the play, so he later provided an epilogue in which he makes it clear that Eliza marries **Freddy Eynsford Hill,** a poor man of noble birth who had fallen in love with her.

Saint Joan (drama, 1923)

The play is set in France in the fifteenth century and relates the life and martyrdom of **Joan of Arc.** For Shaw, she embodied the essential meaning of the Life Force, presaging in her beliefs the creative evolution of ideas and the spirit of a new age. A farmer's daughter, Joan is portrayed as innocent and childlike, a plucky, honest, young girl who had the courage to defy the Catholic Church and to remain true to her own beliefs. Joan's purpose is to drive the English from France and to see the **Dauphin** crowned king. Shaw shows her bravery in battle and the loyalty of her soldiers, and also depicts the political maneuvering that leads to her death.

Joan is accused of heresy because she believes that the ''voices'' who inspire her actions are more important and have more authority than the Catholic Church. Joan's accusers are many, each representing different points of opposition; some dispute her on religious grounds and believe she is a heretic, some discern in her a threat to their comfortable social position, and others want her silenced because she represents a political movement that would endanger their class and its privilege. Although the Dauphin is pleased to have her support in his efforts to become king, he later cautions her to go no further in response to her visions. **The Inquisitor** finds Joan a representative of the Protestant heresy, for she claims that God speaks not through intercessors, but directly to the individual. Accordingly, she must die, not because she is evil, but because she defies doctrine. After she is convicted and sentenced to burn at the stake, Joan is momentarily shaken in her faith. Because she fears the pain of death, she recants, and her sentence is changed to life in prison. But she changes her mind, defiantly tears up her statement, and dies at the stake.

The play ends with a dream epilogue in which Joan returns to witness her canonization in the early twentieth century. Her former persecutors now treat her with reverence, and she considers returning to earth. Yet it is clear that this cannot be—the world is no more ready for a saint in its midst than it was four hundred years ago.

The play's tone is tragic, yet the epilogue offers a humorous perspective on Joan's fate. For Shaw, she reveals society's inability to accept and follow its heroes, those imbued with the Life Force whose higher vision dooms them to be misunderstood.

FURTHER READING

Albert, Sidney P. ''The Price of Salvation: Moral Economics in *Major Barbara.*'' *Modern Drama* 14 (1971): 307-23.

Bentley, Eric. *Bernard Shaw, 1856-1950.* New York: New Directions, 1957.

Brustein, Robert. "Bernard Shaw." In *The Theatre of Revolt: An Approach to the Modern Drama*, pp. 183-227. Boston: Atlantic–Little, Brown, 1964.

Contemporary Authors, Vols. 104, 109. Detroit: Gale Research Co.

Dictionary of Literary Biography, Vols. 10, 57. Detroit: Gale Research Co.

Dukore, Bernard F. *Bernard Shaw, Playwright*. Columbia: University of Missouri Press, 1973.

Frank, Joseph. "*Major Barbara*—Shaw's 'Divine Comedy.'" *PMLA* 71 (1956): 61-74.

Holt, Charles L. "Mozart, Shaw and *Man and Superman*." *Shaw Review* 9 (1966): 102-16.

Mills, John A. *Language and Laughter: Comic Dialectic in the Plays of Bernard Shaw*. Tucson: University of Arizona Press, 1969.

Silver, Arnold. *Bernard Shaw: The Darker Side*. Palo Alto: Stanford University Press, 1982.

Turco, Alfred. *Shaw's Moral Vision: The Self and Salvation*. Ithaca: Cornell University Press, 1976.

Twentieth-Century Literary Criticism, Vols. 3, 9, 21. Detroit: Gale Research Co.

Ward, A. C. *Bernard Shaw*. London: Longmans, Green, 1951.

Watson, Barbara Bellow. "Sainthood for Millionaires: *Major Barbara*." *Modern Drama* 11 (1968): 227-44.

Weintraub, Stanley. "Bernard Shaw's Other Saint Joan." *South Atlantic Quarterly* 64 (1965): 194-205.

Whitman, Robert F. *Shaw and the Play of Ideas*. Ithaca: Cornell University Press, 1977.

Sam Shepard

1943-

American dramatist.

Buried Child (drama, 1978)

The drama takes place on a Midwestern farm. **Dodge** and **Halie** are the aging parents of **Tilden,** a mentally defective man in middle-age, and **Bradley,** a cripple with one leg. As the play begins, Tilden's son **Vince** has arrived with his girlfriend **Shelley** after an absence of six years. No one except Halie appears to recognize or to welcome them. As the play proceeds, a strange and horrifying story begins to unfold, revealing a secret from the family's past: Halie and Tilden had had an incestuous relationship, which produced a child. The child was drowned and buried in the yard by Dodge. The revelation repulses Vince, who leaves the house, ostensibly to buy his grandfather more whiskey, but instead to get drunk himself. When he returns, he storms through the house in a violent rampage, bullying his grandfather into leaving him the farm. At the close of the play, Tilden digs up the corpse of the dead child, which he takes to his mother. Dodge lies dead on the floor, and Vince appears to have taken over as heir.

Buried Child was the second of Shepard's "family plays," in which he focuses on the bitter, unhappy, and in this case horrifying legacy that one generation bequeaths to another. Both Tilden and Bradley are maimed, one mentally, the other physically, the result of the "curse" of the family and its heritage of incest and infanticide. Even the land is affected, for the farm is barren. Yet, when Tilden brings his mother the body of their child, the spell appears to be broken, as if the truth had released them from the grip of the curse, and Halie notes that the corn is growing once again. In contrast to Shepard's earlier drama, the play is more traditional in its narrative design and is considered less experimental and more accessible than his previous work. Shepard was awarded the Pulitzer Prize for *Buried Child* in 1979.

Fool for Love (drama, 1983)

Set on the edge of the Mojave desert, the drama tells the story of the turbulent love affair between **Eddie** and **May.** Their history has been a series of passionate reunions, followed by Eddie's inevitable desertion of May. Now Eddie wants May back, and she won't have him. Their attraction for one another is obsessive, destructive, and violent, and their battles take place in a run-down motel room, where May is living. Eddie is a rodeo rider with a childlike belief in the Old West, and he tries to tempt May to come away with him to share his dreams of a ranch in Wyoming. Although she is tired of his lies and fantasies, she is still passionately attached to him, as he is connected to her. Their personal drama is observed by the **Old Man** on the side of the stage, who sits in a rocking chair drinking whiskey, all the while commenting on the action. He is first introduced as Eddie's father, but as the play progresses, we learn that Eddie and May are half-brother and sister, and that the Old Man is father to both. Thus their relationship is incestual and their love for each other the more desperate. They both have other love interests: Eddie is being pursued by the mysterious "countess" and May has a date with the groundskeeper of the local football field. Eddie does his best to ruin their evening by telling the man about their incestual relationship, which effectively scares him away. Each character tells a version of the relationship in conflicting accounts, leading the viewer to wonder what the truth is. The conclusion, too, is ambiguous, with fire enveloping the motel room, seemingly with the Old Man in the center of the flames. But whether he has been a real person, or only the product of Eddie's and May's imagination, is left to the audience to ponder.

As in *Buried Child,* Shepard deals with the themes of family, obsessive desire, and incest. Another recurrent theme explored here is the West, which offers so many of Shepard's characters the endless promise of the frontier, but in reality has been reduced to a dingy motel on the edge of the desert. The play is divided between the fierce dialogue between May and Eddie and the soul-searching and revealing monologues the characters deliver. As with *Buried Child, Fool for Love* is considered a more accessible work than Shepard's earlier plays, which perhaps accounts for its popularity and wide audience appeal.

A Lie of the Mind (drama, 1985)

Set alternately in California and Montana, the drama relates the tortured relationship of **Beth** and **Jake,** husband and wife. As the play opens, Jake is on the phone with his brother **Frankie,** telling him that he has beaten Beth to death. Beth is in fact alive, but brain-damaged from the ordeal and recuperating with her family in Montana. In parallel scenes throughout the play, we see Jake at home in California with his family, and Beth surrounded by hers; the drama is a revealing portrait of two families warring among themselves and plotting revenge for their wounded daughter and violent son. When Frankie arrives at Beth's home to affect a reconciliation, Beth's father shoots him, thinking he is a dear. This is one of a series of instances where the characters mistake one figure for another; when Frankie sees Beth, she has regressed so far that she mistakes Frankie for Jake and cuddles up to him.

At home with his overbearing mother, Jake is overwhelmed with feelings of jealousy at thoughts of his wife's betrayal, a false assumption that had led to the beating. He recounts his relationship with his father, an alcoholic who deserted the family, and who Jake drove to his death in one marathon evening of drinking. In the concluding scene, Jake has returned to

Beth, driven by his obsessive love for her. He is willing to face humiliation at the hands of her vengeful family.

Once again Shepard treats the themes of family, violence, and obsessive love, indicating that there is no escape from the family and its hold on the individual. For all its violence and despair, the tone of this play is more hopeful than Shepard's previous work, and critics have noted how he blends realistic and fantastic elements and comic and painful emotions in a work considered his most accessible play to date.

FURTHER READING

Asahina, Robert. "The Real Stuff." *The Hudson Review* 37, No. 1 (Spring 1984): 99-104.

Barnes, Clive. "*Fool for Love*—Powerful Play about a Divided U. S." *New York Theatre Critics' Reviews* 44, No. 10 (13-19 June, 1983): 213-14.

Brustein, Robert. "The Shepard Enigma." *The New Republic* 194, No. 4 (27 January 1986): 25-6, 28.

Contemporary Authors, Vols. 69-72; *Contemporary Authors New Revision Series,* Vol. 22. Detroit: Gale Research Co.

Contemporary Literary Criticism, Vols. 4, 6, 17, 34, 41, 44. Detroit: Gale Research Co.

Dictionary of Literary Biography, Vol. 7. Detroit: Gale Research Co.

Earley, Michael. "Of Life Immense in Passion, Pulse, and Power: Sam Shepard and the American Literary Tradition." In *American Dreams: The Imagination of Sam Shepard,* edited by Bonnie Marranca, pp. 126-32. New York: Performing Arts Journal Publications, 1981.

Gilman, Richard. "Introduction." In *Seven Plays,* pp. ix-xxv. New York: Bantam Books, 1981.

Gussow, Mel. "Sam Shepard Revisits the American Heartland." *The New York Times* (15 December 1985): 3, 7.

Rich, Frank. "*Fool for Love,* Sam Shepard's Western." *New York Times* (27 May 1983): 18.

——. "*A Lie of the Mind,* by Sam Shepard." *The New York Times* (6 December 1985): C3.

Simon, John. "Theatre Chronicle: Kopit, Norman, and Shepard." *Hudson Review* 32, No. 1 (Spring 1979): 77-88.

Watt, Douglas. "*Fool for Love* Shows Shepard at His Starkest, Bleakest Best." *New York Theatre Critics' Reviews* 44, No. 10 (13-19 June, 1983): 213.

Mikhail Sholokhov

1905-1984

Russian novelist and short story writer.

The Quiet Don (novel, 1928-1940)

Sholokhov's masterpiece, which appeared in Russian over the years 1928 to 1940, was published in English in two parts as **And Quiet Flows the Don** and **The Don Flows Home to the Sea.**

The Don is a major river which flows through Tatarsk, Russia, an area inhabited by the Cossacks, an agrarian people noted for fiercely guarding their independence. *The Quiet Don* portrays their efforts to protect their way of life during World War I and the Bolshevik Revolution in the years between 1913 and 1920. The main character, **Gregor Melekhov,** is forced to marry **Natalia Korshunov** when his father discovers that he has been having an affair with **Aksinia Astakhova,** the wife of their neighbor, **Stepan Astakhov.** Gregor continues the relationship with Aksinia after his marriage, and they run away to become servants for the wealthy Listnitsky family. When Aksinia bears Gregor a daughter, Natalia attempts suicide; shortly afterward Gregor leaves to join the army.

When he returns home, he learns that Aksinia has been unfaithful to him and that their daughter has died. Gregor reconciles with Natalia, who now has twins, and goes off to war again. Meanwhile, the Bolsheviks are fomenting rebellion against the war and the government of the Czar. Gregor eventually joins the revolutionaries and becomes an officer in the Red Army. When they are defeated by White Army forces, Gregor returns to his village. He is again drawn into the fighting when revolutionary troops approach the Tatarsk, burning and pillaging along the way. After the revolutionary leaders are captured and executed, Gregor returns home in disgust over the brutalities practiced by both sides.

Gregor and his brother **Piotra** join the White Army as the Bolsheviks continue to press their revolutionary ideas upon the Cossacks. A Red sympathizer, **Mikhail Koshevoi,** is put in charge of the government in Tatarsk, and he and his colleagues begin arresting villagers. Gregor escapes when he learns they are coming for him. The Cossacks rebel, and when Piotra is captured in a skirmish, Koshevoi kills him. Gregor returns to fight against the Communists, who are driven back for a time.

Although he is still bitter towards Aksinia, Gregor and his former mistress once again begin their liason. When Natalia hears about it, she is pregnant with Gregor's child and has an abortion, after which she bleeds to death. The Soviet government increases efforts to defeat the Cossacks, who are forced to cross the Don in defense. Aksinia comes to live near Gregor while he is with the White Army, but when the Communists begin to gain ground, they try to escape. Aksinia is taken ill, and Gregor, unable to leave the country, joins the Red Army to fight against the Poles. He and Aksinia eventually return to Tatarsk, where Koshevoi is now the village commissar. Koshevoi tries to have Gregor arrested, but he escapes with Aksinia, who is killed by their pursuers. Gregor throws down his arms, refusing to fight any longer, and returns, asserting the importance of family, home, and love above all else.

The work has been the center of an authorship controversy for years, for many writers and critics believe *The Quiet Don* presents a historical and literary vision beyond Sholokhov's powers, as evidenced in his later writings. Sholokhov's intention in *The Quiet Don* was to portray the land and the people he had known all his life, and was so successful that his novel was used in many Russian school rooms as a history supplement. The scope and characterization of *The Quiet Don* have been described as Tolstoyan in outlook, and despite the controversy it has engendered, it is regarded as a major literary achievement.

FURTHER READING

Contemporary Authors, Vols. 101, 112. Detroit: Gale Research Co.

Contemporary Literary Criticism, Vols. 7, 15. Detroit: Gale Research Co.

Ermolaev, Herman. *Mikhail Sholokhov and His Art.* Princeton: Princeton University Press, 1982.

Solzhenitsyn, Alexander. "Sholokhov and the Riddle of *The Quiet Don.*" *TLS,* No. 3787 (4 October 1974): 1056.

Zhang, Yidong. "Hemingway's and Sholokhov's Viewpoints on War." *International Fiction Review* 14 (Summer 1987): 75-8.

Alan Sillitoe

1928-

English novelist and short story writer.

Saturday Night and Sunday Morning (novel, 1958)

The novel is set in Nottingham, England, and follows the life of **Arthur Seaton,** a young working-class laborer who spends his days at a lathe and his nights getting drunk and womanizing, living by the motto that "it's a great life if you don't weaken." Sillitoe depicts the deadening effects of the life of a factory worker through his protagonist, who has learned to turn his mind off for the hours he works at his machine, and how to deal with the noise, the grease, and the job inspector who is always ready to dock his pay if his rate of production falls off. The author uses both third-person narration and interior monologue to reveal the inner workings of Arthur's mind. He is a young man seething with rage; while he works, he tries to crowd his mind with thoughts of his married mistress, **Brenda,** and of his Saturday nights—"the best and bingiest glad-time of the week"—but his frustration over his life often overwhelms him. While he is described as cocky and rebellious, Arthur is also capable of penetrating insight into his situation, which sets him apart from his fellow workers.

When Brenda gets pregnant, Arthur helps her through an abortion, then spends a wild evening with her sister **Winnie.** Winnie's husband sets out after Arthur, and many months later, Arthur is beaten by a couple of his friends. The beating seems to take the life out of him for awhile, and he gives in to a deep depression. When he recovers, he sees himself as the rebel again, but the same angry thoughts—of violence, destruction, and teeming frustration—crowd his mind. He has given up Brenda and is now seeing a young woman named **Doreen,** a conventional girl looking for a husband. Surprisingly, after all of his talk of rebellion, Arthur is planning on marrying as the novel closes. The fate of generations of laborers—of endless days spent in mindless work, relieved by the debauchery of Saturday night, seem to be his future as well.

The novel is considered to be Sillitoe's finest work and is noted for its simple, straight-forward prose style and credible portraits of working-class life. The dehumanizing nature of factory work and the stultifying English class system are recurrent themes in his work.

"The Loneliness of the Long-Distance Runner" (short story, 1959)

The short story is set in a "Borstal," or reformatory school, and is related by **Smith,** the narrator and protagonist, in language full of working-class and reformatory slang. Like Arthur Seaton of Sillitoe's earlier novel, Smith is a victim of the English class structure and its inequities. He is from a poor working-class home and was sent to the reformatory school for theft, like most of his cousins. Smith is a defiant young man, convinced of the stupidity and hypocrisy of the "in-laws"—the school authorities, the police, and the upper class— and their hostility toward him and the other "out-laws"—those victimized by the social and economic structure. While at the Borstal, Smith becomes a cross-country runner, and the director proudly presents him as the school's hope to win the "Borstal Blue Ribbon Prize Cup For Long-Distance Cross-Country Running." Long before the contest, Smith plans to lose the race; he claims he is not a race-horse or someone's property: "I'm a human being and I've got thoughts and secrets and bloody life inside me." He likes running, and during his early morning training he ruminates on his past, on his parents, and on his life as an "out-law." As he runs, his memories flow in a stream-of consciousness fashion.

Smith loses the race as he planned, and he is relegated to kitchen duty for his efforts. In the conclusion, he's out of Borstal, and has once again become a thief; the money he has stolen has given him the time to write the story we're reading. His hatred and antagonism toward the ruling class has not diminished, nor has he been "reformed" through society's methods. This is one of Sillitoe's finest works of short fiction and is praised for its vivid recreation of reformatory life and its candid portrayal of a life compromised by a rigid class system.

FURTHER READING

Atherton, Stanley S. *Alan Sillitoe: A Critical Assessment.* London: W. H. Allen, 1979.

Contemporary Authors, Vols. 9-12, rev. ed.; *Contemporary Authors New Revision Series,* Vol. 8; *Contemporary Authors Autobiography Series,* Vol. 2. Detroit: Gale Research Co.

Contemporary Literary Criticism, Vols. 1, 3, 6, 10, 19. Detroit: Gale Research Co.

Dictionary of Literary Biography, Vol. 14. Detroit: Gale Research Co.

Hurrell, John Dennis. "Alan Sillitoe and the Serious Novel." *Critique* 4 (Fall-Winter 1960-1961): 3-16.

Nardella, Anna Ryan. "The Existential Dilemmas of Alan Sillitoe's Working-Class Heroes." *Studies in the Novel* 5 (Winter 1973): 469-82.

Penner, Allen Richard. *Alan Sillitoe.* Boston: Twayne, 1972.

Roskies, D. M. "'I'd Rather Be Like I Am': Character, Style, and the Language of Class in Sillitoe's Narratives." *Neophilogus* 65, No. 2 (1981): 308-19.

Staples, Hugh B. "*Saturday Night and Sunday Morning:* Alan Sillitoe and the White Goddess." *Modern Fiction Studies* 10 (Summer 1964): 171-81.

Claude Simon

1913-

French novelist and essayist.

The Flanders Road (novel, 1960)

Based in part on Simon's own experiences in the Battle of the Meuse in 1940, this novel, widely regarded as his finest, relates the recollections of the central figure, **Georges,** from a perspective after the war. The work is a sequence of remembrances, presented in fragmented form, which cohere as the book is read. The themes of eros and thanatos, of love and death, resonate throughout the novel, as Georges endeavors to make sense of the past, particularly the life and death of his officer, **Captain de Reixach.** The narrative takes place within Georges's mind as he makes love to de Reixach's widow, **Corinne.**

Georges is a character who figures in several novels by Simon, including *The Grass,* which focuses on his wife, **Louise.** In that work, Georges's obsession with refuting his aristocratic family had driven Louise from their desolate marriage into the arms of a lover. Like Georges, Corinne despises aristocratic pretense, particularly as it is embodied in her husband. In flashbacks that depict their married life, she is described as an embodiment of feminine beauty and desirability who had often been unfaithful to her husband. Simon unifies his work with a wide range of images and symbols, and Corinne's infidelity links de Reixach in Georges's mind to a recurrent image of a painting that depicts one of the Captain's ancestors, who, it is suggested, was a suicide and a cuckold. Whether de Reixach deliberately allows himself to be shot and killed during the retreat from Flanders and brings about his own death is a matter that obsesses Georges.

Scenes from the war, including the weary retreat of Georges and his comrades and his imprisonment in a concentration camp, are interspersed throughout the text with depictions of the prewar era, offering a glimpse of the aristocracy and a way of life in a state of decadence. Another recurrent image, that of the decomposing body of a dead horse, reinforces Simon's theme of a world in a state of death. In the conclusion, Corinne leaves Georges, for she realizes that he has used her only as a vehicle for his memory. Because of the nature of the text, we are left unsure whether Georges's recollections are real or tempered with dreams and imagination, and the work ends on a note of unresolved ambiguity.

The novel is highly regarded for its vivid imagery and evocative use of language. Simon employs allusions to myth and mythic creatures to lend a sense of the primordial nature of experience. Although he is often linked to the practitioners of the "New Novel" movement in French letters, it is a label that Simon himself eschews, and he is generally regarded as an independent, innovative force in French letters.

FURTHER READING

Contemporary Authors, Vols. 89-92. Detroit: Gale Research Co.

Contemporary Literary Criticism, Vols. 4, 9, 15, 39. Detroit: Gale Research Co.

Fletcher, John. *Claude Simon and Fiction Now*. New York: Calder and Boyars, 1975.

Mercier, Vivian. "Claude Simon: Order and Disorder, Memory and Desire." In *The New Novel: From Queneau to Pinget*, pp. 266-75. New York: Farrar, Straus & Giroux, 1971.

Sykes, S. W. "Claude Simon: Visions of Life in Microcosm." *Modern Language Review* (January 1976): 42-50.

Upton Sinclair
1878-1968

American novelist.

The Jungle (novel, 1906)

Set in the early 1900s in the Chicago stockyards, *The Jungle* is the story of how one immigrant family struggles in vain to maintain their values and survive intact in a hostile, dehumanizing, and criminally unsanitary environment. The novel exposed the disgusting conditions prevalent in the meat-packing industry at that time and led to the passage of the Pure Food and Drug Act of 1906.

The main character, **Jurgis Rudkus,** comes to the United States bringing his father, his fiancée and her family. Lured to America by the high wages being paid in the Chicago stockyards, they are subsequently victimized as they gain passage to the United States, arrive in New York, and purchase a house in Packingtown. Once in Chicago they find the cost of living crippling, the work beyond human endurance, and job security non-existent. Their living conditions offer little relief, for their home is built upon a pool of sewage, and their food is tainted or diluted.

Jurgis and his fiancée, **Ona,** marry after a year in Chicago. Shortly thereafter, his ailing father dies, and Ona has a child, **Antanas.** Later, when Ona becomes pregnant again, Jurgis falls and injures himself at work, and the family finds itself near starvation. When Jurgis discovers that Ona's boss had seduced her, he attacks him and is sent to jail, leaving the family without means of support. When he gains his freedom, Jurgis finds that his family has lost their home and are reduced to begging. Ona dies in childbirth and Jurgis, finding strength in his love for his son, continues as best he can until he returns home one day to find that Antanas has fallen off the sidewalk and drowned in a trench of sewage.

After the death of his son, Jurgis deserts the remnants of his family. He becomes a tramp, a thief, a drunk, a scab and is involved in corrupt political practices. Then, in an effort to keep warm, he wanders into an assembly where he learns about socialism and begins life anew working for the cause.

Sinclair said of *The Jungle* that he "aimed at the public's heart and by accident . . . hit the stomach." His straightforward, dispassionate style emphasizes the horror of the conditions described in the novel and was sufficient to inspire even those with little social conscience to action. But the work failed to rally the American people to the cause of socialism, which was Sinclair's main intent. Still, the novel remains a popular and influential work.

FURTHER READING

Blinderman, Abraham. *Critics on Upton Sinclair: Readings in Literary Criticism.* Coral Gables: University of Miami Press, 1975.

Contemporary Authors, Vols. 5-8, rev. ed., 25-28, rev. ed.; *Contemporary Authors New Revision Series,* Vol. 7. Detroit: Gale Research Co.

Contemporary Literary Criticism, Vols. 1, 11, 15. Detroit: Gale Research Co.

Dictionary of Literary Biography, Vol. 9. Detroit: Gale Research Co.

Harte, James Lambert. *This Is Upton Sinclair.* Emmaus: Rodale Press, 1938.

Yoder, Jon A. *Upton Sinclair.* New York: Ungar, 1975.

Isaac Bashevis Singer

1904-

Polish-born novelist, short story writer, and translator.

"Gimpel the Fool" (short story, 1953)

Set in the village of Frampol, this simple, parabolic tale is one of Singer's most celebrated works. It tells the tale of **Gimpel,** a holy fool, who all of his life has been duped by those around him. Children tease him, the village folk heckle and harass him, and his wife **Elka** deceives him continually with other men, even one of his fellow bakers. His response is a childlike acceptance and belief in all that he hears. He suffers, but he does not become cynical, for he believes in the essential goodness of others no matter how often he is proved wrong. When Elka's deceptions drive him to the rabbis for counsel, he is advised to divorce her. But he loves her deeply and finds one learned father who finds a precedent in scripture that allows them to remain married. On her deathbed Elka confesses that none of their many children are his. While this surprises him, he loves them all regardless.

Gimpel almost succumbs to the temptation of the **Devil,** who tells him to urinate in the bread dough to revenge himself on those who deceive him. He does, but Elka's ghost appears before him and urges him not to choose the way of dishonesty. Realizing the evil in the act, he buries the tainted bread. He leaves his family and becomes a wanderer and a storyteller, a life that reinforces his faith in the incredible and paradoxical in human nature. The story closes as he awaits death, where "even Gimpel will not be deceived."

"Gimple the Fool" brought Singer to the attention of the American audience through Saul Bellow's translation of the work that appeared in the *Partisan Review* in 1953. It depicts a world that recurs throughout his fiction: the shtetl of Eastern Europe, where life is imbued with a magical, mystical quality, where ghosts and devils are commonplace, and where his characters struggle with their fears and their longings. Singer's stories of a vanished way of life have secured his reputation as one of the master storytellers of the twentieth century.

The Magician of Lubin (novel, 1960)

The Magician of Lubin, set in late nineteenth-century Poland, concerns **Yasha Mazur,** master of magic, and his inner conflicts with ethics and morality. Yasha dreams of fame, future conquests, flight, and the devil. He loves five women: **Esther,** his devoted though barren wife; **Magda,** his emaciated aide; **Zeftel,** a deserted, aging Jewess; **Emilia,** a noble, widowed Catholic; and **Halina,** Emilia's fourteen-year-old daughter. Yasha's needs draw him to all women, but always back to Esther. He lives and works for these women and in turn derives his strength from them. Emilia "was the only miracle in his life, his only hope of salvation from the pit he had dug for himself." He promises he will convert to Catholicism and marry her, and then take her and Halina to Italy. Yasha desparately needs money to support himself, his women, and his plans, but when he attempts a simple robbery, he bungles it. Assuming he is being sought by police, he goes to Emilia and confesses his attempt. She states quite simply: "we are dead." In torment, he goes to Shule, questioningly reaffirms his faith, and returns to Magda, to find she has hanged herself and killed his animals. He seeks out Zeftel, only to find her lying with another man. Most of what he has lived for is gone in a day. This desperate, guilt-ridden man wonders whether to turn himself in to the police, flee to Argentina, or commit suicide.

Three years elapse before the next sequence of the novel begins, with Yasha in a self-imposed prison of stone behind his former home. If one cannot see evil, he reasons, one is not tempted. His reclusive behavior has brought him fame, and Yasha is now known as **Jacob the Penitent.** From dawn until dusk people seek his advice and his healing touch. He learns that Zeftel is now the owner of the largest brothel in Buenos Aires, that Emilia has remarried, and that Halina is well. Esther begs him to come out of his shuttered dwelling, but Jacob refuses, for he believes that "a beast must be kept in a cage."

Singer's story relates the tale of a man with a modicum of fame, fortune and respect suddenly upended by deceit, conscience and guilt. Yasha cannot escape the torments of his own mind, nor can his magic help him to elude his self-imposed prison. A holy man to the people surrounding Lublin, Yasha within his cell still dreams of the devil, lusts for Emilia and Halina, pities Esther, suffers guilt for Magda, and fears for Zeftel, but no longer dreams of flight. He has learned that he cannot escape from himself. The novel reflects Singer's recurrent themes of the longing for erotic love and offers another glimpse into the vanished Polish-Jewish past that forms the central focus for his work.

The Slave (novella, 1962)

This dark and passionate story takes place in medieval Poland, where the invading Cossacks take **Jacob,** a scholar and teacher, and sell him into slavery. Jacob is a captive of the lowest form of man, "How can we all be of the same Adam?" he asks. He works the herds in the mountains near a shtetl. He later becomes the property of his owner's widowed daughter, **Wanda,** who brings him sustenance and love. Lust quells his conscience and his God, and Jacob takes Wanda, the pagan. Shortly, Jacob is ransomed, but returns for Wanda. They move to another shtetl, and pass Wanda off as **Sarah,** a deaf mute. However, when she speaks during childbirth, her pagan origins are displayed for all. Sarah gives birth to **Benjamin** (Born of Sorrow), dies, and is interred outside the "proper" cemetery confines. Jacob is arrested, but escapes and returns for Benjamin; the two travel to the Holy Land. Twenty years pass, and Jacob returns for Sarah's bones, so that he may bury them in the Holy Land, where Benjamin is a teacher. Back in Pilitz, Jacob dies, and upon internment, the "lost bones" of a corpse are discovered within the confines of the cemetery; they are Sarah's.

Singer's allegory of slavery is compelling. Jacob is a slave of God, religion, conscience, and deceit. It is a powerful love story, filled with passion, fear, and death, as well as the dybbuks and demons that haunt other Singer stories. The idea of life as time spent merely "dancing on the graves" awaiting the greater glories, be they Heaven or Gemmorah, is central to the story. During our "dance" we are all slaves, Singer implies, and the most harsh masters are those of conscience, love, and God.

FURTHER READING

Allentuck, Marcia. *The Achievement of Isaac Bashevis Singer.* Carbondale: Southern Illinois University Press, 1969.

Buchen, Irving H. *Isaac Bashevis Singer and the Eternal Past.* New York: New York University Press, 1968.

Contemporary Authors, Vols. 1-4, rev. ed.; *Contemporary Authors New Revision Series,* Vol. 1. Detroit: Gale Research Co.

Contemporary Literary Criticism, Vols. 1, 3, 6, 9, 11, 15, 23, 38. Detroit: Gale Research Co.

Dictionary of Literary Biography, Vols. 6, 28, 52; *Concise Dictionary of American Literary Biography, 1941-1968.* Detroit: Gale Research Co.

Hindus, Milton. "An Upright Man on an Eternal Landscape." *The New York Times Book Review* (17 June 1962): 4.

Kahn, Lothar. "The Talent of I.B. Singer, 1978 Nobel Laureate for Literature." *World Literature Today* 53, No. 2 (Spring 1979): 197-201.

Kresh, Paul. *Isaac Bashevis Singer: The Magician of West 86th Street.* New York: Dial, 1979.

Madison, Charles A. "I. Bashevis Singer: Novelist of Hasidic Gothicism." In *Yiddish Literature: Its Scope and Major Writers,* pp. 479-99. New York: Ungar, 1968.

Malin, Irving. *Isaac Bashevis Singer.* New York: Ungar, 1972.

Morrow, Lance. "The Spirited World of I. B. Singer." *Atlantic Monthly* 243 (January 1979): 39-43.

Siegel, Ben. *Isaac Bashevis Singer.* Minneapolis: University of Minnesota Press, 1969.

Aleksandr Solzhenitsyn

1918-

Russian novelist, short story writer, poet, and essayist.

One Day in the Life of Ivan Denisovich (novel, 1962)

The novel is set in a Siberian labor camp in 1951 and chronicles one day in the life of one of the prisoners, **Ivan Denisovich Shukhov.** The work provides a vivid description of the spiritual and physical suffering endured by the millions who were sentenced to the camps during Stalin's reign of terror. Shukhov is a simple man, uneducated and from the peasant class. He had been falsely accused of espionage during World War II, and rather than face a firing squad, he had pled guilty. As the novel begins, he has served eight years of his sentence. The extreme deprivation and cruelty of his experience are described in detail from the perspective of an omniscient narrator, who begins his account as Shukhov awakes on a cold January morning. Food is a major preoccupation among the inmates, for not only are they in a state of near starvation, but food is also a means of bribery and barter. Solzhenitsyn closely describes how Shukhov eats his meager meals, and how food is used by the prison authorities to motivate the men at work, for the amount of food rationed to prisoners is equal to the amount of work done. The work is exhausting, the goals set for the prisoners are impossible, and the working conditions are brutal, as is the staff that guards them and polices their actions.

Shukhov had previously been imprisoned in an even more inhuman camp, where he worked under the leadership of the prisoner **Kuzyomin,** who had been a major influence on him. Throughout the novel, Solzhenitsyn focuses on what these men do to survive their brutal situation, and Kuzyomin provides Shukhov with the philosophy he needs to endure, stressing the importance of maintaining his human dignity. Through his influence, Shukhov learns to wear the mask of the model prisoner and to cloak his inner dignity. He is drawn to both open defiance and complete capitulation, but he remains true to Kuzyomin's code, the only means by which he can survive spiritually and physically.

The novel created an international sensation when it appeared, for it was the first work to reveal the barbarity of the labor camps and the harshness and absurd cruelty of Stalin's rule. Shukhov's story is noted for its understated yet powerful prose, dramatic characterizations, and compelling theme.

The Cancer Ward (novel, 1968)

Set in the cancer ward of a hospital in Tashkent in 1955, this novel tells the story of **Oleg Kostoglotov's** struggle as a victim of both a deadly disease and the oppressive society in which he lives. He is an ex-convict and an outcast, who because of his crime cannot return to his native Leningrad, but is forced to live in exile in a resettlement area. Because of his cancer, he is sent to the hospital, where he encounters a microcosm of Soviet society in his fellow patients. Among them is **Pavel Nikolayevich Rusanov,** a man of wealth and power in the Soviet Union. He is a director of personnel in an industrial concern and is a member of the Communist Party, which insures his continued financial and professional success. Yet he, too, is a victim of cancer. The patients come from different professions, areas, and generations, but their disease makes them equals. Through their conversation, Solzhenitsyn explores the social and political conflicts of the modern Soviet state.

One of the central debates between the patients concerns Tolstoy's *What Men Live By,* and the characters, forced by a death-threatening disease to question the purpose and meaning of life, define themselves through their responses. Solzhenitsyn also illuminates how this simple, powerful book exerts an influence unlike the accepted works of socialist realism approved of by the state. The credibility of modern medicine is also scrutinized in this novel, for the patients are subjected to experimental treatments whose effectiveness and side-effects are unknown. Kostoglotov, a rebel against the authority of the state or organized medicine, learns through the medical student with whom he has fallen in love that the drug to be used on him will cause impotence. Deprived of his freedom by the state, he refuses to be robbed of his ability to pass on life, and he declines the treatment. Yet the doctors are depicted as victims of the medical establishment as well, and they feel deeply for the fate of their patients. Kostoglotov leaves the hospital without being completely cured, and in the final scene he is on his way to exile.

The somber tone of the novel reflects the pain and terror of death and disease, and the cancerous tumors that cause so much suffering are a metaphor for the diseased society under Soviet control.

The First Circle (novel, 1968)

The novel is set in the outskirts of Moscow in 1949 and relates the experiences of **Gleb Vikentyevich Nerzhin** during the time he spends in the *sharashka,* a prison within the Mavrino Institute, a sceintific institution staffed by prisoners, or "zeks" as they are called, and run by the secret police. The sharashka is staffed with scientists, technicians, and engineers, and is referred to as the "first circle" of the Soviet prison system, an allusion to the first circle of hell described in Dante's *Inferno.* The workers in the sharashka are too valuable not to exploit for their expertise and ability, so they are kept in relative comfort, but have lost all freedom. As in his previous works, Sholzhenitsyn deals with the individual struggle for dignity during the terror of the reign of **Josef Stalin.** The novel covers a wide range, for the author depicts the lives of several high-ranking officials in Stalin's government, even the dictator himself.

As the story begins, **Innokenty Artemyevich Volodin,** a government official, tries to warn his old family friend, a physician, that his desire to share medical findings with French doctors could lead to his arrest. Volodin is wirctapped, arrested, and sentenced to a concentration camp. The voice tape used in his conviction had been analyzed by **Lev Grigoryevich Rubin,** a zek philologist and, although a prisoner, a devoted Communist. The prisoners are at work on a telephone coding system for Stalin's personal use, and Solzhenitsyn devotes several chapters to a parodic depiction of the ruler. He is described as stupid, brutal and primitive, a man whose madness and megalomania permeates the entire Soviet system. The zeks are fully aware that their scientific discoveries are being used to destroy innocent victims, and they use sabotage and work slowdowns to protest their involvement. One of the prisioners, **Dmitri Aleksandrovich Sologdin,** a mathemetician, has developed a key portion of the telephone system. Yet rather than aid Stalin, he makes sure that his research is burned with his scrap papers, even though successful completion of the project would have meant freedom. But he later invents another weapon for the secret police to use, and thus sells his integrity for his freedom.

Rubin's situation is ironical: he is a stauch supporter of Stalin and a devoted Marxist, yet he is imprisoned. Although he is a brilliant man, he is unable to see the evil behind the man responsible for corrupting the system he believes in so fervently. Nerzhin is a brilliant mathemetician and a deeply sensitive man. He tries to comprehend what has happened to his country under Stalin and what can be done to remedy the situation. Like Sologdin, he is tempted by the system with offers of amnesty and a more prestigious position to submit. But he refuses, maintaining his humanity and personal dignity. When the officials offer to clear his record, his integrity will not allow it, for he knows that the true criminals are Stalin and his henchmen, not the free-thinking people who are imprisoned for questioning the senseless brutality of the system. For his defiance, he is sent to a more brutal labor camp.

The work is admired for its powerful themes, scathing parody of Stalin, and fearless depiction of the madness of an era. Solzhenitsyn's objective narrator presents a straight-forward evocation of the prisoners' plight, but in the sections describing Stalin, the objectivity gives way to a savage satire on the ruler's imbecility, mocking his rhetorical style. Solzhenitsyn's portrayl of Nerzhin is noted for its compassion and insight.

FURTHER READING

Contemporary Authors, Vols. 69-72. Detroit: Gale Research Co.

Contemporary Literary Criticism, Vols. 1, 2, 4, 9, 10, 18, 26, 34. Detroit: Gale Research Co.

Eagle, Herbert. "Existentialism and Ideology in *The First Circle." Modern Fiction Studies* (Spring 1977): 47-61.

Ericson, Edward E., Jr. *Solzhenitsyn: The Moral Vision*. Grand Rapids, Mich.: Eerdmans, 1980.

Kodjak, Andrej. *Alexander Solzhenitsyn*. Boston: Twayne, 1978.

Lucid, Luellen. "Solzhenitsyn's Rhetorical Revolution." *Twentieth Century Literature* (December 1977): 498-517.

Lukács, Georg. *Solzhenitsyn*, translated by William David Graf. Cambridge: MIT Press, 1971.

Medvedev, Zhores A. *Ten Years after Ivan Denisovich*. New York: Alfred A. Knopf, 1973.

Moody, Christopher. *Solzhenitsyn*. New York: Harper & Row, 1973.

Proffer, Carl R. "Russian Odyssey." *The New Republic* 191, No. 16 (15 October 1984): 35-9.

Rothberg, Abraham. "One Day—Four Decades: Solzhenitsyn's Hold on Reality." *Southwest Review* (Spring 1971): 109-24.

Wole Soyinka

1934-

Nigerian dramatist, poet, and novelist.

A Dance of the Forests (drama, 1959)

This play, commissioned by the Nigerian government to commemorate the nation's independence, is one of Soyinka's most complex and celebrated works. In it, he presents with several themes that recur throughout his drama, such as the importance and influence of the past, the duality of human nature, and the necessity of free will. The play deals with the cycles of history, evoking the past, present, and future in a work whose imagery and allegory are drawn from Soyinka's understanding of the Yoruba myths. The piece opens on the important "gathering of the tribes" as a community prepares for a festival. The people call upon the gods to summon the spirits of their illustrious ancestors. Three members of the village, **Adenebi,** a council orator, **Rola,** a beautiful prostitute, and **Demoke,** an artist, are seen in dual roles, for they are transported to the past and are reincarnated as members of the court of the ancient Nigerian king, **Mata Karibu.** The flashback in time does much to illuminate the true nature of the past, for the ancestors are shown to be small-minded and vain, capable of the jealousies and cruelties that distinguish the contemporary characters as well. This is central to Soyinka's purpose, for he wished to warn his fellow Nigerians against the dangers of viewing the past with sentimentality and romanticism.

Adenebi is a superficial man, insensitive to all the positive values presented in the play. He lacks compassion, pity, and insight into his own nature; he represents the dangers of corruption and complacency and contemporary man's preoccupation with the material world. Rola is a heartless, cruel beauty, contemptuous of the men who are willing to die for her love. Demoke, a wood carver, represents the redemptive power of art, but also the duality of human nature. We learn that he is capable of destruction as well as creation, for he has murdered his apprentice, **Oremole.** It is especially through the character of Demoke that we gain insight into the meaning of the human condition, which, Soyinka stresses, is capable of good and evil, of positive and negative action. The three encounter the **Forest Father,** the creator of humankind, who questions the mortals about their lives. They witness the "welcoming of the dead," who come to induce the living to confront their true natures and the meaning of existence. Adenebi, Rola, and Demoke, masked, become possessed by spirits and speak of the future, bleakly foretelling a reign of destruction, pollution, and exploitation. The **Half-Child** appears, a symbol of this doomed future, and a battle for its fate ensues.

Soyinka's message to his society, beginning a new cycle of history as an independent nation, is to learn from the past, without false sentimentality, the complex, regenerative message of history. *A Dance of the Forests* is especially admired for Soyinka's incorporation of the Yoruba myths, which he finds of vital importance to modern Nigerian culture.

The Trials of Brother Jero (drama, 1960)

This satiric play, one of Soyinka's most popular works, is set in Lagos, Nigeria, in the Bar Beach section, where many religious evangelists live and try to recruit new followers. The central figure, **Brother Jeroboam,** is a false prophet and a charlatan. Jero takes the audience into his confidence, acknowledging his treachery and the necessity of perpetuating the suffering of his followers, in order to insure his own existence. One of the most devout of his disciples is **Chume,** nagged by his unrelenting wife, **Amope.** Chume longs to beat his wife to silence her, but Jero warns him not to, supposedly out of his understanding of Christian tolerance, but actually because he knows he will lose the most faithful of his flock if he allows Chume to achieve happiness.

Meanwhile, Amope, claiming that Jero owes her money, has camped out in front of his house waiting for payment. Not knowing that she is the wife of Chume and hoping to escape her wrath, Jero tries to flee through a window. But Amope removes his mask of pious Christianity, for she knows him for the swindler he is. Further humorous evidence of Jero's human weakness is evident in the lust he feels for a young woman who comes to the beach to bathe each day; another sign, in a play that centers on mistaken identity and masking, of the wolf beneath the lamb's facade. When Jero learns Chume's wife's true identity, he allows his disciple to beat her. When Chume learns that it is Jero who owes his wife money, the prophet is unmasked to his enraged adherent. But Jero has more cunning up his sleeve. He enlists the help of a member of parliament, whom he fills with delusions by telling him he sees a vision of the politician as the Minister of War. Through these machinations, Jero succeeds in getting Chume incarcerated in a mental hospital, thus retaining his power, his mask, and his deluded following. Brother Jero returns in Soyinka's later play, *Jero's Metamorphosis.*

The play's tone is light-hearted and satirical, and the work is peopled with stock characters drawn from the theatrical tradition. When Brother Jero is brought back by his creator fourteen years later, it is with a different, more pessimistic message.

Jero's Metamorphosis (drama, 1974)

This play marks the reappearance of Soyinka's infamous fraud, **Brother Jero,** the false prophet of Bar Beach in Lagos. In this drama, however, the world has grown more sinister, and the light-hearted satire that characterized Soyinka's earlier play is replaced by a darkening of tone. To encourage tourism, the government has transformed Bar Beach into a setting for public executions, causing the displacement of the religious people who lived there. The new building to be erected is to be called the National Public Execution Amphitheater, and the government has chosen the Salvation Army as the religious group that will administer the last rites to the condemned prisoners. Jero, seeing a great opportunity to make money, schemes to get control of the religious ceremonies himself. Through the intervention of a government agent who has become one of his disciples, he gets his hands on secret documents that outline the nefarious dealings regarding the plans for the theater, and he plots to blackmail the officials involved. He succeeds and wins the contract for himself.

Written after Soyinka had been incarcerated for two years because of his outspoken criticism of the Nigerian government, *Jero's Metamorphosis* is considered a harshly satiric view of the state of the author's homeland. Unlike the earlier play in which Jero figured, this drama reflects the bitterness and contempt Soyinka has for the hypocrisy, cruelty, and greed he sees at the heart of the current political situation in Nigeria. The work is considered an indication of a major shift in Soyinka's drama, for it reflects a darker, more pessimistic attitude.

FURTHER READING

Contemporary Authors, Vols. 13-16, rev. ed. Detroit: Gale Research Co.

Contemporary Literary Criticism, Vols. 3, 5, 14, 36, 44. Detroit: Gale Research Co.

Dictionary of Literary Biography Yearbook: 1986. Detroit: Gale Research Co.

Jones, Eldred. *The Writings of Wole Soyinka.* London: Heinemann, 1973.

Laurence, Margaret. "Voices of Life, Dance of Death: Wole Soyinka." In *Long Drums and Cannons: Nigerian Dramatists and Novelists,* pp. 11-76. New York: Holt, Rinehart, and Winston, 1969.

Maclean, Una. "Wole Soyinka." *Black Orpheus,* No. 15 (August 1964): 46-51.

Moore, Gerald. *Wole Soyinka.* London: Evans, 1971.

Ogunba, Ogin. *The Movement of Transition: A Study of the Plays of Wole Soyinka.* Ibadan: Ibadan University Press, 1975.

Roscoe, Adrian A. "Drama." In *Mother Is Gold: A Study of West African Literature,* pp. 13-70. Cambridge: Cambridge University Press, 1971.

Muriel Spark

1918-

Scottish-born novelist, short story writer, and essayist.

The Prime of Miss Jean Brodie (novel, 1961)

This novel, set in an Edinburgh girl's school, is considered Spark's masterpiece. It recounts the life of **Jean Brodie,** a Scottish teacher and spinster, who shares her "prime" years with a select group of her students, molding them with her dominant personality and outlook. The novel cuts backward and forward in time, from the 1930s, when the girls are in grade schoool, to their later adolescence, and, in the case of **Sandy Stranger,** to their middle-age.

Miss Brodie is a fascinating character, dogmatic, unconventional, and captivating. Un-shakable in her belief in herself, her omnipotence, and her plans for her girls, she rejects the commonplace conformity of dreary, middle-class life and urges her girls to do the same. In her orchestration of their lives, she has created roles for them to play. Although she loves the art teacher, **Teddy Lloyd,** who also returns her love, she renounces him and cultivates two of her pupils, **Rose Stanley** and Sandy, to play the parts of lover and informer, respectively. Sandy sees things differently, however, and choses to play the role of mistress herself. Sandy's views of Miss Brodie are a central focus in the novel, and the way in which her opinion of Brodie changes in the course of the work influences our perception. As a young adolescent, secure in her view of Brodie as a manipulative and ultimately evil influence, and motivated by this insight as well as by envy of her mentor, Sandy betrays her teacher, reporting her activities to the school authorities, which results in Brodie's dismissal.

In adulthood, Sandy converts to Catholicism and continues to reflect on her former teacher.

She becomes a cloistered nun and writes an essay on morality, ''The Transfiguration of the Commonplace,'' for which she becomes famous. Spark's themes in this novel are the end of innocence, the complexity of adulthood, and the moral dilemmas one confronts in maturity. Thus, through Sandy, our view of Brodie is transformed, for we share her ability to see the teacher with compassion and understanding, and to apply the moral insight she has gained to our comprehension of this complex woman. The work is highly regarded for its taut prose style and for Spark's effective use of a broken time sequence in which the past and present are juxtaposed. Perhaps Spark's greatest achievement in her best-known work is her creation of Miss Brodie.

FURTHER READING

Berthoff, Werner. ''Fortunes of the Novel: Muriel Spark and Iris Murdoch.'' *Massachusetts Review* 8 (Spring 1967): 301-32.

Contemporary Authors, Vols. 5-8, rev. ed.; *Contemporary Authors New Revision Series,* Vol. 12. Detroit: Gale Research Co.

Contemporary Literary Criticism, Vols. 2, 3, 5, 8, 13, 18, 40. Detroit: Gale Research Co.

Dictionary of Literary Biography, Vol. 15. Detroit: Gale Research Co.

Kelleher, Victor. ''The Religious Artistry of Muriel Spark.'' *The Critical Review* 18 (1976): 79-92.

Kermode, Frank. ''The Prime of Miss Muriel Spark.'' *New Statesman* 66 (27 September 1963): 397-98.

Christina Stead

1902-1983

Australian novelist and short story writer.

The Man Who Loved Children (novel, 1940)

Stead's most famous novel centers on the Pollitt family. **Louisa** is the daughter of **Samuel Pollitt** and his first, now deceased, wife. Louie lives with Sam and his second wife, **Henrietta** and their children in Tohoga House, which they rent from Henny's father in Maryland. The plot covers several years at the end of the 1930s during which Louie grows from adolescence to young adulthood. Sam and Henny have hated each other since the start of their marriage. He is an idealist and dreamer who, when unjustly fired from his job with the Commerce Department, refuses to defend himself or to seek other employment. Sam's disposition is always sunny and optimistic, and he has a special rapport with his several children, fostered by his own childlike nature. Henny, from a well-to-do family, is unable to live within her means after marrying Sam and incurs numerous debts without his knowledge. She sees Sam for what he is, a man unwilling to live in the real world and accept his familial responsibilities, and she takes out her resentment on the children, especially Louie, by being constantly cruel to them. Louie, in her turn, is tormented by the continual arguing between Sam and Henny and longs for escape. This she tentatively achieves through her literary pursuits at home and at school. Matters worsen at the Pollitt home when Henny's father dies and they must sell Tahoga House to settle his debts. The family moves to a poor, dilapidated neighborhood near Annapolis, where the fighting between Sam and Henny escalates. Louie suddenly realizes that the only way she and the other children will ever be free of Sam and Henny is if she kills them. Louie manages to put cyanide in one cup of their morning tea before becoming paralyzed with fear. Henny seems to sense what she has done and deliberately drinks the poisoned tea. When she dies, Louie runs away to her natural mother's family.

When it was originally published, *The Man Who Loved Children* elicited little critical or commercial attention. Upon its reissue in 1965, however, with a laudatory introduction by Randall Jarrell, the novel garnered popular and critical success. The story is a detailed examination of a troubled American family and the social and economical pressures which affect it, and also an exploration of the factors which shape Louie's artistic development. The novel was praised for Stead's keen observations into the workings of a disturbed family and for her realistic social setting.

FURTHER READING

Brown, Denise. "Christina Stead's 'Drama of the Person'." *Australian Literary Studies* 13 (October 1987): 139-45.

Contemporary Authors, Vols. 13-16, rev. ed., 109. Detroit: Gale Research Co.

Contemporary Literary Criticism, Vols. 2, 5, 8, 32. Detroit: Gale Research Co.

Gribble, Jennifer. "The Beauties and Furies." *Southerly* 3 (September 1987): 324-37.

Lidoff, Joan. *Christina Stead.* New York: Ungar, 1982.

Woodward, Wendy. "Writing Differences and the Ideology of Form: Narrative Structure in the Novels of Christina Stead." *Theoria* 68 (December 1986): 49-57.

Gertrude Stein
1874-1956

American novelist, poet and critic.

Melanctha (novella, 1909)

Set in early twentieth-century Baltimore (Bridgepoint), this experimental story analyzes the psychological motivations and love relationships of its mulatto heroine, **Melanctha Herbert.** An eighteen-year-old servant girl, Melanctha is both sensuous and streetwise, schooled by her emancipated companion **Jane Harden.** Melanctha's first serious romantic attachment is to **Dr. Jefferson Campbell,** an attractive black physician who arrives to treat her dying mother. Described as "a serious, earnest, good young joyous doctor," Jeff represents the refinement and wisdom Melanctha wishes to obtain. Their relationship, which forms the focal point of the story, is complex and characterized by uncertain communication and a recurrent ebb and flow of understanding. Although Melanctha succeeds in conveying the volatile, urgent nature of her love so that Jeff is finally able to reciprocate, her interest in him wanes soon after. Her later searches for wisdom and compatible love prove disillusioning. She turns to **Jem Richards,** a gambler, and faces a joyless, desolate future. At the same time he abandons her, Melanctha's close friend **Rose Johnson** abruptly severs contact. Melanctha contemplates though never attempts suicide; instead she endures and, after contracting tuberculosis, dies in a sanitorium.

Melanctha is the most fully realized of the psychological *contes* that comprise *Three Lives,* Stein's first published novel. Virtually unprecedented as a serious attempt by a white author to portray realistic black characters, the story is now recognized as at least partially stereotypic and sociologically inaccurate. Nevertheless, the story's central assumption that human feelings and emotions are oblivious of class and racial distinctions was pioneering in

American letters. Stein's artistic intention was to depict commonplace characters and demonstrate both the drabness and depth of their existence through language that reinforced the themes of circularity and repetition. This early work remains prominent in Stein's canon for its singular advance of the possibilities of language in modern literature and for its penetrating exploration of the inner lives of her characters.

The Making of Americans (novel, 1925)

Stein's self-proclaimed masterpiece, *The Making of Americans* spans three generations in the lives of two wealthy American families, the Dehnings and the Herslands. The two families are linked through the marriage of **Alfred Hersland** and **Julia Dehning.** The 925-page novel is divided into five books and is based loosely on Stein's own German-American family, represented by the Herslands. Huge in conception and unconventional in its abandonment of traditional presentation of scene and development of character, the novel ambitiously attempts to analyze "every kind of men and women, every kind there is of men and women" in America. Consequently, the work cannot be understood through straightforward examinations of plot and character; rather, it must be understood as an elaborate theoretical portrait of Stein's modernist conceptions of time and personality. Indeed, the last book, stripped of both dialogue and characters, is substantially philosophical commentary in support of these conceptions. Central to Stein's thought were William James's propositions regarding consciousness. According to James, the individual perceives the world not in discrete temporal segments of past, present, and future, but as a continuous awareness of the moment being presently lived. In this novel as in her later works, Stein sought to evoke this atemporal sense of a continuous present.

As in *Three Lives,* Stein attempts to underscore the essential repetitiveness of existence. Certain family names as well as family communication patterns are repeated in succeeding generations. The result is fragmented characterization and a confusion of chronological time. What carries the novel slowly forward is Stein's tireless repetition of nearly identical statements in very long paragraphs using only the present tense. Given these characteristics and the fact that the text contains numerous digressions in which Stein records her thoughts, often anxious and uncertain, about the process of writing *The Making of Americans,* there is some doubt whether the work should be considered a novel.

Due to Stein's exceedingly abstract, clinical approach to the psychology of her characters, *The Making of Americans* has received limited critical approval. However, Stein has been credited for her unique attempt to illustrate personality types, revealing the "bottom mature," or essential type, of individuals by depicting their patterns of behavior. Despite the exhausting effects of her redundant style, Stein's epic is remembered not for its content but for the influential force its author exerted upon generations of twentieth-century writers.

FURTHER READING

Contemporary Authors, Vol. 104. Detroit: Gale Research Co.

Copeland, Carolyn Faunce. *Language and Time and Gertrude Stein.* Iowa City: University of Iowa Press, 1975.

Dictionary of Literary Biography, Vol. 4. Detroit: Gale Research Co.

Hoffman, Frederick J. *Gertrude Stein.* Minneapolis: University of Minnesota Press, 1961.

Hoffman, Michael J. *The Development of Abstractionism in the Writings of Gertrude Stein.* Philadelphia: University of Pennsylvania Press, 1966.

——. *Gertrude Stein.* Boston: Twayne Publishers, 1976.

Kostelanetz, Richard. Introduction to *The Yale Gertrude Stein* by Gertrude Stein, pp. xiii-xxxi. New Haven: Yale University Press, 1980.

Stewart, Allegra. *Gertrude Stein and the Present*. Cambridge: Harvard University Press, 1967.

Twentieth-Century Literary Criticism, Vols. 1, 6. Detroit: Gale Research Co.

Weinstein, Norman. *Gertrude Stein and the Literature of the Modern Consciousness*. New York: Ungar, 1970.

John Steinbeck

1902-1968

American novelist, short story writer, and essayist.

Tortilla Flat (novel, 1935)

Set in California's Monterey Peninsula during the 1930s, the novel tells the story of **Danny** and his friends in an episodic structure that Steinbeck modeled on the Arthurian legends of Thomas Malory. His treatment of Danny and his group also parallels Arthur's knights in a manner that is at once humorous and ironic, for unlike Arthur's chivalrous vassals, these are paisanos, men of mixed Spanish, Indian, Mexican, and Caucasian ancestry, who live a life of indolence and roguery. The novel begins as Danny returns to Tortilla Flat following World War I, having inherited two houses from his grandfather. He is a heroic figure: strong, unconventional, challenging and refusing to be fettered by the bourgeois civilization that surrounds him. He invites his friends to live with him in his houses, which they accept. Steinbeck depicts their various "feats" in the tall tales they relate to one another of their exploits, most often focusing on women and wine. But Danny, feeling that home-owning has been a threat to his freedom, escapes into the woods. The paisanos search for him in an ironic reenactment of the search for the Holy Grail. Danny returns and decides to sell the house. His friends get it back, and to enliven his spirits, throw him a party. In the midst of the revelry, Danny becomes fierce and challenges his friends to fight; when they refuse, he goes to the back of the house, to confront an "enemy" worthy of him. Steinbeck never clarifies what it is that Danny encounters, but through it he meets his death. The novel ends with Danny's funeral, which his friends must observe from a distance because they have no suitable clothes to wear; afterwards, they burn Danny's house, destroying all that it symbolized for them, then go their separate ways.

Though some critics have claimed that Steinbeck championed his indolent paisanos, most agree that his purpose here is ironic and satiric. He parodies the middle-class values so affronted by the lazy lives of the paisanos, but they, too, are objects of his satire. The novel is praised as compassionate, insightful, and warmly humorous.

Of Mice and Men (novel, 1937)

The novel is set on a large ranch in the Salinas Valley of California during the Depression where **George Milton** and **Lennie Small** are migrant ranch hands. Lennie, a man governed by impulses he cannot control, is retarded and taken care of by George. Their relationship is one of mutual need: Lennie needs George to restrain him, and George enjoys the power that dominance implies. Together they share a dream of buying a farm of their own, and the narrative recounts George repeatedly retelling the fantasy to Lennie, describing the farm, the animals, and the crops in incantatory tones. Steinbeck depicts them as two innocents in search of a peaceful way of life who are in conflict with the cruel realities of a world motivated by materialism and greed. Their friendship distinguishes them from the hopeless and lonely men who share their lives on the ranches where they find work. As the novel's action begins, Lennie and George are working on a ranch run by a man whose son, **Curly,** a pompous fool, picks a fight with Lennie, in which Lennie crushes his hand. This event foreshadows the novel's violent climax in which Lennie accidently kills Curly's wife. George, fearing that Lennie will be lynched by an angry mob, kills him; when he is discovered, George lies to cover up the truth, claiming that he shot Lennie in self-defense. At the novel's end, George is seen as a shattered, isolated man, for in killing Lennie he has destroyed the innocent in himself, the man unaware of the limitations of life and the one able to live for a dream.

Steinbeck's story is noted for its symbolic and parabolic overtones, rendered in objective and realistic prose. The action of the novel takes place over three days, making it a compact, tightly controlled work. In George and Lennie, Steinbeck created two characters who are victims of forces beyond their control, a theme he will investigate further in *The Grapes of Wrath*.

The Grapes of Wrath (novel, 1939)

Set in Oklahoma and California during the 1930s, the novel depicts the struggles of **Ma** and **Pa Joad** and their family as they become part of the great migration of farmers who left their homes in the Middle West in search of work during the Depression. The novel contains three major divisions: the first section deals with the Joads and their life as sharecroppers in Oklahoma; the second depicts their journey from Oklahoma to California; the third covers their experiences as migrant workers. As the novel begins, **Tom Joad,** recently released from prison, meets **Jim Casy,** a former preacher, on the road to his home in Oklahoma. Casy has fallen away from the Christian faith, believing instead that the greatest good a person can do involves self-sacrifice and caring for one's fellow beings. Tom is a young man whose lack of sensitivity and insight is reflected in his vivid contrast to the character of Casy. When the two arrive at the Joad family farm, they find it vacant; the family has been evicted from their land after the drought had ruined their crops. Tom and Casy find the family enroute to California, the land of promise, where they believe they will find wealth and happiness.

The Joads's individual family saga is interwoven with chapters on a variety of topics that relate thematically to the main narrative, covering such areas as the history of farm ownership in California and the conditions of life for the migrant workers. In this way, Steinbeck provides both a macrocosm and microcosm of the nation and the plight of farm workers during the Depression, for he illuminates the social and economic problems of many people and parallels them to their effect on one particular family. One of Steinbeck's central themes is the disintegration of the family, and the Joads's journey is marred by its tragic evidence: both grandparents die along the way, and both their son, **Noah,** and the husband of their pregnant daughter **Rose of Sharon,** desert the family. The Joads's sense of identity and pride is very much tied to their sense of family, and Ma Joad, one of Steinbeck's most famous characters, is perhaps its foremost exponent. A woman of great courage and strength, she fights tenaciously against the forces that would break up her family up, maintaining a certain misplaced pride in the family's insularity and self-sufficiency.

The family is dealt a further blow when they reach California, for it is not the ''land of milk and honey,'' as they'd dreamed; instead, they are ostracized as outsiders and face a bleak reality: the farms are controlled by property owners who destroy crops to drive prices up and who pit the itinerant workers against one another to avoid paying decent wages. The one hopeful prospect in their new life occurs when they come to live in the Weedpatch, a government camp. Here they discover that they are more than an isolated family and that they are part of the community of migrant workers who care for and share with one another. Casy becomes a labor organizer to better the plight of the workers, but is killed. Tom kills

Casy's murderer to avenge his death. The family flees to protect Tom, who, during his period of hiding, undergoes a transformation. Inspired by the life and philosophy of Casy, he is now determined to devote his life to helping his fellow man. The novel's famous concluding scene depicts Rose of Sharon, whose baby was stillborn, offering her breast to a man starving to death. Although critics fiercely debate the meaning and the success of this scene, many would agree that it suggests a fitting conclusion to the Joads's journey. As Steinbeck describes it, theirs is a voyage of self-knowledge, for they have travelled from an isolated, self-centered existence to an awareness of the plight they share in common with so many others.

Steinbeck's depiction of the Joads is neither idealized nor sentimental; rather, he shows them to be uneducated, crude, and coarse, but also human beings who deserve to be treated with dignity. Their journey is described in epic terms and provides an allegorical vision of the unity of all people, mirrored in the Joads's acceptance of themselves as part of the human family. Stylistically, Steinbeck employs a variety of narrative methods including simple, unadorned prose, documentary, and lush description of nature. *The Grapes of Wrath,* for which Steinbeck was awarded the Pulitzer Prize, is considered a modern masterpiece for its powerful exposition, vivid portraiture, and lasting themes.

East of Eden (novel, 1952)

Steinbeck's canvas is broad in this work, for he chronicles three generations in two families, the Hamiltons and the Trasks, spanning the years between the Civil War and World War I. The Hamiltons are based on Steinbeck's own family, his mother's ancestors, and we follow their journey from Ireland to the Salinas Valley in California. He originally intended the work to be a family chronicle for his sons, and he often addresses them directly as the narrator of the novel. He created the Trask family to provide contrast to the Hamiltons; however, as the novel developed, they became the main focus of the work. Their journey begins in Connecticut, and they, too, finally settle in the Salinas Valley.

Steinbeck examines the nature of good and evil in this work through a parabolic treatment of the story of Cain and Abel. Each generation of the Trask family contains a pair of brothers who compete for their father's affections, and Steinbeck focuses specifically on the rejection of a child's gift by the father and the child's subsequent revenge. **Adam Trask,** the allegorical Adam in search of Eden, meets and marries **Cathy Ames,** knowing little of her background. She turns out to be a figure of evil and is one of the most notorious characters in modern American fiction. She is described as looking like a serpent, and her actions throughout the novel mark her as a satanic figure. Although she is married to Adam, she sleeps with his half-brother, **Charles Trask,** and the twins she conceives are the sons of two different fathers. Adam seeks to create an Eden for himself and his family in California, but after the twins are born, Cathy deserts them all, returning to her life as a prostitute and renaming herself **Kate Trask.**

Adam, left alone with his infant sons, now encounters **Samuel Hamilton,** who helps him to name his boys. As the patriarch and major representative of the Hamilton family, Sam embodies idealism and the will to strive against great odds. Although he is a dreamer and a financial failure, he is a man of depth and goodness. In contrast, the Trasks seem to carry with them a sense of the brooding curse that marks their family. Continuing the jealousy and enmity that characterized the relationship between Adam and Charles, the twins, **Caleb** and **Aron,** carry on the Cain and Abel tradition. Adam favors Aron and rejects Caleb. In a pivotal scene, Adam, after losing money in a business venture, refuses Caleb's offer of help. In a fury of revenge, Caleb tells Aron the truth about their mother, information he knows will ruin his brother. In despair, Aron enlists in the army and is killed during World War I. Caleb, taking responsibility for his brother's death, struggles with the evil within him. Through the Hebrew concept of *timshel,* he learns that humans can choose between good and evil, and thus is able to redeem himself, breaking the curse and its legacy of hatred and revenge. In the conclusion, he is finally reconciled with his father. Kate too has changed. Once the most vicious and sadistic of women, she seeks the solace of religion and eventually commits suicide to escape the evil she has perpetuated.

Although Steinbeck considered *East of Eden* to be the culmination of his career, its initial reception was negative; it has subsequently been reinterpreted and reevaluated, with many modern critics lauding the novel's structure and themes. The work is divided into four parts, three of which begin with essays in the first person. Integrating his own family's story with that of the Trasks, Steinbeck seeks to illuminate the personal in the historical. He intersperses sections of the narrative with essays on the individual characters as well as references to his own family and asides to his sons. As many critics have noted, the sections on the Hamiltons seem irrelevant to the main story of the Trasks, and their interaction is minimal. Yet if the work is considered more as an allegory or romance, the symbolic function of the characters becomes evident and the work can be seen as a unified, complex exploration of good and evil.

FURTHER READING

Benson, Jackson J. "To Tom Who Lived It: John Steinbeck and the Man from Weedpatch." *Journal of Modern Literature* 5 (April 1976): 151-210.

Contemporary Authors, Vols. 1-4, rev. ed., 25-28, rev. ed.; *Contemporary Authors New Revision Series,* Vol. 1. Detroit: Gale Research Co.

Contemporary Literary Criticism, Vols. 1, 5, 9, 13, 21, 34, 45. Detroit: Gale Research Co.

Dictionary of Literary Biography, Vols. 7, 9; *Dictionary of Literary Biography Documentary Series,* Vol. 2. Detroit: Gale Research Co.

Fontenrose, Joseph. *John Steinbeck: An Introduction and Interpretation.* New York: Barnes & Noble, 1963.

French, Warren. *John Steinbeck.* Boston: Twayne, 1961.

Hayashi, Tetsumaro, ed. *Steinbeck's Literary Dimension.* Metuchen, N. J.: Scarecrow Press, 1973.

Levant, Howard. *The Novels of John Steinbeck: A Critical Study.* Columbia: University of Missouri Press, 1974.

Lisca, Peter. *John Steinbeck: Nature and Myth.* New York: Crowell, 1978.

——. *The Wide World of John Steinbeck.* New Brunswick: Rutgers University Press, 1958.

Marks, Lester. *Thematic Design in the Novels of John Steinbeck.* The Hague: Mouton, 1969.

McCarthy, Paul. *John Steinbeck.* New York: Ungar, 1979.

Tedlock, E. W. and C. V. Wicker, eds. *Steinbeck and His Critics: A Record of Twenty-Five Years.* Albuquerque: University of New Mexico Press, 1957.

Timmerman, John H. *John Steinbeck's Fiction: The Aesthetics of the Road Taken.* Norman: University of Oklahoma Press, 1986.

Bram Stoker

1847-1912

Irish novelist.

Dracula (novel, 1897)

Stoker's famous Gothic horror story is set in Romania and England during the Victorian era. The narrative is related in a variety of forms, employing such devices as newspaper clippings, letters and journals. The novel describes an ancient vampire, **Count Dracula,** and details his scheme to make a permanent move from his homeland in Transylvania to England. Constantly in need of fresh blood, the Count believes he has found a country abundant in future victims and sufficiently advanced technologically and culturally to deny the value of superstition and folklore.

As the story begins, **Jonathan Harker** a young solicitor, is sent to the Count's residence to aid him with the purchase of property in England. En route, Jonathan is mystified by the odd reaction of the local natives when they hear of his destination. After spending several days with the Count, Jonathan discovers some unsettling peculiarities regarding his host: he appears only at night, has no reflection in a mirror, and enters and exits the castle by scaling the walls. To his horror, Jonathan finds that he is a prisoner in the castle, but he manages to escape and, after a period of recovery, returns to England.

Prior to Jonathan's return, Dracula arrives in England on a ship whose only apparent occupant had lashed himself to the wheel with a rosary before he died. The vessel's cargo includes several vampires in coffins, which Dracula places in his new home. The ship lands in Whitby where, by coincidence, Jonathan's fiancee, **Mina Murray,** is visiting her long-time friend, **Lucy Westenra.** Soon after the ship lands, Lucy contracts a strange illness which leaves her weak and bloodless. **Dr. John Seward,** one of Lucy's admirers, sends for his mentor, **Dr. Van Helsing,** to attend to her. Van Helsing suspects that Lucy has become the victim of a vampire, but he appears powerless to save her, and she dies. Dracula has transformed her into a vampire, and in order to save her soul Van Helsing convinces Lucy's reluctant fiancé to accompany him to her grave, where they drive a stake through her heart.

Mina has read Jonathan's account of his travels in Transylvania recorded in his journal, and she shares the information with Van Helsing. He encourages the Harkers to return with him to Transylvania to destroy the ruthless vampire, and in a spectacular chase sequence, they capture Dracula and destroy him forever.

Dracula is Stoker's best novel and is considered a fine example of Gothic horror fiction. Despite its reputation as a horror tale, *Dracula* has elicited a wide range of serious critical commentary with interpreters explicating the sexual, religious, and mythic elements in the work. Its notorious central character has become a legendary figure of world literature.

FURTHER READING

Contemporary Authors, Vol. 5. Detroit: Gale Research Co.

Dictionary of Literary Biography, Vols. 36, 70. Detroit: Gale Research Co.

Hennelly, Mark M. "*Dracula:* The Gnostic Quest and the Victorian Wasteland." *English Literature in Transition* 20, No. 1 (1977): 13-26.

MacGillivray, Royce. "*Dracula:* Bram Stoker's Spoiled Masterpiece." *Queen's Quarterly* 79, No. 4 (Winter 1972): 518-27.

Summers, Montague. "The Vampire in Literature." In *The Vampire: His Kith and Kin,* pp. 217-340. Secaucus: University Books, Inc., 1960.

Twentieth-Century Literary Criticism, Vol. 8. Detroit: Gale Research Co.

Wasson, Richard. "The Politics of Dracula." *English Literature in Transition* 9, No.1 (1966): 24-7.

Wolf, Leonard. *A Dream of Dracula: In Search of the Living Dead*. Boston: Little, Brown and Co., 1972.

Tom Stoppard
1937-
Czechoslovakian-born English dramatist.

Rosencrantz and Guildenstern Are Dead (drama, 1966)

This play is based on two minor characters from Shakespeare's *Hamlet* and is at once a comic parody and a deeply philosophical piece. It is concerned with themes central to all of Stoppard's work, including identity, fate, death, and the nature of theatrical reality. Considered Stoppard's first major work, the play is a tour de force, displaying his gift for brilliant wordplay and intellectual probing of ideas central to modern thought.

As the play begins, **Rosencrantz** and **Guildenstern** are on their way to Elsinore, vaguely aware that they have been summoned, but unaware to what purpose. They are flipping coins, which all turn up "heads," even after seventy tosses; thus the themes of chance and the unreliability of the reality we see on the stage are quickly established. The two immediately engage in philosophical speculation about all matter of topics, which continues throughout the play. In keeping with the theme of identity, they are unsure of their own names, and can't recall which of them is Rosencrantz and which Guildenstern. They meet a travelling troop of actors, led by the **Player,** and together they travel to Elsinore. **Ophelia, Hamlet, Claudius** and **Gertrude** come on stage, and Claudius greets Rosencrantz. At this point, Shakespeare's play takes over and the scene is derived directly from the text of *Hamlet*. Suddenly, the focus shifts back to Rosencrantz and Guildenstern alone on the stage, bewildered and wondering what has happened to them. We become aware that we are watching a play-within-a-play, a device that Stoppard uses frequently. The two characters discuss Hamlet, trying to understand Claudius's directive to them—that they try to discern the nature of Hamlet's change of character. Yet they are utterly confused as to their own function and purpose, saying that they've "been caught up" in a situation in which they have no control.

Stoppard purposely focuses on two minor characters from the world's most famous play to examine—through travesty and parody—the nature of reality, autonomy, and the meaning of life and death. Throughout the play, Stoppard's text is interspersed with Shakespeare's, as Rosencrantz and Guildenstern become unwitting accomplices in Claudius's plot to kill Hamlet. In the third act, on a boat to England with Hamlet, they read the letter Claudius has entrusted to them, and realize that they are messengers of death. Later they realize that Hamlet has discovered the plot against him, and has had them killed. Yet how can a character, who only has the life given him by a playwright, die? And how can these two characters have an existence outside the dramatic context of the play? As befuddled as before, they discuss their fate, and then each of them disappear; the final scene of the play is the last scene of *Hamlet,* in which a character announces that "Rosencrantz and Guildenstern are dead." Considered a major work of modern fiction, the play is praised for its subtle and brilliant exposition of theme and the verbal wit and elegance that characterize all of Stoppard's plays.

Travesties (drama, 1974)

During World War I, three prominent forces who shaped twentieth-century art and politics—**James Joyce, Vladimir Ilich Lenin,** and **Tristan Tzara**—were all living in Zurich, Switzerland. Stoppard's plot concocts an imaginary meeting between the three, in which ideas on art, politics, and the place of the artist in society form the focus. He relates his story through the character of **Henry Carr,** who is based on a man drawn from life, an actor from Joyce's English Players theatrical company, who played Algernon Moncrieff in Joyce's production of Oscar Wilde's *The Importance of Being Earnest,* and who was later involved in a legal dispute with Joyce over wages. As the title makes clear, Stoppard once again indulges in parody and the examination of the theme of truth and illusion. Carr speaks from the vantage point of old age, and what we see are recollected flashbacks from his youth, filtered through the consciousness of a befuddled old man who is determined to secure a place for himself among the famous. As Shakespeare's *Hamlet* had served as a parodic point of departure in *Rosencrantz and Guildenstern Are Dead,* so Wilde's *Earnest* provides the focus for travesty in this play. Throughout the work, Carr keeps falling back into the character of Algernon, and he insists that Tzara is John Worthing, the character's friend.

Following Carr's opening monologue, the play begins in the library, where the three great men are gathered. Tzara, dadaist poet and theorist, is snipping pieces of paper and rearranging them to create poetry; Joyce is dictating *Ulysses* to his secretary, **Gwendolyn** (her name derived from Wilde's play); and Lenin is speaking to his wife in Russian, repeating the words "Da, da," ("yes, yes,"), an obvious parody of Tzara and his art. Tzara had been mentioned in Stoppard's earlier play, *Artist Descending a Staircase,* and lines from that play appear in *Travesties.* The theme of the artist's role in society is developed in Carr's conversation with Tzara regarding art, which for Carr must reflect harmony and beauty, but for Tzara indicates the chaos, turmoil, and uncertainty of the modern world. Joyce and Tzara argue about art in a discussion that is drawn from and parodies both *Ulysses* and *Earnest.* For Joyce, art contrives to give meaning to life, even in the face of the chaos of the modern world and the absurdity of human fate.

The second act focuses on Lenin and his political philosophy. He is a revolutionary in politics, as Joyce and Tzara are in art. In Carr's recollection he, Lenin, and Lenin's secretary, **Cecily** (a name also drawn from Wilde) converse in the library. This section contains a further pastiche of Wilde's play, full of coincidence and mistaken identity and paralleling Carr's rather confused remembrance. Lenin appears as an egotistical, power-hungry zealot who believes that art must serve the state. By the conclusion, it is obvious that Joyce is the only one of these three historical giants to emerge as truly great. The play's ending brings the focus back to Carr's old age. Cecily, now his wife, prompts him to tell the truth: he hardly knew these famous men at all. Carr, like Rosencrantz and Guildenstern, is a marginal figure who through his memory is able to create a meaningful past for himself. Richly comic and thematically trenchant, *Travesties* is regarded as one of Stoppard's finest dramas, praised for its thought-provoking analysis of art, politics, and the role of the artist in the twentieth century.

The Real Thing (drama, 1982)

This play, set in contemporary London, focuses on the complexities of modern love. As the drama opens, we witness a scene in which a husband reveals his wife's unfaithfulness. The tone is witty and detached, reminiscent of Noel Coward. Soon we learn that what we've witnessed is a scene from "A House of Cards," written by the protagonist, **Henry,** a dramatist who, like Stoppard, is noted for his verbal wit and detached comedic sense. Once again Stoppard makes use of the play-within-a-play device, and vignettes from Henry's plays are interspersed throughout the drama.

Henry is married to **Charlotte,** the play's leading lady, and is having an affair with **Annie,** also an actress and the wife of **Max,** the play's leading man. The central theme of the play is the education of Henry—brilliant, fastidious, and refined, but convinced that he doesn't "know how to write about love," until life teaches him differently. Annie leaves Max for Henry, and they marry. The second act takes place two years later, when Annie has again strayed and begun an affair with a young actor. Henry, vulnerable at last, is reduced to tears and sobs of entreaty: "please, please, please don't." Thus we learn that Henry has at last experienced the painful ways of passionate attachment. Annie has taken up the cause of a young solider, **Brodie,** who is imprisoned for his involvement as a nuclear activist. She urges to Henry to revise Brodie's badly written play, which Henry does out of love for her, betraying his fidelity to art. The televised version of Henry's rewrite leads to Brodie's release, and Henry wins Annie back.

As in all his work, the play abounds in literary references, especially to the dramas of Ford and Strindberg, for Annie is playing in both *'Tis Pity She's a Whore* and *Miss Julie,* two plays dealing with the emotional ravages of love. Throughout the play Stoppard's perplexed protagonist tries to figure out what is "real" in love, art, or loyalty to one's artistic conscience.

The Real Thing is noted as a departure for Stoppard, for instead of exploring metaphysical or political issues as he had done so brilliantly in his earlier plays, here he lends his characters an emotional richness new to his work. Yet the play still contains the cleverness, wit, and remarkable facility for language that mark all of his drama.

FURTHER READING

Beaufort, John. "Stoppard's *Real Thing* Is Witty—And Warmly Human." *The Christian Science Monitor* (11 January 1984): 21.

Bigsby, C. W. E. *Tom Stoppard.* Essex: Longman Group Ltd., 1976.

Brustein, Robert. "Waiting for Hamlet." *New Republic* (4 November 1967): 25-6.

Contemporary Authors, Vols. 81-84. Detroit: Gale Research Co.

Contemporary Literary Criticism, Vols. 1, 3, 4, 5, 8, 15, 29, 34. Detroit: Gale Research Co.

Dean, Joan Fitzpatrick. *Tom Stoppard: Comedy as a Moral Matrix.* Columbia: University of Missouri Press, 1981.

Dictionary of Literary Biography, Vol. 13; *Dictionary of Literary Biography Yearbook: 1985.* Detroit: Gale Research Co.

Ellmann, Richard. "The Zealots of Zurich." *Times Literary Supplement* (12 July 1974): 744.

Londre, Felicia Hardison. *Tom Stoppard.* New York: Ungar, 1981.

Nightingale, Benedict. "Stoppard as We Never Dreamed He Could Be." *The New York Times* (15 January 1984): 5, 26.

Schwartzman, Myron. "Wilde about Joyce? Da! But My Art Belongs to Dada!" *James Joyce Quarterly* 13 (1975): 122-23.

Sirkin, Elliott. "*The Real Thing.*" *The Nation* (18 February 1984): 200-01.

Taylor, John Russell. "Tom Stoppard—Structure + Intellect." *Plays and Players* 17, No. 10 (July 1970): 16-18.

David Storey
1933-

English novelist and dramatist.

This Sporting Life (novel, 1960)

Set in the industrial north of England, the novel focuses on the life of **Arthur Machin,** a rugby player. The work relates his escape from the tedium of his life as a factory worker and of his ascent to the status of community hero for his athletic prowess. But Machin is plagued by vague despair and loneliness: he doesn't feel he fits in with his fellow athletes, he's not close to his family, and the rootlessness and meaninglessness of his life sometimes overwhelm him. Like the protagonists of many of Storey's works, Machin is a man aware of the division within him; he is a big, powerful man who revels in the physicality of his life as an athlete, but also feels the need to reconcile the physical, sometimes brutal aspects of his nature—his need to dominate, his inability to articulate his needs and feelings or to develop close attachments with others—with the sensitive, thoughtful aspects of his being. This is manifested most tellingly in his relationship with **Valerie Hammond,** a widow who runs the boarding house he lives in. She is a pathetic woman who is lonely and hostile to Machin's attempts to draw her out. They are unable to commit to one another or to abandon their defenses and acknowledge their mutual need and affection. Valerie dies at the end of the novel, never having admitted her true feelings for Machin. The novel's final scene is a bleak one, set at a rugby match. Machin is older now, facing the end of his athletic career and still plagued with the loneliness and uncertainty that have marked his character.

The novel is noted for its simple, straightforward prose style and for its powerful, vivid descriptions of rugby—the sights, smells, and violence of the game. The theme of the novel—the duality of human nature—reflects Storey's own dilemma as a rugby player and artist, with the seemingly irreconcilable demands of a life devoted to athletics and art.

FURTHER READING

Contemporary Authors, Vols. 81-84. Detroit: Gale Research Co.

Contemporary Literary Criticism, Vols. 2, 4, 5, 8. Detroit: Gale Research Co.

Dictionary of Literary Biography, Vols. 13, 14. Detroit: Gale Research Co.

McGuiness, Frank. ''The Novels of David Storey.'' *London Magazine* 3 (March 1974): 79-83.

Mellors, John. ''Yorkshire Relish: The Novels of John Braine and David Storey.'' *London Magazine* 16 (October-November 1976): 79-84.

Taylor, John Russell. *David Storey.* London: Longman, 1974.

August Strindberg
1849-1912

Swedish dramatist, novelist, and essayist.

The Father (drama, 1887)

The play is set in the **Captain**'s country home in Sweden in 1886. The work portrays the battle between men and women for dominance, a recurrent theme in Strindberg's work, seen here in the conflict between the Captain and his wife, **Laura,** for control of their daughter, **Bertha.** The Captain is sympathetically portrayed and is defined as a man of heroic proportions who compares his fate at the hands of his hostile wife to the male victims of female treachery found in the Bible and ancient myth. He is shown to be a man of intelligence and scientific acumen who is brought to the verge of insanity by his wife's cruelty. Laura is a demonic figure, depicted as uncaring, unloving, and unscrupulous in her pursuit of what she wants. Her weapon is her cunning, and in a debate over their daughter's education, she tortures her husband with the suggestion that he might not be her father. This attack on his masculinity unhinges the Captain, and, on the edge of madness, he becomes childlike, babbling in the arms of his former nurse. In the conclusion, he suffers a stroke. The final scene shows Laura and Bertha in an embrace, a visual symbol of the solidarity and perfidy of women. Indeed, all the female characters represent Strindberg's misogynist concept of women and are depicted as primitive, incapable of moral choice, and predatory.

The Father is considered one of Strindberg's most important works and his first successful attempt at drama in the naturalist mode, as evidenced in the depiction of the characters as products of their backgrounds and environments. The work is noted for its taut construction and lack of dramatic convention, which heightens the realism and dramatic power of the play. The tone is one of savage violence and unrelieved hysteria, for the conflict between the Captain and Laura, like the imagery used to describe it, is of mythic dimensions.

Miss Julie (drama, 1889)

The play, Strindberg's most famous work, is set in a Swedish manor house in the 1880s on Midsummer's Eve. It relates the story of **Miss Julie,** the daughter of a count, and her seduction by **Jean,** a valet in her father's service. Once again Strindberg employs his theme of the battle between the sexes, but adds the class struggle for dominance. As the play opens, Jean is returning to the kitchen and in conversation with the cook, **Kristin,** notes that Miss Julie is "crazy again." She has just been jilted by her fiancé, and she is taking part in the servants' revels for the Midsummer celebration. As the festivities continue, Julie is drawn to Jean, and they disappear into his bedroom. Outside the room the peasants perform a ballet interlude, and Kristin chants a mime. When they emerge, Julie and Jean begin to talk. At first they plan to run away together, but as their conversation continues, the inseparable gulf between them becomes apparent. Julie, carried away by the romanticism of the moment, must now face what she has done. Strindberg depicts her as the last of a dying noble line who has fallen from her class, and she is contrasted with Jean, the strong, virile proletarian whose realism and pragmatism mark him as a member of the race that will next predominate. Julie claims that as a result of her upbringing she is half-man and half-woman. Her mother, a believer in equal rights for men and women, through cruelty and unfaithfulness has turned Julie into a man-hater and destroyed her husband's self-respect. As the conversation continues, the two characters vacillate between a servile and a domineering attitude toward one another; at last, Julie determines that she must kill herself to save her honor. At this point, the Count rings for Jean, and as we see him change from the triumphant seducer to the servile valet, Julie takes his razor and leaves the room to commit suicide.

In the play's celebrated preface, Strindberg insisted that his figures are "characterless," and are not determined by a specific set of values. Rather, he stated, they are a blend of old and new, and are fragmented like the age. He specifically states that he wanted to offer a variety of points of view and motives for the characters' actions, which he does with resounding skill and success, for the characters are noted for their depth and wide-ranging, even conflicting emotions. And despite his stated attempt to make Julie an unsympathetic character, she does stir the pity of the audience. The play is not divided into acts, but forms one long sequence of scenes, which Strindberg hoped would enhance the illusory qualities of the drama.

A Dream Play (drama, 1907)

This play, in which Strindberg tried to replicate the sequence and logic of dreams, follows the descent of the **Daughter of Indra,** the Indian God, to Earth, where she is to ascertain whether the complaining of humans is justified. The work is structured like a dream, and Strindberg makes clear in his preface that the characters are the projections of one persona, called "The Dreamer."

The Daughter's journey is a series of loosely connected vignettes. When she first reaches the Earth, she encounters the **Officer,** who is imprisoned in the Castle, a beautiful structure that grows out of manure. The Officer, who isn't sure he wants his freedom, is then seen in a vignette with his mother and later as he waits for his beloved **Victoria,** who never appears. The Daughter then meets the **Lawyer,** a character who is hideous in appearance, for his face and person have been marked by the suffering, crime, and vice of his clients. He and the Daughter marry, but their life soon becomes the scene of domestic despair; here as elsewhere in Strindberg's work, marriage is torment. Throughout her travels, the Daughter is moved by the suffering of all humankind. She learns from her own marriage of the pain of that type of union, and also how often the pleasure of one individual brings pain to another.

In Foulstrand, the Daughter meets the **Poet,** who wallows in the mud to harden his skin. Here he and the Daughter see the suffering of young lovers, and the Daughter is moved to exclaim, as she does throughout the play, that "mankind is to be pitied." With the Poet she visits Fingal's Cave, also called Indra's Ear, where the God listens to the lamentations of mortals. The Daughter decides that she must return to the heavens, but first plans to unlock a secret door, which will reveal the secrets of the universe. It relates the tale of Brahma's desire to propagate and his seduction by Maya, the Earth Mother. This mingling of the earthly and divine has been the source of human misery, for it contains the dichotomy of pleasure and suffering, the joy and sorrow of love, and the conflict of the body and soul. As the Daughter ascends into heaven, she repeats her lament for humankind and for their lot, which is "conflict, discord, and uncertainty."

The play is considered a landmark work for its daring attempt to reproduce the workings of the unconscious mind and has influenced artists of the surrealist and absurd school of theater. Strindberg stated in his preface that in this work "time and space do not exist"; thus it is the association of ideas that lends the work coherence. Whether the Dreamer is the Daughter or Strindberg himself is a matter of debate among critics, but most commentators see this work as the hallmark of his expressionistic era.

The Ghost Sonata (drama, 1908)

This is the most famous of what Strindberg called his "Chamber Plays," written in his expressionist style and reflecting the world of dreams. The work takes its form from the sonata, and like that musical type it is composed of three movements, unified by the restatement of major motifs. In the first part, the **Student Arkenholtz** meets the **Old Man Jacob Hummel** outside a beautiful home. When we meet the inhabitants of the house, we learn that the lovely facade masks a suffocating atmosphere of death, decay, and deceit. Hummel, who seems to know everything about the house and its inhabitants, arranges for Arkenholtz to meet **Adele,** the lovely daughter of the **Colonel,** the owner of the house.

In the second section, Hummel is unmasked and confronted with his true nature at a "ghost supper." In attendance are the Colonel, whom Hummel has revealed to be neither a colonel nor a member of the nobility, and the **Mummy,** the Colonel's wife and Hummel's former lover, by whom she had Adele. It is the Mummy who challenges Hummel, outlining his crimes. He had stolen her soul, as he plans to do with the Student; he had "murdered" the **Consul,** "strangling" him with debts; he is responsible for the death of the **Milkmaid,** who had seen him commit a crime, and who haunts him as a specter. Vanquished by this presentation of his crimes, Hummel takes the rope offered him by the Mummy and hangs himself.

In the final section, Arkenholtz and Adele talk. It is obvious that she is dying, sickened by the atmosphere of "crime and secrets and guilt." We are introduced to the **Cook,** who is like a vampire, draining the life from the inhabitants of the house. Vampirism is a major motif in the play, used to describe the cycle of guilt and suffering that saps life from the characters. In the conclusion, the Student relates the story of his father, who had also hosted a dinner like the one which exposed Hummel, in which he revealed the truth about all present. For his efforts, he was confined to an asylum where he died. He tells the story to Adele as she dies, seeing in her death her release from the "world of illusion, guilt, suffering, and death."

The work is noted for its nightmarish, surrealitic atmosphere, incorporating elements of the grotesque and fantastic. It is considered a major, innovative work of twentieth-century theater, unrelenting in its exposure of the shameful secrets of life.

FURTHER READING

Bentley, Eric. "August Strindberg." In *The Playwright as Thinker: A Study of Drama in Modern Times,* pp. 193-215. London: Reynal & Hitchcock, 1946.

Brustein, Robert. "August Strindberg." In *The Theatre of Revolt: An Approach to the Modern Drama,* pp. 87-134. Boston: Little, Brown, 1964.

Contemporary Authors, Vol. 104. Detroit: Gale Research Co.

Gilman, Richard. "Strindberg." In *The Making of Modern Drama: A Study of Büchner, Ibsen, Strindberg, Chekhov, Pirandello, Brecht, Beckett, Handke,* pp. 83-115. New York: Farrar, Straus, 1974.

Johnson, Walter. *August Strindberg.* Boston: Twayne, 1976.

Krutch, Joseph Wood. "Strindberg and the Irreconcilable Conflict." In *"Modernism" in Modern Drama: A Definition and an Estimate,* pp. 23-42. Ithaca: Cornell University Press, 1953.

Lamm, Martin. *August Strindberg,* edited and translated by Henry G. Carlson. New York: Benjamin Blom, 1971.

Lucas, F. L. "Strindberg." In *The Drama of Ibsen and Strindberg,* pp. 303-463. New York: Macmillan, 1962.

Mortensen, Brita M. E. and Brian W. Downs. *Strindberg: An Introduction to His Life and Work.* Cambridge: Cambridge at the University Press, 1949.

Nicoll, Allardyce. "Strindberg and the Play of the Subconscious." In *World Drama: From Aeschylus to Anouilh,* pp. 547-63. New York: Harcourt Brace & World, 1950.

Reinert, Otto, ed. *Strindberg: A Collection of Critical Essays.* Englewood Cliffs: Prentice-Hall, 1971.

Steene, Birgitta. *The Greatest Fire: A Study of August Strindberg.* Carbondale: Southern Illinois University Press, 1973.

Twentieth-Century Literary Criticism, Vols. 1, 8, 21. Detroit: Gale Research Co.

Williams, Raymond. "A Generation of Masters." In *Drama: From Ibsen to Brecht,* pp. 33-114. London: Chatto & Windus, 1968.

William Styron
1925-

American novelist.

Lie Down in Darkness (novel, 1951)

The novel is set in Port Warwick, Virginia, and recounts the life and death of **Peyton Loftis.** The novel's action takes place on the day of her funeral, and Styron uses flashbacks to tell the story of Peyton's unhappy life and tragic death. She is one of Styron's outsiders, a character type that recurs throughout his fiction. She is an isolated figure, a victim of a tragic family situation. Her father, **Milton,** is a portrait of a ruined life. Once a vital young man with a promising legal career, he allowed his practice to taper off as he began to drink heavily, living off the money his wife, **Helen,** had received as an inheritance. The novel is also a study in the falseness of appearances: their's had seemed a ''perfect match,'' she the daughter of a military man, he a bright young attorney; yet their marriage is empty and full of suppressed hatred.

As Helen and Milton become increasingly estranged, he devotes himself to Peyton, whom he spoils and smothers with affection, a love that is tinged with incestuous desires. Peyton, a beautiful and intelligent young woman, is juxtaposed to her crippled sister **Maudie,** who has become the center of her mother's affections. Peyton rebels against her family, but finds she cannot escape the legacy of self-hatred and self-destruction. Styron records her efforts to distance herself from their negative influence, ending in her marriage to a Jewish artist and a life in New York City. Peyton's final interior monologue, which culminates in her suicide, reveals a tortured psyche. Her confrontation with herself—the realization of her mother's hatred and jealousy of her, as well as her father's incestuous affection—overpowers her, and she throws herself out of a window.

Styron relates Peyton's story as one of tragic inevitability: she and all the characters of the novel are driven by circumstances they cannot control. She is a doomed character, as helpless as her parents to undo the damage of the past and create a new life. Styron presents his narrative through shifting points of view and time sequence.

The Confessions of Nat Turner (novel, 1967)

Nat Turner, the famous leader of the most successful slave rebellion in the United States, is the protagonist of Styron's Pulitzer Prize winning novel. Set in Southampton, Virginia, in the early 1800s, the novel is Styron's fictional interpretation of the life of Nat Turner and an examination of slavery. Based on Turner's own narrative as well as Styron's elaboration, the novel is given in the first person. The story opens after the rebellion has taken place; Nat has been captured, tried, and convicted and now awaits execution. As the narrative moves backwards in time, he gives us, in his own words, the story of his youth. As a young slave on the Turner plantation, his precocious intelligence drew the attention of his master. He was educated and taught a trade by the family and promised his freedom at the age of majority. He is depicted by Styron as an isolated figure, and like Peyton Loftis of *Lie Down in Darkness,* he is an outsider. Separated from blacks by the privilege of his position within a white family, he is equally alienated from the white world by the institution of slavery. He is also isolated sexually, for he dreams of white women and is unable to relate to black ones.

Turner is sold to **Reverend Epps,** a man of great cruelty who works Nat like an animal and sells him again. Knowing that his freedom is in his own hands and inflamed by revenge, Nat plots his rebellion. One of Styron's themes in this novel is Nat's relationship with God, particularly the God depicted in the Old Testament. Thus, the vengeful God of Ezekiel comes to him in a dream, challenging him to lead the revolt. As the rebellion gains credence among the slaves, Nat must also grapple with his love for **Margaret Whitehead,** the white woman he loves and who loves him. Their relationship is marked by the tortured ambivalence that colors Nat's character: she is white, and therefore a beloved object, yet she is also representative of the despised enemy and oppressor of blacks. Also, because she excites him sexually, his feelings are a confusion of desire and revulsion. He murders her, but in the novel's conclusion she appears to him, forgiving him and offering the redemptive message of the New Testament. It is with this feeling of solace that Turner goes to his death.

When the novel first appeared, it was a great financial and critical success, but later became the center of a raging controversy, with many black commentators claiming that Styron was a racist and that his plan to enter the consciousness of a black man was presumptuous. In dealing with the theme of slavery, Styron made a historical correlation that he further developed in *Sophie's Choice:* he portrays the slaves as more acquiescent than moved to revolution, comparing them to the Jews in the Nazi death camps, who have also been brutalized and dehumanized by their enslavement. This has proved to be a point of contention for critics of Styron's last two novels.

Sophie's Choice (novel, 1979)

The novel has a variety of settings, and begins in Brooklyn, New York, where **Stingo,** the first-person narrator, has come to write a book. The novel's main action takes place in the late 1940s, and is given in flashback from the perspective of Stingo as a mature man and successful writer, a character who shares much in common with his creator in background, education, and even of books published. Stingo reflects on his past and particularly on his friendship with **Nathan Landau** and **Sophie Zawistowska.** Styron's narrative purposes are two-fold in this novel, for he juxtaposes the story of the naive Stingo coming of age to the horrifying life story of Sophie as she reveals it to the young narrator.

Nathan and Sophie are Stingo's neighbors in a Jewish section of Brooklyn where they are lodgers in a boarding house. Nathan, a Jewish intellectual, is brilliant, funny, obsessive, and mad. Sophie, a Polish-Catholic and a survivor of Auschwitz, is his lover and a woman obsessed with the guilt of her past. Stingo is irresistibly drawn to them, particularly to Sophie, who embodies his erotic longings. Despite the seriousness of his themes, Styron treats Stingo's preoccupation with sex and losing his virginity with humor throughout the novel. Through Nathan, Sophie, and their friends, Stingo enters a world of sophistication and intellect unlike anything he has ever known, and he revels in the new atmosphere. Yet it is Sophie and her story that most concern him. Gradually she reconstructs her tragic history for him, told in her own words or through the narrator's voice. When the truth is revealed, and Sophie's "choice" is divulged, the horror is overwhelming. Brought to Auschwitz with her two children, she is forced by a sadistic Nazi officer to choose which of them would survive and which would be exterminated. The section of the novel that recounts her ordeal in the concentration camp is a grotesque, nightmarish tale of terror and forms a major section of the work.

Sophie is forced to choose again, this time between Nathan and Stingo at the close of the novel. Nathan's obsessions and violence have driven Sophie away, and she leaves him to go to the South with Stingo. She and Stingo make love, after which she returns to Nathan, knowing she is going to her death.

In his examination of the Holocaust, Styron illuminates the horrors of the past in the personal tragedy of a Polish-Catholic, rather than a Jew, and apprehended through the mind of an innocent, the virginal Stingo. Thus he explores the themes of evil and guilt as they pertain to all peoples confronted by horror and inhumanity. Through Stingo, Styron draws parallels between the Nazi atrocities and the American institution of slavery, a theme that has made the work controversial. Yet it is Styron's most popular and critically successful novel to date.

FURTHER READING

Alter, Robert. "Styron's Stingo." *Saturday Review* 6, No. 14 (7 July 1979): 42-3.

Clark, John H., ed. *William Styron's Nat Turner: Ten Black Writers Respond.* Boston: Beacon, 1968.

Contemporary Authors, Vols. 5-8, rev. ed.; *Contemporary Authors New Revision Series,* Vol. 6. Detroit: Gale Research Co.

Contemporary Literary Criticism, Vols. 1, 3, 5, 11, 15. Detroit: Gale Research Co.

Dictionary of Literary Biography, Vol. 2; *Dictionary of Literary Biography Yearbook: 1980.* Detroit: Gale Research Co.

Friedman, Melvin J. *William Styron.* Bowling Green: Bowling Green University Press, 1974.

Friedman, Melvin J. and Irving Malin, eds. *William Styron's "The Confessions of Nat Turner"—A Critical Handbook.* Belmont: Wadsworth, 1970.

Gardner, John. "A Novel of Evil." *The New York Times Book Review* (27 May 1979): 1, 16-17.

Morris, Robert K. and Irving Malin, eds. *The Achievement of William Styron.* Athens: University of Georgia Press, 1975.

Pearce, Richard. *William Styron.* Minneapolis: University of Minnesota Press, 1971.

Ratner, Marc L. *William Styron.* Boston: Twayne, 1972.

Rosenfeld, Alvin H. "The Holocaust According to William Styron." *Midstream* 25, No. 10 (December 1979): 43-9.

John Millington Synge
1871-1909

Irish dramatist.

Riders to the Sea (drama, 1904)

This one-act play is set on an island off the western coast of Ireland and is considered Synge's finest achievement in tragedy. The drama relates the story of **Maurya,** a woman who has lost a husband and five sons to the sea. As the play begins, we learn that her sixth and last son, **Bartley,** is preparing to go to sea as well, to sell livestock on a neighboring island, while Maurya, with her daughters **Cathleen** and **Nora,** are waiting to hear if the body of the fifth son has washed up on shore. Bartley departs on his horse, with another horse tied behind. Maurya goes to bid him goodbye, but is overcome with a vision: she sees her dead son **Michael** on the back of the second horse. She recounts the story of her losses in a bleak and mournful tone, for she is sure that her last son, too, will perish. Old women appear in Maurya's home, crossing themselves and mourning; neighbors then bring in the body of Bartley, killed when his horse kicked him into the sea and he drowned. The conclusion portrays Maurya resigned to the power and treachery of the sea, which can take nothing further from her.

The play is praised for its economy and power and has been likened in its depth and tragic proportions to Greek tragedy. Mythical and supernatural elements, such as Maurya's vision and Michael's ghost, add to the ominous, sorrowful tone of the play. The work is further noted for its superb structure and Synge's fine ear for dialect.

The Playboy of the Western World (drama, 1907)

This comedy, considered Synge's masterpiece, is set in County Mayo, Ireland. **Pegeen Mike (Margaret Flaherty),** the daughter of **Michael Flaherty,** the owner of a public house, is engaged to marry **Shawn Keogh,** her cousin and a young farmer whose timidity is in vivid contrast to Pegeen's lively exuberance. **Christopher Mahon,** a stranger, enters the pub and mesmerizes the company with the tale that he has killed his father and is on the run. Michael, impressed with his story, offers Christy the job of pot-boy. Michael leaves Christy alone with Pegeen, and he continues to entrance her with tales of his exploits. We learn that Christy is anything but a murderer, for it is only in his imagination that he is the brave, daring hero Pegeen and her father's comrades think he is. Yet here, where he is unknown, he can create the persona he wishes and win the girl of his dreams. When the **Widow Quin** arrives, she and Pegeen seem to vie for the attentions of the new town hero, and even Shawn tries to buy off Christy, offering him clothes and a ticket to leave.

As if out of the grave, **Old Mahon,** Christy's father, appears, looking for his son, whom he describes as a lazy good-for-nothing to the Widow Quin. But Christy, contrary to his nature as pictured by his father, wins all the games and horse races in town, distinguishing himself as the "Playboy of the Western World." In a long scene between Christy and Pegeen in which he asks her to marry him, he even becomes a bit of a poet, describing with lyrical beauty their future together. Old Mahon, whom the Widow Quin had sent out of town, returns and berates his son. Pegeen, seeing her lover transformed into a liar, scorns him. Enraged that Pegeen doesn't want him, Christy turns on his father and seemingly kills him. The riotous comedy of the play dissipates at this point, and the drama darkens. Michael and his comrades prepare to hang Christy for the murder of his father, and Pegeen, too, takes part in his humiliation. But Old Mahon is not dead, and in the conclusion he and Christy leave town together, the son now in the role of the master, his father a "heathen slave," and Pegeen mourning what she has lost, "the only Playboy of the Western World."

The play is noted for its rich comic texture and vivid characterization. Synge's triumph in drama was his believable depictions of peasant characters as revealed in their expressive speech. He often focussed on the necessity of illusion in the lives of his characters, as he does with Christy in *Playboy of the Western World.*

Deirdre of the Sorrows (drama, 1910)

The play is set in the ancient kingdom of Ireland and represents a departure for Synge, for the characters and story are based on Celtic myth. As the play opens, we see **Deirdre,** a young woman of legendary beauty and grace who has been bred from birth to be the wife of old **Conchubor,** King of Ulster, and to be queen. Yet she rejects this role, and against the protestations of her nurse, **Lavarcham,** runs away with **Naisi,** a brave young man, who takes her to the north, where they live in the forests with his brothers. Deirdre risks all this knowing that she is living under a curse, for it is foretold that she would bring "destruction on the world" and that she was born to be the "queen of sorrows." Despite this burden, she and Naisi are happy in their sylvan home for seven years, when a messenger comes from Conchubor bidding them to return to Emain, where he rules. Knowing they are going to their death, Deirdre, Naisi, and his brothers go to meet Conchubor. The old king has Naisi and his brothers killed, and Deirdre, out of love and sorrow, takes her own life.

Within the context of an ancient myth, Synge developed human, believable characters, depicted with realism and compassion. One of his recurring themes was the loneliness and decrepitude of old age, and his young hero and heroine talk about the fear of aging and death, as well as the anxiety of growing weary of each other. Even Conchubor stirs our pity as he says that "there's one sorrow has no end surely—that's being old and lonesome." Thus, Deirdre and Naisi die in their youth, remaining young forever.

Deirdre of the Sorrows is widely admired for its lyric intensity, tragic mood, and fine handling of dialogue. Although the play was finished and revised by Synge before his death, it was never amended to his satisfaction, and is therefore considered incomplete. This last play indicates a new approach to drama in setting, characterization, and language, and some critics speculate that had Synge lived to complete it, it would have been his masterpiece.

FURTHER READING

Bourgeois, Maurice. *John Millington Synge and the Irish Theatre*. London: Constable, 1913.

Contemporary Authors, Vol. 104. Detroit: Gale Research Co.

Corkery, Daniel. *Synge and Anglo-Irish Literature*. London: Mercier, 1931.

Dictionary of Literary Biography, Vols. 10, 19. Detroit: Gale Research Co.

Gerstenberger, Donna. *John Millington Synge*. Boston: Twayne, 1964.

Grene, Nicholas. *Synge: A Critical Study of the Plays*. London: Macmillan, 1975.

Howe, P. P. *J. M. Synge: A Critical Study*. London: Martin Secker, 1912.

Maclean, Hugh N. ''The Hero as Playboy.'' *The University of Kansas City Review* 21, No. 1 (Autumn 1954): 9-19.

O'Casey, Sean. ''John Millington Synge.'' In *Blasts and Benedictions: Articles and Stories,* pp. 35-41. London: St. Martin's Press, 1967.

Price, Alan. *Synge and Anglo-Irish Drama*. London: Methuen, 1961.

Skelton, Robin. *The Writings of J. M. Synge*. London: Thames & Hudson, 1971.

Twentieth-Century Literary Criticism, Vol. 6. Detroit: Gale Research Co.

Paul Theroux

1941-

American novelist, essayist, and critic.

The Mosquito Coast (novel, 1981)

Set in the jungles of Honduras, the novel relates the journey of **Allie Fox,** a disgruntled inventor who moves his family from their Massachusetts home in the pursuit of a simpler, happier life. The novel is narrated by Fox's fourteen-year-old son, **Charlie,** and it is through his eyes that we see Allie, an idealist, perfectionist, and mad genius, who destroys himself and almost ruins his family in his quest.

Allie hates the immoral, materialistic culture of contemporary America—''a dope-taking, door-locking, ulcerated danger zone of rabid scavengers and criminal millionaires and moral sneaks.'' Belligerent and bullying, he is an authority on everything, and his enormous will and ego dominate his family. His wife, only referred to as **Mother** in the novel, is a faceless, nameless embodiment of a helpmate. Charlie's younger brother, **Jerry,** shows some signs of rebelliousness, but is also cowed by his father. The relationship between Charlie and Allie forms the central tension of the novel, as the young man tries to come to grips with the meaning of his father's life and quest.

When they reach Honduras, Allie begins working on his final invention, an ice maker that he believes will transform the jungle. But the machine is a failure, and as it disintegrates it releases noxious gasses into the air. Allie slowly loses his hold on reality, and as his madness grows, the family is helpless. Charlie, once terrified of his father's bullying, is now confronted with a man whose sanity is ebbing away. In the closing section, as the family is slowly starving, Allie dies and is attacked by vultures. The family is rescued and is making its journey homeward as the novel ends, with Charlie sorting out his father's life and legacy, acknowledging the despair and the self-destruction that drove him to his end.

Allie Fox is considered Theroux's finest literary character and the novel is noted for its evocative, realistic description. It reflects the author's keen attention to detail in natural description, honed after years as a writer of well-received travel books, and his insight into the questing American spirit.

FURTHER READING

Busch, Frederick. "Dr. Faustus in the Jungle." *Book World—The Washington Post* (14 February 1982): 1-2.

Contemporary Authors, Vols. 33-36, rev. ed.; *Contemporary Authors New Revision Series,* Vol. 20. Detroit: Gale Research Co.

Contemporary Literary Criticism, Vols. 5, 8, 11, 15, 28, 46. Detroit: Gale Research Co.

Dictionary of Literary Biography, Vol. 2. Detroit: Gale Research Co.

Raban, Jonathan. "Theroux's Wonderful, Bottomless Novel." *Saturday Review* 9, No. 2 (February 1982): 55-6.

Towers, Robert. "Moby-Dad." *The New York Review of Books* 29, No. 6 (15 April 1982): 37.

James Thurber
1894-1961
American short story writer, dramatist, and essayist

"The Secret Life of Walter Mitty" (short story, 1939)

"The Secret Life of Walter Mitty" is the best known of Thurber's short stories. Today **Walter Mitty** is synonymous with a specific type of person: a day-dreamer who escapes from reality into fantasy. Thurber's story is the tale of Walter Mitty, an average man who finds everyday life intolerable. His wife bullies him, his car runs poorly, and he does not excel at anything, but he finds solace in his reveries, where he can be a movie star or a comic-book hero. By the story's end, Mitty is victimized by his dreams; he has driving accidents, and his relationship with others worsens, but he pays no attention.

In "The Secret Life of Walter Mitty" Thurber points to some of his own dilemmas. Thurber, too, did not relate well to women, and he did not relish the mundane aspects of middle class existence. Neither Thurber nor Mitty were the type to attract attention by their appearances, so both men hid in the glamorous alter ego of fantasy characters. While this story is undeniably amusing, it also displays a dark side that often recurs in Thurber's work. Mitty is stifled by his lot in life, and turns to dreams because his pessimism cannot allow for a happy existence in the real world.

"The Catbird Seat" (short story, 1961)

One of Thurber's bleakest stories, "The Catbird Seat" chronicles the existence of **Edwin Martin,** a subservient, innocuous man who works for a brash, crude woman named **Ulgine Barrow.** Tired of her bullying behavior, Martin engenders a scheme to rid the world of Ulgine. In Martin's words, he wanted her "rubbed out," which he thought merely suggested the correction of an error. He begins to act completely out of character in their office, taunting and tormenting Barrow. When she threatens to fire Martin, no one believes her accusations, and she is the one who is forced to leave. Martin sits silently after Barrow is taken away, basking in his ability to change the intolerable.

"The Catbird Seat" is titled thusly because it refers to Martin's position. He is truly in "the catbird seat": a perfect place where he is untouchable. This story also emphasizes Thurber's recurrent theme of the unpleasant relationships between men and women. Barrow's name is intentionally repellent: "Ulgine" sounds like ugly, and "Barrow" connotes a barrel. Thurber's stories occasionally dealt with the fantasy of murder, and he excelled at presenting a horrifying situation in everyday terms. His prose style is subtle and spare, but there is an undertone of psychotic behavior that often seems at odds with his remote, controlled voice.

FURTHER READING

Black, Stephen A. *James Thurber: His Masquerades*. The Hague: Mouton, 1970.

Contemporary Authors, Vols. 73-76; *Contemporary Authors New Revision Series*, Vol. 17. Detroit: Gale Research Co.

Contemporary Literary Criticism, Vols. 5, 11, 25. Detroit: Gale Research Co.

Cowley, Malcolm. "James Thurber's Dream Book." *The New Republic* 112, No. 11 (12 March 1945): 362-63.

Dictionary of Literary Biography, Vols. 4, 11, 22. Detroit: Gale Research Co.

Holmes, Charles S. *The Clocks of Columbus: The Literary Career of James Thurber*. New York: Atheneum, 1972.

Lindner, Carl M. "Thurber's Walter Mitty: The Underground Hero." *The Georgia Review* 38, No. 2 (Summer 1974): 283-89.

Morsberger, Robert E. *James Thurber*. Boston: Twayne, 1964.

Short Story Criticism, Vol. 1. Detroit: Gale Research Co.

Tobias, Richard C. *The Art of James Thurber*. Athens: Ohio University Press, 1970.

J. R. R. Tolkien
1892-1973

English novelist, short story writer, poet, and essayist.

The Hobbit (novel, 1937)

Bilbo Baggins and **Gandalf the Grey** are the principal characters in the novel that prefaced Tolkien's great work of fantasy, *The Lord of the Rings*. In this novel he sets the stage for his monumental trilogy, introducing characters and themes that will continue in his next three novels.

As the novel begins, we are introduced to the world of Middle-earth and its denizens, a land populated by a variety of types: wizards, elves, dwarves, dragons, men, and most particularly hobbits. As illustrated in the character of Bilbo, hobbits are comfort-loving creatures, fond of eating, drinking, smoking, and gardening. Bilbo is an unlikely hero for a tale of adventure, yet Tolkien shows how these little creatures, though small in stature, are capable of great heroism and acts of selflessness, and their innate goodness and steadfast nature are stressed throughout the novels.

Bilbo is drawn from his comfortable home in the Shire by Gandalf the Grey, a wizard, who arrives at his home to talk him into accompanying him and a group of dwarves on a quest for a ring held by a dragon. Bilbo, unaccustomed to the world of conflict, is nonetheless lured into joining the group and journeys with them to Wilderland, where he confronts the terrible dragon, Smaug. The dragon is killed by a member of the party, and Bilbo recovers the lost ring. This same ring saves him during a battle between the gold-thirsty goblins and dwarves, for the ring makes the bearer invisible. Yet it has other, more sinister powers, as Tolkien explains in the later novels. Bilbo's brief insight into its horrible powers is given by the creature **Gollum,** from whom he takes the ring. Gollum is the first of several characters obsessed and ultimately vanquished by the ring's terrible legacy. In the novel's conclusion, Bilbo returns to the Shire, having prepared the way for the trilogy.

"The Lord of the Rings": *The Fellowship of the Ring* (novel, 1954); *The Two Towers* (novel, 1955); *The Return of the King* (novel, 1956)

Like *The Hobbit* which preceded it, the trilogy is set in Middle-earth, at the end of the Third Age. The depth and breadth of Tolkien's imaginary kingdom was only hinted at in *The Hobbit,* for in this series of novels he reveals a remarkably complete fictional world, with, in the words of C.S. Lewis, "its own theology, myths, geography, history, paleography, languages, and orders of beings." It is written in the tradition of the heroic quest, and relates a timeless story of the struggle of good and evil.

The first part of the trilogy, *The Fellowship of the Ring,* recounts **Gandalf the Grey**'s discovery that **Frodo,** the nephew of **Bilbo Baggins,** was in possession of the One Ring, forged in evil by **Lord Sauron** of Mordor, and sought by him and his sinister minions. Gandalf, accompanied by the hobbits Frodo, his servant **Sam Gamgee, Merry,** and **Pippin** leave the comfort of the Shire and journey to Rivendell. At the Council of Elrond, members representing all the peoples of Middle-earth—including men, hobbits, elves, and dwarves—decide that the ring must be destroyed. The truly evil nature of the ring is revealed, for although it endows its wearer with incredible powers, it also corrupts the owner in the ways of evil. The Fellowship of the Ring is formed, with representatives of the different inhabitants of Middle-earth, and Frodo is named Ring-bearer. Thus they begin their journey to the land of Mordor, where Lord Sauron reigns, to destroy the ring in the fires in which it was formed.

During their imperiled quest, Gandalf battles an evil creature and disappears. Thereupon, **Aragorn,** representative of men and revealed to be of illustrious heritage, leads the group. But they are set upon by further disaster, and are separated. The conclusion of the first volume reveals the fellowship torn apart.

In *The Two Towers,* Merry and Pippin, captured by evil orcs, are pursued by Aragorn and the remains of the fellowship. But they have fled their captors and entered the forest of Fangorn, where they meet **Tree-beard** the Ent, certainly one of Tolkien's most beloved and memorable creations. He and the tree-folk ready themselves for their march on Isengard, stronghold of **Saruman,** a wizard who has gone over to the Dark Lord. Aragorn, searching for the hobbits, encounters Gandalf, now transformed into the White Rider. They go to Isengard, where Saruman is held by the Ents. Gandalf overpowers Saruman and breaks his staff. But Pippin comes into possession of a seeing stone, whose seductive powers enchant him, revealing their location to Sauron.

Frodo and Sam continue their quest to Mordor. **Gollum** has found them, but, seemingly subdued by Frodo, leads them through treacherous lands, introducing them to a secret path. There he delivers them into the hands of a hideous spider monster, **Shelob,** who mortally wounds Frodo. Sam takes the ring and continues the quest, but, slipping it on to avoid capture by orcs, he learns that Frodo is not dead, and he tries to save his master, now a prisoner of Sauron. As this action takes place, Sauron has marshalled his forces to begin the War of the Ring, the war that will end the Third Age of Middle-earth.

In *The Return of the King* Frodo and Sam find each other and continue their journey, encountering the ghastly Dead Marshes, a landscape of horror and catastrophe, reflecting the full extent of Sauron's evil. To see the waste that Sauron would wreak should he prove victorious spurs Frodo on in his quest. In a cataclysmic battle, he struggles with Gollum, who plunges into the flames with the ring in his grasp. Then Frodo and Sam witness the destruction of Mordor, as the country is ravaged in a scene of apocalyptic ruin and Sauron disappears into the sky.

Their quest complete, the hobbits return home to find their land ravaged by intruders under the influence of Saruman. They fight for and regain their country, but all know that the end of Sauron's reign also spells the end of the Third Age. Now the Age of Man, our own age, has begun, and Frodo, Gandalf, and others set off across the sea, leaving the world for men.

The work is considered a tour de force, revealing Tolkien's vast knowledge of myth, language, and folklore. Although some consider the work an allegory of the troubled modern world, Tolkien denied that interpretation. It is, however, an avowedly Christian work, and Frodo is a Christ-figure, destined to sacrifice and suffer in his battle against the forces of evil. Frodo, like Bilbo before him, is an unlikely and reluctant hero. Tolkien focuses on the inherent bravery of the hobbits; unchallenged in their daily lives in the Shire, they display courage that surprises their comrades, but especially their enemies. Sauron cannot understand how Frodo can muster the courage to continue his quest and to avoid the seductive powers of the ring, and his underestimating of the hobbit leads to his defeat. "The Lord of the Rings" is a work that has enchanted a generation of readers and in its broad appeal has transcended the category of fantasy. It is considered Tolkien's masterpiece and a major work of twentieth-century fiction.

FURTHER READING

Auden, W. H. "A World Imaginary, But Real." *Encounter* (November 1954): 59-60, 62.

Contemporary Authors, Vols. 17-18, 45-48; *Contemporary Authors Permanent Series,* Vol. 2. Detroit: Gale Research Co.

Contemporary Literary Criticism, Vols. 1, 2, 3, 8, 12, 38. Detroit: Gale Research Co.

Crabbe, Katharyn F. *J. R. R. Tolkien.* New York: Ungar, 1981.

Dictionary of Literary Biography, Vol. 15. Detroit: Gale Research Co.

Helms, Randel. *Tolkien's World.* Boston: Houghton Mifflin, 1974.

Lewis, C. S. "The Gods Return to Earth." *Time and Tide* (14 August 1954): 1082-83.

Lobdell, Jared, ed. *A Tolkien Compass.* La Salle: Open Court, 1975.

Manlove, C. N. "J. R. R. Tolkien (1892-1973) and *The Lord of the Rings.*" In *Modern Fantasy: Five Studies,* pp. 152-206. Cambridge: Cambridge University Press, 1975.

Leo Tolstoy
1828-1910

Russian novelist, short story writer, essayist, and critic.

War and Peace (novel, 1869)

Set in Russia in the years 1803-1813, Tolstoy's epic masterpiece is considered one of the greatest works of world literature and a triumph of realistic fiction. The novel works on many levels, focussing primarily on a group of aristocratic families but also offering a cross-section of Russian society as Tolstoy recounts the national crisis that culminated in the Napoleonic War between Russia and France. The work reflects Tolstoy's historical and religious beliefs: that everything in life is preordained and that one must submit to the inevitable forces of nature and the will of God. He carefully divided his characters between those who eventually submit to the natural processes that govern life and those who embrace the artificial, unnatural, and destructive powers as represented by the sophistication of society or the life devoted to reason.

The heroes of the novel, those that embody the natural in life, are **Pierre Bezuhov, Prince Andrei Bolkonsky, Princess Maria Bolkonskaya, Natasha Rostova,** and **Nicholas Rostov.** Each of these characters undergoes a pilgrimage and experiences suffering, through which they come to understand life and to know their place in it. Each has weaknesses and virtues, which lead them to crises, maturity, and understanding. The Rostov family, members of the aristocracy, represent a fundamental center of the novel. Nicholas and Natasha do not question the meaning of life, but rejoice in it. They represent the uninhibited, spontaneous joy in living that Tolstoy identifies with the natural life force. Natasha, loved by all, becomes spoiled and capricious. She is guilty of egocentricity and too much self-confidence. Although she is engaged to Andrei, she becomes bored during his absence and is easily taken in by the flattery of **Anatole Kuragin,** a reckless rake who nearly ruins her when he coaxes her into eloping with him. Andrei breaks their engagement and Natasha is humiliated. Nicholas is an irresponsible young man who loves the military, in whose conformity and authority he finds an escape from his true responsibilities to family and love.

Both Andrei and Maria have suffered from their father's cruel, uncompromising nature: he refuses to allow Maria to leave him to marry and have a life of her own. She suffers from an excess of spirituality and a sense of self-sacrifice. Andrei is an intellectual, with faith only in ideals and abstractions. He wishes to fit life into an ideal mold rather than letting himself be molded by life.

Pierre is illegitimate, and Tolstoy stresses throughout the novel the importance of family and belonging. He is drawn to the sensuality and dissipation of the Kuragins, both Anatole and his sister **Helene Kuragina.** Pierre marries Helene, who in her sexual promiscuity both before and after marriage represents the perversion of family, love, and life.

Each of the characters' experiences of war challenges and clarifies their understanding of life. Andrei is seriously wounded, and Natasha goes to him and devotes herself to his care during the last days of his life, humbled before God and happy in her submission to His will. Like all the primary characters, Andrei is forced into the realization of his own impotence and insignificance; he forgives Natasha and dies in peace.

Pierre, in an act of supreme egocentricity, plans to kill Napoleon and become the savior of Europe. He is captured by French soldiers and witnesses the terrible human capacity for cruelty. He is nearly executed, and his nearness to death almost destroys him. Yet while in captivity, he meets **Platon Karatayev,** a peasant who teaches him the true meaning of love and self-sacrifice. Platon is the eternal personification of simplicity and truth and submits willingly to the will of God and the natural flow of life.

During the retreat of the Russian army, Nicholas saves Maria from her peasants, who are in rebellion. Her father now dead, Maria is drawn to life and love through Nicholas. Natasha, whose life had seemed meaningless after Andrei's death, is regenerated through her emerging love for Pierre.

Napoleon, the villain who was chosen to fulfill a terrible destiny, is defeated, and Tolstoy ends his main narrative on a note of hope and the promise of regeneration with the emphasis on love, family, and God. The novel concludes with two epilogues which continue the stories of the individual characters, telling of the marriages and lives of Natasha and Pierre and of Nicholas and Maria, and also providing an exposition of Tolstoy's theory of history.

In its size, scope, and moral purpose, *War and Peace* is considered one of the most important novels ever written. Its broad canvas encompasses hundreds of characters, each individually realized. The depth of insight into the psychological and moral makeup of his characters is rendered through the detail that gives significance to their emotional lives. Tolstoy's prose is praised for its transparency and plasticity, whether in the description of the inner workings of his characters' minds or the presentation of war. He realistically depicts the horrifying, sordid nature of conflict, yet also notes how it motivates heroism in men. Tolstoy sought to reveal the ultimate beauty and serenity of life lived under the sway of the forces of nature in this work, yet the reader need not embrace his philosophy to be awed by his consummate artistry and the profundity of his achievement.

Anna Karenina (novel, 1877)

In this work, set in Moscow, St. Petersburg, and the Russian countryside during the 1870s, Tolstoy presents two narrative lines in which he compares and contrasts the lives of **Anna Karenina** and **Constantine Dimitrievich Levin.** Anna's story is one of passion, adultery, and betrayal and ends in her tragic death; Levin, an embodiment of Tolstoy's philosophy and a distinctly autobiographical figure, represents the virtues of conjugal love, family, and devotion to the land. Together they form the story of what is considered Tolstoy's crowning achievement in the field of realistic fiction.

As the novel begins, we see Anna—beautiful, elegant, and charming—in the role of peacemaker for her brother, **Stephan Oblonsky.** He has committed yet another sexual indiscretion, and Anna seeks to reconcile him and his wife, **Dolly.** Thus the theme of infidelity, which will prove to precipitate Anna's tragedy, is introduced in a light, amusing fashion in the early chapters. The Oblonskys also function as the link between Anna and Levin, for Levin is deeply in love with Dolly's sister, **Kitty.** Although Levin has the blessing of Kitty's father, she is infatuated with **Count Alexey Kirilich Vronsky,** a dashing young officer. When Levin proposes to Kitty, she refuses him, and he retreats to his country estate. Vronsky and Anna meet in a railway station, a recurrent setting throughout the novel and one with highly symbolic implications. Anna has been travelling with Vronsky's mother, and now rushes home to her beloved son, **Sergei Alexeyich,** and to her husband, **Alexey Alexandrovich Karenin,** vaguely aware that the young officer is taken with her. Anna and Vronsky meet again and their mutual attraction is evident. Later, aboard a train, Vronsky declares his love for her, and after pursuing her for several months, finally takes her as his mistress. Desperately in love for the first time in her life, Anna risks and loses everything in her affair with Vronsky. Her husband, Karenin, is a cold, ambitious bureaucrat who thinks only of his career. Indeed, when he learns of Anna's affair with Vronsky he regards it only in light of how it will effect his station in the government. Vronsky, described as one of the "gilded youth" of society, is an idler used to a dissolute way of life; yet he is capable of love, and he adores Anna passionately.

The relationship of Anna and Vronsky is paralleled with that of Levin and Kitty, for two years after rejecting his proposal, Kitty agrees to marry him, and the two form a portrait of married happiness. Levin is a complex man, drawn to the peasants and their simple but pure way of life, but also tormented by doubts. He is a passionate, committed, and honest man, always questioning and searching for the meaning of life. He wrestles with his problems as a landowner, trying to give the peasants a greater share in the profits from the land they work. He is also tormented by the fear of death, as is evident in the vivid portrayal of his brother's death from tuberculosis and its profound impact on Levin.

Anna leaves Karenin, giving up her son, her social standing, and her security, and she and Vronsky live together. She bears his illegitimate child and almost dies in childbirth. Tolstoy minutely observes the decay of their love affair, as jealousy and monotony replace their former passion. In despair, Anna commits suicide by throwing herself before an oncoming train. As the novel ends, Vronsky, a broken man, is leaving the city to take part in the

Russo-Turkish war, and Levin is depicted devoted to his family, at peace on his land, yet a part of him still unresolved.

Tolstoy completed *Anna Karenina* shortly before the spiritual crisis that marked the turning point in his career, when he embraced a radical form of Christianity and devoted himself to works of didactic intent. Thus the optimism that marked *War and Peace* is replaced in this novel with a darkening, tragic tone. Once again Tolstoy revealed the inner life of his characters through his detailed descriptions and also made use of symbolism, as in the recurring motifs of the train station, the stories of infidelity that pass between the characters, and repeated dream imagery. Of central concern to the critics who discuss the novel is the ambiguity of Tolstoy's treatment of his heroine, for whether her death is to be read as a fitting punishment for her moral transgression remains unclear. As he had in *War and Peace,* Tolstoy here relentlessly satirizes the hypocrisy and sterility of society and condemns the narrow-mindedness of the social code that leads to Anna's destruction. Yet in his portrait of Levin and Kitty he shows how their love transcends the physical, egocentric level of Anna and Vronsky's affair and reflects an all-encompassing union of two souls. Some critics speculate that Anna, a character who has become one of the most beloved figures of fiction, beguiled her creator as well, and that is why she is drawn with such sympathy and beauty.

"The Death of Ivan Ilych" (short story, 1886)

Tolstoy's most famous short story is a product of his post-conversion phase, and as such it reflects his didactic religious beliefs, rendered in a story that, while not equal to *War and Peace* and *Anna Karenina,* is still a prominent work and an outstanding example of the content and intent of his later work. Tolstoy divided his later short fiction between the simple folk tales that he intended for the uneducated peasants and stories written for the enlightenment of the educated reader. It is in the latter group that this story falls. It is a narrative of conversion, and his protagonist, an average, rather vulgar and self-centered member of the wealthy, educated classes, learns in his confrontation with death the meaning of life, the errors of his past, and the value of love and self renunciation.

The story is related through an omniscient narrator who sees and comments on the actions of the characters. As it opens, we are in the law offices of the late **Ivan Ilych Golovin,** whose close friend **Peter Ivanovitch** reads his obituary notice to his colleagues. Tolstoy stresses how these men are much alike, and their shallowness and selfishness is revealed by the narrator, who relates how each man thinks only of how his position will be altered or enhanced by the death of Ivan Ilych. Tolstoy emphasizes the superficiality of these characters when he describes the funeral. The absence of genuine human emotion is particularly underscored when contrasted to the simple, humane actions of Ivan Ilych's beloved servant, **Gersami,** a poor, uneducated peasant who embodies the natural order and the acceptance of death as part of life. This section is followed by a long segment in which the life of Ivan Ilych is outlined. We learn that he had always been a man of little personal integrity or moral values. Governed by expediency, he makes his way in the legal profession and becomes a judge. He marries **Praskovya Fedorovna Golovina,** and their union is an unhappy, disappointing one. The later sections of the story reveal the final days of the protagonist. Tormented by physical pain, loneliness, and the meaninglessness of his suffering, he at last learns that his entire life had been wrong—"that he had not lived his life as he should have." With this realization, Ivan Ilych is granted the light, a vision of faith that lessens his pain, and in the hour of his passing, he realizes that he has no fear, because "there was no death."

Tolstoy stresses the universality of his protagonist, for in Ivan Ilych, he portrayed an average man, lost to greed and self-interest, who was a perfect vehicle for his moral tale directed at the educated classes. Although his polemical intent weakens the work's overall impact for some, the master storyteller is still in evidence in the attention to detail and the emphasis on the tension of the inner lives of his characters.

FURTHER READING

Baring, Maurice. "Tolstoy and Tourgeniev." In *Landmarks in Russian Literature*, pp. 77-115. London: Methuen, 1910.

Berlin, Isaiah. *The Hedgehod and the Fox: An Essay on Tolstoy's View of History.* New York: Simon & Schuster, 1953.

Cioran, E. M. "The Oldest Fear: Apropos of Tolstoy." In *The Fall into Time,* pp. 141-54. New York: Times Books/The New York Times Book Co., 1970.

Contemporary Authors, Vol. 104. Detroit: Gale Research Co.

Donnelly, John. "Death and Ivan Ilych." In *Language, Metaphysics, and Death,* edited by John Donnelly, pp. 116-30. New York: Fordham University Press, 1978.

Eikhenbaum, Boris. *Tolstoi in the Sixties.* Ann Arbor: Ardis, 1982.

Lavrin, Janko. *Tolstoy: An Approach.* New York: Macmillan, 1946.

Lubbock, Percy. *The Craft of Fiction,* pp. 236-50. New York: Viking, 1957.

Nabokov, Vladimir. "Leo Tolstoy." In *Lectures on Russian Literature,* pp. 137-244. New York: Harcourt Brace Jovanovich, 1981.

Schultze, Sydney. *The Structure of "Anna Karenina."* Ann Arbor: Ardis, 1982.

Steiner, George. *Tolstoy or Dostoevsky.* New York: Knopf, 1959.

Troyat, Henri. *Tolstoy.* New York: Doubleday, 1967.

Twentieth-Century Literary Criticism, Vols. 4, 11, 17, 28. Detroit: Gale Research Co.

Wasiolek, Edward. *Tolstoy's Major Fiction.* Chicago: The University of Chicago Press, 1978.

Wexelblatt, Robert. "The Higher Parody: Ivan Ilytch's Metamorphosis and the Death of Gregor Samsa." *The Massachusetts Review* 21, No. 3 (Fall 1980): 601-28.

Jean Toomer
1894-1967

American short story writer, poet, and essayist.

Cane (short stories, poetry, prose sketches; 1923)

This work is a collection of pieces that together provide a portrait of black American life. Toomer's title is taken from the arduous process by which cane is rendered into syrup; this becomes a metaphor for the hardship endured by black people as they confront racial hatred and subjugation. In the first section, composed of six stories and twelve poems, Toomer explores the lives of six Southern women. Through his depiction of **Karintha, Becky, Carma, Fern, Esther,** and **Louisa,** Toomer reveals how these characters are the victims of racial and sexual oppression. Karintha, an innocent, beautiful girl, becomes a prostitute; Becky, a white mother of two black sons, is ostracized by the community; Carma, accused by her husband of infidelity, drives him to madness; Fern, incapacitated by her passivity, allows herself to be used by men sexually; Esther, light enough to pass for white, becomes obsessed with a black preacher; and Louisa, a black woman with two lovers, one white and one black, witnesses the murder of one and the lynching of the other. This section is noted for its nature imagery, with the repeated symbol of the setting sun providing a motif for Toomer's recurrent theme of the death of the black folk culture in the South.

The second section moves to the North, taking place in Washington, D.C., and Chicago. Toomer here relates the stultifying effects of modern, urban industrial life on a generation of blacks who are severed from their cultural past. In one story, a black man who is consumed with the need to own a house, is shown to be a victim of false bourgeois values.

"Kabnis," the work's third and concluding section, is once again set in the South. **Ralph Kabnis,** an educated black man from the North, takes a job as a school teacher in a rural setting. He is a confused man who wants to understand and embrace the black folk culture that he sees ebbing away, but who must first learn the importance of history. Kabnis must understand and absorb the lesson of the black experience in America, especially the painful legacy of slavery and oppression that have defined the black way of life. But Kabnis's early idealism and quest for self-knowledge are replaced with alienation, dissipation, and despair in the face of the reality of his racial heritage. Other characters, such as **Lewis, Hanby,** and **Father John,** represent different elements of the black experience: Lewis, the Northerner who is able to accept his racial history; Hanby, who plays the role of Uncle Tom for whites and patrician among his own people; and Father John, a former slave who embodies the dignity and strength of a people undiminished by racial bigotry. *Cane* is considered a major work of early twentieth-century American literature and a masterpiece of the Harlem Renaissance of the 1920s, an era in which black literature, music, and art flourished.

FURTHER READING

Benson, Brian Joseph and Mabel Mayle Dillard. *Jean Toomer.* Boston: Twayne, 1980.

Contemporary Authors, Vols. 85-88. Detroit: Gale Research Co.

Contemporary Literary Criticism, Vols. 1, 4, 13, 22. Detroit: Gale Research Co.

Dictionary of Literary Biography, Vols. 45, 51. Detroit: Gale Research Co.

Duncan, Bowie. "Jean Toomer's *Cane:* A Modern Black Oracle." *CLA Journal* 15 (March 1972): 323-33.

Fischer, William C. "The Aggregate Man in Jean Toomer's *Cane.*" *Studies in the Novel* 3 (Summer 1971): 190-215.

Goede, William J. "Jean Toomer's Ralph Kabnis: Portrait of the Negro Artist as a Young Man." *Phylon* 30 (Spring 1969): 72-85.

Short Story Criticism, Vol. 1. Detroit: Gale Research Co.

Mark Twain
1835-1910
American novelist, short story writer, and essayist.

The Adventures of Tom Sawyer (novel, 1876)

The novel is set in the 1840s on the banks of the Mississippi. In the work, based on Twain's own boyhood experiences growing up in Missouri, he created two of the most enduring characters in American fiction, and in **Huckleberry Finn** found the character for his next and greatest work. The novel chronicles the adventures of young **Tom Sawyer,** whose quick intelligence and vivid imagination color all his pranks. In one of the most famous scenes from the book, Tom is forced to whitewash a fence by his **Aunt Polly,** his patient, affectionate, guardian. A natural leader and manipulator, Tom soon has all of his friends around him, who paint the fence for him, feeling privileged to do so. Tom's best friend, Huck Finn, is often his partner in adventure. Unlike Tom, Huck lives outside of society; his only family is his father, who is the town drunk, and Huck, free of the strictures of "civilized" society, smokes a pipe and sleeps in a corn crib. The envy of the other boys, he is an outcast in the grown-up world. **Becky Thatcher** is Tom's girlfriend and the object of his idealized romantic feelings. Among Tom's adventures, the story of **Injun Joe** is perhaps the most vibrant. A cruel and menacing figure, Injun Joe murders **Dr. Robinson,** a crime which Tom sees and relates to the authorities; he later becomes the object of Joe's revenge. The two meet in Joe's hideout in McDougal's cave, but Tom escapes and Joe meets a hideous end, starving to death. Later, while lost in the cave, Tom and Becky stumble on Joe's hidden gold, which Tom splits with Huck.

As the novel draws to a close, Tom urges Huck to go along with the **Widow Douglas** who wants to take Huck in and give him a little respectability. Twain presents Tom as a youthful rebel, who as he ages takes on the trappings of respectability himself; his are the adventures of a youth who becomes more respectable and conventional as he grows older. Huck is different, as Twain demonstrates in *The Adventures of Huckleberry Finn.*

The novel is considered a colorful evocation of boyhood, capturing the flavor of Twain's own young life along the Mississippi. For all its humor, however, there is a dark side to this pleasant representation of boyish adventures, for the presence of evil and death are evident in the Injun Joe subplot, an aspect of life and human nature that Twain developed in his next work.

The Adventures of Huckleberry Finn (novel, 1884)

Once again, Twain sets his work on the banks of the Mississippi in the 1850s. As the novel opens, **Huckleberry Finn** is kidnapped by his father, **Papp Finn,** the town drunk, who has learned that Huck has received half of the gold that **Tom Sawyer** had found in Injun Joe's cave. While they are hiding out, Papp gets drunk, and Huck seizes the opportunity to fake his own death and run off to Jackson's Island. There he meets **Jim,** a runaway slave, and the two set out on a journey down the river, a voyage that is marked by numerous adventures and by Huck's inner growth.

Jim and Huck are two outcasts from society, a fugitive and a boy presumed dead. Their security and solace is their raft, the river, and each other; land is a source of danger and a reminder of the hostile society they are fleeing. Their relationship is deftly developed by Twain. Jim is an honest, trusting man who respects Huck and treats him with a love and concern he had never known before. On their travels, they encounter a wide range of characters, including a pair of con men, **King** and **Duke,** two feuding families, The Grangerfords and the Shepardsons, and the innocent Wilks sisters, the hapless victims of the schemes of King and Duke until Huck's intervention. Through all these adventures, we see Huck grappling with questions of good and evil, learning about the cruelty in human nature through first-hand experience, and growing in understanding. When Jim is caught, Huck is sure of what he must do; despite his earlier thoughts of turning Jim in, he knows he must free his friend. With the help of Tom Sawyer, Huck plots an escape that becomes one of the most humorous episodes in the book, as Tom's imagination transforms the experience into high adventure.

The conclusion finds Huck once again the object of someone's "sivilizing" attempts, but he won't stand for it, claiming "I been there before." This understated declaration of freedom and identity closes the book.

Despite Twain's warning in the book's preface that "persons attempting to find a moral in it will be banished," *Huck Finn* is considered a masterpiece of American literature and, for all its humor, a work of moral seriousness. His examination of the absurdity and cruelty of the institution of slavery is vividly displayed in the relationship between Jim and Huck. Nurtured by Jim's love and respect, Huck undergoes a moral growth that will not allow him to betray his friend. Neither will he conform to society's moral codes, and his growing courage leaves him free at the conclusion to act the way he sees fit. Twain used Huck as the first-person narrator of the work, giving him a language that was colloquial, lively, and free of pretense and that influenced generations of American writers,

A Connecticut Yankee in King Arthur's Court (novel, 1889)

Hank Morgan is a nineteenth-century American factory worker. During a fight, he is struck on the head, and when he awakes, he is in sixth-century Britain at the time of **King Arthur.** Finding himself condemned to death, he uses his American ingenuity to escape his fate: he remembers that the day of his execution is also the day of a solar eclipse, which he predicts and which saves his life. Now an object of awe to King Arthur and his lords, he sets about trying to "improve" the ancient Britons, introducing telephones and six-guns, as well as democracy and industrialization, to his feudal hosts. Twain makes clear that the "civilization" that Hank brings with him also harbors the massive destructive powers of modern technology, as evidenced in the deaths of 25,000 soldiers, blown up with dynamite. He is ultimately defeated, for Arthur loses power and the Church seizes control and undoes all of Hank's "progress." **Merlin,** who had seen Hank as a rival as early as the eclipse, puts Hank to sleep for 1300 years.

Twain's novel, marked by the pessimism of his later works, is a fable about the hypocrisy and evil of the social institutions that Hank brings to the Britons as well as their own structures of power, wealth, and privilege. Twain explores the nature of the human character, pondering whether humankind is capable of improvement, if there is such a thing as progress, or whether, as he will explore in his next major work, *Pudd'nhead Wilson,* we are the victims of our backgrounds and our ancestry.

Pudd'nhead Wilson (novel, 1894)

The novel is set in the early 1800s in the Mississippi river town of Dawson's Landing. It tells a story of mistaken identity involving two young men, **Thomas a Beckett Driscoll** (Tom) and **Valet de Chambre** (Chambers), one black, the other white. Tom, the son of **Percy Driscoll,** a wealthy white landowner, is switched in infancy with Chambers, the son of **Roxanna,** a black slave, who wants her son to have the benefits accorded to a white, privileged heir. Twain makes it clear that the skin color of these two infants makes them appear interchangeable, and that their racial distinction is in society's eyes only. Roxanna's son becomes "Tom," and the true heir becomes "Chambers." Tom develops into the spoiled, nasty son of a rich white man; while Chambers, raised as a black slave, grows to behave in the subservient manner of the other slaves, with no hint of his origin. Twain relates how even as children Tom would bully and punish Chambers, who would accept the humiliation in silence. Tom is a heartless young man, given to gambling and theft; his cruelty even extends to Roxy, whom he sells to another owner when he needs more money.

The true identities of Tom and Chambers become known through the detective work of **David Wilson,** known as **"Pudd'nhead,"** a lawyer whom the townsfolk consider a simpleton, but whose passion for fingerprints solves the final mystery in the novel. Earlier in the work Pudd'nhead had fingerprinted everyone in Dawson's Landing, and when Percy Driscoll is murdered, it is Pudd'nhead who, through the use of his archives, discovers not only that Tom is the murderer, but that he is not Thomas Driscoll and is instead the son of a slave. When Chambers's fortunes change and he is identified as Driscoll's heir, he is unable to fit into white society, for he was bred to look and act like a slave and is illiterate and subservient. But Twain's finest irony is reserved for Tom, who confesses to the murder, and is tried, convicted, and sentenced to prison, only to be reprieved by the governor: as a slave, he is worth more out of jail, and his creditors promptly sell him "down the river."

The novel is one of the most bitter of Twain's later works. His searing satire of slavery exposes a system where generations are trained to accept the absurd notion of racial superiority. Twain also explores in this work the theme of nature and heredity as the determinant of character.

FURTHER READING

Blair, Walter. *Mark Twain & Huck Finn*. Berkeley: University of California Press, 1960.

Brooks, Van Wyck. *The Ordeal of Mark Twain*. New York: Dutton, 1923.

Carrington, George C. *The Dramatic Unity of Huckleberry Finn*. Columbus: Ohio State University Press, 1976.

Contemporary Authors, Vol. 104. Detroit: Gale Research Co.

Dictionary of Literary Biography, Vols. 11, 12, 23, 64; *Concise Dictionary of American Literary Biography, 1865-1917*. Detroit: Gale Research Co.

Fiedler, Leslie A. "Come Back to the Raft Ag'in, Huck Honey!" In *The Collected Essays of Leslie Fiedler, Vol. 1*, pp. 142-51. New York: Stein and Day, 1971.

Gale, Robert L. *Plots and Characters in the Works of Mark Twain*. Hamden: Archon Books, 1973.

Leary, Lewis. *Mark Twain*. Minneapolis: University of Minnesota Press, 1960.

Rubin, Louis D., Jr. "*Tom Sawyer* and the Use of Novels." In *The Curious Death of the Novel: Essays in American Literature*, pp. 88-99. Baton Rouge: Louisiana State University Press, 1967.

Seelye, John. "Introduction." In *The Adventures of Tom Sawyer* by Mark Twain. New York: Viking Penguin, 1984.

Stone, Albert E. *The Innocent Eye: Childhood in Mark Twain's Fiction*. New Haven: Yale University Press, 1961.

Trilling, Lionel. "*Huckleberry Finn*." In *The Liberal Imagination: Essays of Literature and Society,* pp. 104-17. New York: Viking Press, 1950.

Twentieth-Century Literary Criticism, Vols. 6, 12, 19. Detroit: Gale Research Co.

Wagenknecht, Edward. *Mark Twain: The Man and His Work*. Norman: University of Oklahoma Press, 1967.

Warren, Robert Penn. "Mark Twain." *The Southern Review* 8, No. 3 (Summer 1972): 459-92.

Anne Tyler

1941-

American novelist, short story writer, and critic.

Dinner at the Homesick Restaurant (novel, 1982)

The novel begins in contemporary Baltimore at the deathbed of **Pearl Tull,** but the body of the work is an account of Pearl's earlier life, marriage, and children. At thirty, Pearl met and married **Beck Tull,** a handsome and extravagant salesman who saved her from her status as an old maid. In the following years, while continually relocating, the couple had three children, **Cody, Jenny,** and **Ezra.** One day, while they were living in Baltimore, Beck left Pearl explaining that he no longer wanted to be married. In the shock of this sudden abandonment, Pearl found herself incapable of telling her children that their father was not just on another business trip. Over the years times grew harder. Pearl took a job and began breaking down into fits of anger and cruelty towards her children. Cody, Ezra, and Jenny each adjusted in their own way to their unusual home life. Ezra became Pearl's favorite, a blond-haired blue-eyed dreamer who sailed through his rough childhood playing the recorder and ignoring or patching over family problems. Cody, meanwhile, became a rebellious troublemaker, intensely jealous of his mother's special relations with Ezra. Jenny, the middle child, grew to seek compensation for the early nurturing she was denied.

As the years go by, Ezra repeatedly tries to bring the family together for meals that he and his multi-cultural cooks prepare at his establishment, The Homesick Restaurant. These attempts at family unity inevitably backfire when one or more of the family members abandon the effort mid-meal. Contrasted to Ezra's almost unconscious need to love and nurture is Cody's persistent anger and resentment. Despite his personal success, Cody's childhood jealousy toward Ezra seems to intensify with the passing of time. When Ezra finally finds himself a homey bride who shares his passion for cooking and feeding others, Cody stealthfully plots to win her away. She eventually succumbs to his relentless campaign, leaving Ezra to continue cooking for the regular Homesick crowd. Jenny carries her own scars from the past. Seeking love and stability in three marriages, she is oblivious to the instability this kind of searching creates for her children. Distant from this deeper emotional reality, Jenny fills her life with the comfortable hustle and bustle of a third husband, seven children, and a burgeoning pediatrics practice.

Despite wounds from the past, Pearl's children have persevered. Although Ezra is unmarried and childless, he has channeled his caring nature into his restaurant where the food is made with love. And although Cody and Jenny are not perfect parents, they seem far better than Pearl. Pearl herself, in the end, has become more motherly and kind. Aware of her failings, she can only plead that she was not really to blame. Indeed, Tyler seems to suggest that there is no perfect nuclear family and that the concept of home is not that simple. On her deathbed, Pearl searches for a girlhood diary entry about one afternoon when, while kneeling in the earth, she felt perfectly content on "this beautiful green little planet." Having found the entry, she dies in peace. Characteristically, Ezra plans a dinner after the funeral. Having found Beck's address, he invites his father as well. Although Cody's resentment of Beck's abandonment threatens to break up this family meal like all of the others before it, Beck's honest explanation to his son, however simple, allows the meal to go on. Accompanied by their father, Cody, Ezra, and Jenny finish a meal at the Homesick restaurant together for the first time.

Critics commend the verisimilitude with which Tyler conveys family life and the traumatic repercussions when a family is divided and the individual's limitations are laid bare. *Dinner at the Homesick Restaurant* is somewhat darker than Tyler's previous novels and the humor is somewhat grimmer as well. Critics also note the more complicated plot structure and Tyler's artful manipulations of the multiple points of view in the novel.

The Accidental Tourist (novel, 1985)

The story takes place in contemporary Baltimore. The protagonist **Macon Leary** makes his living writing travel guide books for Americans who, like himself, prefer the familiarity of their local fast-food restaurant to the cosmopolitan fare of Paris or Rome. The time is about one year after the death of Macon's only son. Both Macon and his wife **Sarah** are individually struggling to move on despite their profound grief. When Sarah decides that she must leave Macon if she is ever to recover, Macon's coping skills quickly deteriorate. He tries to compensate by increasingly systematizing the already rigid structure of his daily life. He creates time-saving gadgets, but before long his curious strategy backfires and he is caught between his latest contraption and his son's troubled dog, Edward. With a broken leg, Macon is forced to leave the lonely safety of his mechanized household and return to his childhood home. There his three siblings, particularly his sister **Rose,** take care of him.

Edward's strange behavior worsens in this new environment and Macon is driven to seek the help of **Muriel Pritchett** the amorous and somewhat eccentric dog trainer from Meow-Bow Animal Hospital. Muriel is an unusual character with a curious and quirky style of dress and speech and a sickly young son. Although Macon repeatedly deflects Muriels friendly advances, he is finally shamed into explaining his actions and breaks down into tears in her arms. From this point on, their unlikely relationship blossoms and Macon eventually moves out of the controlled serenity of the suburbs into Muriel's ramshackle downtown apartment. He gradually grows to enjoy even the subtlest and strangest aspects of his new neighborhood and companions. However, when Macon's wife Sarah appeals to their past and asks to return home and try again, Macon is draw back to the familiar comfort of her arms. Muriel's strength of character becomes more apparent at this point, for, with all of the money and resolve she can muster, she surprises Macon by accompanying him on his latest trip to Paris. Once there, Macon is bedridden by severe back strain and is faced with yet another surprise, the arrival of his wife brimming with medications and good intentions. At this point, Macon begins to perceive his need for action as well as the depth of the new life he has found with Muriel. The man who once rejected all that was new and foreign willfully says goodbye to Sarah and reembraces Muriel.

The character of Macon has been compared to the characters of Tyler's other novels because of his vacillation between isolated security and the shared comforts of loving relationships. In general, Tyler creates slightly eccentric characters who bumble along, dealing with internal conflicts within the structures of stifling but loving families. The depth and compassion of these character portraits have earned Tyler much respect as a novelist. Critics also praise the author's attention to detail, her warm humor, and her treatment of such themes as family and personal identity and autonomy.

FURTHER READING

Contemporary Authors, Vols. 9-12, rev. ed.; *Contemporary Authors New Revision Series,* Vol. 11. Detroit: Gale Research Co.

Contemporary Literary Criticism, Vol. 7, 11, 18, 28, 44. Detroit: Gale Research Co.

Demott, Benjamin. "Funny, Wise and True." *The New York Times Book Review* (14 March 1982): 1, 14.

Dictionary of Literary Biography, Vol. 6; *Dictionary of Literary Biography Yearbook: 1982.* Detroit: Gale Research Co.

Gornick, Vivian. "Anne Tyler's Arrested Develpment." *The Village Voice* 27, No. 13 (30 March 1982): 40-1.

Johnson, Diane. "Southern Comfort." *The New York Review of Books* 32, No. 17 (7 November 1985): 15-17.

McMurtry, Larry. "Life Is a Foreign Country." *The New York Times Book Review* (8 September 1985): 1, 36.

Updike, John. "Bellow, Vonnegut, Tyler, LeGuin, Cheever." In *Hugging the Shore: Essays and Criticism,* pp. 247-99. New York: Knopf, 1983.

Yardley, Jonathan. "Anne Tyler's Family Circles." *Book World—The Washington Post* (25 August 1985): 3.

John Updike
1932-
American novelist, short story writer, poet, and essayist.

Rabbit, Run (novel, 1960)

The novel is set in Brewer, an imaginary town in Pennsylvania, in the 1950s. As it opens, **Harry Angstrom,** called "Rabbit," is in his late twenties. He is a former high school basketball star, now a gadget salesman, married to his high school sweetheart, **Janice,** and living in a small apartment. The "angst" in Angstrom is a clue to Harry's persona: he is a man in fear—of approaching middle-age, of death, of commitment, and of responsibility. He remembers his high school years, particularly his assured status as a star athlete, with nostalgia. When he compares his former life to his current state, he is filled with hopelessness, for his world seems empty and his life without meaning. He seeks answers to his dilemma in religion, but his minister, **Jack Eccles,** cannot offer comfort for his spiritual distress. Rabbit's marriage also holds no meaning for him, so he seeks release in an extramarital affair with **Ruth Leonard.** Yet even with Ruth, Rabbit is unfulfilled, and, as in response to all of his problems, he flees, "running" from responsibility.

The themes of morality, religion, and sex that shape so much of Updike's fiction are voiced in this work. Rabbit searches for meaning and moral certainty in a modern world that Updike portrays as devoid of values. Contemporary religion, as represented by Jack Eccles, is depicted as sterile and unable to provide solace to its confused adherents. And the sexuality that pervades so much of Updike's fiction is portrayed as a limiting rather than liberating force. Although Rabbit is depicted as inarticulate and insensitive, Updike makes him a sympathetic character whose striving and anguish are believable. Updike has forged a reputation as a consummate prose stylist, and his technical virtuosity in this work has received much praise. The novel is written in the present tense and the narrative is energetic and fast-paced. Updike's detailed descriptions of everyday objects has also been noted, a technique he employs in later works as well. In his minute analysis of mundane objects, he focuses on the topical and the trivial, harkening back to his theme of the vapidness of modern life. Rabbit returns in two sequels, *Rabbit Redux* and *Rabbit Is Rich.*

The Centaur (novel, 1963)

This novel, which earned Updike the National Book Award, is set in the fictional town of Olinger, Pennsylvania, the setting of many of the author's early short stories. **George Caldwell** is a high school teacher and his son, **Peter,** is a high school student. The "centaur" of the title refers to the Greek myths of Chiron and Prometheus, which provides the framework for the novel. In the myth, Prometheus steals fire from the gods and gives it to mortals; his punishment is to suffer eternal physical pain. Chiron, the centaur, was known for his goodness and wisdom and was also a great teacher. In an act of atonement for Prometheus's deed, Chiron sacrificed his immortality and died for him. In the novel, Peter, a fledgling artist, is beset with fears of death and nothingness, an anxiety he shares with many other Updike characters. His father's stance is one of affirmation in the face of the absurdity of existence. Peter is painfully aware of the discrepancy between what his father strives for and what he achieves, and the novel chronicles his struggle to accept and understand him. Updike's method is to use alternate sections to tell the stories of Chiron and the Caldwells in parallel, one illuminating the other. In the novel's conclusion, Peter is a mature artist and finally capable of understanding his father, his art, and the meaning of life and death.

Thematically, the work is closely related to Updike's other novels with its emphasis on death and the nihilism of modern life. The novel's concluding epigram is from the Christian philosopher Karl Barth, whom Updike has acknowledged as a major influence. It offers an image of humankind with one foot in heaven and one on earth, evoking the ambiguity and anxiety of the human condition as Updike views it.

Bech: A Book (short stories, 1970)

Henry Bech is the character who unifies this collection of short stories. Like Rabbit Angstrom, he is a recurrent character, and he appears in several subsequent short stoires by Updike.

Bech is a Jewish writer living in Tarbox, Massachusetts, the fictional counterpart to Ipswich, Massachusetts, Updike's own home for many years and the setting for many of his short stories. As the novel begins, Bech is suffering writer's block. He has produced only three novels and a collection of miscellaneous pieces. Updike uses the block as a metaphor for Bech's dilemma: he is unable to create or to commit to anything, and his life and work are characterized by inertia. Similar to his fellow Updike heroes, Bech is a man afraid, particularly of marriage and success. The stories take place in a variety of locales, chronicling Bech's travels in Europe as well as his encounters with the contemporary American literary scene. Bech is particularly concerned with how authors betray their integrity by writing fashionable books for the marketplace rather than being true to their own voice or vision.

Many critics have noted that Bech serves as something of an alter ego for Updike. They are seemingly unalike—Bech is a Jew, Updike a WASP; Bech is a blocked writer, Updike is one of the most prolific writers of our time; Bech is a bachelor, Updike is very much a family-oriented man and writer. Yet what they have in common and what provides a central focus for these stories is their vocation as writers. Updike uses the Bech stories to explore the nature of the artist, examining his place in modern American life, and especially his relationship with the outside world. And, one concludes, Bech's disgust with the contemporary literary world parallels Updike's own.

Rabbit Redux (novel, 1971)

This novel, like the earlier *Rabbit, Run,* is set in Brewer, Pennsylvania. The year is 1969, the year of the moon landing and the closing year of a decade of social upheaval in America. **Harry Angstrom's** fellow characters in this novel include a hippie, **Jill,** with whom he has an affair. Rabbit's story unfolds against a backdrop of America in chaos: the Vietnam War, drugs, the sexual revolution, and race riots characterize his world. His family life is full of unhappiness and disillusion: Rabbit mourns the death of his infant daughter; his wife, **Janice,** leaves him; and his son, **Nelson,** chides him for being out of touch with modern life.

Rabbit is thirty-six in this novel, and in the middle of the Vietnam era, a hawk, voicing his working-class, politically conservative ideas. He tries to reorient himself to the world of the late 1960s, but he's tired. All of his energy spent in searching for himself has been replaced with inertia, and he is a passive character. Images of decay and sterility permeate the novel, and the world of *Rabbit, Run,* has become even more vapid, meaningless, and despairing in this work. The novel's conclusion offers a picture of destruction and rebirth: the Angstrom's house is burned to the ground, and Jill dies in the fire. Yet Rabbit and Janice are reunited, and we last see them together in a motel, in an embrace.

Rabbit Is Rich (novel, 1981)

Harry Angstrom, protagonist of Updike's earlier novels *Rabbit, Run* and *Rabbit Redux,* makes his third appearance in this work, which won Updike the Pulitzer Prize. The setting is once again Brewer, Pennsylvania, and this time the year is 1979. The Rabbit of this novel differs greatly from the character of the previous works. He is forty-six now, and seems content with his marriage and reconciled to the tragedies of his life, particularly the death of his daughter. As the title indicates, Rabbit has achieved financial success, a result of inheriting his father-in-law's Toyota dealership during the oil embargo. The action of the novel centers on Rabbit's son **Nelson,** who brings home his pregnant girlfriend, marries her against his father's wishes, then deserts her. He is a self-indulgent, callow character whose attitudes toward life and family suggest parallels with Rabbit's own. As he has so often in his fiction, Updike here explores the nature of family relationships, particularly that of father and son, revealing its horrors and joys. The prose style of the novel is characteristically rich, and the tone is noticeably more comic and relaxed than in the previous novels. Updike's recurrent theme of an America in decline is also voiced in this work, evidenced in Rabbit's ironic financial well-being, which takes place during an era when industrial America is struggling with the economic woes brought about by foreign competition and a world-wide oil crisis.

Once again, Updike provides close descriptions of the ordinary products and gadgets that both codify and shape modern life. The dialogue of the novel has received much praise, for Updike is able to replicate the rhythms of family conversation in a manner at once believable and lively.

FURTHER READING

Alder, Renata. "Arcadia, Pa." *New Yorker* (13 April 1963): 182-88.

Contemporary Authors, Vols. 1-4, rev. ed.; *Contemporary Authors New Revision Series,* Vol. 4; *Contemporary Authors Bibliographical Series,* Vol. 1. Detroit: Gale Research Co.

Contemporary Literary Criticism, Vols. 1, 2, 3, 5, 7, 9, 13, 15, 23, 34, 43. Detroit: Gale Research Co.

Detweiler, Robert. *John Updike.* Boston: Twayne, 1984.

Dictionary of Literary Biography, Vols. 2, 5; *Dictionary of Literary Biography Yearbook: 1980, 1982; Dictionary of Literary Biography Documentary Series,* Vol. 3. Detroit: Gale Research Co.

Galloway, David D. "The Absurd Man as Saint: The Novels of John Updike." In *The Absurd Hero in American Fiction: Updike, Styron, Bellow, Salinger,* pp. 17-80. Austin: University of Texas Press, 1981.

Greiner, Donald J. *John Updike's Novels.* Athens: Ohio University Press, 1984.

Hunt, George. *John Updike and the Three Great Secret Things: Sex, Religion, and Art.* Grand Rapids: Eerdmans, 1980.

Hyman, Stanley Edgar. "The Artist as a Young Man." *New Leader* 45 (19 March 1962): 22-3.

Kazin, Alfred. "Professional Observers: Cozzens to Updike." In *Bright Book of Life: American Novelists and Storytellers from Hemingway to Mailer,* pp. 95-124. Boston: Little, Brown, 1973.

Markle, Joyce B. *Fighters and Lovers: Theme in the Novels of John Updike.* New York: New York University Press, 1973.

Myers, David. "The Questing Fear: Christian Allegory in John Updike's *The Centaur.*" *Twentieth Century Literature* 17 (April 1971): 73-82.

Podhoretz, Norman. "A Dissent on Updike." In *Doings and Undoings: The Fifties and After in American Writing,* pp. 251-57. New York: Farrar, Straus, 1964.

Regan, Alfred F. "Updike's Symbol of the Center." *Modern Fiction Studies* 20 (Spring 1974): 77-96.

Suderman, Elmer F. "The Right Way and the Good Way in *Rabbit, Run.*" *University Review* 36 (October 1969): 13-21.

Tanner, Tony. "A Compromised Environment." In *City of Words: American Fiction, 1950-1970,* pp. 273-94. New York: Harper & Row, 1971.

Taylor, Larry E. *Pastoral and Anti-Pastoral Patterns in John Updike's Fiction.* Carbondale: Southern Illinois University Press, 1971.

Uphaus, Suzanne Henning. *John Updike.* New York: Ungar, 1980.

Vickery, John B. *"The Centaur:* Myth, History, and Narrative." *Modern Fiction Studies* 20 (Spring 1974): 29-43.

Mario Vargas Llosa

1936-

Peruvian novelist, short story writer, and essayist.

The Green House (novel, 1966)

As does all his fiction, this novel reflects Vargas Llosa's deep commitment to revealing and exploring the political and social realities of modern day Peru. **Bonifacia,** of Indian descent, is raised and schooled by nuns in Santa Maria de Nieva, a village in the Peruvian jungle. The chapters detailing her childhood and young adulthood are interwoven throughout the text, as we follow her through her years in the mission with the nuns and her later expulsion, when she allows several Indian children, from her own tribe, to escape. After she loses her job, she goes to live in the house of **Adrían Nieves,** whose story forms another major narrative thread. Having escaped from the army, Adrían is involved in the illegal rubber trade of the Japanese convict **Fushía,** a runaway from a Brazilian prison, whose clandestine operation is another focus for the narrative. Through Adrían, Bonifacia meets **Lituma,** a policeman, whom she marries. After his arrest for murder, Bonifacia falls under the corrupting influence of his friend, **Josefino Rojas,** after which she becomes a prostitute in the Green House, an infamous bordello in the city of Piura. The original Green House, founded years ago by a harpist, **Anselmo,** and had been destroyed by the pious hypocrites of the community. The new brothel is placed in a sector of Piura that is devoted to pleasure.

The novel's style has been both praised and criticized, for it is a dense, complex work whose structure and theme do not necessarily become clear to the reader until the conclusion. It contains several narrative strands and focusses on a variety of characters and locales within Peru, and Vargas Llosa emphasizes the dramatic differences presented by a country that contains remote jungle territories, a bridge of mountains that effectively cuts the country in two, and modern cities. Vargas Llosa's method is nonchronological, and he employs a disjointed, fragmented narrative style that reflects his vision of the chaotic nature of Peruvian life.

Vargas Llosa's disjointed narrative style reflects the theme of chaos that symbolizes Peruvian society, a theme he will develop in later works.

Conversation in the Cathedral (novel, 1969)

This novel is set in Lima in the 1950s, the era of Vargas Llosa's own youth, and is a scathing indictment of the corruption of the regime of Manuel Odria, the country's dictator during that decade. **Santiago Zavalita,** a young man from a wealthy, upper middle-class family, and **Don Cayo Bermúdez,** a corrupt official within the Odria government, are contrasted throughout the novel as Vargas Llosa explores his theme of decadence.

A central setting for the work is the Cathedral of the title, a bar and brothel in Lima. There Zavalita and his friend **Ambrosio Pardo** discuss their lives and the state of their country. Once again, Vargas Llosa employs a disjointed narrative structure, using alternate chapters to relate the stories of Zavalita and Bermúdez and often presenting parallel conversations of the two characters on the same page. Zavalita, from a family that has benefited from the corruption of the oligarchic structure of the Odria administration, is an idealistic young student who defies tradition and the wishes of his family to attend the University of San Marcos, a school not for the elite, but for members of the lower classes. But Zavalita soon succumbs to the trappings of the traditional values of his class, marries and becomes a journalist for a paper run by those favoring the current government. Yet the spirit of corruption has affected the Zavalita family in other ways, for we learn that his father, a well-known businessman, is a rather notorious member of the homosexual community. Sexual perversion as a metaphor for the corruption at the basis of society is also revealed in the character of Bermúdez, for he is a man whose world is one of bribery, torture, and aberrant sexual activities.

Vargas Llosa's fragmented style reflects his belief that life itself is a baffling maze, not like a well-made novel in which cause and effect, action and reaction are easily discernable. He stresses the importance of perception in his predominate use of dialogue in the novel. This, the language of present action, displays a society riddled with deceit and corruption, for what is left unsaid reflects each individual's hidden motives. He also examines the image the characters project as opposed to their true natures, especially in describing the Odria government, who have created only the symbols of order: they have instituted controls leading to economic well-being for the country, but have done so through the use of bribery and torture. Vargas Llosa's bitter, pessimistic view is unrelieved in the novel's conclusion, for though he relates the collapse of the Odria regime and the election of President Manuel Prado, nothing truly changes in Peru; compromise and corruption color all human endeavor, and human nature and the natural disorder of Peru will not be changed by a new government.

FURTHER READING

Contemporary Authors, Vols. 73-76; *Contemporary Authors New Revision Series*, Vol. 18. Detroit: Gale Research Co.

Contemporary Literary Criticism, Vols. 3, 6, 9, 10, 15, 31, 42. Detroit: Gale Research Co.

Harss, Luis and Barbara Dohmann. "Mario Vargas Llosa, or the Revolving Door." In *Into the Mainstream: Conversations with Latin American Writers*, pp. 342-75. New York: Harper & Row, 1967.

Kirk, John M. "Mario Vargas Llosa's *Conversation in the Cathedral.*" *The International Fiction Review* 4, No. 1 (January 1977): 11-17.

Luchting, Wolfgang. "Masochism, Anyone?" *Review* (Spring 1975): 12-16.

Moody, Michael. "The Web of Defeat: A Thematic View of Characterization in Mario Vargas Llosa's *La Casa Verde.*" *Hispania* (March 1976): 11-23.

Oviedo, José Miguel. "The Theme of the Traitor and the Hero: On Vargas Llosa's Intellectuals and the Military." *World Literature Today* 52, No. 1 (Winter 1978): 16-24.

Rabassa, Gregory. "'O Tempora, O Mores': Time, Tense, and Tension in Mario Vargas Llosa." *World Literature Today* 52, No. 1 (Winter 1978): 30-3.

Jules Verne
1828-1905
French novelist.

Twenty Thousand Leagues under the Sea (novel, 1870)

As the novel begins, we learn that a giant monster has been attacking ships at sea. **Pierre Aronnax,** a professor from the Museum of Natural History in Paris and the narrator of the novel, is invited to accompany the crew of the *Abraham Lincoln* on a mission to find the beast. With his loyal servant **Conseil,** Aronnax begins his journey. Also on board is the Canadian **Ned Land,** whose harpoon is ready when they sight the monster. But the beast proves to be a submarine under the command of the mysterious **Captain Nemo,** and after a collision between the two vessels catapults them into the ocean, Aronnax, Conseil, and Land are taken aboard as prisoners.

The submarine is the *Nautilus,* a vessel powered by electricity with a continuous oxygen supply that allows her crew to explore the depths of the world's seas. The ship and her captain fascinate Aronnax, a natural scientist. Nemo, whose name means "nobody," is an enigmatic character: he allows the men freedom of movement aboard the vessel, but will not set them free. Although he claims that he has severed ties with all humanity, several of his actions during the voyage belie this declaration. Aboard ship he has a magnificent library, a fine collection of art, and a compilation of zoological specimens that is a wonder to Professor Aronnax. Verne had a great interest in and knowledge of science, and through Aronnax the depths of the sea and its animals and plants are described in scientific detail, as are the processes of electricity and the function of the submarine.

The adventures aboard the *Nautilus* begin, including a "hunt" upon the sea floor, the macabre discovery of sunken ships with corpses, pearl fishing, a viewing of the lost city of Atlantis, and an exciting journey to the South Pole, which Nemo claims for himself. As the voyage continues, Aronnax becomes more captivated with the mysterious Captain. He feels Nemo is possessed by vengeance, but cannot discern why or for whom. Although Nemo claims to be unconcerned with the destiny of humankind, he and his crew loot gold from sunken Spanish galleons and give the money to the oppressed of all lands.

The climax of the novel occurs when a man-of-war spots and pursues the *Nautilus,* and the Captain destroys the vessel. It is an act of vengeance and hatred, and the transformation it causes in Nemo appalls Aronnax, even though Nemo reveals that the nation whose ship he sank is the one who deprived him of family and country and had driven him to his isolated existence. Shortly after this incident, just as the three prisoners are attempting to escape, the boat enters a maelstrom. When Aronnax awakens, he and his companions are safe, but the fate of the *Nautilus* and all on board is unknown.

The novel is considered Verne's masterpiece and is praised for its vivid description and keen characterization. Captain Nemo is regarded as Verne's finest creation. His astonishing prescience in technology and his humanist concerns regarding scientific innovation are reflected here and throughout his work. Modern critics claim that the reason *Twenty Thousand Leagues under the Sea* is considered a children's book is because of poor translations into English, and most expect that a revaluation of his work, based on new translations, will bring Verne the serious consideration he deserves.

FURTHER READING

Angenot, Marc. "Jules Verne: The Last Happy Utopianist." In *Science Fiction: A Critical Guide,* edited by Patrick Parrinder, pp. 18-33. London: Longman, 1979.

Contemporary Authors, Vol. 110. Detroit: Gale Research Co.

Costello, Peter. *Jules Verne: Inventor of Science Fiction.* New York: Charles Scribner's Sons, 1978.

Evans, I. O. *Jules Verne and His Work.* Boston: Twayne, 1966.

Twentieth-Century Literary Criticism, Vol. 6. Detroit: Gale Research Co.

Gore Vidal
1925-
American novelist, playwright, and essayist.

The City and the Pillar (novel, 1948; rev. ed. 1965)

Jim Willard is the protagonist of Vidal's first major literary effort, one of the first American novels to deal with the subject of homosexuality. As the novel begins, Jim is twenty-five years old. In our first glimpse of him, he is sitting in a bar, a distressed young man thinking back over his life. The time shifts back to his late teens, when he has a brief homosexual encounter with a boyhood friend, **Bob Ford.** In his late teens and early twenties, Jim must grapple with the fact that he is repelled by women and that he prefers men sexually. Throughout the novel, Vidal portrays Jim as a simple, normal man, distinguished only by his sexual confusion, which brands him an outsider in his culture. While a tennis coach in California, he becomes the lover of **Ronald Shaw,** a famous movie star. Through Jim's eyes, the reader is given a glimpse into the homosexual underworld. Jim finds the relationship unfulfilling; the memory of the encounter with Bob still recurs to him and seems to offer an ideal of love he cannot find with other men. Jim drifts into an affair with a writer that ends as World War II begins. After the war, Jim meets Bob again, who is now married. When he vehemently rejects Jim's sexual overtures, Jim strangles Bob, murdering him. In the 1965 revision of the novel, Vidal changed the ending: in the later version, Jim forces Bob to have sex, after which they part. Both versions of the novel conclude with Jim in the bar, with the reader now aware of the source of the young man's anguish.

Vidal's treatment of the theme of homosexuality, considered scandalous in 1948, is tame by today's standards. However, his was the first novel to deal openly and candidly with the subject, allowing later writers to treat a previously forbidden topic.

Burr (novel, 1973)

Aaron Burr and **Charles Schuyler** are the major characters in one of Vidal's best known and most popular historical novels, a work that is part of a tetralogy devoted to American history, including *Washington, D.C., 1876,* and *Lincoln: A Novel.*

Set in New York in the 1830s, the novel recounts the life of Aaron Burr, a notorious political figure in American History, particularly remembered as the man who shot Alexander Hamilton in a duel. Schuyler is a young law clerk and writer hired by Burr who becomes his friend and confidant. In the course of their relationship, Burr passes on to Schuyler his own history of the emerging United States, peppered with his unflattering portraits of the Founding Fathers. These famous men—**George Washington, Alexander Hamilton, and Thomas Jefferson** among them—are portrayed as self-serving, venal types, descriptions that surely reflect more about the character of their creator, Burr, than they do about the historical figures themselves. It is certainly a partisan view, with Burr making little of his own faults and much of those of his political rivals. Through his protagonist, Vidal reveals his purpose: to debunk the myths that surround the men and the history of the early America. Burr emerges as an appealing character, as much for his self-proclaimed roguishness as for his elegant language. As he pieces together Burr's life, Schuyler incorporates Burr's writings into his own depiction of the man. One of his assignments from Burr is to write a damaging pamphlet on Vice-President **Martin Van Buren,** in which he claims that Van Buren is Burr's illegitimate son.

The work is centered on the theme of fathers, focusing on the importance of understanding the nation's forefathers and illuminating the character of Charles Schuyler as he searches for a father figure. On the last page of the novel, he discovers that both he and Martin Van Buren are Burr's illegitimate sons. *Burr* is one of Vidal's liveliest and most popular historical novels. Schuyler returns in Vidal's later novel, *1876.*

FURTHER READING

Aldridge, John W. "Gore Vidal: The Search for a King." In *After the Lost Generation: A Critical Study of the Writers of Two Wars,* pp. 170-83. New York: McGraw-Hill, 1951.

Contemporary Authors, Vols. 5-8, rev. ed.; *Contemporary Authors New Revision Series,* Vol. 13. Detroit: Gale Research Co.

Contemporary Literary Criticism, Vols. 2, 4, 6, 8, 10, 22, 33. Detroit: Gale Research Co.

Dick, Bernard F. *The Apostate Angel: A Critical Study of Gore Vidal.* New York: Random House, 1974.

Dictionary of Literary Biography, Vol. 6. Detroit: Gale Research Co.

McLaughlin, Richard. "Precarious Status." *Saturday Review of Literature* 31 (10 January 1948): 14-15.

Marcus, Stephen. "A Second Look at Sodom." *New York Herald Tribune Book Week* (20 June 1965): 5.

Terry, C. V. *"The City and the Pillar." New York Times Book Review* (11 January 1948): 22.

White, Ray Lewis. *Gore Vidal.* Boston: Twayne, 1968.

Kurt Vonnegut, Jr.

1922-

American novelist, short story writer, and dramatist.

Cat's Cradle (novel, 1963)

This novel is a darkly humorous account of the end of the world. The story takes place in contemporary Illium, New York, and San Lorenzo, an island in the Caribbean. The main character and narrator is **John,** or Jonah, as he sometimes refers to himself. He is a free-lance writer who, at the beginning of the novel, intends to write a book called *The Day the World Ended,* alluding to the atomic bombing of Hiroshima. Through research and correspondence, John learns a good deal about the so-called "father of the atomic bomb," **Dr. Felix Hoenikker.** Dr. Hoenikker is described as childlike—his laboratory is stocked with dime-store toys—who has provided the world with technological advances with absolutely no regard for their possible ramifications. While playing with a piece of string, Dr. Hoenikker makes a cat's cradle, symbolic of the emptiness upon which humankind tends to justify life. John also learns that Dr. Hoenikker died while working on a new project. Before his death, he created ice-nine, a substance capable of freezing all water on earth. When the Hoenikker children—**Angela, Frank,** and **Newton**—discover the ice-nine, they divide it among themselves and use it for their own purposes. Angela buys a husband with hers; Newton, a midget, purchases a week-long honeymoon with **Zinka,** a Ukrainian midget who is really a Russian spy; and Frank buys a high-ranking place in government on the island of San Lorenzo.

By coincidence, John also goes to San Lorenzo to work on an article about an American sugar millionaire who founded a free hospital in the jungle. Here, John finds **Papa Monzano,** who is dying of cancer, wearing a vial of ice-nine around his neck. John also meets **Mona Monzano,** the island's sex-symbol, and learns of Bokononism, a religion founded on an admitted pack of lies to which everyone on the island subscribes. The founder, **Bokonon,** realized the need for religion to counteract the misery of reality. In this novel, Bokononism represents all "isms": they are as empty as a cat's cradle.

The end of the novel finds Papa swallowing his vial of ice-nine while John and Mona escape the coming apocalypse temporarily, taking refuge in an underground shelter where they make uninspired love. Later, Mona kills herself by swallowing ice-nine. Vonnegut's first major novel is noted for its satiric treatment of modern philosophy, religion, and mores as well as for its bleak observations on the dangers of contemporary technology.

Slaughterhouse-Five; or, The Children's Crusade (novel, 1969)

The novel tells the story of one man's passive acceptance of a fate predetermined by the indifferent forces that shape the universe. **Billy Pilgrim,** a shell-shocked soldier in war-torn Dresden during World War II, is man who is remarkable only in his mediocrity. He is, as are all of the book's characters, neither good nor bad, simply a victim of circumstances which are beyond his understanding and control.

The novel is a complex story-within-a-story, rendered in a fragmented narrative that parallels the protagonist's schizophrenic journey through time and space. To escape the horror and absurdity of war, Billy "time-trips," visiting the distant planet Tralfamadore, where he is put in a zoo and mated to a former movie star from Earth. The Tralfamadorians tell Billy that time is a continuum in which events are predestined, but that knowing what the future holds does not empower one to alter destiny. They further explain that the concept of free will is one that is peculiar to Earth, and suggest that the best one can do is to ignore disagreeable memories and concentrate on the pleasant ones.

Billy, however, has few gratifying memories; his past and present are full of episodes of violence and loss. During World War II, he is captured by the Germans, but manages to survive the cataclysmic bombing of Dresden by the Allies. After the war, Billy returns to school, marries a woman he doesn't love, and has two children. After surviving a plane crash, Billy learns that his wife has died. Upon leaving the hospital, he decides to devote himself to sharing the wisdom of the Tralfamadorians with the world. While doing so, he is shot and killed.

The fragmented, chaotic narrative is unified through the central focus on Dresden and the absurdity and brutality of war. The novel is admired for its compassionate portrait of Billy, the confused, innocent Everyman whose psychic journeys symbolize the wounded soul in need of relief from the horrors of modern life.

Breakfast of Champions; or, Goodbye Blue Monday! (novel, 1973)

In *Breakfast of Champions* Vonnegut explores many themes familiar from his previous fiction, concentrating on the barren, hypocritical quality of modern American life and the chaotic, mechanistic nature of existence. The focal point of the story centers on a meeting between the novel's two main characters, **Kilgore Trout,** an author of science fiction and one of several characters from Vonnegut's earlier novels who reappear here, and **Dwayne**

Hoover, a successful Pontiac dealer in Midland City. Their meeting comes about through the influence of a wealthy citizen of Midland City, **Eliot Rosewater,** who felt that his favorite author should be invited to speak at the opening of a local art center. In this novel, Trout has become a successful writer, publishing his novels through a pornography press which intersperses his text with irrelevant, graphic, sexual illustrations. His other novels, synopsized here, as well as Vonnegut's asides about himself and his art, add to the parodic flavor of the book. En route from New York, Trout is beaten, robbed, and forced to hitchhike most of the way.

Trout arrives in Midland City and wanders into the Holiday Inn where Dwayne's son **Bunny** is playing the piano and where Hoover and Vonnegut—a character in the novel himself—are waiting. Hoover seizes and speed-reads one of Trout's books entitled *Now It Can Be Told.* The book depicts a world in which only one man has been endowed with free will; all of the other beings are robots, put on Earth by the Creator for His enjoyment. After reading the book, Hoover goes mad, and in a frenzy injures Bunny, bites off part of Trout's ring finger, and breaks Vonnegut's watch crystal and his big toe. In the end, Hoover is taken away by the authorities. Vonnegut now confronts Trout, explaining that up to this point Trout had been a fictional creation, but that now the author is relinquishing control of all of his characters. But Trout wants more than freedom and pleads with his creator to "make me young, make me young."

Described by Vonnegut as his fiftieth birthday present to himself, *Breakfast of Champions* is praised for its spare prose style, the extension of his view of a world plagued by chaos and despair, and his mocking analysis of the author as creator.

FURTHER READING

Contemporary Authors, Vols. 1-4, rev. ed.; *Contemporary Authors New Revision Series,* Vol. 1. Detroit: Gale Research Co.

Contemporary Literary Criticism, Vols. 1, 2, 3, 4, 5, 8, 12, 22, 40. Detroit: Gale Research Co.

Dictionary of Literary Biography, Vols. 2, 8; *Dictionary of Literary Biography Yearbook: 1980*; *Dictionary of Literary Biography Documentary Series,* Vol. 3. Detroit: Gale Research Co.

Fiedler, Leslie A. "The Divine Stupidity of Kurt Vonnegut." *Esquire* (September 1970): 195-204.

Greiner, Donald J. "Vonnegut's *Slaughterhouse-Five* and the Fiction of Atrocity." *Critique: Studies in Modern Fiction* 14, No. 3 (1973): 38-51.

Hartshorne, Thomas L. "From *Catch-22* to *Slaughterhouse-Five:* The Decline of the Political Mode." *South Atlantic Quarterly* 78, No. 1 (Winter 1979): 17-33.

Kennard, Jean E. "Kurt Vonnegut, Jr.: The Sirens of Satire." In *Number and Nightmare: Forms of Fantasy in Contemporary Fiction,* pp. 101-28. Hamden: Archon Books, 1975.

Klinkowitz, Jerome. "The Literary Career of Kurt Vonnegut, Jr." *Modern Fiction Studies* 19 (Spring 1973): 57-67.

Lundquist, James. *Kurt Vonnegut.* New York: Ungar, 1977.

Mayo, Clark. *Kurt Vonnegut: The Gospel from Outer Space (or, Yes We Have no Nirvanas).* San Bernardino: Borgo Press, 1977.

Olderman, Raymond M. "Out of the Waste Land and into the Fire: Cataclysm or Cosmic Cool." In *Beyond the Waste Land: A Study of the American Novel in the Nineteen-Sixties,* pp. 189-219. New Haven: Yale University Press, 1973.

Reed, Peter J. *Kurt Vonnegut, Jr.* New York: Warner, 1972.

Schatt, Stanley. *Kurt Vonnegut, Jr*. Boston: Twayne, 1976.

Tanner, Tony. "The Uncertain Messenger: A Study of the Novels of Kurt Vonnegut, Jr." *Critical Quarterly* 11 (Winter 1969): 297-315.

Alice Walker

1944-

American novelist, short story writer, poet, and essayist.

Meridian (novel, 1976)

The novel is set in the South during the civil rights movement of the 1960s. **Meridian Hill** is a young black woman, and the novel chronicles her quest for self-knowledge and self-awareness. The work is divided into three parts, "Meridian," "Truman Held," and "Ending," but Walker's approach to her narrative is not strictly chronological; instead, scenes of present action are interspersed with recollections throughout the work.

As a teenager, Meridian is married and has a son. Overwhelmed by the realities of motherhood, she gives her child away. Her relationship with **Truman Held,** an artist and civil rights worker, is pivotal to the novel, for it is he who opens her eyes to the importance of the movement for political liberation for blacks, and who encourages her to attend college. But he ultimately leaves her and marries a white civil rights worker. One of Walker's central themes here and throughout her fiction is the victimization of black women by both the racism and the sexism that undermines their self-hood. As such, she explores here the constricting aspects of traditional motherhood in Meridian's decision to give up her child and the sexism that colors her relationship with Truman. She attends college, where she becomes deeply involved with the civil rights movement. However, she becomes disillusioned with the effort, particularly the violence that her friends insist is necessary for liberation, and withdraws. In this sequence of the novel, Meridian grapples with profound challenges to her personal and political beliefs, but emerges from the ordeal reborn and with a new sense of purpose. She leaves college to work with poor southern blacks, turning from political activism to a personal expression of her quest for the betterment of her people.

Walker employs such stylistic elements as interior monologue and recurrent imagery in a method she calls "quilting," in which she seeks to unify the fragments of experience through a variety of narrative modes. Her ability to replicate the cadences of black folk speech has been much praised in this work. Walker's theme of the plight of black women as victims of both racism and sexism recurs in such later works as *The Color Purple*.

The Color Purple (novel, 1982)

Set in the rural South, the novel spans thirty years in the life of the protagonis, **Celie,** chronicling her journey from pain and humiliation to triumph and rebirth. The work is in the epistolary form, composed of letters from Celie to God and to her sister **Nettie,** as well as Nettie's letters to her. Celie's life is one of struggle and despair. A victim of incest, she is raped repeatedly by her step-father, a cruel and violent man, who sells the two children she bears him. The oppressive brutality of her life continues when she marries **Albert,** a widower, who beats her and subjects her to a life of domestic servitude. Nettie also flees her step-father, hoping to take shelter with Celie, but Albert throws her out. Nettie decides to go to Africa to become a missionary, accompanying a family who has adopted Celie's two children. While she is gone, she continues to write to Celie, but Albert hides the letters from her.

The only solace in Celie's life is the love of **Shug Avery,** a blues singer and Albert's mistress. Celie cares for her during an illness, and they develop a mutual love that is expressed physically and emotionally. It is Shug who teaches Celie self-respect through her love. Twenty years after her departure, Nettie's letters are discovered by Celie and Shug in a trunk. Although she is infuriated by Albert's treachery, Celie is grateful to learn that Nettie is alive. She and Shug read Nettie's letters, in which Nettie tells of her life in Africa, where the plight of black women is shown to be shockingly similar to that endured by black American women. Celie's sense of confidence and independence continues to grow, and she leaves Albert to travel with Shug and begin a life of her own. In the novel's conclusion, Nettie returns from Africa with Celie's children, and Celie is seen triumphant, joyful, and whole.

As in her other fiction, Walker here continues her exploration of black women's battle for racial and sexual equality. Although the work was controversial, particularly among reviewers who found Walker's depiction of her male characters to be stereotypical and demeaning, it was a major literary success for Walker and earned her the Pulitzer Prize. Commentators especially praised her use of the epistolary form, noting how in her letters to 'God, Celie, abused and powerless, becomes empowered and eloquent. Walker's evocation of the voices of her characters, superbly rendered in black folk English, has also been much admired.

FURTHER READING

Barthelme, Elizabeth. "Victory Over Bitterness." *Commonweal* 110, No. 3 (11 February 1983): 93-4.

Christian, Barbara. "The Black Woman Writer as Wayward." In *Black Women Writers, 1950-1980,* edited by Mari Evans, pp. 457-77. Garden City: Doubleday, 1984.

Contemporary Authors, Vols. 37-40, rev. ed.; *Contemporary Authors New Revision Series,* Vol. 9. Detroit: Gale Research Co.

Contemporary Literary Criticism, Vols. 5, 6, 9, 19, 27, 46. Detroit: Gale Research Co.

Dictionary of Literary Biography, Vols. 6, 33. Detroit: Gale Research Co.

Harris, Trudier. "Folklore in the Fiction of Alice Walker: A Perpetuation of Historical and Literary Traditions." *Black American Literature Forum* 2 (Spring 1977): 3-8.

Smith, Dinitia. "'Celie, You a Tree.'" *The Nation* 235, No. 6 (4 September 1982): 181-83.

Washington, Mary Helen. "An Essay on Alice Walker." In *Sturdy Black Bridges,* edited by Roseann P. Bell, Bettye J. Parker, and Beverly Guy-Sheftall, pp. 133-49. New York: Anchor Books, 1979.

Watkins, Mel. "Some Letters Went to God." *The New York Times Book Review* (25 July 1982): 7.

Robert Penn Warren
1905-1989

American poet, novelist, short story writer, dramatist, and critic.

All the King's Men (novel, 1946)

The novel is set in an unnamed town in the South and chronicles the spiritual journey of

Jack Burden. He is the assistant of **Willie Stark,** a character who is based indirectly on the notorious Huey Long, governor and U. S. Senator from Louisiana during the 1920s and 1930s. Like Long, Willie is a man who embodies political corruption. Warren shows how he evolved from a naive, idealistic young man into a ruthless, pragmatic political boss who builds a political machine to entrench his power, uses graft to enrich his friends and line his own pockets, and involves himself in public works to appease his constituents.

Jack is both attracted and repelled by Willie. He maintains a distance from his boss and from other characters in the novel, protecting himself and avoiding responsibility for his actions with two philosophical concepts: the Big Sleep and the Great Twitch. The Big Sleep represents Jack's occasional lapses into unconsciousness, a state of mind he seeks when he is confronted with a challenge to his ideals. The Great Twitch embodies Jack's theory that life and the individual's response to it as governed by an involuntary reaction, or "twitch." Thus, he is absolved of responsibility in a meaningless world, where actions and responses signify nothing.

Jack is jarred out of complacency by several key events. Willie tells him to dig up politically damaging evidence on **Judge Monty Irwin,** one of the most respected public officials in town and a man who had always refused to support Willie. Jack does uncover criminal evidence about Irwin, which Willie seeks to use to fend off a blackmail attempt. But rather than help Willie, Irwin commits suicide. His death is doubly wounding for Jack, for not only has he driven a man to suicide, but his mother reveals to him that Irwin was his real father. Willie has also begun an affair with Jack's former girlfriend, **Anne Stanton.** Her brother, an idealistic young man, kills Willie, hoping to protect his sister; he in turn is killed by Willie's chauffeur. In the conclusion, Jack has begun the painful road to self-knowledge, having suffered and endured much.

The work is told in flashback, as Jack, now a historian working on his doctoral thesis, tries to make sense of the past. Warren superbly blends several levels of time in the novel, using flashback at various points to reflect on and illuminate past action and its meaning. In addition to the theme of time, Warren explores the nature of evil and betrayal in the novel, which is considered his finest achievement in prose and for which he received the Pulitzer Prize.

FURTHER READING

Anderson, Charles R. "Violence and Order in the Novels of Robert Penn Warren." *Hopkins Review* 6 (Winter 1953): 88-105.

Bentley, Eric. "The Meaning of Robert Penn Warren's Novels." *Kenyon Review* 10 (Summer 1948): 407-24.

Contemporary Authors, Vols. 13-16, rev. ed.; *Contemporary Authors New Revision Series,* Vol. 10. Detroit: Gale Research Co.

Contemporary Literary Criticism, Vols. 1, 4, 6, 8, 10, 13, 18, 39, 53. Detroit: Gale Research Co.

Dictionary of Literary Biography, Vols. 2, 48; *Dictionary of Literary Biography Yearbook: 1980.* Detroit: Gale Research Co.

Girault, Norton R. "The Narrator's Mind as Symbol: An Analysis of *All the King's Men.*" *Accent* 7 (Summer 1947): 220-34.

Evelyn Waugh

1903-1966

English novelist, essayist, and short story writer.

Decline and Fall (novel, 1928)

Set in early twentieth-century England, the story traces the misfortunes of **Paul Pennyfeather,** an innocent young student of theology at Oxford. Unjustly expelled from the university because of the antics of his less disciplined peers, Pennyfeather is advised to turn to a career in teaching. He finds himself at Llanabba Castle, a poorly rated boarding school in Wales, which is staffed by a generally disinterested, inept, or drunken faculty. There Pennyfeather makes several new acquaintances who enliven the story with their unusual habits and lives. The reigning air of corruption and self-interest at Llanabba Castle effects the students as well as the faculty. Even the school's venerated track and field day, with its tradition of sportsmanship and fair play, is spoiled by dishonesty, fighting, and injury. Within this venal environment, Pennyfeather finds some solace and companionship when he begins courting **Margot Beste-Chetwynde,** the wealthy mother of one of his brightest students. Shortly before the couple's marriage, however, Pennyfeather is unexpectedly arrested and imprisoned for his association with the woman. Apparently, she has amassed her fortune by masterminding an international prostitution ring. In jail, the same vein of chaos and corruption runs throughout all affairs, as those inmates with money or social power play upon their political allies while the management leisurely theorizes about reform. Pennyfeather's death is eventually falsified, and he is free to begin a new life. He returns to Oxford to study the Early Church. This time, however, he seems destined to distance himself from the absurdity and corruption surrounding him.

The satiric tone of this novel is echoed in much of Waugh's later fiction. The outrageous occurrences and moral offenses in *Decline and Fall* are, in fact, conveyed with such cool detachment that the publishers originally requested that Waugh include a disclaimer: "Please bear in mind throughout that [the novel] is meant to be funny." Many critics argue that Waugh is deliberately revealing corruption's destruction of beauty and innocence and suggest that the author intentionally portrays characters who finally distance themselves from the chaos of the modern world.

A Handful of Dust (novel, 1934)

The novel is set in the English countryside on a dilapidated neo-Gothic estate. **Tony Last** is an honorable, decent man who lives at his ancestral home with his much loved-wife **Brenda** and their young son. Although Tony is content with their slow, pastoral life-style, Brenda grows restless and becomes involved with a group of London socialites who encourage her to take a lover. She becomes completely infatuated with a weak and repulsive young man named **John Beaver,** who supports himself by appealing to the affections of women wealthier than himself. Brenda's actions appear to be compulsive, for even when she is capable of reflecting on her downfall, she is powerless to reverse it.

Tony is devastated by his wife's senseless infidelity. Despite his own innocence and discomfort, however, Tony succumbs to legal convention and fabricates evidence of his own unfaithfulness for the purpose of divorce. This pretense leads him on an absurd retreat with a prostitute and her young daughter, which only serves to exacerbate Tony's miserable lonely condition. Upon hearing of his wife's exorbitant settlement proposal, Tony fears the loss of his estate and flees to South America before the divorce is finalized. There he embarks on a symbolic journey in search of a mythical city. Scenes of Tony in the jungle are creatively interspersed with scenes of Brenda's lonely misfortunes in London. While Tony pushes onward to find his ideal in the Amazon, Brenda remarries in an unsuccessful attempt to regain the civility and dignity she had once shared with Tony.

The novel ends when Tony is captured by an illiterate jungle settler, **James Todd,** and is forced to read Dickens aloud to Mr. Todd for the rest of his days. Despite their disparate environments, both Tony and Brenda seem ultimately incapable of finding or recreating the ideal they envision. In its conclusion, the novel directly compares the upper-class English society with the primitive lifestyle of the Amazon in an effort to make the juxtaposition of barbarism and innocence—wherever it may occur—more distinct.

Enriching the successful satiric mode he established in *Decline and Fall* with deeper characterization, Waugh created one of his strongest works with *A Handful of Dust*. Critics note that although Waugh still treats the amorality of modern culture with cool comic detachment, he has tempered this mood with realism and pathos. The novel further differs from *Decline and Fall* in its more obvious identification of good and innocence with Christianity and in the characters' ineffectual idealized visions of the past.

Brideshead Revisited (novel, 1945)

The novel is narrated by **Charles Ryder,** who first appears as a disenchanted English army officer during World War II as he overlooks the lovely estate of Brideshead, home of the Marchmain family. Ryder is looking back to the early 1920s at Oxford University and his relations with the very wealthy and aristocratic Catholic family of his schoolmate **Sebastian Flyte,** the son of **Lord** and **Lady Marchmain.** As a studious undergraduate, Ryder is drawn to the unconventional and carefree lifestyle of Sebastian and his friends. Among the most intriguing of his new-found acquaintances is **Anthony Blanche,** an extremely intelligent aesthete whose perversities and biting criticisms of the world around him have captivated Waugh's critics. Ryder's account of these school days and the affairs of the Marchmain family form the body of the novel and reveal the predominant "spirit of the profane" during this period before the central characters' eventual return to their neglected Catholic faith.

Through Ryder's reminiscences, the lovelessness of the Marchmain family slowly comes to light, casting a shadow over the worldly pleasures described. As the conflict between pleasure-seeking and Catholicism becomes more pronounced in the Marchmains's lives, the individual family members flee from the family and their faith. Sebastian abuses alcohol, **Julia** escapes into an unhealthy marriage, and Lord Marchmain takes a mistress and moves to Italy. When Sebastian visits his father in Venice, the depth of his struggle between easy boyhood innocence and adult acceptance of the responsibility accompanying belief is revealed. The family's solution to his problem is to send Sebastian to a sanatorium. Sebastian resorts to flight once again, but this time he escapes to North Africa where he finds temporary peace and friendship. Several years later, Ryder brings Sebastian back to England amidst great social turmoil so that he can comfort his ailing mother. After her death, the family is furthest from its faith and the Marchmain chapel, a symbol of the family faith, is closed.

Over the years, Ryder becomes a successful architectural painter. He encounters Sebastian's sister Julia on a voyage returning from South America and, although they are both married now, they make love, thus beginning the affair that will work on Julia's Catholic conscience. Meanwhile, Sebastian is living in North Africa at a monastery. Near the close of the novel, Lord Marchmain returns to his home to die. Crossing himself on his deathbed, he triggers Julia's awakened conscience into action and she, repentant, ends her affair with Ryder. Ultimately the novel returns to Ryder's encampment at Brideshead where the story began and where Ryder reveals his own acceptance of Christianity. Nothing remains of the past at the castle but the children's steadfast nanny and a rekindled flame at the Marchmain altar.

Critics have complained that although this is Waugh's first novel to end with a note of promise, the ostensible affirmation of Catholicism is marred by the emphasis on discipline and duty rather than the heartfelt faith of the characters. In this way, they contend, Waugh fails to carry out his stated intent to depict "the operation of divine grace" in the corrupt world of men. Other critics argue that Waugh does not intend to portray the Catholic faith as sacrosanct, but intentionally pokes fun at the exaggerated rituals and superstitions of the faith without seriously questioning its integrity. For these critics, the profane gives way to the sacred at the close of the novel and the central theme—the unavoidable grace of God for the spiritually aware—is revealed.

FURTHER READING

Carens, James F. *The Satiric Art of Evelyn Waugh.* Seattle: University of Washington Press, 1966.

Contemporary Authors, Vols. 85-88; *Contemporary Authors New Revision Series,* Vol. 22. Detroit: Gale Research Co.

Contemporary Literary Criticism, Vols. 1, 3, 8, 13, 19, 27, 44. Detroit: Gale Research Co.

Delasanta, Rodney and Mario L. D'Avanzo. "Truth and Beauty in *Brideshead Revisited.*" *Modern Fiction Studies* 11 (Summer 1965): 140-52.

Dictionary of Literary Biography, Vol. 15. Detroit: Gale Research Co.

Doyle, Paul A. *Evelyn Waugh: A Critical Essay.* Grand Rapids: Eerdmans, 1969.

Hollis, Christopher. *Evelyn Waugh.* London: Longman, 1971.

Joost, Nicholas. "*A Handful of Dust:* Evelyn Waugh and the Novel of Manners." *Papers on Language and Literature* 12 (Spring 1976): 177-96.

LaFrance, Marston. "Context and Structure of Evelyn Waugh's *Brideshead Revisited.*" *Twentieth Century Literature* 10 (1964): 12-18.

Lodge, David. *Evelyn Waugh.* New York: Columbia University Press, 1971.

Sykes, Christopher. *Evelyn Waugh: A Biography.* Boston: Little, Brown, 1975.

Wilson, Edmund. "Splendors and Miseries of Evelyn Waugh." In *Classics and Commercials: A Literary Chronicle of the Forties,* pp. 298-305. New York: Farrar, Straus and Giroux, 1950.

H. G. Wells
1866-1946

English novelist, short story writer, and essayist.

The Time Machine (novel, 1895)

The scientific fantasy begins in late nineteenth-century England at the Richmond home of a professor-inventor, whom the narrator refers to as the **Time Traveler.** Discussion among the Traveler's dinner guests centers upon a four-dimensional theory of geometry the Traveler has conceived and is attempting to elucidate. His assertion that time, properly understood, is simply an unconsidered, additional dimension of space is met with puzzlement and skepticism. Attempting to further demonstrate his theory and satisfy his friend's queries, he displays a small model of his time machine, capable of limitless travel into the past and the future. With the movement of a lever, the machine disappears, traveling at a velocity surpassing the powers of human vision. A week later guests gather for another dinner party; the Time Traveler arrives late, shocking his friends by his bedraggled, haggard appearance.

The story that ensues consists of the Traveler's spellbinding narration of his eight-day encounter with the inhabitants of a dystopian England in the year 802,701 A.D. The first, strange descendants of humanity he meets are the Eloi, short, frail, simple-minded beings who subsist on fruit, play, and love. While their alien language and mental lassitude pose a difficult barrier for the Traveler, he quickly apprehends that the Eloi have an intense fear of darkness. When his time machine disappears the Traveler, accompanied by a young Eloi named **Weena,** canvasses the landscape and encounters the Morlocks. Likewise descendants of humanity, the Morlocks are crafty subterranean dwellers who resemble gigantic spiders. Unlike the Eloi, they are industrious and carnivorous, their only fear being light, which their eyes cannot tolerate. At nighttime Weena perishes and the Traveler escapes death by the Morlocks only because he has inadvertently set a nearby forest ablaze. The next evening he finds his unharmed machine and, closely pursued, departs further into the future. Tracing the devolution of the earth to a point thirty million years beyond the industrial age, he discovers a dying sun and a deathly still planet. The novel closes the day after the dinner party when the narrator returns to the professor's laboratory and watches the Traveler and his machine vanish.

A novelist of ideas, many pertaining to the future of civilization, Wells founded his quintessential classic on three popular theories of his age: biological adaptation to the environment, increasing divisiveness between social classes, and dissipating order and vitality of the universe. These theories mirror the findings of Charles Darwin, Karl Marx, and T. H. Huxley. One of the world's first and most successful scientific romances, *The Time Machine* depicts the impossible with striking verisimilitude and detail. Thus, Wells's debut novel has remained a pioneering inspiration to generations of science fiction writers.

The Invisible Man (novel, 1897)

A riveting scientific mystery set in late nineteenth-century England, *The Invisible Man* illumines the moral descent of **Griffin,** a brilliant young scientist who has discovered invisibility. Outfitted with dark oversized spectacles, fake facial hair, and clothing covering his entire body, Griffin enters the village of Iping, where he secures lodging and attempts to hide his secret. **Mr.** and **Mrs. Hall,** owners of the inn, are among the first to ponder their guest's bizarre appearance and reclusive habits. Unusual occurrences and unsolved thefts arouse the curiosity of the other villagers. Eventually, attempting to evade paying his bill, Griffin unmasks himself, leaving the onlooking innkeeper and town constable horror-stricken. Stories of the Invisible Man's thefts and disappearance reach the newspapers.

The second section of the novel focuses on Griffin's past and the events that led him to his stunning discovery. Obsessed with his theories of light refraction and cell transparency, he stole money from his father to fund his research and experiments. Shortly thereafter, his father committed suicide, for the money had been loaned to him. Once invisible, Griffin became increasingly desperate, ruthless, and remorseless. In the final section, he launches a reign of terror after being betrayed to the police by a former university acquaintance, **Dr. Kemp,** with whom he had sought refuge. Having killed one man and wounded another, Griffin is finally contained by his pursuers and struck down with a spade. Now dead, he slowly materializes, naked upon the ground.

Although less serious in its conception than Wells's earlier novels of ideas, *The Invisible Man* does propound the thesis that unchecked scientific investigation leads to moral vacuousness. Yet Wells avoids an overtly remonstrative tone. The novel endures as one of Wells's most popular and convincing works.

The War of the Worlds (novel, 1898)

The most celebrated of Wells's science fiction novels is set in and around London near the end of the nineteenth century. Nearly devoid of character development, the documentary-like narrative unfolds the action surrounding a Martian invasion. The narrator, an unnamed suburban man with an interest in astronomy, describes how one night at the observatory he viewed Mars and saw small pinpoints of light leaving the planet. Days later a large meteor crashes near his home. A brown creature resembling an octopus, with enormous eyes and tentacles, emerges. More creatures venture forth and begin digging a pit around their craft. As the digging and building continue a few scientists and a neighborhood crowd gather. London newspapers, however, ignore reports of the event. Soon the Martians' project is complete; hundred-feet tall metal tripods scourge the landscape, firing great incendiary rays with devastating effect. Reckless alarm spreads as the militia hopelessly attempts to destroy the rampaging machines. The horrific story concludes when the twelve-day siege ends with the Martians vanquished, destroyed by bacteria.

Capping the first phase of Wells's literary career, *The War of the Worlds* is now inseparable from Orson Welles's radio-broadcast adaptation, which aired on Halloween night, 1938, and fueled panic among countless listeners across the United States. Beyond its immediate shock value, though, the novel pointedly conveys a Swiftian satire of the author's own culture and times. Wells intended for his contemporaries to draw parallels between the relentless, destructive advance of the technologically superior Martians and the one-sided military successes of the British Army over poorly protected peoples during the years of British colonial expansion. Furthermore, Wells meant through his juxtaposition of Eng-landers and Martians to posit the frightful evolutionary destiny of the entire human race.

Tono-Bungay (novel, 1908)

Begun in England during the Edwardian era, the seriocomic novel traces **George Ponderevo's** meteoric rise from lower-class life to fame and fortune. Raised by his mother, a servant housekeeper, George comes to despise his background. George's mother eventually sends him to Sussex to live with his uncle **Edward Ponderevo.** While there his mother dies and the exclamatory Edward, a fortune-seeking chemist, squanders George's trust fund. At twenty-two George enters a South Kensington technical school on a scholarship. There he meets **Marion Ramboat,** whom he later marries. Neglecting his studies and concerned about his future, George seizes an opportunity to work for Edward manufacturing and marketing a new patent medicine. The innocuous quack cure-all, Tono-Bungay, is inexpensive to produce and the Ponderevos, through bold, relentless advertising, quickly acquire great wealth. Marion consents to marry George, but the union ends in divorce when George succumbs to a weekend fling with an office secretary.

Attempting to recover his integrity, severely jeopardized by his broken marriage and a growing cynicism, George devotes himself to aeronautical study and research. Meanwhile, Edward broadens the Ponderevo financial empire, marking his escalating wealth with the purchase of increasingly opulent private estates. Eventually, Edward's speculations doom the corporation and desperate measures must be taken to avoid bankruptcy. George journeys to Mordet Island, off the west coast of Africa, and steals a cargo of quap. The Ponderevos believe the rare mineral can be refined to produce an improved lamp filament and thus salvage their enterprises. The quap's radioactivity causes the plan to backfire and George to mysteriously murder an African native. To avoid creditors and the authorities, the Ponderevos cross the English Channel by night in George's airship. When Edward dies in France, George returns to England and, once absolved of charges, begins designing and testing destroyers for the British Navy.

An ambitious portrayal of social, political, and individual decay, *Tono-Bungay* stands out among Wells's satiric novels and serves as a bridge between his character and expository fiction. Despite its elliptical conclusion, in which George uncertainly ponders the existence of some transcendent truth that counters the overweening degeneracy of the modern world, the work has been called Wells's masterpiece. Perhaps nowhere else has he so successfully blended sweeping moral criticism with spirited British humor and optimism. With the possible exception of George Bernard Shaw, no other author of his day so effectively captured the exuberant sense of release from Victorian conventions and morals.

FURTHER READING

Bergonzi, Bernard. *The Early H. G. Wells: A Study of the Scientific Romances.* Toronto: University of Toronto Press, 1961.

——, ed. *H. G. Wells: A Collection of Critical Essays.* Englewood Cliffs: Prentice-Hall, 1976.

Brooks, Van Wyck. *The World of H. G. Wells,* 1915. Reprint. St. Clair Shores: Scholarly Press, 1970.

Contemporary Authors, Vol. 110. Detroit: Gale Research Co.

Dictionary of Literary Biography, Vols. 34, 70. Detroit: Gale Research Co.

Freeman, John. "H. G. Wells." In *The Moderns: Essays in Literary Criticism,* pp. 53-101, 1917. Reprint. Freeport: Books for Libraries Press, 1967.

Hillegas, Mark R. *The Future as Nightmare: H. G. Wells and the Anti-Utopians.* New York: Oxford University Press, 1967.

Lodge, David. "*Tono-Bungay* and the Condition of England." In *Language of Fiction: Essays in Criticism and Verbal Analysis of the English Novel,* pp. 214-42. London: Routledge and Kegan Paul, 1966.

MacKenzie, Norman and Jeanne MacKenzie. *The Time Traveller: The Life of H. G. Wells.* London: Weidenfeld and Nicolson, 1973.

McConnell, Frank. *The Science Fiction of H. G. Wells.* New York: Oxford University Press, 1981.

Suvin, Darko. "Wells as the Turning Point of the SF Tradition." In *Metamorphoses of Science Fiction: On the Poetics and History of a Literary Genre,* pp. 208-21. New Haven: Yale University Press, 1979.

Suvin, Darko and Robert M. Philmus, eds. *H. G. Wells and Modern Science Fiction.* Lewisburg: Bucknell University Press, 1977.

Twentieth-Century Literary Criticism, Vols. 6, 12, 19. Detroit: Gale Research Co.

Williamson, Jack. *H. G. Wells: Critic of Progress.* Baltimore: Mirage Press, 1973.

Eudora Welty

1909-

American novelist, short story writer, and essayist.

The Robber Bridegroom (novella, 1942)

The setting of the work is the Natchez Trace in old Mississippi in the year 1798. The novella has been called a historical fantasy, and Welty employs elements of fairy tale and folklore in style and characterization. **Jamie Lockhart,** the robber bridegroom of the title, is a merchant by day and a brave and cunning bandit by night. **Rosamond Musgrove** embodies all the characteristics of the typical fairy tale heroine: she is beautiful, virtuous, and adventurous. In an opening scene, Jamie encounters a legendary bandit, **Mike Fink,** who has captured Rosamond's father, **Clement Musgrove.** Jamie saves Clement, who in gratitude brings him home where he meets Rosamond, whom he kidnaps and seduces. But Rosamond falls in love with her captor and stays with him. Unaware of her fate, Clement goes in search of his daughter. Much of the narrative is given through Clement's consciousness, and his musings throughout the book are central to Welty's purpose. The central theme of the novella, the duality of human nature, is presented by Clement as he talks to Rosamond after she has returned home: "All things are double," he tells her, referring to her lover, who is both good and evil, and to humankind in general. True to the fairy tale elements at work in the story, Clement's wife, **Salome,** functions as the "wicked stepmother," who is jealous of and cruel to her beautiful step-daughter, yet she willingly sacrifices herself to save her family in the novel's climax. The conclusion of the story finds Jamie and Rosamond in New Orleans, married and apparently embarked on a life of respectability.

Welty's mock-epic is vibrant with humor and satire. Through comic exaggeration, she makes use of Southern folk lore to create an allegorical fantasy. Welty chronicles the New World in flux, changing and losing its wildness as the hero and heroine leave the wilderness for the civilized world of New Orleans.

Delta Wedding (novel, 1946)

As with most of Welty's fiction, the story is set in Mississippi, this time the delta town of Fairchilds, site of the Shellmound Plantation, in 1923. The novel focuses on the Fairchild family as they prepare for the wedding of **Dabney,** daughter of **Ellen** and **Battle Fairchild,** to **Troy Flavin,** the overseer of the plantation. The narrative is given in a variety of voices and perspectives. The action of the work centers on the preparations for the wedding, full of washing, ironing, cooking, eating, gift-giving, and talking. The Fairchild family is constantly engaged in discussing the family history, which is told and retold throughout the work. Generations of tragedies and triumphs, births and deaths, and fortunate and unfortunate marriages are chronicled, reaching back to the Civil War and up to the present, focusing on Dabney's wedding and Ellen's tenth pregnancy.

A central incident in the story centers on **George Fairchild,** Battle's brother, who saves little **Maureen** from death when her shoe is stuck on a railroad track before an oncoming train. This story is related many times by various family members, for whom George acts as a kind of catalyst to ruminations on family, love, and sacrifice. George is one of the few characters in the novel who is never known to the reader through his own words, but is instead portrayed by a variety of characters who interpret for us the depth of his sensitivity and understanding. Ellen's perspective represents the filtering consciousness of the novel. As one of Welty's "outsiders," a Fairchild by marriage only, she is able to observe and analyze the family and how it works. She is the unifying sensibility of the novel, and in her compassion and insight, clarifies its vision.

Welty's central theme in this, as in so much of her fiction, is the dominion of the family. She examines the way in which the individual is both drawn to and repelled by the power of a large and close-knit family, exploring such topics as identity, responsibility, isolation, and the need to belong. The work has been praised for Welty's deft handling of a variety of narrative perspectives, her ear for dialect, and for the subtlety and complexity of her characterizations.

The Golden Apples (short stories, 1949)

Virgie Rainey is a recurrent figure in a number of short stories from Welty's third collection of short fiction, a work acclaimed as one of her best. The stories were initially published separately, then revised and published in book form.

The setting for all the stories is the delta town of Morgana, Mississippi, and the action spans the forty years between the pre-World War I era and the late 1940s, covering the lives of a core group of characters. Virgie is the central character in two of the most important and best-known stories in the volume, ''June Recital'' and ''The Wanderers.''

In ''June Recital'' the events of the narrative are chronicled through several narrators. **Loch** and **Cassie Morrison,** brother and sister, observe the activity at the abandoned house next door where **Miss Eckhart,** the old piano teacher, scatters papers and sets fire to the house, while upstairs Virgie and a sailor make love. As Cassie watches, she hears the strains of Beethoven's ''Für Elise,'' a piece connected with her childhood and especially with Virgie and Miss Eckhart. She lapses into a reverie, recalling her past and Miss Eckhart's June recitals in the house next door. Virgie was Miss Eckhart's prodigy, the pupil she thought would become a great musician. But Virgie was a rebellious girl and preferred the world of boys and sex to music, and she rejected Miss Eckhart's urgings that she leave Morgana and seek a career in music. Miss Eckhart, of German descent and one of Welty's ''outsiders,'' is a lonely, isolated figure. When she is able to reach out to another, as she does with Virgie, hoping to share her passionate love for music, she is desperately hurt by the rejection and withdraws into deeper isolation. Loch Morrison, described as the all-seeing Argus of myth, watches as Miss Eckhart sets fire to her papers, which become a kind of sacrifice for her wasted life. As two townspeople save Virgie and Miss Eckhart from the fire, Loch rescues Miss Eckhart's burning metronome.

Welty's well-known use of myth is evident in this and all the stories in *The Golden Apples.* The recurrent themes of loneliness and the search for love are also evoked in this work. The multiple perspectives created by the variety of narrators is a feature that brings depth and resonance to the story.

In ''The Wanderers'' Virgie Rainey has returned to Morgana for her mother's funeral. **Katie Rainey** had been the narrator of the first story in the collection, and her death marks its closing. Throughout the wake and the funeral, the citizens of Morgana pass by Virgie, and she notes how they are all old and dying, appearing more like specters than the vibrant men and women of her memory. During the funeral, **King MacLain,** whose amorous wanderings as a young man had been compared to those of Zeus, makes a hideous face at Virgie. She sees it and understands its implications: he, and all of them, know that he will be the next to die. After the funeral, Virgie swims in the Big Black River, a ritual enactment that cleanses her and makes her one with the mysterious natural world. On her way out of town, she is caught in a storm, and taking shelter under a tree, remembers the picture of Perseus and Medusa that hung in Miss Eckhart's studio. The meaning of the myth it depicts becomes vivid for her: the heroic act requires a victim. She finds in the action of Perseus cutting off the Medusa's head a symbol for the loneliness in the severing of the self from another.

Welty's use of myth and ritual in this, as in so many of her stories, elevates and illuminates the mundane world. Thematically, she explores the human need for love, but also the need to explore and to wander, accepting the loneliness inherent in the search for self-knowledge.

The Ponder Heart (novella, 1954)

The story is set in the Beulah Hotel in Clay, Mississippi, where **Edna Earle Ponder** is the manager. The work is given as a monologue as she relates the story of her life, her town, and its inhabitants to a travelling salesman. As narrator, Edna Earle is by turns vivacious, earthy, snobbish, and garrulous, and her portraits of her fellow townspeople are richly comic; few escape her satiric scrutiny. One major focus for her thoughts is the life of her

Uncle Daniel Ponder, a legendary figure in the community. Uncle Daniel, one of Welty's finest portraits of an eccentric, is not terribly bright, but he is a man of great heart and generosity. Despite his limitations, Edna Earle loves him fiercely and tries to protect him from those who would take advantage of this harmless, loving, foolish man. The story of his relationship to **Bonnie Dee** is a central sequence in the story, following their courtship, marriage, separations, and Bonnie Dee's death at the hands of Uncle Daniel, who, trying to distract her from her fear during a thunderstorm, tickles her to death. Uncle Daniel's subsequent trial for his wife's murder is hilariously portrayed, and ends in his acquittal, as he strews the courtroom with the last of his money.

The tone of the novel is lively and humorous, and many critics consider it Welty's finest work in the comic vein. Once again, her recreation of colloquial speech is vividly displayed through the voice of Edna Earle. Her monologue is a brilliant tour de force, heightened by the variety of setting and tone and given at a breathless pace.

The Optimist's Daughter (novel, 1972)

Set for the most part in Mount Salus, Mississippi, the novel is divided into four sections. Part One deals with the death of **Judge Clinton McKelva,** attended by his daughter **Laurel McKelva Hand** and **Wanda Fay Chisom McKelva,** her father's selfish, vulgar second wife. Part Two covers the funeral of Judge McKelva and gives further insight into the vapid, grasping Chisom family. In the third and fourth sections, Laurel's introspective thoughts on her family and her own life are described as she realizes that she must now turn her family's home over to the ruthless Wanda Fay. She immerses herself in remnants of the past—her father's clock, her mother's roses, the breadboard made by her late husband—sifting through a lifetime of memories and learning how to place the past in perspective and live in the present. Her reflections on her family are not all pleasant: her mother was a difficult, headstrong woman who died after a lingering illness; her father, particularly in his marriage to Wanda Fay, could be weak and foolish; and her husband, killed in World War II, died before having a chance to live. Laurel also ruminates on the loneliness that seemed to separate the family members from one another long before their deaths. In the novel's conclusion, Laurel, having confronted and understood her past, leaves the house to Wanda Fay without acrimony and returns to her own life at peace.

As she has so often in her fiction, Welty examines the power of family ties and the nature of filial responsibility. This theme is heightened by Welty's focus on perception and the meaning of memory as Laurel learns to live with the past. Although she is the novel's central figure, Laurel does not truly become known to the reader until the third and fourth sections, for it is not until she can understand herself that she is fully comprehended by us. In her portrait of the vulgar Wanda Fay, Welty juxtaposes the New South with the genteel traditions of the Old South as embodied in Laurel and her family. As in her other works, Welty's deft ear for dialogue is used to discern the cultural difference in her characters. *The Optimist's Daughter,* for which Welty received the Pulitzer Prize, is considered one of her finest achievements.

FURTHER READING

Aldridge, John W. "Eudora Welty: Metamorphosis of a Southern Lady Writer." *Saturday Review* 11 (April 1970): 21-3, 35-6.

Appel, Alfred, Jr. *A Season of Dreams: The Fiction of Eudora Welty.* Baton Rouge: Louisiana State University Press, 1965.

Brooks, Cleanth. "The Past Reexamined: *The Optimist's Daughter.*" *Mississippi Quarterly* 26 (Fall 1973): 577-87.

Bryant, J. A., Jr. "Seeing Double in *The Golden Apples.*" *Sewanee Review* 82 (Spring 1974): 300-15.

——. *Eudora Welty*. Minneapolis: University of Minnesota Press, 1968.

Contemporary Authors, Vols. 9-12, rev. ed.; *Contemporary Authors Bibliographical Series,* Vol. 1. Detroit: Gale Research Co.

Contemporary Literary Criticism, Vols. 1, 2, 5, 14, 22, 33. Detroit: Gale Research Co.

Desmond, John F. "Pattern and Vision in *The Optimist's Daughter.*" In *A Still Moment: Essays on the Art of Eudora Welty,* pp. 118-38. Metuchen: Scarecrow, 1978.

Dictionary of Literary Biography, Vol. 2; *Concise Dictionary of American Literary Biography, 1941-1968.* Detroit: Gale Research Co.

Fleischauer, John F. "The Focus of Mystery: Eudora Welty's Prose Style." *Southern Literary Journal* 5 (Spring 1973): 64-79.

Goeller, Allison. "*Delta Wedding* as Pastoral." *Interpretations: A Journal of Idea, Analysis and Criticism* 13 (Fall 1981): 59-72.

Gross, Seymour L. "Eudora Welty's Comic Imagination." In *The Comic Imagination in American Literature,* edited by Louis D. Rubin, Jr., pp. 319-28. New Brunswick: Rutgers University Press, 1973.

Hardy, John Edward. "*Delta Wedding* as Region and Symbol." *Sewanee Review* 60 (July-September 1952): 397-417.

Holland, Robert B. "Dialogue as a Reflection of Place in *The Ponder Heart.*" *American Literature* 35 (November 1963): 352-58.

Howard, Zelma Turner. *The Rhetoric of Eudora Welty's Short Stories.* Jackson: University and College Press of Mississippi, 1973.

Jones, William M. "Name and Symbol in the Prose of Eudora Welty." *Southern Folklore Quarterly* 22 (December 1958): 173-85.

Manning, Carol S. *With Ears Opening Like Morning Glories: Eudora Welty and the Love of Storytelling.* Westport: Greenwood Press, 1985.

McHaney, Thomas L. "Eudora Welty and the Multitudinous Golden Apples." *Mississippi Quarterly* 26 (Fall 1973): 589-624.

Short Story Criticism, Vol. 1. Detroit: Gale Research Co.

Franz Werfel
1890-1945

Austrian novelist, dramatist, and poet.

The Song of Bernadette (novel, 1941)

The Song of Bernadette, Werfel's most popular work, is a fictional biography of Saint Bernadette. The story takes place in Lourdes, France in the mid-nineteenth century and describes the details and aftermath of a young girl's vision of the Virgin Mary.

As the story opens, **Marie Bernarde Soubirous (Bernadette),** her sister, and a school friend are gathering wood when Bernadette, temporarily isolated from the others, sees a beautiful lady in a grotto. Afterwards, Bernadette confides in the other girls who then inform the neighborhood. Bernadette is depicted as a simple, naive girl, overwhelmed by the attention and antagonism focussed on her as a result of her vision. Considered a stupid, limited girl, she is at first scorned by the villagers. But when the lady in the vision invites

Bernadette to dig in the grotto, a spring appears and roses begin to bloom. Bernadette acquires a following of sorts, which mildly alarms the town magistrates. After a child is miraculously healed at the site, more and more people flock to Lourdes, hoping to witness a miracle. As a result, the Mayor, **Adolphe Lacade,** erects a barricade at the grotto, for he hopes to use the spring water as a source of income for the town and plans to have it bottled and sold. The Church is reluctant to become involved, because any effort spent on what could turn out to be a hoax would threaten its credibility, and also because it is loathe to challenge the state.

Bernadette finds herself both idolized and scorned. She is interrogated by both government and church officials and her relationship with her family and friends becomes strained. In the end, the barricade is removed by order of Napoleon III, sparking a four-year Church investigation into the matter. During the inquiry, Bernadette is sent to the Convent of St. Gildarde, where she lives for the remainder of her life. Seventy-five years after the first miracle, she is canonized as Saint Bernadette.

Thematically, Werfel's novel is a testament to his belief in the innate goodness of humankind. Through the character of Bernadette, he demonstrates his admiration for self-sacrifice and piety. Werfel claimed to have written the novel as a token of thanks after his escape from the Nazis during World War II.

FURTHER READING

Contemporary Authors, Vol. 104. Detroit: Gale Research Co.

Fox, W. H. "Franz Werfel." In *German Men of Letters: Twelve Literary Essays,* edited by Alex Natan, pp. 107-25. New York: Wolff, 1964.

Kohn-Bramstedt, Ernst. "Franz Werfel as a Novelist." *Contemporary Review* 146 (July 1934): 66-73.

Slochower, Harry. "Spiritual Judaism: The Yearning for Status." In *No Voice Is Wholly Lost . . . Writers and Thinkers in War and Peace,* pp. 229-42. New York: Creative Age Press, 1945.

Twentieth-Century Literary Criticism, Vol. 8. Detroit: Gale Research Co.

Warren, Robert Penn. "The Lady of Lourdes." *The Nation* 154, No. 22 (30 May 1942): 229-42.

Nathanael West

1903(?)-1940

American novelist and dramatist.

Miss Lonelyhearts (novel, 1933)

Generally considered West's most artistically accomplished work, *Miss Lonelyhearts* is the story of a newspaper advice columnist who becomes obsessed with the suffering of his correspondents and his inability to help them. Writing for the New York *Post-Dispatch* during the late 1920s, **Miss Lonelyhearts** finds himself the suffering center of a stark, surreal world in which unhappiness and tragedy are commonplace. Originally accepting his job as a joke, he has since recognized the burdensome, painful responsibilities of his position. In his redemptive quests, which populate both his waking and dream worlds, he resembles Christ, an ivory figure of whom rests on his otherwise barren apartment wall. His continual brooding over others' problems has led his boss, **Willie Shrike,** to perpetually invade his consciousness and cruelly taunt him. Lonelyhearts's dull-witted but well-meaning girlfriend, **Betty,** urges him to quit his job. Yet, following a recuperative, passion-filled stay with Betty on a Connecticut farm, he persists in his mission.

He meets **Peter Doyle,** the downtrodden, crippled husband of an advice-seeking woman, **Fay Doyle,** whom he has already met and seduced. After being invited home to the Doyles, he awkwardly attempts to explain the husband's love for his wife. The evening ends sourly when Fay sends her husband on an errand and attempts to seduce Lonelyhearts, who beats her before leaving. Increasingly frustrated with his repellent behavior and because he can neither discern nor create any beauty or gentleness in the world about him, he isolates himself and suffers an emotional breakdown. He envisions himself a rock, impervious to outside feelings. Lonelyhearts's mad reverie is interrupted by Mr. Doyle. Misapprehending Doyle's intention the columnist prepares to greet the cripple, for whom he will perform the obvious miracle. Seeking revenge, However, Doyle shoots and kills Lonelyhearts.

West conceived of *Miss Lonelyhearts* as "a novel in the form of a comic strip," with each chapter the equivalent of a cartoon panel, in which one action instigates many reactions. Although he abandoned this idea, he wrote that "each chapter instead of going forward in time, also goes backward, forward, up, and down in space like a picture." The structurally as well as stylistically innovative novel deals with the loneliness, alienation, despair, and violence that were concomitant with the financial disasters of the Great Depression. Most critics concur that West's decision to identify his protagonist only as Miss Lonelyhearts served to underscore the dehumanizing character of the times.

The Day of the Locust (novel, 1939)

A horrifying story of dreamers, *The Day of the Locust* takes place in Hollywood during the 1930s. After studying at the Yale School of Fine Arts, **Tod Hackett** has come to California to work as a set and costume designer. He meets a variety of people, all of whom search for romance, happiness, and fulfillment in an arid, heartless landscape. As in typical of West's protagonists, Tod obsessively pursues a goal rendered futile by the degeneration of American society. He loves and hopes to win the affection of **Faye Greener,** a beautiful, morally barren, second-rate actress. Lacking money and clout, Tod succeeds only in becoming a voyeur who helplessly watches Faye move from cowboy **Earle Shoop,** to Earle's Mexican friend, **Miguel,** to an innocent, generous Midwesterner, **Homer Simpson.** As the novel unfolds, the characters become increasingly frustrated when they perceive the impossibility of their ambitions, and an atmosphere of violent tension mounts. Homer, a failed and lonely man limited to expressing his emotions through the seemingly detached flexing of his hands, typifies this pervasive anxiety. Tod releases his frustrations through work on an apocalyptic mural, which he titles "The Burning of Los Angeles." At the painting's center is a sexually provocative image of Faye, calm and expressionless as an angry mob approaches her. Tod's apocalypse materializes in the final scene, as a star-crazed crowd impatiently awaits a movie premiere. Pandemonium rapidly erupts when Homer, with machinelike dispatch, murders **Adore Loomis,** a boy who has been teasing him. Tod, nearly submerged by the crowd, confuses his imaginary completion of the mural with the chaotic scene that surrounds him.

Regarded as a stylistic innovator whose works fit no standard literary classification, West combined elements of both traditional literary naturalism and the new technique of surrealism in the two novels for which he is best known, *Miss Lonelyhearts* and *The Day of the Locust.* In the latter, often called the finest novel about Hollywood, West found a representative setting of everything he believed was wrong with American culture. West is noted as one of the earliest progenitors of black humor and the grotesque in modern American fiction.

FURTHER READING

Comerchero, Victor. *Nathanael West: The Ironic Prophet.* Syracuse: Syracuse University Press, 1964.

Contemporary Authors, Vol. 104. Detroit: Gale Research Co.

Dictionary of Literary Biography, Vols. 4, 9, 28. Detroit: Gale Research Co.

Hyman, Stanley Edgar. *Nathanael West.* Minneapolis: University of Minnesota Press, 1962.

Jackson, Thomas H., ed. *Twentieth Century Interpretations of "Miss Lonelyhearts": A Collection of Critical Essays.* Englewood Cliffs: Prentice-Hall, 1971.

Malin, Irving. *Nathanael West's Novels.* Carbondale: Southern Illinois University Press, 1972.

Martin, Jay. *Nathanael West: The Art of His Life.* New York: Farrar, Straus and Giroux, 1970.

——, ed. *Nathanael West: A Collection of Critical Essays.* Englewood Cliffs: Prentice-Hall, 1971.

Reid, Randall. *The Fiction of Nathanael West.* Chicago: University of Chicago Press, 1967.

Twentieth-Century Literary Criticism, Vols. 1, 14. Detroit: Gale Research Co.

Widmer, Kingsley. *Nathanael West.* Boston: Twayne, 1982.

Edith Wharton

1862-1937

American novelist and poet.

The House of Mirth (novel, 1905)

Lily Bart and **Laurence Selden** are the main characters in Wharton's novelistic statement about upper-class Manhattan society at the turn of the century. Born of good family, Lily has beauty and charm but little money. The story is of her struggles to adhere to standards which have been ingrained by her deceased mother: to marry for wealth and maintain her position in a society in which the moral fiber has been weakened by conspicuous spending and trivial pursuits. Her wealthy aunt, **Mrs. Peniston,** provides the proper but temporary environment for Lily's marital game-plan.

Laurence Selden moves in Lily's social circle, but lacks the affluence of his peers; he has chosen to remain outside of the ''gilt cage'' which they occupy and is more realistic than Lily in his regard for integrity and freedom from excess. They are attracted to each other, and although he does not meet her fiscal requirements, their relationship is friendly and open; she trusts him to be honest with her. Later, Selden comes to love Lily and admits it, but fails to convince her that her value system is faulty and that she must change it.

After his admonitions, there follows a series of disastrous events for Lily. The unscrupulous **Gus Trenor,** married to Lily's friend **Judy,** takes advantage of Lily's monetary naïveté, with the result that she soon owes him a debt which she cannot repay. His offer for settlement is that she have an affair with him. Repelled, Lily flees to Europe. Upon her return to receive her inheritance from her aunt, her predicament is compounded; the legacy is delayed, and she is no longer received by her contemporaries, since they feel her behavior has been questionable.

Her now desperate attempts to maintain her position are futile, and she is forced to seek employment for sustenance. When at last she receives her inheritance, her final gesture is to arrange for payment to Trenor and to commit suicide in her boarding-house room. It is only after death that she gains final favor with Selden.

The novel is Wharton's analysis of a society which she felt to be destructive, in that its rules made for choices between right and wrong action, at the same time that the definition of "right" and "wrong" was often obfuscated. It is the story of a beautiful young woman victimized by her lack of character, confused by the only alternatives she perceived to be available to her, and who arrived, too late, at a sense of the integrity which might have saved her.

Ethan Frome (novella, 1911)

Ethan Frome, his wife **Zenobia**, and **Mattie Silver** are the main characters in the novel, set in a rural town in New England at the turn of the century. The opening narrative voice is that of a visitor to the town who becomes fascinated by the lonely cripple Ethan Frome and decides to learn his story.

Ethan is a moral man, dedicated to preserving the farm of his dead father. The farm is poor, the work is hard, and his mother is now dying. He marries Zeena (Zenobia) Pierce, who has seen him through his mother's demise; he is now lonely and cannot realize his dream of becoming an engineer and leaving his impoverished environment.

It is a barren marriage, made so by Zeena's almost immediate reversion to hypochondria and her ungrateful need for constant care. When her young relative, Mattie Silver, is left homeless, Zeena grudgingly allows her a home at the farm to provide herself with two caretakers.

It is a simple story, and plot development is not unexpected. Mattie is young and beautiful, and her innocent ways soon captivate Ethan. The flowering romance is delicately presented as the couple interacts in gentle, loving ways; always self-conscious and guilty, they are too simple and moral to allow their passions to surface. Wharton's technique in presenting the tensions involved as they come to the realization of their feelings is movingly perceptive.

When Zeena becomes suspicious and arranges to dispatch Mattie and her services for a less attractive hired girl, Mattie and Ethan are devastated. In passionate hysteria, they decide on a last, dangerous ride together on a sled. It is ill-fated and they are crippled by the accident which occurs. Ethan is left scarred and lame and Mattie becomes a querulous paralytic. Wharton's use of the ironic mode is masterful, for in the end it is Zeena who must care for Mattie. Ethan, now impoverished in both body and spirit, becomes symbolic of his bleak and uncompromising environment.

In her preface to the work, Wharton noted that the outcroppings of granite so apparent in rural Massachusetts might be a correlative for the protagonist of the piece. She meant the story to be one of poverty and frustration, set in a harsh but often beautiful location, and commentators concur that she succeeded in her attempt. One of her best-known works, the story has been called by some critics an outstanding example of naturalism—an analysis of fortitude in the face of frustration, pain, and psychological alienation.

The Custom of the Country (novel, 1913)

Undine Spragg and **Ralph Marvell** are the main characters in this work. They marry and have a child but their contrasting world views exemplify the clash between the old and new social order in New York at the time the novel was written. Ralph represents the old, elegant, and proper American aristocracy. Ill-prepared for the working world, he is a dilettante who is paralyzed by an unrealistic sense of self and the demise of the society in which he finds himself. Undine, on the other hand, is a member of the *nouveau riche,* ambitious and determined to belong to a social class which she does not understand, but which she feels will provide her with the "best" life there is.

Ralph had been attracted by her beauty and vitality, and initially the marriage is happy. But he is unaware that the unscrupulous **Elmer Moffet** has threatened to expose his earlier, secret marriage to Undine if she does not introduce him to members of the upper class to enhance his business dealings.

Undine soon tires of her prosaic life with Ralph and begins a flirtation with **Peter Van Degen.** Ralph, desperate for money because of Undine's excessive extravagance, capitulates to Moffet's invitation to participate in a questionable business transaction. Undine uses the financial windfall to desert her husband and remove to Paris for a love affair with Peter. This ends when Peter becomes tired of her selfish ways and returns to his wife and the American social class which he had left behind.

Ralph, now divorced from Undine, seeks comfort in his son and his writing; Undine has remained in Europe and has waived all rights to her child, but for a price. She demands money from Ralph to pay for religious annulment of their marriage so that she may marry **Comte Raymond de Celles.** Undine's extortive act drives Ralph to Moffet for financial aid. When Moffet divulges the secret of his earlier marriage to Undine, Ralph commits suicide. Undine, rising to all occasions, gets the money, her French count, and her child.

No one is surprised that she again becomes bored. A chance meeting with Moffet in Europe rekindles her interest in him when it becomes clear that he is now the wealthiest man she has ever met. She returns to America, divorces Raymond to marry Moffet, and is in an ironic trap. It remains for her new husband, so like her in his world view, to keep her ambitious ways in check, for her dreams of more of the "best" there is will no longer come so easily to fruition.

Wharton is again discussing morality in this work, and her technique is one of savage irony. She indicts the old social order now in a state of flux that must renew its energy and moral purpose to sustain itself and prevent invasion by a manipulative, new class system. Undine, unlike the pathetic and naïve Lily Bart, remains relentlessly avaricious and materialistic to the end. She is symbolic of the newcomer to a coterie which has held long and complacent sway in America, and which was destined to end with World War I.

The Age of Innocence (novel, 1920)

This work, considered by critics to be her finest work, won Wharton the Nobel Prize for Literature in 1920. Set in the 1870s, it is the story of **Newland Archer,** a member of an old, established social order, his exposure to the excitement of the European experience, and of his final coming to terms with his own, changing era.

Archer, prototype of the conventional behavior of his class, is engaged to the proper **May Welland** and anxious for the alliance to be consummated. But he is intrigued by her cousin, **Ellen Olenska** who, like a Jamesian heroine, had earlier capitulated to the charms of a Polish count in a marriage which had ended disastrously. While in Europe, she had developed the mannerisms of the culture and presents a beautiful and dazzling change from her provincial cousin. She and Archer are attracted to each other during May's absence to nurse her ailing father, and Ellen comes to represent for Newland a more exciting, sensual way of life than he has ever known. But he also senses danger as his passions are aroused and soon presses May to set a wedding date. When she asks for more time, Archer and Ellen attempt to sort out their tangled emotions. But convention prevails when each receives a telegram from May declaring that she will marry Newland within a month.

One critic has aptly called the second half of the novel a "variation of the original theme."

In it, May and Archer marry and Ellen, having been convinced by him to retain her status as a married lady, drops her suit for divorce. She leaves New York after another delicately described, emotional encounter with Archer, in which they decide again to do the conventional thing. When May becomes pregnant, Ellen returns to Europe and her count. Archer is now able to realistically accept his innate value system of duty to family and career. His earlier fantasies about love, romance, and passion have been symptomatic of a kind of innocence which must be outgrown, and his character is delineated by Wharton as a man who has endured a rite of passage into maturity and full self-realization. In the end, he can reflect that he has been able to accept what life has offered and has made the most of it, in the most exemplary way he knew. He has found contentment.

Newland Archer's character embodies one of Wharton's central themes: he represents the opposing forces at work in the human personality which are in conflict over what one wants and what one ought to do. Archer wins the battle, for he has preserved the old order, even as he has noted and accepted its many and distracting changes.

FURTHER READING

Auchincloss, Louis. *Edith Wharton: A Woman in Her Time.* New York: Viking Press, 1965.

Brennan, Joseph X. "Ethan Frome: Structure and Metaphor." *Modern Fiction Studies* 7, No. 4 (Winter 1961-62): 347-56.

Contemporary Authors, Vol. 104. Detroit: Gale Research Co.

Coxe, Louis O. "What Edith Wharton Saw in Innocence." *The New Republic* 132, No. 26 (27 June 1955): 16-18.

Dictionary of Literary Biography, Vols. 4, 9, 12; *Concise Dictionary of American Literary Biography, 1865-1917.* Detroit: Gale Research Co.

French, Marilyn. Introduction to *The House of Mirth* by Edith Wharton, pp v-xxxviii New York. Berkley Books, 1981.

Hopkins, Viola. "The Ordering Style of *The Age of Innocence.*" *American Literature* 30, No. 3 (November 1958): 345-57.

Howe, Irving. "The Achievement of Edith Wharton." *Encounter* 19, No. 1 (July 1962): 45-52.

Kronenberger, Louis. "Edith Wharton: *The Age of Innocence* and *The House of Mirth.*" In *The Polished Surface: Essays in the Literature of Worldliness,* pp. 246-70. New York: Alfred A. Knopf, 1969.

Lewis, R. W. B. *Edith Wharton: A Biography.* New York: Harper & Row, 1975.

Lubbock, Percy. *Portrait of Edith Wharton.* New York: Appleton-Century, 1947.

Milne, Gordon. "Edith Wharton." In *The Sense of Society: A History of the American Novel of Manners,* pp. 116-49. Rutherford: Fairleigh Dickinson University Press, 1977.

Twentieth-Century Literary Criticism, Vols. 3, 9, 27. Detroit: Gale Research Co.

Walton, Geoffrey. *Edith Wharton: A Critical Interpretation.* Rutherford: Fairleigh Dickinson University Press, 1970.

Wilson, Edmund. "Justice to Edith Wharton." In *The Wound and the Bow,* pp. 195-213. Boston: Houghton Mifflin, 1941.

Wolff, Cynthia Griffin. *A Feast of Words: The Triumph of Edith Wharton.* New York: Oxford University Press, 1976.

Oscar Wilde
1854-1900
Anglo-Irish dramatist, novelist, poet, and essayist.

The Picture of Dorian Gray (novel, 1891)

In this famous novel, set in London at the end of the nineteenth century, Wilde created one of the best-known characters of modern fiction and offered both an explication and a condemnation of aestheticism, the movement with which his name is closely linked. As the novel opens, **Dorian Gray,** a young man of great physical beauty, is visiting the studio of his friend, the painter **Basil Hallward.** As he sits for his portrait, Dorian is introduced to the sinister **Lord Henry Wotton,** a character who will prove to be an evil influence on him. In their discussion, Lord Henry advances his doctrine of "New Hedonism": "To realize one's nature to perfection—that is what each of us is here for." Throughout the novel, Lord Henry acts as a Mephistopheles to Dorian's Faust, as is revealed when Dorian, falling under his spell, states that he would give his soul if he could remain eternally young while his portrait ages. As he later discovers, his wish is granted.

Dorian meets and is attracted to **Sibyl Vane,** an actress. But as Sibyl falls more deeply in love with Dorian, she loses her ability to act; she prefers life to art, and Dorian scorns her for it, saying: "without your art you are nothing." His rejection drives her to suicide. Inspecting the portrait, now hidden away, Dorian notices that the face has altered and now bears a cruel, ruthless expression. Under the influence and manipulation of Lord Henry, Dorian is drawn to a life of corruption and crime. When he is thirty-eight, Basil comes to him and pleads with his friend to quit his life of debauchery. Dorian shows the portrait to him, now grotesquely changed; knowing that he has betrayed his secret, Dorian kills Basil. With the help of a chemist, **Alan Campbell,** Dorian disposes of the body; Campbell later takes his own life.

In the conclusion, Dorian confronts the portrait and slashes it. The servants hear a cry, and going to their master, they find a portrait of the young, handsome Dorian Gray, and lying beneath it a shrivelled old man, a knife through his heart.

The novel was condemned when it was first published as an immoral work, a charge to which Wilde objected strongly, claiming that his novel offered the discernable moral that "all excess, as well as all renunciation, brings its own punishment." The work evinces the influence of a variety of sources, including the Faust legend; *Against the Grain* by J. K. Huysmans, in which the primary character, Des Esseintes, gives himself up to a life of pleasure; and supernatural Gothic tales from the early nineteenth century. Most important-ly, in the person of Dorian, Wilde reveals the attractions as well as the dangers of aestheticism, particularly the tragic, self-destructive consequences of the life devoted to sensation.

The Importance of Being Earnest (drama, 1895)

This society comedy, considered Wilde's finest literary effort, is also acknowledged as one of the most perfectly crafted dramas of the modern era. A vehicle for Wilde's tremendous gift of dialogue, the play incorporates and parodies the comic situation, taken from classical comedy, of the foundling who is revealed to be of noble birth, and also offers social commentary in its satire on the conventional values of Victorian society. Each of his main characters, male and female, reflect Wilde's conception of the dandy, and their conversa-tion is characterized by its wit, elegance, and defiance of societal convention. In particular, Wilde indicates through his characters the preference for aesthetic over moral values, for to them pretense and the ability to lie gracefully are preferred to the truth.

As the play opens, we are introduced to **Algernon Moncrief,** called Algy, an artificial, elegant man of London. To avoid the company of his snobbish, demanding aunt, **Lady Augusta Bracknell,** he has invented a friend, Bunbury, whose frequent illnesses take Algy away from the city scene. In the country, he has fallen in love with **Cecily Cardew,** the ward of his good friend **John Worthing,** called Jack. Cecily, very much taken with the romantic life, keeps a journal full of imaginary happenings. While in the country, Algy poses as Jack's fictional brother, Ernest, described as a wicked reprobate. Meanwhile, Jack has fallen in love with Lady Bracknell's daughter, **Gwendolyn Fairfax,** but Lady Bracknell opposes the marriage, for Jack is a foundling, and she will not allow her daughter to wed someone without parents and a distinguished lineage. Jack is also masquerading as his wicked brother Ernest, which is fine for Gwendolyn, for she had earlier banked her marital happiness on the fact that she would marry someone with that name. The action of the play is devoted to the development of the two love stories and an unravelling of Jack's true ancestry. In the conclusion we discover that Jack is indeed of privileged birth, for we learn that his nurse, the rather scatter-brained **Miss Letitia Prism,** had abandoned him in Victoria Station in a handbag twenty-eight years ago. Jack is really the son of Lady Bracknell's sister, and his true name is Ernest. Thus the impediment to a happy union between Jack and Gwendolyn is removed; even Cecily, although she is disappointed that her lover's name is not Ernest but Algernon, declares she believes she can still love him.

The work is noted for its witty, insouciant tone, its elegant, artificial language, and for Wilde's use of the epigrams for which he is justly famous. The characters and plot are as unrealistic and artificial as the language they speak, reflecting the play's philosophy that: "we should treat all trivial things very seriously, and all the serious things of life with sincere and studied triviality." Whether the play is a light, frivolous, and disarmingly ingenious piece or a work inspired by more deep convictions of philosophy is a matter critics continue to debate, but all agree that with *The Importance of Being Earnest,* Wilde created a comic masterpiece that has secured his name in the history of drama.

FURTHER READING

Contemporary Authors, Vol. 104. Detroit: Gale Research Co.

Dictionary of Literary Biography, Vols. 10, 19, 34, 57. Detroit: Gale Research Co.

Ellmann, Richard. *Oscar Wilde.* New York: Knopf, 1987.

Jordan, Robert J. "Satire and Fantasy in Wilde's *The Importance of Being Earnest.*" *Ariel* 1, No. 3 (July 1970): 101-09.

Nassaar, Christopher S. *Into the Demon Universe: A Literary Exploration of Oscar Wilde.* New Haven: Yale University Press, 1974.

Partridge, E. B. "The Importance of Not Being Earnest." *Bucknell Review* 9, No. 2 (May 1960): 143-58.

Twentieth-Century Literary Criticism, Vols. 1, 8, 23. Detroit: Gale Research Co.

Worth, Katharine. *Oscar Wilde.* New York: Grove Press, 1984.

Thornton Wilder

1897-1975

American playwright and novelist.

The Bridge of San Luis Rey (novel, 1927)

This novel, which won the Pulitzer Prize, takes place in eighteenth-century Lima, Peru and concerns a priest's examination of the lives of five people who fall to their deaths after the collapse of an ancient bridge. Through his exploration, **Brother Juniper** seeks proof of divine intervention; however, his inquiry is ruled heretical and he is burned in the village square at the conclusion.

Each of the five who perished—the **Marquesa de Montemayor, Pepita, Esteban, Uncle Pio,** and **Don Jaime**—shared a common experience: they all sacrificed the very substance of life by allowing themselves to become possessed by an all-consuming love for another. In every case, their terrible longings remained unsatisfied. Ironically, just prior to their deaths, each victim realized his or her plight and resolved to begin life anew.

The Marquesa de Montemayor loved her daughter, **Clara,** to the exclusion of all else. Clara chose to marry and flee to Spain in order to escape her mother's smothering affection. The Marquesa would not be put off and devoted the remainder of her life to writing to Clara in hopes that her devotion would be returned. Pepita, an orphan, was sent to the Marquess by the Abbess, **Madre Maria del Pilar,** for companionship. Pepita longed only to be back at the convent with her beloved Abbess, who was totally unaware of the emotional needs of the girl; the Abbess was interested only in cultivating Pepita as her successor. Esteban, a young man who was also raised in the orphanage by the Abbess, lost his twin brother to blood poisoning. Unhappily, the two were so close that Esteban lacked an identity of his own. Uncle Pio dedicated most of his life to raising and training **Camila** for a career in the theater. Although they were close and loyal friends and she became a brilliant actress, Uncle Pio was shunned by Camila when she decided to give up the theater. Don Jaime, Camila's illegitimate young son, was a beautiful but very sickly child. He worshipped his mother but was never offered the benefit of her courage in his suffering.

Before the bridge collapses, Wilder relates the way in which each of the characters acquires self-awareness. Pepita writes a letter to the Abbess begging to return to the convent. She becomes ashamed of her lack of bravery, however, and never sends it. The Marquesa reads the letter and through it recognizes her own selfishness. She then writes Clara a generous letter and vows to begin life anew. Esteban, in despair over the loss of his twin, had tried to hang himself, but was thwarted in his attempt by a compassionate sea captain who for years had mourned the death of his daughter. Esteban now decides to sail with **Captain Alvarado.** Uncle Pio had made an attempt to fill the void left by Camila's rejection by asking her permission to take Don Jaime for one year. Don Jaime went with him willingly.

In the conclusion, Wilder sums up the theme of his story in the words of the Abbess, who, after reading the Marquesa's final letter, notes that "anywhere you may expect grace," and that between "the living . . . and the dead . . . the bridge is love."

Our Town (drama, 1938)

Wilder won another Pulitzer Prize for this play, set in turn-of-the-century Grover's Corners, a small town in New Hampshire. The play is a celebration of the beauty and wonder of the commonplace occurances in daily life, reflected in the simple plot and characterizations.

The story relates the lives of two middle-class families, the Gibbs and the Webbs. **Dr.** and **Julia Gibbs** have two children, **George** and **Rebecca. Editor** and **Myrtle Webb** also have a boy and a girl, **Wally** and **Emily.** The families share similar values and interests: Mr. Webb and Dr. Gibbs are both history buffs; Mrs. Webb and Mrs. Gibbs share the same daily routines, are both interested in gardening, and sing in the church choir. Their children are wholesome representatives of innocent America and are nearly indistinguishable.

A major character and device in the play is the **Stage Manager,** who acts as narrator, prop man, takes on various minor roles in the play, and comments on the action, interacting with both the characters and the audience. He has the ability to interrupt the time sequence of the story and to foretell the future.

The plot is uncomplicated and is suggested in the titles of each of the three acts: Daily Life, Love and Marriage, and Death. Central to the work is the relationship of George and Emily, who grow up together, fall in love, and marry. Emily dies in childbirth, but is able to return to life through the help of the Stage Manager to relive her twelfth birthday. She finds the experience too painful, however, and returns to the world of the dead, who comment that the living never "realize life while they live it." The Stage Manager agrees, noting the possible exception of saints and poets.

Praised for its simple, life-affirming themes, *Our Town* is acknowledged as a classic piece of twentieth-century American drama.

FURTHER READING

Burbank, Rex. *Thornton Wilder*. Boston: Twayne, 1961.

Cohn, Ruby. "Less than Novel." In *Dialogue in American Drama,* pp. 170-225. Bloomington: Indiana University Press, 1971.

Contemporary Authors, Vols. 13-16, rev. ed., 61-64. Detroit: Gale Research Co.

Contemporary Literary Criticism, Vols. 1, 5, 6, 10, 15, 35. Detroit: Gale Research Co.

Dictionary of Literary Biography, Vols. 4, 7, 9. Detroit: Gale Research Co.

Goldstein, Malcolm. *The Art of Thornton Wilder*. Lincoln. University of Nebraska Press, 1965.

Grebanier, Bernard. *Thornton Wilder*. Minneapolis: University of Minnesota Press, 1964.

Miller, Arthur. "The Family in Modern Drama." *The Atlantic Monthly* 197, No. 4 (April 1956): 35-41.

Stresau, Hermann. *Thornton Wilder*. New York: Ungar, 1971.

Weales, Gerald. "Unfashionable Optimist." *Commentary* 67, No. 19 (7 February 1958): 486-88.

Tennessee Williams
1911-1983
American dramatist, short story writer, and poet.

The Glass Menagerie (drama, 1944)

The play is set in St. Louis during the Depression. The Wingfields are a family struggling through difficult financial and emotional times. **Amanda Wingfield,** mother to **Laura** and **Tom,** is an aging Southern belle whose husband has left her and who lives in the past, obsessed with her former beauty and popularity. Laura is crippled and withdrawn. Her physical deformity parallels her emotional impairment, for she is too fragile and weak to deal with the outside world. Like her mother, she lives in a world of fantasy, as the keeper of a collection of glass animal figurines, the "menagerie" of the title. Tom is an aspiring writer, frustrated with his job in a shoe factory. Amanda urges him to bring home a suitor for Laura, a "gentleman caller," suitable for marriage. Tom agrees to bring home his friend **Jim O'Connor,** and Amanda busies herself with the preparations. Jim and Laura are drawn to each other; after dinner, they dance and accidently run into Laura's glass collection, breaking one of the pieces. As they stoop to pick it up, they kiss. However, the possibilities of the encounter are dashed when Jim reveals that he is engaged and can never return to the

Wingfields. Amanda is enraged with Tom, who storms out of the house. In the play's conclusion, he has left his family, determined to be a writer, yet haunted by his decision.

In this play, Williams established several of the themes and character types that were to recur throughout his dramatic work. Laura is the prototype of the fragile Williams heroine, whose isolation and life of fantasy link her with such characters as Blanche DuBois of *A Streetcar Named Desire*. Amanda is also a character who lives in an unreal world. Tom represents Williams himself, in a work that his been called his most autobiographical. Tom is an artist trapped by circumstance, eager to escape his family and mundane job. The themes of loneliness and the life of illusion that characterize this work are found in all of Williams's later works. Stylistically, the work is marked by a lyrical tone. Also of note is Williams's use of Tom as narrator, speaking directly to the audience between scenes and commenting on the action. *The Glass Menagerie* is considered one of his finest plays and is one of the most popular works of the recent American theater.

A Streetcar Named Desire (drama, 1947)

The play is set in the French Quarter of New Orleans. As the play opens, **Blanche DuBois** has arrived at the home of her sister, **Stella,** and Stella's husband, **Stanley Kowalski.** Blanche and Stanley represent the polarities of human existence that Williams often explored in his drama. Blanche is a faded Southern aristocrat, sexually repressed and drawn to a life of illusion. Stanley is a crude but vigorous figure, sexually dynamic and brutally honest. He sees Blanche as a threat to his relationship with Stella, whom he loves. He also sees behind the hypocritical facade of her gentility. Blanche tells people that she is a schoolteacher on leave, but she has truly lost her job because of an illicit relationship with a teenaged boy. She presents herself as an innocent, virginal young woman, particularly to win the heart of Stanley's friend **Mitch;** yet in truth she is a shattered human being, whose life of illusion masks the horror of her life, for she has lost her husband to suicide, as well as her job and self-respect. She taunts Stanley for his coarse behavior and jealously protects her sister, whom she mistakenly believes needs her care, for Stella loves Stanley and prefers her way of life to the life of delusion represented by her sister. In the play's conclusion, Stanley has revealed the truth about Blanche to Mitch, and she withdraws further into her fantasy. When Stella is away at the hospital having her first child, Stanley rapes Blanche, an act of hatred and defiance. The last scene depicts Blanche in a state of complete emotional collapse, being led away to a mental hospital.

As in *The Glass Menagerie,* Williams here focuses on a character emotionally unable to live in the world of reality, this time juxtaposed to a figure who embodies strength and sensuality. His characters are developed with compassion, for he creates in Blanche a woman capable of love and sacrifice as well as one drawn to a life of artifice. In Stanley, he has developed a character who, despite his coarseness, passionately loves his wife and fights to protect their life together. The themes of death, decay, and the destructive and redemptive power of sexuality that characterize many of his later works were given voice in this work, which is noted for its blend of lyricism and gritty realism, and which won Williams the Pulitzer Prize.

Cat on a Hot Tin Roof (drama, 1955)

The play is set in the Mississippi Delta on **Big Daddy Pollitt**'s plantation, and the central focus of the work is the celebration of his sixty-fifth birthday. **Brick Pollitt** is in his late twenties and an alcoholic. An ex-football star and the favored son, he is a man increasingly isolated from his friends and family. He and his wife, **Maggie,** have stopped sleeping together. The action of the play takes place in their bedroom on the day of Big Daddy's birthday celebration. As they talk, the major thematic concerns of the play are revealed. Big Daddy is dying of cancer, which everyone knows about but he and his wife, **Big Mama.** Brick's brother **Gooper** has always lived in the shadow of his brother; now, he and his wife

Mae and their children are also gathered in the house. For Maggie, they represent the painful failure of her own marriage, for she is childless, and her husband is slipping deeper and deeper into alcoholism. She is a passionate woman, very much in love with Brick, wanting children and a happy marriage. The true reason behind the deterioration of their relationship is hinted at during their conversation. Maggie had been fiercely jealous of Brick's friendship with **Skipper,** now dead, a victim of drugs and alcohol. She had tried to force Skipper to sleep with her, and when he couldn't, guessed that the nature of her husband's relationship with Skipper was homosexual.

Skipper is also the focus of a heated confrontation between Brick and Big Daddy, when in the second act Big Daddy tries to uncover the reason behind his son's drinking. Brick tells him that he is sick of the "mendacity" of existence, the need to live a life of lies. He reveals to his father that he had rejected Skipper just before his death and cannot forgive himself. When his father accuses him of not being able to face the truth, Brick reveals to him the truth about his cancer. Big Daddy explodes and storms off. In the concluding act, the family tells Big Mama the truth about her husband's illness, and the family argues over the their rights to Big Daddy's land. In the conclusion, Maggie enters to announce that she is pregnant. Afterwards, as she and Brick move towards reconciliation, she tells him that she will keep him from drinking until she can make this final lie a truth.

As in his other work, Williams here deals with the themes of truth and illusion, loneliness, sexuality, and death. The work is praised for its realistic dialogue and finely developed characters, and the dramatist received his second Pulitzer Prize for the work.

FURTHER READING

Berkman, Leonard. "The Tragic Downfall of Blanche DuBois." *Modern Drama* 10, No. 2 (December 1967): 249-57.

Clurman, Harold. "The American Playwrights: Tennessee Williams." In *Lies Like Truth: Theatre Reviews and Essays,* pp. 72-80. New York: Macmillan, 1958.

Cohn, Ruby. "Late Tennessee Williams." *Modern Drama* 27, No. 3 (September 1984): 336-44.

Contemporary Authors, Vols. 5-8, rev. ed., 108. Detroit: Gale Research Co.

Contemporary Literary Criticism, Vols. 1, 2, 5, 7, 8, 11, 15, 19, 30, 39, 45. Detroit: Gale Research Co.

Corrigan, M. A. "Memory, Dream, and Myth in the Plays of Tennessee Williams." *Renascence* (Spring 1976): 155-67.

Dictionary of Literary Biography, Vol. 7; *Dictionary of Literary Biography Yearbook: 1983; Dictionary of Literary Biography Documentary Series,* Vol. 4; *Concise Dictionary of American Literary Biography, 1941-1968.* Detroit: Gale Research Co.

Heilman, Robert B. "Tennessee Williams: Approaches to Tragedy." *Southern Review* 1, No. 4 (October 1965): 770-90.

Hirsch, Foster. *A Portrait of the Artist: The Plays of Tennessee Williams.* New York: Kennikat, 1979.

Holditch, W. Kenneth. "Surviving with Grace: Tennessee Williams Tomorrow." *The Southern Review* 22, No. 4 (Autumn 1986): 892-906.

Miller, Jordan Y., ed. *Twentieth-Century Interpretations of "A Streetcar Named Desire": A Collection of Critical Essays.* Englewood Cliffs: Prentice Hall, 1971.

Tharpe, Jack, ed. *Tennessee Williams: A Tribute.* Jackson: University Press of Mississippi, 1977.

P. G. Wodehouse
1881-1975
English short story writer, novelist, and memoirist.

Right Ho, Jeeves (novel, 1934)

This well-known novel features a vintage appearance by Wodehouse's most enduring characters, who comprise one of the greatest comic duos in literature: the loveable British buffoon, **Bertie Wooster,** and his "gentleman's personal gentleman," **Jeeves.** They appeared in numerous novels and short story collections, all set in London in the early twentieth century, produced during Wodehouse's long and prolific career. Bertie is recognized as the prototype of the upper-class twit, a hilariously self-absorbed, dim-witted bachelor whose life revolves around chasing beautiful girls and socializing at the gathering-place of his like-minded cronies, the Drones Club. In spite of his foolishness and endless foibles, Bertie is a good-hearted fellow, a fact tacitly acknowledged by the infinitely patient and sane Jeeves. Wise and seemingly omnipotent, Jeeves exerts a gentle authority over Bertie, always standing by to rescue him with precisely the correct action or words, which often are cleverly turned literary allusions.

While vacationing in Cannes with his **Aunt Dahlia Travers,** Bertie meets **Madeline Bassett,** whom he refers to as "the Basset," and who later turns out to be the enamored of his old school chum, **Gussie Fink-Nottle,** now living on his country estate and devoting himself to the study of newts. In Bertie's absence, Gussie has come to London to see Jeeves, well-versed in aiding Bertie's friends in affairs of the heart.

After their return, an exchange of telegrams between Bertie and Aunt Dahlia reveals that she demands his presence at her country home, Brinkley Court in Market Snodsbury. It seems that she's got to find someone to give an address at a local boys school and wants to line up Bertie. He dutifully goes to the country and coerces Gussie to go with him—the Bassett will be there—and also talks his love-sick friend into giving the speech. Once there, Gussie is stymied by shyness and is unable to approach the object of his affections. True to his character, Bertie makes a hash of everything while trying to play matchmaker, and Jeeves must make everything right. But not before a hilarious scene where Gussie, who had taken several stiff pulls from a bottle of spirits to steel his nerves, arrives to give his speech completely intoxicated, much to the delight of the boys and the horror of Bertie and Aunt Dahlia. Jeeves, as always, can be relied upon to make all rough waters smooth, and the novel ends with the news that Gussie and the Bassett are engaged.

The language of both Bertie and Jeeves is a feature highly praised by critics, particularly the vivid slang of Bertie, in whose incomparable voice his own misadventures are narrated.

FURTHER READING

Aldridge, John W. "P. G. Wodehouse: The Lesson of the Young Master." In *Time to Murder and Create: The Contemporary Novel in Crisis,* pp. 245-59. New York: David McKay, 1966.

Contemporary Authors, Vols. 45-48, 57-60; *Contemporary Authors New Revision Series,* Vol. 3. Detroit: Gale Research Co.

Contemporary Literary Criticism, Vols. 1, 2, 5, 10, 22. Detroit: Gale Research Co.

Dictionary of Literary Biography, Vol. 34. Detroit: Gale Research Co.

Hall, Robert A., Jr. *The Comic Style of P. G. Wodehouse.* Hamden: Archon Books, 1979.

Muggeridge, Malcolm. "For Ever Wooster." *The Observer* (6 August 1967): 17.

Short Story Criticism, Vol. 2. Detroit: Gale Research Co.

Spath, Eberhard. "P. G. Wodehouse's Jeeves: The Butler as Superman." In *Functions of Literature: Essays Presented to Erwin Wolff on His Sixtieth Birthday*, edited by Ulrich Broich, Theo Stemmler, and Gerd Stratmann, pp. 264-81. Tubingen: Niemayer, 1984.

Usborne, Richard. *A Wodehouse Companion*. London: Elm Tree Books, 1981.

Thomas Wolfe
1900-1938
American novelist, short story writer, and essayist.

Look Homeward, Angel (novel, 1929)

Set during the first decades of the twentieth century in the small town of Altamont, North Carolina, this autobiographical novel lyrically details **Eugene Gant**'s birth, family background, upbringing, and growth toward manhood. His keenly sensitive nature and yearning for life assume epic significance when cast against a backdrop of vividly drawn characters, including his acquisitive, overbearing mother, **Eliza Gant,** who runs a boardinghouse and speculates in real estate; his estranged father, **Oliver Gant,** a hopelessly idealistic, alcoholic, monument salesman; his favorite brother, **Ben Gant,** whose early death from pneumonia deeply affects Eugene; and his first serious romantic interest, **Laura James.** While the importance and influence of these characters is unmistakable, it is ultimately Eugene's innate hunger for literature and experience that molds and sustains him. The novel concludes with Eugene, at the age of twenty, approaching a mature vision of life, one which enables him to both accept his past and courageously embark on a career as a writer, leaving Altamont behind him.

Although *Look Homeward, Angel* is an essentially platless novel, and, like Wolfe's major works, has been criticized for excessive sentimentality, wordiness, and occasionally immature outlook, it is nevertheless recognized as an unusually rich and largely successful work in which lush, lively descriptions radiate with perceptive genius. The novel's two composite themes are lost innocence and the rapid flight of time, themes to which Wolfe repeatedly returned in his later novels.

Of Time and the River (novel, 1935)

Continuing the worldly, artistic, and spiritual ascension of **Eugene Gant,** the novel begins with a long train journey, transporting Eugene from his provincial birthplace in the South to New York City. During the trip, present and past fuse as Eugene recalls the memory of his father and his brother **Ben,** whose gift of a watch he still carries with him. Upon reaching New York, Eugene undergoes a process of initiation into urban life which begins in disappointment and disillusion and ends in acceptance and creative maturity. A key friendship develops between Eugene and **Joel Pierce,** whose affluent family appears to Eugene at first as a marvel, but whom he later finds to be tawdry and distasteful. The novel closes with Eugene a mature, Harvard-educated, aspiring author who has acquired a wealth of experience in New York City and abroad.

Despite Eugene's preeminent dramatic stature, Wolfe provides throughout the novel remarkable depictions of several secondary characters. These include **Uncle Bascom Pentland, Oswald Ten Eyck, Abe Jones, Francis Starwick,** and **Robert Weaver,** all of whom, for their strongly etched, eccentric personalities and actions, recall the most colorful characters and scenes of Dickens's best works.

An enormously long novel, *Of Time and the River* is generally considered structurally weak and thematically redundant. Here, more than in any other work, Wolfe recurringly explores the nature of time, its relevance to society, and its impact on the artistic temperament. The ubiquitous motif of a dark, silent river, continually in flux, undergirds this intention. Wolfe's periods of stylistic brilliance are more scarce than in his first novel and his narration of Eugene's yearning soul more prominent. Nevertheless, the novel is praised for its bold experimental prose and a unifying concern with portraying the multifarious American experience through the eyes of a sensitive, intelligent, relentlessly searching protagonist.

The Web and the Rock (novel, 1939)

Like *Of Time and the River,* the novel is largely centered in New York City, though early sections recount **George Webber's** hard youth in North Carolina and latter sections describe his soul-searching escape to Europe. Although replete with several minor characters and a host of urban vignettes, this work is primarily concerned with the tumultuous love affair of George and **Esther Jack,** a compelling woman who first appears at the conclusion of Wolfe's previous novel. George is essentially Eugene Gant renamed, and is another of Wolfe's autobiographical personas. Esther, a prominent set-designer, represents Aline Bernstein, a woman with whom Wolfe carried on a passionate romance for five years. She functions as George's mentor in love, sex, and cosmopolitan life; further, she serves as both a sympathetic soul mate and an intellectual catalyst for George as he suffers through the creative process, trying to write a panoramic novel of American life. The latter part of the story traces the couple's growing difficulties, which lead to a break up, followed by a temporary reconciliation. A drunken brawl leaves George hospitalized and sparks a serious reexamination of his troubled past. As he recovers, he resolves to write another novel, certain that he will now succeed, given his newfound inner peace and acceptance of the world he knows.

Unfinished and disorganized at the time of Wolfe's death, the novel is flawed by the same stylistic excesses that plague much of Wolfe's fiction. Yet it is still considered a highly evocative work which contains some of Wolfe's most graphic and telling depictions of human passion and indulgence.

You Can't Go Home Again (novel, 1940)

Set in depression-era New York as well as abroad, the novel documents **George Webber**'s life as a famous author and his tumultuous relationship with **Esther Jack.** Episodic in arrangement, the story builds in focus as George travels to England and Germany and witnesses the growth of Nazism. He recalls from past trips his strong affinity with German culture, but soon perceives the evil and horror of Hitler. He realizes—as he had upon his earlier, disastrous return to his birthplace in Libya Hill—that you can't go home again, that simpler, happier days are irretrievable.

Nonetheless, George maintains a cautious optimism for the future of the United States, one which is challenged by two of his friends, **Foxhall Edwards** (Wolfe's portrait of his editor and confidant Maxwell Perkins) and **Lloyd McFarg** (based on the successful but embittered author Sinclair Lewis). Concluding that fame and love are not enough to sustain him and have in fact led him to disillusionment, George redirects his attention to the forgotten people, the ordinary and the outcast, and finds in them the inspiration to write with renewed vigor as he tries to reawaken the conscience of his country.

Fragmentary in structure, Wolfe's final novel reexamines his ruling theme, the passage of time. Critics have found his unusual stylistic restraint and more prevalent social commentary admirable, evidence of the novelist's progression toward literary greatness. The novel stands as Wolfe's final affirmation of the experiential life in America, where hope hovers amidst the lost, lonely, and disenchanted.

FURTHER READING

Contemporary Authors, Vol. 104. Detroit: Gale Research Co.

Dictionary of Literary Biography, Vol. 9; *Dictionary of Literary Biography Yearbook: 1985; Dictionary of Literary Biography Documentary Series,* Vol. 2. Detroit: Gale Research Co.

Field, Leslie, ed. *Thomas Wolfe: Three Decades of Criticism.* New York: New York University Press, 1968.

Holman, C. Hugh. *The Loneliness at the Core: Studies in Thomas Wolfe.* Baton Rouge: Louisiana State University Press, 1975.

Johnson, Pamela Hansford. *The Art of Thomas Wolfe.* New York: Charles Scribner's Sons, 1963.

Kennedy, Richard S. *The Window of Memory: The Literary Career of Thomas Wolfe.* Chapel Hill: North Carolina Press, 1962.

McElderry, B.R., Jr. *Thomas Wolfe.* Boston: Twayne, 1964.

O'Rourke, David. "The Lost Paradise of *Look Homeward, Angel.*" *The Thomas Wolfe Review* 7, No. 1 (Spring 1983): 16-23.

Reeves, Paschal, ed. *The Merrill Studies in "Look Homeward, Angel."* Columbus: Charles E. Merrill Publishing Co., 1970.

Rubin, Louis D., Jr. *Thomas Wolfe: The Weather of His Youth.* Baton Rouge: Louisiana State University Press, 1955.

Twentieth-Century Literary Criticism, Vols. 4, 13. Detroit: Gale Research Co.

Watkins, Floyd C. *Thomas Wolfe's Characters: Portraits from Life.* Norman: University of Oklahoma Press, 1957.

Virginia Woolf

1882-1941

English novelist, essayist, and critic.

Jacob's Room (novel, 1922)

Jacob Flanders is the main character of this chronicle, which is not so much the detailed story of his conventional experience from birth to death, but is rather made up of impressionistic glimpses of him as seen by others, combined with his own fragmentary sensory responses to his surroundings. The narrative voice is omniscient and interruptive, often reflective of the past and critical of the British social milieu of Woolf's era.

One of three children of the widowed **Betty Flanders,** Jacob is often misunderstood and lives in his own mysterious world, a worrisome wanderer. His childhood room reflects a love of nature, with his strange collection of butterflies, shells, and an animal skull.

As a student at Cambridge, he becomes immersed in intellectual life, but is known as "Julian the Apostle" by his colleagues, named for the renegade early Roman emperor who renounced his religion and stood apart from his peers. Jacob is often late to tea at his don's home and generally bored by his surroundings. A description of his room at Trinity is masterly; the reader feels at once the impact of his intellect, his disorder and despair in images of an empty room, where the absent Jacob's gloom pervades. On holiday with his school-mate, **Timothy Durrant,** Jacob is seen by others as socially inferior, awkward, and inarticulate, but thought to be distinguished in appearance and so, acceptable to the Durrant family. Timothy's sister **Clara** falls in love with him, but steeped in familial snobbery, she is incapable of showing her emotions.

In London, the young Jacob capitulates (reluctantly, at first) to the sensual with **Florinda,** who is unfaithful to him, and then to **Fanny Elder,** who falls hopelessly in love with him. These are shallow, superficial women who are intrigued by Jacob, but fail to understand him. He abandons them and London for travel to France, Italy, and Greece, after receiving a small inheritance from a little-remembered aunt. On the continent, he is exposed to *avant garde* artists and is mildly impressed by abstract art, somewhat exhilarated by Italy, and moved, by the Acropolis while in Athens. Woolf's use of internal monologue gives fleeting perception of actual events; there is a sense of an existential sadness in Jacob, despite his attraction for and to an older woman who enjoys his intellectuality.

With his return to London, there are presented brief descriptions of him—at the railway station, in Hyde Park under a tree, in Piccadilly Circus, and as accidentally seen by Clara while stalled in a taxi on the way to the London Opera House. This is followed by fragmentary plot indication that World War I in underway.

A final, single page further indicates that he has been in the service of his country and has been killed in action. His close friend, **Richard Bonamy,** is alone in Jacob's last dwelling place. His mental observation is that the disordered accoutrements give evidence that Jacob did not expect to die and that he was probably as surprised at death as he had often seemed by events while alive.

Then follows a repetition of the tiny paragraph that has described Jacob's room while at Cambridge and is part of the omniscient narrative line. These impressions of empty rooms are now metaphorically related to the character of Jacob himself, for readers have had few concrete views of him. There have been instead minute, impressionistic glimpses of him and of everything around him. He has thus been created through the reader's perceptions of him; he is transitory, as is the world around him. This technique will be further and more carefully developed in Woolf's later work.

Mrs. Dalloway (novel, 1925)

Clarissa Dalloway's day of preparation for an important dinner party, which will include England's Prime Minister, provides a relatively firm outline in this novel through which the characters move and act. The setting is in post-World War I London; unity of time is preserved as Big Ben tolls the passing of the hours. However, Woolf's break with tradition in style is again evident with the use of the internal monologues which provide readers with prismatic views of her characters and their responses to experience.

Clarissa's otherwise mundane, external existence is enhanced by her poetic stream-of-consciousness monologue; it allows glimpses of her past and her questions about the future to be presented for emphatic textual dimension. As she begins a day of necessary errands, the narrative begins. She remembers her girlhood and a young lover whom she rejected, and she meets an old friend who will be attending the party and who flatters her and makes her feel young again; this causes more musing about her youthful suitor, **Peter Walsh.** Her thoughts are fragmented as she walks; they include what she is now and what she might have been, anxiety about her young daughter and her future, and thoughts about a limousine which, obviously carrying a member of the royal family, has impact on her and everyone who views. it. At the florist's shop, her sensory impressions of the florist and of the flowers are delicately imagistic.

While Clarissa shops, the character of **Septimus Smith** is introduced, a suicidal young man whom Clarissa does not know and will not meet, but who will later affect her deeply. Symbolic of the war and its devastation, Septimus's monologue depicts the horror of its aftermath and his own personal disintegration.

At home, Clarissa is disturbed to find that her husband will lunch with a social rival, and has a surprise visit from Peter Walsh. They chat civilly, but their thoughts reveal that their early love affair still remains as a strong and loving connection. These thoughts are reiterated by Peter, after accepting an impromptu invitation to the party and departing for a walk through London. In Hyde Park, he passes an unknown young man and his wife and notes that they seem unhappy. The young man is Septimus Smith.

Septimus, now mentally ill, visits **Sir William Bradshaw,** a doctor, as Clarissa rests at home and as Peter ruminates while walking. Simultaneously, **Richard Dalloway** arrives for his luncheon engagement, where the discussion is of Peter Walsh, his old friend. The doctor advises a sanatorium for Septimus; Richard returns home and buys Clarissa flowers on the way.

Septimus and his wife return to their flat in Bloomsbury and it is in his dialogue with his wife and in his internal monologue that readers are painfully aware of his anxiety and his mental deterioration. Woolf has given an implicit verbal impression of the breakdown of his thought processes and his loss of control. A surprise visit from a colleague of Bradshaw drives him impulsively to the window, and to suicide on the ground below. The hall clock is striking six.

As Clarissa's party begins, details of the wines, food, and guests are related through the thoughts of the servants. Guests include the nobility, poor relations, old and new friends, all climaxed by a visit from the Prime Minister. Clarissa is simultaneously happy as well as anxious for social success. When Dr. Bradshaw appears late, because of Septimus's death, she is torn between pity for a young, dead man and rage that his action casts a pall on her happiness. In a solitary internal monologue, we can sense her responses to both the terror and beauty of life, with death as its natural ending.

She returns to her party, and her final appearance fills Peter Walsh with a strange "ecstasy [and] excitement," both of which belie what readers have come to know as a small part of the reality of the persona of Clarissa Dalloway.

This novel shows further development of Woolf's strategy of combining a simultaneity of actions and thoughts of her characters to provide dramatic narrative denouement. The literary pace is quick, impressionistic, and at times poetic. As one critic has noted, Woolf "dramatizes the tensions between life and death . . . [and] intimacy and isolation."

To the Lighthouse (novel, 1927)

This work begins with a discussion of the weather; if it permits, **James** and **Mrs. Ramsay** will take their young son, **James,** to visit the lighthouse keeper in order to provide that lonely soul some sustenance and comfort. Mrs. Ramsay is optimistic—Mr. Ramsay is not, and this continuing syndrome is symbolic of the many differences between two; it will re-echo throughout the work. The novel is divided into three sections; "The Window" is the title of the first.

The Ramsay family, on holiday in the Hebrides, are in company with an artist, **Lily Briscoe,** a poet, **Mr. Carmichael,** a student, **Mr. Tansley,** and **William Bankes,** intimate of Mr. Ramsay, who is a philosopher. Woolf's concept of character reality is conveyed through fragmentary, evanescent rhetorical passages. Thus, when Lily and William Bankes take their regular evening strolls, we are aware of Lily's thoughts, as well as her discussions with William. We learn that she suffers artistic paralysis, that she cannot reproduce what she sees on canvas, and that she adores Mrs. Ramsay and envies her loving, nurturing qualities.

Likewise, it is private monologues which reveal Mrs. Ramsay's frustration with her marriage, her love of beauty and of solitude, and her desire to be exemplary in all she does, as well as Mr. Ramsay's feelings that his wife is lovely, warm, but simplistic and superficial. Readers sense evidence of strong physical attraction, but the relationship is barren of communication. The nuances of life on holiday—social interaction with friends, a love affair for a daughter, and discussions of money and house repairs—are interspersed throughout the interior monologues that dominate the work.

In the section "Time Passes" there are images of a now empty summer home, storm-battered and worn. The house is cursorily tended by **Mrs. McNab,** a servant who is distantly aware of the changes that the years have made, most importantly the deaths of Mrs. Ramsay and two of the children. The maid attempts in a ludicrous way to maintain a home which has been disordered by the erosion of time. When a letter arrives requesting that the house be readied for a visit by some family members and friends, order is painfully restored. Lily Briscoe is the first to arrive.

"The Lighthouse" is the title of the last section. It is through the consciousnesses of Lily, **Camilla Ramsay,** James, and Mr. Ramsay that the story unfolds. Lily has brought paints and easel, in an effort to finish the painting which she had begun of Mrs. Ramsay ten years earlier. She is ambivalent now; she misses and reveres her friend, but is angry and confused at her abandonment, through Mrs. Ramsay's death. Mr. Ramsay, out of grief for his wife and a subtly indicated selfish desire to find a subservient replacement for her, is now prepared to complete the ritual Mrs. Ramsay so long desired and to take Cam and James to the lighthouse. He seems to want to reconcile the differences between himself and his children, who consider him a tyrant, but we are given few of his inner thoughts and see him through the perceptions of the other characters. It is, however, his final action which provides focus for plot resolution.

The journey in the boat is long and tedious. James sullenly works the sail, while Mr. Ramsay reads and discusses the trip with the boatman; James waits for criticism from his father, but now there is none. He reflects that, of the two parents, only his mother could be trusted to tell the truth. As they reach the lighthouse, Cam and James conclude that they will never know what their father really thinks of them, but both realize, when he compliments James on his handling of the boat, that Mr. Ramsay has come to some self-realization, despite his inability to articulate his feelings. As the Ramsays complete their journey, Lily completes her painting—both rituals have been performed; both artistic and emotional catharses have been achieved.

In this novel, Woolf has reworked her theme of the meaning of life and her own presentation of the reality of character; here she has once again richly and poetically exposed the tensions which are set up in a network of interpersonal relationships.

The Waves (novel, 1931)

There are seven characters in this, Woolf's initial experiment in the changing form of the novel which came in her time. Her narrative stance is that of a poet and an observer of the life stages of her characters. They are perceived by readers through their mental experiences; each one has an individual response to life, depending on point of view. There are seven sections; each one is prefaced with a description of the sun as it rises and passes through a path to sunset, and by a description of breaking waves and their sounds as they are affected by the solar tides of a day. Each introduction provides the only firm time chronology in the work.

Readers are first introduced to six characters, as children, and the tone is one of poetic drama. **Neville, Susan, Rhoda, Jenny, Louis** and **Bernard** are at play, and each one describes what is seen, according to individual sensibility. Here a strange tension is set up between the artifice of poetic language and childlike, human attitudes of fear, insecurity, jealousy, and love. This is the beginning of an elusive narrative device which will continue throughout, with little traditional plot development.

The children mature, and accordingly fulfill upper-middle-class convention and are sent away to schools; now girls are separated from boys, except for holidays, when relationships are renewed. The character of **Percival** is introduced at the boy's school. Representative of objective reality, he will become an object of love for some characters and fascination for all as well as a force which will bind them together. A man of action rather than contemplation, he is reminiscent of Mr. Ramsay. He will die a violent death as a young man, and this will affect the others until the end of their lives.

In adulthood, Neville becomes a successful poet, and is tortured by his aesthetic sensibility and his love for Percival. Louis capitulates to convention, marries and has a child, but becomes Rhoda's lover. Susan marries, has children and lives the life of a country woman. Bernard feels steeped in mediocrity and that his life has not been fulfilled, as does Jenny, who has been a superficial wanderer. She will end life a suicide.

In a reunion during their middle-age, each character reflects that with Percival's death, each of them had died a little and that the excitement of life is over; it has been replaced with illusion and inescapable chaos. The final section is given over to Bernard's summation of his life and those of the remaining characters. His internal monologue provides an ending to the novel. This retrospective gives fragmented and often illusory views of himself and his friends. In his view (and Woolf's, as we are now aware), it is impossible to subjectively order forth individuals concretely, since human beings are made up of sensory perceptions as well as physical attributes, weaknesses and fears. He compares his life and those of his friends to a symphony, with each one playing a tune on a different instrument to provide both the discord and harmony of life's experience. Percival, in death, had made each aware of mortal frailty; however, Bernard's final conclusion is that the life force which is symbolized by the relentless rise and fall of waves upon a shore provides an analogy for all human desire for life.

Woolf believed that life was made up of fragmentary experience and that the novelist's goal was to present every aspect of a character's life; without this, there could be no reality of being. Life, she felt, was simultaneously trivial and exciting, desperate and beautiful. Her purpose was to tell the truth. Like Emily Dickinson, Woolf chose to tell it "slant," and it was in the development of this technique that her creative genius lay.

FURTHER READING

Bell, Quentin. *Virginia Woolf: A Biography*. 2 volumes. New York: Harcourt Brace Jovanovich, 1972.

Brower, Reuben Arthur. "Something Central which Permeated: Virginia Woolf and *Mrs. Dalloway*." In *The Fields of Light: An Experiment in Critical Reading*, pp. 123-37. New York: Oxford University Press, 1951.

Contemporary Authors, Vol. 104. Detroit: Gale Research Co.

Daiches, David. "Virginia Woolf." In *The Novel and the Modern World*, rev. ed., pp. 187-218. Chicago: University of Chicago Press, 1960.

Dictionary of Literary Biography, Vol. 36. Detroit: Gale Research Co.

Edel, Leon. *Bloomsbury: A House of Lions*. Philadelphia: Lippincott, 1979.

Freedman, Ralph, ed. *Virginia Woolf: Revaluation and Continuity*. Berkeley: University of California Press, 1980.

Latham, Jacqueline E. M., ed. *Critics on Virginia Woolf*. London: Allen & Unwin, 1970.

Leaska, Mitchell A. *The Novels of Virginia Woolf: From Beginning to End*. New York: John Jay Press, 1977.

Lee, Hermione. *The Novels of Virginia Woolf*. New York: Holmes & Meier, 1977.

Marcus, Jane, ed. *New Feminist Essays on Virginia Woolf.* Lincoln: University of Nebraska Press, 1981.

Miller, J. Hillis. "Virginia Woolf's All Souls' Day: The Omniscient Narrator in *Mrs. Dalloway.*" In *The Shaken Realist: Essays in Modern Literature in Honor of Frederick J. Hoffman,* edited by Melvin J. Friedman and John B. Vickery, pp. 100-27. Baton Rouge: Louisiana State University Press, 1970.

Naremore, James. *The World Without a Self: Virginia Woolf and the Novel.* New Haven: Yale University Press, 1973.

Schlack, Beverly Ann. *Continuing Presences: Virginia Woolf's Use of Literary Allusion.* University Park: The Pennsylvania State University Press, 1979.

Twentieth-Century Literary Criticism, Vols. 1, 5, 20. Detroit: Gale Research Co.

Richard Wright
1908-1960
American novelist, autobiographer, short story writer, and essayist.

"Big Boy Leaves Home" (short story, 1938)

The action takes place in the rural, Jim Crow South of pre-World War II America. The story is the first and, many critics believe, finest in Wright's first published book, *Uncle Tom's Children,* a collection of four long stories. "Big Boy Leaves Home" powerfully sets forth the major theme that was to dominate Wright's writings: the horror and inescapability of racism in the United States. In the first section of the three-part story, four black youths— **Big Boy Morrison, Bobo,** and two friends—enjoy a delicious afternoon of truancy in the woods and a skinny-dip in a creek expressly forbidden to blacks. Their Edenic idyll is disrupted when a young white woman happens upon the naked boys and reacts hysterically, causing Big Boy in the confused aftermath to murder her aggressive fiancé. In the story's final section, the narrative voice shifts from third into first person, as Big Boy, hiding in terror, describes what he observes of the horrifying aftermath of the incident, in which enraged whites hunt down and beat, lynch, and burn Bobo to death. Big Boy himself waits to be carried secretly away by truck to the sanctuary of the North.

The forceful irony of the story is considered to lie in the fact that the bittersweet rite-of-passage traditionally depicted in literature here is a violent baptism of fire into the reality of racism. Wright's strong implication in this and his subsequent works is that for blacks living in twentieth-century America racism is entirely unavoidable.

Native Son (novel, 1940)

Set in Chicago in the mid-twentieth century, Wright's first novel centers around a doomed young black man, **Bigger Thomas,** who is the author's most famous character. Desperate for respite from poverty, Bigger with his street gang briefly considers robbing a white man's delicatessen, but then secures a job as a chauffeur with a wealthy white couple, **Mr.** and **Mrs. Dalton.** Late one night, the blind Mrs. Dalton enters the bedroom of her rebellious young daughter, **Mary,** as Bigger is trying to help the drunken girl into bed before her parents realize her misbehavior. Terrified of the consequences if he is discovered in Mary's room, Bigger claps a pillow over the girl's face to keep her from answering her mother's calls. In the process, he unwittingly kills her, then, panic-stricken, decapitates the body and burns it in the Dalton's furnace. Bigger tries to implicate Mary's Communist boyfriend, **Jan Erlone,** in her disappearance, forging a ransom note which he sends to her parents. But

Bigger subsequently discovers at the Daltons's unburned remnants of Mary's bones and decides he must flee with his lover **Bessie.** In his mounting terror, he decides she is a burden, and he brutally murders her. At this point Bigger implodes into a violent criminal, terrorizing the tenements until police finally capture him.

In Wright's unvarnished depiction of the hopeless and tragic fate of a black youth in a racist society, Wright contributed for the first time in the canon of white American literature a relentlessly honest view of black life in the United States.

FURTHER READING

Abcarian, Richard. *Richard Wright's Native Son: A Critical Handbook.* Belmont: Wadsworth, 1970.

Avery, Evelyn Gross. *Rebels and Victims: The Short Fiction of Richard Wright and Bernard Malamud.* Port Washington: Kennikat Press, 1979.

Bakish, David. *Richard Wright.* New York: Ungar, 1978.

Baldwin, James. "Everybody's Protest Novel." In *Notes of a Native Son,* pp. 85-114. Boston: Beacon, 1955.

Contemporary Authors, Vol. 108. Detroit: Gale Research Co.

Contemporary Literary Criticism, Vols. 1, 3, 4, 9, 14, 21, 48. Detroit: Gale Research Co.

Delmar, P. Jay. "Tragic Patterns in Richard Wright's *Uncle Tom's Children.*" *Negro American Literature Forum: For School and University Teachers* 10, No. 1 (Spring 1970): 3-12.

Dictionary of Literary Biography, Vol. 76; *Dictionary of Literary Biography Documentary Series,* Vol. 2. Detroit: Gale Research Co.

Howe, Irving. "Black Boys and Native Sons." In *A World More Attractive,* pp. 98-110. New York: Horizon, 1963.

Ray, David and Robert M. Farnsworth, eds. *Richard Wright. Impressions and Perspectives.* Ann Arbor: University of Michigan Press, 1973.

Short Story Criticism, Vol. 2. Detroit: Gale Research Co.

Émile Zola
1840-1902

French novelist, short story writer, critic, and essayist.

Nana (novel, 1880)

There are two main characters in Zola's ninth novel of the "Rougon-Macquart" series, **Anna Coupeau,** or **Nana,** and the **Count Muffat de Beuville.**

Our first glimpse of Nana in this novel symbolically foreshadows her entire character throughout the story. She appears on stage in the Théâtre des Variétés, eighteen years old, unknown in Paris, and displaying not a shred of musical or acting ability. She is described as being tall, having masses of blonde hair and rather plump thighs. She carries herself with an air of decided self-assurance and exudes a charisma that men find irresistible. She portrays Venus in an operetta, and by the end of the performance she has completely captivated the audience. They quickly excuse her lack of talent for her manner, spirit, and, especially, her naked body.

Nana's theatrical success immediately vaults her into the midst of Second Empire French society. Her powerful charms allow her to enchant male after male. She has a way of devouring their fortunes then casting them aside for new blood and more money. Her appetites appear to be insatiable.

One of her victims is the Count Muffat. A man with considerable social experience, the Count is a Chamberlain to the Emperor. He is married to the **Countess Sabine** and resides with her, their daughter **Estelle,** and his father-in-law. "Icily dignified," Muffat is also described as being a "decent individual with an upright character." He behaves with "an old-fashioned code of conduct" and has a "lofty conception of his duties at court." Some note that he acted as if he were always in church.

Although he is an unlikely person to take up with Nana, their acquaintance begins with his refusal of her invitation to dine at her flat. "A man of his position did not sit down at the table of a woman like that."

As he accompanies the Emperor to see Nana's performance at the Théâtre, they visit her dressing room. The count can feel himself becoming obsessed with her. This feeling throws his very being into revolt with itself, for the attraction is directly opposed to his pious nature. An internal struggle ensues, but soon his lust renounces and replaces his Catholic frigidity and rigidity. His dignity and ethics give way to his emotions and his entire life becomes consumed and dictated by Nana.

She is never faithful to him; time and again he finds her in compromising situations, but her professions of faithfulness allay his mistrust and anguish. He ultimately spends his entire fortune pleasing her with the gifts and luxuries she demands.

When Nana falls ill, the count keeps vigil outside her lodging. He speaks to no one and appears oblivious to any life continuing on around him. At the news of her death he covers his face with his handkerchief and resumes his stoic demeanor. A man who had cast aside forty years of convictions to enjoy the pleasures of Nana's flesh is left alone and devastated.

Nana became the blatant courtesan in a culture where affairs and trysts were common but not flaunted. Society denounces Nana, but in reality she is condemned by the same people who are a party to her favors. It was these persons who were responsible for her eventual position of power and control surrounded by luxury.

In chronicling Nana's ascent to Parisian demi-monde society, Zola made a sweeping indictment of the decadence and insincerity of the French Empire. Attacked by major critics as foul, indecent, and dull, *Nana* was at the same time heralded by others as ingenious and successful. Whether deemed moral or immoral, classified as realistic or illusionary, or interpreted as an artistic endeavor or pornography, *Nana,* along with *Germinal,* has formed the basis of Zola's reputation in the twentieth century. Zola's characters give us a vivid picture of the moral corruption he saw at the core of French society during the Second Empire. Zola's acceptance of the theories of hereditary determinism form the basis of Nana's character. As a child descended from the Rougon-Macquart line, she was raised in an atmosphere of alcoholism and promiscuity, a background she cannot escape and which affects her character indelibly. As in *Germinal,* Zola chronicles the life of an individual doomed by a hereditary weakness she is incapable of comprehending or changing.

Germinal (novel, 1885)

Étienne Lantier is the principal character of the thirteenth novel of Zola's "Rougon-Macquart" series. Penniless and homeless, Étienne arrives at Montsou to find a job in the Le Voreux mine, located in Northern France. Unskilled in this line of employment, he proves himself to be a hard worker and is easily and readily accepted by the other miners who have been dragging coal out of this pit for generations. As early as his first day in the mine, Étienne recognizes a "feeling of revolt steadily mounting in him." With the threat of a wage decrease pending and his increasing awareness of the discrepancies between capitalist and laborer, Étienne begins to study ideologies and social theories. He refines his instinct to rebel. Popular with the miners, he is influential and articulate and soon is the undisputed leader of a massive strike.

Perhaps for the fist time, the workers begin to see themselves as abused. Étienne inspires in them a feeling of strength to resist the capitalists; he speaks of their rights as humans and points out the profound inequities between themselves and their bosses. As time passes, however, they begin losing this strength. Many die of starvation, and those who survive are weakened by hunger. Étienne falls into disfavor, becoming the scapegoat for the unsuccessful strike. After two long months, the survivors are back in the mine hauling out the coal.

The day work resumes, Étienne leaves for Paris. In spite of the workers' submission, he is hopeful. Though outwardly nothing has been gained, in his heart Étienne feels the seeds of revolution have been sown. The workers have been shown how unbalanced the class divisions are, and the capitalists have been shown that workers do have power in trying to reform an unjust system. In Paris, Étienne will continue his dedication to reform; he will take part in a "war on society," confident that in time, equality will be attained for all.

In this novel, Zola vividly portrays the class divisions of nineteenth-century France. Using in-depth characterizations and graphic situational descriptions he clearly shows the inequities between capitalists and laborers. A strong statement is made for a complete reformation of society, but underlying his polemic is a hope for and belief in the possibility of a better world for all mankind. While Étienne is obviously the main character, the importance of the other characters cannot be overlooked, especially **Maheu** and **Maheude,** a miner and his wife, who, with their seven children embody the exploited victims of a cruel social order. Crowds and masses of people symbolize strength and power; their unity of purpose and commonality of goals reflect Zola's personal vision of a new, more fair and equal social order.

Zola is perhaps best known as an outstanding exponent of literary naturalism, an approach to his art that compelled him to examine, with the scientific study of hereditary determinism as his basis, the effects of heredity and environment on the development of an individual. In the "Rougon-Macquart" series, he endeavored to render the inescapable elements that determine his characters' lives dispassionately and with a scientist's eye to detail. Étienne, like Nana a descendent of the Rougon-Macquart family, is conscious of the horrible legacy he carries, and he is able to control his impulsive, destructive tendencies, to work for the social betterment of the working class, and to act as Zola's eyewitness to the seeds of revolution among the miners.

FURTHER READING

Bédé, Jean-Albert. *Émile Zola.* New York: Columbia University Press, 1974.

Contemporary Authors, Vol. 104. Detroit: Gale Research Co.

Hemmings, F. W. J. *Émile Zola.* Oxford: Oxford University Press, 1953.

Levin, Harry. *The Gates of Horn: A Study of Five French Realists.* New York: Oxford University Press, 1963.

Pritchett, V. S. "Zola." In *Books in General,* pp. 110-22. London: Chatto & Windus, 1953.

Turnell, Martin. "Zola." In *The Art of French Fiction: Prévost, Stendhal, Zola, Maupassant, Gide, Mauriac, Proust,* pp. 91-194. London: Hamish Hamilton, 1959.

Twentieth-Century Literary Criticism, Vols. 1, 6, 21. Detroit: Gale Research Co.

Wilson, Angus. *Émile Zola: An Introductory Study of His Novels.* New York: William Morrow, 1952.

CHARACTER INDEX

461

465

471

Character Index

TITLE INDEX

Title Index

DISCARD